Interpreting Canada's Past

Sixth Edition

Interpreting Canada's Past

A Pre-Confederation Reader

EDITED BY

AMY SHAW
COREY SLUMKOSKI
J.M. BUMSTED

OXFORD
UNIVERSITY PRESS

OXFORD
UNIVERSITY PRESS

Oxford University Press is a department of the University of Oxford.
It furthers the University's objective of excellence in research, scholarship,
and education by publishing worldwide. Oxford is a registered trade mark of
Oxford University Press in the UK and in certain other countries.

Published in Canada by
Oxford University Press
8 Sampson Mews, Suite 204,
Don Mills, Ontario M3C 0H5 Canada

www.oupcanada.com

First Edition published in 1986
Second Edition published in 1993
Third Edition published in 2005
Fourth Edition published in 2012
Fifth Edition published in 2017

Library and Archives Canada Cataloguing in Publication
Title: Interpreting Canada's past : a pre-Confederation reader / edited by Amy Shaw, Corey
Slumkoski, and the late J.M. Bumsted.
Names: Shaw, Amy J. (Amy Jeannette), 1972- editor. | Slumkoski, Corey, 1972- editor. |
Bumsted, J. M., editor.
Description: Sixth edition. | Previous edition edited by Michel Ducharme, Damien-Claude Bélanger,
and J.M. Bumsted. | Includes index.
Identifiers: Canadiana (print) 20200399454 | Canadiana (ebook) 20200399497 | ISBN 9780199038350
(softcover) | ISBN 9780190162023 (EPUB)
Subjects: LCSH: Canada—History. | LCSH: Canada—History—Sources.
Classification: LCC FC170 .I57 2021 | DDC 971—dc23

Cover image: John Poad Drake
The Port of Halifax, c. 1835
oil on canvas, 136.3 × 186.3 cm
Gift of the Canadian National Railways, Montreal, 1963
National Gallery of Canada, Ottawa
Photo: NGC
Cover design: Laurie McGregor
Interior design: Sherill Chapman

Oxford University Press is committed to our environment.
Wherever possible, our books are printed on paper
which comes from responsible sources.

Printed by Sheridan Books, Inc., United States of America

1 2 3 4 — 21 20 19 18

Contents

Preface

This reader provides students of Canadian history with the means to develop and hone important skills in understanding and critically analyzing the past. It brings together primary sources, so that students can engage directly with the voices of people from other eras, and secondary sources, so that students can see some of the ways those documents have been used by historians to interpret the past and understand the concerns of those who lived then. This reader brings in the work of scholars offering exciting new insights and interpretations, but it also draws on some older foundational works, so that students can think about how historians' work builds on each other, and the ways that historiography changes to reflect contemporary concerns.

This reader has been conceived not as a replacement for but rather as a complement to lectures and textbook chapters. It focuses on specific issues that may not have been discussed at length in class. The topics covered in this edition are varied and demonstrate the breadth of questions, approaches, methodologies, and sources inspiring Canadian historians. In choosing them, we have tried to draw out themes and perspectives that sometimes get occluded in more general surveys, which tend to prioritize general political and economic trends.

What this reader offers is a chance for undergraduate students to participate in the work of historians. We have taken great care in choosing primary documents that will help them ask necessary questions about sources: What does this document mean? Why did its creator want to express the ideas it contains? How reliable is it? What does it tell us about change? These questions, and the interpretative skills that develop from asking them, are of course crucial not just to being a historian, but to becoming an engaged citizen.

This edition builds on the work of earlier editions and the considerable scholarship and hard work of previous editors. It also draws on classroom experience and the feedback of thoughtful undergraduate students, and it has been improved by the recommendations of numerous peer reviewers. We are grateful to all of them.

We thank the staff at Oxford, along with previous editors Michel Ducharme, Damien-Claude Bélanger, Len Kuffert, and Jack Bumsted, for their vision for the readers and commitment through the earlier editions. We also wish to thank Mariah Fleetham, Elizabeth Ferguson, and all of the historians and publishers who have generously allowed us to reprint their work.

Amy Shaw, University of Lethbridge

Corey Slumkoski, Mount Saint Vincent University

Introduction to Primary and Secondary Sources

The work of historians is toward a clearer understanding of the past. Those who want to understand how people lived their lives, in all the great variety of pre-Confederation Canada, ask questions about the past. Good history starts with good questions. Once they have decided which questions they find most interesting, and seem most clearly to demand further exploration, they start looking for information to answer them. The first challenge they face is that the people and places they want to study do not exist anymore. While the past has shaped the present, today's context has rendered it distant and, to greater or lesser extents, foreign. The role of the historian is both to reveal and understand the past for its own sake, and to interpret it to those living in today's society.

In order to make sense of the past, historians have to use whatever evidence or testimonies they can find. They call this evidence, produced by the societies they are studying, primary sources or documents. It is by finding primary sources, analyzing them, and comparing them that historians can answer their research questions; they can find out how people lived in the past, establish causal relationships between facts and events, and develop their own interpretations about past societies. Depending on the objects of their inquiries, historians use different kinds of primary sources. Written documents are the most commonly used. Some of these written documents have been created by public institutions such as governments and courts of justice. Others have been produced by individuals or groups of individuals for a public audience: for instance, political treatises, pamphlets, brochures, newspapers, and books such as novels, travel guides, or cookbooks. Other sources are private, created by individuals and private institutions and not intended for public consumption. Internal documents from groups like voluntary associations, religious institutions, and charitable organizations are among these sources. Personal correspondence, journals, and diaries are also private, even if some have been made public over time. While many of these primary sources can be consulted in their original format, some have been reproduced on microfilms, republished, or digitized. Depending of the nature of these sources, historians can access them in archives (public or private), libraries, or online. Although most historians base their research on written documents, some use alternative primary sources such as artistic works (paintings, photographs, and cartoons, for instance) or even architecture and landscapes. Others focus on material culture such as old coins, clothing, and other artifacts. And lastly, historians can also use oral sources. These sources are especially useful to study societies with strong oral traditions such as Indigenous societies, or to think about more contemporary issues. What is important to remember is that all these sources are valid and valuable. The challenge for historians is to find the right sources to examine their own questions and to compare and confront those sources.

Regardless of the type of sources, historians need to analyze them carefully. They need to know exactly what these sources can and cannot tell them, as historians do not want to make unsubstantiated claims. In order to determine the limitations of their sources, historians must first question the documents themselves: What is the origin of these sources? Where are they coming from? Who created them? When were they created? Why were they created? Are they authentic? Once they have answered these questions, then historians can analyze their content: What do they say? What do they not say? What are their underlying assumptions? Lastly, historians can analyze these sources by putting them into dialogue, comparing them, and establishing how they relate to each other.

Once historians have collected all the primary sources they need (or that they can find), analyzed them, and compared them, then they can answer their questions and develop their own interpretations of the past. Their interpretations are embodied in what is known as secondary sources. These secondary sources, produced by historians, may take the form of monographs (books answering one question), book chapters, and journal articles, among other things. Historians use secondary sources for different reasons. They can use them to contextualize their topic, complement their own information, or situate their work within the overall historical production.

As the readers will notice, we have included in this collection a wide variety of primary sources: from artifacts to official documents, from travel accounts to novels and works of art, from personal diaries to transcription of speeches. All these sources include information that historians can use to understand the past. These sources have been paired to historical interpretations that offer an overview of the different questions asked by historians as well as the different approaches used to answer them. By reading these sources together, students will better understand the work of Canadian historians.

Chapter 1

Origins and Contact

READINGS

Primary Documents

Historical Interpretations

INTRODUCTION

As we look into the history of what is now called Canada, understanding the nature and the impact of the contact between Europe and North America requires an acknowledgement that the two sets of people in each contact zone viewed the world and approached knowledge in different ways. One way to appreciate this is to examine accounts of origin. Our first historical source consists of a Cree explanation for the presence of first peoples in the Americas. This narrative, like the biblical story of Adam and Eve, suggests a world with few people in it—a world in which people could communicate with powerful beings who directed and advised them, and who could help them find different places to live. Religious practices varied widely in pre-contact Canada, though most Indigenous people saw themselves as part of a cosmological order that included the land and its animals, the stars, and the sea. Rituals were often centred on maintaining balance between natural forces. Some of the artifacts illustrated here were used in Indigenous rituals, while others, like the famous pictographs from the shores of Lake Superior, represent Indigenous beliefs.

Contact between Europe and North America would profoundly alter the culture and society of both continents, and the historical interpretations included in this chapter show how it produced an array of consequences. In her piece, Susan Hill examines how the Haudenosaunee way of thinking about land and family shaped their wider political relations with both other Indigenous groups and European newcomers. She reveals a remarkable consistency in the way the Confederacy framed its alliances with the British throughout the contact period and the colonial wars. Jean-François Lozier looks at a very different aspect of contact, which he terms "the transatlantic cosmetic encounter." He shows how many Indigenous people came to prefer imported vermilion for body painting over domestic red ochre, and consequently how the former became a valuable trade good throughout North America.

QUESTIONS FOR CONSIDERATION

1. Does the Cree narrative portray the new place to live as a reward, a punishment, or neither? What leads you to this conclusion?
2. Where does archaeology end and history begin?
3. Why is the question of how long Indigenous people occupied the land before contact an important one for scholars and society at large?
4. How did European contact affect the Haudenosanee relationship to land?
5. What significance did Indigenous people give to body painting and how did contact with Europe change their use of pigments?

SUGGESTIONS FOR FURTHER READING

Carlson, Keith Thor. *The Power of Place, the Problem of Time: Aboriginal Identity and Historical Consciousness in the Cauldron of Colonialism.* Toronto: University of Toronto Press, 2010.

Courchene, Thomas J. *Indigenous Nationals, Canadian Citizens: From First Contact to Canada 150 and Beyond.* Montreal and Kingston: McGill-Queen's University Press, 2018.

Dewar, Elaine. *Bones: Discovering the First Americans.* Toronto: Random House Canada, 2001.

Dixon, E. James. *Bones, Boats & Bison: Archaeology and the First Colonization of Western North America.* Albuquerque: University of New Mexico Press, 1999.

Fagan, Brian M. *Ancient North America: The Archaeology of a Continent,* 3rd edn. New York: Thames & Hudson, 2000.

Haynes, Gary Haynes. *The Early Settlement of North America: The Clovis Era.* Cambridge: Cambridge University Press, 2002.

Jablonski, Nina G., ed. *The First Americans: The Pleistocene Colonization of the New World.* San Francisco: California Academy of Sciences, distributed by University of California Press, 2002.

Leavitt, Howard B. *First Encounters: Native Voices on the Coming of Europeans.* Santa Barbara, CA: Greenwood, 2010.

Marshall, Ingeborg. *A History and Ethnography of the Beothuk.* Montreal and Kingston: McGill-Queen's University Press, 1998.

Meltzer, David J. *First Peoples in a New World: Colonizing Ice Age America.* Berkeley: University of California Press, 2009.

Primary Documents

1 From "Where the First People Came From," in *Cree Legends from the West Coast of James Bay*, ed. C. Douglas Ellis (Winnipeg: University of Manitoba Press, 1995), 2–5. Reprinted with permission.

So then, I shall tell another legend. I'll tell a story, the legend about ourselves, the people, as we are called. Also I shall tell the legend about where we came from and why we came . . . why we who are living now came to inhabit this land.

Now then, first I shall begin.

The other land was above, it is said. It was like this land which we dwell in, except that the life seems different; also it is different on account of its being cold and mild [here]. So then, this land where we are invariably tends to be cold.

So that is the land above which is talked about from which there came two people, one woman and one man . . . they dwelt in that land which was above. But it was certainly known that this world where we live was there.

Now then at one time someone spoke to them, while they were in that land of theirs where they were brought up. He said to them, "Do you want to go see yonder land which is below?"

The very one about which they were spoken to is this one where we dwell.

"Yes," they said, "we will go there."

"The land," they were told, "is different, appears different from this one where we dwell in, which you dwell in now during your lifetime. But you will find it different there, should you go to see that land. It is cold yonder. And sometimes it is hot."

"It fluctuates considerably. If you wish to go there, however, you must go see the spider at the end of this land where you are. That is where he lives."

The spider, as he is called, that is the one who is the net-maker, who never exhausts his twine—so they went to see him, who is called the spider.

Then he asked them, "Where do you want to go? Do you want to go and see yonder land, the other one which is below?"

"Yes," they said.

"Very well," said the spider. "I shall make a line so that I may lower you."

So then, he made a line up to—working it around up to, up to the top.

"Not yet, not yet even half done," he said.

Then he spoke to them, telling them, better for him to let them down even before he finished it the length it should be.

Then he told them, "That land which you want to go and see is cold and sometimes mild. But there will certainly be someone there who will teach you, where you will find a living once you have reached it. He, he will tell you every thing so you will get along well."

So he made a place for them to sit as he lowered them, the man and the woman.

They got in together, into that thing which looked like a bag.

Then he instructed them what to do during their trip. "Only one must look," he said to them. "But one must not look until you have made contact with the earth. You may both look then."

So, meanwhile they went along, one looked. At last he caught sight of the land.

The one told the other, "Now the land is in sight."

The one told the other, "Now the rivers are in sight."

They had been told however, that "if one . . . if they both look together, before they come to the land, they will go into the great eagle-nest and they will never be able to get out and climb down from there."

That's where they will be. That's what they were told.

Then the one told the other, "Now the lakes are in sight. Now the grass."

Then they both looked before they arrived, as they were right at the top of the trees. Then they went sideways for a short while, then they went into the great eagle nest. That's where they went in, having violated their instructions. . . .

Then the bear arrived.

So he said to them . . . and they said to him, "Come and help us."

The bear didn't listen for long; but then he started to get up on his hind legs to go and see them. Also another one, the wolverine as he is called. They made one trip each as they brought them down.

But the bear was followed by those people.

That was the very thing which had been said to them, "You will have someone there who will teach you to survive."

This bear, he taught them everything about how to keep alive there.

It was there that these people began to multiply from one couple, the persons who had come from another land. They lived giving birth to their children generation after generation. That is us right up until today. That is why we are in this country.

And by-and-by the White People began to arrive as they began to reach us people, who live in this country.

That is as much as I shall tell.

2 Indigenous Art and Artifacts

Artifact 1.1 This St Lawrence Iroquoian pot uses a fairly elaborate pattern of incised lines and indentations on the collar, with a similar incised design on the shoulder. It is 20 cm high and 20 cm in diameter.

Artifact 1.2 Distinctive pinched face-effigy pipes from the end of the Late Woodland period may represent a Huron shaman, or medicine man, named Tonneraouanont. The pipe has been broken at the base; the existing part measures 9.9 cm in height.

Courtesy of Archaeological Services Inc.

Artifact 1.3 Archaeologists excavating at the Peace Bridge Site recovered a fragment of a slate gorget that bears two incised Thunderbird images. They found the piece in an archaeological feature associated with the historic Neutral or New York Iroquois, from about 1650 CE.

Courtesy of Archaeological Services Inc., Photo by John Howarth

Artifact 1.4 This moose antler comb comes from Teiaiagon (Baby Point), a Seneca village near the mouth of the Humber River in Toronto. Dating to the 1680s, the comb has depictions of significant Indigenous religious symbols including Mishipizhiw, the long panther-like being at the bottom with its head to the right and tail curled under its body to the left.

Munson, Marit K. "Figure 11.8." *Before Ontario.* Ed. Marit K. Munson and Susan M. Jamieson. Montreal: MQUP, 2013. Print.

Artifact 1.5 The famous pictograph site on Agawa Bay, Lake Superior, shows Mishipizhiw, the Underwater Lynx or Panther. One of the serpents who accompanies him is visible below.

Historical Interpretations

3 From Susan B. Hill, *"Teyohahá:ke—Two Roads,"* in *The Clay We Are Made Of: Haudenosaunee Land Tenure on the Grand River* (Winnipeg: University of Manitoba Press, 2017), 79–131.

TEYOHAHÁ:KE—TWO ROADS

The coming of the Europeans to North America certainly caused extreme changes in a very short time, but they were not the first changes experienced by the people of Turtle Island. Like all societies, a continuum of change exists from the beginning of time to today for the Haudenosaunee. [. . .] However, because this study endeavours to understand the impact of European contact upon the Haudenosaunee relationship to land, a thorough discussion of the contact period is necessary. To discuss change, the state of affairs before Europeans came to Iroquoia—the territories of the Haudenosaunee—must first be explored. That quest presents many challenges: There are no written records from the time; the oral record was scattered by the events that followed contact; and the archeological evidence is incomplete. This forces contemporary scholars to piece together the evidentiary fragments that do exist to get a glimpse into the Haudenosaunee world of the sixteenth century. Adding urgency to this work, the historical study of Indigenous societies at "first contact" has become a legal requirement for Aboriginal rights cases. The Supreme Court of Canada has determined that the moment of "first contact" between a Native people and Europeans and the 50 years that follow "contact" are the starting points in assessing whether or not an activity will be recognized as an Aboriginal right as referred to in Section 35 of the Canadian Constitution. [. . .]

CIRCLES OF INFLUENCE

The Haudenosaunee explain their world by using various spheres of existence and temporal boundaries.[1] These realms build upon each other in terms of identity and understanding of one's place in the world. They also represent a Haudenosaunee view of spatial relationships and the connotation of shared spaces—which become more prevalent as one moves out from the centre. These circles of influence have not remained static and were impacted significantly by "contact" and colonization.[2]

The primary realm of Haudenosaunee life on the eve of the arrival of Europeans was the village. On an individual level, the family hearth served as the hub of daily life as well as the primary unit of identity. Each longhouse consisted of several family units that comprised the larger longhouse family, typically all members of an extended matrilineal family or clan (and men of other clans who had married into the family). Two of these small family units would share a fire pit and undoubtedly would have shared in the work and benefits of that primary fire. The relationship that existed between those two families is a basic unit of Haudenosaunee society—the balance and interdependence between two sides "across the fire" from each other. [. . .] The village was a collection of these homes and, as a result, was a collection of families. [. . .]

Surrounding the gardens and fields were open clearings that stretched to the woods: This space is referred to as "the wood's edge" and is important socially, militarily, and diplomatically. On an internal societal level it marked the connection between the forest, primarily the domain of men, and the clearing, primarily the domain of women. [. . .]

The wood's edge served as a critical boundary for determining whether outsiders were approaching a village with intentions of harm or diplomacy. Runners would lead a diplomatic mission, carrying the message that friendly visitors were approaching the village. They would come to the edge of the woods and wait for village representatives to meet them and receive their message. This procedure was followed by people of other Haudenosaunee villages and nations, as well as non-Haudenosaunee.[3] If people entered the clearing without following these protocols, they were assumed to be enemies and the military protection of the village would be called upon. Because the actions taken at the wood's edge boundary determined whether outsiders were friends or enemies, this space became a critical aspect of Haudenosaunee government. The first part of the Condolence Ceremony is referred to as "At the Wood's Edge" and recalls the greetings of friends and relatives at this boundary.

[. . .] The forest provided many resources to the Haudenosaunee. Most hunting took place in the forest, as did the gathering of nuts, berries, and medicinal plants. The forest provided necessary firewood as well as the resources for building and repairing longhouses, palisades, and canoes. It could also be seen as a buffer between villages, and the farther one went into the forest away from the village, the less it was seen as connected to a particular village. As outlined in the Great Law, the forest was shared territory amongst the villages of a nation. It also became shared territory between nations in terms of resources (as determined under the principles of the Dish with One Spoon), but there was recognition of the territories having national identities. [. . .] The diversity of the Haudenosaunee national landscapes provided for collective economic security, as they shared the bounty of the individual territories across the Confederacy.

Besides the internal agreement to share the wealth of the forest among all the nations of the Confederacy, the Haudenosaunee created similar treaties with many of their neighbouring nations. These agreements established shared hunting grounds with allied nations, and, accordingly, those shared spaces were generally safe places for the Haudenosaunee and their allies. In the case of neighbouring nations who were hostile to the Confederacy, the forest separating the nations was deemed to be dangerous territory but was often still used for harvesting. [. . .]

COMING OF THE O'SERONNI[4]

[. . .] The first documented interaction between Haudenosaunee individuals and Europeans was a confrontation on 30 July 1609 at Crown Point along Lake Champlain between French and their allied Native[5] forces and Mohawk warriors. The entire event lasted only moments as the French and their allies shot at the Mohawks with harquebuses; Champlain claimed to have killed three of their targets and asserted they were "chiefs."[6] There does not appear to be an oral record of the event to corroborate Champlain's claims.

The most important aspect of this event was probably the introduction of the Haudenosaunee to firearms, a new technology that would change the way warfare was conducted.[7] While the battle apparently resulted in several deaths, the impact on Haudenosaunee communities was otherwise minimal, with the actual number of Haudenosaunee people having "contact" being extremely small. Despite those facts, however, in *Mitchell v. Canada (Minister of National Revenue)* (2001), the Supreme Court of Canada deems this event to be the one from which the interpretation of Mohawk rights would stem.[8] [. . .]

TERRITORIAL EXPANSION

In the seventeenth century, the Haudenosaunee territorial domain expanded often as they took in refugees from other nations. Typically, these refugees came from neighbouring nations—Mahican, Huron, Algonquin, Erie, Neutral, and others—who already shared hunting grounds with the Haudenosaunee.

The movement of these groups to join the Confederacy brought their families and their lands within the domain and protection of the Great Law. In most cases, the refugees and adoptees moved to the Haudenosaunee homelands, often setting up villages near the established national villages of the original Five Nations. Their presence contributed to the national and Confederacy economies as well as toward rebuilding the decimated populations of the Haudenosaunee. Their lands contributed further territorial jurisdiction to the Haudenosaunee and added to the collective hunting territories.[9] In accordance with the Great Law, the adopted peoples were allowed to maintain their internal political and cultural structures and were accorded representation through their host nations. For example, the Erie people were taken in by the Seneca Nation and allowed to maintain their distinct identity as Erie as long as they chose. [. . .]

FORGING AND MAINTAINING THE COVENANT CHAIN

Shortly after the British took control of Fort Orange (renaming it Fort Albany), they sought a formal trade relationship with their Haudenosaunee neighbours. A treaty council was held in September 1664, resulting in the first recorded agreement between Great Britain and the Five Nations. [. . .] The relationship was further expanded 13 years later in a treaty known as the Covenant Chain of Friendship, also made at Fort Albany. [. . .]

The 1664 treaty stipulated that the British would provide the same goods to the Haudenosaunee as the Dutch had before them. The British also promised to provide refuge to the Five Nations if they were defeated in their war with the "River Indians" (the Mahicans). Additionally, the treaty included stipulations for separate criminal jurisdictions, with both sides accepting responsibility for prosecution of their own citizens should they commit a crime against either Natives or colonists.[10]

[. . .] The 1664 treaty recognized both the British and the Haudenosaunee as sovereigns with their own "subjects" and laid out the principles upon which these two governments would work together but remain distinct as allies, neither becoming subject to the other. [. . .] The [Fort Albany Treaty] negotiations involved provisions of trade, but in accordance with Haudenosaunee diplomatic principles the heart of the treaty involved the formation of the relationship that would flow from the formal agreement. [. . .] This treaty did not negate the previous relationship; it actually used the original treaty as a basis for further development while acknowledging how both sides had been responsible for damaging their agreement and relationship. Like a marriage, the treaty relationship did not end because of violations by either party; instead, the subsequent treaty addressed the wrongdoings and created a means to rectify the wrongs.

[. . .] The Great Law established a framework within which peoples of different blood could become family. Building upon that ideology, familial relations were extended to Haudenosaunee allies in the same way. The idea that the British had become brethren to the Haudenosaunee through their treaty relationships was taken very seriously by the Haudenosaunee. It was seen as an extension of the Great Law, which directed that family members take care of each other and assume responsibilities for each other. The British may not have felt as strongly about the newly formed kinship bonds, but they used the terminology extensively in their relations with the Haudenosaunee and other Indigenous peoples throughout the treaty period.

Peace councils were held in Albany almost annually[11] for a century following the forging of the Covenant Chain. At each meeting, delegates from both the British and the Haudenosaunee would recall the original meetings where their relationship had been formalized.[12] The Haudenosaunee would remind the British that they inherited the position of friendship from their Dutch predecessors, and the British would reaffirm their promises of peace and friendship forever. Presents and wampum belts were often exchanged as symbols of the ever-flowing mutual friendship between the Crown and the Confederacy. This process of reaffirmation gained the metaphorical description of "polishing the chain." [. . .]

As laid out in this summary of the relationship, the Covenant Chain was a critical relationship for both the Haudenosaunee and the British. It demonstrates both the interdependence and the independence central to the relationship. Without this alliance, the British surely would not have succeeded in eliminating their European competition for colonial control over much of North America. [. . .]

THE TREATIES OF 1701: A CALL TO NEW ORDER

The years immediately following the forging of the Covenant Chain were tumultuous for the Haudenosaunee. They were dealing with hostilities between themselves and many of their western neighbours—Native nations allied with the French—over hunting grounds and control of the fur trade. Eventually the French were drawn directly into the fighting, with French military leaders invading several Haudenosaunee villages. The English reluctantly joined the hostilities to assist the Haudenosaunee. [. . .]

Under the provisions of the Covenant Chain, the Five Nations held council with the English regularly. Often during this period, the meetings would include the request for English assistance in their struggles against the French and the western nations. The Haudenosaunee were clear, however, to explain that it was in their hands to make peace with the French if they so chose. At one such meeting in Albany in 1685, the Confederacy spokesman explained to the New York governor: "Where shall I seek the Chain of Peace? Where shall I find it, but upon Our Path? and whither doth Our Path lead us, but unto this

house? this is a House of Peace [. . .] neither Onontio[13] or Corlear is our master, and that no man has the right to command us."[14]

Sovereignty was central to the Haudenosaunee standing at this time, even while under attack by the French and their allies. They clearly understood the need to demonstrate their autonomy and the fact that they were not subjects of the Crown. Under the Covenant Chain, however, they recognized their mutual responsibilities with the English when either was under attack. [. . .]

The Haudenosaunee were weakened by the warfare and attacks on their villages. Around 1693 they began to consider the French offers for a peace meeting. This started with their talks of peace between themselves and the "Dionaondades," allies of the French who included the Wyondot, Huron, Wendat, and others. When the Confederacy spokesmen informed New York governor Fletcher about this potential peace, the governor tried to convince the Confederacy to cease their informal discussions with New France governor general Frontenac.[15] Despite the promises of respect, trust, and peace made in the Covenant Chain, the English failed to see that their recognition of the Haudenosaunee as allies rather than subjects meant that they were free to ally themselves with any other nations they chose, including the French.

The French and English reached a peace agreement in 1697, but the hostilities continued between the Haudenosaunee and the western nations, as they were not included in the treaty negotiations. A year later, a series of peace conferences were held between the Haudenosaunee and the French and several of their Native allies. Again, the British began to rebuff the Haudenosaunee–French discussions. It appears that the British felt they could council with the French but were not willing to recognize the Haudenosaunee right to do the same. In September 1700, the French sponsored a peace conference between themselves, several of their allies, and the Haudenosaunee. A preliminary peace was agreed to between the Five Nations, the Hurons, the Odawas,[16] the Abenakis, the Montagnais, the Sault, and the French.[17] This peace was finalized in August 1701, after several weeks of meetings in Montreal. It became known as the Great Peace of Montreal and, as Paul Kayanasenh Williams and Curtis Arihote Nelson write, accorded the Haudenosaunee over 20 years of relative peace following its signing: "during that generation [of peace], the population of the Confederacy more than doubled, both through natural growth and through adoption of other nations."[18] The peace created through the treaty allowed the Haudenosaunee the opportunity to rebuild their economic and political strength, and, as noted, their longhouses continued to be places of refuge for many other Native peoples. In many ways, this peace allowed the Confederacy time to regroup after the devastation of the epidemics and related warfare of the seventeenth century.

[. . .]

In 1701, the Confederacy assessed the situation they were in: caught between England and France and France's Native allies. They determined what outcome they desired: a recognition by both European powers that the Five Nations were autonomous and had the option of allying with both or neither. Finally, they took the steps to achieve that outcome by treating with both, as well as the other involved Native nations. In this they were extremely practical and pragmatic, making agreements with the English and French (and their Native allies) that were not ideal but that served the primary goal—peace and protection for the Haudenosaunee people.[19]

EIGHTEENTH-CENTURY TERRITORIAL CHANGES

[. . .] Starting in the late 1600s, the Haudenosaunee experienced challenges to their jurisdiction over much of the northern and western hunting grounds. They attempted to address these issues through a series of military actions and eventually secured peace

with many of the Indigenous nations involved, as well as with the French. They also attained British promises to protect the Haudenosaunee interests in those hunting grounds. The Five Nations continued to provide refuge to dislocated peoples in the eighteenth century, but often those refugees did not add to the Haudenosaunee territories as had their adoptee predecessors. The result was an expanding Haudenosaunee population without an equivalent territorial expansion. In fact, the Five Nations were experiencing a reduction in territory and resources. This reduction started in the hunting grounds but eventually made its way into the homelands, thereby affecting the internal aspects of many Haudenosaunee communities.

The largest internal territorial pressures were experienced by the Mohawks, as British colonists pushed their way into the fertile Mohawk Valley.[20] As the easternmost Haudenosaunee nation, the Mohawks had the greatest amount of interaction with Europeans, especially the British. Some of the colonists were invited in by the Mohawks through alliances of friendship. Others bought their way in, often securing fraudulent titles to vast tracts of land. These land swindles became epidemic in the Mohawk Valley and were cause for growing tensions between the Mohawks and the colonists. [. . .]

Often the British responded to Haudenosaunee land claims by offering to build a fort in the neighbouring area so as to monitor the actions of British subjects in the area. One of these British settlements was Fort Hunter, established around 1700. While such forts were built by the British to protect Haudenosaunee land interests, they often had the opposite effect, as they introduced more Europeans to the Haudenosaunee interior. [. . .] In 1712, for example, 2500 Palatine Germans purchased the right to occupy land in the Mohawk Valley at Schoharie.[21] While the Mohawks of the area had consented to this sharing of land with the Palatines, it still led to increased competition for land and resources.

On another front, the Six Nations leadership also let it be known that they were well aware of the value of the lands they had agreed to share with the British colonists. In a famous speech made at the Treaty of Lancaster in 1744, Canasatego, an Onondaga Royaner, declared the following: "We know our lands have now become more valuable. The white people think we do not know their value; but we know that the land is everlasting, and the few goods we receive for it are soon worn out and gone."[22] [. . .]

This "sale" was prefaced by a promise by the British that their future generations would respect their Haudenosaunee peers. In other words, the treaty was only binding so long as the British descendants treated the Haudenosaunee descendants as brethren. [. . .]

TOWN SETTLEMENTS, REFUGEES, AND HOUSING PATTERNS

Most of the written record of this period focuses upon external Haudenosaunee land dealings, especially treaty councils. Less evidence exists regarding the internal impacts of those land deals on the villages and nations of the Haudenosaunee. Information reflected in the written record documents town settlements, the impact of refugees within villages, and shifts in housing patterns.

The Mohawks, as the easternmost nation, faced the largest onslaught of British people and culture. As they made room in their territory for the colonists, they shifted into a more sedentary village pattern. In the previous centuries, they occupied a village from 15 to 50 years and moved once the neighbouring fields lost fertility and nearby resources became scarce. In the eighteenth century, the Mohawks established permanent villages, often referred to in the records as "towns," but continued to inhabit satellite villages.[23] [. . .]

Like all the Five Nations, the Oneidas experienced an influx of refugees in the eighteenth century, including the most well-known of all the refugee nations to the Confederacy, the Tuscaroras. The Tuscaroras originated in the Carolinas and spoke a language similar to those of the Haudenosaunee.[24] When the Five Nations reported the addition of the Tuscaroras to the Confederacy, they were described as follows: "they were of us and went from us long ago, and now are returned and promise to live peaceably among us."[25] British colonists had moved into their homelands, and the Tuscarora efforts to remove them became known as the Tuscarora War. They were defeated by the colonial forces and sought refuge with their northern relatives of the Confederacy.[26] [. . .] The record states the Tuscaroras were officially accepted as the sixth nation of the Confederacy in 1722, and the name "Six Nations" appears in a treaty with the British in the following year.[27] [. . .]

Similar to the Oneidas, the Onondagas also established satellite villages near the main Onondaga town to accommodate their refugee population. [. . .] In the Haudenosaunee oral record, it is explained that these refugee satellite villages allowed the adopted Haudenosaunee to acclimate to their new surroundings and relatives. In accordance with the Great Law, these villages also provided a means by which refugees could maintain their distinct social, political, and religious structures, if they so chose. The Cayugas [also] experienced a population influx as members of the Conoy, Nanticoke, and Tutelo nations sought refuge in their territory.[28]

[. . .]

In the eighteenth century, Seneca political jurisdiction covered their homelands region in the Genesee River Valley and spread into the Confederacy's western hunting grounds of the Ohio River Valley and present-day southern Ontario. In these lands, the Senecas took in peoples from scores of different nations, most of whom adapted to a Seneca identity over time. Like their eastern neighbours in the Confederacy, the Senecas had altered their residential patterns from the centralized large villages of the previous century to smaller, more dispersed settlements.[29] While some longhouses remained in the older settlements,[30] new Seneca villages were comprised mainly of cabin-like structures that accommodated two families who shared a single hearth. While this was a major shift from the longhouses of previous generations—where several families belonging to a larger matrilineal clan shared one housing structure—the shared hearth of the cabins allowed for the primary unit of interdependence—the relationship "across the fire"—to continue. [. . .]

Even though villages, houses, and land holdings had changed, the Haudenosaunee persisted in their view of the land as central to their being. In 1732, in the midst of filing a land claim against Philip Livingston, the Mohawk speaker summed it up best: "then Mr. Livingston has murdered us asleep, for our land is our life."[31] Clearly, the Haudenosaunee not only continued to see the earth as Mother, but still understood their dependence upon her for their survival and the continuation of all life.

TARNISHING THE CHAIN

As evidenced in the various land disputes between the Confederacy and the British, strained relations were commonplace in the eighteenth century. While British officials often tried to make amends to the Haudenosaunee for colonists' encroachments and land thefts, the reality inflicted a toll upon the Covenant Chain. [. . .] In fact, by 1750 it appeared that the Confederacy might back the French in the brewing war between French and British colonial interests. If it were not for Sir William Johnson—and the close bonds he held with many Haudenosaunee leaders— the British might have lost their most important North American ally. Had that occurred, the Crown would certainly have lost much of its territorial interests as well.

Johnson had become a skilled diplomat in his dealings with the Haudenosaunee. By learning the Mohawk language, Johnson gained an important edge in his work with

the Confederacy. He was able to better understand the Haudenosaunee perspective in council meetings and, as a result, developed a much deeper understanding of Haudenosaunee society than any other British official working with the Six Nations. His ability to articulate key aspects of Haudenosaunee philosophy gained him a great deal of trust among the Confederacy leadership of the day. [. . .]

While he did not achieve unanimous trust and support from the Haudenosaunee, Johnson's influence allowed the British to maintain a grasp on the Covenant Chain and the continued alliance of the Haudenosaunee. His ability to "polish the chain" after the actions of British subjects had tarnished it proved absolutely essential to the continuity of the Haudenosaunee–British alliance. [. . .]

In 1755, full-scale war had broken out again between the British and the French, and the Crown sought the assistance of their old allies through the Covenant Chain. Often in their attempts to garner Haudenosaunee support in the war, British officials appealed under both the Covenant Chain and the 1701 Nanfan Treaty. [. . .]

General Braddock asserted similar sentiments to the Haudenosaunee through Johnson:

> as it appears that the French from time to time by fraud and by violence have constructed strong forts within the limits of the aforesaid lands in contravention of the agreements expressed in the said contract and treaty, you will assure the said nations in my name that I have come on the part and in the name of His Majesty to destroy all the said forts and to build some which will suffice to protect the said lands and *to insure them to them and their successors for ever agreeably to the object and the spirit of the treaty. And, for this purpose, summon them to take up the hatchet and to come and take possession of their own lands.*[32]

[This passage] not only notes the desire of the British to gain Haudenosaunee assistance in the war but also demonstrate that the British recognized these lands as being Haudenosaunee territory. [. . .]

The British references to the 1701 Nanfan Treaty, and their oath to protect Six Nations interests as articulated in that treaty, proved successful as the Haudenosaunee joined their war efforts—although reluctantly in many cases—against the French.

It is also important to note that the British were not only aware of the Haudenosaunee affinity for the Nanfan Treaty, but they were also well acquainted with the Haudenosaunee understanding of that treaty. In 1755, Johnson described the Six Nations' viewpoint in this way:

> That memorable and important act by which the Indians put their Patrimonial and conquered lands under the Protection of the King of Great Britain their Father is not understood by them as a cession or surrender as it seems to have been ignorantly or wilfuly supposed by some, they intended and look upon it as reserving the Property and Possession of the soil to themselves and their heirs. This property the Six Nations are by no means willing to part with and are equally averse and jealous that any Forts or Settlements should be made thereon either by us or the French.[33]

Johnson's words are especially important when considering the Crown's later representation of the treaty and its impact upon the Grand River Haudenosaunee following their move there in 1784.

"GREAT FRAUDS AND ABUSES"

Like many of their predecessors, the British colonists of the 1760s pushed farther and farther into Haudenosaunee territory, often without the proper consent from the Confederacy.

The colonists' land encroachments continued to spread in the years following the Seven Years' War. British disregard of their promises to protect Haudenosaunee land interests also grew. Once the French were out of the way, the British appeared less concerned about maintaining the Covenant Chain. Williams and Nelson assert that British policy makers desired to protect the Haudenosaunee interests.[34] Unfortunately, in order to maintain some balance within the colony, those charged with enforcing policies often failed to do so.

[. . .]

In response to the many issues raised to the Crown by various Native nations, including the Haudenosaunee, the King issued a Royal Proclamation on 7 October 1763. Excerpts of the decree follow:

> And whereas, it is just and reasonable, and essential to our Interest, and the Security of our Colonies, that the several Nations or Tribes of Indians with whom we are connected, or who live under our Protection, should not be molested or disturbed in the Possession of such Parts of our Dominions and Territories as, not having been ceded to or purchased by us, are reserved to them, or any of them, as their Hunting Grounds.
>
> And whereas great Frauds and abuses have been committed in purchasing Lands of the Indians, to the great Prejudice of our Interests, and to the great Dissatisfaction of the said Indians. In order, therefore, to prevent such Irregularities for the future, and to the end that the Indians may be convinced of our Justice and determined Resolution to remove all Reasonable Cause of Discontent, We do, with the Advice of our Privy Council strictly enjoin and require, that no Private person do presume to make any purchase from the said Indians of any lands, reserved to the said Indians, within those parts of our Colonies where We have thought proper to allow Settlement; but that, If at any time

any of the said Indians should be inclined to dispose of the said Lands, the same shall be Purchased only for Us, in our Name, at some public Meeting or Assembly of the said Indians, to be held for that purpose by the Governor or Commander in Chief of our Colony respectively within which they shall lie.[35]

There are several key phrases within the Royal Proclamation that are directly relevant to Haudenosaunee issues with the Crown. First, the Proclamation specifies two different types of Crown–Native relations: those with whom they "are connected" and those who "live under [their] Protection." While the British had promised to protect Haudenosaunee interests in their territories, the Haudenosaunee fell under the first category as "connected" nations, meaning that they remained sovereign. This is evidenced directly in many references to the Covenant Chain, with the analogy of "linking arms" metaphorically connecting the two peoples. Second, the idea of "great frauds and abuses" spoke directly to the fraudulent patents in the Mohawk Valley.

[. . .] Finally, in the King's stated desire "to remove all Reasonable Cause of Discontent," he was referencing (among other situations) Pontiac's Rebellion of 1763–64, which had received support from many of the Senecas as well as several allied nations of the Confederacy. It was clear to the Crown that if they did not address the many issues of the Haudenosaunee and their Native neighbours, they were likely to band together against the British and their colonists. It was hoped that the Royal Proclamation would put an end to that possibility. In many ways, it probably did assist in reducing the support for Pontiac's War (both from the Haudenosaunee as well as other nations) against the British, but it actually did nothing to address the past abuses nor did it create a forum that could address them. It was simply crafted as a preventative tool for future situations. [. . .]

As the Crown's representative to the Six Nations, Johnson had the responsibility of disseminating information on the Royal Proclamation to the Confederacy. [. . .] Before the end of January 1764, Johnson had met with each of the Six Nations.[36]

But, as Williams and Nelson have noted, the Royal Proclamation was being used as a tool for both peace and war. They write, "Johnson wanted to reassure the eastern nations of the Confederacy that they 'need be under no apprehension' concerning their lands, to prevent them from joining the war against the British, while at the same time encouraging them to join the British army that would punish the Shawnees and Delawares and others who had fought the British. The situation was delicate: the Senecas had also attacked the British, and the other nations of the Confederacy were reluctant to fight their own people."[37] The above describes the situation prior to the 1764 Niagara Strip Treaty. In many ways, that treaty became a means for both the Haudenosaunee and the Crown to repair part of their very strained relationship. The Senecas offered important parts of their territory to be placed under the protection of the King. Surely, part of their motivation must have been appeasement for the participation of some of their people in Pontiac's efforts. Coupled with the transfer of land to the protection of the King, the Senecas also made a personal gift of the islands in the Niagara River to Johnson.[38] Notably, this "gift" directly violated the Royal Proclamation. The islands were given directly to Johnson and were not first surrendered to the Crown—as required under the proclamation. However, in recent court cases, the "gift" has been upheld and the land remains firmly in the hands of non-Haudenosaunee.[39] [. . .]

Seneca influence with the western First Nations was considered critical for the British in order to gain stability in the Ohio region. For their part, the Senecas trusted in the limitations of the treaty, especially in the fact that they had placed their lands under the King's protection but had not made an actual cession. They believed this would protect their various interests, and they trusted that the British had finally addressed some of their most pressing concerns. Yet, in its limitations, the Niagara Strip Treaty closely resembled the 1701 Nanfan Treaty.

While the 1764 Niagara Strip Treaty brought the Senecas firmly back into the Covenant Chain, issues around the eastern border between the Haudenosaunee and the British still needed to be formally addressed. The line described in the Royal Proclamation was intended to be temporary only, and the responsibility of securing a permanent line with the Haudenosaunee fell upon Johnson. A treaty council was held at Fort Stanwix in October 1768 to achieve this goal. Given past transgressions, the Haudenosaunee were reluctant to relinquish any more territory. During a private Haudenosaunee council at Fort Stanwix, a speaker reminded Johnson of these concerns:

> Brother
> We have been some time deliberating on what you said concerning a boundary line between the English & us, and we are sensible that it could be for our mutual advantage, if it was not transgressed, but daily experience teaches us that we cannot have any great dependence on the white people and that they will forget their agreements for the sake of our lands, however, you have said so much upon it, that we are willing to believe more favourably in their cases.[40]

Johnson's participation in the council and his personal promises carried a great deal of influence toward convincing the Haudenosaunee to consent to the treaty. They did so with an understanding that the Covenant Chain would never again be allowed to tarnish. This they clearly stipulated in their agreement to the treaty: "We now tell the King that we have given him a great and valuable country, and

we know that what we shall now get for it must be far short of its value. We make it a condition of this our agreement concerning the line, that His Majesty will not forget or neglect to show us his favour, or suffer the chain to contract rust, but that he will direct those who have the management of our affairs to be punctual in renewing our ancient agreement."[41] The Haudenosaunee well understood the value of the land they ceded; they did so not for the financial compensation but because of the bonds of family they shared with the British. While the Haudenosaunee ceded "a great territory" they were careful to retain hunting rights within the ceded lands and limited the British from hunting on "our side of the line." This marked a shift in Haudenosaunee–British relations. Previously, in an extension of the principle of the Dish with One Spoon, the Haudenosaunee and the British had agreed to share hunting grounds. This was an obvious attempt on the part of the Confederacy to protect their remaining lands from future encroachment, which often began with colonists hunting on Haudenosaunee lands. This attempt, and the entire treaty, failed to do what it had set out to accomplish. Just five years later, in 1773, British trader George Croghan estimated that 60 000 whites had violated the Fort Stanwix Treaty line and had settled in Haudenosaunee territory (Figure 1.1).[42]

[. . .]

A CALL TO WAR

Beyond its inability to address Haudenosaunee and other Indigenous land grievances, the Royal Proclamation fuelled growing discontent among many of the people of the Thirteen Colonies. Many historians deem it to be a primary impetus of the War of American Independence that started 12 years later. As tempers flared, leaders of both the British and the colonists courted the Haudenosaunee, seeking assistance in the impending struggle.

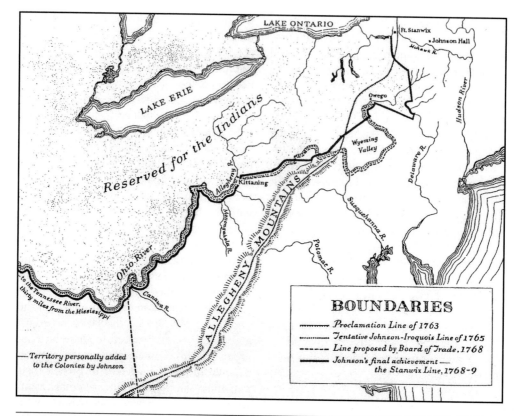

Figure 1.1 Map of 1763 Royal Proclamation and 1768 Fort Stanwix Boundaries.
Source: From the Collection of the Haudenosaunee Standing Committee on Burials and Repatriation.

Initially, the Grand Council favoured neutrality in the war, but eventually determined that each nation would make its own decisions about its individual national participation.[43] Collectively, the Confederacy was deeply affected by the violations of the Fort Stanwix line. They knew it was the colonists[44] actually perpetrating the violations, but they also believed that the Crown had a responsibility to protect Haudenosaunee territory, regardless of who was violating the agreements. Many also felt that the conflict was between "a father and child" and it was not their place to interfere. Others remarked on their esteem for both the British and the colonists and wished not to take sides between two peoples for whom they cared.

At the onset of war, the individual nations attempted to remain neutral. Very quickly, however, many of the Mohawk warriors were enticed to support the British. Shortly after that, several Oneidas (along with some Tuscaroras) joined colonial forces. The Onondagas, Cayugas, and Senecas maintained neutrality until 1779, when the Americans marched into their territories on a rampage ordered by General George Washington. Troops with the Clinton–Sullivan Campaign tore through the western Haudenosaunee villages, destroying all of the major towns with a massive military action.[45] The Haudenosaunee of these villages fled to Fort Niagara, where they took refuge with the British. Facing similar attacks, many of the Mohawk people had fled their homelands, making their way to British protection at Fort Niagara or Lachine. Many Oneidas who did not support the Americans also made their way to Niagara. As might be expected, many of the once-neutral Onondagas, Cayugas, and Senecas joined British forces against the Americans following the Clinton–Sullivan Campaign.

Both before and during the war, British military leaders promised the Haudenosaunee that, in the event of a British surrender (which they never believed would happen), the Crown would compensate any territorial losses (including homes, crops, and land) experienced by their allies. In 1779, General Haldimand (commander-in-chief of British forces in Quebec) echoed an earlier promise made by Carleton:

> Some of the Mohawks of the Villages of Conajoharie, Tujondarago, and Aughwago, whose settlements there, had been upon account of their steady attachment to the King's Service and the Interests of Government Ruined by the Rebels; having informed me, that my Predecessor Sir Guy Carleton, was pleased to promise, as soon as the present Troubles were at an end, the same should be restored at the Expence of Government, and the said Promise appearing to me Just, I do hereby ratify the same, and assure them the said Promise, as far as in me lies, shall be faithfully executed, as soon as that happy Time come.[46]

These promises, along with the refuge provided at Niagara and Lachine, were not products of recent negotiations between the Haudenosaunee and the British but came as the result of the Covenant Chain relationship. The first British–Haudenosaunee treaty, established in 1664, provided that the British would shelter the Five Nations if they were to lose their war against the "River Indians." The 1701 Nanfan Treaty carried similar provisions as the Haudenosaunee placed their hunting grounds under the protection of the King. These promises were echoed in subsequent treaty agreements, demonstrating the continuity of the relationship between the two allies, whereby the Crown guaranteed

the protection of Haudenosaunee interests and, in the event of a war loss, promised to provide adequate financial and territorial compensation for any losses.

However, in 1783, when the British negotiated the Paris Peace Treaty with the Thirteen Colonies, they failed to include provisions for their Haudenosaunee allies in the treaty. In order to make amends for the oversight, General Haldimand set about finding a territory suitable to compensate the Haudenosaunee land losses in the war. Eventually the Haudenosaunee at Fort Niagara selected the lands along the banks of the Grand River as their new homeland; their selection was formalized under an agreement with Haldimand in October 1784.

Ironically, the Americans were even less successful in addressing the needs of their Oneida and Tuscarora war allies than the British had been. Under a series of treaties (several of which were later deemed to be fraudulent) that followed the war, the American colonists eventually claimed practically all Oneida lands in what became New York State. The majority of the Oneida people left their homelands, settling in a number of different places: Onondaga, Grand River (with relatives who had supported the British during the war), Thames River (on land they purchased from their treaty funds), and Wisconsin (territory offered to them in exchange for some of their original lands). Today, their recognized reservation land in New York State consists of just 32 acres.[47] The Tuscarora fared better, as the Senecas offered them land along the Niagara Escarpment not far from Fort Niagara. Many of the Tuscaroras, like their previous host Oneidas, also chose to settle along the Grand River.

Beyond the different territorial impacts felt by the individual nations of the Confederacy, the Haudenosaunee remain affected to this day by the choices of some to enter the war. In the end, those who supported the British and the Americans drew all of their people into the conflict despite the desires of many to remain neutral. Both the British and the Americans failed to adequately provide for their allies after the war was over. The end result was an extremely limited territory within the original Haudenosaunee homelands, a resettlement of many Haudenosaunee into the western and northern hunting grounds, and internal strife that greatly weakened the familial bonds created by the Great Law. In many ways, the Confederacy has spent the last two centuries attempting to rectify the internal problems caused by the decisions to participate in the American Revolutionary War.

The Haudenosaunee–British treaties of this period stand in a continuum under the umbrella of the Covenant Chain and treaties preceding it. British promises of refuge and protection in the event of war losses were made repeatedly but were never necessary until the British defeat in the American Revolutionary War. Under their treaties and other agreements, the British had promised to protect Haudenosaunee interests in their hunting grounds along the Grand River—territory that had been placed under the King's protection eight decades earlier in the Nanfan Treaty. This land was selected by many of the Haudenosaunee to become their new homeland. On 21 May 1783, Joseph Brant, as speaker for the Six Nations, addressed General Haldimand at Quebec in regard to the Crown's responsibilities to the Haudenosaunee:

> Brother,
> We, the Mohawks, were the first Indian Nation that took you by the hand like friends and brothers, and invited you to live amongst us, treating you with kindness upon your debarkation in small parties. The Oneidas, our neighbours, were equally well disposed towards you we fastened your ship to a great mountain at Onondaga, the Center of our Confederacy, the rest of the Five Nations approving of it. We were then a great people, conquering all Indian nations round about us, and you in a manner but a handfull, after which you increased by degrees and we continued your friends and allies, joining you from time to time against your enemies, sacrificing numbers of our people and leaving their bones scattered in your enemies country. At last we assisted you in conquering all Canada, and then again, for joining you so firmly and faithfully, you renewed your assurances of protecting and defending ourselves, lands and possessions against any encroachment whatsoever, procuring for us the enjoyment of fair and plentiful trade of your people, and sat contented under the shade of the Tree of Peace, tasting the favour and friendship of a great Nation bound to us by Treaty, and able to protect us against all the world.[48]

In traditional Haudenosaunee fashion, Brant endeavoured to remind the British of the provisions of the Covenant Chain and demonstrated how the Six Nations had maintained their end of the relationship. Brant was also putting the Crown on notice as to their obligation to compensate the Haudenosaunee for their wartime losses. For many of the Haudenosaunee, that compensation meant land, as much of their territory had been lost, first, to settlers who violated the Fort Stanwix Treaty and earlier treaties and, second, to the Americans when the British signed it over to the United States through the Treaty of Paris.

With their understanding of land as life, the Haudenosaunee were making clear the obligation of the British to secure them in a new homeland where they could once again live alongside the British as stipulated in the Kaswentha and the Covenant Chain. While this new homeland could not replace their old villages, fields, and surrounding forests—the lands that held the bones of their ancestors—they looked with hope toward moving to the hunting grounds and rebuilding their villages there. They knew that their new village sites would continue to provide for them as had the land of their original homes. After all, they had not been failed by creation, they had been failed by their relationships with other peoples. The hope was that the new homeland—carved out of their hunting grounds—and their rights to it would prove to be more respected by the British than their original homelands had been.

NOTES

1. Many of these "circles of influence" persist today, but there are shifts caused by the segmenting of our territories through treaties and other losses of land.

2. The term "contact" is usually seen as an event, but in reality it is a process. The Canadian courts fail to understand that and place emphasis on a moment rather than on relationships.

3. The oral record notes that visitors with peaceful intentions often approached the village singing songs of peace (like those of the Great Law).

4. O'seronni ("they make axes") is a common Mohawk term referring to all people of European extraction. In Cayuga, they are referred to as Hotinyo'oh.

5. Reportedly, Algonquin, Huron, and Montagnais warriors accompanied Champlain on this expedition.

6. Matthew Dennis, *Cultivating a Landscape of Peace: Iroquois–European Encounters in Seventeenth-Century America* (Ithaca, NY: Cornell University Press, 1993), 72 (he notes "2 chiefs" were killed); Francis Jennings, ed., *The History and Culture of Iroquois Diplomacy: An Interdisciplinary Guide to the Treaties of the Six Nations and Their League* (Syracuse, NY: Syracuse University Press, 1985), 233.

7. Tuscarora historian Richard W. Hill, Sr, has noted, "Previously, they had met in an open field, and hand to hand combat determined the victor. When a force was overcome, the fighting stops and the weaker forces were made prisoners. With the introduction of guns, open field fighting made no sense, so the Iroquois turned to guerrilla style warfare, with surprise attacks, swift hit-and-runs" (Richard Hill, "The Cultural History of Iroquois Sovereignty" [unpublished manuscript, 1999]).

8. *Mitchell v. Canada (Minister of National Revenue)*, [1999] 1 C.N.L.R. 112. Paul Williams, an attorney for Mike Mitchell, has called this the "bullet to the head school of first contact." Personal communication.

9. As noted, most of these lands were already accessed by the Haudenosaunee in shared hunting relationships, but when many of their neighbours became Haudenosaunee their prior competition for furs ceased to exist. For further discussion, see Francis Jennings, *The Ambiguous Iroquois Empire* (New York: Norton, 1984).

10. For a detailed discussion of this, see Paul Williams, "The Chain" (LLM thesis, University of Toronto, 1982).

11. There were periods when the relationship weakened and the meetings did not happen.

12. This follows Haudenosaunee protocols. For example, when a new Royaner is to be condoled, the process begins with a recollection of the beginning of the Confederacy (the Peacemaker's journey). The idea of "refreshing" one's memory of the past is seen to be critical before one can make decisions for the future with a good mind.

13. Onontio—"nice/good hill"—is the Haudenosaunee title given to the French governor. It has been erroneously translated as "big mountain," which would be "Onontawenen."

14. As cited in Hill, "Cultural History."

15. Jennings, *Iroquois Diplomacy*, 163.

16. The historic record often refers to this nation as the "Ottawas," but I use the contemporary spelling, which is a better match for the name these people are known by in their own language.

17. Jennings, *Iroquois Diplomacy*, 164–65.

18. Paul Kayanasenh Williams and Curtis Arihote Nelson, "Kaswentha," January 1995, Research report prepared for the Royal Commission on Aboriginal Peoples, in *For Seven Generations: An Information Legacy of the RCAP* (Libraxus, 1997), unpaginated.

19. In fact, Seneca historian John Mohawk asserts that Haudenosaunee traditional philosophy is an example of progressive pragmatism. He explains this in a discussion of the Great Law: "'Now we put our minds together to see what kind of world we can create for the seventh generation yet unborn.' . . . [It lays] out the

idea that we are now going to put our minds together to create some kind of desirable outcome. And pragmatism is entirely about outcome. To begin with, you lay out the outcome and then you step back and negotiate the steps to go from here to the outcome that you want." John Mohawk, "What Can We Learn from Native America about War and Peace?: The Progressive Pragmatism of the Iroquois Confederacy," *Lapis Magazine Online*, http://www.lapismagazine.org/what-can-we-learn-from-native-americaabout-war-and-peace-by-john-mohawk.

20. While British subjects, the ethnic background of these colonists varied from Dutch to English to German to Scottish.

21. Deborah Doxtator, "What Happened to the Iroquois Clans? A Study of Clans in Three Nineteenth Century Rotinonhsyonni Communities" (PhD diss., University of Western Ontario, 1996), 116.

22. Julian Boyd, ed., *Indian Treaties Printed by Benjamin Franklin, 1736–1762* (Philadelphia: Historical Society of Pennsylvania, 1938), 78; as cited in Ronald Wright, *Stolen Continents* (Toronto: Penguin Books, 1992), 128.

23. This section refers to the Mohawks of the Mohawk Valley. I have not attempted to address the village patterns of the northern Mohawk communities at this time.

24. The Tuscarora language belongs to the Southern Iroquoian linguistic family.

25. As cited in Hill, "Cultural History."

26. Not all of the Tuscaroras fled north at the end of the war. Many attempted to stay in their southern homelands. In the decades that followed, those who had moved north returned home to entice their relatives to migrate back with them to Haudenosaunee territory.

27. Hill, "Cultural History." While the Tuscarora are seen as the sixth nation, they do not have their own representation in the Grand Council. Originally their interests were voiced by the Oneidas as their host nation. Today, their chiefs sit with the Royaner of the Younger Brother nations, but officially their issues are raised by the Tonawanda Seneca Royaner.

28. Officially the Tutelo Nation no longer exists, but many Grand River families (especially within the Cayuga Nation) continue to identify as Tutelo descendants and maintain some of their major ceremonies.

29. For a description of Seneca villages of this period see Kurt A. Jordan, "Seneca Iroquois Settlement Pattern, Community Structure, and Housing, 1677–1779," *Northeast Anthropology* 67 (2004): 23–60.

30. Tooker, "Iroquois since 1820," in *The Handbook of North American Indians: Vol. 15: Northeast*, ed. Bruce G. Trigger (Washington: Smithsonian Institution, 1978), 449–65; and Anthony F.C. Wallace, *The Death and Rebirth of the Seneca* (New York: Random House, 1972 [1969]), 194, note that the Clinton–Sullivan Campaign of 1779 destroyed all of the longhouses in the Onondaga, Cayuga, and Seneca villages.

31. Cited in Doxtator, "Iroquois Clans," 55.

32. Emphasis added. *The Papers of Sir William Johnson* [SWJP], II (Albany: University of the State of New York, 1965): 234.

33. E.B. O'Callahan, *Documents Relative to the Colonial History of the State of New York* [hereafter referred to as NYCD], XXXIII: 18, as cited in Williams and Nelson, "Kaswentha."

34. Williams and Nelson, "Kaswentha."

35. As cited in Williams and Nelson, "Kaswentha."

36. Library and Archives Canada [LAC], RG 10, Vol. 1825, 61.

37. Williams and Nelson, "Kaswentha."

38. SWJP, XI.

39. For example, see *Seneca Nation v. State of New York*, United States Court of Appeals for the Second District, decided 9 September 2004, http://caselaw.findlaw.com/us-2nd-circuit/1033184.html. On 5 June 2006 the United States Supreme Court refused without comment to hear the appeal.

40. SWJP, XII: 617–31; also in NYCD, VIII: 113–34.

41. SWJP, XII: 617–31.

42. Hill, "Cultural History."

43. The discussion of the American Revolution here is only an overview, with an emphasis on Haudenosaunee territorial impacts only. For a detailed discussion of Haudenosaunee participation in the war, see Barbara Graymount, *The Iroquois in the American Revolution* (Syracuse: Syracuse University Press, 1972).

44. The specific colonies involved were Massachusetts, New York, and Pennsylvania; however, "colonists" from many different British colonies crossed the Fort Stanwix line and homesteaded in Haudenosaunee Territory.

45. This is sometimes also referred to as the "Sullivan Campaign" or the "Sullivan–Clinton

Expedition." For a discussion of the impact of the campaign, see Wallace, *Death and Rebirth of the Seneca*, 141–44; Tooker, "Iroquois," 449–65; Doxtator, "Iroquois Clans," 124; and Barbara Graymont, *Iroquois*, 192–222.

46. LAC, RG 19, F1, Vol. 2, 89–90.

47. In the 1990s, the Oneidas of New York purchased lands within their land claim area of their traditional homeland territory. Some of that land was transferred into "trust status" by the U.S. Bureau of Indian Affairs, but the recent *Sherrill v. Oneida* decision in U.S. Federal Appeals Court calls into question the legality of other lands owned by the Oneida Nation of New York—primarily the land where the Turning Stone Casino is built—as being eligible for reservation status. *City of Sherrill v. Oneida Indian Nation of New York*, 544 U.S. 197 (2005).

48. PRO, CO 42, Vol. 44, 133–35.

---

4 From Jean-François Lozier, "Red Ochre, Vermilion, and the Transatlantic Cosmetic Encounter," in *The Materiality of Color: The Production, Circulation, and Application of Dyes and Pigments, 1400–1800*, eds Andrea Feeser, Maureen Daly Goddin, and Beth Fowkes Tobin (Farnham: Ashgate, 2012), 119–38. Reproduced with permission of Taylor & Francis Books UK.

The Europeans who approached North America from the final decade of the fifteenth century onwards could not help but notice that the inhabitants of this New World were scantily clad but abundantly decorated. The Taino encountered in the Caribbean islands by Columbus and his companions used pottery stamps coated with red, white, and black pigments to paint their bodies with lavish designs.[1] The Spanish explorers who in the decades that followed ranged into the North American southeast came across peoples with "their bodies, legs, and arms painted and ochred, red, black, white, yellow and vermilion in stripes" or, more commonly, "painted with a kind of red ointment."[2] The whalers and cod fisherman who began to visit the shores of Newfoundland too caught glimpses of men, women, and children whose bodies were painted red.[3] These, decidedly, were painted peoples.

Though the claim that it was due to early encounters with red-painted people that all Native Americans became "red-skinned" in Western eyes has been disproved in recent years, there is no doubting that body paint was of considerable socio-cultural importance among the inhabitants of the New World.[4] The same might be said, for that matter, of the inhabitants of the Old. Artificially whitened faces and reddened checks and lips were a common sight throughout early modern Europe. Leaving aside the related topics of tattooing and scarification, this article investigates the roots and ramifications of the meeting of Aboriginal and European skin-painting cultures—what might be termed the transatlantic cosmetic encounter—between the early sixteenth and late eighteenth centuries. In Europe this period was marked by the rise of face painting and of new pigments, which were accompanied by a heated polemic regarding the propriety of the painted face. On North America soil, painted faces also become a site of anxiety and innovation, with missionaries making tentative challenges to longstanding Indigenous practices and Indigenous practices making room for new transatlantic commodities. From locally sourced ochre, the following pages thus lead us to imported vermilion.

In Aboriginal North America, the search for good colours was assiduously pursued. To paint themselves, explained one commentator, the original inhabitants prepared colours "with several sort of Herbs, Minerals, and Earths, that they get in different parts of the Country where they Hunt and Travel."[5]

The red pigments that dominated the palette might be extracted from a number of vegetal and mineral sources. In the east, bloodroot (*Sanguinaria canadensis*, also known as blood-wort of puccoon root) found widespread medicinal and decorative use. John Smith reported that the Powhatans of Virginia made great use of this root which they called *pocones* and "which being dried and beate in powder turneth red." It reduced swellings and aches, or, mixed with oil, was used to paint faces and garments.[6] Ochre was preferred, however, for the brightness of its hues and by its excellent colour fastness.

Ochre—the term can refer to a variety of red or reddish pigments processed from iron ores, mainly namely hematite and limonite—is associated with human activity in the archaeological record as early as the time of *Homo erectus*, approximately 300 000 BCE. The persistence of practices and regularity in patterns in the use of ochre in prehistoric and contemporary non-literate societies are such that one anthropologist describes it as being "like a red thread" woven through human history.[7] Red ochre has been found with regularity at the sites of the earliest human occupation throughout the US, much of Canada, and northern Mexico. Paleoindian habitation areas often reveal traces of ochre, while ochred human skeletal remains and associated red-stained artifacts are a common feature of that lithic period's burials and caches. So abundant was the use of powdered red ochre in the mortuary traditions of some regions that archaeologists speak of a "Red Paint People" on the north Atlantic coast (since renamed the "Moorehead Burial Tradition," circa 3000 BCE), and a "Red Ochre Culture" around the Great Lakes (circa 1000–500 BCE).[8] That ochre was used during this period to adorn the living, and not only the dead, can be inferred with confidence.

This prehistoric predilection for red ochre has been attributed by some to the substance's function as an external and internal healing agent: The iron salts found in ochre are effective antiseptics, have an astringent effect, and tend to arrest hemorrhaging.[9] More significantly perhaps, this predilection has been linked to a partiality, inferred from the prehistoric archaeological record and solidly documented by modern ethnography, for the colour red. Observing that all languages contain terms for black and white (or "light" and "dark") and that if a language distinguished a third colour it is necessarily "red," according to which the terms to describe these colours were the first to emerge in human languages everywhere. The other basic colour terms, yellow, blue, and green, appeared only at later stages, followed by terms for brown, orange, pink, purple, or grey.[10]

Victor Turner and others since have argued that the primacy of black, white, and red as basic colours follows from their cognitive relationship with body emissions—semen, milk, water, feces, blood—and with the associated physical experiences and heightened emotional states.[11] Linguistic evidence leaves no doubt of the connection between blood and the colour red among the Indigenous cultures of North America. In Proto-Algic, the reconstructed proto-language which would have been spoken from Atlantic Canada to the Rocky Mountains several thousand years ago and from which subsequent Algonquian languages derived, the word for red derives from a verbal root meaning "bleed" or noun meaning "blood." The connection persists in many modern languages: In Algonquin, *miskwi* means blood, and *misko* means red; in Mohawk, *onekwensa* means blood, while *onekwentara* means red.[12] Through its relationship with blood, the colour red is linked with physical and physiological excitement. It was closely connected with the rituals and symbol of life and death, of reproduction and violence, with festivities and joy. What one writer remarked of the inhabitants of the western Great Lakes in the 1860s—"Red is not only their joy, but also their favorite colour"—could have been said just about anywhere on the continent.[13]

* * *

Deposits of ochre—hematite, mainly—are abundant throughout North America. Bodies of water whose banks were known to be rich in ochre were often named accordingly: In the Algonquian-speaking northeast, names such as Aramoni, Olamon, Onaman, Oulaman, Osanaman, etc. dotted the landscape. European explorers and settlers in turn translated these diverse names into "Vermillon" Lake or River (in French, or Anglicized to Vermilion), or "Paint" River or Creek.[14] Depending on circumstances and cultural context, the ethnographic record suggests that specific sites of extraction might be kept secret from outsiders or shared with them. In recent years an otherwise friendly and co-operative Yuma informant explained to Paul Campbell that "no one divulges their source for red ochre." Meanwhile, Naskapi tradition held that all comers, regardless of their band affiliation, could take as much ochre as they needed for their personal use from the deposits near Lake Chibougamau, Quebec, without asking for permission from the band on whose hunting territory the resource was located or providing payment to them. The only constraint was that its sale was strictly forbidden.[15]

Restrictions on the sale of ochre or the divulgation of its source point to the highly sacred nature of this resource, which like most natural resources was thought to be controlled by supernatural beings. The extraction of ochre, accordingly, was generally accompanied by rituals and offerings aimed at honouring and appeasing these spirits. Several thousand years ago the Paleoindians who exploited the ochre deposits at the Powars II Site in Wyoming left behind successfully used stone projectile points and bifaces as an offering. In more recent times the Gwich'in or Loucheux of the Northwestern Territories, Yukon, and Alaska, were known to leave pieces of sinew when they extracted ochre from the earth. The Piegan Blackfeet of Montana would for their part "pray and sing and go through their religious activities."[16]

It is also possible that the processing of ochre had a ritual dimension. The technical components of this processing depended largely on the nature of the deposit. While ochre-bearing clays extracted from riverbanks required only minimal processing, stone-like chunks of ochre taken from the earth could be easily processed by scraping or crushing. Certain varieties of ochre may have been heat-altered, to facilitate their pulverization or to enhance their hues. Grease, water, sap, or spit was used as a binding agent before ochre was painted on the body, with more or less ceremony depending on the circumstances. The body-painting pottery stamps of the Taino had few if any parallels in North America, where paint was applied with hands, fingers, sticks, and rudimentary brushes. Fingers and sticks might then be used to scrape or remove paint to embellish designs with negative spaces.[17]

As might be expected, the practices and meaning associated with face and body painting varied form one Aboriginal culture to another continent. For those peoples who usually went about naked or almost naked, full-body painting had the practical advantages of keeping away mosquitoes and gnats, and in northern climes to serve "in winter as a mask against the cold and the ice."[18] Additional layers of meaning, related to concerns with beauty, spirituality, and self-identification, were common. Among the Beothuks of Newfoundland, the ochring of every member of the band—conducted at a site that still bears the name Red Indian Lake—called for a ceremony, and the application of the first coat in infancy was regarded as a sign of initiation.[19]

While in some groups it was common for both women and men to paint themselves, the European newcomers discovered with some amusement that in the Eastern Woodlands it was to the men that paint tended to afford the greatest opportunities for self-expression. Women painted themselves sparingly in comparison, though it was customary for them too to paint their faces black to display grief in times of mourning. To European eyes, the garish designs adopted by men during celebrations, councils, and on the war path seemed to follow personal fancy. In attempting to describe the face paintings of the Iroquois one Jesuit drew on the vocabulary of facial features most familiar to him and to his European readers: some "appear artistically bearded," while others "seem to wear spectacles."[20]

When questioned about the meaning of such garish designs, warriors admitted to the quizzical foreigners that "not being master of their nature, their enemies could perceive on their face some air of pallor and of fear." Face paint concealed these signs of weakness, as well as "extremes of youth or age, which might inspire strength and courage in the adversary." Conversely, warriors found that paint "adds to their Courage and strikes a terror in their Enemies."[21] Though settlers were wont to believe that paint acted as a "disguise" which also concealed the identity of treacherous warriors, one Jesuit's statement that each warrior had "in this matter his own style of livery, so to speak, which he retains through life," suggests that the intent was quite the contrary.[22] While some warriors may indeed have sought to gain an advantage from the fact that paint covered up their identity, others used paint to proudly proclaim it.

Such personal "liveries" may very well have been inspired by visionary experiences. Though the spiritual significance of face and body painting tended to elude the European newcomers to the Eastern Woodlands and in the southwest during the early modern period, ethnographical information collected in the Plains in the late nineteenth and early twentieth centuries make it clear that colour and design preferences were generally inspired by visions and dreams in which supernatural entities imparted powers that protected the wearer from harm. Thus the Hidatsa chief Black Shield might "wet some gunpowder and paint his face" before going into battle, applying "white paint on his lips and eyes just as he has seen these things in his dream."[23] [. . .]

* * *

Although the European newcomers to North America found Indigenous manipulation of skin colour repulsive, or at the very least strange and unsettling, the practice was not entirely foreign to them. To those among them who had benefitted from a humanistic education, the classical authors offered a natural point of reference. After describing the painted breasts and arms of the Chiriguaná women of what is today Columbia, the sixteenth-century Spanish historian Gonzalo Fernández de Oviedo y Valdés had asked: "How can we blame them, when we look at other nations of the world who are now prosperous and live in a Christian republic, like the English of whom Julius Caesar writes?"[24]

The Jesuit Joseph-François Lafitau, who, after living among the Iroquois of what is now Canada between 1712 and 1717, penned *Moeures des Sauvages américains comparées aux moeurs des premiers temps* (1724) in an effort to provide reciprocal illumination of the customs of the inhabitants of the New World with those of the Old, found the adornment of the body with tattoos and paint to be a fecund point of comparison. On the subject of peoples who reddened their entire bodies, Lafitau was expansive. "As a rule," he writes, "the ancient writers tell us this about the [East] Indians, the Africans, the Picts, the Geloni, the Agathyrses and a number of other peoples," including the Ethiopians, about whom Pliny "assures us that they coloured themselves with vermilion from head to foot." Deducing that these people were doubtless the same who when about naked, Lafitau goes on to point out that even the Romans painted the statues of their gods during feasts in red, "because this colour better simulates that of fire," and that they did the same to the bodies of their victorious generals during their triumphal processions. Other societies, meanwhile, such as the Persians, had applied paint around the eyes. Noting that the inhabitants of North America had the habit of applying vermilion to their hair, Lafitau pointed out that "all the barbarian peoples of antiquity took pleasure in greasing it well and adorning it with artificial colours."[25]

Antiquity was not alone in offering points of comparison, for Europe itself has experienced a revival of face paint during the Age of Discovery. By most accounts, the cosmetic arts had been pushed out of fashion throughout most of the continent during the medieval period. While the Church followed the lead of Saint Augustine who, citing as precedent Saints Cyprian and Ambrose, exhorted against "women who colour, or discolour, their features with paint," the breakdown of trade routes restricted access to the cosmetic staples common in antiquity.[26] The Crusades and escalating activity of Italian merchants, who brought various perfumes, unguents, and recipes associate with beautification from the East, triggered a revitalization of cosmetic practices beginning in the thirteenth century.[27] [. . .]

Italy, unsurprisingly perhaps, emerged as the centre of the face-painting renaissance. Already in the early thirteenth century, the poet and jurist Cino da Pistoja could place in the mouth of an attentive mother the following admonition: "Never leave home without face paint, little girl."[28] If a tad of irony was implied, it nevertheless was an accurate reflection of what was becoming a prevailing fashion. [. . .] Caterina de'Medici was credited with bringing the practice of wearing white and red *fards* to France when she travelled there to become queen in 1533. In England, the preparation and use of what were called *fucus* increased dramatically during the second half of the century, as a result of the increased trade with the continent and of the example set by Queen Elizabeth who used them openly and increasingly with age. The *Siglo de Oro* also saw face paint become fashionable in Spain.[29]

By the early seventeenth century, the painted woman and the professional beautician had become familiar figures and—as with "Doctor Plaster-Face" in John Marston's play *The Malcontent*—stock characters on the stage.[30] Fashionable gentlemen were also wont to experiment with face paint.[31] The cosmetic convention was for women to whiten the skin of their faces and, as sartorial fashions evolved, shoulders and bosoms with variety of preparations centered on flour, alum, alabaster, talcum, etc. Because of their bright hues, because they clung well to the skin and because they did not require a heavy application, artists' pigments found new uses. White lead (lead carbonate or lead oxide), widely referred to as *ceruse*, generally came to be preferred to other whiteners.[32] [. . .]

* * *

Though women from all rungs of society indulged in white and red face paint to brighten their complexion, it emerged as a sign of aristocratic identity and a hallmark of the court culture which thrived in France and emanated from there throughout Europe. Given the theatrical way in which paint was worn at court, with white applied in a thick layer across the face so as to erase all signs of aging and disease, and red generously daubed on the lips and cheeks, there could be no question of its being intended to pass off as natural. Rather, paint was a power statement, a demonstration of the aristocratic elite's ability to force the boundaries of fashion beyond the norms of nature. To be sure, the face-painting excesses in vogue among the entourage of Louis XIV and Louis XV were widely exotic by comparison to those of the British court. In the mid-eighteenth century Horace Walpole was able to spot an Englishwoman at the Paris opera by the fact that she wore "no rouge."[33]

To wear or not to wear face paint was a question about which women across Europe had struggled for centuries. Italian, Spanish, French, and English men of letters, meanwhile, had expended profuse quantities of ink on the matter. Picking up the old patristic arguments which held that the use of cosmetics deformed God's work and contributed to shifting the emphasis away from the soul to the body, and fusing them with new

humanist concerns about the relationship between nature, truth, artifice, and falsehood,
these late medieval and early modern authors
opposed an almost universally negative response to the cosmetic revival.

In England a puritanical current of reform, coupled with the death of that patron
of face paint, Queen Elizabeth, and the perceived cosmetic excesses of the Jacobean
period, unleashed a veritable flood of misogynistic polemics and satire, much of which
took aim at cosmetic practices. John Donne
and Richard Brathwait criticized the woman
who took "the pencill out of God's hand" to
hold it in her own "impudent hand." Thomas
Tuke devoted an entire tract to the subject,
entitled *Treatise against Painting and Tincturing
of Men and Women* (1616).[34] Face painting was
perceived to be a peculiarly feminine vice.
Though men who indulged in face painting
might be decried as effeminate fops—the en-
amored Benedick in *Much Ado About Nothing*,
for example, is teased for washing, shaving,
and painting his face—it was women who
bore the brunt of the criticism.[35] [. . .]

Such misogynistic flights, which be-
trayed considerable anxiety with respect to
women's lack of readability, appear to have
been particularly virulent in England. Among
their avalanche of complaints the English
critics pointed to the fact that most cosmetics substances were imported and thus costly,
but also foreign and corrupting.[36] Nonetheless, the critique of face painting was a theme
which crossed national and linguistic boundaries. In Spain as well as in France, that
bastion of face painting, men of letters disparaged and mocked the use of cosmetics.[37] Beyond that theological and moral arguments,
critics everywhere pointed to the paradoxes
of these substances which, though meant to
enhance beauty, in fact damaged it. The cor-
rosive effects of many ingredients used in face
paint were already known in the fourteenth
and fifteenth centuries, when the authors of
some of the earliest treatises on beautification
warned their readers against the deleterious
effects of the very cosmetic recipes which

they supplied. Still, though, it was widely
known that substance such as white lead and
vermilion (a compound of mercury, it will be
remembered) were damaging to beauty and
health, they continued to find wide use until
the second half of the eighteenth century.[38]

* * *

Even if the meanings and practices of face
and body painting in the New World mapped
only imperfectly onto those of face painting in
the Old, colonial commentators naturally recognized parallels between the two. William
Strachey thus remarked how the inhabitants
of Virginia "annoynt" their bodies with colored dyes, "as doe out great Ladies their oyle
of Talchum, or other Paynting white and
redd." On one point of comparison, at least,
Strachey found that the analysis favoured the
locals. The Virginian woman was not as se-
cretive with her cosmetic recipes as her English counterpart: she "preserves yt not yet so
secret, and pretious unto her self, as doe out
great Ladies . . . but they friendly communicate the secret, and teach yt one another."[39]
More often than not, though, the newcomers
tended to view Indigenous decorative habits
as the result and proof of a collective deficiency in character. Like European women,
Aboriginal men seemed overly preoccupied
with their appearance. "The young people,
absorbed in their vanity and desire to please,
have recourse to art to embellish themselves,"
wrote Lafitau of the Iroquois. "[T]hey put in-
finite time on it and it occupies them as much
as it does European ladies and much more
than it does their own [women] who appear
persuaded that charity, decorum and their
domestic work require more modesty and
simplicity."[40]

To the missionaries who wished to convert and civilize the "barbarous" inhabitants
of the New World, face painting represented
more or less of an obstacle to overcome. Roger
Williams, the Protestant theologian and
founder of the colony of Rhode Island, held
opinions in line with those of the English

polemicists of his time. It was with some regret indeed that he conceded that it was the "foolish Custome of all barbarous Nations to paint and figure their Faces and Bodies (as it hath been to out shame and griefe, wee may remember it of some of our Fore-Fathers in this [English] Nation)." In his *Key into the Language of America* (1643), Williams provided phrases by which his readers might attempt to dissuade the Narragansetts from painting themselves: "Cummachiteoûwunash kuskeé-suchquash," meaning "You spoil your face"; and "Mat pitch cowahick Manit keesiteonckqus," meaning "The God that made you will not know you."[41] [. . .]

The Jesuit missionaries operating in the Saint Lawrence valley during the same period also attempted to rebuke their Montagnais, Algonquin, and Huron neophytes for the "mischievous custom" of face and body painting.[42] When he built and decorated a chapel in the mission-village of Lorette, near Quebec, patterned after the Santa Casa of Loreto in Italy, Father Pierre-Joseph-Marie Chaumonot was careful that the statue of Saint Mary be painted in flesh tones rather than in the dark tones that characterize the original in Loreto. "We did this for fear lest, if we exposed for the veneration of our Savages an image entirely black," explained Chaumonot, "we might cause them to resume the custom which we have made them abandon, of blackening and staining their faces."[43] In the decades that followed, however, the Jesuits of New France relaxed their attitudes toward face and body painting. Acknowledging the impossibility of effecting a wholesale transformation of Indigenous society, the missionaries came to believe that these customs, like other forms of adornment and dress, language, and music, were innocuous and compatible with the fundamentals of the Catholic faith. [. . .]

The Franciscan missionaries toiling in New Mexico similarly exhibited a great deal of tolerance of painting, even as they fought against idolatry and attempted to reform habits of nakedness. In 1714, the colony's Governor Juan Ignacio Flores Mogollón conducted an investigation into whether or not the Pueblos should be allowed to continue to paint themselves in a traditional manner. The friars to whom he turned for advice explained that the people of the Pueblos described the painted body as being akin to a "beautiful suit," and that "body paint is their fancy dress." Fray Salvador Lopez reminded the governor that the use of paint by their wards was little different from Spanish women's practice of painting their own faces with white shell powder. Because the Spanish used powder, colour, ribbons, and feathers "among themselves to adorn their bodies" and because this was not judged sinful, he reasoned that they could not prohibit the Pueblos from doing the same. "I have seen the painting and the plumes many times," declared Fray Antonio Miranda of the Pueblos, "and they have told me because among the Spanish it is not a bad thing to put on the hats, feathers and ribbons [that] . . . they don't use these things for bad things either."[44]

Anxieties about painted neighbours were not merely theological. Governor Flores's investigation had been prompted by the concern that Spaniards could not tell the friendly Pueblos apart from the other, "heathen" and hostile, inhabitants of the regions such as the Apaches. It was feared that the Pueblos, painted and dressed so as to be unrecognizable from the enemy, were free to mischievously steal livestock and murder settlers.[45] [. . .]

At the same time, colonists were only too happy to don the Aboriginal "disguise" when it suited their purpose. Taking to hearth the precept that "When in Rome . . . ," French and British officials and military men cultivated habits of self-presentation that allowed them to interact most fruitfully with their Aboriginal interlocutors. It was "dressed and painted after the manner of an Indian War Captain" that the trader and diplomat Sir William Johnson entered the city gates of Albany at August of 1746, at the head of a Mohawk delegation "likewise dressed and painted, as is usual when they set out in War."

A willingness to display a face painted according to Indigenous conventions on certain key occasions, much like a familiarity with their languages, was a means of demonstrating solidarity with trading partners and allied warriors, of acquiring and maintaining a measure of influence among them.[46]

In difference circumstances, putting on the painted disguises allowed colonists to register political protest under the cover of anonymity. "I immediately dressed myself in the costume of an Indian," recalled George Hewes of his involvement in the Boston Tea Party of 1773. "[A]fter having painted by face and hands with coal dust in the shop of a blacksmith," he fell in "with many who were dressed, equipped and painted as I was," before reaching Griffin's wharf. This thinly veiled impersonation of "Indians" (Mohawks to be more precise) fooled no one. But then again, these colonists were less concerned with passing off as something other than what they were than about registering their protest in flamboyant and symbolic style. Painted faces and hands embodied both an expression of longstanding colonial anxieties centred on Indigenous neighbours beyond the frontier and of more recent anxieties centred across the Atlantic, on Great Britain. The painted Indian, representing the antithesis of King George's tyranny, was a convenient symbol of the emerging American identity.[47]

* * *

The rise of the transatlantic fur-trading markets in the seventeenth and eighteenth centuries transformed cosmetics use among the Indigenous peoples of North America. Mirrors, by facilitating the precise application of paint to one's own face, may have entailed a true revolution in face-painting practices, allowing for the more careful self-application of paint.[48] The introduction of copper vessels may have made the collection of manufactured pigments such as verdigris, red lead, and, more importantly, vermilion. By all accounts, Aboriginal consumers exhibited a marked preference for vermilion over ochre. As Lafitau explained, the locally sourced pigments produced "a rather nice red, but that is not worth our vermilion."[49]

When and how, exactly, the transatlantic trade in pigments began must remain a matter of conjecture. Oral tradition among the French residents of Canada during the mid-eighteenth century had it that vermilion had been traded from the colony's earliest days. "Many persons have told me," reported the Swedish naturalist Pehr Kalm, in the mid-eighteenth century, "that they had heard their fathers mention, that the first Frenchmen who came over here got a great heap of furs from the Indians, for three times as much cinnabar [vermilion] as would lie on the top of a knife."[50] Though this suggests that vermilion had been traded since the first decade of the seventeenth century, it is not until the century's final decades that the earliest sure evidence of a transatlantic trade in red pigment emerges. In 1684, Cavelier de La Salle listed vermilion among the "small articles" which he was trading in the Great Lakes and asked for 50 pounds of it to be sent from France to "drive a profitable trade." By the turn of the century, the French chronicler Bacqueville de La Potherie stated that a "great commerce" in vermilion was conducted in Canada.[51] [. . .] Vermilion was abundantly traded and offered as diplomatic presents by French, British, and Spanish merchants in every frontier zone throughout the eighteenth century.

The rise of the transatlantic vermilion trade at the end of the seventeenth century may have something to do with technical advances. Since antiquity, vermilion had been derived from powdered cinnabar. "Vermilion mines" in Galicia continued to produce through the Middle Ages and early modern period.[52] A process for synthesizing vermilion from mercury and sulphur was recorded in Europe as early as the eighth century, plausibly after having been carried from China via Arabia. Form the twelfth century onwards, synthetic vermilion was used throughout Europe as an artist's pigment.[53] In the seventeenth century

Amsterdam emerged as the centre of production of vermilion using the "dry" process, which involved combining mercury with molten sulphur and heating it to the point of sublimation.[54] In 1687, a German named Gottfried Schultz invented a new "wet" process which entailed heating a mixture of mercury and sulphur in a warm, caustic solution of ammonium or potassium sulphide. This more efficient and cheaper process was adopted in Amsterdam, which retained its dominance as a centre of vermilion production until the early nineteenth century.[55] [. . .]

Red lead, on the other hand, was something that Britain produced increasingly as the seventeenth and eighteenth centuries wore on. One source from 1670 mentions the presence of red lead mills at the lead mine in Cariganshire, and four decades later others are mentioned in Glamorganshire.[56] Given the lower value of red lead compared to vermilion, it is no surprise that it found its way into the hands of Britain's allies and trading partners in North America. Governor Dongan's 1684 enumeration of "Indian Goods" included not only vermilion, but also red lead. In 1711, Governor Robert Hunter of New York presented to Schagticoke headmen "5lb Red lead and half a pound of Vermilion for Paint." [. . .] Though lists of trading goods sometimes allude to both vermilion and red lead, and though they occasionally allude to "vermilion mixed" of "paint," there is good reason to believe that the pigments described simply as "vermilion" in the records were not always pure mercuric sulphide.

For traders there were good profit margins to be made in "vermilion," which by volume and weight was one of the most expensive commodities of the North American fur-trading market. The nineteenth-century historian François-Xavier Garneau's claim that "as much as 800 franc have been obtained for a pound of vermilion!" was most probably an exaggeration.[57] A pound of vermilion which cost Antoine Crozat only 5 livres in France was sold at his store in Mobile for more than three times as much in

1715.[58] The Hudson Bay Company's standard of trade through most of the eighteenth century hovered around 1 to 1.5 ounces (28 to 42 grams) of vermilion per beaver skin. To put this in perspective, a list of the value of various goods traded by the Hudson's Bay Company in 1749 indicates that a beaver skin could buy a full pound (450 grams) of heads, gunpowder, shot, or thread.[59] [. . .]

* * *

The impact of the introduction of vermilion on Indigenous customs is exceedingly difficult to ascertain. Evidence of ochre use for a variety of ceremonial purposes, including face and body painting, through the nineteenth century and in a limited context to this day, is abundant in the ethnographic record. Vermilion, it is plain, did not entirely replace ochre. The high cost of the imported pigment, like the fact that some groups lived at a great distance from trading posts and maintained relatively little contact with outside traders, may explain why ochre continued to be used. In addition, it is tempting to think that notwithstanding the oft-stated Indigenous preference for the vibrant hues of vermilion, some individuals and communities continues to prefer ochre because they could control the ritual dimensions of its extraction and thus maintain a relationship with the supernatural forces that inhabited the landscape. Imported vermilion or red lead, because it was decontextualized from the environment, may in some ritual circumstances have seemed rather poor ersatz.

The high price of vermilion should not be measured only in economic terms, for the impact of mercury- and lead-based pigments on the health of their Aboriginal users gives cause for pause. From the earliest days of the cosmetics revival, the deleterious effects of these substances were a concern to specialists. By the second half of the eighteenth century, these effects were almost universally recognized in Europe. With respect to women's use of vermilion on their cheeks, Antoine

Le Camus' *Abedeker, ou l'Art de conserver la beauté* (1754) explains that it is "very dangerous; for by using it frequently they may lose their Teeth, acquire a stinking Breath, and excite a copious Salivation."[60] It was in no small part due to the intervention of medical professionals that the popularity of white and red face paint underwent a sharp decline in favour of a more naturalistic aesthetic. Still, in distribution and trade of vermilion in North America continued unabated. Perhaps the missionaries and officials who sought at various times to dissuade their Aboriginal wards and allied from painting themselves evoked this argument, but if that is the case it left no trace in the record. Only in 1902 do we find a Commissioner of Indian Affairs, William A. Jones, attributing "the majority of the cases of blindness among the Indians of the United States" to face painting in an attempt to bring about its end in the country's reservations.[61]

It was during the nineteenth and early twentieth centuries, rather than the seventeenth or sixteenth, that the most fundamental transformation of Aboriginal cosmetic culture occurred. On the one hand, the prized vermilion became more affordable and a wide variety of new pigments were introduced to the inventories of traders: Prussian blue, yellow lead chromate, green chromium oxide, ivory black or bone char, and zinc oxide of Chinese white.[62] On the other, new power dynamics undermined political and cultural autonomy as never before. In the years that followed the War of 1812, as the strategic importance of allied warriors waned, the British and American governments ceased to distribute presents of arms, ammunition, and other accessories of war among which vermilion had featured prominently until then. Warrior culture, for which imperial powers vying against one another had found uses in the seventeenth and eighteenth centuries, now represented a threat to the stability and progress of the American and British (later Canadian) nations in their westward expansion.

The nineteenth-century institution of reservations and increasingly rigid civilizing policies of the state allowed missionaries and government officials an unprecedented repressive power. The naturalistic shift taken by Western cosmetic culture left little room for the tolerance of Indigenous face- and body-painting customs, nor did the rising concern with hygiene. Missionaries now objected to these customs with reviewed vigour. Though vermilion continued to be traded well into the twentieth century to serve in various crafts, its use on the body was discouraged. Traders operating on many reservations were instructed not to sell pigments that could be used for face or body paint. At Metlakala in British Columbia, the factor was told that "No red paint or other articles of heathenism were to be offered for sale."[63] Painted peoples were now seen as belonging to the past.

NOTES

1. Julia Tavares, *Guide to Caribbean Prehistory* (Santo Domingo: Museo del Hombre Dominicano, 1978), 15–16; Lesley-Gail Atkinson, *The Earliest Inhabitants: The Dynamics of the Jamaican Taino* (Kingston, Jamaica: University of the West Indies Press, 2006), 148–9.

2. Edward Gaylord Bourne, ed., *Narratives of the Career of Hernando de Soto in the Conquest of Florida* (New York: Barnes, 1904), vol. 1, 108, 113; vol. 2, 56, 136.

3. Ingeborg Marshall, *A History of Ethnography of the Beothuk* (Montreal: McGill-Queen's University Press, 1998), 14–24.

4. James P. Howley seems to have been among the first to conclude, without supporting evidence, that the fifteenth-century explorers of Newfoundland called the locals "red," a claim that was repeated by the authoritative *Handbook of North American Indians*. See James P. Howley, *The Beothuks or Red Indians:*

The Original Inhabitants of Newfoundland (Cambridge: Cambridge University Press, 1915), 2–3, 10; and Barrie Reynolds, "Beothuk," in William C. Sturtevant and Bruce G. Trigger, eds, *Handbook of North America Indians* (Washington, DC: Smithsonian Institution, 1978–2008), vol. 15, 101, 107.

5. John Brickell, *The Natural History of North-Carolina* (Dublin: James Caron, 1737), 316. See also Joseph-François Lafitau, *Customs of the American Indians Compared with Customs of Primitive Times* (Toronto: Champlain Society, 1977), vol. 2, 32.

6. John Smith, *Generall Historie of Virginia, New England, & the Summer Isles* (Glasgow: James MacLehose and Sons, 1907), vol. 1, 55, 71, 76.

7. Ernst E. Wreschner, "Red Ochre and Human Evolution: A Case for Discussion," and Comments and Reply by Ralph Bolton, Karl W. Butzer, Henri Delporte, Alexander Häusler, Albert Heinrich, Anita Jacobson-Widding, Tadeusz Malinowski, Claude Masset, Sheryl F. Miller, Avraham Ronen, Ralph Solecki, Peter H. Stephenson, Lynn L. Thomas, Heinrich Zollinger, all in *Current Anthropology* 21, 5 (October 1980): 631–44; Erella Hovers et al., "An Early Case of Color Symbolism: Ochre Use by Modern Humans in Qafzeh Cave," *Current Anthropology* 44, 4 (August–October 2003): 491–522; Chris Knight, *Blood Relations, Menstruation and the Origin of Culture* (New Haven: Yale University Press, 1991), 435–49; Rebecca Morris, "A Shroud of Ochre: A Study of Pre-Contact Mortuary Ochre Use in North America" (unpublished Master's thesis, University of Leicester, 2007).

8. Michael D. Stafford et al., "Digging for the Color of Life: Paleoindian Red Ochre Mining at the Powars II Site, Platte County, Wyoming, U.S.A.," *Geoarchaeology* 18, 1 (2003): 71–90; D.C. Roper, "Plans Paleoindians Red Ochre Use and Its Possible Significance," *Current Research in the Pleistocene* 4 (1987): 82–4; D.C. Roper, "A Comparison of Contexts of Red Ochre Use in Paleoindian and Upper Paleolithic Sites," *North American Archaeologist* 12, 4 (1991): 289–301; D.C. Roper, "Variability in the Use of Ochre in the Paleoindian Period," *Current Research in the Pleistocene* 13 (1996): 40–2; Robert E. Ritzenthaler and George I. Quimby, "The Red Ochre Culture of the Upper Great Lakes and the Adjacent Areas," *Fieldiana Anthropology* 36, 11 (March 1962): 243–75; Morris, "A Shroud of Ochre."

9. On ochre as a healing agent, see Joseph Velo, "Ochre as Medicine: A Suggestion for the Interpretation of the Archaeological Record," *Current Anthropology* 25, 5 (1984): 674; A.R. Piele, "Colours that Cure," *Hemisphere* 23, 4 (1979): 214–17.

10. Brent Berlin and Paul Kay, Basic Color Terms: Their Universality and Evolution (Stanford CA: CSLI 1999).

11. Victor W. Turner, "Colour Classification in Ndembu Ritual," in Michael Banton, ed., *Anthropological Approaches to the Study of Religion* (New York: Praeger, 1966), 80–1; Knight, *Blood Relations*.

12. Paul Proulx, "Algic Color Terms," *Anthropological Linguistics* 30, 2 (Summer 1988): 135–49; Jean-Andre Cuoq, *Lexique de la langue Iroquoise* (Montreal: J. Chapleau, 1882), 33.

13. Johann Georg Kohl, *Kitchi-gami: Life among the Lake Superior Ojibway* (London: Chapman & Hall, 1860).

14. Jean-François Lozier, "Rouge Amérique: Le toponyme vermillon au Canada et aux Etats-Unis," unpublished paper presented at the annual meeting of the Canadian Society for the Study of Natives, Montreal, May 2010.

15. Paul Douglas Campbell, *Earth Pigments and Paint of the California Indians* (Los Angeles: Sunbelt, 2007), 32; Julian Lips, *Naskapi Law* (Philadelphia: American Philosophical Society, 1947), 443, 485.

16. Stafford et al. "Digging," 88; Richard Slobodin, "Kutchin," in William C. Sturtevant and Bruce G. Trigger, eds, *Handbook of North American Indians* (Washington, DC: Smithsonian Institution, 1978–2008), vol. 6, 517; Lloyd James Dempsey, *Blackfoot War Art: Pictography of the Reservation Period 1880–2000* (Norman: University of Oklahoma Press, 2007), 44–5.

17. See for example Reuben Gold Thwaites, ed., *Maximilian, Prince of Wied's Travels in the Interior of North America, 1832–1834* (Cleveland: A.H. Clark, 1906), vol. 22, 328.

18. Andrew White, "*A Briefe Relation of the Voyage unto Maryland,*" in Clayton Colman Hall, ed., *Narrative of Early Maryland* [1633–1684] (New York: Charles Scribner's & Sons, 1910), 42–3; George Percy, "Discourse," in Philip L.

Barbour, ed., *The Jamestown Voyages under the First Charter, 1606–1609* (Cambridge: Cambridge University Press, 1969), 1: 130; *JRAD*, vol. 38, 253.

19. Marshall, *History*, 287–8.

20. *JRAD*, vol. 38, 249. See also *JRAD*, vol. 5, 23; John Heckewelder, *History, Manners, and Customs of the Indian Nations who Once Inhabited Pennsylvania and the Neighboring States* (Philadelphia: Historical Society of Pennsylvania, 1876), 203–5.

21. Claude Charles Le Roy Bacqueville de La Potherie, *Histoire de l'Amerique Septentrionale* (Paris: Jean-Luc Nion et François Didot, 1722) vol. 3, 43–4; *JRAD*, vol. 38, 253; Brickell, *Natural History*, 316; *NYCD*, vol. 3, 714.

22. Brickell, 316; *JRAD*, vol. 41, 111–13.

23. Alfred W. Bowers, *Hidatsa Social and Ceremonial Organization*, Smithsonian Institution, Bureau of American Ethnology, Bulletin 194 (Washington, DC: Government Printing Office, 1965), 239.

24. Quoted by Sabine McCormac in Frank Salomon and Stuart B. Schwartz, *The Cambridge History of the Native Peoples of the Americas: South America* (Cambridge: Cambridge University Press, 1999), vol. 1, 149.

25. Lafitau, *Customs*, vol. 2, 38.

26. Augustine of Hippo, *De doctrina christiana: On Christian Doctrine* (New York: Macmillan, 1958), 150, 157.

27. Jacques Pinset and Yvonne Deslandres, *Histoire des soins de beauté* (Paris: Presses Universitaires de France, 1960), 44–8; also see Denis Menjot, ed., *Les soins de beauté: Moyen Age— début des temps modernes. Actes du IIIe Colloque international, Grasse (26–28 avril 1985)* (Nice: Centre d'études médiévales, 1987).

28. Quoted in E. Rodocanachi, *La femme italienne à l'époque de la Renaissance: Sa vie privée et mondaine, son influence sociale* (Paris: Hackette, 1907), 106.

29. Catherine Lanoë, *La poudre et le fard. Une histoire des cosmétiques de la renaissance aux Lumières* (Seyssel: Champ Vallon, 2008); Carroll Camden, *The Elizabethan Woman* (New York: Appel, 1952), 175–215; Neville Williams, *Powder and Paint: A History of the Englishwoman's Toilet* (London: Longmans, 1957); Farah Karim-Cooper, *Cosmetics in Shakespearean and Renaissance Drama* (Edinburgh: Edinburgh University Press, 2006); Jesús Terrón González, *Léxico de cosméticos y afeites en el Siglo de Oro* (Salamanca: Servicio de Publicaciones de la Universidad de Extremadura, 1990); Elizabeth Teresa Howe, "The Feminine Mistake: Nature, Illusion, and Cosmetics in the Siglo de Oro," *Hispania* 68, 3 (September 1985): 443–51.

30. John Marston, *The Malcontent*, ed. George K. Hunter (Manchester: Manchester University Press, 1988), 61–2.

31. James Cleland, *The Institution of a Young Nobleman* (Oxford: Barnes, 1607), 216; Annette Drew-Bear, *Painted Faces on the Renaissance Stage: The Moral Significance of Face-Painting Conventions* (Cranbury: Associated University Presses, 1994), 29–31, 73–82, 118; Frances E. Dolan, "Taking the Pencil Out of God's Hand: Art, Nature, and the Face-Painting Debate in Early Modern England," *PMLA* 108, 2 (March 1993): 224–39.

32. On the production of cosmetics in the early modern period, see Catherine Lanoë, *La poudre et le fard* and "La céruse dans la fabrication des cosmétiques sous l'Ancien Régeme (XVIe–XVIIIe siècles)," *Techniques and Cultures* 38 (2002), http://tc.revues.org/index224.html, accessed 15 January 2010; Moraig Martin, *Selling Beauty: Cosmetics, Commerce, and French Society, 1750–1830* (Baltimore: Johns Hopkins University Press, 2009).

33. Horace Walpole, *Letters of Horace Walpole, Earl of Orford, to Sir Horace Mann* (Philadelphia: Lea & Blanchard, 1844), vol. 2, 402.

34. George R. Potter and Evelyn M. Simpson, eds, *The Sermons of John Donne* (Berkeley: University of California Press, 1955), vol. 2, 343; Richard Brathwait, *Ar't asleepe Husband? A Boulster Lecture* (London: R. Bishop, 1640); Thomas Tuke, *A Treatise against Painting and Tincturing of Men and Women* (London: Tho. Creed and Barn. Allsope, 1616).

35. Drew-Bear, *Painted Faces*, 102.

36. Dolan, "Taking the Pencil," 229.

37. Lanoë, *La poudre et le fard* and "La céruse"; Martin, *Selling Beauty*, 73–96; Howe, "The Feminine Mistake."

38. Lanoë, *La poudre et le fard* and "La céruse"; Martin, *Selling Beauty*, 73–116; Rodocanachi, *La femme italienne*, 107.

39. William Strachey, *The Historie of Travell into Virginia Britania*, Louis B. Wright and Virginia Freund, eds (London: Hakluyt Society, 1953), 70–1.

40. Lafitau, *Customs*, vol. 2, 41.

41. Williams, *Key*, 192–3.

42. *JRAD*, vol. 18, 153; *JRAD*, vol. 29, 129; *JRAD*, vol. 59, 231.

43. *JRAD*, vol. 60, 93.

44. Quoted in Tracy Brown, "Tradition and Change in Eighteenth-Century Pueblo Indian Communities," *Journal of the Southwest* 46, 3 (Autumn 2004): 468–9.

45. Ibid.

46. *A Treaty between his Excellency . . . George Clinton . . . And the Six . . . Nations* (New York: James Parker, 1746), 8; Timothy J. Shannon's "Dressing for Success on the Mohawk Frontier: Hendrick, William Johnson, and the Indian Fashion," *The William and Mary Quarterly*, 3rd ser., 53 (January 1996): 13–42.

47. John Warner Barber, *The History and Antiquities of New England, New York, New Jersey, and Pennsylvania* (Hartford: H.S. Parsons & Co. 1842), 389; Bruce E. Johansen, *The Native Peoples of North America: A History* (Westport, CT: Praeger, 2005), vol. 2, 169–71.

48. *JRAD*, vol. 38, 253. Compare, tentatively with *JRAD*, vol. 4, 205.

49. Lafitau, *Customs*, vol. 2, 32 (retranslated by author).

50. Peter Kalm, *Travels into North America* (Barre: Imprint Society, 1972), 491.

51. *NYCD*, vol. 9, 220; Bacqueville de La Potherie, *Histoire*, vol. 1, 365; vol. 3, 43; Louis Armand de Lom d'Arce de Lahontan, *Mémoires de l'Amerique septentrionale en la ou la suite des voyages de M. le baron de Lahontan* (La Haye: Fréres l'Honoré, 1704), 70.

52. Jacques Savary de Brûlons and Philémon-Louis Savary, *Dictionnaire universel de commerce d'histoire naturelle & des arts* (Copenhagan: Claude Philibert, 1765), vol. 5, 879, 848.

53. Rutherford J. Gettens et al., "Vermilion and Cinnabar," *Studies in Conservation* 17, 2 (May 1972): 47–8; Pamela H. Smith, "Vermilion, Mercury, Blood, and Lizards: Matter and Meaning in Metalworking," in Ursula Klein and E.C. Spary, eds, *Materials and Expertise in Early Modern Europe Between Market and Laboratory* (Chicago: University of Chicago Press, 2010), 29–49.

54. A.F.E. Van Schendel, "Manufacture of Vermilion in Seventeenth-Century Amsterdam: The Pekstok Papers," *Studies in Conservation* 17, 2 (May 1972): 70–82.

55. Gettens et al., "Vermilion and Cinnabar," 50, *Encyclopédie méthodique* (Paris: Panckoucke, and Liège: Plomteux, 1789), vol. 6, 764; Jacques Accarias de Serionne, *La richesse de la Holland: Ouvrage dans lequel on expose l'origine du commerce & de la puissance des Hollandois . . .* (London: Compagnie [de Indes orientales], 1778), vol. 1, 66; Théodore Château, *Technologie du bâtiment spécialement destiné aux ingénieurs, architectes . . .* (Paris: A. Morel, 1866), vol. 2, 625.

56. William Henry Pulsifer, *Notes for a History of Lead* (New York: D. Van Nostrand, 1888), 56, 74, 276–83; David John Rowe, *Lead Manufacturing in Britain: A History* (Beckenham: Associate Lead, 1983), 5–18.

57. François-Xavier Garneau, *Histoire du Canada depuis sa découverte jusqu'à nos jours* (Quebec: P. Lamoureax, 1859), vol. 2, 153.

58. Review of Duclos' report by the Conseil de la Marine, September 1716, Archives nationales (France), Archives de la Colonie, C13A 4, fol. 271.

59. Elizabeth Mancke, *A Company of Businessmen: The Hudson's Bay Company and Long-Distance Trade, 1670–1730* (Winnipeg: Rupert's Land Research Centre, 1988), 56; *A Short State of the Countries and Trade of North America Claimed by the Hudson's Bay Company* (London: J. Robinson, 1749), 25–6.

60. Antonie Le Camus, *Abdeker au l'Art de conserver la beauté* (Paris: 1754) 82; Solange Simon-Mazoyer, "Le conflit entre les excès de la mode et de la santé au XVIIIe siècle, 'L'habillage' du visage," in Vincent Barra and Micheline Louis-Courvoisier, eds, *La médecine des Lumières Tout autour de Tissot* (Geneva: Georg, 2001), 41–53; Martin, *Selling Beauty*, 67–117.

61. Charles F. Lummis, "In the Lion's Den," *Out West* 16, 2 (February 1902): 189–91.

62. John Wesley Powell, *Fourth Annual Report of the Bureau of Ethnology, 1882–1883* (Washington, DC: Government Printing Office, 1886), 52.

63. Jean Usher, *William Duncan of Metlakatla: A Victorian Missionary in British Columbia* (Ottawa: National Museums of Canada, 1974), 43, 67.

Chapter 2

Missionaries and Indigenous People

READINGS

Primary Documents

Historical Interpretations

INTRODUCTION

With the French determination to stay and colonize a corner of North America came a determination to make the Indigenous people living in what came to be called New France into faithful Christians. The belief system that had conquered Europe and had also led its faithful into battle during the Middle Ages was, by the mid-sixteenth century, undergoing its own crisis in the form of the Protestant Reformation. The Jesuit order that emerged as one of Catholicism's weapons during the struggle was well-suited (at least in the eyes of church leaders) to undertake missionary work in the new world. After their arrival in the early 1610s, the Jesuits and other orders took some time to set their missionary work in motion, not really becoming effective until the 1630s. Part of the problem for them was that the French colonial claim to the region was not yet at its strongest.

We include one primary source, the *Jesuit Relations*, which has been the richest account of the Jesuits' work. In the *Relations*, essentially a massive collection of reports, the missionaries reflect upon the successes and failures in their work, and try to describe some of the characteristics of life among a wide variety of Indigenous peoples. Their contact with the Huron, or

Wendat, people was especially significant, as disease and the Wendat alliance with the French and Jesuits would result in the nation's destruction and dispersal by 1650.

The other primary source comes from the same era, but from a member of a female order, the Ursulines. The Ursulines arrived in Quebec in 1639. Their initial objectives were to convert and educate Indigenous girls. In order to do so, they opened the first learning institution in New France shortly after landing in the colony. Their convent soon afterward began to provide education to the daughters of the French colonists. The Ursulines eventually also provided care for the sick. As Roman Catholic nuns, the Ursulines took great pleasure in the news of religious conversions among Indigenous people.

We have scant evidence of suspicion among these missionaries that their work may have been harming its targets. Why would they doubt the faith when having faith in its eternal truth was part of their "job description"? The historical interpretations, looking into the records of these missionary groups, cast a different light on the interaction between missionaries and Indigenous peoples, interpreting the presence of missionaries as a disruption to the livelihoods and long-term physical and psychological or spiritual health of these societies. Carole Blackburn examines the relationship between the Wendat and the Jesuit missionaries who lived among them, and offers motivations for both acceptance of and resistance to the French conversion efforts. Mairi Cowan's focus is on the Ursulines, whose mandate included the education of Indigenous girls. She shows how what that entailed shifted over time according to mandates from France and a changing attitude about the necessary connection between Christianity and the acceptance of European culture.

As you read the historical interpretations included here, try to hold these two perspectives in mind: the missionaries' eagerness to deliver salvation and the often tragic results of that effort. It is a theme that would be repeated much closer to our own time.

QUESTIONS FOR CONSIDERATION

1. The simplest and most obvious answer to the question "What motivated the missionaries?" is probably "faith." Is there a better answer—one that addresses missionaries' earthly goals for the Indigenous people they lived with?

2. What aspects of Indigenous life did those who compiled the *Jesuit Relations* consider worthy of their attention? Why?

3. Why do you think missionaries needed to live for extended periods among Indigenous people? Could they just have visited once in a while?

4. What might have led the Huron/Wendat to distrust the missionaries among them, or to believe that a higher power favoured them?

5. How did the Ursulines approach educating Indigenous girls? How successful were they?

SUGGESTIONS FOR FURTHER READING

Blackburn, Carole. *Harvest of Souls: The Jesuit Missions and Colonialism in North America, 1632–1650*. Montreal and Kingston: McGill-Queen's University Press, 2000.

Dunn, Mary. "Bedside Manners: Sickness and the Jesuit Mission in Early Modern New France." *Journal of Jesuit Studies* 5, no. 4 (2018): 567–85.

Englebert, Robert, and Guillaume Teasdale, eds. *French and Indians in the Heart of North America, 1630–1815*. Winnipeg: University of Manitoba Press, 2013.

Greer, Allan. *Mohawk Saint: Catherine Tekakwitha and the Jesuits*. New York: Oxford University Press, 2005.

Labelle, Kathryn Magee. *Dispersed But Not Destroyed: A History of the Seventeenth-Century Wendat People*. Vancouver: UBC Press, 2013.

Parkman, Francis. *The Jesuits in North America in the Seventeenth Century* (many editions).

Parmenter, Jon. *Edge of the Woods: Iroquoia: 1534–1701*. Winnipeg: University of Manitoba Press, 2014.

Peace, Thomas, and Kathryn Labelle, eds. *From Huronia to Wendakes: Adversity, Migration, and Resilience, 1650–1900*. Norman: University of Oklahoma Press, 2016.

Thwaites, Reuben Gold, ed. *The Jesuit Relations and Allied Documents: Travels and Explorations of the Jesuit Missionaries in New France, 1610–1791* (73 vol. in 35). New York: Pageant Books, 1959.

Trigger, Bruce. *The Children of Aataentsic: A History of the Huron People to 1660*. Montreal and Kingston: McGill-Queen's University Press, 1976.

Primary Documents

1 From *The Jesuit Relations and Allied Documents: Travels and Explorations of the Jesuit Missionaries in New France, 1610–1791*, ed. Reuben Gold Thwaites (Cleveland: Burrows, 1898), 103–21.

CHAPTER VII. OF THE HURONS WHO WINTERED AT QUEBEC AND SILLERY

The Seminary of the Hurons, which had been established at nostre-Dame des Anges some Years ago, in order to educate children of that nation, was interrupted for good reasons, and especially because no notable fruit was seen among the Savages; our experience in beginning the instruction of a people with the children, has made us recognize this fact. Here is an occasion which has obliged us to reëstablish a Seminary in a new fashion, as it were,—but easier, and in behalf of persons, older, and more capable of instruction. God grant that the incursions of the Hiroquois may not hinder us from continuing.

[104] A young man, of those who had formerly been at the first Seminary of the Hurons at Nostre Dame des Anges, happening to be in a great storm, in the midst of their great lake, made a vow to God, if he escaped, to lead a more regular and orderly life. His vow is heard,—he is delivered, contrary to every human probability; he goes to find our Fathers who were with the Hurons, and imparts to them his vow and his resolution. They think thereon; they deliberate; they finally resolve to take him out of his own country, where he was in greater danger, and to send him down here, so that he should be better aided, and that he might see the example of the French and of the Algonquins of Sillery. They gave him for companion another Huron young man, who desired to become a Christian; both these arrived at

Sillery last year, in the month of September. It was on that occasion that I again detained Father Jean de Brebeuf, who had wintered here in the preceding year, and who had not yet gone up again, in order to instruct them and to take charge of them. Several other Huron young men, who had come down to trade, presented themselves [105] also to us, in order to be received and instructed; but, the scanty provisions that we have not permitting us to admit any more, part of them were constrained to return to their own country, and the others, to join the Algonquins in order to go during the winter to the hunt or to the war with them.

Nevertheless, the charity of Monsieur the Governor and of the Hospital Mothers has given us means to add three to the first two, and to baptize those with us who were not baptized. With the help that I have mentioned, we have lodged and maintained four of them, and toward the Spring, a sixth, who came unexpectedly. Generally speaking, all have greatly edified us; they were always among the first at Mass and at prayers, and were the last to leave, both at evening and in the morning. They failed not to say their prayers, quite long, on both knees, whether they were at home or hunting in the woods. Several times in the day they went to the Chapel, to pray to God and salute the blessed Sacrament; they would take care not to begin anything [106] without having first made the sign of the Cross. All, since their baptism, have not failed to Confess themselves and receive Communion at least every Sunday; and several of them went to Confess themselves as soon as they thought they had committed any notable fault. Throughout the winter, they went every Sunday to Quebec, in order to attend high Mass, from which they have not been absent, whatever the state of the weather,—although the distance is about two leagues, and though they were usually obliged to start before daylight, during the rigor of the winter; but the desire of pleasing God, and the satisfaction that they received

in seeing the devotion of our French, assembled in the Church, caused them to find nothing difficult. Moreover, the peace and unity in which they have lived together, and with our French and the Algonquin Savages, and the services which they willingly rendered, showed well enough what the power of faith and of the divine grace can do when it has gained possession of even Savage hearts. The foregoing is what was common to all; here follows what is individual. The one who [107] gave occasion for the whole enterprise is a certain Armant Andewaraken, who has aided not a little, by his deeds and his words, in the instruction of the others, and in encouraging them to do well. Our Lord has imparted to him, at intervals, great desires for his salvation,—and sometimes even to forsake the world and to enter into Religion, which he knows very well, and separates from the common life; but it requires a long probation,—to be a Savage and to be a Religious are things which seem very repugnant; nevertheless, the grace of God, and time, will avail to compass everything. This young man came one day of last Winter to find Father Brebeuf, at the end of his Mass, and spoke to him as follows: "My Father, I have great desire to do right and to save myself; I have wholly resolved that, for I fear those fires which burn incessantly beneath the earth, and which are never extinguished. In order to attain what I desire, I would like to live always with you, and not return to the Hurons, where there is great difficulty in saving oneself,—the opportunities for sin are frequent in our villages, [108] and the liberty in them is great. I am nevertheless determined to obey, and to do everything which the Father Superior shall order. If he commanded me to go to the Hyroquois, I would go very willingly, without any escort; and even if he commanded me to cast myself, at the loss of life, into this river which passes yonder before us, I would do so at once." Thus he spoke, not looking at the thing which in itself is illicit, but simply at the command.

"Moreover," he said, "let the Father Superior tell me what I ought to do; I am sure that it will be the will of God, and therefore I shall acquiesce therein. Archiendassé"—that is to say, Father Hierosme l'Allemant, who is Superior among the Hurons—"has addressed me to him. I know well that you have still other Superiors in France; but it is he who here takes the place of God, and who will tell me what I must do." The Father Superior sent him word that he greatly praised his design and his devotion; that he should persevere courageously; that we would always have a most special care for him; that, with reference to living down there with us, we would think of it, [109] and we would recommend the matter to God, and that he, on his part, should do the same. There was a consultation after prayers were done, and it was found best that he should return again to his own country,—that God-fearing, as he is, and assisted by our Fathers, this would be the best for him and for his fellow Countrymen. He has mightily applied himself to the mortification of his impulses and inclinations; often he felt himself prone to dispute, and sometimes he would grow angry at certain words; but straightway he would return to himself, and stop short in silence, remembering that he had resolved to do right. One day, having had some difference with one of our Frenchmen, he not only went straightway to Confess, but he went to ask pardon of the one whom he had offended, embracing him tenderly; and since then he has rendered him all the services in his power.

The first to profit by these examples has been a young man named Saouaretchi, who had come down with him; he is of an excellent disposition,—gentle, peaceable, obedient, industrious,—and endowed with a good mind, by means of which he has quickly [110] learned all the prayers. He was baptized on Christmas eve, in the Chapel of the Ursuline Mothers, and named Ignace, by Monsieur Martial Piraube. On the very night of that great Feast, he received his first Communion;

and since that time he has always continued to confess himself and receive Communion every Sunday, with much devotion: his desire to be instructed has notably appeared in this point. His comrades, toward the beginning of Lent, having taken the resolution to go hunting for the Moose, he said that, for his part, he would not go; and that he had not come from so far in order to go hunting, but in order to know God, and learn to serve him, and that he made account of no other thing than that; that it was this which he aspired to carry away at his return, and not skins of Moose, or other things. His particular devotion has been to fast every Saturday, in order to prepare himself for Sunday Communion, and for the prompt performance of all that was commanded him. The Baptism of this young man causes us to hope for the Conversion of many others; [111] for, besides that he is very exemplary and very zealous, he belongs to one of the largest and most numerous families of the Hurons, which already is thoroughly attached to the faith, and which awaits, it seems, only the Baptism of this young man in order to plunge after him into those blessed waters.

About the middle of January, one of the other Hurons, who had gone to live among the Algonquins of the Island, and who until then had remained with them near the fort of Richelieu, came down to Sillery, expressly to be instructed in the faith. The village of which he is native is named Arrente,[1] and he is nephew to one of the Captains; but what commends him still more, is his extreme gentleness and docility in every respect. He has very good wit and judgment; mild and thoroughly obedient.

The Hospital Mothers have lodged and fed him, with a charity which embraces all sorts of nations. It is remarkable how much satisfaction he has given them in all the services which have been desired of him; these he has rendered with a cheerfulness, promptness, and constancy that [112] would cause shame to many Frenchmen.

His affection toward the faith has made itself noteworthy,—not only in that he constantly came, evening and morning, to find the Father, in order to be instructed; but also in that, having been instructed in some new prayer or lesson, he would repeat and meditate upon it, and that so much and so long, that he knew it before going away. Hence there was no need of telling him the same thing twice over. He failed not to go into the Chapel of the Hospital every evening and every morning, in order to say his prayers there; and stayed there a good space of time. He was baptized at the Hospital, the 8th of March, and was named Pierre by Monsieur de Repentigny, who since then has ever shown him much affection.

About the middle of February, two other Huron young men—natives of the same village as the preceding, and impelled by the same desire to have themselves enrolled in the number of the Christians—also abandoned the Algonquins at the fort of Richelieu, in order to come in quest of Father de Brebeuf, so as to be instructed by him. [113] We received them, moreover, at our abode; for want of room we were constrained to lodge them with our workmen; one was named Atarohiat, and the other, Atokouchiouani. The longing to be baptized as soon as possible, so greatly kindled in them the desire to be instructed, that they had learned all the prayers and the Catechism in a very little while; and one of them, moved with this vehement desire to learn, was not willing to divert himself by going to the hunt with his Comrades, saying: "The time that we have for staying here is too short: I desire to employ it in obtaining instruction; and then, besides, I have not the happiest memory in the world. I have not come down here to go hunting; and, as for eating meat, if I had cared to eat any, I had only to stay with the Algonquins up there at Richelieu, where the hunt is much better than here." Seeing that they knew the prayers well, they requested Baptism so ardently,—saying, among other things, that they feared lest, going often into the woods, upon the waters, and into other dangerous places, there might happen to them some misfortune,—[114] that finally it was granted them. It was in the Church of Quebec where they were baptized, very solemnly, the day of the Annunciation of our Lady, when they also received Communion for the first time, according to the custom of the Church. Monsieur de saint Sauveur[2] gave the name of Joseph to Atarohiat; and Monsieur de la Vallée, that of René to Atokouchiouani.

I have said that they had been baptized as solemnly as possible,—and this designedly, because that has much effect upon the minds of the Savages, and is to them, not a slight incentive to belief. To this end, after the baptism of these two latter, Father de Brebeuf—having led all the Hurons before Monsieur the Governor, in order to thank him for so much kindness and honor as he did them—asked them in his presence, all in succession, what that is which touched them the most, and most inclined them to embrace the faith. The first said, that what struck him chiefly was, to consider the omnipotence of God, with whom nothing is impossible; and to think of the [115] marvelous works which he has done, from the beginning of the world,—as, to have drawn so many creatures out of nothing; to have caused the children of Israel to pass through the red sea with dry feet; to have fed them with the Manna for the space of forty years; to have satisfied several thousand persons with five loaves and two fishes; to have raised Lazarus from the dead, four days after death; and countless other like wonders.

Another said that what touched him very strongly was, to see men and Religious maids leave their own country, where they were much at their ease, and without danger, in order to come to places where there is nothing but dangers and incredible inconveniences,—and all that in order to instruct them, and win them to God.

But the most part answered that what mainly attracted their attention was, to see all that was done to honor God. "When we see," said they, "every one assemble here on Sundays and Feasts, in order to hear the Mass and to pray to God; when we see Confessions and frequent Communions, [116] observed with so much devotion; when we consider what is done for the Savages,—how fields are prepared for them, how houses are built for them, how they are assisted in body and soul,—that is what makes us say that faith is something important, and that what you teach is true." Toward Spring there arrived a sixth, who had been baptized in passing through Montreal, together with some Algonquins. He lodged, as a rule, at the Hospital, with Pierre, his Comrade, and tried to compensate with his fervor for the little time that he should have, and to become instructed before his Baptism. He has given every sort of contentment to Father Brebeuf, in the short time that he could have him for his Teacher. Such has been the status of our five or six Huron boarders, who no doubt would be more numerous if the means were greater. Howbeit, one thing has caused them fear and given them pain,—to wit, the return to their country; "For," they said, "while we shall be here among you, it [117] is hardly possible for us to offend God, seeing so many good examples of virtue, and no vices: but in our own country, it is quite the contrary,—one knows not what it is to do right; it is a chaos of confusion and of disorder." "And then," said the one last baptized, "there is as yet scarcely any one in our village, or in those round about, who has solidly embraced the faith. We are the first and the only ones." Thus they spoke, and represented the danger wherein they believed themselves to be, of offending the divine Majesty. In fact, they have just cause to fear, and we also; and if, indeed, some one of them should happen to stumble, we must not be surprised. Nevertheless, we hope in the divine goodness that it will preserve them, and that it will perfect what it has begun. They all went away toward the middle of June, in order to return to their own country, in the company of about six-score other Hurons, who had come for trade. This plan of Seminary is easy, and can be realized at small expense, and is excellent,— choosing a number of young men, of twenty [118] or twenty-five years, of good will and good intelligence, and training them one Autumn and one Winter among our French and our Algonquin Christians; causing them to see and to taste the profession of Christianity among us, and among people of their very country; and then sending them away, under the Guard and the guidance of our Fathers who are with the Hurons. But I know not whether the rage of the Hiroquois will not deprive us of this consolation; and them, of so great a good fortune. If the Hurons were won over, the nation of the Neutrals, and others neighboring, would hardly be slow to follow. The Hurons who have come for trade have told us that these who are being instructed are, at present, the principal men of the country.

NOTES

1. For location of Arent (Aronte), vol. x, *note* 23.
2. Jean le Sueur, a secular priest, came to Canada in 1634, with Giffard (vol. vi, *note* 8); his other title was derived from a parish in Normandy, which he had served, Saint Sauveur de Thury. In 1645–46, he was missionary at Côte de Beaupré, and later officiated in the chapel at Côteau Ste. Genevieve. In March 1646, he became joint proprietor, with Jean Bourdon, of the fief St. Francis (vol. xi, *note* 11). *The Jounr. des Jesuits* frequently mentions him, up to 1660. One of the suburbs of Quebec is named St. Sauveur, for this priest.

2 From *Word from New France: The Selected Letters of Marie de l'Incarnation*, ed. Joyce Marshall (Toronto: Oxford University Press, 1967), 122–6, 387–8. Permission conveyed through PLSclear.

17. NEWS OF JOGUES

TO HER SON.
Quebec, 30 SEPTEMBER 1643
My very dear and well-loved son:
May the love and life of the King of nations consume your heart with the ardour with which he transports the hearts of our converts.

You ought now to have received the letters I wrote to you in the month of July last and in which I gave you a brief account of what happened last year in New France and in the new Church of Jesus Christ. [. . .]

But I must not waste time; let us begin to speak of our converts. The first foundations of the Church have been laid this year at Miscou,[1] which is a French settlement solely for traffic in furs. Ten leagues beyond the settlement, a chapel has been built and a large mission established for the Savages to the north, who have been drawn to the Faith by the conversation of our Montagnais Savages from Tadoussac. This mission promises great fruit, for the material is ready. It is about a hundred and fifty leagues from here, going in your direction.

A hundred leagues to this side of it is the Tadoussac mission, where marvels have been seen this year, a great many Savages, who live more than twenty days' journey by land away, having come there to be instructed and then baptized. They have such religious sentiments and perform such Christian acts that they make us ashamed and surpass us in piety. This is the fruit of the zeal of our good settled Christians, for they go in one direction and the other expressly to win souls to Jesus Christ. All these nations are from the regions to the north; and Tadoussac, where they assemble, is forty leagues or thereabouts from here, going towards Miscou.

Sillery is one league above Quebec and we are midway.[2] Some of our settled Savages are at Sillery and the others at Quebec, where trade is carried on.

Last year the Attikamegue nation came here to be instructed and more than half of them were baptized. The first baptism was held in our church, and the first marriage also, for when a man and woman are baptized they are at the same time united before the Church. Several others were afterwards baptized and married. I must confess that the joy my heart feels when I see a soul washed with the blood of Jesus Christ cannot be expressed.

These good people were instructed every day in our chapel. After Mass we made them a feast of peas or sagamite—Indian corn with dried plums—after which they spent almost all the day at our grille, to receive some instruction or learn some prayer. It was a prodigy to see with what promptness and facility they learned everything they were taught.

One poor woman, who had a slightly duller mind than the others, grew angry with herself and said as she prostrated herself, "I shall not get up, from this day, unless I know my prayers." She kept her mouth pressed against the ground all day and God so blessed her fervour that, when she arose, she knew everything she had wished to learn. Fervour is universal and we are overjoyed to see great men coming eagerly to see us so that we may teach them to make interior acts and jaculatory orisons, which they employ when required.

The chief of this nation was a great sorcerer and the most superstitious man alive. I listened to him uphold the virtue of his charms and superstitions, and soon afterwards he came to see the Father with whom he had disputed, bringing his charms and the drum he had used in his enchantments, and declared that he intended never to use them again. I am sending the drum to you so you may see how the devil beguiles and seduces this poor people with a child's device, for you will know that it is used to cure sickness, to predict things to come, and for similar extraordinary things. After this change of heart, we had the consolation of seeing all the drums of this nation sacrificed to God in a single day.

Later they all went back, hunting, to their own county [the upper St Maurice valley], so as to arrive there in the spring. And because they are newly instructed, one of our new Christian women of Sillery went with them in terrible snowy cold to make them repeat their prayers each day for fear they might forget them. We have learned that they are leading an admirable life.

It is a marvel to see the fervour of our good converts. They are not satisfied with believing in Jesus Christ, but their zeal so carries them away that they are not content and think they only half believe if all do not believe as they do. The chief of the Abnakiouois [Abenakis] left his country and his people to come to settle here so he could be instructed and afterwards win his people to the Faith of Jesus Christ. He was baptized yesterday and married to one of our seminarians, named Angèle, of whom the *Relations* spoke last year with great praise. His zeal will carry him even further for he is resolved to carry the Gospel into many other nations. "I shall not be content," he told me, "to bring my people and my young men to faith and prayer, but as I have been in several other nations and know their tongues, I shall make use of this advantage to go to visit them and bring them to believe in God."

It is not only the men that are on fire with this zeal. A Christian woman went to a very distant nation expressly to catechize those that live there and succeeded so well in this that she brought them all here, where they were baptized. She needed an apostolic

courage to face the dangers to which she exposed herself in order to render this service to Our Lord. We often see like fervour in our good converts who, to be quite truthful, put those that were born of Christian parents to shame.

There is no prominent person among the Hurons that does not wish to be a Christian. Four chapels have been built in their country this year and hitherto they would scarcely suffer one. The Iroquois, nevertheless, persecute this poor nation greatly. They captured and killed a great number of them two years ago and but a fortnight since they defeated their fleet again.[3]

You know that last year they captured the Reverend Father Jogues, some Frenchmen, and one of our seminarians. They killed the old men[4] and made captives of the others. The Reverend Father was beaten into insensibility and stripped naked upon his arrival in their country. His thumb was cut off and his index finger gnawed to the joint. The ends of his other fingers were burned and then he was made to suffer a thousand ignominies. As much was done to a Frenchman [Guillaume Couture], his domestic, and another [René Goupil], who was also in his service, had his head split by the blow of a hatchet.[5] The poor Father, believing that the same would be done to him, go down on his knees to receive the blow and offer his sacrifice, but nothing further was done to him. The same was done to the greater number of the captives as to the Father, and then all their lives were spared. Our seminarian, Thérèse, has suffered no injury and has courageously continued to profess the Holy Gospel and to pray in public. The Reverend Father is at present preaching the Gospel among the Iroquois; he is the first to have that honour, and God has so blessed his labour that he has baptized more than sixty persons in his captivity.[6]

I must speak a little of our seminarians, who give us all possible satisfaction.

One said to me a little while ago, "I often speak to God in my heart. I get great pleasure from naming Jesus and Mary. Ah, what beautiful names they are!"

We sometimes hear them conversing together about God and making spiritual colloquies. One day among others they were asking one another for what they believed they were most greatly obliged to God.

One said, "It is because he made himself a man for me and suffered death to deliver me from hell."

Another replied, "It is because he made me a Christian and placed me, by baptism, in the number of his children."

A little girl, who is but nine years old and has been receiving communion for a year and a half, raised her voice and said, "It is because Jesus gives himself to us as meat at the Blessed Sacrament of the altar."

Is this not delightful in girls born in barbarism?

They never fail to make their examination of conscience or to accuse one another of their offences, which they do with matchless simplicity. They sometimes ask to be punished so they can pay the penalty to God for their sins while they are still in this world. When one of them had been punished, we asked her what she thought of the chastisement she had been given.

"I thought," she said, "that you must love me, since you punished me to bring me to my senses, for I have no sense yet. I, who have been instructed, am much much more guilty than my companion, who was not."

You see our employments. I beg you to be very mindful of the kingdom of Jesus Christ. Pray for the conversion of the Iroquois, who hinder it greatly and close the passages lest the more distant nations come here to be instructed. The Iroquet nation was not allowed to pass through the lands of these barbarians, who fired more than a hundred shots at them, but God so well protected them that there was not a single one of them wounded.[7]

I am writing to you at night because of the pressure of letters and the imminent departure of the vessels. My hand is so weary that I can scarcely govern it—it is this that makes me finish by begging you to excuse me if I do not reread my letter.

NOTES

1. The Jesuits had maintained two priests at Miscou—an island off the northeast coast of New Brunswick at the entrance to the Baie des Chaleurs—since 1634 for the benefit of the Frenchmen who came there in connection with the fur trade. Marie de l'Incarnation's use of the words "first foundations of the Church" refers to the building of the chapel and a mission devoted exclusively to the Indians.

2. The Ursulines had occupied their new monastery in the upper town of Quebec since 21 November 1642. It was situated just west of the fort and was the first building encountered by the Indians of Sillery as they came along rue Saint-Louis (Grande Allée). This is undoubtedly Marie de l'Incarnation's meaning, though her use of the word "milieu," middle, is somewhat ambiguous. At the time there was no direct access to Sillery from the lower town except by boat.

3. As the result of this most recent capture, of a fleet that was attempting to carry supplies to the Huron missions, the Jesuits in Huronia were deprived for the second year in a row of the necessities of food and clothing that they were accustomed to receive annually from Quebec.

4. According to Jogues's own account, only one old man had been killed.

5. Goupil was killed 29 September 1642 at Ossernenon (now Auriesville, New York), on the order of an old man, who was angered because Goupil had made the sign of the cross over a child. Couture was adopted by a Mohawk family to replace a dead relative, according to a common Indian custom.

6. News of these things had been brought to Quebec by Thérèse's uncle, Joseph Teondechoren, who had escaped with some of the other prisoners. Jogues himself had managed

to send a letter to France and to have others delivered to Quebec. Within weeks of his capture, Arendt van Corlaer, the Dutch commandant of Fort Orange (Albany, New York), had tried without success to ransom him from the Mohawks.

7. The *Relation* (*JR* XXIV) tells a different story. A group of Algonkian Iroquets, who had sought refuge at Montreal, was sent out to parley with some Iroquois that had approached the settlement. The Iroquois then fired upon them, though none of the Iroquets was injured. The Iroquets, who lived above Montreal between the St Lawrence and the Ottawa Rivers, had no occasion to traverse the Iroquois country.

Historical Interpretations

3 From Carole Blackburn, *Harvest of Souls: The Jesuit Missions and Colonialism in North America, 1632–1650* (Montreal and Kingston: McGill-Queen's University Press, 2004), 105–28, 153–5.

CONVERSION AND CONQUEST

The Jesuits hoped to promote the obedience and submission that was a necessary attribute of Christian life by reconfiguring Aboriginal social and political relationships. Conversion itself, however, and the Jesuits' ability to gain compliance most frequently occurred after a process of chastisement and humiliation that had been brought about by disease or the consequences of warfare. The Jesuits described the misfortunes that were increasingly experienced by Native people during the 1630s and 1640s as afflictions and crosses, and they wrote that these afflictions had an especially beneficial effect in inducing conversion and generating the humility and obedience that were appropriate to Christian behaviour. Le Jeune, for example, wrote that affliction "opens the eyes of the understanding" (14:183). He and other Jesuits argued that suffering was necessary in order to reduce the pride and independence that kept people from recognizing the necessity of submission and their obligations to God and the Jesuits. This understanding was pointedly expressed in the *Relation* for the years 1642 and 1643, which stated: "Humiliations are the harbingers that mark the dwellings of the great God; and tribulation attracts us more strongly and with much more certainty than does comfort. It is necessary to abase the pride and the haughtiness of these people, in order to give admission to the faith" (25:39).

THE HAND THAT SMITES THEM

Shortly after the Jesuits arrived in Huron country, many of the villages were stricken with a disease of European origin. This was the first of a series of epidemics that further reduced the Huron population by almost half over a period of six years (Trigger 1987, 499). Although the Jesuits and other French also became ill during the initial epidemic, they recovered and remained relatively unaffected as the outbreaks of disease recurred. This was in sharp contrast to the inability of large numbers of Huron to withstand the diseases, and it suggested to many of them that the French had some effective means of prevention and cure. The Jesuits were accordingly asked to help stop the sickness—at which point, they took the opportunity to insist that all Huron pray and believe in God, presenting this as "the true and only means of turning away this scourge of heaven" (13:159). While many people were initially prepared to adopt the Jesuits' terms, most did not realize the exclusive nature of the priests' demands, and they continued to seek other remedies, leaving the Jesuits to accuse them of hypocrisy and backsliding (13:165, 177).

As the diseases continued unabated, the Jesuits' proposed cures were soon discredited, though most Huron continued to believe that the priests had the power to protect themselves from the illnesses—a belief that was reinforced when the Huron observed the Jesuits spending so much time with the sick yet remaining "full of life and health" (19:93). For the Huron, withholding assistance from someone who was ill violated community reciprocity, and as a sign of disregard for the welfare of others it could only be motivated by hostile intentions. Such behaviour was easily interpreted as a sign of complicity in a disease that had been caused by witchcraft, which was believed to be the most common cause of incurable illnesses and the most frequent expression of antisocial, hostile sentiments (Trigger 1987, 66–7). Although the residents of most Huron villages first sought to identify and eliminate possible witches among themselves, the majority came to the conclusion that the French, and particularly the Jesuits, were causing the diseases through sorcery.

This interpretation of the Jesuits as witches was encouraged by the priests' reputation as successful and potentially powerful supernatural practitioners. Evidence that the Jesuits possessed power had already been apparent in their success in praying for rain and their ability to predict lunar eclipses (15:139, 175), as well as by a number of the technologies they had brought from Europe. Brébeuf had been involved in a successful bid for rain during his first years with the Huron, before the English defeat of the French and the removal of the missionaries to France (10:43–9). This was not forgotten by those Huron

who knew Brébeuf, and during the very dry spring and summer of 1635 they asked the Jesuits to pray for an end to the drought. The efforts of Huron *arendiwane* to do the same had been unsuccessful. One shaman in particular blamed the Jesuits for his failure and demanded, much to the chagrin of the priests, that they take down the cross they had erected in front of their cabin in Ihonatiria (10:37–43). The Jesuits not only refused to remove the cross but they twice enjoyed seeing their prayers and processions followed by a significant amount of rain, as well as by the admiration and respect of many people.

Suspicion about the Jesuits' involvement in the diseases also stemmed from the fact that most Huron did not completely understand the priests' intentions in wanting to live among them (17:125). While it was accepted that traders and warriors had occasion to live with allies or trading partners, the missionaries' evangelical purpose, based as it was on a universalist belief, had no precedent and consequently was open to local interpretation (Trigger 1987, 534). As the diseases spread, the Jesuits' teaching and habits were easily shaped into indisputable proof of hostile intentions and sinister activities, whose ultimate objective was the destruction of the Huron people.

This was particularly the case with behaviour that was culturally alien and either oddly inappropriate or more directly suggestive of the stinginess and unco-operative spirit which the Huron associated with witchcraft. The priests' habit of closing their door at certain times of the day for private meditation, for example, fell within the range of antisocial behaviour, and many Huron believed that the Jesuits needed this privacy in order to practise their sorcery (15:33). Their practice of speaking to those who were sick about death and the afterlife was similarly unusual and inappropriate (15:23, 69). Most people found the priests' continual references to death disturbing and morbid, and they suspected that the Jesuits were concerned not with an individual's recovery but solely with sending him or her to heaven. The Jesuits attempted to aid the sick as much as possible, hoping to advance the cause of Christianity by discrediting the cures offered by the shamans and setting an example of Christian charity (15:69). However, at the same time as they were diligently attempting to bring people some relief, their stern criticism of Native curing rites and their refusal to participate in them were viewed by most Huron as socially unco-operative behaviour and interpreted as further evidence that the priests actually wanted to prevent people from recovering. In this way, although the priests cast their behaviour in the benevolent idiom of Christian charity and sacrifice, the Huron interpreted it through the divergent idiom of harmful intent and sorcery. Some Huron even suggested that the Jesuits' wish to see them in heaven as soon as possible caused them to shorten the lives of those whom they felt were best prepared for the afterlife (19:241).

The unfamiliar material and technological features of the mission were similarly subject to interpretation by the Huron, who saw in them further evidence of the Jesuits' sorcery. The act of writing, especially, was subject to a variety of appropriations that challenged the Jesuits' own understanding and their expectation of its significance. Writing was the Jesuits' most potent technology, both as the source of their universal truths and because Native people admired their ability to communicate silently through pieces of marked paper. The Jesuits based much of their faith in the truth of Christianity and its universal relevance on the authority of their written tradition. In their attempt to persuade people to convert, they lost no opportunity to assert the value of the Bible as a written document containing the authentic and undistorted Word of God. They argued that while oral traditions were subject to the fallibility of memory and the accumulation of lies and stories invented for the sake of entertainment, the basis of their

own faith in the Word, not just spoken but recorded, was indisputable (11:153; 17:135). Le Jeune quickly identified the word used by the Montagnais to speak of the distant past, *nitatohokan*, as meaning "I relate a fable, I am telling an old story invented for amusement" (6:157). By comparison, when some Huron asked Brébeuf how the Jesuits "knew there was a Hell, and whence we obtained all that we told about the condition of the damned," he replied "that we had indubitable proofs of it, that we possessed it through divine revelation; that the Holy Ghost himself had dictated these truths to certain persons, and to our Ancestors, who had left them to us in writing, and that we still carefully preserved the books containing them" (13:51–3).[1]

The Jesuits' faith in the Bible as a written document was deeply embedded in an assumption that all truth and knowledge was textually dependent (Mignolo 1992, 318). The proof of God himself could be "read" in nature. As one of the priests explained, "The reality of a God was . . . so clear that it was only necessary to open the eyes to see it written in large characters upon the faces of all creatures" (13:173). I have already noted that the Jesuits' mission in New France depended, in large part, on an oral practice and that the early history of Christianity was itself strongly oral, relying on an oral praxis of preaching and teaching the Word. However, the Jesuits came to North America after the Renaissance, when an ideology of the letter had emerged which emphasized the primacy of writing as well as the physical form of the book itself, both as the essential repository of knowledge and as its principal means of transmission (Mignolo 1992, 311, 318). While Christ himself was originally the Word of God embodied (11:169), the authority of this Word came to be the authority of the Book. Indeed, in an especially interesting gloss on Christ's physical embodiment of textual authority, Le Jeune referred to Christ as "the living Book" (16:123). Writing, knowledge, and the material form of the book convened in an ideology and philosophy of writing that had considerable effect on interpretations of the New World and its peoples; the absence of a system of alphabetical writing quickly came to be interpreted as a sign of the absence of civilization and as evidence of the inferiority of New World peoples (Mignolo 1992, 317–18).

The priests knew that "the art of inscribing upon paper matters that are beyond sight" (15:121) visibly impressed the people they were trying to convert. Notes sent between Jesuits from one village to another caused the Native people to think that the priests could predict the future and read minds at a distance, something that only shamans could similarly claim to do (Axtell 1988, 93). In 1635 Brébeuf wrote that the Huron admired the lodestone, prism, and joiner's tools, "but above all . . . writing, for they could not conceive how, what one of us, being in the village, had said to them, and put down at the same time in writing, another, who meanwhile was in a house far away, could say readily on seeing the writing. I believe they have made a hundred trials of it" (8:113). He added: "This serves to gain their affections, and to render them more docile when we introduce the admirable and incomprehensible mysteries of our Faith; for the belief they have in our intelligence and capacity causes them to accept without reply what we say to them" (8:113).

However, while the technology of writing contributed to the aura of power and prestige which the Jesuits' were trying to cultivate, they could not control the whole meaning of the relationship between writing and power in the minds of Huron who suspected them of witchcraft. This relationship was quite different from the priests' understanding of the power of writing as a privileged vehicle of knowledge and the permanent repository and record of the Word of God. While it constituted proof that the Jesuits were figures of some unusual skills and power, it was precisely this power that would have enabled the Jesuits to harm people by causing inexplicable diseases through sorcery. That the Jesuits represented themselves as men who had come to North America only for the good of the Huron was irrelevant, since the Huron believed that powerful individuals did not use their power for good or evil exclusively but could put it to use for both purposes.

Thus, although writing initially contributed to the respect with which the priests were treated, as fears of the Jesuits' sorcery grew it also came to be suspected as a means by which the Jesuits targeted people for illness or otherwise spread the contagion. Lalemant explained in 1639 that if the fathers "asked the name of some one, in order to write it in the register of our baptized ones, and not lose memory of it, it was (they said) that we might pierce him secretly, and afterward, tearing out this written name, cause the death, by this same act, of him or her who bore that name" (19:129). Similarly, when Fathers Antoine Daniel and Simon Le Moyne visited the eastern Arendarhonon villages, some inhabitants of the principal village of Contarea claimed to have seen these fathers in dreams, "unfolding certain books, whence issued sparks of fire which spread everywhere, and no doubt caused this pestilential disease" (20:33). Dreams were not random occurrences for the Huron; they were prophetic of events, as well as of the innermost desires of the soul, and the Huron paid close attention to them (Sioui 1994, 297). In these instances, the symbolic significance of writing and its associated technologies slipped their moorings in the Jesuits' ideology and received altered significance at the hands of the Huron. Accusations that linked writing to witchcraft subverted the Jesuits' position as benefactors concerned with saving people rather than destroying them. In this way, they displaced the equivalence which the Jesuits were trying to convey between themselves and health and life. These accusations also denied the ideology of the letter that informed the priests' reliance on the book. By contesting the authority of writing, Aboriginal people acknowledged its power but denied its hegemonic function as the embodiment of a universal truth; in this way, if only temporarily, they refused the translation of colonial signifying practices and the authority embedded in them.[2]

In other instances, the ritual and pictorial symbolism of Christianity was appropriated and resisted in ways the Jesuits could neither control nor possibly have predicted. Many Huron had initially interpreted and received baptism as a healing rite; but as the diseases intensified, the Jesuits' sacrament of life came to be viewed as one of the ways in which they perpetrated their witchcraft. Many people refused it on the grounds that it was certain to kill them or their children. Others incorporated a facsimile of baptism into their own healing rituals, to the great annoyance of the Jesuits. This particular innovation first occurred in 1637, when it was introduced by a shaman who had fasted for ten days in an attempt to acquire insight into the cause and cure of the prevailing disease, and it involved sprinkling water on the sick (13:237–43). It appeared again in 1639, after a Huron man had a vision of Iouskeha, a central Huron deity, in which Iouskeha blamed the Jesuits for the disease and prescribed a healing ritual that involved drinking ritually prepared water from a kettle (20:27–9). The Jesuits roundly condemned the vision as the work of demons who were trying to defend their territory against the Jesuits, and they described the practitioners of the prescribed healing rite as "masqueraders" and "physicians from hell" (20:31).

The Jesuits' vigorous condemnation of these acts suggests the degree to which they frustrated their objectives. These acts also show the ambivalence of Huron resistance. The Huron did not wholly reject the content of the Jesuits' practices or the authority linked to them, nor did their actions leave Huron and French cultural meanings and systems of signification intact, within imaginary boundaries, with their contents unimplicated in

each other (Bhabha 1994, 110). The Huron men and women who participated in these rites engaged the potential power of baptism as a healing ritual. In doing so, they allowed some of its significance while disallowing the Jesuits' monopoly over the meaning and potentially life-saving effects of the ritual and its water (20:29–31).

This time of illness and death was, understandably, fraught with the search for signs of the cause of disease. The life-size paintings of Christ and the Virgin Mary displayed by the Jesuits in their chapel in Ossossané were believed to possess magical qualities and to be two of the instruments through which the priests were causing illness among Huron who were unfortunate enough to have looked at the pictures (15:19). Paintings of hell, detailing the torments of the damned—intended to inspire fear and to encourage people to convert—were interpreted as literal representations of the sufferings of those whom the Jesuits had afflicted with disease. Le Mercier explained that "on the day of the baptism of Pierre Tsiouendaentaha," the Jesuits "exhibited an excellent representation of the judgment, where the damned are depicted,—some with serpents and dragons tearing out their entrails, and the greater part with some kind of instrument of their punishment" (14:103). While "many obtained some benefit from this spectacle," some "persuaded themselves that this multitude of men, desperate, and heaped one upon the other, were all those we had caused to die during this Winter; that these flames represented the heats of the pestilential fever, and these dragons and serpents, the venomous beasts that we made use of in order to poison them" (14:103).

In this instance, the Jesuits' teaching about heaven, hell, and punishment was deflected and was returned to the Jesuits with new and contrary meanings. Even the communion wafers became suspect. As a general principle, the priests had been careful to reveal the doctrine of transubstantiation (whereby the wafers became the body of Christ) only to the few Christian Huron whom they felt most trustworthy in the faith (15:33). In spite of this precaution, the host soon featured in a rumour suggesting that the Jesuits were causing the diseases through a corpse they had brought from France and were hiding in their residence (15:33).

Several years later, after the diseases had largely run their course, stories began to circulate among the Huron of dreams and visions through which people had learned that the Jesuits' teachings were not only wrong but were dangerous. In one story, the soul of a recently deceased woman returned, after having journeyed to heaven, to warn the Huron that all who had become Christian were being tortured in heaven as prisoners of war, by the French, just as war captives were tortured by the Huron and their enemies (30:29). This warning was especially subversive because it situated the Jesuits as enemies whose objective in making converts was to take prisoners, rather than as people who had come to give the secret of eternal life. It also completely overturned the division between heaven and hell, which many Native people found especially problematic. These incidents demonstrate the decentring that can occur when signs that are supposed to stand for the authority of the colonizers—or, in this case, the missionaries—are exposed to interpretation and appropriation by the colonized; they also illustrate competition for control over the interpretation of events and for what passes as the truth. As assertions of Native beliefs that make sense of Christian symbolism and Christian figures in the context of these beliefs, they are also an ideological response in kind to the Jesuits.

However much the Jesuits were required to argue over meaning with the Huron while they were in the Huron villages, their own understanding of the cause of the diseases was forcibly and categorically expressed in the pages of the *Relations*. It revolved around the influence of the devil in inspiring the persecution against them (19:91) and the biblically precedented interpretation of disease as divinely instigated punishment and trial. After the initial accusation of witchcraft in 1636, Le Jeune wrote that the growing hostility toward the Jesuits was a positive sign that the demons—hitherto unchallenged as the masters of the country—had been "powerfully attacked, since they put themselves vigorously on the defensive" (11:41). A few years later, Father Le Mercier characterized the accusations and general hostility as part of "the war that the powers of darkness have openly declared against us" (14:109). The Jesuits described their work with the sick and their unflagging attempts to teach and baptize people in the midst of threats as a literal struggle against the forces of evil (17:191; 20:51). In view of the Jesuits' own understanding of their mission, the allegation that it was they who were manipulating supernatural powers for harm could only be understood and represented as a fundamental misinterpretation of their activities and proof of the blindness of their accusers. Jérôme Lalemant responded to the accusations brought against the Jesuits with righteous indignation, writing that the words of their accusers were "often only blasphemies against God and our mysteries, and insults against us, accompanied with incredible evidences of ingratitude,—hurling at us the reproach that it is our visits and our remedies which cause them to sicken and die, and that our sojourn here is the sole cause of all their troubles" (17:15).

The Jesuits soon came to represent the diseases as punishment sent by God in response to people's initial refusal to heed the Word and to accept their opportunity for salvation.[3] Once spoken in the New World, the Word of God erased the legitimacy of previous religious practices and, significantly, exposed Aboriginal people to their ignorance as well as to the full force of the consequences of their sin. The words spoken by the Jesuits left a permanent mark, inhabiting the spaces where they had been spoken with a kind of ominous finality. To ignore them and the truths they announced was to make the fatal choice between salvation and condemnation to greater punishment in this life and the next. In a letter to Mutio Vitelleschi, general of the Society of Jesus at Rome, Lalemant explained: "While they were sound in body, they did not hear; it therefore pleased God to pull their ears through a certain kind of pestilence, which spread over the whole country, and adjudged many to the grave" (17:227).

At the beginning of the epidemics, Le Jeune compared the situation in which the priests found themselves with the persecution suffered by the first Christians and, reversing the accusations made against the Jesuits, attributed the diseases to God's justice: "All the misfortunes, all the pests, wars, and famines which in the early ages of the infant Church afflicted the world, were formerly attributed to the faith of Jesus Christ, and to those who embraced or preached it. What occurred in this regard in the primitive Church can be seen every day in new France, especially in the Huron country. There is no black malice of which we are not accused. Here are the causes of it. As the contagion caused a great many Hurons to die, these people, not recognizing therein the justice of God, who takes vengeance for their crimes, imagined that the French were the cause of their death" (12:85).

While the Jesuits attributed all power over the diseases to God and continually urged the Huron to have recourse to the faith, most Huron abandoned Christianity completely in an attempt to dissociate themselves from the priests' teachings and, by association, from the diseases. The few who had converted and who remained Christian during the epidemics were warned by their relatives of the injustice of the Jesuits' God and his powerlessness to assist them or to preserve their lives (19:211, 235). But while resistance to the Jesuits became more imperative for the majority of Huron men and women, it situated them in a more perilous position according to the Jesuits' understanding of the epidemic and its

causes. The Huron's rejection of Christianity as the only possible cure and their continual search for cures among those offered by the shamans and curing societies confirmed the Jesuits' in their belief that the devil influenced these people's behaviour (15:71). According to this view, such behaviour made them more deserving of retribution for denying the opportunity for their salvation. In the same way, the threats and accusations that the Huron made against the priests—who believed themselves to be there as the instruments of the Huron's salvation—compounded the "measure of their sins" (13:161) and, consequently, the measure of their punishment. The Jesuits met the active resistance of the Huron with an intensification of their threats of punishment, rhetorically moving the Huron's refusal to comply into the realm of the worst blasphemy. While the Jesuits and many Huron apportioned blame for the disease to each other they did so according to divergent cultural and ideological premises that enabled them to find significant, incontrovertible meaning in their respective actions. The result was a duel over signification, in which each became grist for the other's worst accusations as they struggled—if not for life and death itself—at least for the meaning of life and the cause of death.

The first serious outbreak of disease occurred during the autumn of 1636 and lasted through the winter. After this, the Jesuits moved their principal residence from the village of Ihonatiria, where many people had lost their lives to the disease, to the more southern and less afflicted village of Ossossané. The Jesuits had been publicly accused of practising witchcraft in Ihonatiria that winter and were aware that their lives were at risk. Le Mercier, the author of the Huron *Relation* for that year, identified one family as having been most active in these accusations. According to Le Mercier, it was when the priests' lives were most threatened that "the scourge fell upon that wretched family that had said the most against us. This chastisement had been for a long time due them on account of the contempt they had always shown for our holy mysteries" (13:217). Lalemant later explained that the move from Ihonatiria was necessary because its population was "nearly all . . . scattered or dead from the malady, which seems to be, not without reason, a punishment from Heaven for the contempt that they showed for the favour of the visit that the divine goodness had procured for them" (17:11). The following autumn, when it appeared that a council of confederacy headmen in Ossossané would sanction the Jesuits' death, Brébeuf reiterated the priests' assumption that their lives would be preserved or disposed of solely as God willed. Their deaths would prevent the salvation of those they were trying to save, and Brébeuf believed that if God allowed the Jesuits to be killed, this in itself would be a form of punishment: "And yet I fear that divine Justice, seeing the obstinacy of the majority of these Barbarians in their follies, may very justly permit them to come and take away the life of the body from those who with all their hearts desire and procure the life of their souls" (15:63).

Crop failures, the escalation of the war with the Iroquois, and famines were also represented as the punishments of God. When Jérôme Lalemant described the destruction of one of the outlying Huron villages by an Iroquois war party, he associated this disaster with the village's previous rebelliousness: "It was the most impious of the villages, and that which had been most rebellious against the truths of the faith in all these countries; and its inhabitants had more than once told the Fathers who had gone to teach them that, if there were a God who avenged crimes, they defied him to make them feel his anger, and that, for anything less than that, they refused to acknowledge his power" (26:175). Similarly, Father Dequen explained to the Montagnais residing at Sillery that the capture of a group of Huron traders and the Jesuit father accompanying them, as well as "so many other misfortunes," were "the effects of God's anger, who was justly irritated by the wickedness of bad Christians and of the infidels who would not obey his word" (25:149).

Of course, the few who remained or became Christian during the epidemics were equally likely to suffer from the diseases. Similarly, as more people converted to Christianity after the diseases had run their course, they—like the non-Christians—were caught up in the punitive effects of escalating warfare and famine (25:105; 26:217). Inequities in the distribution of suffering are not unaccounted for in the Judeo-Christian tradition, and the Jesuits drew on well-established precedents when they represented these afflictions as having been sent by God for the improvement and redemption of those he had elected to save (26:217). Such was the argument offered to a group of Huron who complained that the Iroquois, who did not pray, were prospering and that since prayer had been introduced among the Huron, they themselves were perishing from warfare and disease. These Huron were told that God was behaving toward them "like a Father toward his child; if his child will not have sense, he punishes it, in order to give it some; having corrected it, he throws the rods into the fire. A Father does not put himself to so much trouble about his servants as about his children. God regards you as his children: he wishes to give you sense; he uses the Iroquois as a whip, in order to correct you, to give you faith, to make you have recourse to him. When you shall be wise, he will throw the rods into the fire; he will chastise the Iroquois, unless they reform" (25:37).

The Jesuits had precedents for this language and did not have to invent it for use in North America. However, such language assumes particular potency when used in a situation of evolving political and economic inequality, and in conjunction with what was frequently an aggressive rhetoric of political imperialism, which compared the spread of Christianity in the New World to a territorial conquest. These Huron replied that they had enough sense and suggested it might have been better if God had begun with the Iroquois. The Jesuits advised them that their greater misfortunes were due to the greater love God bore them and that, however much the Iroquois appeared to be prospering, it was certain that, as unbelievers, they would not enjoy the rewards of the next life. The Jesuits' representation of suffering reflects an assumption that the appropriate response to it could only be submission and endurance, undertaken with an understanding of the presence of a superior will to which one must be subordinate, and with the hope of rewards to come (Bowker 1970, 54). This complete abnegation of the self, along with submission before a greater will, was a feature of the Jesuits' training. While the Jesuits' interlocutors frequently appeared unmoved by a God who apparently benefitted people through their affliction, for the Jesuits suffering reduced neither the possibility of God nor the justice of God. Those who endured with strength and patience would be recognized and potentially rewarded—"for one is approved if, mindful of God, he endures pain while suffering unjustly" (1 Peter 2:19).

When sent as trials, misfortunes were a tool for separating those who were firm in the faith and willing to submit from those who were not (32:189). It is significant that in the *Relations* these trials were frequently represented as a necessary and important step in the establishment of Christianity in North America, just as they had been in Europe and Asia, where the faith of Christians had been tested through political persecution. While describing the hardships suffered by the Montagnais in the vicinity of Quebec, Le Jeune asserted: "The Faith must propagate itself as it has been planted,—namely, in calamities. And because there are here no Tyrants who massacre our Neophytes, God provides for them otherwise, deriving proof of their constancy from their afflictions, sore indeed" (16:219). The repeated use of this historical reference situates the experiences

of Native peoples in the St Lawrence region—for whom the signature events of Christianity were the remote occurrences in the life of an unknown prophet referring to the deity of an unknown people in a remote and alien land—within the frame of a universal, exclusively Christian and ultimately hegemonic vision of global history. In 1643 Barthélemy Vimont described the general condition of the Christians of New France:

> The condition to which this nascent Church is now reduced is such as to bring to the eyes of all who love it tears both of sorrow and of joy. For, on the one hand, it is pitiful to see these poor peoples perish before our eyes as soon as they embrace the Faith; and, on the other, we have reason to console ourselves when we see that the misfortunes which assail them on all sides serve but to arouse a desire for the faith in those who had hitherto despised it, and to strengthen it and make it shine with still greater glory in the hearts of those who had already received it. We see very well that God is the Founder of this Church, as well as of the primitive one; for he has caused the former to be born, like the latter, in travails, and to grow in sufferings, in order to be crowned with her in glory. (25:105)

By the summer of 1649 most Huron villages had been destroyed or significantly depopulated by warfare and the accompanying famine and disease. The priests and surviving Huron took refuge on an island in Georgian Bay, where they were temporarily safe from Iroquois raiding parties but lacked provisions for the coming winter. "Then it was," according to Paul Ragueneau, that the missionaries "were compelled to behold dying skeletons eking out a miserable life, feeding even on the excrements and refuse of nature" (35:89). Conditions reached such an extreme that people were reduced to exhuming bodies for food. Ragueneau nevertheless wrote:

"It was in the midst of these desolations that God was pleased to bring forth, from their deepest misfortunes, the wellbeing of this people. Their hearts had become so tractable to the faith that we effected in them, by a single word, more than we had ever been able to accomplish in entire years" (35:91).

The upheavals in Huron society in the final years of the Jesuits' mission among them made them more dependent on the Jesuits and enabled the priests to exact at least an outward compliance with Christianity. Lalemant had foreshadowed this role of affliction in creating subject relations of dependency, when he wrote of the general condition of Christianity in New France in the *Relation* for the years 1643–44: "We have, however, great reason to praise God because he reaps his glory from the affliction of these poor peoples and makes it serve still more for their conversion. Although there is not in the world a nation poorer than this one, nevertheless there is none prouder than they. When they were prosperous, we could hardly approach them; the French were dogs, and all that we preached them were fables. But since affliction has humiliated them, and necessity has made them more dependent upon the French, and has made them experience the effects of Christian charity, their eyes are opened; and they see more clearly than ever that there is no other Divinity than he whom we preach to them" (25:111). Lalemant's comment also reveals the strong sense of cultural superiority that characterized Aboriginal people's initial response to Europeans.

The Jesuits also represented affliction as the enactment of a more final and inevitable justice. In the Huron report of 1640 Lalemant explained that many "villages and cabins were much more populous formerly, but the extraordinary diseases and the wars within some years past, seem to have carried off the best portion; there remaining only very few old men, very few persons of skill and management" (19:127). To this he added, "It is to be feared that the climax of their sins is approaching, which moves divine justice to exterminate them as well as several other nations" (19:127). People who resisted conversion or actively argued against the Jesuits and who then suffered misfortune or death frequently figured in the *Relations* as examples of God's justice, however far removed this would have been from these people's own interpretation of their death or misfortune. The punishments featured in these incidents are in sharp contrast to the joy and gratitude which the Jesuits generally associated with conversion. In 1634 Paul Le Jeune attributed the miserable death of a "blasphemer" to the "just and terrible vengeance of the great God" (7:283). Ten years later Lalemant described the punishment of three Algonkin men who had come down to Trois-Rivières and were "placing some obstacles against the expansion of the Faith" by openly retaining more than one wife (31:257). Lalemant asserted that these three "refractory ones" (31:257) were the victims of "a thunderbolt hurled from Heaven" (31:257), all dying ignoble or miserable deaths.

One of these men, on becoming ill, blamed Christianity and in so doing was said to have revolted "more than ever against the arm which struck him only to cure him" (31:263). The Jesuits warned him of the punishment that would come in the next life if he did not open his eyes and accept baptism, but he replied unrepentantly "that a Law which made men die was abominable" (31:261). He died in this refutation of the faith, a resistance that became, under Lalemant's pen, the "rage" that was "the Catastrophe of his life" (31:263). Another of these men especially annoyed the Jesuits by his persistence in attributing a recent outbreak of disease to the effects of Christianity, and when he too fell sick Lalemant described this as an attack by God (31:263). Lalemant referred to this man, who bore the name Joseph Oumosotiscouchie, as an apostate who was unusually "proud and insolent" because he had been given the name used by several former leaders in his country (31:261).

Oumosotiscouchie publicly denied the utility of prayer to heal, blaming his sickness on the faith, and he undertook to cure himself in a healing ceremony that involved the fulfillment of three dream wishes. On completion of the ceremony, he publicly claimed to be cured, at which point, according to Lalemant, "a violent fever seizes him in the midst of his triumph, prostrates him to the earth, throws him into a wreck and into torments so unusual that he foamed like one possessed. Those of his cabin—frightened, and fearing lest he might beat some one to death—having tied him, threw over him a blanket, so as to conceal his fury and his rage; behold my blusterer much humbled" (31:265). When the Jesuits and the surgeon arrived, they found the man "stone-dead" and all who had witnessed the event astonished at "so awful a spectacle" (31:265). This man was later "flung into a hole like a common sewer, for fear that he might infect the air with his body, as he had polluted it with his vices and his apostasy" (31:275). After this punishment, Lalemant stated with some satisfaction that no one "dared longer open his lips against the Faith; it was now spoken of only with a dread and respect that altogether pleased us" (31:267).[4]

Those who physically harmed Jesuits could also be situated in the *Relations* as victims of divine punishment. One man, for example, kicked a priest while the latter was baptizing a child, and "some time after that, he was carried off by a disease as grievous as it was strange" (14:227). The woman who cut off the thumb of Father Jogues while Jogues was a captive in an Iroquois village apparently "had no long career after that rage" (29:229). Likewise, wrote Lalemant: "They who gnawed his fingers and those of his companions, and who treated them with most fury, have been killed by the Algonquin in their latest combats" (29:229). The "same justice" was applied to the Iroquois who tortured Father Bressani when he was held captive among them, although this punishment was in the form of diseases that would "perhaps . . . give true health to that poor people" (29:229).

NOTES

[Editor's note: Parenthetical references in the text are to volume and page number in Reuben Gold Thwaites, *Jesuits Relations and Allied Documents*, 73 vols (Cleveland: Burrows Bros. 1896–1901).]

1. In an especially interesting literal play on the Jesuits' insistence that the Bible was the unmediated, directly transmitted Word of God, Le Jeune reported: "When I told them that we had a book which contained the words and teachings of God, they were very anxious to know how we could have gotten this book,—some of them believing that it had been let down from the Sky at the end of a rope, and that we had found it thus suspended in the air" (11:209).

2. Indeed, while the smallpox epidemics ultimately passed, Native critiques of writing were not without prescience of the larger ramifications of entering history. One man, upon being told that his people were dying as a result of the overconsumption of the brandy used in the fur trade, retorted: "It is not these drinks that take away our lives, but your writings; for since you have described our country, our rivers, our lands, and our woods, we are all dying, which did not happen until you came here" (9:207). The Jesuits denied these deleterious consequences of writing the New World into a history that embraced the inhabitants with alien pathogens at the same time as it was supposed to proffer them the means of salvation, by explaining to this man that they "described the whole world" without similarly harmful effects (9:207).

3. A recent attribution of these diseases to the Europeans' abandonment of the "laws of nature" and more general alienation from the natural world (Sioui 1992, 3–7) is as embedded in the assumption of a universally applicable schema of laws, causes, and effects as

the attributions of the Jesuits. While it may be meant to refute such statements as the priests initially made and to represent the real truth, it matches them in the assumption that the cultural and religious dictates of one people—including an understanding of the natural world and the appropriate human relationships with it—are not, in effect, creations but represent reality as a given, and that, as such,

they can be universally binding as a yardstick with which to judge and understand the history, behaviour, and beliefs of other peoples.

4. Aboriginal people who reportedly resisted or abused Christianity were nor the only victims of God's anger and punishment in the *Relations*. The Jesuits represented the untimely death of French Protestants in a similar manner (5:233; 6:105–7).

REFERENCES

Axtell, James. (1988). *After Columbus: Essays in the Ethnohistory of Colonial North America.* New York and Oxford: Oxford University Press.

Bhabha, Homi. (1994). *The Location of Culture.* London and New York: Routledge.

Bowker, John. (1970). *Problems of Suffering in the Religions of the World.* Cambridge: Cambridge University Press.

Mignolo, Walter D. (1992). "On the Colonization of Amerindian Languages and Memories: Renaissance Theories of Writing and

the Discontinuity of the Classical Tradition," *Comparative Studies in Society and History* 34, 4: 301–30.

Sioui, Georges. (1994). *Les Wendats: Une civilisation méconnue.* Sainte-Foy: Presses de l'Université Laval.

Trigger, Bruce. (1987). *The Children of Aataenstic: A History of the Huron People to 1660,* 2 vols. Montreal and Kingston: McGill-Queen's University Press.

4 From Mairi Cowan, "Education, Francisation, and Shifting Colonial Priorities at the Ursuline Convent in Seventeenth-Century Quebec," *Canadian Historical Review* 99, no. 1 (March 2018): 1–29.

The Ursuline nuns who disembarked at the small French settlement of Quebec in 1639 placed the Christian education of Indigenous girls at the heart of their mission. As the convent's foundation contract states, the Ursulines were to be held in perpetuity to instruct the "little Indian girls of New France" in "knowledge of the Catholic, Apostolic, and Roman religion, to teach them to read and, if it seemed good, to write, to teach them also the catechism and generally all that is necessary to know for a true and faithful Catholic Christian."[1] [. . .] Indigenous students formed a majority of the student population in the convent's early years. Mostly Algonquin and Innu (Montagnais) at the start, they were soon joined by Wendat (Huron) and, later, Haudenosaunee (Iroquois) and Abenaki.

Some were "séminaristes passagères" who received instruction at the school but lived elsewhere, and others were "séminaristes sédentaires" who boarded at the school and lived cloistered with the nuns.[2]

In providing Indigenous students with instruction in religion, language, and domestic skills, the Ursulines were playing a role in the wider colonial project through their contribution to the program of *francisation*. This policy of assimilation was never laid out in precise terms by the architects of French colonial policy, and it was envisioned and enacted somewhat differently by different people. At its core, though, its goals were religious conversion to Christianity and cultural adaptation to French norms.[3] Evidence of the ideals and implementation of francisation at Quebec's Ursuline Convent is found in a variety of colonial sources, including the Ursulines' financial accounts, the Jesuit *Relations*, correspondence between royal agents in the colony and the metropole, and letters from the nuns. The process of francisation as presented in these sources was complex, and even Marie de l'Incarnation, the Canadian Ursulines' most famous writer, appears to have changed her mind about its achievements. In letters written during her first years in New France, Marie expressed confidence in the efficacy of the Ursulines' instruction. To a noblewoman in 1640, for example, she boasted of how the girls were making great progress in learning about religion, manners, and work. That same year, Marie wrote to her brother that as soon as the girls were washed with the waters of baptism, they lost all that they had of the "sauvage." They even exceeded French girls in some respects, being more pliable to learn whatever the nuns taught them.[4] Marie's later letters conveyed a much different outlook. In 1668, she said that "it is very difficult, if not impossible, to Frenchify or civilize" the Indians, and she estimated that only seven or eight students had been *francisées* in all the years of the school's existence.[5]

[. . .] Marie de l'Incarnation's optimism did not cease after a few years in Quebec, nor even after a couple of decades. The change in 1668 was abrupt. [. . .] To interpret this seemingly sudden change of heart requires a consideration of continuities in the Ursulines' mission style and changes to French colonial policy. The Quebec Ursulines' efforts remained rooted in a belief that the Indigenous girls should learn French skills at the convent and add these skills to what they already knew. The Ursuline teachers were well aware of their students' retention of significant aspects of their Indigenous cultures, and they also accommodated their pedagogy and daily routines to their students' expectations. This additive and accommodationist approach, favoured by the Ursulines since their arrival

in New France, fell increasingly out of step with changes to colonial policy piloted by the Crown. In the 1660s, royal authorities in France and their agents in New France started to insist more forcefully upon the replacement of Indigenous identities with a French one. Then, toward the end of the century, they took a sharp turn away from their earlier stance, so that instead of presuming that Indigenous inhabitants of New France could be made into French subjects, they questioned whether Indians could ever become French at all. Marie de l'Incarnation's modulated tone acquires a new meaning when set against this shifting backdrop of colonial policy. While acknowledging limits to the francisation program at her convent, she did not perceive these limits as insurmountable obstacles until the French state's receding horizon of francisation demanded a more complete assimilation of Indigenous peoples into colonial society than what the Ursulines were willing to attempt. Their choice to continue with an approach that was open to the possibilities of a negotiated and hybrid francisation reminds us that the French colonial experience in North America during the mid-seventeenth century was variegated and dynamic. [. . .]

* * *

The idea of francisation began in Europe, but its development was shaped by experiences in North America. Strong and diverse local identities in France hindered the formation of a single national identity in the early seventeenth century, and it was contact with Indigenous cultures in Canada that helped to crystallize the language of what constituted "Frenchness" on both sides of the Atlantic.[6] A well-known example of how the emerging French identity drew upon North American encounters is found in the 1627 foundation charter of la Compagnie des Cent-Associés, which stipulates that a person could live in New France as either a descendant of the French or as an Indian who has made profession of Catholicism and be counted among the "natural French."[7]

At the time of the Ursulines' arrival at Quebec, therefore, francisation in New France required first and foremost a conversion to Catholic Christianity. Many colonial authorities embraced a broader ideal, hoping that francisation would prepare Indigenous inhabitants of New France to lead a full French civil life. This project of integration included not only conversion to Catholicism but also the adoption of French cultural habits (such as sedentism, dress, and trades) and eventually miscegenation with French settlers.[8] An anticipated result of such acculturation, as Samuel de Champlain famously declared, was that the boys of the French would marry the girls of the Natives, and they would become one people.[9] Such a project was obviously designed for North America rather than Europe, but it nonetheless fit well with the goals of Ursuline schools in France, which emphasized Christian training for girls who would become wives and mothers.[10] [. . .]

The Ursulines in Quebec adhered to the basic requirement of religious conversion while remaining fairly flexible about the need to adopt outward signs of Frenchness. Although the replacement of Indigenous practices with French ones was sometimes desired, it was not, for the most part, required. Marie de l'Incarnation and her Ursuline sisters supported their students' retention of languages and foodways and allowed their alterations to Christian practices. The nuns reshaped their pedagogical approaches to suit the realities of North American life, and even in the grooming and dressing of students— probably the area of daily life at the school where the students retained the least of their traditional Indigenous practices—they made concessions to the girls' tastes.

* * *

Within a few years of the school's start, Indigenous students were speaking, reading, and writing in French.[11] Francisation in language notably did not mean an abandonment of Aboriginal tongues, since the girls also sang, conversed, and wrote letters in Indigenous languages.[12] In fact, multilingualism was encouraged among the students. [. . .] Multilingualism was also recommended for the Ursuline nuns, whose *Constitutions* said that the sisters were to make it a particular part of their vocation to study Indian languages from books and to practise them with the help of their students.[13] They continued their efforts right through the 1660s. In August 1668, Marie wrote to her son that she had recently been working on a book about sacred history in Algonquin, along with a dictionary and catechism in Iroquois, and that the previous year, she had written an Algonquin dictionary in the French alphabet.[14] The nuns may have learned Indigenous languages for practical reasons of pedagogy—as Le Jeune explained in his *Relation* of 1635, knowledge of Indian languages was needed to make progress in instruction[15]—but whatever the motivations, the convent became a polyglot space where students and teachers added new languages to those they already knew.

Foodways at the school were likewise additive. Visitors were regularly fed *sagamité*, a corn-based stew that was a staple of Aboriginal cuisine in the area.[16] French missionaries knew that this dish was enjoyed by Indigenous peoples around Quebec and thought that it might be good for their health.[17] Alongside familiar Indigenous dishes, students were also given foods from Europe selected according to what the nuns and their donors thought would be appealing. In the Jesuit *Relations*, missionaries often recounted stories of Indigenous people seeking sweet foods such as candied lemon peel, jam, and raisins.[18] Perhaps responding to such reports, wealthy French donors to the convent sent sugar, dried fruits, marmalades, and jams, which they designated specifically for Indigenous girls.[19] [. . .] Financial accounts of the convent show that the nuns, too, ate a diet consisting of foods from both Europe and North America. They consumed foods that would have been familiar to Europeans, such as beef, pork, lard, olive oil, cloves, cinnamon, nutmeg, and pepper, but they also purchased foods that were distinctly North American, such as moose muffles (the upper lip and nose) and tongues.[20]

Instruction at the school was based in European expectations, but, like diet, it was moulded onto North American realities. The *Constitutions'* statement that the nuns were to teach the girls all that was good for their condition—to read, write, count, calculate, sew, and "other exercises proper to their sex"—sounds much like a typical Ursuline education back in France.[21] Although nothing like a detailed curriculum survives for Quebec, Marie de l'Incarnation's report in a letter from 1640, that an Algonquin girl aged 12 was making progress in the knowledge of religious mysteries, in good behaviour, in reading, and in playing the viol, leaves a vivid impression of what was being taught.[22] As French as this curriculum may sound, the musical life of the convent took on an Indigenous timbre: The girls regularly danced "in the way of their country" and were joined on at least one occasion by the convent's founder and benefactor, Madame de la Peltrie.[23]

The Ursulines altered their pedagogy at deeper structural levels as well. [. . .] Travel, business, and even fire and the threat of military attack meant that the nuns often had to leave the convent. Strict enclosure was also impractical for the nuns' teaching role in New France, and in their Quebec house, they could go to the parlour as often as they liked in order to teach those who came for instruction, without distinction of sex. [. . .] That the Ursulines in Quebec were less strictly enclosed than their sisters in Europe is in line with arguments that restrictive gender ideologies more broadly were slower to take hold in New France than they were in France, and that female spirituality in New France was very traditional but also shaped by innovations and

variations.[24] The Ursulines' adjustments to pedagogy may have been influenced by their recognition of how much authority women, including their students, could have in Indigenous communities.[25] Thérèse Khionreha, as they knew, convinced other Wendat to accept Christianity while she was still at the convent school, and later, when living as a captive among the Iroquois, she became a leader in her longhouse and provided instruction in Christian prayers.[26]

As Khionreha's activities suggest, religious conversion was another additive, and possibly combinative, process.[27] Seminarians were given new names at baptism, which befit the Christian theology of rebirth in the rite. It may have suggested a new French identity as well, but the basic practice of renaming was a familiar one in Indigenous societies. Names could be changed when passing from childhood to adolescence, from adolescence to maturity, and from maturity to old age, and a person sometimes also took a new name after escaping from danger or coming out of sickness, or as a result of a dream.[28] Moreover, the students' names at the convent usually included both French and Indigenous elements, creating what Allan Greer calls "a badge of layered identity."[29] In a similar kind of layering, students modified the religious environment of the cloister. [. . .]

When Thérèse Khionreha took an interest in the nuns' spiritual exercises, she retired to a little grove of trees in the cloister and prayed to God. Some of her companions found her and decided to do the same. They made a little house of leaves, enclosed themselves in this greenery, and kept silence together. Marie de l'Incarnation found it a very strange thing that Indians born in such liberty should hold themselves captive and keep a voluntary solitude.[30] What she seems not to have considered was that these students, through careful negotiation, were adapting and adjusting French Catholic customs into a state of co-existence with their own Indigenous practices.[31]

Unlike the additive type of francisation in language and diet, and the combinative francisation of religion, the francisation in hygiene and clothing aimed more at replacing Indigenous customs with French ones. Smearing the skin with fat from seal, bear, and moose had very practical purposes in the eastern North American woodlands. It insulated against heat and cold, acted as a waterproof coating for hair, and, perhaps most importantly, offered protection from biting insects.[32] So notorious were these tiny masticators that the governor of Trois-Rivières, in ranking the inconveniences of Canada, placed mosquitoes in second place: not as bad as attacks by the Iroquois, but worse than the five-month-long winter.[33] However annoying the insects, though, French colonists generally did not adopt the Aboriginal means of protection against their bites. Jérôme Lalemant wrote of how insects did not let him write a single syllable without pain, but he described the scent of the protective grease as "wounding the nostrils."[34] When Indigenous girls arrived at the convent school, they were washed to remove the grease that covered their bodies. During the process, which could take several days, the nuns did not think that they were simply helping the girls substitute one kind of grooming for another in a neutral sense; the Ursulines were trying to improve the students—to move them toward what they saw as a civilized way of presenting themselves.[35] [. . .] After the removal of grease, the girls' hair was restyled "a la françoise," and they were clothed in dresses of red camelot, an expensive fabric, with red shoes and mittens.[36] [. . .] The students, for their part, were not just passive wearers of French clothing; they had their own clear opinions, not all of which necessarily came from an inclination toward francisation. When Jérôme Lalemant asked some students whether everything was going well, they answered that he could see their dresses were old and used, which made them sad. Lalemant could not stop himself from laughing,

but Marie de l'Incarnation took the students' response more seriously. She immediately went to get beautiful red serge, and she tied it on to all their dresses and mittens.[37] While the girls' behaviour in this instance could have appeared to some observers as a sign that francisation was working,[38] the students' desire for these specific French items might have had little or nothing to do with eagerness to become *francisées*. Their preference for the newer, unfaded cloth is consistent with other seventeenth-century evidence about Indigenous people in the vicinity of Quebec favouring bright colours, and reds in particular.[39] Whether from their own products or from trade goods, bright red colours appealed not just to European but also to Indigenous consumers.[40] [. . .]

The Ursulines' efforts to groom and dress the seminarians according to French custom, even when modified to appeal to the girls' preferences, came from a deeply held belief about the relationship between culture and progress. European colonizers shared in their imaginations a theoretical hierarchy of societies, placing those that were sedentary and Christian at the top. But for the Ursulines—as for the Jesuits [. . .] it was the society, not the individual people within it, that was categorical: Any human being had the capacity to move into different levels of civilization, and the society of New France had the potential to exceed Old France in its Christian perfection.[41] This potential had to be carefully nurtured, the nuns recognized, because people move in multiple directions between cultures. [. . .]

In this belief system, francisation was attainable by all people, and for Marie de l'Incarnation, outward appearance was not the most important consideration. As she wrote to an Ursuline nun at Tours, the souls of the French and the Indians cost the same to the son of God.[42] The francisation as undertaken by the first Ursulines in Quebec created in the convent school a "hybrid space," as described by Natalie Zemon Davis,[43] a kind of "bricolage" like what Gilles Havard had found in French politics regarding Indigenous peoples in French North America more generally, with strategic accommodations and adaptations to Indigenous customs, as well as tension between the discourse of subordination and the realities of local constraints.[44] [. . .]

* * *

Marie de l'Incarnation's letter to her son of 1 September 1668 offers important information about why, after promoting it for 30 years, she declared francisation to be difficult or impossible. [. . .] Marie de l'Incarnation's first reason for the limitations of francisation was that the girls left the convent: "They climb over our fence and go running in the woods with their families, where they find more pleasure than in all the amenities of our French houses."[45] This activity was certainly different from what the Ursulines tolerated in France. When students entered French Ursuline monasteries, they were not supposed to leave again over the course of their education. Their stay in the cloister, therefore, could last for years, and nuns sometimes refused to let girls return if they departed, even if for just a short time.[46] [. . .] Yet departures and re-entries were not uncommon for Indigenous students. The sisters Agnès Chabdikouchich and Anne-Marie Uthirchich were at the convent for three months before accompanying their parents on the winter hunt in 1641–2. They remained in contact with the Ursulines through letters, and afterwards they returned to the seminary. [. . .] There were still other children, Marie de l'Incarnation said, who left by whim or caprice, climbing like squirrels over the palisade and running into the woods.[47] Students at the Ursuline school maintained a prerogative to stay or go largely as they pleased.[48]

Marie de l'Incarnation linked the students' desire for freedom to their dispositions, or, as she articulates it in seventeenth-century fashion, their "humours." This was her second reason for why francisation was not working: the "Indian humour" is made in such a way that "they cannot be constrained, if they are, they become melancholic, and melancholy makes them sick."[49] [. . .]

The third reason that Marie de l'Incarnation offered in 1668 for the difficulty of francisation was that Indigenous and European expectations for discipline were so different: "The Indians love their children extraordinarily, and when they know that they are sad they go beyond all consideration to have them back, and [the children] must be returned."[50] The Ursulines' approach to discipline was actually quite restrained when compared to that of other seventeenth-century Europeans, and self-consciously so. Their *Constitutions* for Quebec advise a middle way between gentleness and severity, a moderation of impatience and anger in encounters with children. Corporal punishment was admitted as a possibility, but with strictures: It could only be administered by order of the superior or the nun who was taking her role, and only in the manner that she judged most appropriate after having given everything careful consideration. Moreover, the nuns were to take special care to say nothing injurious to the schoolgirls, both out of respect for charity and also to avoid offending their families.[51] In the Indigenous societies from which the girls came, by contrast to even the most mild of Ursuline approaches, any corporal punishment of children was fundamentally unacceptable. [. . .] Paul Le Jeune knew that the conflict between an Indigenous value of gentleness toward all children and a French insistence on physical correction would cause serious problems, because the Indians' unwillingness to punish a child or even to see one being punished would give the French trouble in their intention of instructing young Native children.[52] In this, at least, Le Jeune was correct: Parents did pull their children out of the convent because of discipline, and the students quite often left of their own accord.[53] [. . .]

These concerns with the Crown's designs for francisation are echoed in other letters of Marie's from the fall of 1668. [. . .] In all the years that the Ursulines had been in Canada, Marie said, they had not been able to francise more than seven or eight girls; the others, a large number, all returned to their families, even though they were very good Christians. She then explained that the students preferred their Indigenous way of life, which they considered superior to the French. "The Indian life is so charming to them because of its liberty," she wrote, "that it's a miracle to be able to captivate them with the ways of acting of the French, which they consider unworthy of them." She went on to suggest that different ideas about gender may have been influential, that children learn all this starting at birth, and that the women and girls canoe just like the men. "Judge from this," she instructed her son, whether it is easy to change habits learned from infancy "and which are as if natural to them."[54] In each of these letters, she emphasized the importance of families and liberty. Conversion could remain true even after a departure from the convent, but family bonds endured through conversion, and any practice at the convent that triggered objections by the girls' families would fail.

The schoolgirls' freedom of movement, their antipathy for constraint, their parents' unwillingness to tolerate harsh discipline, and the strong ties between the students and their families all pushed against the assimilationist policy of the Crown—or at least against its recent innovations. The core of this policy was not new in 1668. Since the time of Champlain, the basic French ideal of making colonists and Indians into "one people" was proposed as a way for the colony to increase its population.[55] The development that interfered with the Ursulines' efforts was a growing insistence among French and colonial officials that francisation include compulsion and exclusion: Native peoples should be required take on French customs, abandon Indigenous ways, and become entirely subsumed in the colonial population.[56] This insistence can be observed in a series of letters between Jean-Baptiste Colbert, minister to Louis XIV, and Jean Talon, intendant of New France. It was already under way in 1666 when Colbert said that nothing would contribute more to growing the colony than an attempt to "civilize" the Indians who had embraced Christianity and dispose them to establish themselves in community with the French and raise their children in French manners and customs.[57] Talon replied that he had attempted to regulate the ways of Indians and form their customs after those of the French, but he admitted that he had not been entirely successful. He added that they should long ago have taught Indians the French language rather than require the king's subjects to study theirs in order to communicate.[58] The following year, Colbert's letter to Talon made very plain how the standard of francisation was shifting. He said that they had, up to that point, been little worried about order and civil life among the Indians, who had for a long time submitted to the domination of the king, and that they had been making few efforts to detach Indians from their own customs and oblige them to adopt French customs or language. Colbert went on to say that Talon had begun to remedy this "long negligence" and that he was to try to attract these peoples, especially those who had embraced Christianity, to live next to the French habitations and, if possible, mix the peoples together.[59] Colbert was acknowledging, in effect, that he was abandoning an earlier approach to francisation, one that was largely unconcerned with cultural assimilation and instead focused on conversion to Christianity and the establishment of political loyalty to the French Crown. [. . .] In a letter written to Talon in February 1668, Colbert again stressed the distance between religious conversion and full acculturation. He reminded Talon of the importance of growing the colony and repeated that the Jesuits and others had not done enough to "civilize" the Indians while they were converting them, whether in joining them by marriage to the French, attracting their families to reside among the French and obliging them to leave their "lazy and idle" lives and cultivate lands next to French habitations, or drawing their children from their families' hands to teach them the French language and raise them according to French customs.[60]

Here was the context in which Marie de l'Incarnation started emphasizing the difficulties with francisation: Colbert's assertion that religious conversion, political allegiance, and some adoption of French customs were no longer sufficient, and his insistence that missionaries needed to do more to force Indigenous people to abandon their traditions and adopt French ways. [. . .]

The main problem that Marie de l'Incarnation had with the new form of francisation was that it was meant to compel the imposition of Frenchness to the exclusion of Indigeneity. The king and Colbert wanted to force Indigenous people to replace their Indigenous customs with French ones; the Ursulines, by contrast, perceived a fluidity of identity that did not require an abandonment of all Indigenous elements in becoming French.[61] As for why the Ursulines did not challenge the Colbertian view directly, two factors likely to have influenced their response were a need for funds and the limitations imposed by the cloister. [. . .]

French policy on francisation continued to harden during the years after Marie de l'Incarnation's death. In 1673, the governor of New France, Louis de Buade de Frontenac, wrote to Colbert that he was scandalized to find Indians only two leagues from Quebec who knew as little French as if they had never seen French people, whereas the English in New England provided a good example by forcing the Indians to learn their language and even their trades.[62] King Louis XIV wrote to Frontenac in 1675 that he was "well satisfied" with what Frontenac had done to attract the children of Indians, including the girls to be

raised by the Ursulines, because there was nothing that could contribute more to the good of religion and the augmentation of the colony than diminishing the number of those who lived as Indians.[63] [. . .] In 1682, the intendant Jacques De Meulles wrote that Indian girls should not be instructed like they were with the Ursulines, where they learn only to pray to God and to speak French. Instead, they should be taught how to live as French villagers, which is to say that they should know how to spin, sew, knit, take care of beasts, milk the cows, and other duties of the countryside. He had no doubt that if married to Indian men, the girls would subtly introduce this way of life to their husbands and in time remove "cet Esprit de Sauvage."[64] [. . .]

By the end of the century, with the development of a theory among Europeans and Euro-Americans that differences between French and Indigenous peoples were not cultural but biological, colonizers increasingly assumed that Indigenous people were inherently inferior to the French.[65] It was surely not a coincidence that at this same time, the critiques of the Ursuline program of education became especially vicious. When Antoine Laumet de Lamothe Cadillac proposed to establish a permanent settlement at Detroit in 1700, Governor Louis-Hector de Callière and Intendant Jean Bochard de Champigny rejected the plan to include an Ursuline school for the education of Indigenous girls and articulated their reasoning in shocking terms. For them, "experience shows that the Indian girls educated by the Ursulines, and who learn the French language, are the most awful whores because they do not only tempt away the Indians but even the French."[66] As Guillaume Aubert has pointed out, marriages between French and Indigenous people had never been designed to create a Métis population, but rather to assimilate Native populations, diluting "Indian blood" into the French "race." By the start of the eighteenth century, however, most colonial officials had turned to opposing French–Indian intermarriage in terms of biological integrity from fear of mixing "bad" and "good" blood.[67] It was no longer Native culture that the French considered a block to assimilation, but Native nature. [. . .] The governor and intendant's position against intermarriage was contrary to that of their predecessors, and fundamentally incompatible with an education meant to help prepare Indigenous girls to live as French women.

Francisation for the Ursulines sometimes aimed for the replacement of an Indigenous custom with a French one, at least temporarily (such as in the personal grooming of the students), but it was also additive (such as when students learned French in addition to Indigenous languages, and when they sang French songs but danced Aboriginal dances) and combinative (such as when students undertook religious devotions by themselves in their sylvestrian constructions). Writing her letters from the swirling centre of changing means and ends to francisation, her political agency limited by the cloister and by her community's endless need for funds, Marie de l'Incarnation may have been presenting her concerns with francisation not as a straightforward evaluation of the Ursulines' work but rather as a veiled critique of a misguided change in policy. The Ursulines in Quebec were, to be sure, agents of colonization. But as autonomous agents in a complex and contingent process, they were to a large degree accommodationist when it came to their interactions with Indigenous students, yet unwilling to accommodate the unrealistic expectations of Cobertian assimilation.

NOTES

1. "Contrat de Madame Chauvigny de la Peltrie pour la fondation des Ursulines en Nouvelle-France," 1/A,2,1,3,1, Archives des Ursulines de Québec (AUQ), 1–2, 4. All translations from French, unless indicated otherwise, are my own. I use "Indian" as a translation for "sauvage"; it is a less jarringly offensive rendering than the more obvious cognate, "savage," and, since it is a geographically inaccurate label, it conveys something of the misunderstandings common among European observers in seventeenth-century North America. Sometimes "sauvage" is rendered as "Native" in instances where I think that the early modern author meant to emphasize a North American origin. When providing a more modern interpretation or perspective, the word "Indigenous" is preferred.

2. Marcel Trudel, *Les écolières des Ursulines de Québec, 1639–1686* (Montreal: Cahiers du Québec Collection Histoire, 1999), 20–1, 42–8, 50–3, 57.

3. Saliha Belmessous, *Assimilation and Empire: Uniformity in French and British Colonies, 1541–1954* (Oxford: Oxford University Press, 2013), 14–15, 31–6. On how early modern states used an idea of universal mission to claim spiritual powers beyond the borders of their civil authority, see Luke Clossey, "Faith in Empire: Religious Sources of Legitimacy for Expansionist Early-Modern States," in *Politics and Reformations: Communities, Polities, Nations, and Empires*, eds Christopher Ocker, Michael Printy, Peter Starenko, and Peter Wallace (Leiden: Brill, 2007), 571–87.

4. Marie de l'Incarnation, *Correspondance*, ed. Guy Oury (Solesmes: Abbaye Saint-Pierre, 1971), 96, 102, 104, 112, 119.

5. Marie de l'Incarnation, *Correspondance*, 809, 828.

6. Saliha Belmessous, "Être français en Nouvelle-France: Identité française et identité coloniale aux dix-septième et dix-huitième siècles," *French Historical Studies* 27, no. 3 (2004), 510–15, 539; Gilles Havard, "'Les forcer à devenir Cytoyens': État, Sauvages et citoyenneté en Nouvelle-France (XVIIe–XVIIIe siècle)," *Annales. Histoire, Sciences Sociales* 64, no. 5 (2009), 989–1000; Belmessous, *Assimilation and Empire*, 28–30.

7. *Édits, ordonnances royaux, déclarations et arrêts du Conseil d'État du roi, concernant le Canada,*

vol. 1 (Quebec: Imprimés par P.E. Desbarats, 1803), 7.

8. Belmessous, *Assimilation and Empire*, 29; Dominique Deslandres, *Croire et faire croire: Les missions françaises au XVIIe siècle (1600–1650)* (Paris: Fayard, 2002), 364, 376; Dominique Deslandres, "L'éducation des Amérindiennes d'après la correspondance de Marie Guyant de l'Incarnation," *Studies in Religion* 16, no. 1 (1987): 92–4, 99; Trudel, *Les écolières*, 56; Gilles Havard, "Introduction: Singularités franco-amérindiennes," in *Un continent en partage: Cinq siècles de rencontres entre Amérindiens et Français*, eds Gilles Havard et Mickaël Augeron (Paris: Les Indes savantes, 2013), 16–18; Cornelius J. Jaenen, "Education for Francization: The Case of New France in the Seventeenth Century," in *Indian Education in Canada: The Legacy*, vol. 1, eds Jean Barman, Yvonne Hébert, and Don McCaskill (Vancouver: UBC Press, 1986), 47.

9. Often missing from accounts of this speech is that Champlain's Indigenous audience responded with laughter to his suggestion. *Monumenta Novae Franciae* II (Rome: Monumenta hist. soc. Jesu; Quebec: Les Presses de l'Université Laval, 1979), 452–5.

10. Laurence Lux-Sterritt, "Between the Cloister and the World: The Successful Compromise of the Ursulines of Toulouse," *French History* 16, no. 3 (2002): 253; M.A. Jégou, *Les Ursulines du faubourg Saint-Jacques à Paris 1607–1662: Origines d'un monastère apostolique* (Paris: Presses Universitaires de France, 1981), 55–6.

11. Marie de l'Incarnation, *Correspondance*, 152, 161–2, 718; Trudel, *Les écolières*, 55.

12. Marie de l'Incarnation, *Correspondance*, 103; *Monumentae Novae Franciae* (MNF) V: 65, 432, 436.

13. *1647 Constitutions*, 68r, 77r–77v; Marie de l'Incarnation, *Correspondance*, 108; Trudel, *Les écolières*, 49–50.

14. Marie de l'Incarnation, *Correspondance*, 801.

15. MNF III, 52.

16. Marie de l'Incarnation, *Correspondance*, 200; *Annales des Ursulines de Québec 1639–1822*, 1E,1,1,3,2,1, AUQ, 13v.

17. MNF II, 412, 476–77; MNF III, 615. Some may have thought that a diet based on *sagamite´* was better for the French, as well. In 1648, Paul Ragueneau wrote that Indian corn ground in a mortar, boiled in water, and seasoned with some smoked fish furnished them with a health less subject to sicknesses than did the richness and variety of foods from Europe. MNF VII, 373.

18. MNF II, 473; MNF III, 230, 744; MNF IV, 154, 215. For a discussion of the various biological and historical factors contributing to cross-cultural transmission of tastes in a colonial context, see Marcy Norton, "Tasting Empire: Chocolate and the European Internalization of Mesoamerican Aesthetics," *The American Historical Review* 111, no. 3 (2006): 660–91.

19. *Dons*, 1E,3,4,6,1, AUQ, 3r, 5v; *Annales des Ursulines de Québec 1639–1822*, 7r.

20. *État de comptes 1672–1750*, 1E,3,3,1,2, AUQ, 7r–7v.

21. *1647 Constitutions*, 64r–64v. The *Constitutions* for the Ursulines in Toulouse state that the principal aim of the order was to instruct girls in Christian doctrine and in good morals according to the study that is proper and suitable to their sex. To teach the girls Christian doctrine, piety, and practice of Christian virtues, the nuns were to instruct the girls how to read, write, and sew—in short, all sorts of work suitable for a well-raised girl. In Valréas, the nuns were to spend most of their time showing the girls how to read, write, and do other works suitable to their sex, while remembering that Christian doctrine was the principal thing they were to teach. Communities in Provence and Comtat-Venaissin had as their primary mission to catechize rather than instruct. Chantal Gueudré, *Histoire de l'ordre des Ursulines en France*, vol. ii (Paris: Éditions Saint-Paul, 1960), 229–30; Lux-Sterritt, "Between the Cloister and the World," 252; Claude-Alain Sarre, *Vivre sa soumission: L'exemple des Ursulines provençales et comtadines, 1592– 1792* (Paris: Publisud, 1997): 297, 301.

22. Marie de l'Incarnation, *Correspondance*, 96.

23. *Les Ursulines de Québec, depuis leur établissement jusqu'à nos jours*, Vol. I (Quebec: C. Darveau, 1863), 41, 114–15.

24. Jan Noel, *Along a River: The First French Canadian Women* (Toronto: University of Toronto Press, 2013); Timothy G. Pearson, "'I Willingly Speak to You about Her Virtues': Catherine de Saint-Augustin and the Public Role of Female Holiness in Early New France," *Church History* 79, no. 2 (2010): 305–33.

25. Leslie Choquette, "'Ces Amazones du Grand Dieu': Women and Mission in Seventeenth-Century Canada," *French Historical Studies* 17

(1992), 642, 654–5; Allan Greer, "Women of New France," in *Race and Gender in the Northern Colonies*, ed. Jan Noel (Toronto: Canadian Scholars, 2000), 97–8; Mary Dunn, "When 'Wolves Became Lambs': Hybridity and the 'Savage' in the Letters of Marie de l'Incarnation," *Seventeenth Century* 27, no. 1 (2012), 104–20, especially p. 115; Deslandres, "L'éducation des Amérindiennes," 105.

26. Marie de l'Incarnation, *Correspondance*, 165–6; Trudel, *Les écolières*, 118–19; Deslandres, *Croire et faire croire*, 406–7; Deslandres, "L'éducation des Amérindiennes," 94, 105; Vincent Grégoire, "L'éducation des filles au couvent des Ursulines de Québec à l'époque de Marie de l'Incarnation (1639–1672)," *Seventeenth-Century French Studies* 17, no. 1 (1995), 91. For an example of women in the 1670s who had previously been students at the Ursuline school and then withdrew themselves from traditional religious practices once they returned to their Native communities, see Tracy Neal Leavelle, *The Catholic Calumet: Colonial Conversions in French and Indian North America* (Philadelphia: University of Pennsylvania Press, 2012), 143.

27. On "combinatory American Religion" more generally, see Catherine Albanese, "Exchanging Selves, Exchanging Souls: Contact, Combination, and American Religious History," in *Retelling U.S. Religious History*, ed. Thomas Tweed (Berkeley: University of California Press, 1997), 200–26.

28. *MNF* V, 473.

29. Allan Greer, *Mohawk Saint: Catherine Tekakwitha and the Jesuits* (New York: Oxford University Press, 2005), 102.

30. Marie de l'Incarnation, *Correspondance*, 165–6; *MNF* V, 433–4. Contrast the (presumably) local plants used in the girls' cabin with the European flowers depicted in the seventeenth-century altar frontal analyzed by Christine Turgeon and Louise Lalonger, "La broderie d'art chez les Ursulines de Québec," *Bulletin du CIETA* 74 (1997): 134–45.

31. Greer, *Mohawk Saint*, especially pp. 108–11; Stuart B. Schwartz, *All Can Be Saved: Religious Tolerance and Salvation in the Iberian Atlantic World* (New Haven, CT: Yale University Press, 2008), 171.

32. *MNF* I, 499; *MNF* II, 144, 308.

33. Pierre Boucher, *Histoire véritable et naturelle des mœurs & productions du pays de la Nouvelle France, vulgairement dite le Canada* (Paris: Chez Florentin Lambert, 1664), 153–4.

34. *MNF* IV, 129; *MNF* VII, 335.

35. Ursulines in France made rules about the dress and presentation of their students too, by prohibiting an open throat and powder, for example. Gueudré, *Histoire de l'ordre des Ursulines en France*, ii, 246.

36. Marie de l'Incarnation, *Correspondance*, 220; Trudel, *Les écolières*, 53–4.

37. *Les Ursulines de Québec*, Vol. 1, 138–9.

38. Marcel Trudel describes the girls' behaviour in this episode as "coquetterie" and interprets their desire for the clothing as proof that they were beginning to *franciser* themselves. *Les écolières*, 54–5.

39. *MNF* II, 144, 303, 416; Marie de l'Incarnation, *Correspondance*, 122.

40. Dutch merchants and traders also catered to a taste for red in cloth and beads in the northeastern woodlands. De Rasiere to the Amsterdam Chamber of the West India Company, 23 September 1626, in *Documents Relating to New Netherland, 1624–1626, in the Henry E. Huntington Library* (San Marino, 1924), 228–31, cited in William Howard Carter, "Chains of Consumption: The Iroquois and Consumer Goods, 1550–1800," PhD diss., Princeton University, 2008, 248–9; George R. Hammel, "The Iroquois and the World's Rim: Speculations on Color, Culture, and Contact," *American Indian Quarterly* 16, no. 4 (1992): 451–69. My thanks to Peter Olsen-Harbich for these references.

41. Sara E. Melzer, "The Role of Culture and Art in France's Colonial Strategy of the Seventeenth Century," in *Jesuit Accounts of the Colonial Americas: Intercultural Transfers, Intellectual Disputes, and Textualities*, eds Marc André Bernier, Clorinda Donato, and Hans-Jürgen Lüsebrink (Toronto: University of Toronto Press, 2014), 170–2; Brigitte Caulier, "'Bâtir la Jérusalem des Terres froides': Réflexion sur le catholicisme français en Nouvelle-France," in *Mémoires de Nouvelle-France: De France en Nouvelle-France*, eds Philippe Joutard and Thomas Wien (Rennes: Presses universitaires de Rennes, 2005), 235–49.

42. Marie de l'Incarnation, *Correspondance*, 507.

43. Natalie Zemon Davis, *Women on the Margins: Three Seventeenth-Century Lives* (Cambridge, MA: Harvard University Press, 1995), 120. Hybridity and conversion in the context

of New France are also discussed by Mary Dunn, who writes of how the Indigenous convert "draws attention to the production of hybridization as the effect of colonial power" in Marie de l'Incarnation's letters. See Dunn, "When 'Wolves Become Lambs,'" 112. It may also have been somewhat like the "cultural conversions" described by Tracy Neal Leavelle, those "hybrid cultural forms and religious practices that reflected simultaneously the movement and the persistence of boundaries" after several generations of cultural encounter in the Upper Great Lakes and the Mississippi Valley. Neal Leavelle, *The Catholic Calumet*, 8.

44. Havard, "'Les forcer à devenir Cytoyens,'" 985–8. Contrast with Cornelius J. Jaenen, who writes that "little by little, there was a realization on the part of the educators that Amerindian cultures were not easily eradicated, that traditional beliefs were well rooted, and that the colonial environment favoured many of the Amerindian customs and practices." Jaenen, "Education for Francization," 59.

45. Marie de l'Incarnation, *Correspondance*, 809.

46. Gueudré, *Histoire de l'ordre des Ursulines en France*, ii, 241–2; Grégoire, "Malentendus culturels," 113; Deslandres, *Croire et faire croire*, 375; Jégou, *Les Ursulines du Faubourg St-Jacques*, 151.

47. Marie de l'Incarnation, *Correspondance*, 802.

48. On the Wendat in particular, see Kathryn Magee Labelle, *Dispersed but Not Destroyed: A History of the Seventeenth-Century Wendat People* (Vancouver: UBC Press, 2013), 165.

49. Marie de l'Incarnation, *Correspondance*, 809.

50. Marie de l'Incarnation, *Correspondance*, 809.

51. *1647 Constitutions*, 64v–65v. In their directions on corporal punishment, the Québec constitutions closely resembled those of communities in France. See Gueudré, *Histoire de l'ordre des Ursulines en France*, ii, 244–5; Sarre, *Vivre sa soumission*, 301.

52. *MNF* II, 458–9.

53. Marie de l'Incarnation, *Correspondance*, 95, 161–2; Trudel, *Les écolières*, 54–5.

54. Marie de l'Incarnation, *Correspondance*, 828–9.

55. Guillaume Aubert, "'The Blood of France': Race and Purity of Blood in the French Atlantic World," *William and Mary Quarterly* 61, no. 3 (2004): 439–78; Gilles Havard, "'Nous ne ferons plus qu'un peuple'. Le métissage en Nouvelle-France à l'époque de Champlain," in *Le Nouveau Monde et Champlain*, eds Guy Martinière et Didier Poton (Paris: Les Indes Savantes, 2008), 85–107.

56. Belmessous describes "three concrete measures" adopted to advance the assimilation of Indigenous peoples: encouragement to move into the St Lawrence Valley, education of children, and replication of European gender norms. *Assimilation and Empire*, 35–6. On the unusualness of France's assimilationist strategy, see Sara E. Melzer, *Colonizer or Colonized: The Hidden Stories of Early Modern French Culture* (Philadelphia: University of Pennsylvania Press, 2012), 102–9.

57. "Lettre du Ministre Colbert à Talon (5 janvier et 5 avril 1666)," *Rapport de l'archiviste de la province de Québec* (*RAPQ*) (1930–1), 45.

58. "Lettre de Talon au Ministre Colbert (13 novembre 1666)," *RAPQ* (1930–1), 58.

59. "Lettre du Ministre Colbert à Talon (5 avril 1667)," *RAPQ* (1930–1), 72.

60. "Lettre du Ministre Colbert à Talon (20 février 1668)," *RAPQ* (1930–1), 94–5.

61. Even from within the cloister, Marie de l'Incarnation recognized the importance of Indigenous peoples maintaining their traditional ways of life as critical to the economy and even the survival of the colony. In 1665, she wrote to her son about Christian Algonquin people whose hunt caught many beavers, moose, and other animals. In this, the Indians and the French mutually assisted one another—the French defending the Indians and the Indians feeding the French with the flesh of the country. *Correspondance*, 760.

62. "Lettre du Gouverneur de Frontenac au Ministre Colbert (13 novembre 1673)," *RAPQ* (1926–7), 34–5.

63. "Lettre du Roi au Gouverneur de Frontenac (22 avril 1675)," *RAPQ* (1926–7), 82–3.

64. Quoted in Havard, "'Les forcer à devenir Cytoyens,'" 999.

65. Belmessous, *Assimilation and Empire*, 15–16, 27.

66. Aubert, "'The Blood of France,'" 458.

67. Aubert, "'The Blood of France,'" 439–478.

Chapter 3

The Seigneurial Regime in New France

READINGS

Primary Documents

1 From "Memoir of Jacques Raudot, Intendant, to M. de Pontchartrain, Minister of Marine, on the Growth of Seigneurial Abuses in Canada, November 10, 1707," Jacques Raudot; D.C. Bélanger, trans. and ed.

2 From *Travels into North America: Containing Its Natural History and a Circumstantial Account of Its Plantations and Agriculture in General . . .* , Peter Kalm

Historical Interpretations

3 From "Seigneurial Landscapes," in *The Metamorphoses of Landscape and Community in Early Quebec*, Colin M. Coates

4 From "The Feudal Burden," in *Peasant, Lord & Merchant: Rural Society in Three Quebec Parishes 1740–1840*, Allan Greer

INTRODUCTION

The seigneurial system stands as one of the defining aspects of the colonial experience in New France. Under this system of land tenure, large land grants were made by the French Crown to prominent subjects called *seigneurs* who were required, in turn, to grant strips of land to tenants called *censitaires* (also known as *habitants*) in exchange for the perpetual payment of rent and dues. Land was not to be sold to the censitaires, who owned their farms, and they were tied to their seigneur through a complex system of mutual obligations. A seigneur could become wealthy if he succeeded in attracting censitaires to the land, and it was assumed that paternalism and self-interest would guide him to provide the services necessary for settlement and encourage his tenants to work hard.

The seigneurial system defined everyone's duties clearly, but it required a great deal of management. Was this seigneur doing his part? Was that tenant using land or resources without permission? The first primary source is an excerpt from a memoir written by the intendant

Jacques Raudot addressed to the French Minister of Marine in 1707. In his memoir, Raudot highlights many problems relative to the working of the seigneurial system in New France and suggests many reforms to make it more effective. When Peter Kalm travelled through New France in 1749, he noted another effect of the system: the orderly arrangement of tenants' houses that were not in a village, but situated to allow the tenants to exploit their land and the transportation corridors offered by the St Lawrence and its tributaries. He also noted the poverty among the censitaires, whose happiness was tied directly to how well or poorly their crops fared in a particular year. With tenants living in this fashion, it was almost inevitable that the system would influence the social interactions between tenants, between tenants and seigneurs, and between seigneurs. As Colin Coates demonstrates, for seigneurs, the priorities were enlarging their holdings and establishing themselves as indispensable to the colonial effort. They renamed geographical features in their seigneuries, served in the military (French and British), allocated land to tenants, sued tenants, and played the role of social elite very well, maintaining their positions despite the considerable upheaval that accompanied the Conquest. In the final selection, Allan Greer studies the importance of the rents due to the landlords, arguing that these rents could be quite burdensome to the censitaires. He shows that it was difficult for the latter to accumulate wealth in the way that seigneurs could and did. For most colonists, survival was the priority.

QUESTIONS FOR CONSIDERATION

1. What do you find most remarkable or surprising about the way the seigneurial system worked?
2. What were the main abuses of the seigneurial system in New France according to Raudot, and how could the Minister of the Marine remedy them?
3. It is fairly well known that lands within the seigneuries were laid out in relation to rivers. How might this distribution affect the way people socialized?
4. List some examples of the ways in which the Lanaudière family consolidated its power under the seigneurial system.
5. What kinds of dues did seigneurs extract from their censitaires? How lucrative were they for the former and burdensome for the latter?

SUGGESTIONS FOR FURTHER READING

Dechêne, Louise. *Habitants and Merchants in Seventeenth-Century Montreal*. Montreal and Kingston: McGill-Queen's University Press, 1992.

Greer, Allan. *Peasant, Lord & Merchant: Rural Society in Three Quebec Parishes 1740–1840*. Toronto: University of Toronto Press, 1985.

———. *The People of New France*. Toronto: University of Toronto Press, 1997.

Grenier, Benoit. *Brève histoire du régime seigneurial*. Montreal: Boréal, 2012.

Kennedy, Gregory. *Something of a Peasant Paradise? Comparing Rural Societies in Acadie and the Loudunais, 1604–1755*. Montreal and Kingston: McGill-Queen's University Press, 2014.

Munro, William Bennett, ed. *Documents Relating to the Seigniorial Tenure in Canada, 1598–1854*. Toronto: The Champlain Society, 1908.

Trudel, Marcel. *The Seigneurial Regime*. Ottawa: Canadian Historical Association, 1971.

Primary Documents

1 From Jacques Raudot, "Memoir of Jacques Raudot, Intendant, to M. de Pontchartrain, Minister of Marine, on the Growth of Seigniorial Abuses in Canada, November 10, 1707," D.C. Bélanger, trans. and ed.

Correspondance Générale, XXVI, 7.

My Lord,

The spirit of enterprise, which has always, as you know, far more deviousness and chicanery than truth and righteousness, has begun to appear here recently and increases daily in a most negative way. If we could curb its undesirable side, *this spirit could augur well for the future*, though the simple life of bygone years would be far better. But the past is past, and to my mind there is nothing more pernicious than this spirit and more harmful to the repose and the tranquility that one must give to the people of a colony, which can only be upheld and increased by the labour of its inhabitants, and which they must not be given the occasion to turn away from.

Since almost none of the commerce that they have conducted followed the rules, the notaries, bailiffs, and even judges are all ignorant, especially those who were trained in this colony, as they have for the most part worked their lands *without proper assurances from those who conceded them*, there is no property against which one cannot find a fault, no division which is uncontestable, no widow that could not sued into a common state,[1] and no guardian who could not be brought to court for the accounts that he kept for his wards. It is not that things were done in bad faith, but rather that ignorance and a lack of observance for the rules in all these affairs has produced disorder, which would become worse if those who are imbued with the spirit of enterprise, either of their own accord or under the council of others, brought various matters to court. There would be more trials in this country than there are persons; and since judges are obliged to follow the law, which they are beginning to get a sense of, as they apply it to cases where ignorance of the law insured that it was not followed, they would be obligated to perpetrate a thousand injustices, which I would have been forced to do myself, My Lord, if I had followed the strict letter of the law in many of the cases that were brought before me.

For all these reasons, My Lord, I believe that you could not do greater good to the inhabitants of this country than if you could obtain from His Majesty *a declaration that would guarantee permanent ownership over land* following existing property lines for those *who have been in possession of said property for five years* or who have laboured therein or held a title, in any form, that validates all present divisions, and which would forbid parties from initiating legal proceedings regarding guardianship agreements and legal waivers that wives have had to make to their husband's community, and which would forbid judges from accepting cases of this nature. Also, My Lord, the declaration would validate all the decrees that have come to pass and all other acts, as well as contracts that have been passed up to the present and the rights that individuals have obtained from each other, *except in odious cases*, for instance in acts and contracts where evidence of usury, misconduct, or fraud is present, or in cases of appropriation through violence or abuse of authority.

Only in this way My Lord, can you put this country at peace and tranquility, which without this just precaution will always be unhappy and unable to grow, as its inhabitants, who should be busy cultivating their land, will instead be forced to occupy themselves with spurious litigation. I know this evil, My Lord, through all the business that is continually brought before me and which has overwhelmed me since I have arrived here; because these poor inhabitants have found me easy to deal with and do not need to dip into their purse to plead their case, scarcely a day goes by where I do not issue several ordinances to straighten out various matters that were concluded before I arrived. There are even those who, fearing trials, come to see me to ask that I prevent such trials from occurring, their ignorance making them fearful of the smallest threats from those who are as ignorant as they.

I am honoured to tell you, My Lord, that if His Majesty gives them the declaration that I have the honour to ask for them, it will be necessary to insure the ownership over land to its rightful owners that it contain a clause that covers cases of simple possession because formalities were often not followed here when land grants were made. Many *habitants* have toiled on the mere word of the *seigneurs*, others on simple bills that did not properly lay out the dues related to their grant. Out of this has come much abuse, where *habitants* who have worked without a valid title have been subjected to arbitrary rents and contracts, which they are forced to accept because otherwise they will lose the fruits of their labour. This has created a situation whereby in almost all of the *seigneuries'* rights and obligations are different; some pay in one way, others in another way, all following the whim of the *seigneur* who made the grant. They have even introduced in almost all the contracts *a retrait roturier that is not contained in the Custom of Paris*,[2] but that has become customary in this country and which stipulates that a *seigneur*, when land is sold, can take back the land that he granted *en roture* for the sale price, and in

so doing they have abused of the *retrait conditionnel*[3] that is stipulated in the Custom of Paris and which is sometimes contained in contracts of sale where the seller reserves the right to buy back the property, though it is not established between *seigneurs* and tenants; this preference, My Lord, hinders all land sales.

There are concessions where the capons[4] that are paid to the *seigneurs*, are in fact paid in kind or in cash at the whim of the *seigneurs*; these capons are appraised at 30 sols but are only in fact worth 10 sols; the *seigneurs* then force their tenants to give them money, which is extremely burdensome for them because they often do not have the means to pay, because while 30 sols might not seem like a lot of money, it is in fact a great deal of money in this country where specie is rare, aside from the fact that it seems to me that whenever there are accounts payable, when there is a choice, that choice should be made to the advantage of the debtor, as owing specie is a burden when he cannot pay in kind.

The *seigneurs* have also introduced in their fiefs the right of the *four banal*,[5] which the *habitants* cannot profit from because their homes are often quite far from the *seigneur*'s house, where this oven must be placed, and which cannot be placed anywhere more convenient, no matter what, because most homes are far from each other and it would not be possible to bring the dough to the oven in all seasons; in winter it would freeze before it could be brought there. The *seigneurs* are vexed by these circumstances and do not exercise their full banal rights at present, but they will no doubt turn these into a title that must be bought for a large sum, and in so doing they will acquire a right that does not in any way benefit the *habitants*. This is called, My Lord, to give oneself a title in order to cause future vexation. [. . .]

I thus believe, My Lord, according to your pleasure, that to bring some semblance of order and to give justice to the *habitants* in a way that the *seigneurs* have not done at present and to prevent future abuse, that it is necessary for His Majesty to *make a declaration that will reform* and that will settle for the future the rights and obligations that the *seigneurs* have given themselves and that they will give themselves in the future, and that His Majesty will order in the future; and that His Majesty will order that they only take by arpent granted, one sol of rent and one capon by arpent of frontage, or twenty sols, at the discretion of the debtor; that the preference clause that *seigneurs* have given themselves in the sale of *héritages roturiers* be removed; that the right of *four banal* be removed; that in areas where fishing is practised the seigneurial rights be diminished to a simple tenth, without further conditions; and that the *droit de banalité* be maintained, and that a mill be built in all seigneuries within a year, without which the right will be considered to have fallen into disuse, and the *habitants* will not have to mill their grain at the seigneurial mill thereafter; without this, My Lord, we will never be able to get the seigneurs to build mills, a situation which causes much suffering among the *habitants*. [. . .]

I remain, with profound respect, My Lord, your most humble, your most obedient, and your most obligated servant,
Raudot
At Quebec, on this 10th of November 1707.

NOTES

1. That is, "no widow whose dower right might not be contested."
2. The *retrait rotutier* was the right of the seignior, when a habitant sold his farm, to exercise an option of buying in the land at the sale price.
3. The Custom of Paris recognized the *retrait conditionnel*, or *jus retraiteur*, whereby a dominant seignior might, within 40 days after any sale of a sub-seigniory, buy it in by tendering the sale price to the purchaser (*Coutume de Paris*, Article XX.).
4. The reference is to the seigniorial *rentes*, which were usually paid in poultry and grain.
5. The Custom of Paris (Article LXXI.) recognized the seignior's right to erect a seigniorial oven, and, when he had so stipulated in the title-deeds given to his censitaires, to compel the latter to make use of such oven at a fixed toll. This toll was usually one twenty-fourth of the bread. The nature and extent of this right is discussed in a paper on "The Droit de Banalité during the French Régime in Canada," in American Historical Association, *Report*, 1899, I. 205–28.

2 From Peter Kalm, *Travels into North America: Containing Its Natural History and a Circumstantial Account of Its Plantations and Agriculture in General . . .*, vol. 2 (London: T. Lowndes, 1773), 242–4, 330–1.

All the farms in *Canada* stand separate from each other, so that each farmer has his possessions entirely distinct from those of his neighbour. Each church, it is true, has a little village near it; but that consists chiefly of the parsonage, a school for the boys and girls of the place, and of the houses of tradesmen, but rarely of farm-houses; and if that was the case, yet their fields were separated. The farm-houses hereabouts are generally built all along the rising banks of the river, either close to the water or at some distance from it, and about three or four *arpens* from each other. To some farms are annexed small orchards: but they are in general without them; however, almost every farmer has a kitchen-garden.

[. . .]

The farm-houses are generally built of stone, but sometimes of timber, and have three or four rooms. The windows are seldom of glass, but most frequently of paper. They have iron stoves in one of the rooms, and chimneys in the rest. The roofs are covered with boards. The crevices and chinks are filled up with clay. The other buildings are covered with straw.

There are several *Crosses* put up by the road side, which is parallel to the shores of the river. These crosses are very common in *Canada*, and are put up to excite devotion in the traveller. They are made of wood, five or six yards high, and proportionally broad. In that side which looks towards the road is a square hole, in which they place an image of our Saviour, the cross, or of the holy Virgin, with the child in her arms; and before that they put a piece of glass, to prevent its being spoiled by the weather. Those crosses, which are not far from churches, are very much adorned, and they put up about them all the instruments which they think the *Jews* employed in crucifying our Saviour, such as a hammer, tongs, nails, a flask of vinegar, and perhaps many more than were really made use of. A figure of the cock, which crowed when *St. Peter* denied our Lord, is commonly put at the top of the cross.

The country on both sides was very delightful to-day, and the fine state of its cultivation added greatly to the beauty of the scene. It could really be called a village, beginning at *Montreal*, and ending at *Quebec*, which is a distance of more than one hundred and eighty miles; for the farm-houses are never above five arpens, and sometimes but three, asunder, a few places excepted. The prospect is exceedingly beautiful, when the river goes on for some miles together in a strait line, because it then shortens the distances between the houses, and makes them form exactly one continued village.

[. . .]

August 26th. [. . .] The common people in the country seem to be very poor. They have the necessaries of life, and but little else. They are content with meals of dry bread and water, bringing all other provisions, such as butter, cheese, flesh, poultry, eggs, &c. to town, in order to get money for them, for which they buy clothes and brandy for themselves, and dresses for their women. Notwithstanding their poverty, they are always chearful, and in high spirits.

August 29th. By the desire of the governor-general, marquis *de la Jonquiere*, and of marquis *de la Galissonniere*, I set out, with some *French* gentlemen, to visit the pretended silver-mine, or the lead-mine, near the bay *St. Paul.* I was glad to undertake this journey, as it gave me an opportunity of seeing a much greater part of the country than I should otherwise have done. This morning therefore we set out on our tour in a boat, and went down the river *St. Lawrence.*

The prospect near *Quebec* is very lively from the river. The town lies very high, and all the churches and other buildings appear very conspicuous. The ships in the river below ornament the landscape on that side. The powder magazine, which stands at the summit of the mountain on which the town is built, towers above all the other buildings.

The country we passed by afforded a no less charming sight. The river *St. Lawrence* flows nearly from south to north here; on both sides of it are cultivated fields, but more on the west side than on the east side. The hills on both shores are steep and high. A number of fine hills, separated from each other, large fields, which looked quite white from the corn with which they are covered, and excellent woods of deciduous trees, made the country round us look very pleasant.

Historical Interpretations

3 From Colin M. Coates, "Seigneurial Landscapes," in *The Metamorphoses of Landscape and Community in Early Quebec* (Montreal and Kingston: McGill-Queen's University Press, 2000), 13–31, 171–6.

Land was no longer free as air or light,
A fixed division mark'd each owner's
right.

Ovid, *Metamorphoses*, 12

In the 300 years following Jacques Cartier's first sighting of the area that became the seigneuries of Batiscan and Sainte-Anne de la Pérade, the landscape underwent irrevocable change. In contrast to the shields of forests that had confronted the early European explorers and settlers, it became possible by the early nineteenth century to compare the land to European landscapes and to use European artistic conventions to capture it on paper. The changes that occurred were long-term ones caused by different perceptions and uses of the land. At least in the areas close to the St Lawrence, the landscape became essentially European, with a visible hierarchy of land use.

The appropriation of the landscape by French settlers involved the importing of new animal and plant species and obviously a new race of humans. This process entailed the distancing of the native animals, plants, and humans from the new settlements. There was a dual process in the transformation of the landscape. In the first place, the French colonial state and the seigneurs played important roles in an overall restructuring of the land; the respective importance of the seigneurs and the state varied over time. Even more important, the practical labour of generations of habitants irrevocably altered the bases of society.

REDEFINING THE LAND

Naming

One of the most important ways in which the colonial state initially made its presence felt in Batiscan and Sainte-Anne de la Pérade was through attempts to redefine the land, to draw and redraw borders around the areas.[1] The first act of appropriating the territories in the name of the French king was to name them (or properly speaking, rename them).

The origins of the word "Batiscan" are obscure, though it doubtless has an Amerindian derivation. Samuel de Champlain first mentioned "a river called Batiscan" in his account of his 1603 voyage.[2] Among the various geographical phenomena that he saw during his explorations, he found rivers particularly noteworthy. This interest illustrates the bias of the typical explorer, intrigued by geographical phenomena which demarcate journeys as well as those which promise future explorations.[3] However, the ambiguous chronology surrounding its mention in the account leaves open the possibility that the name does not necessarily refer to the same river as today. Indeed, Champlain's 1612 map placed the "contrée de bastisquan" to the west of the Rivière Saint-Maurice. By contrast, Marc Lescarbot's map of 1609 illustrated and named the "R. Batescan" in the same area as the present one. Even if, in reporting the earthquake of 1663, the Jesuits alluded to "the river which the barbarians call Batiscan,"[4] it was a French decision whether or not to adopt the name.

The river with the Algonquin name formed the symbolic locus of future French settlement. The title "Batiscan" was extended to the seigneury, indicating that early French interest in the area lay, not in the land itself, but in the river and the transportation that it provided into the interior and into fur-trading areas. Over time, French settlers populated the territory and placed more importance on the land than the river. They even occasionally domesticated the Aboriginal origin of the name. In 1783, for example, the habitants living along the river drew up a petition in which the name was given as "Baptiste Camp."[5]

In his account of the 1609 voyage and on his 1612 map, Champlain had named the river to the east of the Batiscan the Sainte-Marie. This name later came to refer to the seigneury on the west bank of the river, and the river itself took on the name of an island at the mouth, Île Sainte-Anne.[6] As in Batiscan, the river's name was extended to both the seigneury on the east bank and the parish, which included settlers on both sides. The names Sainte-Marie and Sainte-Anne, linked as they were to Christian beliefs and particularly to the Marian cult of the Catholic Counter-Reformation, illustrated another imperial aim: the propagation of the faith.

But the region owed its territorial names not only to explorers and their imperial initiatives. Local seigneurs also made their imprint. To distinguish it from the other Sainte-Annes in the colony, the seigneurial patronymic La Pérade gradually replaced près Batiscan (near Batiscan) in the eighteenth century. Likewise, in Batiscan the choice of the Jesuit pioneers for the parish names of Saint-François-Xavier and Saint-Stanislas surely reflect the order's ownership. Finally, when the Jesuits' agent sold businessman Thomas Coffin an arrière-fief (a fief within a larger seigneury) in Batiscan in 1795, it is not difficult to imagine the inspiration for the name Saint-Thomas. In these ways seigneurs replicated for their own purposes the state's initial process of imposing names on the region.

Distributing Fiefs

Conceded as seigneuries at different times, Batiscan and Sainte-Anne illustrate two important moments in the distribution of fiefs during the seventeenth century. According to its charter, the Compagnie de la Nouvelle-France was compelled to establish a French population in the colony. In 1636 it conveyed ten leagues of land downstream from the Rivière Saint-Maurice to Jacques de La Ferté, the king's confessor. Three years later, La Ferté conceded part of the immense tract in arrière-fief to the Jesuits. The shape of Batiscan seigneury resembled other land grants of the period: a long trapezoid with relatively little waterfront.[7]

Jacques de La Ferté "for the love of God" conveyed the area around the Rivière Batiscan to the Jesuits, the religious order leading the Counter-Reformation and one of the largest landholders in the colony. The Jesuits' deed stipulated the width of the seigneury—from one-quarter league beyond the Batiscan to one-quarter league beyond the Rivière Champlain—but left its depth ill-defined.[8] It may have been Champlain's reference to an Aboriginal population in the Batiscan area that led to the decision to concede it to the Jesuits. According to the deed, the seigneury was intended for Christianized Amerindians, but their lack of interest and hostility delayed settlement for decades. The Jesuits' intention was clearly to create a new France in the New World, preferably with converted Natives. However, agents of the order did not perform the ritual taking symbolic possession of the seigneury until 1662.

Batiscan seigneury represented one of the larger land grants in the colony. Nonetheless, the exact boundaries were not immediately defined. In 1667 the Jesuits claimed, in vague fashion, ownership of "a space of land between the Rivière Batiscan and the Rivière Champlain."[9] Ten years later it was acknowledged that the breadth consisted of two leagues of river frontage from the east

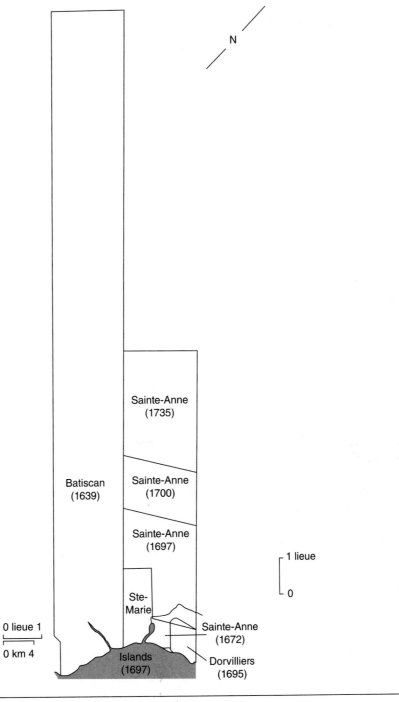

Figure 3.1 Seigneurial boundaries, Sainte-Anne and Batiscan

bank of the Rivière Champlain to a quarter league beyond the Rivière Batiscan.[10] The seigneury extended 20 leagues into the interior, representing some 282 240 arpents (1 arpent equals 0.342 hectares). Batiscan did not appear in the colonial census of 1663, but many settlers received land grants in the following decade.[11] According to the seigneurs, confirmed deeds of settlement had been delayed by two main factors, the Iroquois menace and the absence of established authority—"having no regular or established form of justice in the area."[12] From the beginning, European settlement required the authority of the colonial state.

Changes in royal policy account for the difference in size of the concessions of Batiscan and Sainte-Anne. After Louis XIV assumed direct control of the colony in the 1660s, he expressed the desire to limit the size of seigneurial grants and to curtail the granting of seigneuries to religious orders. The details of the granting of Île Sainte-Anne to Michel Gamelain, probably in 1666, are not known,[13] but it is clear that the seigneury extended over only a tiny area. Gamelain used this property to establish a fur trade post, but he nonetheless did concede some land on the island.[14]

Intendant Jean Talon pursued the king's policy more thoroughly, granting smaller seigneuries, many of them to officers of the Carignan regiment.[15] This desire to facilitate the creation of a noble military-seigneurial class led to Talon's approval of the purchase of Gamelain's land by Edmond de Suève and Thomas de Lanouguère. In 1672 the intendant officially recognized the purchase and further conceded land to a depth of one league between the Rivière Sainte-Anne and the seigneury of Grondines to the two noble officers. As he stated, this grant was given "in consideration of the good, useful, and praiseworthy services that they have rendered to His Majesty in different places, both in Old France and in New France since they passed to the

latter on His Majesty's order, as well as in consideration of the services that they intend to render in the future."[16] The intendant explicitly justified the officers' status as seigneurs by mentioning their service to the monarch. Members of the de Lanouguère family subsequently carved out a long career of service to their king, regardless of the throne on which he sat.

The co-owners of Sainte-Anne divided the seigneury into two distinct sections. In 1695 de Suève willed his half to Edmond Chorel de Champlain, who passed it into the hands of his brother, François Chorel d'Orvilliers. As in the western part of Sainte-Anne, the seigneurial family names over time came to identify the area. However, the seigneurs who owned the eastern section did not reside there. The d'Orvilliers family lived principally in Champlain seigneury during the French regime, and subsequent seigneurs of Sainte-Anne Est in the early nineteenth century were also absentee owners: Moses Hart, a merchant in Trois-Rivières, and Pierre Charest, a merchant at Saint-Joseph de Soulanges.[17]

From time to time boundary disputes set the seigneurial families of the two parts of Sainte-Anne against each other, but by the 1730s it was clear that de Lanouguère's son, Pierre-Thomas Tarieu de La Pérade, enjoyed greater local prominence. He and his mother had successfully petitioned for the extension of the original boundaries in 1697, 1700, and 1735.[18] The two smaller fiefs on either side, Dorvilliers to the east and Sainte-Marie to the west, found themselves bounded on the north by the expanded seigneury. By 1735 Sainte-Anne seigneury encompassed some 60 square leagues. Although the Tarieu de Lanaudière family was by no means always present at its seigneury, it seems to have participated actively in local issues. Like the Jesuits in Batiscan, its members exercised their seigneurial privileges at certain times and provided a link to the world of the colonial state.

Hierarchy in the Landscape

In contrast to the Aboriginal occupation of the territory, the French landholding system entailed a hierarchical view of society. The king, in whom ultimate title rested, distributed tracts of land to seigneurs and preserved certain rights on that land, particularly concerning minerals and timber. The seigneur in turn distributed lots to tenants (*censitaires*) but placed limits on the tenants' control of their property.

When the seigneurs began to distribute land in their seigneuries, it was of course impossible for them to know that immigration would remain negligible over the next century. They could not know that future population growth and the concomitant increase of their seigneurial revenues would depend almost exclusively on natural demographic trends. Therefore in an examination of the way in which seigneurs preferred their landscape to take shape, the earliest years of French settlement are the most revealing.

The seigneurs' attempts to structure their space appear most clearly in their decisions concerning manors, mills, and churches. In both Batiscan and Sainte-Anne the early seigneurs first directed their proprietorial interest toward small islands in the St Lawrence, perhaps because these were more defensible. In Batiscan the *aveu et dénombrement* (list of landholdings) of 1677 designated Île Saint-Éloi, along with a nearby concession on the mainland, as the "demesne and seigneurial manor."[19] The first windmill, constructed in 1668, and the parish church were erected nearby on the mainland. Since this tract of land lay in the middle of the concessions along the St Lawrence, we can speculate that the Jesuits attempted thereby to provide a symbolic centre for the early seigneury, one dominated by the religious power of the church, the practical economic functions of the windmill, and the legal authority of the seigneur. An early deed of concession referred to this area as "le village de batiscan," which,

given the low density of settlement at that date, represented more a wish than a reality.[20]

In Sainte-Anne, Michel Gamelain first granted concessions on Île Saint-Ignace, at the mouth of the river. He reserved Île des Plaines for himself, and over time, subsequent seigneurs regained most of Île Saint-Ignace for themselves.[21] These islands would remain in the hands of the seigneurs for the next century and a half, but they chose to establish their manor on the mainland. Unlike Batiscan—or for that matter, neighbouring Sainte-Marie and Dorvilliers—none of the habitants' concessions fronted on the St Lawrence. In Sainte-Anne the seigneurs reserved this privilege to themselves, establishing their manor a short distance away from the river and only sharing the frontage with a common.[22] Consequently, from the perspectives afforded by the rivers, the seigneurs of Sainte-Anne dominated their landscape: Anyone sailing along the north shore of the St Lawrence or travelling up the Sainte-Anne would first come into view of seigneurial lands. The Lanouguères enjoyed the clearest view of the St Lawrence from their land, while the principal axis for the habitants' concessions would be the Rivière Sainte-Anne.[23]

The seigneurs of Sainte-Anne also encouraged the founding of a village. Disputing the location of the parish church with the seigneur of adjacent Sainte-Marie, they were ultimately able to establish the church on the east bank of the river.[24] In 1691 de Suève granted to the parish land for a church and a presbytery and permitted the construction of a village on the remaining property, transferring the rents for this land to the church.[25] By the time of James Murray's 1760 map, a rather diffuse village had taken shape, largely to the south of the parish church.[26] It probably owed its existence in part to chance: It served as an important relay post along the royal road, one day's journey from Quebec. In general, the habitants in both Sainte-Anne and Batiscan avoided dense settlement.

Given the fact that Lanouguère, de Suève, and the Jesuits could not have known how slow the rate of settlement would be, we must speculate as to the nature of the ideal landscape that they wanted to establish. It was one in which the seigneurs wished to occupy central and strategic places. From the land that they maintained as a demesne, they could closely watch over the development of their respective seigneuries. The Jesuits' control centred around the church and the mill; that is, it was based on both religion and economy. The lay seigneurs of Sainte-Anne dominated the view of the St Lawrence and therefore the access to the external world.

After Gamelain's initial, and short-lived, focus on fur-trading activities, subsequent seigneurs turned their attention to a local agrarian economy. But the early attempts to structure the landscape illustrate their desire to assert their ascendancy and reveal the symbolism of land distribution.

SEIGNEURS AND THE STATE

The Lanaudière Family

The local elite ensured the connection of their society to the external world: Seigneurs, priests, local state officials (judges, notaries, bailiffs, and militia captains), and military officials all played a role, but in Sainte-Anne the seigneurs enjoyed pre-eminence during the French regime. The colonial state relied on this noble elite to represent it in rural areas and provided privileged access to patronage and favours. For the Tarieu de Lanaudière family, this treatment persisted into the British regime.

For many seigneurial families, military commissions and concomitant fur trade privileges provided the economic basis of their status. The Lanaudières always remained a military family. All the adult males up to the early nineteenth century held commissions in either the French or the British army, and

a couple of the women were famous for their exploits with firearms too.[27] Through the five generations of Lanaudières who owned Sainte-Anne, the family profited from its connections to governing officials to obtain trade licences and other lucrative privileges.

After Sainte-Anne was granted to de Suève and Thomas de Lanouguère, the former managed the seigneury while the latter, with Governor Louis de Buade de Frontenac's support, participated in the fur trade and exercised the military command in Montreal.[28] From an early date the seigneurs defended their rights; in 1673 they appealed to their seigneurial judge to force their tenants to pay their dues.[29] After his death in 1678, Lanouguère's widow, Marguerite-Renée Denys, assumed control of the western half of the seigneury. A 1685 census enumerated 114 residents. In 1704 Denys abandoned, in exchange for annual payments of 400 livres, ownership to her second son, Pierre-Thomas, under the assumption that his long-absent elder brother was dead.[30]

In the 1720s and 1730s Pierre-Thomas and his wife Madeleine de Verchères initiated a number of court cases as they attempted to enforce their legal rights and ensure their social and economic prominence in the growing seigneury. In 1728, for example, they accused the local priest and several habitants of contravening the requirement to take grain to the seigneur's gristmill. The judgment in this case validated the seigneur's seizure of wheat and required the habitants to take their grain to the seigneurial mill in the future. To add prestige to the economic gain, the intendant ordered that the seigneur should serve as arbiter in any disputes over measurement.[31] In other cases, the family sought confirmation of its exclusive rights over fishing and hunting and for the privilege of first pew in the parish church.[32]

During this time it appealed to the government for other concrete recognitions of its status. In 1731 Madeleine de Verchères requested, through the governor and the intendant, an increase in the royal pension that she received for her youthful heroism in defending her family fort at Verchères from the Iroquois.[33] Although Pierre-Thomas's application in 1729 for the position of chief road officer and his request the following year for a military promotion were not granted,[34] he continued to hold military posts, which he was able to use to profit from trade. Despite his activity outside the seigneury, Pierre-Thomas and in particular his wife were very active in local social relations. Their heirs, however, became less involved in the seigneury.

In the last decades of the French regime, Pierre-Thomas's son, Charles-François de Lanaudière, became even more closely tied to state officials in Quebec. Diarist Élisabeth Bégon described his wife as the intendant's "princesse."[35] Charles-François and his younger brother formed part of Intendant François Bigot's retinue, following him on his travels through the colony.[36] Charles-François, while serving as an officer in the colonial troops, earned the cross of the order of Saint-Louis in 1759. He served the governors on a number of occasions in a police capacity: compiling a roll of militiamen and requisitioning provisions from the peasantry for the sustenance of French troops during the Seven Years' War.[37] He also participated in the fur trade, establishing lucrative accounts with merchants in La Rochelle, selling seal furs and oil, and importing wine and brandy.[38] In 1750 Lanaudière was granted the seigneury of Lac-Maskinongé, presumably in recognition of the successes of his military career. The official favour that Lanaudière enjoyed in the period before the Conquest confirmed his status in society, but it also drew him away from the seigneury of Sainte-Anne. The estate inventory drawn up after the death of his first wife in 1762 noted that there was no seigneurial manor.[39]

After the Conquest, Sainte-Anne might have passed out of the hands of the Lanaudière family. Charles-François and his only surviving child, Charles-Louis, both sailed to France following the military defeat. However, they did not emigrate definitively. Charles-François, like others in his situation, discovered the difficulties of acquiring a good position in the French army, of maintaining his trade contacts in the newly redefined North America, and of establishing a son who lived more expensively than he could afford. With the direct trade to Canada blocked, Charles-François pursued trading possibilities through the French island of Miquelon off Newfoundland and through Louisiana, dealing in merchandise such as cloths, nails, and sealing lines, but this venture took many years to come to fruition and proved less lucrative than he had foreseen. Charles-François's subsequent correspondence with La Rochelle merchants focused on investing his capital in securities. He hesitated for a while about settling in France, but the news that Canadian officers found it difficult to acquire positions in the French army must have been discouraging.[40]

Charles-François returned to Canada in 1762, after the death of his first wife. Two years later he married Marie-Catherine Le Moyne de Longueuil, with whom he had ten children. Over time, his eldest son, Charles-Louis, developed an interest in Sainte-Anne seigneury, one which appeared to be tied up with noble sentiments and with an assertion of his position among his father's offspring.

[. . .]

Charles-Louis had returned to Canada by 1768, apparently because he was an inveterate gambler and had racked up so many debts that he had to leave France to escape his creditors. During his stopover in London he ran into more troubles and had to make a hasty return to Quebec.[41]

Back at home Charles-Louis de Lanaudière was able to acquire a position as aide-de-camp to General Guy Carleton, a position he relished. As he informed his father in 1770, "one cannot be happier than I am with my sire the general."[42] In this position, he returned to England and Europe on many occasions, during which he attempted to enhance his trading activities. [. . .]

According to Charles-Louis, a hunting trip with three English friends awakened his interest in the paternal estate of Sainte-Anne. The English aristocratic predilection for country estates and in particular for hunting privileges is well recognized.[43] Charles-Louis de Lanaudière undoubtedly came to share these tastes. He asked his father for title to the seigneury, which was granted to him less Île des Plaines (or Île Sainte-Marguerite) in an agreement signed in 1772.[44] Nonetheless, he did not establish permanent residency at Sainte-Anne. His activities led him to spend much of his time in Quebec, but the letters that Charles-Louis wrote from Sainte-Anne indicated that his presence at the seigneury was not restricted to any one season.[45] [. . .]

Despite his occasional notable appearances on his seigneury, Lanaudière paid much less day-to-day attention to its administration. He entrusted the management of the seigneury to the Gouin family. By the 1810s he was concentrating his demesne farming on sheep, hay, and wheat.[46] Nonetheless, he still maintained a paternalistic interest in his tenants.

Obviously, Lanaudière would have appreciated the steady, if not elevated, income that the seigneury provided. However, his main projects, such as fur-trading ventures, took place elsewhere.[47] But his principal field of activity was his connection with the new rulers of the colony. He was appointed to the sinecure of surveyor general of forests and rivers in 1771. He demonstrated his loyalty to the British crown in 1775 when he tried to raise militia to fight the American invaders and provided protection for Governor Carleton. Charles-Louis received his share of patronage and social recognition as a result, being appointed to the Legislative Council and to the position of overseer of highways. Like British grandees of the period,[48] he saw the position of surveyor general as an opportunity to bend rules to his own profit. In 1778, for example, he sent a proposal to his cousin, François Baby, to cut timber from his seigneury and the neighbouring ones for sale in Quebec. Taking advantage of his position and his connections to the government, he suggested supplying the garrison in Quebec with wood: "As the government must use its authority to cut the wood—I propose this, if I can be given the parishes of Deschambault, Grondines, Sainte-Anne, and all of Batiscan—which never supply wood, with the power to command the men whom I will require for this work."[49] The government's ability to demand a corvée (required labour) would even release him personally from the necessity of hiring workers to cut the trees. He added in a subsequent letter, "in conducting government business, I must also do my own."[50] For Lanaudière, state and personal affairs were not just compatible; they were mutually reinforcing.

He and other members of the family continued to use whatever influence they could muster to support the colonial government. In the 1792 elections for the House of Assembly, for example, Lanaudière campaigned in favour of William Grant, a candidate who favoured strong British rule.[51] Almost two decades later, his half-brother Xavier-Roch presented himself for election in Sainte-Anne, an act which sister Agathe applauded in trying to convince her other brother Gaspard to do the same: "it is the duty of all men who are attached to their king to make this effort."[52]

The Lanaudière family, in particular Charles-Louis, had obviously made an easy transition to the new regime. It is possible that its members counted among the most successful French nobles in this regard.[53] In doing so, Charles-Louis adopted many of the viewpoints of the new rulers, in particular those concerning land tenure.

[. . .]

In 1790 Lanaudière submitted his opinions on seigneurial tenure to the Executive Council. After drawing a somewhat exaggerated picture of seigneurial privileges, he concluded, "The honorary, as well as pecuniary duties and dues are evidently complex, arbitrary, injurious. Can anything further be necessary to induce a benevolent monarch and nation to destroy them, and to grant in their stead that certain and determinate tenure of King Charles the Second, free and common socage, which the other subjects of His Majesty King George the Third enjoy, and with so much reason boast of."[54] The printing of Lanaudière's petition in 1791 in the *Gazette de Québec* launched a heated public debate with Abbé Thomas-Laurent Bédard over the advantages of free and common socage. Lanaudière reviewed the movement of settlers to other parts of North America and claimed that if he could not alter the tenure on his lands, "I ran the risk of remaining alone with my family and the few *habitans* who have settled themselves on it; and that the remaining part might lie uncultivated." Lanaudière continued his appeal by referring to the superiority of English social and economic conditions: "An english farmer discovers liberty in his very figure and air . . . He consumes more in one month than three fourths of your farmers [i.e., habitants], even of those at their ease, in six."[55] Of course, Lanaudière's wish was not granted. Nonetheless, he did not give up on his idea of abolishing seigneurial tenure on his lands.

In the meantime he defended his seigneurial privileges, for example, justifying his rights over the Sainte-Anne ferry by exhibiting his titles.[56] But in 1810 he renewed his petition, "having always ardently wished to hold his land in free and common socage in preference to feudal tenure."[57] In this light, Lanaudière occupies a rather singular place as an anti-seigneurial Canadian seigneur, preferring English land tenure to French.

A number of visitors to the colony met with Lanaudière and recorded his pro-British sentiments. John Lambert commented that Lanaudière "is sincerely attached to the British government, and in his conduct, his manners, and his principles, appears to be, in every respect, a complete Englishman."[58] He certainly was one noble with close connections to the government, and he tried to use these to his best advantage. As it had during the French regime, the Lanaudière family supported the colonial rulers and benefitted from its connections. For instance, just as the colonial government and the English elite tried to encourage hemp growing, Lanaudière addressed an appeal to his tenants to grow the plant, offering to purchase all their production at the highest market prices.[59] During his intermittent presences in Sainte-Anne, Charles-Louis worked hard to defend the policies of the British rulers. No French seigneur could have better represented the British colonial state.

The Jesuits

While a noble seigneur's ties to the state are readily apparent, the role of a corporate religious seigneur is more complex. The relationship between tenants and such a seigneur was obviously different from the personal connections that one might have with a powerful family. Nonetheless, the Jesuit owners of Batiscan were no less implicated in the running of the colonial state. In their general relations with the colonial government, they defended a specific elitist and state-oriented view of the social order, one in which religion represented the supreme virtue. Like that of the Lanaudière family, the history of the Jesuits' seigneurial title was linked to their relations with the colonial government.

Historians have shown that ecclesiastical seigneuries were managed with much astuteness and flexibility. This generalization applies to Batiscan also, at least during the French regime. The first concessions there date from 1664, and they multiplied thereafter. The Jesuits had begun to comply with the royal edicts compelling them to see to the settlement of their lands. According to the

census of 1685, 261 people lived in the seigneury by that date.

Early riverfront concessions to individuals in the eastern part of the seigneury
often accompanied grants of land in the
western part. "The Jesuits," concludes the
most detailed analysis of Jesuit policy in
Batiscan, "could thus solidly establish the
colonists by assuring them from the beginning a plot on which to settle their sons."
An agent (*procureur général*) for the Jesuits' interests resided in Batiscan during the
French regime. By the eighteenth century
the order had taken advantage of a larger
population base to enforce control over
land-granting practices, not conceding land
in pioneer zones until some clearing had occurred.[60] The seigneurial court, established
definitively at Batiscan after 1726, provided
a means for ensuring adherence to the Jesuits' policies. In 1745, for instance, the agent
summoned Antoine Trottier to the court in
order that he be dispossessed of land that
he had worked without proper title for the
previous five years.[61]

The Jesuits also constructed mills on
their seigneury. A map from about 1726 depicts two windmills along the St Lawrence
and a sawmill situated in the depths of settlement on the Rivière Batiscan. The Murray map of 1760 indicates the existence of
a windmill on the St Lawrence and a watermill on the Batiscan. As shown by their
land-granting policy and their construction
of mills, the Jesuits' active role in the running
of the seigneury continued up to the time of
the Conquest.

Although the Conquest did not lead to
a fundamental redefinition of land title and
obligations in the old seigneuries, when the
British abolished seigneurial courts, they destroyed a powerful instrument for enforcing
the seigneur's will at the local level. Moreover,
the Jesuits suffered more than other seigneurs
when Canada was lost.[62] General Jeffery
Amherst, the supreme British military commander in North America at the time of the

Conquest, refused to grant protection to the
property of the Jesuits and the Recollets until the Crown had pronounced on the future
status of those orders in the colony. British
aversion to the Jesuits in particular was reinforced by the movement in other countries
to suppress the order. In 1764 a royal decree
dissolved the Jesuits throughout France and
its colonies. Nine years later Pope Clement
XIV suppressed the entire order. The consequences for Jesuit properties in Canada were
complex. In 1775 the British government
outlined a policy concerning the Jesuits. Although the order was suppressed, the surviving members would be provided for during
their lifetimes. Ultimately, this policy came to
mean that they were to enjoy the profits from
their properties, but that title would revert to
the Crown on the death of the last member
of the order.

Meanwhile, General Amherst had requested a grant of the Jesuit lands in recognition of his services to the Crown, and King
George III had promised him this recom-
pense. Subsequent attempts to acquire the
titles persisted beyond his own lifetime. His
nephew and heir, the second Lord Amherst,
pressed the claim in the declining years of
the last Jesuit, Father Jean-Joseph Casot. Ultimately, the second Lord Amherst received
monetary compensation for the king's promise, but he never acquired title to the estates
themselves. In 1800, upon Casot's death, the
lands previously belonging to the Jesuits reverted to the Crown.

During this period of uncertainty over
the disposition of the Jesuit estates (which
launched a century-long political debate
concerning the use of public funds for education and the relationship between church
and state), the Jesuits continued to employ
agents to manage their seigneuries. The
principal agent for Batiscan, François-Xavier
Larue, lived in Pointe-aux-Trembles, near
Quebec. In general, the Jesuits now seem to
have been less attentive to the management
of Batiscan than in the period before the

Conquest. However, they were more vigilant than the government itself would be when it ultimately took control.

Judging by the mills, the single most lucrative of the seigneurial privileges, the Jesuits through their agents continued to attend to their property. The 1781 *aveu et dénombrement* made reference to a mill in the process of being built in the seigneury.[63] The windmills along the St Lawrence were replaced over time by watermills along the Batiscan. A report prepared at the end of the Jesuits' administration noted two mills in operation, one built of stone on the northeast shore of the Rivière Batiscan at Sainte-Geneviève and the other built of wood on the Rivière des Envies.[64] The mills apparently remained functional and at least partially fulfilled the needs of the habitants: a seigneurial agent later reported that the mills "still worked and were in relatively good order at the time of the last Jesuit."[65] In providing relatively lucrative banal mills, the Jesuits maintained a traditional seigneurial monopoly, one that offered at least a minimum of required services to their tenants.

However, the Jesuits were much less attentive in their management of land grants in Batiscan seigneury. The numbers of titles conceded provide at least a general overview of their stewardship. From 1763 to 1790 only 22 concessions were awarded.[66] The Jesuits' agents were no longer facilitating settlement of the seigneury.

Another measure of the Jesuits' interest in their property is provided by their collection of seigneurial dues. Information concerning the amount collected is available for only a few scattered years. In 1768 the Jesuits acknowledged receiving 1291 *livres tournois* in rents. Thirteen years later, in 1781, different copies of the general recapitulation of the Jesuits' properties indicate between 988 and 1285 *livres tournois* in *cens et rentes*.[67] The reasons for the discrepancies in these figures, which relate to the same document, are not clear. It is possible that land-granting policy

limited the amount of seigneurial dues paid up to that point. However, by 1790 the revenues had about doubled, although the population had increased by only about 40 per cent. Batiscan earned about £94 sterling in *cens et rentes*, or 2256 *livres tournois*. The banal mill earned another 1200 livres tournois. Even with this increase, Batiscan was not a particularly lucrative Jesuit seigneury: it provided less than 7 per cent of the total receipts for the estates, much less than other properties such as La Prairie and Sainte-Geneviève near Montreal and Notre-Dame-des-Anges near Quebec.[68]

In the final years of life of the last Jesuit, the land-granting policy changed dramatically. A large portion of the seigneury fell into the hands of English-speaking entrepreneurs. In the 1790s the rhythm of concessions picked up markedly. Between 1795 and 1800, 83 concessions were granted, 53 in 1798 alone. Most of these involved small amounts of land and probably entailed the recognition of land already occupied by tenants. However, among the concessions were huge grants to businessman Thomas Coffin, made under the dubious circumstances surrounding the disposition of the Jesuits' properties. In 1795 Coffin received the *arrière-fief* of Saint-Thomas, comprising all of the seigneury north of the Rivière des Envies, in exchange for 300 sols annual rent. In 1798 he added three ill-defined "compeaux" of land, "being the remainders between conceded land, that he [Coffin] is obliged to have surveyed, and pay one 'sol' per arpent."[69]

This vast land grant, with its timber and iron resources, held much promise for profit, since Coffin and his partner, the deputy commissary general John Craigie, were able to establish a new ironworks. Not all colonial officials were pleased with such land grants. In July 1799, before the death of Father Casot, the attorney general, Jonathan Sewell, protested against the land grant, expressing to the agent, Desjardins, "the disapprobation of Government not only of that Concession but of all others (except perhaps the common Concession en roture to Habitans of small lots at the accustomary cens et rentes)."[70] Likewise, the local agent for the Jesuits' estates protested that Coffin had begun employing men to cut wood in the seigneury without permission.[71] Nonetheless, the owners of this Batiscan land were too well connected to be in danger of losing it.

When Father Casot died in 1800, title to the Jesuit estates reverted to the Crown, which appointed a commission to oversee the management of the property. Coffin and Craigie soon acquired a new partner in the Batiscan ironworks, Thomas Dunn, a former administrator of the colony, who sat on the Board of Commissioners of the Jesuit Estates. Lord Amherst's brother-in-law, John Hale, who anxiously watched over the family's interests in the colony, resigned from the Board of Commissioners when it became apparent that the property was not likely to be turned over to Amherst.[72]

[. . .]

For their part, the Jesuits' role in Batiscan seigneury had changed over time. Following their active involvement in its administration during the French regime, the complicated post-1763 struggle over the order's estates in Canada led to an increasing indifference toward Batiscan. As title shifted from the Jesuits to the Crown, a large section of the seigneury fell into private hands.

CONCLUSION

Seigneurial control over the land was undoubtedly an important aspect of the changes in landscape. It gave the localities their broad outlines, though it did not strictly speaking determine the nature of land use. This responded more to the exigencies of small-scale, family-oriented agricultural production. Superficially, the landscape projected a seigneurial presence, even though this faded the closer and the later one looked.

Since the mid-eighteenth century, commentators have argued over the degree to which seigneurial tenure was incompatible with profitable economic development.[73] But as Françoise Noël has demonstrated, "seigneurial tenure . . . could be used by large proprietors to monopolize scarce resources."[74] The founding of the Batiscan ironworks rested upon seigneurial privileges granted in *arrière-fief* by an increasingly irrelevant seigneur.

Thus, the lack of attention that seigneurs showed to their seigneuries could be equally determinant as when they did try to direct matters firmly. The increasing inattention during the British regime gave more rein to local elites to exercise control over social relations. It was during this latter period that the seigneurs had the least impact on the local landscape, marginalized as they increasingly became from local affairs.

NOTES

1. For the importance of naming and drawing boundaries in the appropriation of land, see Paul Carter, *The Road to Botany Bay: An Exploration of Landscape and History.* New York: Alfred A. Knopf, 1988.

2. H.P. Biggar, ed., *Works of Samuel de Champlain.* 6 vols. Toronto: Champlain Society, 1920–36, 1: 132.

3. Carter, *The Road to Botany Bay*, 47–54.

4. Reuben Gold Thwaites, *The Jesuit Relations and Allied Documents.* 74 vols. Cleveland: Burrows Brothers, 1896–1901, 48: 215.

5. Baby Collection, Université de Montréal (UM-Baby), mf. 2584, Requête des habitants de Baptiste Camp à François Baby, 15 février 1783. John Knox recorded the name as "Batiste camp" (Arthur G. Doughty, ed., *An Historical Journal of the Campaigns in North American for*

the Years 1757, 1758, and 1760. By Captain John Knox. Vol. 2. Toronto: Champlain Society, 1914, 2: 478).

6. Raymond Douville, *Les premiers seigneurs et colons de Sainte-Anne de la Pérade, 1667–1681*. Trois-Rivières: Éditions du Bien Public, 1946, 9–10.

7. Marcel Trudel, *Les débuts du régime seigneurial au Canada*. Montréal: Fides, 1974, 20–1; Richard Colebrook Harris, ed., *Seigneurial System in Early Canada*. 2nd edn. Montreal: McGill-Queen's University Press, 1984, 23–5.

8. Fonds Seigneuries (FS), Archives nationales du Québec à Québec, vol. 3, Batiscan, Acte de Concession de Messire Jacques de La Ferté aux Pères Jésuites, 3 mars 1639.

9. National Archives of Canada (NA), France, Archives des colonies, Des limites et des postes, Transcriptions, MG 1 série c 11 E (mf. F-409), 14, Estat des Terres que les Reverends Peres Jesuistes Possedent en Canada suivant leurs declarations du 26e novembre 1667.

10. Archives nationales du Québec à Montréal (ANQ-M), Seigneurie Batiscan, P220/1, Aveu et dénombrement, 29 décembre 1677.

11. Philippe Jarnoux, "La colonisation de la seigneurie de Batiscan aux 17e et 18e siècles: L'espace et les hommes." *RHAF* 40, no. 2 (1986), 169.

12. "Ayant pas meme sur les Lieux aucune Justice formée ni assurée" (Terres et forêts, Biens des Jésuites (BJ), ANQ-Q, vol. 70, Title Deeds, Jesuits Estates, 82–4, Acte de Monsieur de Bouteroue Intendant pour suppleer au defaut d'insinuation des Donnations des fiefs Batiscan & Champlain, 27 nov. 1668).

13. Douville, *Les premiers seigneurs et colons*, 13–36.

14. C.-M. Boissonault, "Gamelain de La Fontaine, Michel," *Dictionary of Canadian Biography* (*DCB*), 1: 320–1.

15. Harris, *Seigneurial System*, 26–31.

16. "en Considera[ti]on des bons utils et louables services quil[s] ont rendus a sa ma[jes]te en differents endroicts tant en lancienne France que dans la nouvelle depuis quils y sont passez par ordre de sa ma[jes]te et en veue de ceux quils temoignent encore vouloir rendre cy apres" (FS, vol. 52, Sainte-Anne de la Pérade [Ouest], Acte de concession par Jean Talon, 29 octobre 1672).

17. Ibid., Sainte-Anne de la Pérade (est), Extrait d'un Contrat de vente par Moses Hart à Pierre Charay [sic] et uxor, 26 février 1816.

18. Hale Collection, National Archives of Canada (NA-Hale), vol. 2, Acte de foi et hommage, 23 décembre 1819.

19. ANQ-M, Seigneurie Batiscan, P220/1, Aveu et dénombrement, 1.

20. UM-Baby, MF. 2104–5, Contrat de concession d'une place au village de Batiscan, 13 septembre 1674.

21. Douville, *Les premiers seigneurs et colons*.

22. Carte de Catalogne, 1709, in Marcel Trudel, *Atlas de la Nouvelle-France/Atlas of New France*. Quebec: Presses de l'Université Laval, 1968, 169. This map does not, in fact, indicate the presence of a common in Sainte-Anne, though one was established.

23. Louis-Edmond Hamelin, "Le rang d'arrière-fleuve en Nouvelle-France," *Géographe canadien/Canadian Geographer* 34, 2 (1980): 113–14, notes that the St Lawrence formed the principal axis for concessions in the majority of cases. Still, according to Catalogne's map of 1709, other seigneurs also assured themselves of the most prominent geographic positions.

24. Douville, *Les premiers seigneurs et colons*, 122–8.

25. NA, Sainte-Anne de la Pérade, Transcriptions, MG 8, F 83, 10–13, Copie du contrat de donation faite par feu messire de Suève, 8 août 1691.

26. National Map Collection (NMC), National Archives of Canada, NMC-10842, Murray Map (1760), section FI.

27. For the male Lanaudières' military activity, see P.-G. Roy, *La famille Tarieu de Lanaudière*. Lévis: [n.p.], 1922. As for the women, besides Madeleine de Verchères, Philippe Aubert de Gaspé discussed his aunt, Agathe de Lanaudière, in his Mémoires, 402–4.

28. Raymond Douville, "Lanouguère, Thomas de," *DCB*, 1: 417–18.

29. Douville, *Les premiers seigneurs et colons*, 56, 62.

30. FS, vol. 52, Sainte-Anne de la Pérade (Est) [sic], Acte d'abandon et cession de la seigneurie de Sainte-Anne par Marguerite-Renée Denys à Pierre-Thomas Tarieu de la Pérade (Greffe Genaple), 4 novembre 1704.

90 Chapter 3 ❧ The Seigneurial Regime in New France

31. "Ordonnance qui déclare bonne et valable la saisie . . . ," in *Pièces et documents relatifs à la tenure seigneuriale*. Quebec: E.R. Fréchette, 1852, 120–4.

32. ANQ-M, Conseil supérieur, Registres, M9, (mf. 1197), vol. 28, folio 39r–v, Esmond et Jean Tessier et al. versus Thomas Tarrieu de la Pérade, 18 août 1721; vol. 32, folio 51v–52v, François Chorel Dorvilliers vs Thomas Tarrieu de la Pérade, 12 mars 1725.

33. NA, Nouvelle-France, Correspondance officielle, 3e série, MG 8, A1, vol. 12, 2657–8, Lettre de Beauharnois et Hocquart au ministre, 15 octobre 1731.

34. Ibid., vol. 11, 2427–8, Lettre de Beauharnois et Hocquart au ministre, 25 octobre 1729; NA, France, Archives des colonies, Lettres envoyées, MG 1, série B, vol. 54, folio 423½, Lettre du ministre à Beauharnois, 4 avril 1730.

35. Élisabeth Bégon, *Lettres au cher fils: Correspondance d'Élisabeth Bégon avec son gendre (1748–1753)*. Montreal: Hurtubise HMH, 1972, 53.

36. Ibid., 72; Louis Franquet, *Voyages et mémoires sur le Canada*. Montreal: Éditions Elysée, 1974, 129, 141.

37. Baby Collection, National Archives of Canada (NA-Baby), vol. 1, 511a, Beauharnois à Lanaudière, 22 juillet 1744; vol. 3, 1722–3, Marquis de Vaudreuil à Mr de Lanaudière, 23 juillet 1759.

38. Ibid., vol. 30, 18725–61, Inventaire des biens de La communauté entre de La Perrade [Lanaudière] et feue Geneviève de Boishébert, sa première épouse, 5 juillet 1762 (according to this document, Lanaudière held some 63 000 livres in France in the hands of various merchants); Tarien de Lanaudière (TL), ANQ-Q, vol. 1, Accord entre M. de Lanaudière et M. Varin, 16 octobre 1753, and Cession de Gaultier, 4 avril 1754.

39. NA-Baby, vol. 30, 18759, Inventaire des biens de la communauté entre de La Perrade [Lanaudière] et feue Geneviève de Boishébert, sa première épouse, 5 juillet 1762.

40. Ibid., vol. 4, 2139–40, Thouron & Frères à Lanaudière, 22 avril 1764.

41. NA-Baby, vol. 5, 2652–8, Thouron & frères à Lanaudière, 10 mars 1768.

42. "On ne peux pas être plû heureux que je le sui avec Mr Le generalle" (ibid., 2968, Lanaudière à son père, 14 septembre 1770).

43. E.P. Thompson, *Whigs and Hunters: The Origins of the Black Art*. Harmondsworth: Penguin, 1977.

44. NA-Baby, vol. 30, 19052, Inventaire et procès-verbal de vente des biens de la succession de Lanaudière, avril 1788.

45. Letters in NA-Baby between 1774 and 1783 were written in March, July, September, October, and December.

46. Hale Family Collection (UT-Hale), Thomas Fisher Rare Book Library, University of Toronto, E.F. Hale to Lord Amherst, 17 September [1819].

47. NA-Baby, vol. 6, 3570–1, Lanaudière fils à Vercher, 24 juillet 1773.

48. Roy Porter, *English Society in the Eighteenth Century*. London: Penguin Books, 1977, 73–8.

49. "Comme nesséscairement il fautdra que le gouvernement fasse, Dotorité faire, faire le bois,—je propose sesi, si lon veux me dormer les paroisses—Déchambaut, grondine, *St anne* & tous batiscand—qui ne fournisse jamais du bois, avec pouvoir de commender Les hommes dont jorei besoin pour bucher" (NA-Baby, vol. 8, 4398–9, Lanaudière à M. François Baby, 17 septembre 1778; emphasis in original).

50. "En fesant l'affaire Du gouvernement il faut que je fasse les miéne" (ibid., vol. 8, 4406, Lanaudière à François Baby, 30 septembre 1778). Evidence that the enterprise was undertaken is shown by a further letter in the same collection (4736–7, Lanaudière à F. Baby, 6 mars 1781).

51. See the criticism of Charles de Lanaudière in the handbill *Commentaire sur le discours de l'honorable Chas. Delanaudiere (qui a paru hier)*, reprinted in John Hare, *Aux origines du parlementarisme québécois 1791–1793*. Sillery: Les Éditions du Septentrion, 1993, 177–9.

52. "Cest le devoir de toutes hommes quis est atachés a son rois de faire c'est [cet] effort" (TL, vol. 2, Agathe de Lanaudière à Gaspard Lanaudière, 2 avril 1810).

53. Roch Legault, "Les aléas d'une carrière militaire pour les membres de la petite noblesse seigneuriale canadienne de la révolution américaine à la guerre de 1812–1815." Mémoire de maîtrise, Université de Montréal, 1986, 113–15.

54. "Answers submitted by Charles de Lanaudière to various Questions relating to the Seigniorial

System, October 11, 1790," in W.B. Munro, *Documents Relating to the Seigniorial Tenure in Canada, 1598–1854*. Toronto: Champlain Society, 1908, 273.

55. *Gazette de Québec*, 24 mars 1791; supplément, 28 avril 1791.

56. Archives nationales du Québec à Trois-Rivières (ANQ-TR), Cour de banc du roi (dossiers), T25, Terme de septembre 1808, no. 1, Pierre Bureau vs Jos. Riv[ar]d Lanouette et L'Honorable De Lanaudière.

57. "Ayant toujours ardemment désiré de tenir ses Terres en franc et commun Soccage en préference de Féodalité" (NA, Lower Canada Land Papers, RG 1 L 3 L, vol. 188 [mf. C-2538], 57763–4, Petition de Charles de Lanaudière à Sir James Craig, 21 décembre 1810).

58. John Lambert, *Travels through Canada and the United States of North America in the Years 1806, 1807 & 1808*. 2nd edn. London: C. Cradock and W. Joy, 1814, 461. Lord Selkirk was similarly impressed with Lanaudière: "a very gentlemanly old Canadian Officer, & a man of reflexion" (NA, Selkirk Papers, MG 19, E 1, Lord Selkirk's Diary, 19749).

59. *Gazette de Quebec*, 22 juillet 1802.

60. Jarnoux, "La colonisation," 173–75, quotation from 173. See also Raymond Douville, "Les lents débuts d'une seigneurie des Jésuits," *Cahiers des dix* 25 (1960): 249–76.

61. BJ, vol. 97, St-Agnian vs Antoine Trottier, 29 avril 1745. See also Collection des pièces judiciaires et notariales (ANQ-Q), Mesager vs François Massicot, 6 avril 1748. Lavallée notes that the Jesuit seigneurs of La Prairie became more vigilant in the 1730s, launching a number of court cases for nonpayment of dues in the following decade (*La Prairie*, 100).

62. The following section dealing with the disposition of the Jesuit estates is summarized from Roy J. Dalton, *The Jesuits' Estates Question 1760–1888: A Study of the Background for the Three Seigneurial Regime in New France Agitation of 1889*. Toronto: University of Toronto Press, 1968, chaps. 1–6.

63. NA, Executive Council and Land Committee, RG 1, L 7, Jesuit Estates, vol. 38, 11, Extrait de l'aveu & dénombrement des Fiefs & Seigneuries des Jésuites, 12 décembre 1781.

64. BJ, vol. 96, Rapport de l'Etat actuel des Moulins situés en les Seigneuries qui appartenoient ci devant au Jesuites, dans le District des Trois-Rivières . . . (no date; probably July 1800).

65. "Marchoient encore et étoient en assez bon ordre Lors de lextinction des Jesuites" (ibid., vol. 103, Moulin de la Seigneurie, 1824–28, L. Guillet à John Stewart, 2 juin 1826).

66. Ibid., vol. 99, Liste des Concéssions qui ont été faites dans les Seigneuries qui appartenoient ci devant à l'ordre des Jésuites dans le District des Trois Rivières, en la Province du Bas Canada, depuis la conquête de ce pays, fait par l'agent des ditte Seigneuries dans le dit District en conséquence des ordres des Commissaires pour l'adminstration des dits Biens, Suivant une Lettre du secretaire en date du 18 janvier 1802.

67. NA, Earl Amherst Papers, MG 12, WO 34, packet 47 [mf. C-1215], Compte que rendent les Jesuites du Canada à Mr Guy Carleton, le 7 avril 1768; Executive Council and Land Committee, RG 1, L 7, Jesuit Estates, vol. 35, General Recapitulation . . . ; ibid., vol. 38, Extrait de l'aveu & dénombrement des Fiefs & Seigneuries des Jésuites, 12 décembre 1781; Haldimand Papers, MG 21 [mf. A-779].

68. UT-Hale, John Hale to Lord Amherst, 6 May 1802.

69. "Étant des restant entre des terres concédées, qu'il est obligé de faire mesurer, à payer un sol par arpent en Superficie" (BJ, vol. 99, Liste des concessions . . . 18 janvier 1802). The government finally was able to ascertain the extent of the three "grands compeaux" in 1828: 169 arpents behind the falls, 480 arpents behind the ironworks, and 420 arpents near the Rivière à Veillet (ibid., L. Guillet à J. Stewart, 24 septembre 1828).

70. Ibid., vol. 75, Lettres, 1787–1800, Jonathan Sewell to H. Ryland, 27 February 1800.

71. Ibid., vol. 99, Trépagny à Larue, 22 décembre 1799; vol. 257, Larue, 18 juin 1800.

72. UT-Hale, John Hale to Lord Amherst, 5 December 1800.

73. David Milobar, "The Origins of British-Quebec Merchant Ideology: New France, the British Atlantic and the Constitutional Periphery, 1720–70." *Journal of Imperial and Commonweath History* 24, 3 (1996): 370.

74. Françoise Noël, *The Christie Seigneuries: Estate Management and Settlement in the Upper Richelieu Valley, 1760–1854*. Montreal and Kingston: McGill-Queen's University Press, 1992, 136.

4 From Allan Greer, "The Feudal Burden," in *Peasant, Lord, and Merchant: Rural Society in Three Quebec Parishes 1740–1840* (Toronto: University of Toronto Press, 1985), 122–39. © University of Toronto Press, 1985. Reprinted with permission of the publisher.

Were seigneurial and ecclesiastical exactions nothing more than a minor nuisance to the early Canadian peasantry? How exactly was wealth transferred from the agricultural producers to the dominant classes? Was the basis of appropriation fixed or was it at all changeable or arbitrary? Finally, how significant an impact did these feudal dues have on the habitant family economy? In attempting to answer these questions, I shall concentrate on the more problematic seigneurial economy.

SEIGNEURIAL DUES

The most important mechanism of transfer in most Canadian seigneuries was the "cens et rentes," an annual payment in money, produce, or labour, exacted on all lands in the "mouvance" at a rate proportional to the size of each lot. The cens alone was a small payment, considered a token of the "commoners'" form of tenure, which carried with it subjection to a number of dues, such as the "lods et ventes," outlined in the Custom of Paris. Rente was a lucrative charge added to and deliberately confused with the cens in order to subject the inhabitant to the penalties prescribed by law for late payment of the latter.[1] The term "rent" will be used here in the feudal sense, as it was in the past, to refer to the total of these two charges.

The annual rent on each lot was established at the time of concession and it could not legally be altered, although variations in the value of money and grain had the effect of changing the effective burden of this charge. The edict of 1711 moreover, in ordering seigneurs to make new concessions at the prevailing rates of cens et rentes, implied that a standard rate should apply in each seigneurie, if not throughout the colony, on lands granted at any time after that date. A

legalistic bias has led some historians to assume that rents on new concessions therefore remained stable during the French régime and only rose after the Conquest when a French government was replaced by a British one less sympathetic to the habitants. In fact, a clear pattern of ever-increasing rent scales on newly settled sections of the mouvance is evident in seventeenth-century Montreal.[2] Similarly, in St Ours, new rents rose steadily throughout the French régime, but remained stable after the 1750s, just the opposite of the pattern suggested by the traditional view. Apparently, the development of the region's agricultural productivity led seigneurs to insist on a proper share of the expanding peasant surplus.

But how did the seigneurs of St Ours manage to defy official policy in this way? An examination of St Ours concession deeds suggests that the rise was the outcome of a subtle policy of altering the combination of cash, produce, and livestock in the annual rents, substituting pseudo-equivalents so as to change the value of payments while appearing to alter only their form. Cash was substituted for capons, and then wheat was put in the place of the money; also area measurements were substituted for linear frontage. The switch to payments largely in wheat in the years after 1720 was partly a reflection of the emergence of an agricultural economy in the Lower Richelieu, but it was also a clever hedge against erosion of fixed money rents. The seigneurs' imposition of altered rates made a mockery of legislation intended to protect the peasantry; the eighteenth-century rise in grain prices, joined to biased alterations in the form of payment were such that, at early-nineteenth-century wheat prices, a 90-arpent farm conceded in the seventeenth century would owe about 6 livres per year, while one conceded after 1754 (this included the majority of St Ours farms) would owe 27 livres.[3] The trouble that the French régime seigneurs of St Ours took to adjust their rent scales suggests that they did not regard these revenues as "token payments."

Less is known about the evolution of cens et rentes in Sorel and St Denis. Toward the end of the French régime, the charge seems to have been a roughly equivalent combination of money and wheat to that exacted in St Ours, although every lot in Sorel owed an additional levy of one day's corvée labour.[4] (Note that corvée was simply a form of payment, labour rather than money or produce, and not a separate variety of seigneurial exaction, as many have suggested. The corvée in mid-eighteenth-century Sorel seems to have been an element of the cens et rentes, whereas Pierre de St Ours exacted a day's work from the habitants for use of a common pasture.) However, the seigneurs of Sorel and St Denis, both of them absentees probably anxious to simplify accounts and collection procedures, converted all charges in labour and kind to a single annual cash exaction. This change occurred around 1770 in Sorel and probably much earlier in St Denis, with the effect that rents there were greatly devalued by the long-term inflation of the eighteenth century. In the early nineteenth century, a 90-arpent farm was charged about 13.5 livres in St Denis, 18 livres in Sorel, and between 16 and 32 livres in St Ours, depending on the price of wheat.[5] The seigneur of St Ours tended to benefit in the long run by their adherence to rents in kind. The relative advantage of seigneur and habitant in each seigneurie changed, in opposite directions, with fluctuating grain prices. Moreover, the positions of the two parties reverse as one moves from St Ours to Sorel or St Denis; that is, a rise in wheat prices favoured St Ours seigneurs and Sorel habitants, while a price decline tended to favour Sorel seigneurs and St Ours habitants.

In addition to the cens et rentes, Canadian seigneurs benefitted from a variety of lucrative charges, including the lods et ventes, a mutation fine amounting to one-twelfth of the purchase price owed by the buyer of land in the mouvance. In France, and in some Canadian seigneuries, purchasers who paid promptly were charged a third or a quarter less than the legal rate, but this discount was not universal and St Ours seigneurs invariably demanded the full amount.[6] [. . .] To realize its full value, the right of lods et ventes required that a seigneur be aware of the details of land transactions in his fief and it was therefore closely tied, in its practical application, to the various official and unofficial aspects of his control over people and lands. In addition to his role as the main repository of land title records, the seigneur disposed of the retrait seigneurial to guarantee the proper reporting of prices. Of course the co-operation of the local notary, who officiated at transactions and kept their records, was invaluable, but what notary could risk offending the seigneur, normally his most important client?

Several minor exactions were added to the basic feudal rent and mutation fines. One of these was the annual fee for admission to the common pasture; such "droit de commune" was demanded of all Sorel habitants until the late eighteenth century and of the residents of the St Lawrence section of St Ours until the end of seigneurial tenure. The situation here was not what it was in Old Régime France, where commons were generally controlled by peasant communities whose possession was only partially usurped by aggressive seigneurial offensives.[7] [. . .]

Although they profited through the above-mentioned exactions from habitant grain-growing, livestock raising, and property sales, the seigneurs of the Lower Richelieu were not prepared to let even minor ancillary productions go untaxed. In Sorel, there was a levy on maple sugar-making as well as a fishing fee. In the eighteenth century, choice locations on islands in the St Lawrence were farmed out to habitants for 78 livres annually, as much as the rents of a dozen farms. A document dated 1809 mentions an exaction of two fish from each netful of shad caught.[8] There was no basis in law for this "droit de pêche," but this seems to have escaped the seigneurs' notice.

Seigneurs benefitted, not only from these direct exactions, but also from various monopolies, above all the "banalité" (grist mill monopoly), which will be discussed later. These privileges are quite different from the dues mentioned so far in that they were not lucrative in themselves, even though they could be used to enrich the seigneur at the habitants' expense. The banal mill was a protected enterprise with a captive market, but it did provide a service; the milling toll was therefore unlike the almost entirely parasitic cens et rentes as it went partly to defray expenses. Only a portion of this fee was profit for the seigneur and only part of that could be attributed to the effects of protection from competition.[9] Collecting the milling toll was a simple matter of withholding one-fourteenth of the grain processed, whereas seigneurs experienced considerable difficulty in securing payment of annual dues and mutation fines.

PAYMENT

Seigneurial dues were notoriously difficult to collect (frontier or no frontier, Canada was exactly like France in this respect).[10] Most habitants were a few years in arrears on occasion and many fell behind more seriously and were never able to get out of debt. Behind this backlog was probably a combination of inability to pay, unwillingness to pay, and a calculated postponement based on the knowledge that it was not worthwhile for the seigneur to take action to recover small debts. Some habitants lived so close to the edge of subsistence that chronic debt to the seigneur must have been almost unavoidable; whereas others, normally able to pay regularly, must have experienced temporary distress that put them slightly in arrears now

and then. Most likely, there was also a certain amount of passive resistance to seigneurial exploitation expressed in the failure to pay promptly. Figure 3.2 shows that only 15 per cent of Sorel's lands had rent arrears of more than four years in 1809. By 1855, however, this figure had risen to 25 per cent, reflecting the general distress of the seigneurie's habitants in the period when fur trade employment had disappeared.[11] Accumulated arrears seem to have been disproportionately great in recently conceded lands, probably because many of them were not fully cleared and productive for several years. In Sorel, and presumably in other seigneuries, payments of current and overdue rents fluctuated from year to year with the harvests, the general economic situation, and the varying pressure exerted by the seigneur (see Table 3.1).[12]

Arrears of lods et ventes were more common and of much longer duration than arrears of rents. The former charge usually amounted to a relatively substantial sum due all at once, and many habitants found themselves unable to pay it for years, or even generations, even if they could make the more moderate rent payments year by year. "Quitte excepté les lods" is a recurrent phrase in the St Ours estate rolls. From the seigneur's point of view then, the actual revenue in any one year was never even close to the total value of the dues to which he was legally entitled. By about 1840 the censitaires of Sorel and St Ours owed their seigneurs at least 92 000 and 71 158 livres respectively. Of course many of these arrears would never be paid at all. The notaries who drew up the inventory of 1841 following the death of François Roch de St Ours judged that one-third of the arrears of the seigneurie should simply be written off since they were owed on uncleared lots of very little value.[13]

Extracting payments of arrears from indebted habitants was a delicate task requiring, on the part of the seigneur or his agent, a thorough acquaintance with the individuals and the productive capacities of

Table 3.1 Seigneurial Rents and Arrears Paid, Sorel 1798–1805

Year	Annual Rent Due	Rent and Arrears Received	Percentage
1798	2 643	1 817	69
1799	2 787	1 988	71
1800	2 874	2 268	79
1801	2 930	1 523	52
1802	2 942	2 572	87
1803	3 407	3 564	105
1804	3 407	2 213	65
1805	3 407	2 493	73

more promising candidate. This sometimes required an expensive and time-consuming lawsuit to obtain a judicial seizure.[14] Seigneurs naturally preferred the various procedures mentioned above—repossession for failure to develop and "voluntary" abandonment—that weeded out undesirables with much less inconvenience. For less serious cases, they were inclined to show a certain amount of patience in the hopes of eventually recovering overdue rents. Paternalistic attitudes may have had something to do with it, but there were also more practical motives for forbearance. Since habitant agriculture was often quite unproductive and short harvests were common, rigid insistence on immediate payment would clearly be unreasonable and self-defeating in many cases. As long as a habitant made a visible effort to make good back dues and as long as his farm was valuable enough to bear the

their lands. If the seigneur was convinced that the debtor would never pay, he would generally take steps to have him removed so that the land could be turned over to a

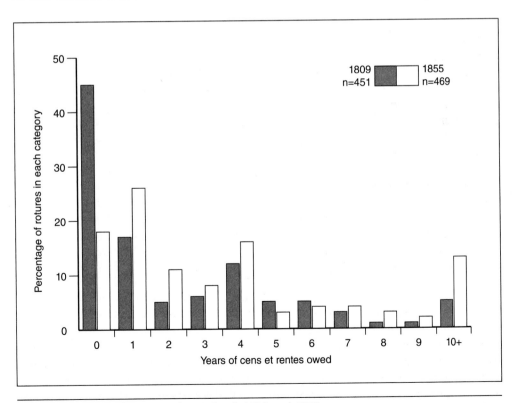

Figure 3.2 Arrears of seigneurial rent, Sorel, 1809 and 1855

debt, he could usually feel safe. In the end, a seigneur could take advantage of his position as legally privileged creditor to claim arrears from the estate when his debtor died. Prompter payment was certainly preferable, however, and seigneurs used a variety of strategies, threatening, cajoling, setting deadlines, and accepting payments in unusual forms, in order to wring as much as possible out of peasants who had the slimmest of surpluses and who were disinclined to part with them. Always it was the threat, implied or stated, of being deprived of their homes and livelihood that encouraged such marginal cases to turn over what they could.

[. . .]

Documents from St Ours suggest that seigneurial dues were acquitted in a great variety of forms. There were always a large number of habitants who apparently paid punctually and in the money and wheat specified in their title deeds but, for poorer censitaires, these commodities were only accounting abstractions. Products offered for rents and lods et ventes between the 1790s and the 1840s include oats, barley, peas, lumber, firewood, maple sugar, hay, cattle, and homespun cloth. Labour was also a common means of payment, even though officially there was no corvée in St Ours after about 1720. The estate rolls show that censitaires received a certain amount of credit for each day spent working on roads and fences or on the construction of a mill. When a gristmill on the Yamaska River was planned in 1814, the contract with the seigneur required the builder to employ, as far as possible, St Ours habitants who would be paid half their wages in cash and the other half in coupons to be applied to their accounts with the seigneur.[15] Once again it seems clear that the form in which feudal dues were officially set down was of no essential importance; what was appropriated was the surplus labour of the peasant, either in its raw form, or as agricultural produce or as produce converted into cash.

SEIGNEURIAL MONOPOLIES

As an outgrowth of seigneurial judicial powers, Canadian landlords enjoyed certain privileges and monopolies over the territories of their estates and the people who lived there; long after they had ceased to act as local judges, the seigneurs of Sorel, St Ours, and St Denis continued to insist on the lucrative perquisites of the position. The most important of these was the gristmill monopoly and it was more widespread and more stringent in Canada than it was in most parts of Old Régime France.[16] Here, it was often an important source of seigneurial revenues, and a real inconvenience to habitants. The Custom of Paris only allowed seigneurs to require their vassals to grind the wheat they needed for domestic consumption at the seigneurial watermill and only in cases where the right was sanctioned by written titles or ancient custom. A royal edict of 1686 enlarged the Canadian seigneur's rights in this regard by declaring banal every mill, whether water- or wind-driven, and without any need for stipulation in title deeds.[17]

Nevertheless, every St Ours deed mentioned the mill monopoly, in order to spell out the habitant's obligations and to specify penalties for infractions. The trend over the course of the eighteenth century was toward more extensive obligations and more stringent penalties. In the seventeenth century, only grain used for home consumption had to be ground at the seigneur's mill and the fine for processing flour elsewhere was the equivalent of the milling toll on the amount of grain. By the 1790s, the formula in concession deeds subjected all grain grown to the banalité, whether it was consumed at home or sent abroad, and piled penalty on top of penalty: Not only would a fine equal to the milling toll be exacted, the illicit flour could also be seized and additional arbitrary fines imposed. This evolution in title deed clauses seems to reflect a wider trend toward a more careful and exacting style of estate management. Note, however, that, right from the beginning, the seigneurs of St Ours assumed the right to subject all varieties of grain to their monopoly even though the law of the land limited the banalité to wheat alone, and only to the amount needed for domestic consumption.[18]

There is a long-established myth in Canadian historiography to the effect that the law of 1686 giving all seigneurial mills monopoly privileges was as much a burden for the seigneurs as it was for the habitants, since it also forced the former to build mills within a year or forever forfeit their right of banalité.[19] In fact, many seigneurs easily retained their privileges even though they only opened a mill long after that date. Pierre de Sorel had a mill built in 1670, no doubt as much to contribute to the development of his estate as in anticipation of future profits, but Pierre de St Ours waited until 20 years after the law of 1686 before erecting a windmill, and his banal privileges were never revoked. Worse still, the absentee seigneurs of St Denis left their peasants with no mill until after the Conquest, noting all the same in concession deeds that granted lands would be, "sujette au moulin de ladte. seigneurie lorsqu'il y en aura un de construit."[20] Two small seigneurial mills, one wind-driven and the other water-driven, were eventually built in the late eighteenth century, but the seigneurs of St Denis found they did not even have to bother investing in milling facilities to profit from their banalité. [. . .]

After a period of severely fragmented ownership around the middle of the eighteenth century, the seigneurs of St Ours showed a greater willingness than their neighbours to establish their own mills and profit directly from the monopoly. This was partly because the fief was well supplied with good hydraulic sites, but also because the seigneurs generally lived on the estate for at least part of the year and took a personal hand in managing it. In addition to Pierre de St Ours's old windmill on the St Lawrence, there was a water-driven mill on the Richelieu, built in 1773 and, following the development of the rear sections of the seigneurie, another watermill was established in 1815, this one on the Yamaska River. This last mill was the largest in St Ours and it contained three pairs of stones with bolts, as well as a fulling mill; in 1842 the building and machinery were insured for 10 000 livres.[21]

The milling toll in early Quebec was set by law at one-fourteenth of the grain ground but of course expenses claimed a considerable portion of the gross revenue. Mills were always leased out to a miller, either for a set annual rent or, more commonly, for a proportion of the proceeds; in various contracts this amounted to one-half, one-third, or one-quarter of the revenues.[22] The seigneur also had to pay for major repairs and for a portion of the operating expenses. This left, according to one optimistic estimate, about two-thirds of the milling tolls, or 4.8 per cent of all the grain processed, as the seigneur's net profit.[23] In Sorel, badly served by two decrepit windmills, net profits were only 160 minots of wheat (worth 480 livres) in 1782–3, but the big gristmills of St Ours were worth 1500 minots of grain (value about 3000–7000 livres) annually to their seigneur around 1840.[24]

[. . .]

A source of revenue to the seigneur, the banalité appeared from the habitant's point of view as a double restriction, preventing him both from having his grain ground where he wished and from establishing a gristmill of his own. In practice, it was the latter restriction that was most effectively enforced and economically most important. Although they always insisted on their right to prevent habitants from taking unground grain outside the fief, seigneurs were unable to police movements of this sort; contraventions seem to have been common.[25] On the other hand, it was impossible for interlopers to build unauthorized gristmills and escape detection. Two St Denis residents built mills on their own land but the seigneur promptly sued them and, in an out-of-court settlement, imposed the annual tribute mentioned earlier as the price of allowing them to continue operations; a less accommodating seigneur might have had the offending mills razed, with the full backing of the law. The lack of competition did not affect the cost of services to the habitant, since this was set by law at a moderate rate. On the other hand, the quality of flour and the regularity of service may have suffered. More serious was the inconvenience of having to carry grain to seigneurial mills that were, for many users, far from home. In France, only peasants within a certain distance, usually one league, were subject to the mill monopoly but, in Canadian seigneuries, which were generally quite vast, there was no such limit and farmers had to transport their grain many leagues to the banal mill.

[. . .]

FEUDAL EXACTIONS AND THE PEASANT HOUSEHOLD ECONOMY

If we add the ecclesiastical payments to the seigneurial dues enumerated here, it becomes clear that eighteenth-century habitants were subject to a diverse array of rents, tithes, fees, and fines. And yet, according to many historians, these all added up to an aggregate "feudal burden" that was paltry indeed.[26] The people of the Lower Richelieu, on the other hand, were more inclined to take these matters seriously. We have seen the heated disputes that often arose between priests and parishioners over pew rents and assessments for construction projects. Think also of the great pains that seigneurs took to adjust rent scales and to levy the full mutation fine on every imaginable transaction, and of the risks that many habitants ran in allowing backrents to accumulate even when they were in danger of losing their farms. These exactions mattered both to exploiters

and to exploited because the wealth at stake was significant.

What exactly was the material weight of feudalism on the peasantry? This is a question that has bedeviled historians of both Canada and Europe; many have attempted estimates but results have always been controversial and generally unsatisfactory.[27] Source deficiencies—the absence of reliable figures on agricultural production and aristocratic revenues—are only part of the problem. More serious are a number of thorny conceptual issues, many of them connected to the diversity of the forms of feudal exactions. It is very difficult to construct a single index out of the various dues when some were paid in cash, some in kind, and others in labour. Furthermore, some—tithes, pew rents, and seigneurial rents, for example— were due on a regular annual basis, while others—mutation fines and ecclesiastical assessments, for instance—had to be paid only on certain occasions. A further problem has to do with the fact that many payments to priests and seigneurs were at least partially compensation for a genuine service. Mill tolls fall into this category since only part of the fee can be attributed to the seigneur's privileged position. Finally, there is the question of whether the demands of the state—taxes, military service, road work—should be counted as part of the feudal burden. All this makes it next to impossible to measure the feudal economy with any precision or to make meaningful comparisons between different periods or between different countries.

Beyond these methodological dilemmas loom some options more theoretical than technical. Researchers wishing to determine the economic importance of feudalism must consider the questions, important for whom? and according to what criteria? The tendency is often to ignore the distinctions between capitalist and pre-capitalist economies and treat seigneurs and habitants as though they were landowners and agricultural entrepreneurs. From this point of view it makes sense to divide seigneurial revenues by the area of the censive to find a rate of seigneurial exactions amounting to so many livres per arpent. A similar procedure consists of estimating peasant agricultural income and dividing by the total of seigneurial and ecclesiastical revenues; this gives a percentage figure representing the proportion of habitant harvests absorbed by the feudal classes. This would be fine if the agriculturalists in question were genuine farmers engaged in a profit-making enterprise, selling all or most of what they grew and paying ground-rent as one of the expenses of doing business. Eighteenth-century habitants were of course nothing of the sort; they were peasants and their economy centred on production for domestic consumption. Thus there was a fairly inflexible minimum supply of many crops that habitant families needed to survive and to reproduce themselves. Ignoring this basic characteristic of pre-capitalist agrarian society allows one to conclude that "seigneurial dues . . . were very low, representing 10 per cent of the produce of their concessions,"[28] but it does not tell us much about the realities of the feudal economy since the "produce" of peasant lands remains an abstract quantity. In fact, the figure of 10 per cent does not seem so low, especially when we realize that it does not include the tithe or other ecclesiastical dues, but that is not the point. The problem with this approach is that we do not know what the loss of 10 per cent of its harvest would mean for an habitant family, whether, for example, this would simply leave it with a little less wheat to sell or whether it would threaten its very survival by cutting into the stock needed for seed and for subsistence.

A better way of evaluating feudal exactions is therefore to consider them in relation to habitant *surpluses*. This requires estimating, not only how much peasants grew annually, but also how much they needed to retain in order to last the year. Because of the methodological and source difficulties mentioned above, I am not in a position to set up a complete "model" of the habitant economy in the eighteenth century but I do have enough information to make a rough estimate of production, surplus, and exactions for wheat alone. Thus, only one aspect of Lower Richelieu agriculture is covered, although wheat was surely the most important element. Data [from the 1765 census on grain sown] can now be used to estimate the wheat production of all the habitants of St Ours. Census figures on the population of adults and children, along with information from deeds of gift on flour consumption, allow us then to calculate roughly the amount of wheat needed for home consumption. Taking the difference between production and consumption gives the estimated wheat surplus of each habitant family in the parish. It is then a simple matter to evaluate the impact on this surplus of the tithe and the wheat portion of seigneurial rents (see Table 3.2).[29]

According to this model then, almost half (44 per cent) of the wheat grown by the habitants of St Ours in 1765, beyond what was needed to maintain the growers, would have been owed to the local seigneur and curé just to pay those feudal exactions that were set down in terms of wheat. This of course does not give us a complete picture of the relationship between peasant surpluses and aristocratic exploitation. Habitants raised many products other than wheat, but most of these were exclusively for domestic use and therefore not part of a saleable surplus. On the other hand, many important feudal dues—mutation fines, pew rents, church assessments, and the cash portion of seigneurial rents, to name a few—do not enter into our calculations. If anything therefore, this partial estimate underestimates the feudal burden.

It should be noted that this is a "model" and not a detailed description of reality. In fact, harvests varied greatly from year to year, and so therefore did the relative weight of fixed dues; the seed-yield figure of 1:5.8 is simply one historian's estimate of the

Table 3.2 Habitant Surpluses and Feudal Exactions, Wheat Only, St Ours 1765

"Habitant" Households		99
Production		
(a) grain sown	2098 minots	
(b) wheat sown (2/3a)	1399 minots	
(c) yield per seed	5.8	
(d) wheat harvested (b x c)	8112 minots	8112 minots
Deductions		
(e) wheat seed for next year	−1399 minots	
(f) mill toll (1/14)	−358 minots	
(g) total	−1757 minots	−1757 minots
Domestic Consumption		
(h) adult population	238	
(i) boys under 15	158	
(j) "girls"	134	
(k) adult rations (h+i/2+3j/4)	417.5	
(l) consumption (12k)	5010 minots	−5010 minots
(m) surplus (d − g − l)		1345 minots
Exactions		
(n) wheat portion seign. rent	276 minots	
(o) wheat tithe (d/26)	312 minots	
(p) total	588 minots	588 minots
Feudal exactions = 588/1345 = 44% of habitant wheat surplus		

"normal" return. Also, some families no doubt ate more wheat than others and thus the 12-minot ration would not have been strictly uniform. [. . .] But, for the moment it is important to recognize that, imprecise and partial though this aggregate model may be, it does indicate that feudal dues deprived the Lower Richelieu peasantry of a substantial portion—probably more than half—of its agricultural surpluses.

Beyond this "average" experience, individual returns from the 1765 census make it clear that the production, surplus, and feudal burden varied greatly from one St Ours household to the next. For half the cases it is impossible to compute the percentage of wheat surpluses drained by tithe and seigneurial rent, since 48 of the families had no surplus at all once the exactions were subtracted. Of these households, 11 grew less than five minots of wheat per "adult equivalent"; evidently marginal grain-growers, these families may have been artisans or day-labourers. The other 37 who apparently lacked a wheat surplus must have had to scramble to get by, perhaps making do with less bread than their neighbours or earning a little money as hired hands at harvest time. These are no doubt the habitants who let their rents go unpaid for long stretches and who paid the seigneur, when they could, in lumber, cloth, and labour. Feudal dues must have been a serious problem for these families, but also for those, slightly better off, who grew enough in good years to retain a small surplus after they had paid the landlord and the curé. Table 3.3 shows that the wealthier half of the St Ours peasantry generally owed a substantial portion of their excess wheat to the aristocrats. Only 2 paid less than 10 per cent, whereas 28 paid more than 30 per cent of their surplus, some losing their entire surplus to feudal dues. For a handful of the richest peasants, on the other hand, tithes and rents were a much less significant drain. The three largest producers had a net wheat surplus after deductions, exactions and consumption of 110, 122, and 122 minots respectively. After them came ten others with 50 to 100 minots surplus. Feudal dues did not exceed 20 per cent of the excess of any of these 13 prosperous families. They normally had substantial quantities of grain to sell and were the section of the community that grain dealers were most interested in.

This "model" of wheat surpluses by household demonstrates, not only the differing impact of feudal exactions, but also the variety of economic positions within the Lower Richelieu peasantry. As to the economic impact of feudal dues, it seems fair to conclude that they were an obstacle to the accumulation of capital in peasant hands. Certainly tithes, rents, and assessments did not absolutely prevent a habitant from amassing wealth, but generally they were a significant drain and particularly so for modest habitants like the Allaires who had a good deal of trouble in keeping above the subsistence line.

If extra-economic exactions and a prevalence of subsistence agriculture are the two primary characteristics of the feudal economy, here then is one connection between them. The first feature tended to reinforce the second by depriving peasants of part of the fruits of their labour. Seigneurial and ecclesiastical dues helped prevent the formation of an agrarian bourgeoisie by working against the accumulation of capital in habitant hands.

Instead, a large portion of the agricultural surplus was delivered to priests and landlords who showed little inclination to invest their revenues in the land. Farms therefore remained relatively small and unproductive. Obviously feudal exploitation was not the only factor responsible for this state of affairs. The limited market for agricultural produce in the early years of the Lower Richelieu settlement also discouraged investment and egalitarian inheritance customs counteracted any long-term concentration of property. Moreover, the limitations on peasant ownership inherent in seigneurial tenure could be an obstacle to enterprise in some cases. Thus, although it would be an exaggeration to say that tithes, rents, and so on by themselves prevented the development of agriculture, it is nevertheless clear that they were a real burden for the habitant household, one that added its influence to other factors in making large-scale market-oriented production unlikely.

In other words, many of the basic characteristics of Lower Richelieu social and

Table 3.3 Proportion of Wheat Surplus Devoted to Tithe and Seigneurial Rent (Wheat Only) by Habitant Household, St Ours 1765

	Households	Per Cent
No surplus left after exactions	48	48
Exactions require 0–10% of surplus	2	2
Exactions require 10–20% of surplus	21	21
Exactions require 20–30% of surplus	11	11
Exactions require 30–50% of surplus	11	11
Exactions require 50–100% of surplus	4	4
Exactions require 100% + of surplus	2	2
TOTAL	99	99

economic life were mutually reinforcing. The habitant majority lived and worked in family units, with household production organized mainly around the direct satisfaction of household consumption needs. This self-sufficient peasantry found a significant portion of its surplus drained off to support local priests and seigneurs, the latter constituting a local aristocracy whose political ascendancy guaranteed its economic privileges. This combination of peasant self-sufficiency, together with aristocratic appropriation through extra-economic compulsion, is the basically "feudal" configuration that is essential to an understanding of this rural society.

NOTES

1. Louise Dechêne, "L'évolution du régime seigneurial au Canada: le cas de Montréal aux XVIIe et XVIIIe siècles," *Recherches sociographiques* 12 (May–August 1971): 152.

2. Ibid.; cf. William Bennett Munro, *Documents Relating to the Seigniorial Tenure in Canada, 1598–1854* (Toronto: Champlain Society 1908) 74.

3. The assumption here is that wheat is valued at 10 livres per minot and that the hypothetical farm measures 3 arpents frontage by 30 arpents depth. The earliest concessions were fixed at one sol per arpent of area plus one capon (value 10 sols in 1709) for each arpent of frontage. The rate applied from 1754 on was one sol per arpent plus one-half minot of wheat for each 20 arpents (PAC, St Ours seigneurie, vol. 1, concession deeds). The evolution of rents in the seigneurie of Longueuil was almost exactly parallel, except that the rise in rates occurred rather earlier. Louis Lemoine, "Une société seigneuriale: Longueuil: méthode, sources, orientations" (MA thesis, Université de Montreal 1975) 145.

4. PAC, de Ramezay papers, pp. 1532–42, estate roll, Sorel, n.d. (1761–3).

5. ANQM, St. Denis seigneurie, 22RS7, list of arrears, 1840; PAC, Sorel seigneurie, vol. 11, estate roll, 1795.

6. PAC, Sorel seigneurie, vol. 12, accounts of the seigneurie of Sorel, 1840–7. Cf. William Bennet Munro, *The Seigniorial System in Canada: A Study in French Colonial Policy* (Cambridge: Harvard University Press 1907), 96; Dechêne, "L'évolution du régime seigneurial," 157–8.

7. Marc Bloch, *French Rural History: An Essay on Its Basic Characteristics*, trans. J. Sondheimer (Berkeley: University of California Press 1966), 180–9; Régine Robin, *La Société française en 1789: Sémur-en-Auxois* (Paris: Plon 1970), 153–4; Pierre de Saint-Jacob, *Les paysans de la Bourgogne du Nord au dernier siècle de l'ancien régime* (Paris: Université de Dijon 1960), 75–92, 377–80.

8. PAC, Haldimand papers, Add. Mss 21885, pt. 2, fols. 217–18; PAC, RG8, C, 278: 196–7, petition of Jean-Baptiste Veilleux, 22 July 1809.

9. Louise Dechêne makes this point in "L'évolution du régime seigneurial," 164. Other historians, on the other hand, include mill tolls, sometimes with operational expenses deducted, in lists of seigneurial revenues. This gives a misleading impression of the weight of seigneurial exactions. Habitants would have had to pay a charge to have their grain ground into flour even if there had been no seigneurial régime and it is difficult to say how much, if any, they would have saved had they not been subject to the banalité. Cf. Marcel Trudel, *The Seigneurial Régime,* Canadian Historical Association booklet 6 (Ottawa: CHA 1956), 13; R.C. Harris, *The Seigneurial System in Early Canada: A Geographical Study* (Madison: University of Wisconsin Press 1966), 78.

10. Cf. Jean Bastier, *La féodalité au siècle des lumières dans la région de Toulouse (1730–1790)* (Paris: Bibliothèque nationale 1975), 274–9.

11. PAC, Sorel seigneurie, vol. 13, "Rent Roll of His Majesty's Seigniory of Sorel for the year 1809," 24 March 1810; ibid., "Sorel Seigniory, abstract of arrears," 31 March 1858.

12. PAC, RG8, C, 279: 131, "Report on the Accounts of Mr Robert Jones Agent of His Majestys Seigniory of Sorel" (amounts shown are in livres).

13. ANQ, AP.G.–288 PAC, MG11, Q, 240–1: 190–5.

14. The disadvantages of this procedure did not stop the seigneur of St Ours from successfully suing ten habitants between 1839 and 1842. *Pièces et Documents relatifs à la tenure seigneuriale, demandés par une adresse de l'Assemblée législative, 1851* (Quebec: E.R. Fréchette 1852), 150.

15. Ibid., agreement between Charles de St Ours and Bazile Bourg, 2 November 1815.

16. Dechêne, "L'évolution du régime seigneurial," 164.

17. François-Joseph Cugnet, *Traité de la Loi des Fiefs* (Quebec: Guillaume Brown 1775), 36–7.

18. Munro, *The Seigniorial System* 117–19.

19. Trudel, *The Seigneurial Régime,* 15; Harris, *The Seigneurial System,* 72.

20. ANQM, gr. Deguire, concession par M. de Contrecoeur à Jacques Coder, 8 December 1758.

21. Azarie Couillard-Desprès, *Histoire de la seigneurie de St-Ours,* 2 vols. Montreal: Imprimerie de l'institution des sourds-muets 1915–1917, vol. 1: 292–3; PAC, St Ours seigneurie, vol. 5, agreement between Charles de St Ours and Bazile Bourg dit Canic, 2 November 1815; ibid., vol. 10, Aetna Insurance Company, policy no. 3580, Mme R. de St. Ours, 11 November 1842.

22. ANQM, gr. Jehanne, lease by Monsieur de la Bruyère Montarville to Gabriel Chabot, 1 October 1779; ANQM, gr. Michaud, lease by Mr de la Bruyère Montarville to Sr Joseph Bourque dit Canique, 21 October 1799; PAC, St Ours seigneurie, vol. 5, agreement between Charles de St Ours and Bazile Bourg dit Canic, 2 November 1815.

23. PAC, Haldimand Papers, Add. Mss 21885, pt. 2, fol. 217–18, "Etat actuel des rentes et autres revenus de la seigneurie de Sorel, suivant les deux dernières Recettes en 1782 et 1783."

24. Ibid.; ANQ, St Ours collection, estate inventory of François Roch de St Ours, 19 June 1841. The seigneur's cash revenues cannot be estimated with any precision since a variety of grains with different values were ground.

25. *Edits, ordonnances, déclarations et arrêts relatifs à la tenure seigneuriale, demandés par une adresse de l'Assemblée Législative, 1851* (Quebec: E.R. Fréchette, 1852), 139–40; PAC, documents légaux des seigneuries, vol. 971, testimony of Joseph Mignault, 16 June 1860.

26. See Fernand Ouellet's critical discussion of this position in two articles: "Libéré ou exploité! Le paysan québécois d'avant 1850," *Histoire sociale/Social History* 13 (November 1980) 339–68; "La formation d'une société dans la vallée du Saint-Laurent: d'une société sans classes à une société de classes," *Canadian Historical Review* 62 (December 1981): 407–50.

27. Harris, *Seigneurial System* 78; Lise Pilon-Lê, "L'endettement des cultivateurs québécois: une analyse socio-historique de la rente foncière (1670–1904)" (PhD thesis, Université de Montréal 1978) 168–9; Guy Lemarchand, "Féodalisme et société rurale dans la France moderne," in *Sur le féodalisme,* 86–105 (see also Jacques Dupâquier's comments in ibid. 107); Albert Soboul, "Sur le prélèvement féodal," in *Problèmes paysans de la révolution (1789–1848): études d'histoire révolutionnaire* (Paris: François Maspero 1976), 89–115; Bastier, *La féodalité au siècle des lumières,* 258–9.

28. W.J. Eccles, *France in America* (Vancouver: Fitzhenry and Whiteside 1973), 79.

29. Only 99 of the 107 local households are included in this "model," the remaining 8 being eliminated either because data were evidently missing from their entries or because they had no land and were therefore apparently priests, artisans, or labourers. The assumptions underlying this estimate are that two-thirds of the census-recorded grain sown was wheat, that the seed-yield ratio of wheat was 1: 5.8, that the 11 037 arpents held by these 99 families were subject to the prevailing rate of seigneurial rent which included a levy of "one half minot of wheat for every 20 arpents," that adults required 12 minots of wheat a year (the lowest individual ration commonly found in eighteenth-century pensions alimentaires), while children needed only half that amount and "girls" (unmarried females not differentiated by age in the census) ate, on the average, three-quarters of an adult ration.

Chapter 4

The Expulsion of the Acadians

READINGS

Primary Documents

Historical Interpretations

INTRODUCTION

In today's society, we venerate the ideals of harmony and trust, yet—collectively at least—we frequently fail to embody them. Eighteenth-century colonial North America was one place where similar failures occurred. The early eighteenth century brought significant change to the continent as French-speaking residents of Acadia (today's Nova Scotia and New Brunswick) found themselves under British control, thanks to a peace treaty in which the French "traded away" this territory. The 1713 Treaty of Utrecht gave the British a region that, a century earlier, had been one site of French colonial hopes. The new owners expected loyalty, but had demonstrated little patience with their Roman Catholic subjects elsewhere and knew little about the local Indigenous people. As in most conflicts, each side had some merit to its case. Acadians who largely wished to go about their lives unaffected by questions of colonial jurisdiction were urged to swear allegiance to the British monarch. Those who had to govern the region faced a population of Acadians who seemed to be stubbornly refusing to acknowledge British power and hoping for a return to the French fold.

For over 40 years, this was the pattern: an uneasy co-existence. In 1755, it came as a rather rude shock to the Acadians when longstanding suspicions about their disloyalty were followed up by British action. When the Acadians failed to convince British administrators that they had not been covertly aiding the French, they were handed an expulsion notice. Harmony and trust were impossible in Acadia with the larger conflict between colonial powers affecting the way that governors and governed related to one another.

The deportation was a process that lasted from 1755 to 1762. The Acadians of Minas Bassin and Beaubassin were the first to be evicted, followed by the ones from Louisbourg and Île St-Jean. In total, nearly 12 000 Acadians were deported to the Thirteen Colonies, Britain, and France. The primary documents describe that moment to show us the resolve of Governor Charles Lawrence along with Acadian disbelief and desperation. As for the historical interpretations, Geoffrey Plank discusses how the British authorities were reassessing their attitudes toward cultural and religious diversity in Nova Scotia after the Scottish uprising of 1746 and the War of the Austrian Succession. Naomi Griffiths argues, however, that the Deportation was not the result of a long-planned program, but of the decision of the local then–Lieutenant Governor Lawrence. When the Acadians left, they went or were sent to a variety of places, none of which had agreed to accommodate them.

QUESTIONS FOR CONSIDERATION

1. What sort of behaviour did the British seem to expect from the Acadians?
2. What do the Acadians appear not to understand about their situation, and how are British suspicions confirmed later in the summer of 1755?
3. Do you think that the Acadians posed a real threat to British rule in Nova Scotia?
4. How different are Griffiths's and Plank's interpretations about the influence of British politics in the decision to deport Acadians?
5. Do you agree with Griffiths that the expulsion had not been planned long in advance?

SUGGESTIONS FOR FURTHER READING

Daigle, Jean, ed. *The Acadians of the Maritimes: Thematic Studies.* Moncton: Centre d'études acadiennes, 1982.

Faragher, John Mack. *A Great and Noble Scheme: The Tragic Story of the Expulsion of the French Acadians from their American Homeland.* New York: W.W. Norton & Co., 2005.

Griffiths, N.E.S. *From Migrant to Acadian: A North American Border People 1604–1755.* Montreal and Kingston: McGill-Queen's University Press, 2005.

Hodson, Christopher. *The Acadian Diaspora: An Eighteenth-Century History.* Oxford: Oxford University Press, 2012.

Johnston, A.J.B. *Endgame 1758: The Promise, the Glory and the Despair of Louisbourg's Last Decade.* Sydney, NS: Cape Breton University Press, 2007.

Lockerby, Earl. "The Deportation of the Acadians from Île St. Jean, 1758." *Acadiensis* XXVII (Spring 1998): 45–94.

Parmentier, Jon, and Mark Power Robinson. "The Perils and Possibilities of Wartime Neutrality on the Edges of Empire: Iroquois and Acadians between the French and British in North America, 1744–1760." *Diplomatic History* 31, 2 (April 2007): 167–206.

Plank, Geoffrey. *An Unsettled Conquest: The British Campaign Against the Peoples of Acadia.* Philadelphia: University of Pennsylvania Press, 2001.

Primary Documents

1 From "1755 Council Minutes," in *Acadia and Nova Scotia: Documents Relating to the Acadian French and the First British Colonization of the Province 1714–1758,* ed. Thomas B. Akins (Halifax, 1870), 247–57.

At a Council holden at the Governor's House in Halifax on Thursday the 3rd July 1755.

PRESENT—

The Lieutenant Governor.

Councs.: Benj. Green, Jno. Collier, Willm. Cotterell, Jonn. Belcher.

The Lieutenant Governor laid before the Council the two following Memorials, Signed by the Deputies and a number of the French Inhabitants of Minas and Pisiquid, and delivered to Capt. Murray the Commanding Officer there, by whom they had been transmitted to His Excellency.

[Translated from the French.]

"MINES June 10th. 1755."

"To His Excellency CHARLES LAWRENCE, Governor of the province of Nova Scotia or Acadie, &c. &c.

"Sir,—

"We, the Inhabitants of Mines, Pisiquid, and the river Canard, take the liberty of approaching your Excellency for the purpose of testifying our sense of the care which the government exercises towards us.

"It appears, Sir, that your Excellency doubts the sincerity with which we have promised to be faithful to his Britannic Majesty.

"We most humbly beg your Excellency to consider our past conduct. You will see, that, very far from violating the oath we have taken, we have maintained it in its entirety, in spite of the solicitations and the dreadful threats of another power. We still entertain, Sir, the same pure and sincere disposition to prove under any circumstances, our unshaken fidelity to his Majesty, provided that His Majesty shall allow us the same liberty that he has granted us. We earnestly beg your Excellency to have the goodness to inform us of His Majesty's intentions on this subject, and to give us assurances on his part.

"Permit us, if you please, Sir, to make known the annoying circumstances in which we are placed, to the prejudice of the tranquillity we ought to enjoy. Under pretext that we are transporting our corn or other provisions to Beausejour, and the river St. John, we are no longer permitted to carry the least quantity of corn by water from one place to another. We beg your Excellency to be assured that we have never transported provisions to Beausejour, or to the river St. John. If some refugee inhabitants at the point have been seized, with cattle, we are not on that account, by any means guilty, in as much as the cattle belonged to them as private individuals, and they were driving them to their respective habitations. As to ourselves, Sir, we have never offended in that respect; consequently we ought not, in our opinion, to be punished; on the contrary, we hope that your Excellency will be pleased to restore to us the same liberty that we enjoyed formerly, in giving us the use of our canoes, either to transport our provisions from one river to the other, or for the purpose of fishing; thereby providing for our livelihood. This permission has never been taken from us except at the present time. We hope, Sir, that you will be pleased to restore it, especially in consideration of the number of poor inhabitants who would be very glad to support their families with the fish that they would be able to catch. Moreover, our guns, which we regard as our own personal property, have been taken from us, notwithstanding the fact that they are absolutely necessary to us, either to defend our cattle which are attacked by the wild beasts, or for the protection of our children, and of ourselves.

"Any inhabitant who may have his oxen in the woods, and who may need them for purposes of labour, would not dare to expose himself in going for them without being prepared to defend himself.

"It is certain, Sir, that since the savages have ceased frequenting our parts, the wild beasts have greatly increased, and that our cattle are devoured by them almost every day. Besides, the arms which have been taken from us are but a feeble guarantee of our fidelity. It is not the gun which an inhabitant possesses, that will induce him to revolt, nor the privation of the same gun that will make him more faithful; but his conscience alone must induce him to maintain his oath. An order has appeared in your Excellency's name, given at Fort Edward June 4th, 1755, and in the 28th year of his Majesty's reign, by which we are commanded to carry guns, pistols etc. to Fort Edward. It appears to us, Sir, that it would be dangerous for us to execute that order, before representing to you the danger to which this order exposes us. The savages may come and threaten and plunder us, reproaching us for having furnished arms to kill them. We hope, Sir, that you will be pleased, on the contrary, to order that those taken from us be restored to us. By so doing, you will afford us the means of preserving both ourselves and our cattle. In the last place, we are grieved, Sir, at seeing ourselves declared guilty without being aware of having disobeyed. One of our inhabitants of the river Canard, named Piere Melançon, was seized and arrested in charge of his boat, before having heard any order forbidding that sort of transport. We beg your Excellency, on this subject, to have the goodness to make known to us your good pleasure before confiscating our property and considering us in fault. This is the favour we expect from your Excellency's kindness, and we hope that you will do us the justice to believe that very far from violating our promises, we will maintain them, assuring you that we are very respectfully,

> Sir,
> Your very humble and obt. servants,"
> Signed by twenty-five of the said
> inhabitants.

"MINES, June 24, 1755."
"To his Excellency CHARLES LAWRENCE, Esq., Governor of the province of Nova Scotia or Acadie.
"Sir,—

"All the inhabitants of Mines, Pisiquid and the river Canard, beg your Excellency to believe that if, in the petition which they have had the honor to present to your Excellency, there shall be found any error or any want of respect towards the government, it is intirely contrary to their intention; and that in this case, the inhabitants who have signed it, are not more guilty than the others.

"If, sometimes, the inhabitants become embarrassed in your Excellency's presence, they humbly beg you to excuse their timidity; and if, contrary to our expectation, there is anything hard in the said petition, we beg your Excellency to do us the favour of allowing us to explain our intention.

"We hope that your Excellency will be pleased to grant us this favour, begging you to believe that we are very respectfully,

Sir,

Your very humble and very obedient servants,"

Signed by forty-four of the said inhabitants in the name of the whole.

The Lieutenant Governor at the same time acquainted the Council that Capt. Murray had informed him that for some time before the delivery of the first of the said memorials the French Inhabitants in general had behaved with greater Submission and Obedience to the Orders of the Government than usual, and had already delivered into him a considerable number of their Fire Arms, but that at the delivery of the said Memorial they treated him with great Indecency and Insolence, which gave him strong Suspicions, that they had obtained some Intelligence which we were then ignorant of, and which the Lieutenant Governor conceived might most probably be a Report that had been about that time spread amongst them of a French Fleet being then in the Bay of Fundy, it being very notorious that the said French Inhabitants have always discovered an insolent and inimical Disposition towards His Majesty's Government when they have had the least hopes of assistance from France.

The Lieutenant Governor likewise acquainted the Council that upon his receipt of the first Memorial, he had wrote to Captain Murray to order all those who had Signed the same, to repair forthwith to Halifax to attend him and the Council thereon, and that they were accordingly arrived and then in waiting without.

The Council having then taken the Contents of the said Memorials into Consideration, were unanimously of Opinion That the Memorial of the 10th of June is highly arrogant and insidious, an Insult upon His Majesty's Authority and Government, and deserved the highest Resentment, and that if the Memorialists had not submitted themselves by their subsequent Memorial, they ought to have been severely punished for their Presumption.

The Deputies were then called in and the Names of the Subscribers to the Memorial read over, and such of them as were present, ordered to Answer to their Names, which they did to the number of fifteen, the others being Sick, after which the Memorial itself was again read, and they were severely reprimanded for their Audacity in Subscribing and Presenting so impertinent a Paper, but in Compassion to their Weakness and Ignorance of the Nature of our Constitution, especially in Matters of Government, and as the Memorialists had presented a subsequent one, and had shewn an Appearance of Concern for their past behaviour therein, and had then presented themselves before the Council with great Submission and Repentance, The Council informed them they were still ready to treat them with Lenity, and in order to shew them the falsity as well as Impudence of the Contents of their Memorial, it was ordered to be read Paragraph by Paragraph, and the Truth of the several Allegations minutely discussed, and Remarks made by the Lieutenant Governor on each Paragraph, to the following Effect, vizt.

It was observed in Answer to this Paragraph of their Memorial of the 10th of June

"That they were affected with the Proceedings of the Government towards them."

That they had been always treated by the Government with the greatest Lenity and Tenderness. That they had enjoyed more Privileges than English Subjects, and had been indulged in the free Excercise of their Religion. That they had at all times full Liberty to consult their Priests, and had been protected in their Trade and Fishery, and had been for many Years permitted to possess their Lands (part of the best Soil of the Province) tho' they had not complied with the Terms, on which the Lands were granted, by Taking the Oath of Allegiance to the Crown.

They were then asked whether they could produce an Instance that any Privilege was denied to them, or that any hardships, were ever imposed upon them by the Government.

They acknowledged the Justice and Lenity of the Government.

Upon the Paragraph where

"They desire their past Conduct might be considered."

It was remarked to them that their past Conduct was considered, and that the Government were sorry to have occasion to say that their Conduct had been undutifull and very ungratefull for the Lenity shown to them. That they had no Returns of Loyalty to the Crown, or Respect to His Majesty's Government in the Province. That they had discovered a constant disposition to Assist His Majesty's Enemies, and to distress his Subjects. That they had not only furnished the Enemy with Provisions and Ammunition, but had refused to supply the Inhabitants, or Government, with Provisions, and when they did Supply, they have exacted three times the Price for which they were sold at other Markets. That they had been indolent and Idle on their Lands, had neglected Husbandry, and the Cultivation of the Soil, and had been of no use to the Province either in husbandry, Trade or Fishery, but had been rather an Obstruction to the King's Intentions in the Settlement.

They were then asked whether they could mention a single Instance of Service to the Government. To which they were incapable of making any Reply.

Upon reading this Paragraph,

"It seems that your Excellency is doubtfull of the Sincerity of those who have promised fidelity, That they had been so far from breaking their Oath, that they had kept it in spight of terrifying Menaces from another Power"

They were asked What gave them Occasion to suppose that the Government was doubtfull of their Sincerity? and were told, that it argued a Consciousness in them of insincerity and want of Attachment to the Interests of His Majesty and his Government. That as to taking their Arms, They had often urged that the Indians would annoy them if they did not Assist them, and that by taking their Arms by Act of Government, it was put out of the Power of the Indians to threaten or force them to their Assistance. That they had assisted the King's Enemies, and appeared too ready to Join with another Power, contrary to the Allegiance they were bound by their Oath to yield to His Majesty.

In Answer to this Paragraph,

"We are now in the same disposition, the purest and sincerest, to prove in every Circumstance Fidelity to His Majesty in the same manner as we have done, Provided that His Majesty will leave us the same Liberties which he has granted us"

They were told that it was hoped, they would hereafter give Proofs of more sincere and pure dispositions of Mind, in the Practice of Fidelity to His Majesty, and that they would forbear to Act in the manner they have done, in obstructing the Settlement of the Province, by Assisting the Indians and French to the distress and Annoyance of many of His Majesty's Subjects, and to the Loss of the Lives of several of the English Inhabitants. That it was not the Language of British Subjects to talk of Terms with the Crown, to Capitulate about their Fidelity and Allegiance, and that it was insolent to insert a *Proviso*, that they would prove their Fidelity *Provided* that His Majesty would give them Liberties.

All His Majesty's Subjects are protected in the Enjoyment of every Liberty, while they continue Loyal and faithfull to the Crown, and when they become false and disloyal they forfeit that Protection.

That they in particular, tho they had acted so insincerely on every Opportunity, had been left in the full Enjoyment of their Religion, Liberty and Properties, with an Indulgence beyond what would have been allowed to any British Subject, who could presume, as they have done, to join in the Measures of another Power.

They were told in answer to the Paragraph where,

"They desire their Canoes for carrying their Provisions from one River to another and for their Fishery"

That they wanted their Canoes for carrying Provisions to the Enemy, and not for their own use or the Fishery, That by a Law of this Province, All Persons are restrained from carrying Provisions from one Port to another, and every Vessel, Canoe or Bark found with Provisions is forfeited, and a Penalty is inflicted on the Owners.

They were also told in Answer to the following Paragraph,

"They Petition for their Guns as part of their Goods, that they may be restored to defend their Cattle from the Wild Beasts, and to preserve themselves and their Children, That since the Indians have quitted their Quarters, the Wild Beasts are greatly increased"

That Guns are no part of their Goods, as they have no Right to keep Arms. By the Laws of England, All Roman Catholicks are restrained from having Arms, and they are Subject to Penalties if Arms are found in their Houses.

That upon the Order from Captain Murray many of the Inhabitants voluntarily brought in their Arms, and none of them pretended that they wanted them for defence of their Cattle against Wild Beasts, and that the Wild Beasts had not increased since their Arms were surrendered. That they had some secret Inducement, at that time, for

presuming to demand their Arms as part of their Goods and their Right, and that they had flattered themselves of being supported in their Insolence to the Government, on a Report that some french Ships of War were in the Bay of Fundy. That this daring Attempt plainly discovered the falsehood of their Professions of Fidelity to the King, and their readiness has been visible upon every Intimation of force or Assistance from France, to insult His Majesty's Government, and to join with his Enemies, contrary to their Oath of Fidelity.

Upon reading this Paragraph,

"Besides the Arms we carry are a feeble Surety for our Fidelity. It is not the Gun that an Inhabitant possesses, which will lead him to Revolt, nor the depriving him of that Gun that will make him more faithful, but his Conscience alone ought to engage him to maintain his Oath."

They were asked, what Excuse they could make for their Presumption in this Paragraph, and treating the Government with such Indignity and Contempt as to Expound to them the nature of Fidelity, and to prescribe what would be the Security proper to be relied on by the Government for their Sincerity. That their Consciences ought indeed to engage them to Fidelity from their Oath of Allegiance to the King, and that if they were sincere in their Duty to the Crown, they would not be so anxious for their Arms, when it was the pleasure of the King's Government to demand them for His Majesty's Service. They were then informed that a very fair Opportunity now presented itself to them to Manifest the reality of their Obedience to the Government by immediately taking the Oath of Allegiance in the Common Form before the Council. Their Reply to this Proposal was, That they were not come prepared to resolve the Council on that head. They were then told that they very well knew these Six Years past, the same thing had been often proposed to them and had been as often evaded under various frivolous pretences, that they had often been informed that sometime or other it would be required of them and must be done, and that the Council did not doubt but they knew the Sentiments of the Inhabitants in general, and had fully considered and determined this point with regard to themselves before now, as they had been already indulged with Six Years to form a Resolution thereon. They then desired they might return home and consult the Body of the People upon this subject as they could not do otherwise than the Generality of the inhabitants should determine, for that they were desirous of either refusing or accepting the Oath in a Body, and could not possibly determine, till they knew the Sentiments of their Constituents.

Upon this so extraordinary a Reply they were informed they would not be permitted to Return for any such purpose, but that it was expected from them to declare on the Spot, for their own particular, as they might very well be expected to do after having had so long a time to consider upon that point. They then desired leave to retire to consult among themselves, which they were permitted to do, when after near an hour's Recess, They returned with the same Answer, That they could not consent to take the Oath as prescribed without consulting the General Body, but that they were ready to take it as they had done before, to which they were answered, That His Majesty had disapproved of the manner of their taking the Oath before, That it was not consistent with his Honour to make any conditions, nor could the Council accept their taking the Oath in any other way than as all other His Majesty's Subjects were obliged by Law to do when called upon, and that it was now expected they should do so, which they still declining, they were allowed till the next Morning at Ten of the Clock to come to a Resolution. To which Time the Council then adjourned. . . .

The Council being met according to Adjournment, the french Deputies who were Yesterday Ordered to Attend the Council, were brought in, and, upon being asked what Resolution they were come to in regard to the Oath, They declared they could not consent to Take the Oath in the Form required without consulting the Body. They were then informed that as they had now for their own particulars, refused to Take the Oath as directed by Law, and thereby sufficiently evinced the Sincerity of their Inclination towards the Government, The Council could no longer look on them as Subjects to His Britannick Majesty, but as Subjects of the King of France, and as such they must hereafter be Treated; and they were Ordered to withdraw.

The Council after Consideration, were of Opinion That directions should be given to Captain Murray to order the French Inhabitants forthwith to Choose and send to Halifax, new Deputies with the General Resolution of the said Inhabitants in regard to taking the Oath, and that none of them should for the future be admitted to Take it after having once refused so to do, but that effectual Measures ought to be taken to remove all such Recusants out of the Province.

The Deputies were then called in again, and having been informed of this Resolution, and finding they could no longer avail themselves of the Disposition of the Government to ingage them to a Dutifull Behaviour by Lenity and perswasion, Offered to take the Oath, but were informed that as there was no reason to hope their proposed Compliance proceeded from an honest Mind, and could be esteemed only the Effect of Compulsion and Force, and is contrary to a clause in an Act of Parliament, I. Geo. 2. c 13. whereby Persons who have once refused to Take the Oaths cannot be afterwards permitted to Take them, but are considered as Popish Recusants; Therefore they would not now be indulged with such Permission; And they were thereupon ordered into Confinement.

2 From "Extracts from Col. John Winslow's Journal" [1755], in *Report Concerning Canadian Archives for the Year 1905* (Ottawa: S.E. Dawson, 1906), vol. II, Appendix A, Part III, 19–29.

Septr. 3rd—This Day had a Consultation with the Captains the Result of which was that I Should Give out my Citation to the Inhabitants to morrow Morning.

1755, September the 4th—This Morning Sent for Doctor Rodion and Delivd him a Citation to the Inhabitants with a Strict Charge to See it Executed, which he Promist Should be Faithfully Done.

September 5th—Att Three in the afternoon The French Inhabitants appeard agreable to their Citation at the Church in Grand Pré amounting To 418 of Their Best Men upon which I ordered a Table to be Sett in the Center of the Church and being attended with those of my officers who were off Gaurd Delivered them by Interpretors the King's orders In the Following words:

GENTLEMEN,—I have Received from his Excellency Governor Lawrance, The Kings Commission which I have in my hand and by whose orders you are Convened togather to Manifest to you his Majesty's Final resolution to the French Inhabitants of this his Province of Nova Scotia, who for almost half a Century have had more Indulgence Granted them, then any of his Subjects in any part of his Dominions. what use you have made of them, you your Self Best Know.

The Part of Duty I am now upon is what thoh Necessary is Very Disagreable to my Natural make & Temper as I Know it Must be Grevious to you who are of the Same Specia.

But it is not my Business to annimedvert, but to obey Such orders as I receive and therefore without Hessitation Shall Deliver you his Majesty's orders and Instructions vizt.

That your Lands & Tennements, Cattle of all Kings and Live Stock of all Sortes are Forfitted to the Crown with all other your Effects Saving your Money and Household Goods and you your Selves to be removed from this his Province.

This it is Preremtorily his Majesty's orders That the whole French Inhabitants of these Districts, be removed, and I am Throh his Majesty's Goodness Directed to allow you Liberty to Carry of your money and Household Goods as Many as you Can without Discomemoading the Vessels you Go in. I shall do Every thing in my Power that all Those Goods be Secured to you and that you are Not Molested in Carrying of them of and also that whole Familys Shall go in the Same Vessel, and make this remove which I am Sensable must give you a great Deal of Trouble as Easy as his Majesty's Service will admit and hope that in what Ever part of the world you may Fall you may be Faithful Subjects, a Peasable & happy People.

I Must also inform you That it is his Majesty's Pleasure that you remain in Security under the Inspection & Direction of the Troops that I have the Honr. to Command.

and then declared them the Kings Prisoner's.

And Gave out the following Declaration.
GRAND PRÉ, September 5sh, 1755.

All officers and Soldiers and Sea Men Employed in his Majesty's Service as well as all his Subjects of what Denomination Soever, are hereby Notified That all Cattle vizt. Horsses, Horne Cattle, Sheep, goats, Hoggs and Poultry of Every Kinde, that was this Day Soposed to be Vested in the French Inhabitants of this Province are become Forfeited to his Majesty whose Property they now are and Every Person of what Denomination Soever is to take Care not to Hurt, Kill or Destroy anything of any Kinde nor Rob Orchards or Gardens or to make waste of anything Dead or alive in these Districts without Special order. Given at my Camp the Day and Place abovesd.
JOHN WINSLOW.

To be Published Throhout the Camp and at Villages where the Vessels lye.

After Delivering These Things I returned to my Quarters and they the French Inhabitants Soon Moved by their Elders that it was a Great Grief to them that they had Incurred his Majty's Displeasure and that they were Fearfull that the Surprise of their Detention here would Quite over Come their Familys whome they had No Means to apprise of these their Maloncolly Circumstances and Prayd that parte of them might be returned as Hostages for the appearance of the rest and the Biger number admitted to Go home to their Families, and that as some of their Men were absent they would be obliged to Bring them in. I informed them I would Consider of their Motions and reporte.

And Immediately Convened my officers, to advise, who with Me all agreed that it would be well that they them Selves should Chuse Twenty of their Number for whome they would be answerable vizt Ten of the Inhabitants of Grand Pré & Village & other Ten of the River Cannard and Habitant and they to acquaint the Families of their Districts how Maters where and to assure them that the women & children should be in Safety in their absence in their Habitations and that it was Espected the Party Indulged Should take Care to Bring in an Exact Account of their absent Bretheren & their Circumstances on the Morrow.

Historical Interpretations

3 From Geoffrey Plank, "Île Royale, New England, Scotland, and Nova Scotia, 1744–1748," in *An Unsettled Conquest: The British Campaign Against the Peoples of Acadia* (Philadelphia: University of Pennsylvania Press, 2001), 106–22. Permission conveyed through the Copyright Clearance Center.

In 1739, after a series of disputes arising out of Spanish efforts to regulate trade in the Caribbean, Britain went to war with Spain. Sir Robert Walpole had tried to settle his government's differences with Spain peacefully, but domestic opposition to his foreign policy forced his hand. The Walpole ministry's opponents rallied a significant portion of the British public in support of war with Spain in part by associating the interests of British merchants abroad with the political liberties of Britons at home. They cited the government's willingness to negotiate with the Spanish as evidence of Walpole's corruption and an indication that he was willing to sacrifice British liberty and subordinate himself to the Catholic powers to advance his own political ends. At public rallies and in the press, the supporters of war called themselves "patriots," and by linking domestic liberty with power overseas, they created a new, broader base of political support for British imperial expansion.[1]

The inhabitants of North America's eastern maritime region followed these events with great interest, assuming that the Anglo-Spanish conflict would broaden into a larger conflagration and that Britain and France would soon be at war. One result was a precipitous decline in the number of New England fishermen visiting Canso. The New Englanders feared a French attack on the island, and many abandoned it after 1739. It turned out that the fishermen were right, though Europe's diplomats staved off war between the British and the French longer than the colonists anticipated. The War of the Austrian Succession, Britain's war with

France, began only in 1744, after Walpole had been driven from power. It started far from the coasts of Nova Scotia, but the French on Île Royale exploited the outbreak of hostilities almost immediately by joining forces with Mi'kmaq allies and attacking the British settlement on Canso after the word arrived from Europe that war had been declared.

In response to the attack on Canso, Massachusetts entered the conflict, first by sending reinforcements to defend the garrison at Annapolis Royal, and then in 1745 (acting alongside forces from elsewhere in New England) by seizing Louisbourg. The New Englanders sent most of the French colonial population of Île Royale to France, but the French military remained active in the region nonetheless, particularly in the eastern part of peninsular Nova Scotia.

The fighting disrupted the conditions that had allowed for relative peace in Nova Scotia over the previous 18 years by forcing almost all the inhabitants to answer questions that many of them had previously been able to avoid. The Mi'kmaq and the English-speaking colonists, especially on the Atlantic coast, had to define in clearer terms the meaning of Mi'kmaq claims to the land. The Acadians throughout the province had to determine under what circumstances they were obliged to support the British colonial government or resist demands made on them by the government's French and Mi'kmaq opponents. Persons of mixed ancestry, and others whose way of life defied simple categorization as "French," "British," or "Indian," had to decide for official purposes in which community they belonged.

Almost every facet of daily life became politically significant. Growing crops and raising livestock in certain areas served the war efforts of the Mi'kmaq and the French and left the Acadians vulnerable to British reprisals. Other activities such as worshipping alongside Native warriors or French soldiers, dancing with the men or helping Mi'kmaq women care for their children, acquired new importance in the context of the war. And even those who avoided contact with the fighting men or their families had reason to monitor and re-evaluate their habits because the British used behavioural cues to determine whether a person was Mi'kmaq. From 1744 onward the Massachusetts government offered prizes for the scalps of the Native people.

The New England colonists who participated in military action in and around Nova Scotia in some respects closely resembled those of earlier generations who had fought in the maritime region, and the War of the Austrian Succession only served to intensify existing patterns of interracial violence. But in other respects the mid-eighteenth-century New Englanders were very different from their predecessors. Partly under the influence of the new brand of imperial patriotism, which had spread across the Atlantic since the start of the war with Spain, many New England colonists saw their actions as part of a larger imperial project, one they embraced without the misgivings of the old Puritans. Following their victory at Louisbourg the colonists celebrated in a way they had never done before.[2]

After 1745 political developments in Britain helped recast the terms of the debate surrounding the Acadians. In 1746, in the aftermath of an uprising in Scotland on behalf of the Stuart claimant to the throne, the British government debated a series of measures designed to pacify broad stretches of the Scottish Highlands and culturally assimilate the Highlanders. Ideas originally developed as a solution for perceived problems in Scotland were considered as policy options for the Acadians. Perhaps the most important idea that reached America in this way was a proposal to move suspect populations within the British Empire. Before the pacification of the Highlands, those who had proposed moving the Acadians imagined that they would be expelled altogether from the British colonies (as the New Englanders sent the

French colonists from Île Royale to France in 1745). But from 1746 forward, under the influence of proposals developed in the Scottish context, the debate shifted as policy makers considered forced migrations designed to incorporate the Acadians into the communal life of British North America.

In the years following the outbreak of the War of the Austrian Succession, events far from Nova Scotia had profound effects on the lives of the peoples of the province. This article highlights the influence of groups who came to the colony from elsewhere in the British and French Empires. It begins with the decision of the French colonial administrators on Île Royale to attack the British fishery at Canso, and proceeds with an analysis of the military response of the New Englanders and the impact of the imperial war on the lives of the Mi'kmaq and the Acadians.

When the French colonial authorities began the large-scale settlement of Île Royale in 1714, they had hoped that the island colony would attract most, if not all, of the Mi'kmaq and the Acadians. The French succeeded in convincing some Acadian families to move, though fewer than they expected. Similarly, Île Royale attracted fewer Mi'kmaq than the French would have preferred, and many of those who went only visited. Nonetheless, even without a wholesale migration of Mi'kmaq and Acadians from Nova Scotia, the French colony on Île Royale prospered. By the early 1740s, Louisbourg alone had nearly 2000 inhabitants; three-quarters were civilians, including the families of soldiers, fishermen, colonial officials, merchants, artisans, and labourers. The island as a whole had a population approaching 5000.[3]

Though the French could not entice all the Mi'kmaq or Acadians to move to Île Royale, various French missionaries and colonial officials remained interested in the affairs of the peoples of Nova Scotia. They continued to think of the Acadians as compatriots, and they thought of the Mi'kmaq

as a client people, dependent on the French for pastoral care, trade, and a measure of political direction. As early as 1734, Joseph Saint-Ovide de Brouillan, the governor of Île Royale, made tentative plans to retake Nova Scotia in the event of a war.[4] His advisors assured him that all of the Acadians and most of the Mi'kmaq would greet the French forces as liberators. Subsequent administrators continued to hold similar views.[5] The outbreak of the War of the Austrian Succession presented the colony's officials with an apparent opportunity to bring the Mi'kmaq and the Acadians back within the borders of the French Empire. Instead of asking them to move, the French would try to shift the boundary and drive Britain's colonial administration away.

The French attack on Canso was intended as a first step toward recapturing all of Nova Scotia. There were several reasons for striking the fishing settlement first. Driving the British from Canso foreclosed any possibility that the island could be used as a base for privateers. The French also hoped to cripple the British fishery in the North Atlantic and thereby acquire a larger share of the world market in fish. Canso seemed vulnerable, and since some of the British settlers there had well-furnished homes, the possibility of plunder made it easier for the French to recruit volunteer troops in Louisbourg. Furthermore, many of the Mi'kmaq continued to resent the British presence on the Atlantic coast, and thus the attack on Canso helped secure a wartime Franco–Mi'kmaq alliance.[6]

The decision to start with an attack on the fishing settlement appears in retrospect to have been a strategic mistake, however, because it had the effect of bringing New Englanders into the conflict from the moment the fighting began.[7] Though they had lost Canso, New England's fishermen and privateers could reach the waters off Nova Scotia from other bases, and the Atlantic fishing banks soon became a battle zone, as New Englanders sought retaliation against the

French, and the French responded in kind. In a matter of months hundreds of fishing vessels were taken or destroyed.[8] Within Massachusetts, fishermen supported Governor William Shirley's decision to reinforce the garrison of Annapolis Royal, and fishermen were among the earliest proponents of his project to seize Île Royale.[9]

More than anyone else it was Shirley who defined and directed New England's response to the renewal of conflict in the maritime region. In many ways he personified an increasingly dominant, cosmopolitan outlook among active members of New England's political elite.[10] He was an English-born lawyer who had trained in London; he had lived in Massachusetts only since 1731, and remained equally at ease on both sides of the Atlantic Ocean. Shirley secured the Massachusetts governorship in 1741 with the help of his patron, Secretary of State Thomas Hollis-Pelham, the duke of Newcastle, and he entered office at a time when Massachusetts was badly divided. Economic disruptions associated with the war with Spain, political struggles over the emission of paper money, and religious upheavals associated with revivalism had combined to divide the colonial population into a complex set of mutually antagonistic groups.[11] Shirley never gained the support of all the colonists, but, as several historians have shown, his military ventures gave him the patronage power he needed to secure political support from the competing factions and govern Massachusetts effectively.[12] Self-interested merchants and office-seekers supported Shirley and his campaign against the French, as did a broad cross-section of the colonial public, including evangelical preachers, conservative Congregationalists and Anglicans, fishermen, and young men eager to advance their prospects through military service and the acquisition of land. The New England churches abandoned their earlier reticence and endorsed Shirley's actions.[13] It helped that the French and the Mi'kmaq appeared to be the aggressors.

The early reports of combat appearing in the Massachusetts newspapers emphasized the participation of Mi'kmaq warriors and presented them in the worst possible light. In June 1744 a correspondent to the *Boston Gazette* indicated that the Mi'kmaq who took part in the attack on Canso had pleaded with the French for permission to slaughter the English-speaking residents of the town and that the French had struggled to restrain them.[14] Similar stories were repeated often during the war and served to convince many New Englanders that the Mi'kmaq were innately irrational and violent.[15]

Such beliefs had long circulated in Massachusetts, and they inspired the New England colonists during the War of the Austrian Succession to adopt a stance toward the Mi'kmaq similar to the one they had adopted in their previous wars. But in 1744 and 1745 the colonists were mobilized for war in the maritime region on an unprecedented scale.

On 20 October 1744 the government of Massachusetts officially declared war on the Mi'kmaq.[16] Five days later the Massachusetts General Court offered a bounty of £100 (provincial currency) for the scalp of any adult male member of the Mi'kmaq nation. For the scalps of women and children, the legislature offered £50.[17] Similar rewards were available for Mi'kmaq prisoners taken alive. Recognizing that it would be difficult to identify scalps by tribe, on 2 November Shirley announced that he would grant a reward for any "Indian" killed or captured east of the St Croix River, regardless of his or her language group. By necessity he made an exception for Native warriors serving under the Anglo-American military command.[18]

There is no record of Jean-Baptiste Cope's activities during the war, but the mission near his home on the Shubenacadie River became a centre of Mi'kmaq resistance. The resident missionary at the Shubenacadie mission, Jean-Louis Le Loutre, served as the principal intermediary between the French forces and the Mi'kmaq on peninsular Nova Scotia. It was Le Loutre who informed the Mi'kmaq in the interior of Nova Scotia of the plan to strike at Canso, and, acting on the advice of the governor of Louisbourg, he also sent them directions to lay siege to Annapolis Royal in the weeks immediately after that attack. Le Loutre accompanied Mi'kmaq warriors to the British colonial capital and played an active role as an advisor to the Mi'kmaq in the first three years of the war.[19] Pierre Maillard, another missionary working among the Mi'kmaq, also travelled with the bands on the peninsula of Nova Scotia and at Île Royale. He provided advice and delivered speeches aimed at strengthening the warriors' discipline and resolve.[20] After disease struck the Mi'kmaq in 1746, the missionaries told them that the British had deliberately infected them by distributing contaminated cloth.[21]

Le Loutre and Maillard may have argued more strenuously than necessary, because the scalp-bounty policy, by itself, was enough to foreclose easy reconciliation between the Mi'kmaq bands and the British. At least among those living within the traditional bands, almost all of the Mi'kmaq supported the war effort. They were fighting not just for land but for survival, and men, women, and children overcame severe hardships to keep the warriors afield. [. . .]

After their seizure of Louisbourg, the New Englanders transported the French-speaking population of Île Royale to France.[22] That decision inspired a brief debate within the provincial council of Nova Scotia over the possibility of similarly expelling the Acadians, though the option was ultimately rejected as impractical.[23] Proponents of deportation argued that the Acadians had not taken valid oaths of allegiance and that their refusal to contemplate military service undermined the credibility of their professed loyalty to Britain. The councilmen also cited the Acadians' recent behaviour. Those who favoured removing them argued that they

had helped supply the French army and Mi'kmaq warriors and refused to sell provisions to the British except at exorbitant prices. The Acadians had seemed slow to inform the British about French and Mi'kmaq military preparations, and the councilmen assumed that they provided the French and the Mi'kmaq useful intelligence. Along with providing information and logistical support, the Acadians behaved in ways that boosted enemy morale. According to a report of the provincial council, when Mi'kmaq warriors and French soldiers first laid siege to Annapolis Royal, Acadian "men, women and children frequented the enemy's quarters at their mass, prayers, dancing and all other ordinary occasions."[24]

As the debate over expelling the Acadians made clear, the outbreak of armed hostilities increased the political ramifications of many aspects of the Acadians' lives. When Acadian merchants and farmers raised the price of food, the men in the garrison interpreted the action as a show of support for the king of France. When Acadian women danced with French soldiers, provincial councilmen took it as evidence of sedition. In part because their daily behaviour came under scrutiny, many Acadians who had formerly worked closely with the provincial government fled Annapolis Royal when the fighting began.[25] [. . .]

Acadian men and women reacted to the pressures of living in wartime in various ways, and it is difficult to generalize about their behaviour. A few young men left their homes and went to fight alongside Mi'kmaq warriors.[26] Others hired themselves out as civilian workers for the British army.[27] At least one merchant who had formerly traded with the British garrisons offered his services to the French military and spent the war ferrying men and equipment to French-controlled regions at the eastern end of the Bay of Fundy.[28] [. . .]

If there was anything "typical" about the Acadians' pattern of behaviour, it was that almost none of them could hold a consistent political stance. [. . .]

By 1746 the policy debates surrounding the Acadians had changed. Early in the conflict, Shirley and various members of Nova Scotia's provincial council had contemplated mass deportations or large-scale retributive raids, especially against the Acadian villagers at the eastern end of the Bay of Fundy, who seemed to have given the most assistance to the French and their Native allies.[29] In 1745, writing to his commander on Île Royale, Shirley had wistfully complained, "It grieves me much that I have it not in my power to send a part of 500 men forthwith to Menis [Minas] and burn Grand Pré, their chief town, and open all their sluices, and lay their country waste."[30] But by the winter of 1746 Shirley had shifted his efforts and began to seek ways to gain the Acadians' co-operation and ultimately win their hearts.

Several factors contributed to this change in thinking. In the previous summer a French fleet sent to recapture Louisbourg foundered on the Atlantic coast of Nova Scotia, and from that time forward the British military position seemed more secure, particularly at Annapolis Royal. Disease had swept through the Mi'kmaq community, killing hundreds and weakening the military power of the survivors.[31] Equally important, the New Englanders within the garrison at Annapolis Royal gradually changed their outlook toward the Acadians. Given more time to interact with the villagers outside the context of an immediate military crisis, they began to believe that they could gain the Acadians' friendship. The soldiers depended on Acadian farmers and merchants for food and firewood, and the social environment encouraged the men to seek the company of Acadians outside the context of trade.

In the first year of the war relations between the garrison and the community had deteriorated. Most of the Acadians in Annapolis Royal had shunned the English speakers

in their village when French or Mi'kmaq forces were in the area. In any event there were fewer English speakers in the French-speaking village; most of the married officers and soldiers at Annapolis Royal had sent their wives and children to Boston for protection, and the departure of their families helped cut the men off from the Acadian community, at least temporarily.[32] Over time new bonds were formed, however, and by the last two years of the war, official British discussions of the Acadians returned repeatedly to the issue of intermarriage between the soldiers and Acadian women.[33]

Overcoming significant cultural obstacles, by 1747 a few New England soldiers managed to court and marry Acadian women in Annapolis Royal.[34] According to reports that reached Shirley, the women who married the New England men were punished with excommunication from the Catholic Church. Shirley complained bitterly about the church's reaction. Though he hoped that the women would leave the church eventually, he knew that church-imposed sanctions would humiliate them and isolate them from their neighbours; excommunication was a strong deterrent to intermarriage. Shirley objected not only for the sake of the soldiers and their spouses, but also because he believed that the church's policy deterred British settlement in Nova Scotia. Almost certainly exaggerating the influence of the policy, he claimed that it "has had so general an effect as to prevent the settlement of any one English family within the province."[35]

When Shirley referred to "English" families, he meant families in which the husband spoke English. This is evident, not only in the context of his concern over the marital fortunes of the soldiers, but also in light of long-term proposals he was developing to promote marriages between Acadian women and English-speaking settlers in Nova Scotia. Intermarriage became a central feature of Shirley's project to transform the Acadians culturally. He wanted to convert them to Protestantism, teach them English, and make them loyal British subjects. As part of that program, he wanted to change the composition of the Acadians' families by encouraging soldiers to settle permanently in Nova Scotia and providing Acadian women with incentives to marry English speakers and Protestants. He also wanted to force the Acadian women to send their children to English-language schools so that their descendants would become, as he succinctly put it, "English Protestants."[36]

Shirley advanced this plan in response to the experiences of the soldiers at Annapolis Royal. Though only a few marriages had taken place between the men of the garrison and Acadian women, he saw those unions as a model for social development in the entire colony. In 1747 Shirley began designing a project to intermingle soldiers and Acadians throughout the eastern Bay of Fundy region, to facilitate integration and gradual assimilation. Annapolis Royal gave him inspiration, but he was also responding to contemporary events in Britain, where the ministry was engaged in a similarly forceful effort at cultural assimilation.

During the winter of 1745, Charles Stuart led an uprising in Scotland in an effort to place his father on the British throne. Though he was ultimately defeated, he received considerable support in certain parts of the Scottish Highlands. Charles was a Catholic and he had counted among his supporters a disproportionate number of Catholics and "nonjurant" Anglicans, communicants in a conservative wing of British Protestantism. It also seemed from the perspective of British policy makers that his support had been strongest among impoverished Highlanders who came from remote pastoral regions where the clans maintained their own juridical traditions and where a considerable amount of economic activity depended on barter and other forms of non-monetary exchange. After defeating the Stuart forces, the British government adopted a set of measures designed to "pacify" the Scottish Highlands by destroying the economic and cultural conditions that they believed underlay support for Charles.[37]

Beginning in 1746, Parliament outlawed Highland dress, made it illegal for the Highlanders to carry weapons, abolished the local court system, and confiscated the property of all those who had fought for the Stuart cause. Missionaries were sent to the Highlands along with land speculators and other investors with the aim of establishing model towns where, through a combination of educational work, economic coercion, and government regulation, the Highlanders could be converted to authorized forms of Protestantism and taught to participate in the market economy. One individual involved in the pacification program summed up the theory as follows: "Make then the Highlanders as rich and industrious as the people of Manchester and they will be as little apt to rebel."[38]

In 1746 Admiral Charles Knowles, who had helped guard the sea lanes to Britain during the Stuart uprising, became governor of British-occupied Île Royale.[39] After he moved to America he continued to participate in the policy debates surrounding the pacification of Scotland, and he brought William Shirley into the debates. Knowles endorsed an idea advanced by William Augustus, duke of Cumberland, that entire Highland clans should be sent to America, and he suggested that space should be cleared for them in Nova Scotia. The Acadians, he argued, could be moved to make room.[40]

When he first learned of this proposal Shirley opposed it, but after a raid against New England troops stationed in Minas in the winter of 1746–7, he entered into an extensive correspondence with Knowles, and the two men worked out a plan to relocate at least part of the Acadian population.[41] They agreed to abandon the idea of replacing the villagers with Highlanders, but endorsed the general theory behind that plan, that shifting peoples within the empire would be an effective way to control them. In a joint letter to the secretary of state they recommended using military force to expel the most "obnoxious" Acadians and replace them with Protestant immigrants. [. . .] The governors predicted that the introduction of immigrants, and the creation of a cosmopolitan society, would transform the Acadians and turn them into loyal subjects. They did not believe that all of the newcomers had to come from Great Britain. Citing the history of Pennsylvania, they claimed that Swiss and German settlers could serve effectively as promoters of British imperial culture.

In spite of his original misgivings, Shirley soon discovered that he liked the idea of directing the process of migration with the purpose of transforming Acadian society, and he began developing more elaborate plans. In the summer of 1747 he proposed sending 2000 New England troops to the isthmus of Chignecto, to clear the region of its inhabitants and settle on the vacated land. The dispossessed Acadians would be taken to New England and placed in scattered towns in Rhode Island, Connecticut, Massachusetts, and New Hampshire.[42] If everything proceeded as Shirley anticipated, the New England settlers in Nova Scotia would intermingle and intermarry with the Acadians. Similarly, the relocated Acadian families would get absorbed into New England.[43] Shirley was ready to proceed with this experiment, but his superiors in London stopped him. As long as the war with France continued, the ministers opposed the relocation program on the grounds that it would divert scarce resources from other projects, and when the war ended in 1748 the military justification for moving the Acadians lost its force.[44]

The Treaty of Aix-la-Chapelle ending the War of the Austrian Succession ceded Île Royale back to France.[45] The cession was controversial in Britain and even more so in Massachusetts, where hundreds of families had lost husbands, sons, and fathers in military service on the island.[46] The Massachusetts government had also nearly bankrupted itself and destroyed the value of the provincial currency financing the Louisbourg expedition, an aborted 1746 expedition to Canada, and the reinforcement of Nova Scotia.[47] After the terms of the treaty were announced Shirley tried to soften the blow by getting the ministry to reimburse the Massachusetts government for its expenses. He also asked the imperial authorities to sponsor an effort to resettle and fortify Nova Scotia so that it could be prosperous, secure, and self-sufficient. A central element of Shirley's project was to assimilate the Acadians into a new, cosmopolitan, British colonial society, and he hoped to accomplish this feat by directing a series of large-scale migrations.

In the winter of 1748 Shirley commissioned a survey of the eastern end of the Bay of Fundy. He wanted to identify hills and islands appropriate for forts, and farmland that could be confiscated to support new immigrants.[48] [. . .] Shirley sent his surveyor's report to London in February 1749, along with a proposal to resettle Nova Scotia with farmers from England, Germany, Switzerland, and other parts of Europe. He did not intend to send any of the Acadians out of Nova Scotia to make room for the new settlers. He suggested instead that some of the Acadians should be moved within the colony. Shirley considered short-distance moves necessary, because he wanted to intermingle European immigrants with Acadians. If all the current inhabitants of Nova Scotia were allowed to stay where they were, the province would remain divided, with a geographically separate French-speaking Catholic community.[49]

The proposal to settle Nova Scotia with Protestants from continental Europe helped Shirley politically in Massachusetts. At least since 1747, in serialized publications and newspapers, the governor's opponents in Boston had complained that the Louisbourg expedition and the reinforcement of

Annapolis Royal had drained New England's labour supply.[50] Citing treatises on political economy, they had generalized from recent experience and argued that population density was the source of economic and military strength. By scattering the population, any effort to expand the territories of the British Empire in North America risked leaving the existing colonies underpopulated, poor, and vulnerable.[51]

[. . .]

British political elites as well as New Englanders had taken an interest in Île Royale in the long months of negotiation leading up to the conclusion of the Treaty of Aix-la-Chapelle.[52] It was a measure of the new importance of imperial issues in British politics that the government's opponents in Parliament and in the press hoped to exploit the cession of the island back to France as an embarrassment to the ministry. In an effort to limit political damage at home, alleviate the social ills associated with demobilization, and placate restive New Englanders, in 1749 the Board of Trade appointed Edward Cornwallis, a veteran of the pacification of the Scottish Highlands, as governor of Nova Scotia, and Parliament allocated a large sum of money to encourage Protestant settlement in the colony.[53] The British government offered veterans free transportation, land, tools, and a year's worth of provisions, and asked nothing in return except that they take the trip to Nova Scotia. It offered the same terms to carpenters, bricklayers, and other labourers with economically valuable skills.[54] In 1749 the ministry spent over £40 000 to encourage the settlement of province.[55] In addition to recruiting in England, agents of the government travelled to France, the valley of the Rhine, and Switzerland in search of Protestants willing to move.[56]

The Board of Trade directed Cornwallis to establish a Protestant town at Chebucto Harbor (present-day Halifax) and then disperse some of the new colonists in Acadian-dominated regions around the Bay of Fundy.[57] The board also instructed him to make sure that the new townships included both Protestants and "French Inhabitants" (Acadians), "to the End that the said French Inhabitants may be subjected to such Rules and Orders as may hereafter be made for the better ordering and governing the said Townships."[58] The governor was also told to establish "Protestant schools," "to the end that the said French inhabitants may be converted to the Protestant religion and their children brought up in the principles of it."[59] Following Shirley's advice, the Board of Trade directed Cornwallis to encourage intermarriage between Acadians and Protestants, and to apprehend, try, and punish any Catholic priest who censured his parishioners for marrying out of the faith.[60] If everything had gone as the ministers wished, within a few generations the Acadians would have converted to Protestantism and joined the new colonists as equals in a single society.

The project of resettling Nova Scotia with a diverse Protestant population, and the articulation of the plan to absorb Acadians into the cultural mix, reflected political developments beyond the shores of the colony. In many parts of the British Empire, public officials were rethinking what it meant to be a British subject and trying to devise new ways to incorporate persons of varying cultural backgrounds into a single political community. The eighteenth-century "British" nation had always been an aggregation of peoples with distinctive histories and traditions. As Linda Colley has argued, the promoters of British nationalism accommodated themselves to the existence of cultural differences in part by concentrating on a few ideals that Britons were presumed to share, such as opposition to Catholicism and loyalty to the Crown.[61] The opening of the British colonies to Protestant immigrants from continental Europe reflected a growing confidence that such settlers would adopt these minimal necessary attributes of "Britishness." Nonetheless, the recent events in the Scottish Highlands served as an object lesson on the dangers that could arise when culturally distinct communities within the realm refused to adhere to the necessary ideals.

NOTES

1. See Kathleen Wilson, "Empire, Trade and Popular Politics in Mid-Hanoverian Britain: The Case of Admiral Vernon," *Past and Present* 121 (1988): 74–109; Gerald Jordan and Nicholas Rogers, "Admirals as Heroes: Patriotism and Liberty in Hanoverian England," *Journal of British Studies* 28 (1989): 210–4.

2. See *Boston Evening Post*, July 8, July 15, 1745; *Boston Postboy*, July 8, 1745; Charles Chauncey to William Pepperell, July 4, 1745 in *Collections of the Massachusetts Historical Society* 1st ser. 1 (1792): 49; Thomas Hubbard to Pepperell, in *Collections of the Massachusetts Historical Society* 6th ser. 10 (1899): 308–9; Daniel Edwards to Roger Wolcott, July 9, 1745, in *Collections of the Connecticut Historical Society* 11 (1907): 334–7.

3. Christopher Moore, "The Other Louisbourg: Trade and Merchant Enterprise in Île Royale, 1713–1758," *Histoire sociale/Social History* 12 (1979): 79–96; John Robert McNeill, *Atlantic Empires of France and Spain: Louisbourg and Havana, 1700–1760* (Chapel Hill: University of North Carolina Press, 1985), 20–4.

4. McNeill, *Atlantic Empires of France and Spain*, 84.

5. See George Rawlyk, *Yankees at Louisbourg* (Orono: University of Maine Press, 1967), 6.

6. Ibid., 2–4.

7. For accounts of the attack, see David B. Fleming, *The Canso Islands: An Eighteenth-Century Fishing Station* (Ottawa: Parks Canada, 1977), 45; William Shirley to Newcastle, July 7, 1744, in Charles Henry Lincoln, ed., *Correspondence of William Shirley* (New York: Macmillan, 1912), 1:133; J.S. McLennan, *Louisbourg from Its Foundation to Its Fall, 1713–1758* (London: Macmillan, 1918), 111; Mascarene to Philipps, June 9, 1744, Add. Mss. 19,071, doc. 45; *Boston Postboy*, June 11, 1744.

8. For accounts of New England vessels taken, see *Boston Evening Post*, June 11, June 25, 1744; *Boston Newsletter*, September 20, 1744; *South Carolina Gazette*, July 4, 1744. For New England's attacks on the French fishery, see *Boston Evening Post*, September 24, October 22, November 26, 1744; *Boston Gazette*, August 21, 1744; *Boston Newsletter*, August 16, September 20, September 27, October 25, 1744; *Boston Postboy*, September 24, October 22, 1744; *New York Gazette*, October 1, 1744; William Douglass, *A Summary, Historical and Political, of the First Planting, Progressive Improvements, and Present State of the British Settlements in North America* (2 vols. Boston: Evans 6307/6663, 1749/1751), 1:339.

9. See Alexander Hamilton, "The Itinerarium of Dr. Alexander Hamilton," in *Colonial American Travel Narratives*, ed. Wendy Martin (New York: Penguin, 1994), 261. See also Rawlyk, *Yankees at Louisbourg*, 37, 38; John A. Schutz, *William Shirley: King's Governor of Massachusetts* (Chapel Hill: University of North Carolina Press, 1961), 90. It was a fisherman who first alerted Boston of the attack on Canso, but the printer of the *Boston Evening Post* chose not to publish the story because it was "looked upon as fishermen's news." Only after a merchant confirmed the report was it placed in the paper. *Boston Evening Post*, May 28, 1744. For the reaction of the legislature, see *Journals of the House of Representatives of Massachusetts* 21: 8–11, 29, 42; *Boston Postboy*, June 4, 1744; *Boston Newsletter*, June 14, 1744.

10. See Schutz, *William Shirley*.

11. Ibid., 23–44; Rosalind Remer, "Old Lights and New Money; A Note on Religion, Economics, and the Social Order in 1740 Boston," *William and Mary Quarterly* 3d ser. 47 (1990): 566–73.

12. See, for example, Schutz, *William Shirley*, 80–103; Bernard Bailyn, *The Origins of American Politics* (New York: Vintage, 1967), 116–17; but see William Pencak, *War, Politics, and Revolution in Provincial Massachusetts* (Boston: Northeastern University Press, 1981), 115–47.

13. Nathan Hatch, "Origins of Civil Millennialism in America: New England Clergymen, War

with France, and the American Revolution," *William and Mary Quarterly* 3d ser. 31 (1992): 492–508.

14. *Boston Gazette*, June 26, 1744.

15. See, for example, *Boston Newsletter*, June 6, 1745; *Boston Evening Post*, July 29, 1745.

16. *Boston Evening Post*, October 22, 1744.

17. *Journals of the House of Representatives of Massachusetts* 21: 99, 106–7; *Boston Evening Post*, November 5, 1744.

18. *Boston Evening Post*, November 11, 1744; using a contemporary term, Shirley called the St Croix the Passamaquodi River.

19. Normand Rogers, "Abbé Le Loutre," *Canadian Historical Review* 11 (1930): 105–28; Jean-Louis Le Loutre, "Autobiography," translated by John Clarence Webster, in John Clarence Webster, ed., *The Career of the Abbé Loutre in Nova Scotia* (Shediac: Private printing, 1933), 33–50, 35; See also Rawlyk, *Yankees at Louisbourg*, 7–11.

20. Pierre Maillard, "Lettre," in Abbé Henri-Raymond Casgrain, ed., *Les Soirées canadiennes* (Quebec: Brousseau, 1863), 289–426, 322–28; Webster, *Career of the Abbé Le Loutre*, 10.

21. "Motifs des sauvages mickmaques et marichites des continuer la guerre contre les Anglois depuis la dernière paix," in Gaston du Bosq De Beaumont, ed., *Les Derniers jours de l'Acadie* (Geneva: Slatkine-Megariotis, 1975), 248–53, 251.

22. Ian K. Steele, "Surrendering Rites: Prisoners on Colonial North American Frontiers," in *Hanoverian Britain and Empire: Essays in Memory of Philip Lawson*, Stephen Taylor, Richard Connors, and Clyve Jones, eds (Rochester: Boydell Press, 1998) 152–3; *Boston Evening Post*, July 15, July 22, August 5, September 2, October 21, 1745; *Boston Postboy*, July 22, September 9, September 30, 1745; *Boston Newsletter*, September 12, 1745.

23. Mascarene to Shirley, December 7, 1745, CO 217/39, doc. 316, Public Record Office (hereafter PRO); Shirley to Newcastle, December 23, 1745, RG1, vol. 13, doc. 21, Public Archives of Nova Scotia (hereafter PANS); Shirley to Newcastle, February 11, 1746, RG1, vol. 13A, doc. 5, PANS; see Barry Morris Moody, "A Just and Disinterested Man: The Nova Scotia Career of Paul Mascarene, 1710–1752" (PhD diss., Queen's University, 1976), 334–42.

24. "State of the Province of Nova Scotia," November 8, 1745, CO 217/39, doc. 320, PRO.

25. For accounts of the general wartime migration to French-controlled territory, see Andrew Hill Clark, *Acadia: The Geography of Early Nova Scotia to 1760* (Madison: University of Wisconsin Press, 1968), 278, 285, 291; Muriel K. Roy, "Settlement and Population Growth in Acadia," in *The Acadians of the Maritimes: Thematic Studies*, Jean Daigle, ed. (Moncton: Centre d'études acadiennes, 1982), 151–2; Jean Daigle, "Acadia from 1604 to 1763: An Historical Synthesis," in *Acadia of the Maritimes: Thematic Studies from the Beginning to the Present*, Jean Daigle, ed. (Moncton: Chaire d'Etudes Acadiennes, 1995), 36.

26. Report of Jean Luc de La Corne, September 28, 1747, RG1, vol. 3, doc 89, PANS; Statement of Honore Gautrol, December 13, 1749, in Thomas B. Akins, ed., *Selections from the Public Documents of the Province of Nova Scotia* (Halifax: Charles Annand, 1869), 177; *Boston Evening Post*, January 15, 1750; John Salusbury, *Expeditions of Honour: The Journal of John Salusbury in Halifax, Nova Scotia, 1749–53*, Ronald Rompkey, ed. (Newark: University of Delaware Press, 1980), 76; Edward Cornwallis to Board of Trade, March 19, 1750, CO 217/9, doc. 188, PRO.

27. Mascarene to Philipps, June 9, 1744, Add. Mss. 19,071, doc. 45; Mascarene to Secretary of State, June 15, 1748, CO 217/40, doc. 22, PRO; Mascarene to Gorham, August 6, 1748, Add. Mss. 19,071, doc. 119; Mascarene to?, September 29, 1749, Add. Mss. 19,071, doc. 99.

28. Mascarene to Shirley, spring 1745, in Placide Gaudet, "Acadian Genealogy and Notes," in *Report Concerning Canadian Archives for the Year 1905* (Ottawa: National Archives of Canada, 1906), 38; Council minutes, May 2–4, 1745, in Charles Bruce Fergusson, ed., *Minutes of his Majesty's Council at Annapolis Royal, 1736–1749* (Halifax: Public Archives of Nova Scotia, 1967), 68–70; Council minutes, November 14, 1746, in Fergusson, *Minutes*, 94; Shirley to Newcastle, May 22, 1746, in Lincoln, *Correspondence of William Shirley*, 1: 150; see also E.B. O'Callaghan, ed., *Documents Relative to the Colonial History of the State of New York* (15 vols. Albany: Weed, Parsons, 1850–83), 10:

155; "Relation d'une expedition faite sur les anglois dans le pays de l'Acadie, le 11 fevrier 1747, par un détachement de canadiens," in Abbé Henri-Raymond Casgrain, ed., *Collection des documents inédits sur le Canada et l'Amérique* (3 vols. Quebec: L.-J. Demers and Frère, 1888), 2:10–16, 15; "Journal de la compagne du détachement de Canada à l'Acadie et aux mines, en 1746–47" in Casgrain, *Collection*, 2: 16–75, 47, 51–52. For evidence of the merchant's earlier co-operation with the government, see Mascarene to William Douglass, July 1740 and August 20, 1741, Mascarene Family Papers; Abbé Henri-Raymond Casgrain, *Pèlegrinage au pays d'Evangéline* (Quebec: L.-J. Demers and Frère,1888), 519; Council minutes, August 17, 1736, in Archibald M. MacMechan, *Original Minutes of His Majesty's Council at Annapolis Royal, 1720–1739* (Halifax: Public Archives of Nova Scotia, 1908), 361–62.

29. See Mascarene to Deputies of Mines, Pisiquid and River Canard, October 13, 1744, in Akins, *Selections*, 137; Shirley to Board of Trade, October 16, 1744, in Lincoln, *Correspondence of William Shirley*, 1:150; Shirley to Newcastle, October 16, 1744, RG1, vol. 12, doc 37, PANS.

30. Shirley to Pepperell, May 25, 1745, in *Collections of the Massachusetts Historical Society* 6th ser. 10 (1899): 219.

31. "Journal de la campagne," 1746–47, in Casgrain, *Collection*, 2: 16–75, 44, 48; *Boston Evening Post*, December 1, 1746; see also *Boston Evening Post*, November 3, November 17, 1746; William C. Wicken, "Encounters with Tall Sails and Tall Tales: Mi'kmaq Society, 1500–1760," PhD diss, McGill University, 1994, 184–205. For a vivid description of the epidemic, see "Journal," July 25, 1748–September 14, 1748, AC, F3, vol. 50, doc. 447, National Archives of Canada (NAC).

32. *Boston Evening Post*, May 28, 1744.

33. See, for example, Shirley to Newcastle, October 20, 1747, RG1, vol. 13A, doc. 32, PANS; Shirley to Newcastle, November 21, 1746, RG1, vol. 13, doc. 33, PANS; Charles Knowles and Shirley to Newcastle, April 28, 1747, RG1, vol. 13A, doc. 25, PANS; Shirley to Newcastle, July 8, 1747, RG1, vol. 13A, doc. 27, PANS.

34. See "Journal de la campagne," 1746–47, in Casgrain, *Collection*, 2: 16–75, 48.

35. Shirley to Newcastle, October 20, 1747, RG1, vol. 13A, doc. 32, PANS.

36. Shirley to Newcastle, November 21, 1746, RG1, vol. 13, doc. 33, PANS; Knowles and Shirley to Newcastle, April 28, 1747, RG1, vol. 13A, doc. 25, PANS; Shirley to Newcastle, July 8, 1747, RG1, vol. 13A, doc. 27, PANS.

37. See Allan I. Macinnes, *Clanship, Commerce, and the House of Stuart, 1603–1788* (East Lothian: Tuckwell Press, 1996), 210–41; Charles W.J. Withers, *Gaelic Scotland: The Transformation of a Cultural Region* (New York: Routledge, 1988).

38. "On the subject of civilising the Highlands," 1748, GD248654/1, Scottish Record Office.

39. John Knox Laughton, "Knowles, Sir Charles," in *Dictionary of National Biography* (DNB) (London: Oxford University Press, 1882) 11:293; see also Laughton, "Martin, William" (DNB), 12:1185; Jeremy Black, *Culloden and the '45* (New York: St. Martin's Press, 1997), 89, 124–5.

40. Shirley to Newcastle, November 21, 1746, RG1, vol. 13, doc. 33, PANS. See Duncan Forbes, "Some Considerations on the Present State of the Highlands of Scotland," in Duncan Warrand, ed., *More Culloden Papers* (Vol. 5. Inverness: R. Carruthers and Sons, 1930), 5:98–103; W.A. Speck, *The Butcher: The Duke of Cumberland and the Suppression of the '45* (Oxford: Blackwell, 1981), 168; John Prebble, *Culloden* (London: Penguin, 1967), 232.

41. Brenda Dunn, *The Acadians of Minas* (Ottawa: Parks Canada, 1985), 19; *Boston Evening Post*, November 24, 1746, March 2, March 9, September 28, 1747; *Pennsylvania Gazette*, December 16, 1746, March 3, March 10, 1747; Report of Pierre de Chapt, Chevalier de la Corne, September 28, 1747, RG1, vol. 3, doc. 89, PANS; Report of Jean Baptiste Le Guardier de Repentigny, November 1, 1747, RG1, vol. 3, doc. 90, PANS; *Journals of the House of Representatives of Massachusetts*, 23: 313–15, 319; Knowles and Shirley to Newcastle, April 28, 1747, RG1, vol. 13A, doc. 25, PANS; see also Knowles to Shirley, May 24, 1747, HM 9712, Huntington Library.

42. Shirley to Newcastle, July 8, 1747, RG1, vol. 13A, doc. 27, PANS.

43. Shirley to Newcastle, July 8, 1747, RG1, vol. 13A, doc. 27, PANS.

44. John Russell, duke of Bedford, to Newcastle, September 11, 1747, RG1, vol. 13A, doc. 30, PANS; Newcastle to Shirley, October 3, 1747, RG1, vol. 13A, doc. 31, PANS.

45. Jack M. Sosin, "Louisbourg and the Peace of Aix-la-Chapelle, 1748," *William and Mary Quarterly* 3d ser. 14 (1957): 516–35. The final decision to cede Île Royale back to France was not made until the end of the negotiations in 1748, but the ministry had considered the island a bargaining chip from the moment it learned of New England's conquest. See Newcastle to ?, August 18, 1745, Add. Mss. 32,705, doc. 65.

46. More than 1000 New England men died, most of disease after an epidemic struck the New England garrison at Louisbourg after the French surrendered. See George Rawlyk, *Nova Scotia's Massachusetts: A Study of Massachusetts–Nova Scotia Relations, 1630 to 1784* (Montreal: McGill-Queen's University Press, 1973), 177; Gary B. Nash, *The Urban Crucible: Social Change, Political Consciousness, and the Origins of the American Revolution* (Cambridge, MA: Harvard University Press, 1979), 172; William Pencak, *War, Politics, and Revolution in Provincial Massachusetts* (Boston: Northeastern University Press, 1981), 127; Gary B. Nash, "Failure of Female Factory Labor in Colonial Boston," *Labor History* 20 (1979): 165–88. For London newspaper pieces urging the retention of Île Royale, see General Advertiser, February 21, 1746 (quoted in the *Boston Evening Post*, June 2, 1746); *General Evening Post*, July 26, 1746 (quoted in the *Boston Evening Post*, October 13, 1746); *Daily Gazetteer*, October 16, 1746 (quoted in the *Boston Evening Post*, March 2, 1747); *British Spy*, October 25, 1746 (quoted in the *New York Evening Post*, January 19, 1747); *London Magazine*, December 1746 (quoted in the *Maryland Gazette*, July 28, 1747).

47. The value of the province's notes dropped by one-half. See Douglass, *Summary*, 1: 357; *Boston Evening Post*, September 25, 1749.

48. Mascarene to Joseph Gorham, August 6, 1748, in Adam Shortt, V.K. Johnston, and Gustave Lactot, eds., *Documents Relating to Currency, Exchange and Finance in Nova Scotia, with Prefatory Documents, 1675–1758* (Ottawa: J.O. Patenaude, 1933), 274–6.

49. "Report by Captain Morris to Governor Shirley," 1749, in *Report of the Archives Branch for 1912, 79–83*; Shirley to Bedford, February 18, 1749, RG1, vol 13, doc. 45, PANS; see also Mascarene to Board of Trade, October 17, 1748, CO 217/32, doc. 103, PRO.

50. See especially Douglass, *Summary*; *Independent Advertiser*.

51. See, for example, *Independent Advertiser*, February 8, 1748; William Douglass, "To the Publishers of the *Independent Advertiser*," *Independent Advertiser*, July 4, 1748; *Independent Advertiser*, February 13, 1749. Political economists had been advancing this argument against imperial expansion at least since 1670. See Roger Coke, *A Discourse of Trade* (London, 1670. Reprint, New York: Arno Press, 1972), 7; *The Royal Fishery Revived* (London, 1670).

52. See, for example, *London Evening Post*, March 27–29, 1746.

53. James Henretta, *"Salutary Neglect": Colonial Administration under the Duke of Newcastle* (Princeton: Princeton University Press, 1972): 287–90. See also *Pennsylvania Gazette*, October 28, 1748; *Boston Evening Post*, May 1, 1749; Instructions for Edward Cornwallis, May 2, 1749, in Gaudet, "Acadian Genealogy and Notes," 49–51.

54. *Boston Evening Post*, May 1, 1749.

55. *Boston Evening Post*, June 5, 1749; Cornwallis to Bedford, March 9, 1750, CO 217/33, doc. 17, PRO.

56. Winthrop Pickard Bell, *The "Foreign Protestants" and the Settlement of Nova Scotia: The History of a Piece of Arrested Colonial Policy in the Eighteenth Century* (Toronto: University of Toronto Press, 1961), 284.

57. Instructions for Cornwallis, May 2, 1749, in Gaudet, "Acadian Genealogy and Notes," 49–51.

58. Ibid., 49.

59. Ibid., 51; see also Board of Trade to the Society of the Propagation of the Gospel (SPG), C/Can NS 1, iv, Records of the SPG.

60. Instructions for Cornwallis, May 2 1749, in Gaudet, "Acadian Genealogy and Notes," 51.

61. Linda Colley, *Britons: Forging the Nation, 1707–1837* (New Haven: Yale University Press, 1992).

4 From N.E.S. Griffiths, "The Decision to Deport," in *From Migrant to Acadian: A North American Border People, 1604–1755* (Montreal and Kingston: McGill-Queen's University Press, 2005), 431–64, 574–81.

One of the earliest historical accounts, as distinguished from the contemporary reports in newspapers, of the events of 1755 was published by Abbé Guillaume Raynal in 1766.[1] In his opinion, the Acadians had been deported because of the prevailing climate of the time, a period of "national jealousies, and of that greed of government which devours country and man."[2] But, Raynal concluded, the British had committed a great crime in removing an innocent pastoral people from their lands. Two years later, a work by a certain William Burck appeared in translation in Paris. He believed that, while the deportation was justifiable, in terms of the Franco-British conflict at the time, it involved actions that any "humaine and generous heart only takes with regret."[3] These differing opinions, one an explicit condemnation of a crime, the other a regretful verdict that what had taken place had been a cruel necessity, were only the first of many, increasingly bitter, disagreements over how the deportation of the Acadians should be judged.[4] By the middle of the twentieth century, more than 200 articles, books, and pamphlets had been published on the subject and since then a great many more have seen the light of day.[5] As was the case with Raynal and Burck, a significant number of the authors have made their judgment of what happened in 1755 the pivotal question of their work, spending relatively little time on a close analysis of the way in which the decision was reached or the immediate situation in the region at the time when the actual decision was made. The emphasis has been placed less on what is usually the first step of historical inquiry—"How did this happen?"—than on a search to discover the guilty. [. . .]

My approach is different. The focus in what follows is upon the actual experiences of those who lived in Nova Scotia in 1755, whether British administrators, French officials, military officers, or the Acadians themselves. More than anything else, this analysis has sought to present the realities of everyday eighteenth-century life for people of the North Atlantic world. In many ways, the argument I have with a number of colleagues rests as much upon an interpretation of the norms of eighteenth-century life as it does upon questions of ideology. The crucial debate turns upon whether the deportation was the result of a planned policy flowing from ethnic hatred or something that occurred as a consequence of local military action at a time of intense rivalry between competing empires. My interpretation suggests that short-term decision making is central to what happened, the personal convictions of the individuals in question being the framework for their actions but of less immediate significance than the immediate problems that had to be solved.

Of major influence upon the course of events leading to the deportation was the way in which the relationship between Lawrence and the Acadians developed between the late summer of 1754 and the capture of Beauséjour on 16 June 1755 (Figure 4.1). Throughout these months, whenever Lawrence considered the problem of Nova Scotia security, the reliability of the Acadians during an attack by the French was always a major concern for him. The information Lawrence received about the international situation, the knowledge he had of the balance of power between Massachusetts and Île Royale, Louisbourg and Boston, and his opinion of the reality of Acadian neutrality governed many of his reactions to Acadian matters. The Acadians' response to his internal administration of the colony, toward requests made by his forces for food and labour, as well as the intelligence he received about the strength of the forts at Beauséjour and Gaspereau were major

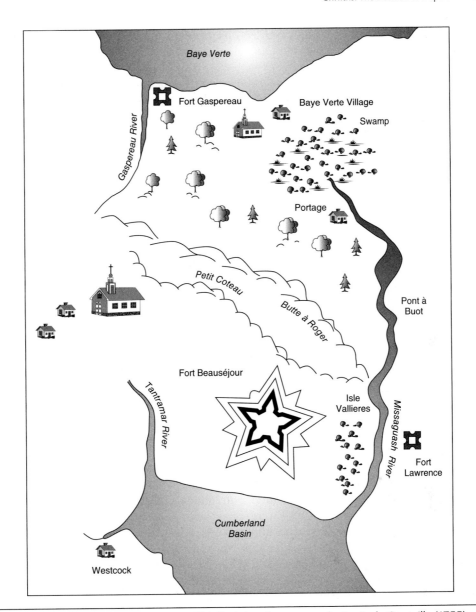

Figure 4.1 The region of Beauséjour, 1755. Redrawn from a map by Louis de Courville (1755), reproduced in Stanley, *New France*.

considerations in his thinking. When the steps he took to bolster his command of the colony showed some success, Lawrence was encouraged to continue along the same lines. His organization of the forts, the co-operation of the Acadians with requests for wood for the local garrisons, tentative peace proposals from the Mi'kmaq, and some lessening of the trade between Acadian farmers and Louisbourg and Port Lajoie—all confirmed Lawrence's belief in the wisdom of his tactics. From August 1754 on, one can see Lawrence becoming more and more confident in his office. He began to take decisions without waiting for less than clear-cut directions to reach him from London. This penchant for independent action was strengthened by Governor Shirley's support of his plan to attack Beauséjour as well as by their common interpretation of the freedom of action accorded them by the imperial authorities.

In many ways, of course, Lawrence had no alternative but to act independently, decisively, and with dispatch on matters that were brought either directly to his attention or to his notice through meetings of the Council: [. . .] It usually took five months, and often more, before Lawrence received an answer to his letters to London. But Nova Scotia was ruled by a governor and Council, which he appointed to advise him. Lawrence was charged with the day-to-day administration of a sparsely settled colony, with a minimum of troops and his few councillors. Together, they were responsible for the way in which the civil administration of the colony was carried out and for the security of its settlements. The questions confronting them involved not only the usual difficulties of colonial administrations with matters of local government but also the complex relationship of the British administration with the Mi'kmaq and the Acadians. As well, there was the constant problem of France's strength on the borders of the colony and its influence upon the Acadian population. While clashes with French land forces during the last months of 1754 were rare, two priests, Le Loutre at Beauséjour and Henri Daudin at Pisiquid, did everything in their power to stir up both the Mi'kmaq and the Acadians against the British.[6] [. . .]

Information about events in North America had arrived in London and Paris throughout the spring and summer of 1754. The reaction in London was both stronger and more immediate than that of France. The influence of Governor Dinwiddie of Virginia and Governor Shirley of Massachusetts was far greater upon the course of British politics than that of any French North American colonial official on French policies. As well, at this time, the French were more deeply concerned with European affairs than with matters across the Atlantic, whereas the British saw North American issues of considerable moment. [. . .] The Duke of Newcastle, who had come to power in March 1754, had considerable sympathy with the colonists. [. . .] There is no doubt that there was a general consensus among the political elite that British interests, whether in Europe or in North America, had to be defended. The debate between the different factions centred, of course, upon how, when, and where action should be taken.

Newcastle had chosen Sir Thomas Robinson as secretary of state and leader of the House of Commons.[7] On 5 July 1754 Robinson wrote to both William Shirley and Charles Lawrence. [. . .]

Both Lawrence and Shirley considered that these letters gave them the liberty to mount a joint expedition against the French in the Saint John valley and in the Chignecto isthmus. For Lawrence, Massachusetts cooperation was crucial. Without Shirley's permission to raise volunteers from Massachusetts, without loans from Apthorp and Hancock, Boston merchants and bankers, Lawrence had neither the manpower nor the money to undertake any major military enterprise, let alone one that would require at least an additional 2000 men to serve in Nova Scotia. Shirley [. . .] was convinced that war was imminent and [. . .] believed that, should Nova Scotia be lost, "the Eastern parts of the Province of Massachusetts Bay, and the whole Province of New Hampshire . . . together with the Rivers of St. John's, Pentagoet, and Kennebeck with the whole fishery to the Westward of Newfoundland" would soon be in French hands. It was this conviction that fuelled Shirley's support of Lawrence and ensured a sympathetic reception for the latter's request for assistance when it reached him in the first week of December.

[. . .]

Shirley's rhetoric on the opportunity for "ridding the Province of its dangerous Neighbours, with all the Mischiefs that threaten'd it from their remaining so near"[8] was not the sole argument in favour of Massachusetts endorsing the governor's proposal for raising 2000 volunteers. There was also the matter of the immediate financial benefits to Boston merchants, since it was they who would provide supplies and services for the men. There would also be further economic advantages to the Commonwealth, flowing from the terms under which the men would serve. They were promised "the King's Bounty Money, pay, uniform, Cloathing (the most that can be got here) and Arms, and have everything provided for them which is necessary for their comfortable Subsistence." The question of security and the possibility of financial gain proved useful arguments for John Winslow, who was given the rank of lieutenant-colonel and put in charge of recruiting for the new regiment. [. . .] The commander-in-chief of the expedition remained Lieutenant-Colonel Monckton, aged 29, a regular army officer who would end his career as a lieutenant-general, governor of Portsmouth, England, and an MP.[9] [. . .]

During the months that Monckton had spent in Boston, overseeing the preparations for the expedition, Lawrence had been considering what would follow the capture of Beauséjour. The lieutenant-governor had been aware that those Acadians who had lived in the area, some only since Beaubassin had been set on fire in 1750, would present political difficulties. Many of the Acadians had established farms on land which had previously been under British supervision but which had not yet been surveyed. As a result, the Nova Scotian administration considered their title to the land dubious at best. As far as Lawrence was concerned, the attitude of these Acadians could be expected to be the same as that of those who had asked to be re-admitted to British-controlled territory: argumentative, disputatious, and motivated by a strong belief that they had political rights that the British must respect. But, as will be seen, Lawrence in January 1755 was still unclear as to what

would be the appropriate measures to take once the fort was captured. When he had written to the Board of Trade at the beginning of August 1754, he had tentatively stated that, should these Acadians refuse the unmodified oath of allegiance, when the opportunity to take it was given to them, he was of the opinion that it would be "better if they were away."[10] The lieutenant-governor had hedged this suggestion by remarking that he "would be very far from attempting such a step without your Lordships approbation." The Board of Trade did not compose a response to this letter until 29 October 1754.[11] Their dispatch arrived in Halifax at the beginning of January 1755.[12] It was not, in any way, a clear directive for decisive action. [. . .] The best advice they could offer was that the matter should be referred to Chief Justice Jonathan Belcher, who had taken the oaths of office at the Council meeting of 21 October 1754.[13] [. . .] In sum, in shaping his policy toward the Acadians, Lawrence was left to his own devices and to what guidance and recommendations members of the Council could offer.

Their lordships were aware, of course, of the parameters within which Lawrence would work. He was a successful regular army officer, whose career showed the extent to which he accepted the ideas of the politically and socially powerful of the time. Eighteenth-century society, French or British, Germanic or Hispanic, was hierarchical and brutal and paid considerable attention to hereditary rights.[14] Government measures taken to control dissidents differed from state to state but were, without exception, ruthless, without mercy. [. . .] In Britain, transportation of the indigent, vagrants, and children without visible means of support had begun in the reign of James I. In 1617, for example, a hundred children were dispatched from London to Virginia, their passages paid for by collections from various parishes, where they were considered a burden.[15] [. . .] For those transported as punishment, bonded service could be little better than slavery. The English Civil

War provided the greatest impetus to the practice of removing difficult subjects from the care of the home government to the colonies. In 1648, when Cromwell's forces were unquestionably victorious, transportation for the defeated Stuart forces became commonplace.[16] From this time on, the English colonies in North America, as well as in the West Indies, received diverse groups of dissidents, Scottish covenanters, youngsters from Ireland, and Scottish military exiles. The return of the monarchy did not end the practice. [. . .] Thus, by the middle of the eighteenth century, British authorities, civil and military, colonial and imperial, were accustomed to transporting a motley collection of subjects, under varying regulations, from one jurisdictional area of the realm to another.

Further, Lawrence would have been aware not only of the general use of transportation but of the deportation of some 2000 French and Acadian inhabitants of Île Royale to France in 1745 and of the forced French relocation of a minimum of 1500 Acadians from the Beaubassin area to Île Saint-Jean after 1750. And so there was nothing original, in late 1754 and early 1755, in Lawrence considering deporting the Acadians in the Beauséjour region, and it is clear from his correspondence with Monckton that the lieutenant-governor was, indeed, thinking seriously about such a possibility. In a letter to Monckton written on 30 January 1755, Lawrence told him that, once the fort had surrendered, he would not have the oaths of allegiance proposed to "the French Inhabitants" of the Chignecto area "as their taking them would tye our hands and disqualify us to extirpate them, should it be found (as I fancy it will) ever-after necessary."[17] Lawrence, at this point, was in the process of making up his mind over the best way to secure Nova Scotia. He was hopeful of populating the Beaubassin area with English-speaking Protestants, concluding his letter to Monckton with the suggestion that, if any of the

Massachusetts troops had the "least disposition" to settle in the lands that were already controlled by the British but had been deserted since the burning of Beaubassin, they should be told that they would receive "all the encouragement" he had the power to offer. [. . .]

At the same time [Lawrence's] attitude toward the Acadians was reinforced by the appointment of the chief justice, Jonathan Belcher, as a Council member. It was Belcher who, on the day that Nova Scotia Council resolved to deport the Acadians, wrote the legal and political defence of the action.[18] Belcher had been born in 1710 to an established New England family, his mother's father having been lieutenant-governor of New Hampshire. His other grandfather had been a successful Boston merchant and member of the Massachusetts Council. His own father was governor of Massachusetts and New Hampshire from 1730 to 1741 and governor of New Jersey from 1747 to 1757.[19] [. . .] Until his appointment as the first chief justice of Nova Scotia, at the age of 44, Belcher had spent his working life outside North America but his childhood and early adulthood had been as a privileged member of the New England elite. [. . .]

The absence of any major discussion about the Acadians during this period by the Council is no indication of the actual relationship that existed at the time between the Acadians within Nova Scotia and the British administration. The rancour of the previous autumn continued. News about the lives of relatives on the Chignecto isthmus and along the Memramcook, the Petitcodiac, and the Shepody, where Le Loutre was active, served to sharpen Acadian ambivalence. Le Loutre was engaged not only in overseeing the building the dyke on the Aulac River in the Beauséjour area but also in encouraging the construction of smaller dykes on the Memramcook and the Shepody.[20] His aim was to stabilize the Acadian settlements, within the territory controlled by the French, by strengthening the development of traditional Acadian farming practices. At the same time, he worked to persuade the Acadians to recognize his authority to confirm their rights to the lands they farmed. The Acadians were hesitant, especially those who had their lands granted to them before 1710. Many had no wish to accept greater regulation of their affairs from any source, whether from the military at Beauséjour or from Le Loutre personally.[21] As well, the abbé demanded that they swear loyalty to Louis XV, their "legitimate sovereign,"[22] a demand that the French government had made ever since 1751 with respect to the Acadians who came under their control.[23] [. . .] All this activity seemed to presage French determination to remain an effective power in the region and perhaps the possibility of French reoccupation of Nova Scotia.

But the most important determinant of the attitude of many of the Acadians, in the spring of 1755, must have been the manner and policies of the French officials in the region. There were four administrators, the most senior being Augustin de Boschenry de Drucour, who had arrived to take charge at Louisbourg in 1754. That same year, Gabriel Rousseau de Villejouin had been appointed as major and commandant of Île Saint-Jean. Charles Deschamps de Boishébert et de Raffetot, who had played such an important role in the engagement at Grand Pré in 1747, was at mouth of the Saint John River as commandant of Fort La Tour, and Louis Du Pont Duchambon de Vergor was the commandant of Beauséjour. [. . .] Vergor was joined at Beauséjour by the appointment that same year, 1754, of Louis-Thomas Jacau de Fiedmont as the chief engineer for the fort, and Louis-Léonard Aumasson de Courville as notary for the Acadian settlements in the area. Jacau left an account, from a military perspective, of the fall of Beauséjour and Gaspereau which, as Webster points out, sought to place the blame everywhere except upon his own shortcomings as the man in charge

of the defences of the fort for the two previous years.[24] The memoir of Aumasson de Courville is a much longer work and includes a wide variety of comments on Vergor and Le Loutre.[25] Together with the journal of Thomas Pichon (Tyrell), a British spy who had somehow attached himself as a commissary officer to Beauséjour, these works provide a vivid picture of the disorganization among the officers stationed there and the general state of disrepair of the fort in 1755.[26] Vergor himself was convinced until the day the British force arrived that there would be no major fighting in the region that year, so nothing had been done to prepare a defence against an attack.[27] There had been no concerted effort during the last weeks of winter and the first weeks of more clement weather to recruit Acadians to strengthen the fort or to assemble those who had been given militia responsibilities.

So, before the anchoring of the Boston fleet in Annapolis Bay, little had taken place that would have alerted the Acadians to the possibility of a major outbreak of warfare in their lands. Evidently, only the vaguest of rumours about the recruitment of volunteers in Massachusetts for an expedition against Beauséjour had reached the Acadian population. Certainly, the possibility of a major disruption of Acadian life throughout the Acadian villages of Nova Scotia would not have entered their minds. As Lawrence prepared to make Nova Scotia a completely secure outpost of the British Empire in North America and to establish once and for all British control of the colony, the Acadian population, as a whole, still believed that British administrators of Nova Scotia continued to take Acadian reactions into account when making policy decisions. The existence of Halifax, of a Protestant population within the colony that was more than ten times what it had been a decade before, was not something that had made the Acadians consider any revision of their political stance. For the majority of the population, the need to alter their religious beliefs and linguistic heritage in order to remain on their lands would have unimaginable. Even if the French never reclaimed Nova Scotia, the strong French presence in the region meant visible support for Acadian retention of their customs and traditions. French control of Île Royale and Île Saint-Jean did not appear to be weakening at this time, especially after the return of Louisbourg to France in 1748. Since then, the build-up of French forces in the Chignecto area had served to strengthen the conviction, among the British as well as among the Acadians, that France was prepared to defend its presence in the area and probably had plans to expand the territory under its control.

The rapid conquest of Beauséjour [in June 1755], followed by the fall of Fort Gaspereau, and the lack of any immediate French response fundamentally altered the military situation in the region. As a consequence, the political options for the British administration at Halifax were broadened and those of the Acadians narrowed. [. . .]

The establishment of Halifax and the founding of Lunenburg had presaged a decision, on the part of London, to make Nova Scotia as much a British colony as the other British colonies in North America. From the moment he was appointed as lieutenant-governor, Lawrence was eager to make this decision a reality. We have a great deal of information on how Lawrence saw his own policy. He wrote, at length, to Governor Shirley of Massachusetts, to other governors of British colonies in North America, and to the authorities in London. By the summer of 1754, Lawrence had decided that those Acadians who refused to take an unqualified oath of loyalty to the British Crown were a major stumbling block to fulfilling his plans.[28] At the same time, he saw that the French control of the Chignecto isthmus was both a constant encouragement to those Acadians who were dissatisfied with the British government and a potential military threat to British control of Nova Scotia. While the attack on Beauséjour was taking place, his view of the unreliability

of Acadian neutrality was strengthened. As has been previously mentioned, Lawrence had taken steps to prevent any major aid being sent to Beauséjour by the Acadians under his jurisdiction. He also had made an attempt to disarm the Acadians of the Minas Basin and Captain Murray had issued orders to this effect from Fort Edward in the first week of June.[29] As well, a number of Acadian canoes were confiscated. The extent to which the Acadians complied has been a matter of debate among historians but the evidence shows that the majority of them did surrender at least some of their guns. Judge Isaac Deschamps, who was in Pisiquid at the time, stated that just under 3000 guns had been brought in.[30] The strongest evidence for their compliance, however, is the petition of the Acadians for the return of their guns, which was presented to Captain Murray on 10 June and forwarded to Lawrence within the week. It is hardly likely that the Acadians would have taken time and effort to ask for their guns back had they not given up sufficient to make the request worthwhile.

[. . .]

On 24 June the Acadians arrived with another communication to the captain, this one much shorter and signed by 44 of the settlers "in the name of them all."[31] Obviously, the news of Beauséjour's capitulation on 16 June had reached the Minas Basin for in this communication "the Inhabitants of Mines, Pisiquid and the river Canard" begged Lawrence to understand that "if there shall be found any error or want of respect towards the government" in their recent memorial this was "intirely contrary to their intention."[32]

It is unlikely that this memorial would have reached Lawrence until just before the Council meeting of 3 July. Certainly, he could not have received it before 25 June, on which day he sent a dispatch to Monckton about the treatment to be accorded to the Acadian settlers in the Chignecto area. In this communication, Lawrence showed his continued concern for the security of the colony, his exasperation with the settlers in the Chignecto isthmus, and the policy he wished to pursue toward them as well as the uncertainty he had about implementing that policy. He was convinced that "unless we remain in possession undoubtedly the French will return and re-establish and we can never expect a lasting peace with the Indians, without first totally extirpating the French who incite make war . . ." [. . .] There is no doubt that Lawrence had a great wish to solve the Acadian problem, once and for all, but he hesitated over the imposition of truly Draconian measures. As well, he obviously considered that an unqualified oath of allegiance was something which would have to be taken into account. [. . .] Thus, on 3 July 1755, when Lawrence met with 15 Acadian leaders from the Minas area who had been summoned to Halifax to explain their reasons for the petition of 10 June, the lieutenant-governor was a man still unsure of the military security of his colony, wanting unequivocal proof that the Acadians had accepted the reality of British government of Nova Scotia and of their role as British subjects. He was also aware that, however inconvenient it might be, the Acadians had some civil rights under British law.

Nevertheless, Lawrence had written to the Board of Trade, four days before this Council meeting, about what he intended to do with the Acadians settled in the isthmus. His dispatch first reported the surrender of Beauséjour and Gaspereau and then went on to state that "the deserting French" were surrendering their arms, after which they were "to be driven out of the country," although they might very well be put to repairing Fort Beauséjour, now renamed Fort Cumberland, before they were sent into exile.[33] While there is no evidence that, at this point, Lawrence contemplated the wholesale deportation of the Acadian population, the possibility of the dispersal of a significant number of Acadians was definitely in his mind.

The attitude of the Acadians at the Council meeting of 3 July was in keeping with their past behaviour over close to a century. It did nothing to make Lawrence reconsider his position. [. . .] In fact, as the minutes of the Council meetings throughout the month of July 1755 show, Lawrence and his advisors considered the Acadians not only politically unreliable but also socially impertinent, lacking in proper deference to their betters.

It is not surprising, then, that the atmosphere at the Council meetings in the first week of July was one of mutual incomprehension.[34] Colonel Lawrence chaired this and all other Council meetings during July. There were four other Council members present on the meetings of the 3rd and 4th of the month. [. . .] None of them had any personal acquaintanceship with the Acadians, knowing them only as a French-speaking, Catholic people who claimed to be different from the French but whose behaviour in the face of French intrusions on the borders of the colony was, at best, unreliable.

It was clear from the outset that the councillors found the Acadians' rhetoric deeply offensive. Before the Acadians were called into the meeting, Council members had come to the unanimous conclusion that the memorial was "highly arrogant and insidious, an insult upon His Majesty's Authority and Government, and deserved the highest Resentment . . . "[35] Once the Acadians were present, it became quickly apparent that the two parties were at complete odds. The Acadians had composed their petition in the belief that Lawrence and the Council regarded them as people to be accorded consideration. The inhabitants had tried to explain, in the second paragraph of their communication, their difficulties. "Permit us, if you please, Sir, to make known the annoying circumstances in which we are placed, to the prejudice of the tranquillity we ought to enjoy," words that showed that, in their own eyes, they had every right to complain to those governing them.[36] They went on to ask the Council to take their past conduct into consideration as proof of their loyalty to the British. To this, the councillors answered that "their past Conduct was considered, and that the Government were sorry to have occasion to say that their Conduct had been undutifull and very ungrateful for the Lenity shown to them." From that point on, the minutes show that the councillors were united in demonstrating to the Acadians that the latter had shown a "constant disposition to Assist His Majesty's Enemies, and to distress his subjects."

[. . .] Toward the end of the meeting, the essence of the administration's position became clear: the Acadians were told that their loyalty and obedience could best be properly demonstrated by "their immediately taking the Oath of Allegiance in the Common form before the Council." Until this point, and including the request for the oath, the members of Council, while more abrasive than their predecessors, had acted much as former administrations had done. But when the Acadians responded, as they had done in the past, by saying that "they had not come prepared to resolve the Council on that Head," they were then informed that for "these Six Years past, the same thing had often been proposed" and that they must have "fully considered and determined this point with regard to themselves before now." The Acadians next asked to return and "consult the Body of the People . . . as they were desirous of either refusing or accepting the Oath in a Body." The councillors rejected this reply as "extraordinary" and gave them an hour to consult among themselves. On their return, the Acadians were of the same mind but offered to take the oath "as they had done before." The councillors answered that "His Majesty had disapproved of the manner of their taking the Oath before" and that any such compromise was now unacceptable. At this point the meeting was adjoined until the next day at ten o'clock.

The next morning, the Acadians repeated their decision that they could not take the oath without consulting their communities. At this point, Lawrence and the Council, composed of the same people as the day before, informed the Acadians that they had now provided enough evidence to make the Council consider them "no longer as Subjects of His Britannick Majesty, but as Subjects of the King of France, and as such they must hereafter be Treated; and they were Ordered to Withdraw."[37] The minutes record that the Council members then decided among themselves that Captain Murray should order the "French Inhabitants forthwith to Choose and send to Halifax new Deputies with the General Resolution of the said Inhabitants in regard to taking the Oath, and that none of them should for the future be admitted to Take it after having once refused to do but that effectual Measures ought to be taken to remove all such Recusants out of the Province." The 15 Acadians were now required to return to the meeting and were told of this decision. They then offered to take the oath but were informed that "they would not be indulged with such Permission, And they were thereupon ordered into Confinement."

It is striking that the Council decided, at this point, that refusal to take the oath of allegiance as offered would deprive the Acadians of their status as British subjects. In fact, it was a judgment that even Belcher and Lawrence would not repeat. It went against the tradition of international law, which had been accepted, particularly in the case of the Acadians after Utrecht, by both France and Great Britain, that peoples whose territories changed governments through treaties became unequivocally subjects of their new rulers.[38] In also went against all previous arguments by British administrators, including Cornwallis, on the status of Acadians. Finally, it contradicted English legal tradition since before the Tudors, as it had evolved with the linking of Wales and Ireland to England. By the time of Henry VIII, those born on territory ruled at the moment of their birth by England were considered as natural-born subjects.[39] The majority of the Acadian population within peninsular Nova Scotia had by this time, 42 years after Utrecht, been born on British territory. Belcher's influence on the matter is difficult to assess. His experience in Ireland ought to have prevented him making a judgment that the Acadians' status as subjects depended on an oath of allegiance. By the end of month, when he wrote a defence of the decision to deport the Acadians en masse, he based his opinions upon the question of their loyalty as subjects, rather than upon their position as aliens. This is the argument that would be used in the future to defend the deportation.

The legal argument over the link between the oath of allegiance and the rights of the Acadians as British subjects had little import for the immediate circumstances of the Acadians in July 1754. At that time, their fate depended upon the designs of Lawrence and the Council, designs that become clear when the complete records of the Council meetings for 4, 14, and 15 July are read. The brief minutes of the meeting of 4 July alone leave some question in one's mind as to whether the decision to remove out of the province those who refused the oath referred to just certain individuals from the Minas area or to the Acadians as a whole. [. . .]

On 9 July, Admiral Edward Boscawen dropped anchor in Halifax harbour. On 14 July, Lawrence called another Council meeting; it was attended by the same people who had attended the meetings of 4 and 5 July.[40] Lawrence informed the Council that he had received instructions, which had been sent from the secretary of state to all governors on 15 April, requesting them to co-operate with Admiral Boscawen and provide him with all obtainable intelligence.[41] [. . .] At the meeting that took place on the 15 July, once more attended by those members who had been present at the meetings earlier in the month but with the addition of the two admirals, Lawrence laid out "the proceedings of the Council in regard to the French Inhabitants, and

desired their opinion and advice thereon."[42] The admirals agreed that "it was now Time to oblige the said Inhabitants to Take the Oath of Allegiance to His Majesty, or to quit the Country." At this meeting, it was also decided that it was "absolutely necessary for the Good of His Majesty's Service and the Security of this His Province, to retain in pay the Two Thousand New England Troops . . . "

[. . .]

The support of the admirals for Lawrence was precisely that: support. Obviously, they had not arrived in Nova Scotia with instructions to take over the administration of the colony, nor did they have either the requisite knowledge or the interest to do so. What they did provide was an agreement by senior British naval personnel that the policy being pursued by the administration of Nova Scotia seemed sensible, considering the overall military situation. Boscawen's presence at Halifax until October 1755, and the presence of the fleet in the region, obviously encouraged Lawrence.[43] But Lawrence remained the person in charge of the colony and ultimately the one responsible for its security. [. . .]

Lawrence wrote to the Board of Trade, presenting his view of the situation that confronted him. Neither in this dispatch nor in any other of his letters to London did Lawrence suggest that anyone else was responsible for the evolution of his policy toward the Acadians. Of course, he sought, and gained, the approval of the Council at each stage of its development; it was not a policy that the lieutenant-governor had fashioned against the general beliefs and attitudes of his advisers. However, essentially, it was his policy and the administrations of Cornwallis and Hopson had shown that it would have been possible to pursue another course. One of its most important antecedents was Shirley's proposal after the capture of Louisbourg in 1745, but no dispatch from London, whether from the Board of Trade or from any of the secretaries of state, suggested anything similar. Ever since 1713 the policy of the British government was one of determined refusal to admit that there was any great necessity to resolve the issue, one way or another, of the oath of allegiance. Further, Britain had consistently argued against sending the Acadians out of the colony and these arguments were repeated again in a letter from the secretary of state, Robinson, to Lawrence on 13 August 1755.[44] In it Robinson wrote that "it cannot, therefore, be too much recommended to you, to use the greatest Caution and Prudence in your Conduct, towards these neutrals, and to assure such of Them, as may be trusted, especially upon their taking the Oaths to His Majesty and His Government, That they may remain in quiet Possession of their Settlements under proper Regulation . . . " This dispatch was in reply to one sent by Lawrence on 28 June 1755, in which he had broached the possibility of deporting Acadians, primarily from the Beauséjour region. Unfortunately, Robinson's dispatch arrived in Halifax only in late October 1755. As has already been mentioned, Lawrence's dispatch of August 1754, in which he pleaded for guidance on the issue, had received no other answer than that the problem he raised was, indeed, interesting and he should seek the advice of Belcher, the newly appointed chief justice of the colony.

Now, on 18 July, Lawrence reported his actions to his superiors.[45] It is a highly intelligent dispatch and guilty less of direct lying than of suppressing evidence and suggesting misleading implications. In relating what had happened at the Council meetings of 4 and 5 July, he omitted to mention that he had not, in fact, informed the Acadians clearly, before the final request to take an unqualified oath of allegiance, that their refusal would see them imprisoned and deported to France at the first opportunity. Moreover, he concluded the dispatch by saying that he was "determined to bring the Inhabitants to compliance, or rid the province of such perfidious subjects." There is no evidence whatsoever to suggest that Lawrence was then determined to exile

not only the 15 men from the Minas Basin but also the Acadians who had settled in the Chignecto area, let alone all the Acadians settled elsewhere. Indeed, the information in his dispatch concerning the incarceration of the deputies on George's Island, until they could be sent to France, increases the impression that Lawrence was considering only a small group of the population for exile. It is possible, of course, that Lawrence was convinced that the Acadian population, especially those of the Annapolis region, would not prove obdurate.[46] The dispatch of 18 July, however, quite plainly ruled out any possibility of negotiation with those who did prove recalcitrant. Any softening of this position became less than likely when rumours of Braddock's defeat reached Halifax on 23 July.[47]

In the meantime, of course, from the moment the men from Minas had been detained at Halifax, the Acadian communities had been forced to consider their position on the oath. They responded to the demand for their presence at Halifax, 30 men from Annapolis Royal arriving there on 25 July and 70 from the Minas settlements on 28 July. The written response brought by the Annapolis group emphasized their past conduct, asserting that "several of us have risked our lives to give information to the government concerning the enemy; and have also, when necessary, laboured with all our heart on the repairs of Fort Annapolis."[48] The memorial stated that the deputies had been "charged strictly to contract no new oath."[49] [. . .] Their answer was discussed at the Council meeting of 25 July. [. . .] On this occasion, the Acadians were told clearly that "if they once refused the Oath, they would never after be permitted to Take it, but would infallibly lose their Possessions." They were then dismissed but required to attend another Council meeting on Monday, 28 July.

The same men were present at this meeting as had been in attendance three days earlier. Belcher presented to this meeting a memorial bringing together his ideas as to why the Acadians should be expelled. It was not sent to London until the spring of 1756.[50] It was a mean-minded document, full of historical inaccuracies and of specious arguments. In it the Acadians were accused of outright and continuous support of the French since 1713, and it was implied that all British administrators since 1713 had acted contrary to "the spirit and letter of His Majesty's Instructions." Belcher went on to assert that, to allow the Acadians to take the oath once they had refused to do so, would defeat "the Intention of the Expedition to Beau Sejour." He went on to say that the Acadian presence "may retard the Progress of Settlement . . . since the French at Lunenburgh and the Lunenburghers themselves . . . are more disposed to the French than to the English." In any case, Belcher wrote, even if the Acadians did take the oath, "it is well known, that they will not be influenced" by it "after a [papal] Dispensation."[51] He concluded by remarking that the presence of Massachusetts forces in the colony had provided an opportunity to remove the Acadians which, "once the armament is withdrawn," would be lost. At that point, the Acadians would "undoubtedly resume their Perfidy and Treacheries and with more arts and rancour than before." Belcher therefore advised that "all the French inhabitants may be removed from the Province" from "the highest necessity which is lex temporis, to the interests of His Majesty in the Province."

And so, when the Acadians were called before the Council on 28 July, their fate had already been decided. [. . .]

There had been no attempt made, in any of the Council meetings, to persuade the Acadians that taking the oath would guarantee them the peaceful possession of their lands. From the beginning, Lawrence had treated the Acadian population as a liability and something to control by fear. His policy had been one of accusation and demand. He had a fundamental disbelief in the possibility of the Acadian population being of any value to Nova Scotia and thus his communications with the various settlements were always threatening: "this will happen if you do not conform to my orders." Such a policy was bound to be less than successful, given that the Acadians had heard threats of exile and eviction from British administrators before. For more than 40 years, such threats had been no more than words. It was unlikely that the Acadians were disposed to take Lawrence seriously at this point, even with the presence of much greater military resources in the colony than they had ever known. As well, their forced exile would have seemed an almost unimaginable possibility—they could not conceive of a worse fate than transportation to France. Thus, the Acadian delegates unanimously refused the request to take the oath. They were sent into confinement and the minutes record that "as it had been before determined to send all the French Inhabitants out of the Province if they refused to Take the Oaths, nothing now remained to be considered but what measures should be taken to send them away, and where they should be sent to." The final paragraph of the minutes of this momentous meeting noted that, "after mature Consideration, it was unanimously Agreed That to prevent as much as possible their Attempting to return and molest the Settlers that may be set down on their lands it would be most proper to send them to be distributed amongst the several Colonies on the Continent, and that a sufficient Number of Vessels should be hired with all possible Expedition for that purpose."

An understanding of the sequence of events that led to the deportation leaves unanswered a great many questions. But it goes a long way to answering how such a catastrophe, the destruction of an established community of people, who had built a thriving society over more than a century and a half, occurred. It even goes some of the way to disentangling the complex of ideas and decisions that turned the possibility of the removal of Acadians from Nova Scotia, broached at the time of the Treaty of Utrecht, into the reality of exile. Insistence upon the context of eighteenth-century European life leads to a greater place being given to the contemporary realities of communication through time and across space. It provokes questions about how the belief and opinions of the elites affected the actions of those who lived on the periphery of the European empires in North America. Above all, the reconstruction of who actually did what and when brings to the fore the political and social conventions that were widespread at the time.

The Acadian deportation, as a government action, was of a pattern with other contemporary happenings, from the deportations after the 1745 rebellion in Scotland to actions on the European continent during the War of the Austrian Succession. It was, in many ways, quintessentially an act of a time when the state rested its authority upon the hereditary right of the monarch and when, as Dummett and Nicol have pointed out, there was "a vertical relationship between monarch and individual, not a horizontal one between the members of a nation or the citizens of a body politics."[52] But this conclusion, that the Acadian deportation was not essentially an extraordinary incident, does little more than scratch the surface of the questions posed. There are at least three ways in which the events of 1755 were significantly different from the other such occurrences. First, as we have seen, the possibility of removing the Acadians from the colony had been a matter of discussion by both French and English from the time of Treaty of Utrecht in 1713.[53] It had a long history as a proposition whereas the other deportations were the immediate consequence of particular actions, the solution to recent and immediate problems. Secondly, the actual pressure for the deportation came as much from a neighbouring territory as from within the jurisdiction itself. The Commonwealth of Massachusetts and its governor, Shirley, were as fully implicated in the event as were the officials in

place in Nova Scotia. Further, as has already been mentioned but bears repeating, the final authority, London, had consistently argued against such action since 1713 and reiterated this argument once more in a letter sent from Whitehall on 13 August 1755. Thirdly, the enterprise itself was significantly different from the deportations that followed the Monmouth and Jacobite rebellions. Those were organized after battles had been fought against those sent into exile and were the result of judgments made in a law court about individuals. As well, the number deported was, in each case, only a fraction of the communities concerned. The Acadian deportation involved the removal of almost an entire society, which had been judged as a collectivity. People were dispatched to other communities with a letter of recommendation by the man in charge of the operation, suggesting that, since the deportation would divide Acadian strength, "they May be of some Use as Most of them are Healthy Strong People; And as they Cannot easily collect themselves together again, it be out of their Power to Do any Mischief And they May become Profitable and it is possible, in time Faithful subjects."[54]

Finally, of course, the greatest difference between the Acadian deportation and the other events is what happened afterwards: Neither Jacobite nor Huguenot went into exile with the capacity to retain a coherent identity. The Acadians did. They had always been involved in shaping their own lives. In 1713, when "Acadia or Nova Scotia" was transferred to Great Britain, the Acadians themselves, as much as the French or the English, decided that they would remain as subjects of the British Empire rather than move to Île Royale, territory that the French still held.[55] In fact, the Acadians' stance represented two political beliefs that confronted the principles of hereditary power. The first was their conviction that they were indeed a people, distinct from the French of France and therefore with different political ambitions. The second belief was that, despite the actions of empires and the decisions of princes, the Acadians had every right to debate and present ideas about how and where they should live to those who claimed them as subjects. However skeptical others have been about the existence of Acadian identity, the Acadians themselves never seem to have doubted it. In considering their history, one has to give this "obstinacy" its due, particularly when "what happened next," the aftermath of the deportation, is examined. The Acadians had not been a collection of uneducated, illiterate, and ignorant peasants—the goods and chattels of others—before July 1755.

NOTES

1. *Histoire philosophique et politique de l'établissement des Européens dans les deux Indes*, 1766 edn, 7 vols.

2. "des jalousies nationales, de cette cupidité des gouvernements qui dévorent les terres et les hommes": ibid., 6:364.

3. "font telles qu'un coeur humain & généreux ne les adopte jamais qu'à regret": William Burck, *Histoire des colonies européennes dans l'Amérique en six parties . . .* (Paris: Merlin 1767), 2 vols, 2:319. My translation.

4. For a collection of opinions on the issue, see N.E.S. Griffiths, *The Acadian Deportation: Deliberate Perfidy or Cruel Necessity?* (Toronto: Copp Clark 1969).

5. For the nineteenth-century debate, see Francis Parkman, *Montcalm and Wolfe* (2 vols. Boston: Little, Brown 1884) and *A Half-Century of Conflict* (2 vols. Boston: Little 1897); and H.R. Casgrain, *Un pèlerinage au pays d'Evangéline* (Quebec: Demers 1887). The debate was continued in the twentieth century by a great number of writers, most recently by Robert Sauvageau, *Acadie: La guerre de Cents Ans des Français d'Amérique aux Maritimes et en Louisiane, 1678–1769* (Paris: Berger-Levrault 1987); Yves Cazaux, *L'Acadie: Histoire des Acadiens du XVIIe siècle à nos jours* (Paris: Albin Michel 1992); and Geoffrey Plank, *An Unsettled Conquest: The British Campaign Against the Peoples of Acadia* (Philadelphia: University of Pennsylvania Press, 2001). The bibliographies produced by the Centre d'études acadiennes, at the Université de Moncton, New Brunswick, are the first place to begin a survey of this literature. See, in particular, *Inventaire général*, vol. 2, *Bibliographies acadienne . . . à 1975* (n.d.), and various supplements. Worthwhile consulting, too, is N.E.S. Griffiths, "The Acadian Deportation: A Study in Historiography and Literature" (MA thesis, University of New Brunswick 1957), which provides a critical survey of what was published before 1956.

6. A full account of their actions is found in Micheline Dumont-Johnson, *Apôtres ou agitateurs: la France missionnaire en Acadie* (Trois-Rivières: Boréal Express 1970), 116–28.

7. Robinson had been secretary to the embassy at Paris from 1723 to 1730 and plenipotentiary at the peace negotiations leading to the Treaty of Aix-la-Chapelle in 1748. He was appointed a member of the Board of Trade in 1748–49. See Alan Valentine, *The British Establishment, 1760–1784: An Eighteenth-Century Biographical Dictionary* (Norman: University of Oklahoma Press 1970), 2:743–4.

8. For Governor Shirley's speech in February 1755, see *Doc. Hist. St. Maine*, 12:350–62.

9. I.K. Steele, "Robert Monckton," *Dictionary of Canadian Biography* (1974), 4:540–2.

10. National Archives of Canada (NAC), CO 217, 15, Lawrence to the Board of Trade, 1 Aug. 1754; Thomas Beamish Akins, ed., *Acadia and Nova Scotia: Documents relating to the Acadian French and the first British colonization of the province, 1714–1758* (Cottonport: Polyanthos 1979. Rpt of Halifax: Charles Annand 1869 edn), 213.

11. NAC, CO 218, 5, Board of Trade to Lawrence, 29 Oct. 1754; partially printed in Akins, *Acadia*, 235–7.

12. NAC, CO 217, 15, Lawrence to the Board of Trade, 12 Jan. 1755.

13. NAC, CO 220, NS (B), 8, f.126, Council minutes.

14. A short corrective to present-day visions of the eighteenth century as a time of highly civilized and compassionate behaviour, epitomized by

the glorious music of Bach and Mozart and the paintings of Fragonard, is found in M.S. Anderson, *War and Society in Europe of the Old Regime, 1618–1789* (Montreal and Kingston: McGill-Queen's University Press 1998). See also R.R. Palmer, *Age of the Democratic Revolution: A Political History of Europe and America 1760–1800* (2 vols. Princeton: Princeton University Press 1964).

15. Abbott Emerson Smith, *Colonists in Bondage: White Servitude and Convict Labor in America, 1607–1776* (New York: W.W. Norton 1971), 148.

16. Ibid., 92.

17. NAC, Vernon-Wager Papers, printed in Griffiths, *The Acadian Deportation*, 108. It is clear from the body of Lawrence's correspondence that he is using the word "extirpate" to mean "to clear away persons from a locality" and not in the sense of "to kill." See *Oxford English Dictionary*.

18. Included in a letter of 14 April 1756 from Secretary Fox to the Lords of Trade, printed in PAC *Report*, 1905, app. B, 63–5. As lieutenant governor of Nova Scotia, Belcher displayed a harsh attitude toward the Acadians: see C.J. Townshend, "Jonathan Belcher, First Chief Justice of Nova Scotia," *Collections of the Nova Scotia Historical Society* XVIII (1914), 25–57.

19. Susan Buggey, "Jonathan Belcher," *Dictionary of Canadian Biography* (DCB), 4:50–4.

20. See Abbé de L'Isle-Dieu to Pontbriand, 25 March 1755, in "Lettres et mémoires de l'abbé de l'Isle-Dieu," RAPQ, 1935–36.

21. Pichon to Surlaville, 12 Nov. 1754, in Gaston Du Boscq de Beaumont, *Les derniers jours de l'Acadie (1748–1759), correspondances et mémoires: extrait du portefeuille de M. le Courtois de Surlaville, lieutenant-général des armées du roi, ancien major des troupes du l'Île Royale, mis en ordre et annotés* (Genève: Slatkine-Megariotis Reprints 1975), 130.

22. "légitime souverain": R. Rumilly, *Histoire des Acadiens* (2 vols. Montreal: Fides 1955), 1:436.

23. John B. Brebner, "Canadian Policy Towards the Acadians in 1751," *Canadian Historical Review* 12, 3 (1931): 284. This includes the proclamation of La Jonquière on the subject, as does Griffiths, *The Acadian deportation*, 82–3.

24. See excerpts and analysis in J.C. Webster, *The Forts of Chignecto: A Study of the Eighteenth*

Century Conflict between France and Great Britain in Acadia (Shediac 1930), 58–60.

25. Aumasson de Courville, *Mémoires sur le Canada, depuis 1749 jusqu'à 1760*, LHSQ ed. (Quebec: Imprimerie de T. Cary 1838).

26. For an account of Pichon's career, with references to those of his papers held in PANS, see J.C. Webster, *Thomas Pichon, "the Spy of Beauséjour," an Account of his career in Europe and America* (Sackville: Tribune Press 1937). For a précis of the sort of information that Pichon sent the British, see T.A. Crowley, "Thomas Pichon," DCB, 4:630–2.

27. J.C. Webster, ed., *Journals of Beauséjour: Diary of John Thomas, journal of Louis de Courville* (Halifax: Public Archives of Nova Scotia 1937), 16, 17, and 100.

28. Akins, *Acadia*, 212–14.

29. PAC *Report*, 1905, app. B, 60; a description of the disarming is in *Coll. Doc. Inédits*, 1:138–9.

30. See, in particular, the evidence of Judge Isaac Deschamps in NAC, Brown Papers, Mss. 19073, item 52; and Grace M. Tratt, "Isaac Deschamps," DCB, 5:250–2.

31. "Signé par quarante-quatre des susdits habitants, au nom de tous": Council minutes, 5 July 1755, ff.166–7, printed in full in French in PAC *Report*, 1905, app. A, pt. 3, and in English in Akins, *Acadia*, 249–50.

32. "si dans la Requette qu'ils ont eu l'honneur de présenter à votre Excellence il se trouvoit quelque faute ou quelque manque de respect envers le gouvernement, que c'est contre leur intention . . . ": ibid.

33. NAC, CO 217, 15, Lawrence to the Lords of Trade, 28 June 1755.

34. John Brebner believes that the British, clearly irritated, attempted to make the Acadians declare themselves unequivocally: *New England's outpost: Acadia before the conquest of Canada* (Hamden: Archon 1927), 215ff. L.H. Gipson maintains that the British judiciously presented their position to the Acadians: *The British Empire before the American Revolution* (New York: Alfred A. Knopf 1942), 6:255ff.; Emile Lauvrière is convinced that the meeting was a Machiavellian inquisition, designed to make the Acadians appear guilty: *La tragédie d'un peuple: histoire du peuple acadien de ses origines à nos jours* (2 vols. Paris: Editions Brossard 1922), 1:428ff.

35. NAC, CO 220, NS (B), 8, Council minutes, 3 July 1755; printed in Akins, *Acadia*, 250.

36. "Permettez-nous, s'il vous plait, d'exposer ici les circonstances genantes dans lesquelles on nous retiens au prejudice de la tranquillité dont nous devons jouir": ibid.

37. NAC, CO 220, NS (B), 8, Council minutes, 4 July 1755; printed in Akins, *Acadia*, 256.

38. See N.E.S. Griffiths, *From Migrant to Acadian: A North American Border People 1604–1755* (Montreal and Kingston: McGill-Queen's University Press), chapter 6 for a discussion of the decision by French jurists that the British Crown was justified in demanding an oath of allegiance.

39. Anne Dummett and Andrew Nicol, *Subjects, Citizens, Aliens and Others: Nationality and Immigration Law* (London: Wiedenfield and Nicholson 1990), 45.

40. Ibid., 14 July 1755; printed in Akins, *Acadia*, 257.

41. NAC, CO 218, 5, Secretary of State Robinson's circular to all governors, 15 April 1755.

42. NAC, CO 220, NS (B), 8, Council minutes, 15 July 1755; printed in Akins, *Acadia*, 258–9.

43. W.A.B. Douglas, "Nova Scotia and the Royal Navy, 1713–1766," PhD thesis, Queen's University 1973, 242.

44. CO 5, 211, British Library (BL), Mss. 19073, f.42, Robinson to Charles Lawrence, 13 Aug. 1755; printed in full in Griffiths, *The Acadian Deportation*, 111.

45. NAC CO 217, 15, Lawrence to the Lords of Trade, 18 July 1755.

46. In much the same way that officials in France were shaken in 685 when Protestants chose exile rather than conversion.

47. Brought by one of the ships, the brig *Lily* out of New York. See J. Macdonald, "The Hon. Edward Cornwallis," *Collections of the Nova Scotia Historical Society*, vol. XII, p. 42.

48. "nous pouvons bien assurer votre Excellence que plusieurs d'entre nous se sont risqué la vie pour donner connoissance au gouvernement de l'ennemis et aussi lorsqu'il a été nécessaire de travailler pour l'entretien du Fort d'Annapolis . . . nous nous y avons porter de tout notre coeur": NAC, CO 220, NS (B), 8 Council minutes, 25 July 1755; PAC *Report*, 2, app. A, pt. 3, app. C, 61.

49. "nous leurs enjoignons de ne contracter aucun nouveaux serment": ibid., 61.

50. This memorial was not sent to the Lords of Trade until 24 Dec. 1755. It was included in a dispatch from Belcher, the main body of which was concerned with the need for an assembly for Nova Scotia: NAC, CO 217,16; printed in full in PAC *Report*, 1905, 2, app. A, Pt. 3, app. C, 63–5.

51. Belcher obviously believed that the Catholic hierarchy might proclaim that oaths sworn to a Protestant monarch were not binding. Such a position was extreme, but, when one recalls that Belcher had lived in United Kingdom during the Stuart rebellion of 1745, which had been openly financed by France, it becomes understandable.

52. Dummett and Nicol, *Subjects, Citizens, Aliens*, 22.

53. For the French view, and their wish to have the Acadians as settlers on Île Royale, see NAC, AC, IR, C11B, 1, f.123, Costebelle to the minister, 1715; for the English view, and their fear that the departure of the Acadians would strip Nova Scotia of its population, see NAC, NS/A, 5:1, Caulfield to the Lords of Trade, 1715.

54. NAC, CO 217, 15, Lawrence, "Circular letter to the governors of certain colonies," 11 Aug. 1755; printed in PAC *Report*, 1905, 2, app. B, 15–16.

55. See Antoine Bernard, *Le drame acadien depuis 1604* (Montreal: Clercs de Saint Viateur 1936), 247–85.

Chapter 5

The Conquest and Integration of Quebec

READINGS

Primary Documents

1   From "Governor Murray to the Lords of Trade, Quebec 29th Octr 1764," and "Petition of the Quebec Traders," in *Documents Relating to the Constitutional History of Canada 1759–1791*

2   From *The History of Emily Montague*, Frances Brooke

Historical Interpretations

3   From "A Different Kind of Courage: the French Military and the Canadian Irregular Soldier During the Seven Years' War," Martin L. Nicolai

4   From "Loyalty, Order, and Quebec's Catholic Hierarchy," Damien-Claude Bélanger

INTRODUCTION

The Seven Years' War shaped the area that would become Canada significantly. After years of fighting and a devastating death toll, *la guerre de la Conquête* ended with the Treaty of Paris (1763), and New France became British North America. The repercussions of the conflict, and the years of conciliation, repression, and adaptation after its close, were equally important to Canada. Although the British had reason to celebrate their victory over the French, their celebration was short-lived. The conquest of the French colony in North America quickly created problems for the British government, now responsible for the entire region. Some of these issues had to do with the Indigenous rebellion led by Pontiac, south of the Great Lakes. Others concerned British policies toward the Thirteen Colonies to the south. The decisions made by the British government to prevent American expansion westward, to tax the American colonists without their consent, and to leave troops in the colonies, even without any external threat, exasperated the colonists and eventually pushed them on the path of rebellion. The conquest of New France and its integration into the British Empire also raised the issue of diversity within this empire. British identity had been created after 1707 in opposition to France and rested on Protestantism and commerce. The integration of the *Canadiens*, French Roman Catholic subjects who were mainly peasants, into the Empire represented a huge challenge for the British authorities and for the British American merchants (called *Bostonnais* by the Canadiens) who came to the colony after the Conquest.

The first set of primary documents includes a dispatch from James Murray, governor of the newly created Province of Quebec, to the lords of trade who managed colonial affairs for the British government. In it, Murray complains about the fanaticism demonstrated by local British traders toward French subjects. His sympathy is clearly with the latter. This set also includes a petition from the British local merchants to the king that illustrates their attitude toward their French fellow subjects. The second document comprises excerpts from an epistolary novel written by Frances Brooke, a British author who lived in Quebec for a few years in the 1760s. Close to the British traders (also called the English party), Brooke used her characters to express their and her prejudices toward French subjects. Many of these attitudes were tenacious and would poison French–English relationships in the colony for decades to come.

Nicolai's article shows that in their generations away from France, the Canadians had developed forms of and attitudes toward combat that resembled their Indigenous allies (and foes). He discusses French attitudes to this, and the military hierarchy's efforts to bring the two styles together into an effective fighting force during the Seven Years' War. In his article, Damien-Claude Bélanger looks at different cultural groups coming together in Quebec just a few years later, but in markedly different circumstances. Bélanger examines the years just after conquest and the decision of Catholic Church leaders in Quebec to work with their new English rulers. He shows that these French Catholic officials played an integral role in the integration of the colony into a Protestant British empire.

QUESTIONS FOR CONSIDERATION

1. Do you consider literature and works of art to be reliable historical documents? What about photographs?
2. What kinds of prejudices are illustrated in the traders' petition and Brooke's novel? What important aspects of eighteenth-century British identity do they highlight?
3. Why did Murray dislike the people he called "the Licentious Fanaticks Trading" so much?
4. Why did the Canadiens fight differently from the soldiers of France? Is this evidence of a distinctive cultural identity?
5. According to Bélanger, what role did the clergy play in integrating the French and Roman Catholic subjects in the Province of Quebec into the British Empire?

SUGGESTIONS FOR FURTHER READING

Anderson, Fred. *Crucible of War: The Seven Years' War and the Fate of Empire in British North America, 1754–1766*. New York: Knopf, 2000.

Buckner, Phillip, and John G. Reid, eds. *Remembering 1759: The Conquest of Canada in Historical Memory*. Toronto: University of Toronto Press, 2012.

————, eds. *Revisiting 1759: The Conquest of Canada in Historical Perspective*. Toronto: University of Toronto Press, 2012.

Burt, A.L. *The Old Province of Quebec*, 2 vols. Toronto: McClelland & Stewart, 1968.

Christie, Nancy, ed. *Transatlantic Subjects: Ideas, Institutions, and Social Experience in Post-Revolutionary British North America*. Montreal and Kingston: McGill-Queen's University Press, 2008.

Fyson, Donald. *Magistrates, Police, and People: Everyday Criminal Justice in Quebec and Lower Canada, 1764–1837*. Toronto: University of Toronto Press, 2006.

Lawson, Philip. *The Imperial Challenge: Quebec and Britain in the Age of the American Revolution*. Montreal and Kingston: McGill-Queen's University Press, 1994.

Miquelon, Dale. *Society and Conquest: The Debate on the Bourgeoisie and Social Change in French Canada, 1700–1850*. Toronto: Copp Clark Publishing, 1977.

Viau, Roland. "Careful Coexistence: The Canadians and the British in Montreal prior to 1800." In *Montreal: The History of a North American City*, edited by Dany Fougeres and Roderick Macleod. Montreal and Kingston: McGill-Queen's University Press, 2017.

Primary Documents

1 From "Governor Murray to the Lords of Trade, Quebec 29th Octr 1764," and "Petition of the Quebec Traders" in *Documents Relating to the Constitutional History of Canada 1759–1791*, vol. 1 (Ottawa: J. de L. Taché, 1918), 231–4.

GOVERNOR MURRAY TO THE LORDS OF TRADE

QUEBEC 29th Octr 1764
MY LORDS

The inclosed papers will shew you the situation of affairs here and how necessary it is for me to send Mr Cramahé to London that your Lordships may have the most Minute and Clearest Acct of every thing relating to this Province. An immediate Remedy seems necessary. To any thing I can write doubts may arise and misrepresentations may be made (which I find too frequently to be the case) the necessary delay to clear up such Doubts and misrepresentations by letters, may be dangerous. Mr Cramahé will answer every purpose, if properly attended too, he is thoroughly informed of all I know, no Man has the good of this Colony more at heart, no Man is more zealous for the Kings service and

certainly there doth not exist a Man of more Integrity and Application.

Little, very little, will content the New Subjects but nothing will satisfy the Licentious Fanaticks Trading here, but the expulsion of the Canadians who are perhaps the bravest and the best race upon the Globe, a Race, who cou'd they be indulged with a few priveledges which the Laws of England deny to Roman Catholicks at home, wou'd soon get the better of every National Antipathy to their Conquerors and become the most faithful and most useful set of Men in this American Empire.

I flatter myself there will be some Remedy found out even in the Laws for the Relief of this People, if so, I am positive the populer clamours in England will not prevent the Humane Heart of the King from following its own Dictates. I am confident too my Royal Master will not blame the unanimous opinion of his Council here for the Ordonnance establishing the Courts of Justice, as nothing less cou'd be done to prevent great numbers from emigrating directly, and certain I am, unless the Canadians are admitted on Jurys, and are allowed Judges and Lawyers who understand their Language his Majesty will lose the greatest part of this Valuable people. [. . .]

I have the Hon[r] to be with the greatest truth & regard.
My Lords,
Your Lordships' mo. Ob[t], &[ca].
The Lords of Trade & Plant[n], (Signed)
JA MURRAY
[. . .]

PETITION OF THE QUEBEC TRADERS

To the King's Most Excellent Majesty

The Humble Petition of Your Majesty's most faithful and loyal Subjects, British Merchants and Traders in behalf of themselves and their fellow Subjects, Inhabitants of your Majesty's Province of Quebec
MAY IT PLEASE YOUR MAJESTY.

Confident of Your Majesty's Paternal Care and Protection extended even to the meanest and most distant of your Subjects, We humbly crave your Majesty's Gracious Attention to our present Grievances and Distresses.

We presume to hope that your Majesty will be pleased to attribute our approaching your Royal Throne with disagreeable Complaints, to the Zeal and Attachment we have to your Majesty's Person and Government, and for the Liberties & Priviledges with which your Majesty has indulged all your Dutifull Subjects.

Our Settlement in this Country with respect to the greatest part of us; takes it's date from the Surrender of the Colony to your Majestys Arms; Since that Time we have much contributed to the advantage of our Mother Country, by causing an additional Increase to her Manufactures, and by a considerable Importation of them, diligently applied ourselves to Investigate and promote the Commercial Interests of this Province and render it flourishing.

To Military Government, however oppressive and severely felt, we submitted without murmur, hoping Time with a Civil Establishment would remedy this Evil.

With Peace we trusted to enjoy the Blessings of British Liberty, and happily reap the fruits of our Industry: but we should now despair of ever attaining those desirable ends, had we not Your Majesty's experienced Goodness to apply to.

The Ancient Inhabitants of the Country impoverished by the War, had little left wherewith to purchase their common necessaries but a Paper Currency of very doubtfull Value: The Indian War has suspended our Inland Trade for two years past, and both these Causes united have greatly injured our Commerce.

For the redress of which we repose wholly on your Majesty, not doubting but the Wisdom of your Majesty's Councils will in due time put the Paper Currency into a Course of certain and regular Payment, and the Vigour of Your Majesty's Arms terminate that War by a peace advantageous and durable.

We no less rely on your Majesty for the Redress of those Grievances we suffer from the Measures of Government practised in this your Majesty's Province, which are

The Deprivation of the open Trade declared by your Majesty's most gracious Proclamation, by the Appropriation of some of the most commodious Posts of the Resort of the Savages, under the Pretext of their being your Majesty's private Domain.

The Enacting Ordinances Vexatious, Oppressive, unconstitutional, injurious to civil Liberty and the Protestant Cause.

Suppressing dutifull and becoming Remonstrances of your Majesty's Subjects against these Ordinances in Silence and Contempt.

The Governor instead of acting agreeable to that confidence reposed in him by your Majesty, in giving a favourable Reception to those of your Majesty's Subjects, who petition and apply to him on such important Occasions as require it, doth frequently treat them with a Rage and Rudeness of Language and Demeanour, as dishonorable to the Trust he holds of your Majesty as painful to those who suffer from it.

His further adding to this by most flagrant Partialities, by formenting Parties and taking measures to keep your Majesty's old and new Subjects divided from one another, by encouraging the latter to apply for Judges of their own National Language.

His endeavouring to quash the Indictment against Claude Panet (his Agent in this Attempt who laboured to inflame the Minds of the People against your Majesty's British Subjects) found by a very Worthy Grand Inquest, and causing their other judicious and honest Presentments to be answered from the Bench with a Contemptuous Ridicule.

This discountenancing the Protestant Religion by almost a Total Neglect of Attendance upon the Service of the Church, leaving the Protestants to this Day destitute of a place of Worship appropriated to themselves.

The Burthen of these Grievances from Government is so much the more severely felt, because of the natural Poverty of the Country; the Products of it been extremely unequal to support its Consumption of Imports.

Hence our Trade is miserably confined and distressed, so that we lye under the utmost Necessity of the Aids of Succours of Government, as well from Our Mother Country as that of the Province, in the Place of having to contend against Oppression and Restraint.

We could enumerate many more Sufferings which render the Lives of your Majesty's Subjects, especially your Majesty's loyal British Subjects, in the Province so very unhappy that we must be under the Necessity of removing from it, unless timely prevented by a Removal of the present Governor.

Your Petitioners therefore most humbly pray your Majesty to take the Premises into your gracious Consideration, and to appoint a Governor over us, acquainted with other maxims of Government than Military only; And for the better Security of your Majesty's dutiful and loyal Subjects, in the Possession and Continuance of their Rights and Liberties, we beg leave also most humbly to petition that it may please your Majesty, to order a House of Representatives to be chosen in this as in other your Majesty's Provinces; there being a number more than Sufficient of Loyal and well affected Protestants, exclusive of military Officers, to form a competent and respectable House of Assembly; and your Majesty's new Subjects, if your Majesty shall think fit, may be allowed to elect Protestants without burdening them with such Oaths as in their present mode of thinking they cannot conscientiously take.

We doubt not but the good Effects of these measures will soon appear, by the Province becoming flourishing and your Majesty's People in it happy. And for Your Majesty and your House your Petitioners as in Duty bound shall ever pray, &ca &ca

Saml Sills	John Danser.	Geo. Allsoopp.	Alex^r McKenzie
Edwd Harrison	Ja^s Jeffry.	Wm Mackenzie	Geo. Measam
Eleaz^r Levy	Ja^s Johnston.	B Comte.	Jⁿ A. Gastineau
Ja^s Shepherd	Thos Story.	Peter Faneuil.	Ph. Payn.
John Watmough.	Danl Bayne	Geo. Fulton.	
John Ord.	John Purss.		

2 From Frances Brooke, *The History of Emily Montague* (London: Printed for J. Dodsley, in Pall Mall, 1769), 4 vols.

LETTER 22: FROM A. FERMOR TO MISS RIVERS (SILLERI, SEPT. 25)

I have been rambling about amongst the peasants, and asking them a thousand questions, in order to satisfy your inquisitive friend. As to my father, though, properly speaking, your questions are addressed to him, yet, being upon duty, he begs that, for this time, you will accept of an answer from me.

The Canadians live a good deal like the ancient patriarchs; the lands were originally settled by the troops, every officer became a seigneur, or lord of the manor, every soldier took lands under his commander; but, as avarice is natural to mankind, the soldiers took a great deal more than they could cultivate, by way of providing for a family: which is the reason so much land is now waste in the finest part of the province: those who had children, and in general they have a great number, portioned out their lands amongst them as they married, and lived in the midst of a little world of their descendants.

[. . .]

The corn here is very good, though not equal to ours; the harvest not half so gay as in England, and for this reason, that the lazy creatures leave the greatest part of their land uncultivated, only sowing as much corn of different sorts as will serve themselves; and being too proud and too idle to work for hire, every family gets in its own harvest, which prevents all that jovial spirit which we find when the reapers work together in large parties.

Idleness is the reigning passion here, from the peasant to his lord; the gentlemen never either ride on horseback or walk, but are driven about like women, for they never drive themselves, lolling at their ease in a calache: the peasants, I mean the masters of families, are pretty near as useless as their lords.

You will scarce believe me, when I tell you, that I have seen, at the farm next us, two children, a very beautiful boy and girl, of about eleven years old, assisted by their grandmother, reaping a field of oats, whilst the lazy father, a strong fellow of thirty two, lay on the grass, smoking his pipe, about twenty yards from them: the old people and children work here; those in the age of strength and health only take their pleasure.

A propos to smoking, 'tis common to see here boys of three years old, sitting at their doors, smoking their pipes, as grave and composed as little old Chinese men on a chimney.

[. . .]

They [the Canadiens] sow their wheat in spring, never manure the ground, and plough it in the slightest manner; can it then be wondered at that it is inferior to ours? They fancy the frost would destroy it if sown in autumn; but this is all prejudice, as experience has shewn. I myself saw a field of wheat this year at the governor's farm, which was manured and sown in autumn, as fine as I ever saw in England.

I should tell you, they are so indolent as never to manure their lands, or even their gardens; and that, till the English came, all the manure of Quebec was thrown into the river.

[. . .]

Adieu! I am tired of the subject.

Your faithful,

A. Fermor.

LETTER 72: FROM WILLIAM FERMOR TO THE EARL OF —— (SILLERI, FEB. 20)

My Lord,

Your Lordship does me great honor in supposing me capable of giving any satisfactory account of a country in which I have spent only a few months.

As a proof, however, of my zeal, and the very strong desire I have to merit the esteem you honor me with, I shall communicate from time to time the little I have observed, and may observe, as well as what I hear from good authority, with that lively pleasure with which I have ever obeyed every command of your Lordship's.

The French, in the first settling this colony, seem to have had an eye only to the conquest of ours: their whole system of policy seems to have been military, not commercial; or only so far commercial as was necessary to supply the wants, and by so doing to gain the friendship, of the savages, in order to make use of them against us.

The lands are held on military tenure: every peasant is a soldier, every seigneur an officer, and both serve without pay whenever called upon; this service is, except a very small quit-rent by way of acknowledgement, all they pay for their lands: the seigneur holds of the crown, the peasant of the seigneur, who is at once his lord and commander.

The peasants are in general tall and robust, notwithstanding their excessive indolence; they love war, and hate labor; are brave, hardy, alert in the field, but lazy and inactive at home; in which they resemble the savages, whose manners they seem strongly to have imbibed. The government appears to have encouraged a military spirit all over the colony; though ignorant and stupid to a great degree, these peasants have a strong sense of honor; and though they serve, as I have said, without pay, are never so happy as when called to the field.

They are excessively vain, and not only look on the French as the only civilized nation in the world, but on themselves as the flower of the French nation: they had, I am told, a great aversion to the regular troops which came from France in the late war, and a contempt equal to that aversion; they however had an affection and esteem for the late Marquis De Montcalm, which almost rose to idolatry; and I have even at this distance of time seen many of them in tears at the mention of his name: an honest tribute to the memory of a commander equally brave and humane; for whom his enemies wept even on the day when their own hero fell.

I am called upon for this letter, and have only time to assure your Lordship of my respect, and of the pleasure I always receive from your commands. I have the honor to be,
My Lord,
Your Lordship's, &c.
William Fermor.

LETTER 117: FROM WILLIAM FERMOR TO THE EARL OF —— (SILLERI, APRIL 8)

Nothing can be more true, my Lord, than that poverty is ever the inseparable companion of indolence.

I see proofs of it every moment before me; with a soil fruitful beyond all belief, the Canadians are poor on lands which are their own property, and for which they pay only a trifling quit-rent to their seigneurs.

This indolence appears in every thing: you scarce see the meanest peasant walking; even riding on horseback appears to them a fatigue insupportable; you see them lolling at ease, like their lazy lords, in carrioles and calashes, according to the season; a boy to guide the horse on a seat in the front of the carriage, too lazy even to take the trouble of driving themselves, their hands in winter folded in an immense muff, though perhaps their families are in want of bread to eat at home.

The winter is passed in a mixture of festivity and inaction; dancing and feasting in their gayer hours; in their graver smoking, and drinking brandy, by the side of a warm stove: and when obliged to cultivate the ground in spring to procure the means of subsistence, you see them just turn the turf once lightly over, and, without manuring the ground, or even breaking the clods of earth, throw in the seed in the same careless manner, and leave the event to chance, without troubling themselves further till it is fit to reap.

I must, however, observe, as some alleviation, that there is something in the climate which strongly inclines both the body and mind, but rather the latter, to indolence: the heat of the summer, though pleasing, enervates the very soul, and gives a certain lassitude unfavorable to industry; and the winter, at its extreme, binds up and chills all the active faculties of the soul.

Add to this, that the general spirit of amusement, so universal here in winter, and so necessary to prevent the ill effects of the season, gives a habit of dissipation and pleasure, which makes labor doubly irksome at its return.

Their religion, to which they are extremely bigoted, is another great bar, as well to industry as population: their numerous festivals inure them to idleness; their religious houses rob the state of many subjects who might be highly useful at present, and at the same time retard the increase of the colony.

Sloth and superstition equally counterwork providence, and render the bounty of heaven of no effect.

I am surprized the French, who generally make their religion subservient to the purposes of policy, do not discourage convents, and lessen the number of festivals, in the colonies, where both are so peculiarly pernicious.

It is to this circumstance one may in great measure attribute the superior increase of the British American settlements compared to those of France: a religion which encourages idleness, and makes a virtue of celibacy, is particularly unfavorable to colonization.

However religious prejudice may have been suffered to counterwork policy under a French government, it is scarce to be doubted that this cause of the poverty of Canada will by degrees be removed; that these people, slaves at present to ignorance and superstition, will in time be enlightened by a more liberal education, and gently led by reason to a religion which is not only preferable, as being that of the country to which they are now annexed, but which is so much more calculated to make them happy and prosperous as a people.

Till that time, till their prejudices subside, it is equally just, humane, and wise, to leave them the free right of worshiping the Deity in the manner which they have been early taught to believe the best, and to which they are consequently attached.

It would be unjust to deprive them of any of the rights of citizens on account of religion, in America, where every other sect of dissenters are equally capable of employ with those of the established church; nay where, from whatever cause, the church of England is on a footing in many colonies little better than a toleration.

It is undoubtedly, in a political light, an object of consequence every where, that the national religion, whatever it is, should be as universal as possible, agreement in religious worship being the strongest tie to unity and obedience; had all prudent means been used to lessen the number of dissenters in our colonies, I cannot avoid believing, from what I observe and hear, that we should have found in them a spirit of rational loyalty, and true freedom, instead of that factious one from which so much is to be apprehended.

It seems consonant to reason, that the religion of every country should have a relation to, and coherence with, the civil constitution: the Romish religion is best adapted to a despotic government, the presbyterian to a republican, and that of the church of England to a limited monarchy like ours.

As therefore the civil government of America is on the same plan with that of the mother country, it were to be wished the religious establishment was also the same, especially in those colonies where the people are generally of the national church; though with the fullest liberty of conscience to dissenters of all denominations.

I would be clearly understood, my Lord; from all I have observed here, I am convinced, nothing would so much contribute to diffuse a spirit of order, and rational obedience, in the colonies, as the appointment, under proper restrictions, of bishops: I am equally convinced that nothing would so much strengthen the hands of government, or give such pleasure to the well-affected in the colonies, who are by much the most numerous, as such an appointment, however clamored against by a few abettors of sedition.

I am called upon for this letter, and must remit to another time what I wished to say more to your Lordship in regard to this country.

I have the honor to be,

My Lord, &c.

Wm. Fermor.

LETTER 138: FROM WILLIAM FERMOR TO THE EARL OF —— (SILLERI, MAY 12)

It were indeed, my Lord, to be wished that we had here schools, at the expence of the public, to teach English to the rising generation: nothing is a stronger tie of brotherhood and affection, a greater cement of union, than speaking one common language.

The want of attention to this circumstance has, I am told, had the worst effects possible in the province of New York, where the people, especially at a distance from the capital, continuing to speak Dutch, retain their affection for their ancient masters, and still look on their English fellow subjects as strangers and intruders.

The Canadians are the more easily to be won to this, or whatever else their own, or the general good requires, as their noblesse have the strongest attachment to a court, and that favor is the great object of their ambition: were English made by degrees the court language, it would soon be universally spoke.

Of the three great springs of the human heart, interest, pleasure, vanity, the last

appears to me much the strongest in the Canadians; and I am convinced the most forcible tie their noblesse have to France, is their unwillingness to part with their croix de St. Louis: might not therefore some order of the same kind be instituted for Canada, and given to all who have the croix, on their sending back the ensigns they now wear, which are inconsistent with their allegiance as British subjects?

Might not such an order be contrived, to be given at the discretion of the governor, as well to the Canadian gentlemen who merited most of the government, as to the English officers of a certain rank, and such other English as purchased estates, and settled in the country? and, to give it additional lustre, the governor, for the time being, be always head of the order?

'Tis possible something of the same kind all over America might be also of service; the passions of mankind are nearly the same every where: at least I never yet saw the soil or climate, where vanity did not grow; and till all mankind become philosophers, it is by their passions they must be governed.

The common people, by whom I mean the peasantry, have been great gainers here by the change of masters; their property is more secure, their independence greater, their profits much more than doubled: it is not them therefore whom it is necessary to gain.

The noblesse, on the contrary, have been in a great degree undone: they have lost their employs, their rank, their consideration, and many of them their fortunes.

It is therefore equally consonant to good policy and to humanity that they should be considered, and in the way most acceptable to them; the rich conciliated by little honorary distinctions, those who are otherwise by sharing in all lucrative employs; and all of them by bearing a part in the legislature of their country.

The great objects here seem to be to heal those wounds, which past unhappy disputes have left still in some degree open; to unite the

French and English, the civil and military, in one firm body; to raise a revenue, to encourage agriculture, and especially the growth of hemp and flax; and find a staple, for the improvement of a commerce, which at present labors under a thousand disadvantages.

But I shall say little on this or any political subject relating to Canada, for a reason which, whilst I am in this colony, it would look like flattery to give: let it suffice to say, that, humanly speaking, it is impossible that the inhabitants of this province should be otherwise than happy.

I have the honor to be,

My Lord, &c.

William Fermor.

Historical Interpretations

3 From Martin L. Nicolai, "A Different Kind of Courage: The French Military and the Canadian Irregular Soldier during the Seven Years' War," *Canadian Historical Review* 70, no. 1 (1989): 53–75.

In recent decades, two historians of Canada during the Seven Years' War, Guy Frégault and William J. Eccles, have attacked their predecessors' adulation of Louis-Joseph, Marquis de Montcalm, by portraying him as a poor strategist, a mediocre tactician, and a defeatist. However true this might be, they also portray the French officer corps, including their commander, as contemptuous of Canadians and irregular warfare.[1] During the course of the Canadian campaign, Montcalm and his officers did demonstrate a general lack of respect for the petty raiding of *la petite guerre* and an ambiguous attitude toward the Canadian soldier. This, however, was less a rejection of irregular warfare than an expression of their belief that a more structured and sophisticated use of irregular tactics was necessary when the enemy was no longer simply a colonial militia but a large, well-organized army complete with highly trained regiments of heavy and light infantry. As Ian Steele makes clear, the Seven Years' War in North America marks the end of the days of small-scale raiding and the advent of professional armies on the continent. The war, he states, was won by conventional, European-style battles and sieges, not by skirmishes in the woods.[2]

At first complacent in their use of Canadian irregulars, relying on local practice and their knowledge of the use of light troops in Europe during the War of the Austrian Succession, the French eventually attempted to bring Canadian soldiers onto the conventional battlefield not simply as sharpshooters roaming on the flanks but as actual light infantry operating on the central line of battle in close co-operation with the heavy infantry of the French *troupes de terre*. There is every sign that the Frenchmen finished the campaign convinced by the success of Canadian light troops that units of properly led and disciplined light infantry were a valuable part of a European army.

[. . .]

The exposure of many members of the officer corps to irregular warfare in Europe made them appreciate the effectiveness of this type of military activity. Irregulars could severely hamper reconnaissance, slow an army's advance, and harry an enemy's communications so severely that large numbers of fighting men had to be withdrawn from the main body simply to guard the army's baggage and lines of supply and communication. There was, as a result, a general recognition among military men by the end of the 1740s that ir-regular troops, fortunately or unfortunately, had a role to play in wartime, if only to defend one's own force against enemy irregulars.

What impressions did French officers have of Canadian soldiers during the first few years of the Seven Years' War? One prom-inent characteristic of the Canadian *habi-tants*, noted by all of the officers, was their willingness to perform military service, an attitude which was in striking contrast to that of the average French peasant. The long wars against the Iroquois in the seventeenth century, which forced all Canadian males to take up arms and learn Indian methods of ir-regular warfare, engendered a military ethos among Canadians which was fostered by in-termittent campaigns against the English in company with Canada's Indian allies.[3] The reputation of Canadians as a "race of soldiers" was confirmed by the French officers, whose constant refrain in their writings was to con-trast the Canadians' skill and courage with their indiscipline.[4] Colonel François-Charles de Bourlamaque, for instance, believed that Canada possessed far more "naturally cou-rageous men" than any other country, and although Canadian militiamen were not ac-customed to obedience, when they found firmness and justice in their officers they were quite "docile."[5] They possessed a differ-ent "kind of courage," wrote Louis-Antoine de Bougainville, for like the Indians, Cana-dians exposed themselves little, organized ambushes, and fought in the woods behind a screen of trees, defeating in this way an en-tire British army under General Braddock.[6] Despite his criticisms of Canadian indisci-pline, Bougainville was careful to qualify his remarks: "God knows we do not wish to disparage the value of the Canadians . . . In the woods, behind trees, no troops are com-parable to the natives of this country."[7] Some of the least charitable comments on Cana-dians came from the Baron von Dieskau's second-in-command, Pierre-André de Gohin, Chevalier de Montreuil, who, blaming the

irregulars for his commander's humiliating defeat at Lake George in 1755, declared sarcas-tically that the "braggart" Canadians were well adapted for skirmishing, being "very brave be-hind a tree and very timid when not covered."[8]

[. . .]

Constant contact with Indian allies in wartime and the success of their tactics re-sulted in Canadians adopting not only Indian methods of fighting but also their attitudes toward war, such as the idea that victory in-volved inflicting losses on the enemy with-out incurring any and that the campaigning season was over when a victory, however in-substantial, had been achieved and honour gratified. In addition, native ritual boasting of prowess in war may have encouraged some Canadian soldiers to advertise their military talents in a flagrant manner. French officers noticed these characteristics, and generally realized that they were cultural borrowings from the Indians, but they were too ethno-centric and accustomed to professional mili-tary conduct to sympathize very much with this type of behaviour.

The Canadian penchant for boasting was of minor concern. Boasts "after the Cana-dian fashion, that one of their number could drive ten Englishmen" only boosted morale, and this behaviour was considered no more than a minor annoyance.[9] The Canadian and Indian custom of returning home en masse every time a "coup" was made, however, was subjected to considerably more criticism. La Pause recounted how the comical race of Ca-nadians departed after the Battle of Carillon, rushing off in their boats within hours, mov-ing "day and night, forgetting, losing and often leaving people behind if they did not embark fast enough." After visiting their families, he noted, they would return at an exceedingly leisurely pace to resume the campaign.[10] At other times, as when muskets had to be fired in an attempt to stem the exodus of Cana-dian officers and men after the fall of Fort William Henry—a factor which may have in-fluenced Montcalm's decision to discontinue the offensive—the French were even less amused.[11] This behaviour at Oswego and on other occasions decidedly undermined the French officers' respect for Canadian soldier. Even though they recognized the special nature of the Canadian "race," they expected them, as Frenchmen, to be more amenable to discipline than the Indians.

During the early years of the war, the French officer corps simply accepted the traditional role of their Canadian militia and Indian allies. The recent battle on the banks of the Monongahela proved that the Canadians already had considerable potential, and there did not seem to be any immediate need to do more than instill Canadians with obedience and a basic orderliness. Captain Pierre Pouchot regarded Braddock's defeat on the Monongahela as an "impressive lesson'" for regular troops who could not fire steadily and were unacquainted with the style of fighting of their opponents, although he did not believe that properly organized and trained regular soldiers should be defeated by irregulars.[12] Training Canadians as heavy infantry was pointless because they already performed satisfactorily as scouts, raiders, and sharpshooters, duties which admirably suited the "natural spirit" of the local people.[13] French officers, accustomed to the mosaic of provinces which made up their country, each with its own distinct culture and identity, saw Canadians as a very peculiar set of fellow Frenchmen. It was easiest to adapt to their particular nature and use their skills rather than try to make them more like other Frenchmen and amenable to European-style heavy infantry training. As Pouchot's companion-in-arms Captain Nicolas Sarrebource de Pontleroy of the Royal Corps of Engineers pointed out, Canadians were brave, but without discipline they could not be expected to fight in open fields against regular troops; they were not even equipped for such an eventuality.[14] The war was not yet desperate enough to require a complete rethinking of the role of irregular troops.

[. . .]

The Marquis de Montcalm, who arrived in New France in 1756 to take command of the French forces, was by a combination of experience, necessity, and advice persuaded to employ the regulars and irregulars in the separate roles to which they were most accustomed. The Chevalier de Montreuil, who condemned the "blind confidence" of Dieskau in his Canadian advisers, made certain to instruct Montcalm to rely upon his regulars and to employ his Canadians and Indians only in harassing the enemy.[15] Montcalm viewed raiding expeditions, especially those directed against military targets, as useful in harassing enemy troops and lowering their morale. He also believed that successful raids maintained the offensive spirit in his troops and encouraged the Canadian civilian population, although he abhorred the atrocities committed by his aboriginal allies just as he had hated the tortures inflicted on prisoners by the Slavic Pandours and Italian *barbets*.[16]

Irregulars were perceived to have a particular role: They tied down large numbers of enemy militia on the frontiers and lines of communication, carried out reconnaissance, ambushed detachments of enemy troops, and provided some firepower during sieges and other engagements. Both Captain Jean-Nicolas Desandroüins and Lévis wrote approvingly concerning the contributions of the militia during the sieges of Oswego in 1756 and Fort William Henry the following year. Desandroüins found that the Canadians and Indians showed great enthusiasm at Oswego, and while they wasted a great deal of ammunition firing all day, they did succeed in lowering the garrison's morale. It obviously did not occur to him, however, that they might have captured the fort by themselves, or that the irregulars were anything more than auxiliaries.[17]

The year 1758 was a turning point in the war and in French tactics. For this campaign the British massed an army of 6000 regulars and 9000 provincials at Fort William Henry and advanced on Fort Carillon. [. . .] These regular soldiers, probably the pickets from each of the battalions, skirmished all day with the enemy's abundant light troops, and successfully held them at bay while the abattis was hastily completed. Just as the battle opened, the French *volontaires* withdrew to the protection of the abattis or to the army's left flank.[18] A group of 300 Canadians who were present were ordered to leave the protection of the abattis and open independent fire on the flank of one of the attacking British columns, but refused to do so. A few had to have shots fired over their heads to prevent their fleeing the field, although in the latter case Bougainville admitted that "It is true that these were not Canadians of the good sort."[19] Canadians were not accustomed to fighting on the open battlefield and, having only *habitant* militia officers and occasionally a Canadian colonial regular officer of the *troupes de la Marine* to lead them, could not easily be coerced into exposing themselves to enemy fire. Even worse than the refusal of the Canadians at Carillon to follow orders was the rout of Canadian troops during a forest encounter in August 1758 with Roger's Rangers.[20]

Montcalm resolved at the end of this campaign that a higher level of discipline and co-operation was needed from his Canadian soldiers. His aide-de-camp and close friend Bougainville concluded, correctly, that "Now war is established here on a European basis of campaign plans, armies, artillery, sieges, battles. It is not a matter of making *coup*, but of conquering or being conquered. What a revolution! What a change!"[21] Indeed, the arrival of large regular armies in America had changed the nature of war on the continent. Montcalm believed that a concentration of his forces was necessary to confront the English along the major invasion routes, and he advocated a release of as many of the troops in the garrisons in the west as possible without undermining the Indian war effort. He saw that the Indians tied down large numbers of enemy militia on the frontiers, but doubted

that a major French presence in the west had much effect in diverting British regular troops—the chief danger to New France, in his opinion—away from the central front.[22] The British were better able to respond to attacks by irregulars, and raids against military targets in the Lake George area were becoming more and more costly. Irregulars now found it more difficult to defeat regulars without the support of French or French colonial heavy infantry, and these troops had to be conserved for the principal engagements. Montcalm felt that large-scale raids no longer paid off in terms of the manpower, supplies, and effort invested, and he hoped that the Indians and small numbers of Canadians could maintain sufficient pressure on the English to keep them more or less on the defensive. By the fall of 1758 Montcalm knew that no ambush or raid was going to stem the advance of massive English armies against Montreal or Quebec; what he needed were large numbers of regular soldiers and disciplined light infantry who could be depended on to fight in a series of conventional battles.[23]

Montcalm believed that masses of poorly equipped and undisciplined Canadian militiamen who consumed his extremely limited food supplies were of minimal assistance to his army; rather, he needed regulars to reinforce his depleted battalions, which even at full strength were outnumbered approximately four to one by the British.[24] He therefore obtained Vaudreuil's consent to select 4000 of the best militiamen and divide them into three groups. The first group was to be incorporated into the regular battalions of the line, the second into the *troupes de la Marine*, and the third was to be organized separately in the customary militia brigades. A total of approximately 3000 Canadians were intended for the incorporations.[25]

This reorganization was intended to serve several purposes. First, each company of the *troupes de terre* and *troupes de la Marine* would be augmented by 15 men, and would therefore add good shots, canoeists, and workers to the existing body of regulars, improving the ability of these troops to fight, travel, and build fortifications. Montcalm hoped to have the French and Canadian soldiers teach each other what they knew, making the regulars better woodsmen and the Canadians more dependable infantrymen. The Canadians, who customarily fell sick in large numbers on campaign because they lacked clothing, proper shelter, and enforced camp sanitation, would now live with the regulars in tents and receive uniforms, food, and other supplies. In addition, there had always been a serious lack of officers among the militia—sometimes only one for every 200 men—which resulted in a lack of supervision, discipline, and leadership in battle. Incorporated troops would receive abundant attention from the numerous officers and sergeants of the French line troops and *troupes de la Marine*, thereby, it was hoped, improving discipline and reducing desertion. Montcalm and his fellow officers claimed to have no worries that Canadians would be mistreated in their new companies, for "They live very well with our soldiers whom they love," and their complaints would be addressed by the general himself.[26] The militia and the French-recruited *troupes de la Marine* already camped together, so it was not expected that there would be any serious difficulty in uniting Canadians and the *troupes de terre*.[27]

The 1000 remaining militiamen would be organized in their customary "brigades" of approximately 150 men, each theoretically comprising five companies of 30 men. Three soldiers of the *troupes de la Marine* were usually attached to each company as sergeants, and they gave the Canadians a modicum of discipline and military training.[28] According to Montcalm's plans for 1759, his picked militiamen would be placed under the best militia officers, subjected by special ordinance to the same rules of discipline as the regulars, and since there were fewer militiamen on continuous service, they could be better fed, clothed, armed, and even possibly paid for their longer period on campaign. As a further incentive, Montcalm proposed that distinguished Canadian soldiers receive marks of honour, including gratuities, and that small pensions be granted to those crippled by their wounds. The rest of the militia would remain at home prepared at a moment's notice to assemble and join the troops in the field.[29] All of these ideas centred around an attempt to organize and obtain the most efficient performance possible from irregular troops, either as raiders or as sharpshooters on the edges of the battlefield.

[. . .]

Montcalm's intention to create a new army for the campaign of 1759, however, was only partially fulfilled. The *levée en masse* of the Canadian militia and the need to arm, feed, and supply thousands of these soldiers resulted in an abandonment of the plan to organize a set of elite militia brigades. [. . .] The planned militia incorporations, however, did take place in the late spring, just before the arrival off Quebec of the first ships of a fleet bearing a large British and American colonial army under Major-General James Wolfe. The number of Canadians actually incorporated is unknown, but it is doubtful whether more than 500 or 600 men joined the 3000 or more regulars at Quebec.[30] Montcalm had only three months to train his Canadian regulars, simply an insufficient amount of time to produce the kind of soldier he wanted. Judging by the behaviour of the incorporated Canadians on the Plains of Abraham, it seems that very little effort had been made to drill them at all, and the abysmal performance of the regulars suggests that drill was not a high priority in the French army in Canada. After the battle, one of Montcalm's aides wrote in Montcalm's journal that "The French soldier no longer knew any discipline, and instead of molding the Canadian, he assumed all of his faults."[31]

[. . .]

On the morning of 13 September 1759, as Wolfe's army assembled on the Plains of

Abraham and the French brought up their main force, platoons from the districts of Quebec, Montreal, and Trois-Rivières were detached from their militia brigades and sent forward with the pickets of the Régiment de Guyenne to harass the British troops from behind rocks and bushes all along the front of their line. After pushing back some British advance posts, these soldiers kept up a galling fire on the British regulars. Canadian militia and some Indians scattered in the woods on the two edges of the battlefield also kept up a steady fire from the cover of trees and underbrush.[32] Then, at about ten in the morning, Montcalm ordered the advance.

[. . .]

The officers lost control of their men almost immediately. The enthusiastic soldiers surged forward at an excessively fast pace, and as they marched over the rough terrain without pausing to dress ranks, they quickly lost cohesion.[33] As they approached the British line they began to collide with the advanced platoons of Canadian militia, which because of the rapidity of the advance had no time to retire in the intervals between the columns, two of which had very wide frontages. This caused further havoc in the French formations.[34] The columns began to move obliquely toward the British flanks, and at a distance of about 130 metres, extreme musket range, the French troops came to a sudden halt and fired several ineffectual volleys. The incorporated Canadians dropped to the ground to reload, as was their custom in an exposed position, and as the French officers urged the troops to advance, many if not all of the Canadians suddenly deserted their units and retired to the right where the platoons of skirmishers were joining the Canadians and Indians who lined the woods on the British flank.[35] This unorthodox behaviour—which left the regular officers somewhat nonplussed—demonstrates just how little instruction the Canadian troops had received or accepted.

Pouchot commended the resistance of the militiamen on the right flank, but he also explained that the main attack "confused the [incorporated] Canadians who were little accustomed to find themselves out of cover." This was, however, the kindest assessment of the incorporated Canadians to be made by the French officers whose records are extant. Malanie accused them of cowardice, and others blamed them for setting the French regulars in disarray and abandoning their proper place in the line. The Canadians were shielded from further criticism by the fact that almost immediately after the Canadians left the ranks, the French regulars, who advanced in places to within approximately 40 metres of the enemy line, broke under the impact of devastating British volleys and fled madly to the walls of Quebec and across the St Charles River.[36]

At the conclusion of the Battle of the Plains of Abraham, as the French regulars abandoned the battlefield in complete disorder, the Canadians went far in redeeming themselves for their somewhat weak performance during the main encounter, this time in their traditional role as irregular soldiers. A quarter of Fraser's Highlanders were shot down as they attempted in vain to drive the Canadian rearguard from the woods, and they were obliged to retreat and regroup. [. . .] Pouchot and several other officers mentioned this resistance with approval, although they deplored the indiscipline among the Canadians in the columns.[37]

The French officers had underestimated the extent to which Canadians were attached to the tactics which they had practised for over four generations. Like the Indians, Canadians firmly believed that they should fight in their traditional manner, even if they recognized that conventional heavy infantry tactics might be appropriate for Europeans. Pre-industrial societies are extremely resistant to change because survival is so closely linked to practices—passed on by an oral tradition—which have been proven effective by generations of experience. Also, unlike the American colonists to the south,

Canadians had no tradition of training in conventional tactics to make them open to such ideas. As usual, Canadians did their best in their traditional role fighting as skirmishers, and this would be taken into account when the tactical role of Canadians was reassessed for the next campaign, that of 1760.

The Chevalier de Lévis was not present at the Battle of the Plains of Abraham, but the news of the Canadian rearguard action confirmed his already high opinion of the effectiveness of Canadian militiamen when they fought under conditions for which they were trained. Ever since his arrival in Canada he had shown great interest in the use of irregular troops, and this goes far to explain why he was so popular with Vaudreuil and the Canadian officers. As early as 1756, Lévis had outlined the role he expected his light troops to play. In a directive he specified, first, that the "troupes de la Marine and those of the colony will fight in their manner on the flanks of the troupes de terre."[38] This role of light troops in guarding the flanks was relatively orthodox in the French army, and was practised from Fontenoy to the middle of the Seven Years' War in both Europe and Canada. Second, Lévis attempted to work out a system whereby regulars and irregulars could support each other in battle and compensate for their respective weaknesses. Of particular significance is the fact that he designated some regular troops to serve as light infantry: "M. de Montreuil will also detach all the good shots of his regiment, who will fight à la canadienne, and will keep together only a part of his detachment to receive those who fight a la canadienne, so that, in case they were obliged to withdraw, they could do so with security behind the detachment, which, being in order, would face the enemy and give the troops who had fought as skirmishers [à la légère] time to rally and recommence the fight."[39] Light infantry depended on line troops for protection on the open battlefield because they lacked the density to deliver

the concentrated firepower of a large body of men. In the days when one musket meant one bullet, a few men could do little harm to an advancing infantry unit unless they continually retreated to a new position and renewed their fire.

[. . .]

In the spring of 1760 the Chevalier de Lévis incorporated 2264 Canadian militiamen into his eight battalions of troupes de terre and two battalions of troupes de la Marine.[40] A full 38 per cent of the rank and file of the average battalion was Canadian, with 226 Canadians and 361 regulars in this "average" unit combining to raise its strength to 587 men. [. . .] At the Battle of the Plains of Abraham, the incorporated Canadians had constituted only about 10 per cent of the regulars present. Lévis's militiamen, who wore their traditional costumes and were accompanied by their Canadian habitant militia officers and French regular NCOs under the command of French regular officers, were organized in units separate from the French troops in the battalions and, of course, were not officially enlisted in the regular army. [. . .]

On both sides of the Atlantic, French military men faced the problem of how to increase the efficiency of irregular soldiers while retaining their special attributes of initiative and independence and their unique fighting skills. On each continent they met the problem in a similar way by giving their irregulars more discipline and better leadership, while at the same time cultivating their special esprit de corps. Conventional discipline and irregular tactics were combined to produce a new soldier with the ability to deal with a variety of opponents and battlefield situations. They also increased the co-operation between conventional and light troops until the latter, instead of being employed in a completely auxiliary role as scouts and raiders, became an effective tool on the classic, eighteenth-century battlefield.

The French officers who served in Canada during the Seven Years' War were obliged to fight under conditions which were very different from those which they had known in Europe, but their past experience and awareness of important trends in military tactics helped to prepare them for this new campaign. The growing ability of the enemy to deal with irregulars on their line of march and the likelihood of major encounters between the British and French armies meant that Canadians had to expand their skills by learning to fight on the conventional battlefield against enemy light and heavy infantry. Montcalm displayed a lack of judgment in filling the ranks of his regulars with undrilled

Canadians, and was not sufficiently imaginative or ambitious enough to develop a closer co-operation between his regulars and irregulars. This job was left to Lévis to accomplish by placing militia units under regular officers and carefully linking these new light infantry units to his regular battalions so as to ensure close mutual support between these two corps—a change which paralleled reforms taking place simultaneously in the French army in Germany. The result was a decisive victory at Sainte-Foy, and this accomplishment justified the faith French officers had in the potential of Canadian militiamen to become what even they might have considered professional soldiers.

NOTES

1. For historians who favour Montcalm see Francis Parkman, *France and England in North America*, part 7: *Montcalm and Wolfe*, 2 vols (Boston 1884), Henri-Raymond Casgrain, *Guerre du Canada, 1756–1760: Montcalm et Lévis*, 2 vols (Quebec 1891); and Lionel-Adolphe Groulx, *Histoire du Canada depuis la découverte*, 2 vols (Montreal 1950). For highly critical perceptions of the French general see Guy Frégault, *La Guerre de la conquête* (Montreal 1955); William J. Eccles, "The French Forces in North America during the Seven Years War," *Dictionary of Canadian Biography* (DCB), III, xv–xxiii, W.J. Eccles, "Montcalm, Louis-Joseph de, Marquis de Montcalm," DCB III: 458–69; and W.J. Eccles, "Rigaud de Vaudreuil de Cavagnial, Pierre de, Marquis de Vaudreuil," DCB IV: 662–74. Charles P. Stacey, *Quebec, 1759 The Siege and the Battle* (Toronto 1959), and George G.F.G. Stanley, *New France: The Last Phase, 1744–1760* (Toronto 1968), maintain a more neutral attitude.

2. Ian K. Steele, *Guerrillas and Grenadiers: The Struggle for Canada, 1689–1760* (Toronto 1969). I use the term "irregular" to denote light troops without extensive formal military training. "Light infantry" I define as formally trained light troops, who were often regulars rather than militia or auxiliaries.

3. See William J. Eccles, "The Social, Economic, and Political Significance of the Military Establishment in New France," *Canadian Historical Review* 52 (1971): 1–22, for an examination of the impact of war and the military establishment on Canada's inhabitants.

4. Georges-Marie Butel-Dumont, *Histoire et commerce des colonies angloterres dans l'Amerique septentrionale, où l'on trouve l'état actuel de leur population, & des details curieux sur la constitution de leur gouvernement, principalement sur celui de la Nouvelle-Angleterre, de la Pensilvanie, de la Caroline & de la Géorgie* (Paris 1755), 40.

5. François-Charles de Bourlamaque, "Mémoire sur le Canada," *Lévis* MSS, V, 102. See also James Johnstone, "The Campaign of Canada, 1760." *Collection de manuscrits contenant lettres, mémoires, et autres documents historiques relatifs à la Nouvelle-France, recueillis aux archives de la Province de Québec ou copiés à l'étranger* (MRNF), IV, 254, 262; Pierre Pouchot, *Memoir Upon the Late War in North America between the French and English, 1755–60*, 2 vols., ed. and trans. Franklin B. Hough (Roxburt, MA 1866), II, 45; Louis-Guillaume de Parscau du Plessis, "Journal de la campagne de *la Sauvage* frégate du Roy, armée au port de Brest, au mois de mars 1756 (écrit pour ma dame)," *Rapport de l'archiviste du Province de Québec* (RAPQ)

(1928–9); 221; and Peter Kalm, *Travels into North America*, trans. John R. Foster (Barre, MA 1972), 492, for further comments on the warlike spirit of Canadians.

6. Louis-Antoine de Bougainville, "Mémoire sur l'etat de la Nouvelle-France," RAPQ (1923–4), 58.

7. Bougainville to Mme Hérault, 20 Feb. 1758, Louis-Antoine de Bougainville, *Adventure in the Wilderness: The American Journals of Louis-Antoine de Bougainville, 1756–1760*, ed. and trans. Edward P. Hamilton (Norman, OK 1964), 333.

8. Montreuil to d'Argenson, Montreal. 12 June 1756, *Documents Relative to the Colonial History of the State of New York* (NYCD), ed. E.B. O'Callaghan (Albany 1859), X, 419. See also anonymous, "Situation du Canada en hommes, moyens, positions," RAPQ (1923–4), 9, a memoir probably by Bougainville, and the account by La Pause, who uses almost the same words as this anonymous officer in describing the inability of Canadians to "defend themselves with countenance" Jean-Guillaume-Charles Plantavit de La Pause, chevalier de La Pause, "Mémoire et observations sur mon voyage en Canada," RAPQ (1931–2), 66.

9. Pouchot, *Memoir,* I, 35, 37, and II, 45.

10. La Pause, "Mémoire et observations sur mon voyage en Canada," 66.

11. Bougainville, *Journals,* 174; Stanley, *New France,* 162; Steele, *Guerillas and Grenadiers,* 108; La Pause, "Journal de l'entrée de la campagne 1760," RAPQ (1932–3), 384; and Lévis, *Journal,* I, 12.

12. Pouchot, *Memoir,* I, 41–3.

13. This common philosophy of the time was best illustrated by Montesquieu, who in *De l'esprit des lois* explained the idea that people in a particular environment develop a special character which the laws had to be made to fit rather than making people fit the laws.

14. Nicolas Sarrebource de Pontleroy, "Mémoire et observations sur le project d'attaquer les postes ennemis en avant de Québec, et sur celui de surprendre la place ou de l'enlever de vive force," 18 Jan. 1760, Lévis MSS, IV, 199.

15. Chevalier de Montreuil, "Detail de la marche de Monsieur de Dieskau par Monsieur de Montreuil," MRNF IV, 1–4; Montreuil to d'Adabie, St Frédéric, 10 Oct. 1755, MRNF, IV, 9;

Montreuil to d'Argenson, Montreal, 2 Nov. 1755, MRNF, IV, 13, and Montreuil to d'Argenson, Montreal, 12 June 1756, NYCD, X, 419. Montcalm, La Pause, and Pouchot shared similar ideas regarding the cause of Dieskau's defeat. See Montcalm to d'Argenson, 28 Aug. 1756, National Archives of Canada (NA), MG 4, A1, vol. 3417, no. 208; La Pause, "Mémoire et observations sur mon voyage en Canada," 20; and Pierre Pouchot, *Memoir,* I, 46–7.

16. Montcalm to Moras, Quebec, 19 Feb. 1758, NYCD, X, 686–7. See also Bougainville, *Journals,* 42.

17. Charles Nicolas Gabriel, *Le Maréchal de camp Desandrouins, 1729–1792 Guerre du Canada, 1756–1760, Guerre de l'indépendance américaine, 1780–1782* (Verdun 1887), 50–64, and W.J. Eccles, "Lévis," DCB, IV, 477–82.

18. Bougainville, *Journals,* 230. In the French army, pickets were not selected on a rotational basis; instead, they formed permanent units which were often detached for special duties.

19. Bougainville, *Journals,* 238. See also Gabriel, *Desandrouins,* 182, and Doreil to Belle-Isle, Quebec, 28 and 31 July 1758, RAPQ (1944–5), 138 and 150–2. In these last two letters, war commissary André Doreil passed on to the minister of war confidential information which he had obtained from Montcalm.

20. For French reactions to this incident see Gabriel, *Desandrouins,* 203–6; Bougainville, *Journals,* 261–2, and Montcalm to Moras, Montreal, 11 July 1757, MRNF, IV, 105–6. In 1756, 1900 Canadian militiamen served in the ranks, but another 1100 were needed for transport work and for building fortifications. By 1758, 1500 Canadians were employed on the western supply routes alone. George F.G. Stanley, *Canada's Soldiers: The Military History of an Unmilitary People,* rev. edn (Toronto 1960), 23.

21. Bougainville, *Journals,* 252. Henderson believes that Bougainville may have copied passages from Montcalm's journal into his own, rather than the contrary, since duplicated passages often have a later date in Bougainville's journal. In my opinion, however, Bougainville authored parts of the general's official journal, then copied his handiwork into his own a few hours or days later. The style of the common

passages seems more characteristic of Bougainville than of Montcalm. I have therefore ascribed the quoted passage to Bougainville and not to Montcalm, who also records it: Montcalm, *Journal, Lévis* MSS, VII, 419. Susan W. Henderson, "The French Regular Officer Corps in Canada, 1755–1760: A Group Portrait" (PhD thesis, University of Maine, Orono, 1975), 115–16.

22. Stanley, *New France,* 220–1; Steele, *Guerillas and Grenadiers,* 109; Henderson, "The French Regular Officer Corps in Canada," 102; Montcalm to Vaudreuil, Carillon, 26 July 1758, NYCD, X, 760–1; Montcalm to Cremille, Montreal, 12 April 1759, MRNF, IV, 224–5; and Montcalm to Le Normand, Montreal, 12 April 1759, NYCD, X, 966.

23. Montcalm, "Réflexion générales sur les mesures à prendre pour la défense de cette colonie," 10 Sept. 1758, *Lévis* MSS, IV, 45–6, and Stanley, *New France,* 220–1. Eccles claims, incorrectly, that Montcalm believed that "the guerrilla warfare on the English colony's frontiers had to cease." Eccles, "Montcalm," 463.

24. Bougainville, *Journals,* 199.

25. Montcalm, "Réflexions générales sur les mesures à prendre pour la défense de cette colonie," 45–8.

26. Ibid.; anonymous, "Milices du Canada: inconvenients dans la constitution de ces milices qui empêchent leur utilité; moyens d'en tirer parue, la campagne prochaine," Jan. 1759, RAPQ (1923–4), 29–31; and anonymous, "The Siege of Quebec in 1759," *The Siege of Quebec in 1759: Three Eye-Witness Accounts,* ed. Jean-Claude Hébert (Quebec 1974), 52. Canadian officers of the *troupes de la Marine* were especially plentiful, for at the beginning of the war 60 of them commanded 900 soldiers. Stanley, *Canada's Soldiers,* 27.

27. Jean-Baptiste d'Aleyrac, *Aventures militaires au IXVIIIe siècle d'après les mémoires de Jean-Baptiste d'Aleyrac,* ed. Charles Coste (Paris 1935) 33, 58.

28. Montcalm, "Réflexions générales sur le mesures à prendre pour la defense de cette colonie," 45–8, and d'Aleyrac, *Aventures militaires,* 58.

29. Montcalm, "Réflexions générales sur les mesures à prendre pour la defense de cette colonie," 45–8, and anonymous, "Milices du Canada," 29–31.

30. See Lévis, *Journal,* I, 209, and H.-R. Casgrain, *Montcalm et Lévis,* II, 97, for an indication of the numbers incorporated; Casgrain suggests several hundred. See Arthur C. Doughty and G.W. Parmelee, *Siege of Quebec and the Battle of the Plains of Abraham* (Quebec 1901), III, 154, and John Knox, *An Historical Journal of the Campaigns in North America For the Years 1757, 1758, 1759, and 1760,* ed. Arthur G. Doughty (Toronto 1914), II, 105–6, for estimates of the size of the French army on the Plains of Abraham.

31. Montcalm, *Journal,* VII, 613.

32. Armand Joannès (Hermann Johannes), "Mémoire sur la campagne de 1759 depuis le mois de mai jusqu'en septembre," Doughty and Parmelee, *Siege of Quebec,* IV, 226, and Marcel, "Journal abrégé de la campagne de 1759 en Canada," ibid., V, 296.

33. H.-R. Casgrain, *Montcalm et Lévis,* II, 249; Lévis, *Journal,* I, 209; and Marcel, "Journal abrégé de la campagne de 1759 en Canada," Doughty and Parmelee, *Siege of Quebec,* V, 296.

34. Joannès, "Mémoire sur la campagne de 1759," 226, and Marcel, "Journal abrégé de la campagne de 1759 en Canada," 296.

35. Joannès, "Mémoire sur la campagne de 1759," 226, and Anne-Joseph-Hippolyte de Maurès de Malartic, Comte de Malartic, *Journal des campagnes au Canada de 1755 à 1760 par le comte de Maurès de Malartic,* ed. Gabriel de Maurès de Malartic and Paul Gaffarel (Paris 1890), 285.

36. Pouchot, *Memoir,* I, 217, Malartic, *Journal,* 285; Joannès, "Mémoire sur la campagne de 1759," 226; and Marcel, "Journal abrégé de la campagne de 1759 en Canada," 296.

37. Pouchot, *Memoir,* I, 217.

38. Lévis, *Journal,* I, 51.

39. Ibid.

40. Data derived from table in Lévis, *Journal,* I, 257. Lévis lists 6910 troops, including 2264 incorporated militia and militia officers (who were *habitants,* not professionals) 3610 regulars, and 266 regular officers. There was also a battalion of Montreal militia, 180 Canadian cavalry, and 270 Indians.

4 From Damien-Claude Bélanger, "Loyalty, Order, and Quebec's Catholic Hierarchy," in *Violence, Order, and Unrest: A History of British North America, 1749–1876*, ed. Elizabeth Mancke et al. (Toronto: University of Toronto Press, 2019), 36–52.

After the Conquest, various policies designed to hamper the practice of Roman Catholicism in Quebec were central to British plans to assimilate the *Canadiens*. The British focused their efforts on Protestantizing the *Canadiens*, rather than on anglicizing them, because religious practice and identity were regarded as paramount before the twentieth century. However, in spite of their efforts to suppress the Catholic Church, British officials also believed that they could govern Quebec with the active collaboration of the clergy, which they sought and readily obtained. The clergy indeed played a key role in fostering the general acceptance of British rule that gradually came about in late eighteenth-century Quebec and that facilitated the colony's integration into the British Empire. Much like under the French regime, the Catholic clergy acted as the administrative and political auxiliaries of the colonial state under the British.

As part of this process, the clergy developed a loyalist discourse that urged French-speaking Catholics to accept and, later, to celebrate British rule. This discourse was present in clerical thought and writing for over a century, and it was especially prevalent among the higher clergy, whose responsibilities often required close interaction with British officials.[1] Many of these officials understood that clerical loyalty was a pillar of British rule, and they frequently turned to the clergy for support. In the context of the British regime, loyalty implied a faithfulness to the Crown. It could be active, expressing itself through a willingness to uphold and defend British rule, or passive, which involved eschewing movements that sought to undermine British power. In this sense, both the *Canadiens* who fought against the invading Americans in 1775–6 and those who merely refused to join or aid the rebels can equally be considered to have expressed their loyalty to the Crown.

Loyalism, by contrast, is a positive doctrine. It is the reasoned expression of the idea of loyalty and, in French Canada, it expressed a sincere devotion to the Crown, to British rule, and to British institutions. It rested first and foremost on the idea that the British Conquest had been providential in nature; that it had been ordained by God and had proven to be a fortunate event. Loyalists also believed that the British authorities acted with reasonable munificence and that British political institutions were superior not only to the various republican systems that arose in continental Europe and the Americas but also to those of pre-revolutionary France.

Loyalism was first articulated by the clergy and the seigneurial class, and it was integral to nascent French-Canadian conservatism in the 1770s. However, as Jerry Bannister has noted, "loyalty to the Crown encompassed different political traditions" in British North America and it was not synonymous with reaction.[2] Indeed, by the beginning of the nineteenth century, a liberal loyalism was fast developing among the French-Canadian bourgeoisie and, for a time, a loyalist consensus characterized French Canada's middle and upper classes. This consensus was thrown into disarray in the 1830s, but loyalism remained present in liberal and conservative thought until the late nineteenth century, when the rise of imperialism in Britain and English-speaking Canada began to seriously undermine loyalist discourse in French Canada. Loyalist sentiment declined sharply during the conscription crisis of the First World War and had more or less disappeared by the Quiet Revolution. The Roman Catholic clergy's last great act of loyalty occurred in September 1914, when the bishops of Quebec issued a pastoral letter "sur les devoirs des catholiques dans la guerre actuelle."

The nature and intensity of loyalism differed significantly in English- and French-speaking Canada, and the loyalists of Quebec should not be confused with the United Empire Loyalists of Upper Canada and New Brunswick. The former adhered in a general sense to a doctrine, while the latter were a socio-political group born out of the turmoil of the American Revolution. As Donal Lowry notes, French Canadians can be counted among the "ethnic outsiders" of the British Empire; their loyalism could not contain an ethnic and racial element, and its religious component could not be based on a shared faith.[3] French Canadians could participate in the British imperial project, but only in an ancillary sense, and they were ultimately far more likely to suffer than to perpetrate British colonialism. And yet, loyalty to Britain was among the hallmarks of conservative thought in Quebec for well over a century. Even Henri Bourassa, the consummate anti-imperialist, admired British institutions and regarded the British Conquest as ultimately beneficial for French Canada.[4]

French-Canadian loyalists articulated a vision of Britishness that was essentially civic in character. Bourassa, for instance, was fond of referring to Canada as a "British community," by which he meant that the dominion was an (Anglo-French) state whose fundamental institutions and liberties were British in nature. He believed, moreover, that "the very basis of our British institutions" rested not on racial or religious precepts but rather on the idea "that there shall be perfect equality before the law for all nationalities and for all religions."[5] This conception of Britishness was not widely shared among English-speaking Canadians, who tended to regard Canada's status as a "British community" as implying that the dominion was to be a Protestant and English-speaking nation, one whose leading citizens should be of British birth or ancestry. This logic was deployed relentlessly during the Jesuit Estates controversy, and also during the schools crises in

Manitoba and Ontario, so that by the end of the First World War it had become painfully evident in Quebec that civic notions of Britishness were not likely to prevail in Canada. Loyalist sentiment withered accordingly.

[. . .]

Clerical loyalism expressed a complex and sometimes contradictory set of motivations. Yvan Lamonde perhaps put it best when he wrote that the Roman Catholic Church had followed a policy of loyalty "par conviction et par intérêt."[6] The church's woes under the British Regime are well documented, and I do not wish to delve too deeply into the factors that forced the clergy to co-operate with the British authorities.[7] Instead, I intend to explore the underlying convictions that fostered loyalty among the clergy.

To this end, I have examined the *mandements* and the circular and pastoral letters of the bishops of Quebec issued between the Conquest and Confederation that relate to British rule. These were public documents meant, for the most part, to be read out loud during church services; they reflected the official stance of the church on various matters, especially current events, but they could be issued under some measure of duress. For instance, Msgr. Briand's May 1775 *mandement* "au sujet de l'invasion des Américains" was originally intended to be a mere *lettre circulaire* until Governor Carleton pressed for a more authoritative statement to be issued.[8] For this reason, the *mandements* and *lettres* have been examined alongside relevant correspondence and secondary sources.

From the Conquest to Confederation, *mandements* and pastoral letters reveal a clerical hierarchy that increasingly regarded Britain as an ally in upholding Quebec's Catholic social order, most notably in the face of republicanism and revolutionary turmoil. By Catholic social order, I mean a social, legal, and political order structured according to Christian principles, and one in which the Roman Catholic Church plays a leading role—an order that likewise repudiates secularism and moral relativism. In the 1760s, assertions of loyalty rested on basic biblical principles; within a decade, however, leading clerics began to develop a more profound doctrine of loyalism, one which would persist in clerical writing for over a century.

As others have noted, the loyalty of the clergy can be attributed both to conviction and realism. Catholic doctrine advocates the submission to God's will and to legitimate authority. The church hierarchy in Quebec interpreted the British Conquest as divinely ordained and, once it became apparent that London would not deport the Canadien population or outlaw Catholicism, the clergy began to preach submission to the British Crown. The clergy also viewed the power of the British authorities as divinely sanctioned. In Catholic doctrine, authority is sanctioned by God, and to refuse to submit to legitimate authority is to refuse submission to God.

Even before the formal cession of Canada, the higher clergy had called upon its flock to submit to British rule. In a *mandement* dated 14 February 1762, Jean-Olivier Briand, general vicar and future bishop of Quebec, quoted from the epistles of Peter and Paul, which would often be cited by the clergy to justify British rule. "Le Dieu des armées qui dispose à son gré des couronnes," he wrote, had decided that Canada was to fall "sous la domination de Sa Majesté Britannique." He reminded his flock that Saint Peter, "le prince des apôtres, dans sa première Épître ordonne d'être soumis au Roi et à tous ceux qui participent à son autorité," and he noted that Saint Paul had called upon Christians to honour and respect their sovereigns. There was little doubt in Briand's mind that British rule was divinely ordained and thus legitimate, and he ordered that prayers for the king said during Mass be amended to specifically refer to King George III.[9]

But the clergy's loyalty also reflected the Catholic Church's vulnerability in the face of British power. After the Conquest, the institution's legal status was in limbo. The British governor interfered with clerical appointments, and various restrictions were placed on clerical recruitment and on relations with France and Rome. The Crown had also interfered with clerical appointments during the French regime, but the longstanding Gallican policies of a Catholic monarchy were no doubt regarded as less invasive by the church than those formulated by a Protestant power.

Moreover, the church's title over its extensive property was not fully recognized by the colonial authorities. The Crown seized the Jesuit estates, for instance, in 1800. The clergy thus preached loyalty to Britain, in part, because it wished to ingratiate itself to the colonial authorities in the hope that London would eliminate or at least mitigate the various measures that constrained Catholicism in Quebec. Many clerics also reasoned that anything less than open loyalty would result in further constraints.

Clerical loyalism intensified after the 1774 Quebec Act expanded Catholic rights, and it intensified further still during the American and French Revolutions, when the divine nature of the British Conquest became more readily apparent to many clerics. It was assumed that British power protected Quebec from annexation and that the Conquest had spared the province the horrors of the French Revolution. Clerical loyalism thus acquired a new dimension. It no longer simply reflected basic theological imperatives and strategic calculations; leading clerics increasingly regarded British power and institutions as a means to uphold a Catholic social order in Quebec.

In the early 1770s, religious indifference was a growing problem in the colony. Sunday services were sparsely attended, and the Catholic Church, as an institution, was in shambles. Its financial situation was dire and future status uncertain. The Quebec Act brought with it the promise of redress, but the rebel invasion that soon followed struck fear in the heart of the clergy. The rebels held "des motifs qui choquent la raison, la justice, l'équité, l'ordre établi," wrote Msgr. Briand. Revolution, to be sure, represented a far more immediate threat to Quebec's Catholic social order than did religious indifference. The rebels proposed to abolish tithing and seigneurialism and sought to establish a secular and republican system of government in the St Lawrence valley. Moreover, noted the bishop of Quebec in a 1776 *mandement*, "nulle autre secte n'a persécuté les romains comme celle des Bostonnais."[10] The rebels threatened to upend the religious, social, and political order of Quebec, but British power had held back the tide of revolution.

[. . .]

The French Revolution furthered this logic among the clergy. Msgr. Joseph-Octave Plessis, bishop of Quebec from 1806 to 1825, argued, for instance, that the interests of the Catholics of Lower Canada "n'étaient pas distingués de ceux de la Grande-Bretagne."[11] His predecessor, Msgr. Pierre Denaut, did not hesitate to refer to the French as "nos ennemis" in a 1798 *mandement* celebrating the British victory in the Battle of Aboukir Bay, and to insist that God "s'est déclaré pour la justice de notre cause. Il a exaucé les vœux de son people, qui le priait d'humilier cette nation superbe qui ne veut que la guerre: Ps. 67. *dissipa gentes quae bella volunt*."[12]

The advent of the French Revolution underscored the providential nature of the British Conquest. Clerics argued with increasing frequency that the Conquest was part of a divine plan to preserve Catholicism in Quebec. The French, like the American rebels before them, were portrayed as the agents not only of political mayhem but also of religious and social disorder. Revolutionary France, argued Msgr. Denaut in 1802, sought "la destruction de tous les trônes et de tous les autels." The clergy not only embraced and, indeed, celebrated British rule, it now clearly regarded British power as integral to the maintenance of Quebec's Catholic social order. [. . .]

During the War of 1812, the protective nature of British rule was highlighted with even greater enthusiasm. Leading clerics by then regarded British power not only as integral to Lower Canadian order and stability but also as a global force for order and righteousness, indeed as a bulwark against global radicalism. [. . .]

Clerical loyalty reached its high-water mark in the years following the War of 1812. The church's adaptation to British rule, and especially to British institutions, was far-reaching. Msgr. Briand had praised British criminal justice, and most notably the presumption of innocence, in a 1776 *mandement*.[13] Later, Msgr. Plessis acclaimed the "constitution libérale, sur le modèle de celle du Royaume-Uni" that had been granted to Lower Canada in 1791.[14]

The church's loyalism nevertheless reflected the institution's natural distrust of democracy, by which I mean a system of government deriving its legitimacy from the people rather than from God. The church praised British parliamentarism, but it also benefitted from Lower Canada's authoritarian structure of government because it hampered the growing power of the bourgeoisie. In the early nineteenth century, this class was beginning to challenge the leadership role that the clergy and seigneurs had assumed since the French regime. The bourgeoisie increasingly embraced democratism, a doctrine that the church held in very low regard. As early as 1810, Msgr. Plessis warned the clergy of Lower Canada against the "idées trompeuses d'une liberté inconstitutionnelle que chercheraient à lui insinuer certains caractères ambitieux."[15] As both a system of government and an ideal, democracy is disruptive to divinely ordained hierarchies. It promised most notably to lessen clerical power and influence.

The Roman Catholic Church condemned the 1837–8 rebels and refused them the sacraments. Most clergymen (a couple did voice support for the Patriotes) reminded their parishioners that to rebel against legitimate British authority was to rebel against God, since British rule was divinely sanctioned. [. . .]

Clerical loyalty diminished after the rebellions, and this can be attributed, in part, to the 1840 Act of Union, which the clergy abhorred and lobbied against.[16] But it was also a result of actions taken by the Special Council of Lower Canada in the wake of the rebellions, which confirmed the title of the church's extensive property. The intensity of loyalist sentiment diminished along with the church's sense of vulnerability in the face of British power, but the sense of attachment to Britain did not disappear from clerical discourse until the twentieth century.

The clergy continued to view British rule and, especially, British institutions, as bulwarks against radicalism and revolution. [. . .] Unease and outright fear at the prospect of revolutionary disorder were widespread and potent among nineteenth-century Canadian elites. This was especially true for Quebec's Catholic clergy, who regarded the Victorian era's emerging liberal order with far less anxiety than it viewed the radical challenge posed by republicanism, and most notably by the Parti rouge. The European turmoil of 1848 struck fear in the hearts of Quebec's leading clerics, as did the 1849 burning of the colonial parliament buildings at Montreal and the subsequent agitation in favour of annexation. The Archdiocese of Quebec, which had not issued an ultra-loyalist statement in several years, prepared an address of loyalty to Queen Victoria within a week of the attack on Parliament:

> Nous prions . . . Votre Majesté de compter sur la loyauté, la fidélité et l'attachement de ses sujets catholiques de cette partie de la province du Canada, ci-devant appelée le Bas-Canada, et nous osons assurer Votre Majesté qu'ils regardent comme un bienfait de la divine providence de vivre sous le gouvernement de Votre Majesté, dans un temps où presque toutes les nations civilisées sont en proie aux révolutions, et à tous les malheurs qui en sont la suite inévitable.[17]

The protective nature of British power was highlighted again in a number of *mandements* and pastoral letters issued during the turbulent 1860s, when annexation and the possibility of American aggression preoccupied leading clerics once more. In a letter reminding the clergy of his diocese to assist in the organization of militia levies, Msgr. Ignace Bourget of Montreal noted that the British army and navy formed the backbone of Canadian defence: "Notre gouvernement, après avoir donné à ce pays des institutions si libérales qu'il en a fait vraiment le plus heureux pays du monde, lui offre aujourd'hui pour l'aider à se protéger contre l'invasion ennemie dont il est menacé, sa puissante épée."[18] And Confederation gave several clerics the opportunity to reflect on the value of British rule and institutions. In a *mandement* calling upon his flock to accept the British North America Act, Msgr. Charles-François Baillargeon, the auxiliary bishop of Quebec, reminded Catholics "combien nous avons à nous féliciter de vivre sous l'égide de l'Empire Britannique. Il est peu de pays au monde qui ait marché aussi rapidement que le nôtre dans la voie du véritable progrès, et nous n'en connaissons aucun où la religion jouisse d'une plus grande liberté, et exerce une plus large part d'influence."[19]

[. . .]

The Roman Catholic Church was nevertheless an ambiguous ally for the British. It acted as a bulwark against sedition and agitation, but it also lobbied for reform. [. . .] Clerical submission did not preclude legitimate attempts to temper colonial rule. The church lobbied the colonial authorities on a number of matters, most notably in hopes of preventing the 1840 Union of the Canadas. The church resisted attempts to assimilate the Catholic population and colonial interference in clerical matters. When Governor Craig sought to further subjugate the church by forcing the bishop of Quebec to accept formal British control over ecclesiastical nominations—the bishop would have, in exchange, received greater recognition from the Crown and a generous salary—Msgr. Plessis refused to consent to this arrogation of power.[20] [. . .]

Yet clerical loyalism was alienating the church from the general population. At the beginning of the nineteenth century, the *habitants*, who, by and large, did not hate the British, appear nevertheless to have regarded the intensity of clerical loyalty with a measure of skepticism. Later, in the 1830s, democratic rhetoric and anger at British policies, most notably those related to immigration and settlement, drove an increasing wedge between the *habitants* and their clergy. The aftermath of the Lower Canadian rebellions, however, led both the clergy and the general population to reconsider their relationship to British rule.

Clerical loyalism played a key role in fostering the wider adaptation of French Canadians to British rule and, especially, to British institutions. British power and institutions were largely accepted, indeed, often embraced, because they served the interests of various groups within French-Canadian society. For the Roman Catholic Church, loyalism was strategic, reflecting the institution's vulnerability in the face of British power, but it also proceeded from genuine belief. Many ultra-loyalist *mandements* were issued at the prompting of the British authorities, to be sure, but the available evidence generally indicates that these requests were acceded to with enthusiasm, and that their content was sincere. And the depth of this sincerity becomes more evident after the Special Council of Lower Canada solidified the legal status of church property and again when responsible government significantly diminished the power of the British authorities over Canadian affairs. Msgr. Bourget was not pressed to issue a *mandement* calling for prayers during the Indian Mutiny of 1857,[21] nor were the bishops of Quebec compelled to issue calls for loyalty in the 1860s; they did so because they genuinely believed that British power and institutions had become integral to the preservation of Quebec's Catholic social order.

NOTES

1. Indeed, the fervent loyalty of the higher clergy was not necessarily shared by many parish priests, especially during the 1760s. It is for this reason that Msgr. Jean-Olivier Briand of Quebec felt the need to include the following instruction in a 1768 letter to the clergy of his diocese: "Nous devons certainement soutenir les vérités de la foi, même au péril de notre vie, les prêcher et en instruire les peuples; mais il ne convient ni à la religion de la faire avec aigreur ni à la gloire de Dieu de le faire avec mépris. Vous éviterez donc soigneusement de vous servir de termes offensants et injurieux pour ceux des sujets du Roi qui sont d'une autre religion; ceux de *protestants* et de *frères séparés* seront les seuls dont vous vous servirez, lorsqu'il sera absolument nécessaire de le faire pour expliquer notre croyance. Une autre conduite ne ferait qu'aliéner les cœurs, troubler la bonne harmonie qui doit régner entre les anciens et les nouveaux sujets, ne ferait pas de prosélytes, et pourrait engager le gouvernement à retirer la protection et la liberté qu'il veut bien accorder à notre sainte religion." Jean-Olivier Briand, "Lettre circulaire faisant connaître aux curés les intentions du gouverneur au sujet des cabarets, sur l'union entre les anciens et les nouveaux sujets du roi et sur le 1er rang à être accordé aux bailiffs (15 octobre 1768)," in *Mandements, lettres pastorales et circulaires des évêques de Québec*, vol. 2, ed. Henri Têtu and Charles-Octave Gagnon (Quebec City: A. Côté, 1888), 214. Please note that in all quotations modern French spelling and grammar have been employed.

2. Jerry Bannister, "Canada as Counter-Revolution: The Loyalist Order Framework in Canadian History, 1750–1840," in *Liberalism and Hegemony: Debating the Canadian Liberal Revolution*, ed. Jean-François Constant and Michel Ducharme (Toronto: University of Toronto Press, 2009), 126.

3. Donal Lowry, "The Crown, Empire Loyalism, and the Assimilation of Non-British White Subjects in the British World: An Argument against 'Ethnic Determinism,'" *Journal of Imperial and Commonwealth History* 31 (2003): 99.

4. See, for instance, Henri Bourassa, *Les Canadiens-Français et l'Empire britannique* (Quebec City: Demers, 1903), 13–17.

5. Canada, House of Commons, *Debates* (1 March 1901), 747 (Henri Bourassa, MP).

6. Yvan Lamonde, *Histoire sociale des idées au Québec*, vol. 1, *1760–1896* (Montreal: Fides, 2000), 47.

7. For an overview of British interference with Quebec's Catholic Church, see Marcel Trudel, "La servitude de l'Église catholique du Canada français sous le Régime Anglais," *Report of the Annual Meeting of the Canadian Historical Association/Rapports annuels de la Société historique du Canada*, 42 (1963): 42–64.

8. Ibid., 47.

9. Jean-Olivier Briand, "Mandement pour faire chanter un *Te Deum* en action de grâce du mariage du roi George III (14 février 1762)," in Têtu and Gagnon, eds, *Mandements*, 2: 160–1. No doubt anticipating resistance to this change from some parish priests, Briand appended a revealing note to his *mandement*: "Monsieur . . . Peut-être blâmerez-vous quelques-uns des articles de mon mandement; s'il m'avait été possible, j'eusse demandé sur une matière aussi difficile, le sentiment de messieurs les curés; je m'en suis rapporté à celui du clergé de la ville, qui pense presque unanimement qu'il n'est point défendu dans les prières publiques de nommer un hérétique non dénoncé. Au reste, je vous prie d'expliquer à vos paroissiens dans quel sens nous pouvons prier pour ceux qui sont hors de l'Église." Jean-Olivier Briand to the clergy of the Diocese of Quebec, in ibid., 162. In a subsequent letter to the general vicar of Montreal, Étienne Montgolfier, Briand acknowledged that he had hesitated before ordering the change and that it had been met with skepticism by various clerics. However, he wrote, "Je n'ai pas souffert qu'on m'apportât pour raison qu'il est bien dur de prier pour ses ennemis, etc., etc. Ils sont nos maîtres, et nous leur devons ce que nous devions aux Français lorsqu'ils l'étaient. Maintenant l'Église défend-elle à ses sujets de prier

pour leur prince? Les catholiques du royaume de la Grande-Bretagne ne prient-ils point pour leur roy? C'est ce que je ne puis croire." Jean-Olivier Briand to Étienne Montgolfier, Quebec City, February 1762, *Rapport de l'archiviste de la province de Québec* (1929): 50.

10. Jean-Olivier Briand, "Mandement aux sujets rebelles durant la guerre américaine (juin 1776)," in Têtu and Gagnon, eds, *Mandements*, 2: 273, 275.

11. Joseph-Octave Plessis, "Mandement pour des actions de grâces publiques (16 septembre 1807)," in *Mandements, lettres pastorales, et circulaires des évêques de Québec*, vol. 3, ed. Henri Têtu and Charles-Octave Gagnon (Quebec City: A. Côté, 1888), 31.

12. Pierre Denaut, "Mandement prescrivant des actions de grâces après la victoire de l'amiral Nelson (22 décembre 1798)," in Têtu and Gagnon, eds, *Mandements*, 2: 516. The *mandement* was issued at the suggestion of Governor General Prescott. It should be noted furthermore that Msgr. Denaut did not call for a high mass to celebrate the naval victory. In a letter written shortly after his *mandement*, he informed his auxiliary bishop, Msgr. Plessis, that he did not wish to create a precedent by ordering a high mass, and that a day of thanksgiving would do. Pierre Denaut to Joseph-Octave Plessis, Longueuil, 24 December 1798, *Rapport de l'archiviste de la province de Québec* (1931): 155; Plessis to Denaut, Quebec City, 27 December 1798, *Rapport de l'archiviste de la province de Québec* (1927): 220. For his part, Plessis would use the day of thanksgiving as an opportunity to deliver one of the most loyalist sermons in French-Canadian history, possibly to mollify the governor general, who appears to have urged the church to grant greater solemnity to the celebration. "Ne vous parait-il pas dur," he asked his congregation, "d'être obligés d'appeler ennemi un peuple auquel cette colonie doit son origine?" No, he continued, since revolutionary France was the quintessence of evil, while Britain, by contrast, had emerged as God's instrument on earth. The British Conquest of Canada was surely divinely ordained, Plessis concluded. His lengthy sermon was subsequently published and distributed by parish authorities at Quebec. Joseph-Octave Plessis, *Discours à*

l'occasion de la victoire remportée par les forces navales de sa majesté britannique dans la Méditérrannée le 1 et 2 août 1798, sur la flotte française, prononcé dans l'église cathédrale de Québec le 10 janvier 1799 (Quebec City, 1799), 3.

13. Briand, "Mandement aux sujets rebelles," 270–2.

14. Plessis, "Mandement pour des actions de grâces publiques," 30.

15. Joseph-Octave Plessis, "Lettre circulaire à messieurs les curés (21 mars 1810)," in Têtu and Gagnon, eds, *Mandements*, 3: 44. This *lettre* was issued in the midst of a political crisis orchestrated by Governor General Craig, who insisted that the bishop warn the clergy against supporting the Parti canadien in a forthcoming election. Msgr. Plessis, whose relationship with Craig was difficult, to say the least, allowed a proclamation from the governor general to be read in the Catholic churches of Lower Canada and warned his clerics not to appear disloyal to the administration. In a letter to the general vicar of Trois-Rivières, he noted tellingly that the clergy could not "encourir la disgrâce du gouvernement puisque c'est de sa protection que dépend la liberté du culte catholique dans la Province." Joseph-Octave Plessis to François Noiseux, Quebec City, 22 March 1810, *Rapport de l'archiviste de la province de Québec* (1927): 273.

16. As early as February 1838, the clergy of the Diocese of Quebec petitioned Queen Victoria against a possible revival of the 1822 project to unite Upper and Lower Canada. See "Adresse du clergé du diocese de Québec au parlement imperial contre le projet d'unir la Bas et le Haut-Canada sous une même legislature," in Têtu and Gagnon, eds, *Mandements*, 3: 378–81.

17. "Adresse du clergé de Québec à la reine (2 mai 1849)," in Têtu and Gagnon, eds, *Mandements*, 3: 541–2.

18. Ignace Bourget, "Circulaire de Mgr l'évêque de Montréal à son clergé, sur les bruits de guerre et la nécessité de s'y préparer (25 décembre 1861)," in his *Fioretti vescovilli, ou extraits de mandements, lettres pastorales, et circulaires de monseigneur Ignace Bourget* (Montreal: Le Franc-Parleur, 1872), 121.

19. Charles-François Baillargeon, "Mandement à l'occasion de la confédération des provinces du Canada (12 juin 1867)," in *Mandements, lettres pastorales, et circulaires des évêques de Québec*, vol. 4, ed. Henri Têtu and Charles-Octave Gagnon (Quebec City: A. Côté, 1888), 581.

20. See Joseph-Octave Plessis, "Conversations entre son excellence sir James Henry Craig et l'évêque catholique de Québec (mai–juin 1811)," in Têtu and Gagnon, eds, *Mandements*, 3: 59–72.

21. See Ignace Bourget, "Mandement ordonnant des prières pour le succès de la guerre des Indes (21 novembre 1857)," in his *Fioretti vescovilli*, 97.

Chapter 6

The Loyalists, the War of 1812, and Memory

READINGS

Primary Documents

1   Material Culture of the Black Loyalists

2   "The Petition of 55 Loyalists," 22 July 1783, and "A Memorial of Samuel Hakes and 600 Others," 15 August 1783, in *Vindication of Governor Parr and His Council*

Historical Interpretations

3   From "Freedom Denied," in *The Black Loyalists: The Search for a Promised Land in Nova Scotia and Sierra Leone, 1783–1870*, James W. St G. Walker

4   From Karim M. Tiro, "Now You See It, Now You Don't: The War of 1812 in Canada and the United States in 2012"

INTRODUCTION

The characteristic of loyalty that distinguished some North Americans from others during and after the American Revolution is often invoked to explain some of the most significant differences between Canadians (especially Upper Canadians and Maritimers) and Americans, and the resulting divergence in their values. The decision made by the Loyalists to leave the new republic and seek safety, food, and comfort in other parts of the British Empire certainly affected their lives. However, was loyalty to the British monarch during and after the revolution the only factor that mattered in their decision? Might they have been just as loyal to, or eager to maintain, the positions they held as merchants or tradesmen regardless of who ruled over them?

One way of trying to gauge this, and to understand the experiences of the Loyalists more broadly, is to look at some of the objects they have left behind. Historians have traditionally focused on written documents, but material history offers additional important insight into past lives. Objects reveal additional aspects of people's experiences, especially for groups—like these Black Loyalists—who often have little voice in traditional documents. They also often offer an important emotional connection to the past. It is important for historians to think about how to "read" these images and objects, and to be attentive to how they complement or challenge written documents.

The historical interpretations here look into the diversity and inequality of Loyalist experience and the challenges of memory and nationalism. In his contribution, James W. St G. Walker discusses the fate of the Black Loyalists in Nova Scotia. Even if the British authorities had promised them freedom if they joined the fight against the rebellion, the British never considered granting them equality. Relocated to poor areas, given smaller lots than white settlers, and treated as second-rate subjects, their lives in Nova Scotia were so difficult that many black settlers eventually left North America altogether for Sierra Leone. Karim Tiro addresses the War of 1812, about which Loyalist narratives have played a prominent role, from a public history perspective. He raises important questions about how history is presented to broader society, and the contemporary political goals and pressures that shape historical monuments and commemorations.

QUESTIONS FOR CONSIDERATION

1. What do the material culture artifacts of the Black Loyalists represented here add to our understanding of their lived experiences?
2. What was the purpose of the petition?
3. Do you think the Loyalists were acting primarily out of loyalty to the Empire? What else might have affected their decisions?
4. What were the challenges faced by the free black settlers in Nova Scotia after the American Revolution?
5. Does Tiro's argument about why the War of 1812 is commemorated differently in Canada and the United States work for the memorials and celebrations of other historical events?

SUGGESTIONS FOR FURTHER READING

Bannister, Jerry, and Liam Riordan, eds. *The Loyal Atlantic: Remaking the British Atlantic in the Revolutionary Era*. Toronto: University of Toronto Press, 2013.

Condon, Ann Gorman. *The Envy of the American States: The Loyalist Dream for New Brunswick*. Fredericton: New Ireland Press, 1984.

Errington, Jane. *The Lion, the Eagle, and Upper Canada: A Developing Colonial Ideology*. Montreal and Kingston: McGill-Queen's University Press, 1994.

Graymont, Barbara. *The Iroquois in the American Revolution*. Syracuse, NY: Syracuse University Press, 1972.

Jasanoff, Maya. *Liberty's Exiles: American Loyalists in the Revolutionary World*. New York: Vintage Books, 2012.

Kimber, Stephen. *Loyalists and Layabouts: The Rapid Rise and Faster Fall of Shelburne, Nova Scotia, 1783–1792*. Toronto: Doubleday Canada, 2008.

Knowles, Norman. *Inventing the Loyalists: The Ontario Loyalist Tradition and the Creation of Usable Pasts*. Toronto: University of Toronto Press, 1997.

MacKinnon, Neil. *This Unfriendly Soil: The Loyalist Experience in Nova Scotia, 1781–1791*.

Montreal and Kingston: McGill-Queen's University Press, 1986.

Potter-MacKinnon, Janice. *While the Women Only Wept: Loyalist Refugee Women.* Montreal and Kingston: McGill-Queen's University Press, 1993.

Walker, James W. St G. *The Black Loyalists: The Search for a Promised Land in Nova Scotia and Sierra Leone 1783–1870.* Toronto: University of Toronto Press, 1992.

Whitehead, Ruth Holmes. *Black Loyalists: Southern Settlers of Nova Scotia's First Free Black Communities.* Halifax: Nimbus Publishing, 2013.

Whitfield, Harvey Amani. *North to Bondage: Loyalist Slavery in the Maritimes.* Vancouver: UBC Press, 2016.

Primary Documents

1 Material Culture of the Black Loyalists

HIP/Art Resource, NY. Found in the Tate Britain Archive.

Figure 6.1 *The Death of Major Pearson* by John Singleton Copley, 1782–1784

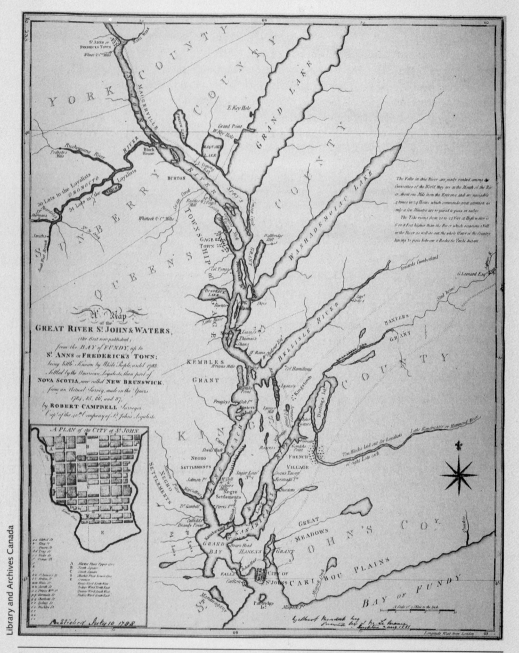

Figure 6.2 *Map of the Great River St. John & Waters* by Robert Campbell, 10 July 1788

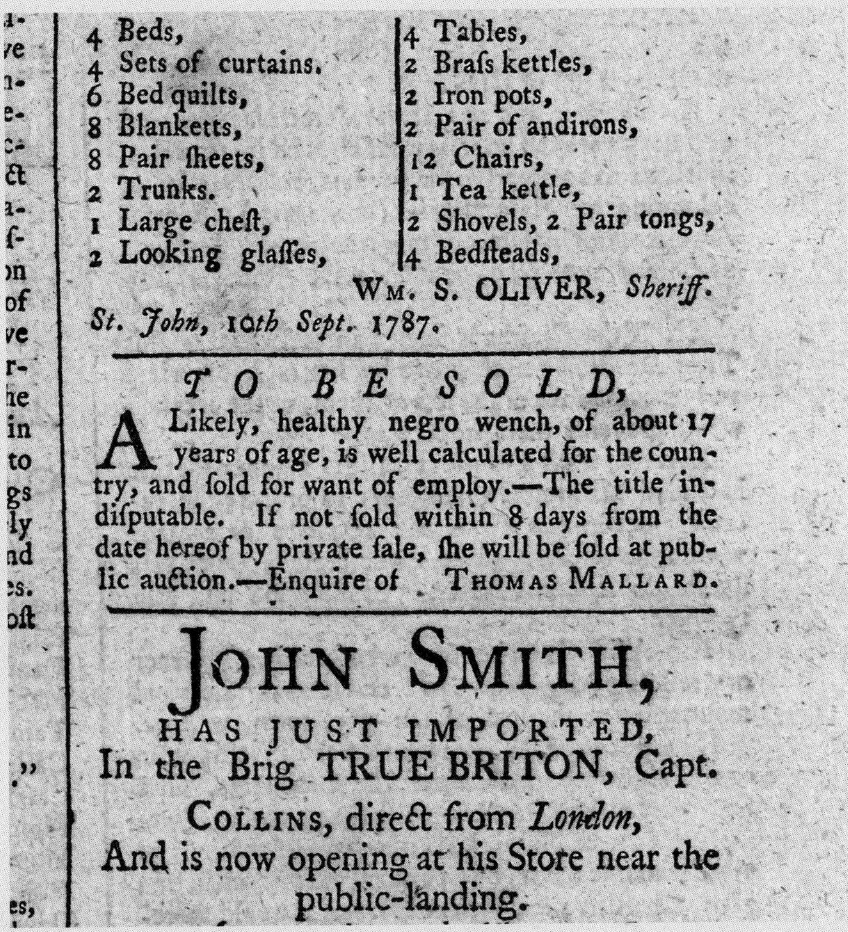

4 Beds,	4 Tables,
4 Sets of curtains.	2 Brafs kettles,
6 Bed quilts,	2 Iron pots,
8 Blanketts,	2 Pair of andirons,
8 Pair fheets,	12 Chairs,
2 Trunks.	1 Tea kettle,
1 Large cheft,	2 Shovels, 2 Pair tongs,
2 Looking glaffes,	4 Bedfteads,

WM. S. OLIVER, *Sheriff.*

St. John, 10*th Sept.* 1787.

TO BE SOLD,

A Likely, healthy negro wench, of about 17 years of age, is well calculated for the country, and fold for want of employ.—The title indifputable. If not fold within 8 days from the date hereof by private fale, fhe will be fold at public auction.—Enquire of THOMAS MALLARD.

JOHN SMITH,

HAS JUST IMPORTED,

In the Brig TRUE BRITON, Capt.

COLLINS, direct from *London*,

And is now opening at his Store near the public-landing.

Figure 6.3 *Royal Gazette and New Brunswick Advertiser,* Saint John, New Brunswick, 11 September 1787, p. 3

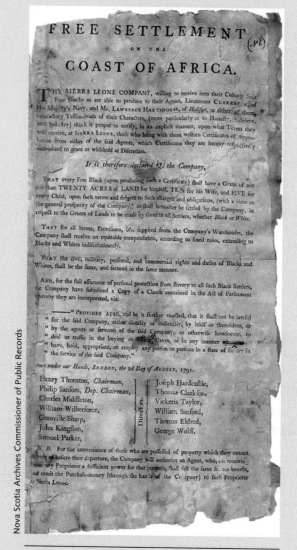

Figure 6.4 Advertisement for the settlement of Black Nova Scotians in Sierra Leone, 2 August 1791

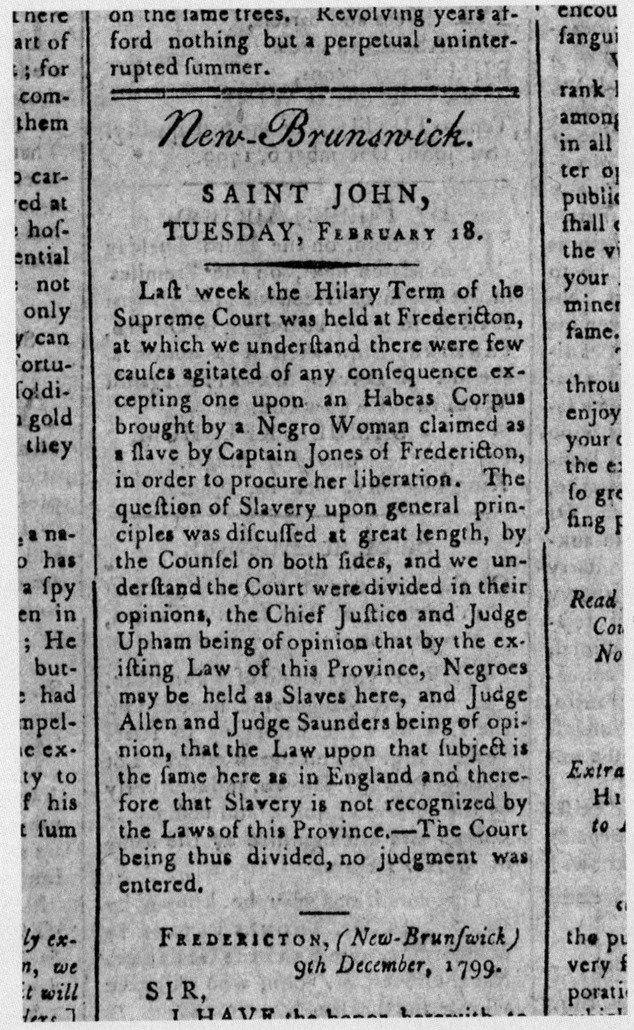

on the ſame trees. Revolving years afford nothing but a perpetual uninterrupted ſummer.

New-Brunswick.

SAINT JOHN,

TUESDAY, February 18.

Laſt week the Hilary Term of the Supreme Court was held at Frederiƈton, at which we underſtand there were few cauſes agitated of any conſequence excepting one upon an Habeas Corpus brought by a Negro Woman claimed as a ſlave by Captain Jones of Frederiƈton, in order to procure her liberation. The queſtion of Slavery upon general principles was diſcuſſed at great length, by the Counſel on both ſides, and we underſtand the Court were divided in their opinions, the Chief Juſtice and Judge Upham being of opinion that by the exiſting Law of this Province, Negroes may be held as Slaves here, and Judge Allen and Judge Saunders being of opinion, that the Law upon that ſubjeƈt is the ſame here as in England and therefore that Slavery is not recognized by the Laws of this Province.—The Court being thus divided, no judgment was entered.

Fredericton, *(New-Brunſwick)*
9th December, 1799.

SIR,

I HAVE the honor herewith to

Figure 6.5 *Royal Gazette and New Brunswick Advertiser*, Fredericton, New Brunswick, 18 February 1800, p. 3

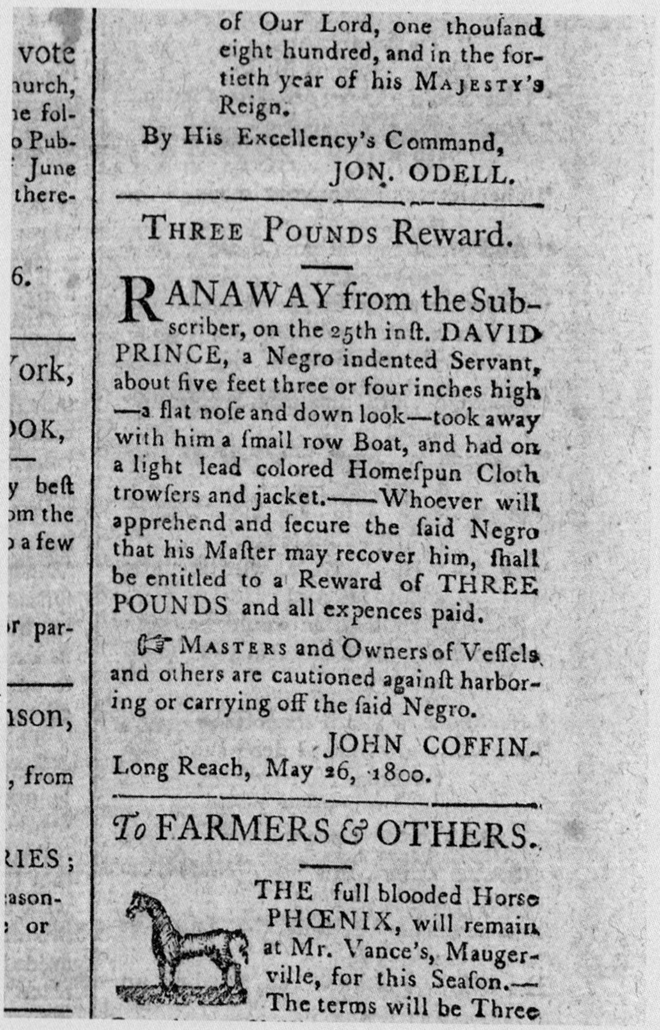

of Our Lord, one thousand eight hundred, and in the fortieth year of his MAJESTY'S Reign.

By His Excellency's Command,

JON. ODELL.

THREE POUNDS Reward.

RANAWAY from the Subscriber, on the 25th inst. DAVID PRINCE, a Negro indented Servant, about five feet three or four inches high —a flat nose and down look—took away with him a small row Boat, and had on a light lead colored Homespun Cloth trowsers and jacket.——Whoever will apprehend and secure the said Negro that his Master may recover him, shall be entitled to a Reward of THREE POUNDS and all expences paid.

☞ MASTERS and Owners of Vessels and others are cautioned against harboring or carrying off the said Negro.

JOHN COFFIN.

Long Reach, May 26, 1800.

To FARMERS & OTHERS.

THE full blooded Horse PHŒNIX, will remain at Mr. Vance's, Maugerville, for this Season.— The terms will be Three

University of New Brunswick Archives & Special Collections

Figure 6.6 *Royal Gazette and New Brunswick Advertiser,* Fredericton, New Brunswick, 26 May 1800, p. 3

Figure 6.7 Slave Collar owned by Abraham DeMill, Sussex, New Brunswick, before 1834

Figure 6.8 *Bedford Basin near Halifax* by Robert Petley, 1835

2 "The Petition of 55 Loyalists," 22 July 1783, and "A Memorial of Samuel Hakes and 600 Others," 15 August 1783, in *Vindication of Governor Parr and His Council* (Halifax: 1783).

THE PETITION OF 55 LOYALISTS (22 JULY 1783)

The affairs at Nova Scotia and New York went on amicably among the Loyalists till August 1783, when it was discovered that the Rev. John Sayre, with fifty-four other persons, had privately presented to Sir Guy Carleton the following letter:

NEW-YORK, JULY 22, 1783.

SIR,

Your Excellency's kind attention and offers of your support to us demand our warmest thanks, which we beg the favour of you to accept.

The unhappy termination of the war obliges us, who have *ever been steady in our duty, as loyal subjects*, to leave our homes; and being desirous of continuing to enjoy the benefits of the British constitution, we mean to seek an asylum in the province of Nova Scotia.

Considering our several characters, and our former situation in life, we trust you will perceive that our circumstances will probably be the contrast to which they have been heretofore; especially as, from our respective occupations, we shall be unable *personally* to obtain the means of a tolerably decent support, unless your Excellency shall be pleased to countenance us by your recommendation in the following proposals; which are, with the utmost deference, submitted to your Excellency's consideration.

1. That a tract or tracts of land, free from disputed titles, be laid out for us in Nova Scotia, in such part of that province as one or more gentlemen, whom we propose to send forward for that purpose, being first approved of by your Excellency, shall pitch upon for us.

2. That this tract be sufficient to put us on the same footing with field-officers in his Majesty's army, with respect to the number of acres.

3. That, if possible, these lands may be exonerated of quit-rents.

4. That they be surveyed and divided at the expence of Government, and the deeds delivered to us as soon as possible, remitting the fees of office.

5. That, while we make this application to your Excellency, we wish not to be understood as soliciting a compensation for the losses we have sustained during the war, because we are humbly of opinion, that the settling of such a number of Loyalists of the most respectable characters, who have *constantly* had great influence in his Majesty's American dominions, will be highly advantageous in diffusing and supporting a spirit of attachment to the British constitution, as well as to his Majesty's royal person and family.

We have only to add our earnest request of your Excellency's aid and support in carrying this matter into execution, as soon as it shall comport with your leisure; and to assure your Excellency, that we are, with great respect, your Excellency's most humble and obedient servants,

Signed by, Addison, Henry (and 54 others). . . .

A MEMORIAL OF SAMUEL HAKES AND 600 OTHERS (15 AUGUST 1783)

The Loyalists about this time (mid-August) discovered the art and designs of the

Fifty-five: a meeting of them was held immediately; when they agreed upon . . . a Memorial to the Commander in Chief:

The Memorial of the Subscribers,
Humbly sheweth,
That your Memorialists, having been deprived of very valuable landed estates, and considerable personal properties, without the lines, and being also obliged to abandon their possessions in this city, on account of their loyalty to their Sovereign, and attachment to the British constitution, and seeing no prospect of their being reinstated, had determined to remove with their families, and settle in his Majesty's province of Nova Scotia, on the terms which they understood were held out *equally* to all his Majesty's persecuted subjects.

That your Memorialists are much alarmed at an application which they are informed Fifty-five persons have joined in to your Excellency, soliciting a recommendation for tracts of land in that province, amounting together to *two hundred and seventy-five thousand acres*, and that they have dispatched forward Agents to survey the unlocated lands, and select the most fertile spots and desirable situations.

That, chagrined as your Memorialists are at the manner in which the late contest has been terminated, and disappointed as they find themselves in being left to the lenity of their enemies, on the dubious recommendation of their leaders, they yet hoped to find an asylum under British protection, little suspecting there could be found, among their fellow-sufferers, persons ungenerous enough to attempt engrossing to themselves so disproportionate a share of what Government has allotted for their common benefit, and so different from the original proposals.

That your Memorialists apprehend some misrepresentations have been used to procure such extraordinary recommendations, the applications for which have been most studiously concealed, until now that they boast its being too late to prevent the effect. Nor does it lessen your Memorialists surprize to observe, that the persons concerned (several of whom are said to be going to Britain) are most of them in easy circumstances, and, with some exceptions, more distinguished by the repeated favours of Government, than by either the greatness of their sufferings, or the importance of their services.

That your Memorialists cannot but regard the grants in question, if carried into effect, as amounting nearly to a total exclusion of themselves and families, who, if they become settlers, must either content themselves with barren or remote lands, or submit to be tenants to those, most of whom they consider as their superiors in nothing but deeper art and keener policy.—Thus circumstanced,

Your Memorialists humbly implore redress from your Excellency, and that enquiry may be made into their respective losses, services, situations, and sufferings; and if your Memorialists shall be found equally entitled to the favour and protection of Government with the former applicants, that they may be all put on an equal footing; but should those who first applied be found, on a fair and candid enquiry, more deserving than your Memorialists, then your Memorialists humbly request that the locating their extensive grants may at least be postponed, until your Memorialists have taken up such small portions as may be allotted to them.

And your Memorialists, as in duty bound, shall ever pray, &c.
New-York, Aug. 15, 1783.

Signed by Samuel Hake,
and above 600 others.

Historical Interpretations

3 Modified version of James W. St G. Walker, "Freedom Denied," in *The Black Loyalists: The Search for a Promised Land in Nova Scotia and Sierra Leone 1783–1870* (Toronto: University of Toronto Press, 1999), 40–63. © University of Toronto Press, 1999. Reprinted with permission of the publisher.

THE BONDAGE OF DEPENDENCE, 1783–91

The Nova Scotia that offered a haven to fleeing American slaves was not itself innocent of the evils of slavery. It has been reported that slaves participated in the building of Halifax in 1749, and one of them, Peter, with his wife and daughter, was included in the muster of original settlers. A list of settlers there in 1750 contained at least 14 different persons specified as "Negro."[1] A slave girl named Louisa, the first in Annapolis County, was sold in July 1767 for £15. That year throughout Nova Scotia the census showed 104 slaves in a total population of 3,022, the largest number, 54, being in the city of Halifax. Returns later in the 1770s included small numbers of slaves, one of them owned by the Reverend James Logon, Nova Scotia's first Presbyterian minister.[2]

It was only with the arrival of the Loyalists, however, that slavery assumed any numerical significance in the province. An estimated 1,232 slaves, often designated "servants" or "servants for life," were brought by Loyalists from the former American colonies.[3] Shelburne in particular, host to the largest body of Loyalists, received hundreds of slaves along with the free blacks being settled there. Shelburne settler Andrew Barclay brought 57 slaves with him; Stephen Shakespeare brought 20, and Charles Bruff 15. Simeon Perkins had two male "servants" and later added a female. The new settlement of Digby counted slaves as well as free blacks among the first pioneers to arrive there in 1783, and some slaves were carried as far as Cape Breton.[4] John Wentworth, former governor of New Hampshire, appointed Surveyor-General of the King's Woods in 1783 and later to become governor of Nova Scotia, included black slaves among the baggage he salvaged from his American estate. Finding them less useful in Halifax, he sent 19 slaves to his cousin Paul Wentworth to be employed on the latter's plantation in Dutch Guiana. "They are all American born and well seasoned," Wentworth wrote to his cousin's agent, "and all are perfectly stout, healthy, sober, industrious and honest. . . . The Women are stout and able, and promise well to increase their numbers."[5]

Other Halifax residents, unwilling like Wentworth to support uneconomic slaves, would sometimes turn "their slaves out of doors to maintain themselves and family, if the family should be so large as to become burthensome to the Master." Then if the slaves' services were required again, or if an opportunity arose to sell them, the master could reclaim them at will. Still others sent six slave children, ranging in age from 5 to 19 years, to the black school established by the Associates of the late Dr Bray. Perhaps they were moved by a genuine humanitarian sentiment, or they may have been seeking to increase their slaves' earning capacity so that they could join that large group of enterprising slave owners who were able to rent their slaves out, particularly if they possessed marketable skills, and pocket the salary that would normally have been paid to the worker.[6] Though many Nova Scotians, most prominent among them Chief Justice Thomas A. Strange and Attorney-General S.S.

Blowers, sought to make perpetual bondage illegal, slavery remained a fact throughout the 1780s and 1790s. It was legally recognized that slaves could be bequeathed as part of an estate, and when Provincial Secretary Richard Bulkeley's slave James was married his status was duly recorded in the Halifax Marriage Bonds.[7]

The presence of so many free blacks in Nova Scotia after 1783 naturally presented a problem to slave owners. With slave and free mingling in schools and markets it was difficult to maintain the notion, in the slave's own mind, that he deserved to be in servitude because of his colour. It was equally difficult for whites to identify a wandering black as a runaway, since a black face could no longer be assumed to be a badge of bondage. Birchtown became a haven to which slaves from all over the province could flee,[8] and once safely hidden there it was extremely unlikely that a master could retrieve them. Advertisements were placed in the newspapers, characteristically accompanied by a representation of a black fugitive carrying a stick, offering rewards for the return of a runaway.[9] Despite the relative insignificance of slavery in the province, and the difficulties involved in retaining a slave at all and then keeping him economically employed, still Nova Scotia was a slave society displaying the crude traits of all such societies. This placed severe limitations on the freedom and opportunities of the Black Loyalists. In a society conditioned to thinking of blacks as slaves, their claims for equality were not always to be taken seriously by white individuals or even by white officialdom. American slavery, fundamentally, had meant the exploitation of black labour. To the Nova Scotian of European descent, therefore, blacks were usually considered to be nothing but a source of labour. It was this economic attitude taken by white people, rather than any identifiable belief in racial interiority, that was to cause the most discriminatory situations experienced by Black Loyalists during the 1780s.

Ironically, labour was in scarce supply during the decade following the Loyalist influx. With most people pioneering their own farms, larger landowners and urban employers were pressed for workers to make their assets productive. As a consequence wages rose until, according to Legislative Assembly Member Alexander Howe, they were "higher than in any other Part of the World." Governor Parr complained to Lord Sydney of the "High Price" of "Every kind of labour in this Country," and even the Rector of St Paul's reported the "exorbitant price of Labour" in a letter to England. A petition to the Secretary of State from a group of large proprietors noted that "The greatest inconvenience which [we] lye under at present is the scarcity of Labourers," and that the demand had driven wages into the range of 2s. 6d. to 4s. per day for unskilled workers.[10]

The existence of a large body of free blacks, forced into the labour market through their lack of land or other means of support, appeared to offer a solution to the labour shortage. They had no choice but to offer their skills and muscles to the nearest employer, and as prevailing opinion considered them an exploitable labour pool, in desperate supply from any other source, they were in a poor position to bargain for the privileges and bounties freely accorded to white Loyalists. [. . .] White employers came to depend on the cheap services of the Black Loyalists until they formed "in many Parts of this Province, the Principal Sources for Labour and Improvement."[11] Besides providing the only group of inexpensive workers the Black Loyalists, being landless, had to buy their food in the open market and therefore helped to increase the prices that could be charges for the staple items of diet. Their value as a buying force in a slim market was noted in the Preston–Dartmouth area, where their departure in 1792 caused a serious decay in local trade, and in Shelburne, where the threat of a black exodus brought about a decline in the price of potatoes from 1s. 3d. to a mere 2½ d. per bushel.[12] It did not escape official notice that the free blacks, in such circumstances, constituted a valuable addition to the provincial economy.

The intention of the British government had been that no Loyalist should be required to become a wage-labourer in order to survive. Provisions were promised to Loyalists, partly as a reward for their loyalty and a compensation for their losses, but primarily to sustain them during their first few years in Nova Scotia until their new farms should become productive and enable them to support themselves. Official policy was that all Loyalists should receive, free from government, full rations for their first year as refugees, two-thirds rations for the second year, and one-third rations for the third year.[13] In the meantime, it was presumed, they would be clearing their land, planting first crop and awaiting a harvest of their own.

[. . .]

Though the Black Loyalists had been given the same promises of government support, and though their claim for government protection was subsequently confirmed by Whitehall,[14] generally speaking they fared as badly with provisions as they had with land. John Clarkson reported to William Wilberforce in 1791 that he could "bring innumerable witnesses (all of whom were parties concerned) who have not received one year's provisions though they were allowed three . . . nay, many of these have neither received a mouthful of provisions, or so much as an implement of husbandry (though these articles were allowed also)."[15]

When the disbanded Black Pioneers first arrived at Digby in May 1784 Sergeant Thomas Peters was placed in charge and it was to him that government provisions were to be delivered. Digby Commissary Thomas Williams eventually issued 12 096 pounds of flour and 9 352 pounds of pork, representing 80 days' full rations for 160 black adults and 26 children, but this was not done until December 1784 and Williams stated bluntly,

"it is all they are to git for the winter." Though Peters may have taken delivery of another 61 days' worth of rations for distribution among the Pioneers, the flour and pork above-mentioned was sent not to Peters but to the Reverend Edward Brudenell. Brudenell, once described as "a particular friend of the Governor's," was one of those Digby agents later to come under criticism for his inefficiency and favouritism. Rather than distributing the rations directly to the blacks, Brudenell stored them in a cellar belonging to one Richard Hill and gave them out only to those blacks who performed work on the township's roads. Most of the people, with no other means of support, agreed to do so, and 11 980 pounds of the flour and 9 209 pounds of the pork were eventually handed over to them by agent John Donnally. No further supplies were ever issued.[16] The Digby blacks, therefore, received provisions only for a few months, not for the three years they had a right to expect; and for these they were forced to work. This labour requirement was not a condition placed on white Loyalists in Digby in order to receive their government support.

David George was given six months' provision by Governor Parr in July 1784, and if he received no further supplies it may be that he failed to fulfill the labour requirement. In Shelburne all Loyalists, whatever their colour, were expected to perform six days of statute labour annually in exchange for rations that "were issued daily to all and sundry."[17] However, since most of the blacks were already engaged in labour through their companies of Pioneers, and gaining their subsistence thereby, the statutory labour period simply meant that they worked those days without pay. Unlike the whites, they did not receive provisions on the basis of their status as Loyalists plus six days' work. The blacks of Preston were also expected to "Work a Proportion of Time on the Road,"[18] and it may have been in exchange for rations inferior to those granted to whites, as was certainly the case in Halifax. "Codfish, molasses and hard biscuit were the principal items" in the Halifax Loyalist diet, with occasional additions from "a very limited supply of meat." But this was for whites only. "Meal and molasses sustained the negroes."[19] In St John at least some of the blacks evidently were issued with government provisions, though these supplies ceased before 1785.[20]

There were also many disappointed white Loyalists who were inadequately supplied with provisions. They had left most of their possessions in the United States, and some of them owned little else than the clothes on their backs. In 1785 Parr wrote to General Campbell for "any Kind of Clothing or Blankets in the King's Stores" that could be distributed to the destitute Loyalists in his care. Time and again the harassed governor had to request extra supplies, since so many of the people were completely dependent on the Royal bounty. The partial allowances issued after the first year were not enough, as few people were yet in a position to contribute to their own support. Some destitute souls, with no food or clothing but confident in the government's generosity, were actually taking credit with local merchants against the eventual receipt of their provisions. By the time those provisions arrived, the recipients would again be destitute.[21]

In Halifax the earliest Loyalists were housed, in winter, in tents, bark shelters, and public buildings, and fed on the streets. Others had to remain in the cramped holds of their transport vessels, unable to find any room ashore.[22] Every available building in Annapolis, including the church, was used for shelter, yet hundreds of people remained without a roof. Some of the more fortunate families there had "a single apartment with sods, where men, women, children, pigs, fleas, bugs, mosquitoes and other domestic insects, mingle in society."[23] Many of those people, moreover, were not receiving the authorized issue of provisions. [. . .]

Clearly, the blacks had no monopoly on poverty and unfulfilled promises. The numbers of Loyalists and the confusion they caused meant that the limited resources of the province could not be strained to satisfy all. But once again the Black Loyalists fared worst in a generally bad situation. Without farms and without provisions they had no choice but to grasp at any opportunity, however unfair, to keep themselves alive. Though almost all the whites were settled within three years of their arrival or, if not, at least had the option, in many cases, of returning to the United States, the blacks continued to depend on whatever they could earn in a labour market prepared to take advantage of them. No deliberate conspiracy is suggested but it is possible that many agents in charge of land and provisions, aware that black services as labourers might not be available if they were to become self-supporting, were inclined, as Brudenell evidently was, to place them last on the list of recipients in both cases.

One common fate of Black Loyalists with neither land of their own nor government support was that they were "obliged to live upon white-mens property which the Govr has been liberal in distributing—and for cultivating it they receive half the produce so that they are in short in a state of Slavery."[24] Akin indeed to slavery or serfdom, the system of "share-cropping" tied the tenant to the land of another and to the landowner himself. The proprietor could take his percentage from the gross produce of the land, leaving his tenant with responsibility for seeding and cultivating a new crop, and therefore, on the marginal farmlands of Nova Scotia, with no hope of accumulating any savings to begin a farm of his own. John Clarkson wrote of one such tenant that the system had "reduced them to such a state of indigence, that in order to satisfy their landlord and maintain themselves, they have been obliged to sell their property, their clothing, even their very beds."[25] [. . .] Of that majority of Black Loyalists who received no land or did so only in uneconomic quantities, hundreds became tenants in circumstances such as these.

For those incapable or unprepared for life as a tenant farmer, a favourite choice was to become a servant or day labourer in an urban centre, particularly Halifax. Those with enough land on which to build a house, particularly if they were near the sea, would supplement the produce of a small garden with seasonal fishing. This was the case the Preston blacks, who contributed to their region's meagre food by selling fish in the local markets. [. . .]

The ever-present Atlantic, of course, offered other opportunities besides fishing. Birchtowners Luke Jordan, Thomas Godfrey, and John Thomas were among those from their community to become members of ships' crews. Black Anthony sailed out of Liverpool on the merchant ship *Good-fortune* as a crewman at 35s. per month. When the schooner *Pilgrim* was lost only one man aboard, Black Jack, "was qualified to Navigate a vessel." Mulatto Jack Peterson commanded 40s. per month as a ship's cook, a salary matched by ordinary seaman Black Philip. Black Harry, Prince Harris, and Black Boston were evidently of exceptional talents, the latter eventually gaining a sailor's salary of 75s. per month. Small wonder that many graduates of the Shelburne black school "have taken to follow the sea."[26] Perhaps the experience of so many black veterans as pilots during the American war qualified them for equal pay afloat. Certainly sailing was one area of employment into which, short of the press gang, black workers could not be coerced. Joining the ships freely, and their navigational skills in great demand in a maritime province, they were also free to bargain for a just wage.

It was noted previously that large numbers of the former slaves had been trained in specific skills on their home plantations. In Nova Scotia they often had an opportunity of following their own trades. Boston King was a carpenter and boat-builder in Shelburne, one of 21 men in Birchtown who described themselves as carpenters. Twelve more were sawyers, of masons, coopers, and caulkers there were three each, and two blacksmiths, a tailor, a sadler, a baker, a shoemaker, a block-maker, a barber and a weaver. [. . .] If Boston King's experiences were at all typical, however, pay rates on shore fell far short of those within a sailor's grasp, and employment was much less regular. Even a skilled carpenter could expect no more than one shilling for a day's work.[27]

There seems to have been considerable resistance on the part of many white people to any black attempts at equality or self-improvement. When David George first arrived in Shelburne to preach and teach, he "found the White people were against me." He persisted in his efforts "but the White people, the justices, and all, were in an uproar, and said that I might go out into the woods, for I should not stay there." At Tracadie the Acadian Roman Catholics kept both relief and religion from the blacks, and a white from Digby reported haughtily that the blacks there "are so wonderfully proud-spirited, that the females think they must dress, when they attend Church, in quite a superior stile to white Ladies."[28] Evidently Loyalist Nova Scotia had a "place" for black people, and though it was usually an improvement on condition of slavery still it meant that a black's true function was a lowly worker to serve the white establishment. Of course, whole classes of white people were in an equivalent position in Europe and North America, but the blacks of Nova Scotia derived their class from their colour and its associations with slave labour. [. . .] The vulnerable blacks were fair game for any exploitive employer, and to keep them so a society dominated by class interests had to restrict their independence.

White workers were equally resentful of the Black Loyalists' vulnerability, but as is so often the case they blamed not those responsible for the oppression but the blacks who accepted the lower wages and thereby monopolized certain categories of work. On 26 July 1784 Benjamin Marston reported from Shelburne:

Great Riot today. The disbanded soldiers have risen against the Free negroes to drive them out of Town, because they labour cheaper than they—the soldiers. [27 July] Riot continues. The soldiers force the free negroes to quit the town—pulled down about 20 of their houses.[29]

Two days later Simeon Perkins heard the news "that an Extraordinary mob or Riot has happened at Shelburne. Some thousands of Assembled with Clubs and Drove the Negroes out of the Town." To David George's Shelburne home "40 or 50 disbanded soldiers . . . came with the tackle of ships, and turned my dwelling house, and every one their houses, quite over." Later they came and beat him with sticks and drove him into a swamp. Along with others of his colour George sought refuge in Birchtown, but even here they were unsafe. While the force of the riot continued in Shelburne for at least 10 days, incursions into Birchtown were reported for up to one month.[30]

Although they, like other post-war immigrants, were entitled to government support and grants of land, the ordinary soldiers had to wait until their betters were served first. In the meantime, they were forced into the labour market with the blacks, but employers were unwilling to pay standard wages as long as blacks could be had at one-quarter the price. Governor Parr blamed Nova Scotia's first race riot exclusively on the soldiers' delay in obtaining land, and indeed he placed responsibility directly on Surveyor Marston, who was dismissed for not preparing the grants more quickly.[31] Parr was undoubtedly correct in assessing the riot's cause as the soldiers' inability to support themselves. The incident is important not so much as an illustration of racial hostility than as an indication of how serious was the economic predicament of those Nova Scotians who had not received lands on which to support themselves.

Outside Shelburne, and without its black companies and organized labour corps, individual blacks often lacked the opportunity to enter a competitive workforce. For them the choices were between starvation and indentured servitude, sometimes termed apprenticeship. Indenture was an established system in Nova Scotia long before the arrival of free blacks, and conditions among white indentured servants differed little from that of outright black slaves. They were liable to the same harsh punishments, the same pervasive authority of a master, as were blacks, but usually for a limited and specified term. James Walch, a white, the indentured servant to Patrick Wall, was sentenced to ten lashes with the cat-o'-nine tails by Shelburne magistrates merely for applying to be discharged from his master's service. Runaways were sought through advertisements and returned to their masters, though the court seems have presumed the right to punish them, rather, than leaving it to the individual who happened to hold the indenture. There is at least one case on record in Shelburne in which a master, Edward Elliott, was charged with maltreating his apprentice.[32]

Many Black Loyalists had to accept positions as indentured servants since there was often no other way to ensure support. The master might then hire them out, as was done with slaves, and retain his servants' earnings as compensation for the subsistence he guaranteed.[33] For the blacks, indenture or apprenticeship was not infrequently the route to a return to actual slavery. Impoverished black parents, unable to sustain their families, would bind their children out for limited terms. When the indenture had run its course, however, the master might claim the child as his legitimate slave or demand of the parents payment for the child's board, during the period of indenture, before turning him free. Molly Roach met such a demand from a Mr Jenkins of Green Harbour when she went to reclaim her child, and Caesar Smith's daughter Phoebe, put to work by a Mr Newman in the dock yards, was claimed as a slave.[34]

The case of Lydia Jackson is perhaps informative, for it was recorded as a typical example of the experience of many unfortunate Black Loyalists. Lydia was living in great distress in Manchester when Henry Hedley invited her to work for him. After several days he demanded payment for her board or, as an alternative, her indenture to him for seven years. Though Lydia refused the seven-year term she was eventually persuaded to place her mark on an agreement for a one-year term. Hedley, however, took advantage of her illiteracy to substitute a term of 39 years in the articles of indenture. She was then sold for £20 to a Dr Bulman of Lunenburg who, with his wife, beat her with fire tongs and kicked her in the stomach, though Lydia was then eight months pregnant. A court case on her behalf, brought by a Lunenburg attorney; was dismissed by the magistrates. After three years with Bulman Lydia learned of his intention to sell her as a slave in the West Indies. To avoid this fate was worth the risk of capture and punishment as an escapee, so she left Bulman's farm and fled to Halifax. John Clarkson, the passionate Abolitionist who interviewed Lydia Jackson, said he had met "many others of a similar nature," and cited five by name.[35]

Though it evidently happened on occasion, an indentured servant could not legally be sold to anyone outside Nova Scotia. The Shelburne court ordered the cancellation of the indenture of Robert Conner when his master, John Harris, was apprehended in an attempt to sell his black servant to a non-resident. The courts took a similar stand when whites detained or attempted to sell black children without holding the properly authorized documents of indenture. Timothy Mahan tried to sell a boy he claimed had been given him by the boy's parents, but the magistrates declared that this did not constitute an indenture. James Cox was ordered to set a boy at liberty whom he claimed, but could not prove, to be legally indentured.[36]

These attempts to enslave free blacks were stopped by the authorities, but the fact that attempts were made at all may be taken as an indication of the insecurity in which the Black Loyalists lived. In fact, the fear of being returned to slavery was a prominent reason offered by numerous people anxious to leave Nova Scotia in 1791. Apprenticeship was only one threat. Direct kidnapping for sale in the United States or the West Indies was another. Shelburne was particularly vulnerable, and many blacks were seized there illegally and carried off as slaves.[37] In 1789 this situation drew the attention of the Legislative Assembly where, in a draft bill, reference was made to the need to prevent the practice of carrying free blacks "out of the Province, by force and Strategm, for the scandalous purpose of making property of them in the West Indies contrary to their will and consent."[38]

Above all, there remained the threat of being claimed, in the courts and with the full sanction of the law, as a legal slave. Four Black Loyalists, all of them with war service, were claimed by Captain Hamilton on the grounds that he had owned them years before in North Carolina. In Halifax Michael Wallace granted Hamilton a warrant to seize the four in question and sell them in the Bahamas. Fortunately, their ship put in to Shelburne, where they managed to have word carried to the court that they were being held without a hearing. Presiding judge Isaac Wilkins decided that Hamilton's claim was insufficient, and the blacks were set free. Black Loyalists Pero and Tom were claimed by Joseph Robins, and though they were not freed at least Robins was required to bring further proof, within one year, of his ownership. Mary Postell was brought to court and claimed, together with her children, by Jesse Gray. While Black Loyalists Scipio and Dinah Wearing were in court testifying in Mary's behalf, their home was set on fire and one of their children killed. Mary had been the slave of a rebel officer and still had General Birch's Certificate in her possession, but again the court granted the alleged master one year to prove his ownership.[39] These people had been free for 10 or more years and could produce documents and witnesses in their own support, but this was not automatically accepted by the law as constituting free status. If a master could prove a prior claim, of however long standing, the black was liable to be returned to slavery.

Such were the sufferings, insecurity, and injustice inflicted upon Black Loyalists by their fellow-refugees in the land of their new liberty. As conditions in Nova Scotia became worse during the late 1780s, and all sorts and conditions of men were brought low by famine and disease, the blacks' position fell correspondingly lower. Hailed as an example of what could be achieved by good and faithful citizens under properly constituted authority, the province failed to develop as quickly or to become as prosperous as most people had expected in 1783. Roads remained unmade and farms uncleared, and trade was not diverted to Halifax and Shelburne in the volume anticipated. In May 1788 the province was still not producing its own food, and a law had to be passed permitting the importation of essential supplies such as food, livestock, and lumber, from the United States.

[. . .]

Shelburne, meanwhile, was suffering unique problems of its own. [. . .] In a city of traders, there was no one with whom to trade. Business stagnated, resulting in unemployment and removal to areas with a healthier economy. From its heyday during the period 1784 to 1787, when its population reached 10 000 and it was not only the largest British American city but the fourth largest city anywhere in North America, Shelburne experienced a sharp decline. [. . .]

The conditions of famine in 1789 and the decline of Shelburne naturally struck hardest at the black people of the district. Unemployment wiped out the black companies of Birchtown. Many were forced to indenture their families and some even sold themselves as slaves. Blacks died of starvation and exposure after parting with all their belongings in exchange for temporary nourishment.

Birchtown, like Shelburne, lost some of its most ambitious residents as they left in search of employment and food. Always at a bare subsistence wage, the black labourers had no savings or property to cushion their fall.[40] Only those with farms or with jobs in the fisheries, and of course the indentured servants and share-croppers, were able to make a meagre living in Shelburne County. Those who drifted to Halifax met conditions scarcely better. The shortage of food and retarded trade affected the capital city too, and few jobs were available. Soon it became impossible for a Halifax resident to walk the streets without being approached by a black beggar.[41] No part of Nova Scotia remained unaffected. [. . .]

But for the charity of their white neighbours and certain well-wishers in England, many more blacks would have died of starvation or exposure during those harrowing years. [. . .]

Public support was also available to paupers in Nova Scotia, though not always generously. In 1789 the people of Halifax preferred to contribute the passage money for 20 white paupers to return to England, rather than maintain them on relief in Nova Scotia. Various acts were passed by the Assembly during the 1780s and 90s to provide for the support of the poor and the maintenance of a poor house, and commissioners and overseers were appointed to ensure that the allocated budget was wisely spent. [. . .]

Black paupers were often included on the relief rolls. Sometimes black vagrants in Shelburne were sent by the court to Birchtown, there to subsist on whatever charity that impoverished community might be able to afford them. A proclamation of that court in 1786 ordered the overseers to be more attendant to the binding out of poor black children, though some black adults appear to have been allowed to remain free while on relief. It was possible for citizens to take black paupers from the poor house as indentured servants, if they reimbursed the overseers for their past support by the public.[42] [. . .]

The life of the Black Loyalist was filled with fear, for his continued freedom, for his subsistence, and for his peace from the interference of discriminatory acts by white individuals and officials. A last desperate move on the part of Shelburne merchants to sustain their economy by making their city a free port for trade with the United States, brought the blacks' fear to a climax in that they expected their former American masters would then be able to enter British territory and reclaim them as slaves.[43] Seldom was it possible, from his very arrival in Nova Scotia, for a Black Loyalist to feel secure in the freedoms and privileges of a British subject.

Either as veterans or as Loyalists, the free blacks had a right to expect treatment as full citizens. They had been promised as much, and these promises were reinforced by statements of officials in London and Halifax.[44] On the one hand, they were required to perform the duties of citizenship, on the other, their rights fell short of equality. Clarkson recorded that the blacks were required to pay taxes, and for Sydney County at least the poll tax returns indicate that some of them did so. A black militia company was formed in Halifax which Governor Wentworth described as "an able, daring, and faithful Body of Men," and he also praised the Black Pioneers attached to the Royal Nova Scotia Regiment. The Digby militia had its black company as well, "of good able Stature and Countenance as any other Men."[45]

While fulfilling these responsibilities, the blacks were "entirely deprived of the privileges of British subjects, particularly trial by jury."[46] From New Brunswick Governor Thomas Carleton gave the opinion that the blacks, "having come within the British Lines with no other View than to escape from the service of their American masters, cannot be considered as intituled to claim anything from Government further than personal protection and freedom from servitude" and therefore "they have not been admitted to vote in Elections for Representatives the General Assembly."[47] In addition to their lack of

the vote and trial, the blacks often suffered restrictions on their private lives as well. In Shelburne hand bills were published by the magistrates "forbidding Negro Dances, and Negro Frolicks in this Town." When this by-law was contravened the offending blacks were charged with "Riotous behaviour" and sent to the house of correction. A second offence might mean being "ordered out of their home for keeping a disorderly house."[48]

When a black was brought before the court for breaking a law, the treatment he received at the hands of the justices was not always equal to that for whites convicted of the same crime. In Guysborough County (Lower Sydney County) between 11 October 1785 and 8 February 1791 no white suffered corporal punishment. Theft slander, assault, "keeping a house of ill fame," even riot, were punished by fines. But when a Black Loyalist woman, Sarah Ringwood, stole some butter, she was "ordered for Punishment to receive Thirty nine stripes on her naked back, at the Public Whipping Post in Manchester." Another black woman, Eleonar Bourke, received the same punishment plus a week's imprisonment "for being a Vagrant, Idle, Disorderly Person." This was during the famine of 1789. In one year, four black men were whipped for stealing food, and another black woman "for abusive, Lewd and Indecent behaviour."[49]

The Shelburne court records bear cruel testimony to the harsh inhumanity of the late eighteenth century. Prince Frederick received 78 lashes and a month's hard labour for stealing a pair of shoes, Daniel Anderson 39 lashes and John Russel 100 lashes for thefts valued at one shilling each. One black woman named Dianna, convicted on two counts of petty larceny, suffered the incredible sentence of "Two hundred lashes at the Cart's Tail, next Saturday, at 12 o'clock, at noon, for the first Offense, and One hundred and fifty lashes on the following Saturday, at the Cart's Tail, for the second offense." The unfortunate Alicia Wiggins received 39 lashes in April 1792 for theft, and in July, for a second offence involving 3s. 11d. worth of used clothing, she was sentenced to be hanged. Alicia pleaded a stay of execution on the grounds of pregnancy but "twelve Matrons or discreet women," on examining her, found that she was "not four months gone with child," so she was executed as ordered. All these sentences were inflicted on black people. As in Guysborough County, Shelburne whites were often, though not always, fined for similar offences. [. . .][50] In Halifax County punishments generally were milder, and even blacks were allowed to pay fines for their misdemeanours. [. . .][51]

Without doubt the last two decades of the eighteenth century represent a heartless and difficult period in the history of Nova Scotia. No man or woman of low station could avoid the constant threat of physical suffering. It also appears quite evident that for black Nova Scotians, as a group, the threat was greater and more frequently realized than for any others. In a slave society they took their status not from the body of Loyalists, to which they belonged, but from the mass of slaves whose African race they shared. In many ways their life as freemen was not altogether different from the life of slavery that they had left behind. As share-croppers, indentured servants, or subsistence day-labourers they were still completely dependent upon white people and subject to the whims and prejudices of their white employers. The law deemed them equal privileges and services yet expected as much of them as of any other resident, and when they strayed, they were corrected with greater severity. They were regarded as little more than physical beings, whose function was to fill the lowest levels of the labour force.

The Black Loyalists faced, with other Loyalists, all the hardships of a pioneering situation in a new country. They were also pioneering in a sense unique to themselves. The vast majority of them had been born and raised in slavery, a condition which sapped their initiative, resourcefulness, and self-reliance. An attitude of dependence had developed in these people, long accustomed to direction in labour and sustenance in living. Now they were expected to find some inner spring of resourcefulness within themselves, and to fend for themselves in a climate calling for expensive shelter and with a scarcity of food. More than any other group of immigrants the blacks needed special assistance during a period of transition for their new lives as free and self-supporting citizens. Instead, that same "slave mentality" was perpetuated and reinforced by their experiences in Nova Scotia. They continued to feel dependent on whites, in the economic sphere, neither encouraged nor capable to strike out on their own.

NOTES

1. T. Watson Smith, "The Slave in Canada," *Collections of the Nova Scotia Historical Society* 10 (1898): 9; T. Akins, "History of Halifax City," *Collections of the Nova Scotia Historical Society* 8 (1895): Appendix F, p. 246, "List of Families, original settlers, 1749."

2. Charlotte Isabella Perkins, *The Romance of Old Annapolis Royal* (Annapolis, 1934), 108; Public Archives of Nova Scotia (PANS), vol. 443, "A General Return of the Several T-ownships in the Province of Nova Scotia for the first day of January 1767" and "Poll Tax and Census Rolls, 1767–1794"; W.R. Riddell, "The Slave in Canada," *Journal of Negro History* V, 3 (July 1920): 362.

3. Smith, "The Slave in Canada," 23, 32.

4. J. Plimsoll Edwards, "The Shelburne That Was and Is Not," *Dalhousie Review* (April 1922): 132; C.B. Fergusson (ed.), *The Diary of Simeon Perkins*, vol. III, 1790–96 (Toronto, 1961), pp. 50, 196, 394; Isaiah W. Wilson, *A Geography and History of the County of Digby, Nova Scotia* (New Haven and Montreal, 1971), 74; C.W. Vernon, *Bicentenary Sketches and Early Days of the Church in Nova Scotia* (Halifax, 1910), 237.

5. Sir Adams Archibald, "Life of Sir John Wentworth, Governor of Nova Scotia 1792–1808," *Collection of the Nova Scotia Historical Society* XX (1921): 53, letter of John Wentworth, 24 February 1784.

6. PANS, Family Papers. Clarkson, Clarkson's Mission to America, p. 230, diary entry for 7 December 1791; *An Account of the Designs of the Associates of the late Dr Bray, with an Abstract of their Proceedings, Abstract for 1787*, p. 31; Simeon Perkins, *Diary of Simeon Perkins*, eds H.A. Innis, D.C. Harvey, and C.B. Fergusson (Toronto, 1948–67, 4 vols), vol. III, p. 85.

7. Riddell, "The Slave in Canada," pp. 367–9; I. Allen Jack, "The Loyalists and Slavery in New Brunswick," *Transactions of the Society of Canada* (2nd Series), IV (1898): section II, pp. 142, 149–50; PANS, Shelburne Records, Early Wills 1784–92, will of Thomas Robinson, 10 August 1787; New Brunswick Museum (NBM), Hazen Collection, Shelf 88, Box 2, Folder I, "Schedule of Goods and Chattels" accompanying will dated 2 May 1791; NBM, Jarvis Papers, Shelf 86, Box 21, Items 19 and 20, sale certificates; Public Archives of Canada (PAC), MG 23 D1, Lawrence Collection, vol. 19, Business Papers, memo of 9 February 1805; PANS, Marriage Bonds, 1763–99, 20 May 1794.

8. PANS, Shelburne Records, General Sessions, 5 July 1791.

9. For example, *Royal Gazette and Nova Scotia Advertiser,* 7 September 1790, 1 March, 7 June, 5 July, 19 and 22 November 1791, 10 and 17 January, 19 May 1792.

10. Public Records Office (PRO), CO 217/68, Howe to Quarrell, 9 August 1797; PANS vol. 47, doc. 51, Parr to Sydney, 17 October 1785; Society for the Propagation of the Gospel (SPG), Dr Bray's Associates' Minute Books, vol. III, 1768–1808, 3 February 1785, quoting Breynton to Associates, 15 November 1784; PRO, CO 217/64, Proprietors of Lands to Henry Dundas, 16 May 1793.

11. PRO, CO 217/68, Howe to Quarrell, 9 August 1797.

12. PANS, Bishop Charles Inglis, Letters, 1791–99, number 3, p. 58, memo to the Archbishop of Canterbury, 3 May 1794; Clarkson's Mission, p. 109, letter to Henry Thornton, 6 November 1791.

13. PANS, vol. 366, doc. 33, George Rose to Haldimand, 17 March 1784.

14. PANS, vol. 359, doc. 65, "The Humble Petition of the Black Loyalists," 21 August 1784; PANS, vol. 33, doc. 12, Sydney to Parr, 5 October 1784; Clarkson's Mission, pp. 98–100, diary entry for 31 October 1791.

15. Ibid., p. 188, Clarkson to Wilberforce, 27 November 1791.

16. PRO, CO 217/63, Bulkeley to Dundas, 19 March 1792, enclosure, "Enquiry into the Complaint of Thomas Peters, a Black Man," evidence given before the enquiry by Thomas Peters, 16 and 19 November 1791; Appendix E, Thomas Williams to the Secretary to Dr Brudenell, 11 December 1784; Appendix G, "State of the Provisions sent the Rev. Mr Brudenell for the use of the Blacks at Digby"; PANS, vol. 394, doc. 52, Morris to Major Studholme, 20 August 1783.

17. David George, "An Account of the Life of Mr. David George (as told to Brother John Rippon)," *Baptist Annual Register,* vol. I (1790–3), 478; PANS, Shelburne Records Special Sessions, 6 August 1787 and 23 September 1789; Edwards, "The Shelburne that Was," p. 189.

18. PANS, Halifax County Quarter Sessions, 1766–1801, 7 June 1791.

19. James S. MacDonald, "Memoir of Governor John Parr," *Collections of the Nova Scotia Historical Society* XIV (1910): 54.

20. Public Archives of New Brunswick (PANB), Colonial Correspondence, New Brunswick, III, Carleton to Dundas, 13 December 1791.

21. PANS, vol. 137, Parr to Campbell, April 1785, Parr to Commodore Sawyer, 29 June 1785, Parr to Campbell, 18 and 30 November 1785; PANS, vol. 367½, doc. 34, Stephen Tuttle to Major Matthews, 26 April 1784.

22. James S. MacDonald, "Memoir of Governor John Parr," *Collections of the Nova Scotia Historical Society* (1910), 47, 52, 55, 56.

23. SPG Journal, vol. 23, p. 284, Jacob Bailey to Society, November 1783; Vernon, *Bicentenary Sketches,* p. 145, quoting Jacob Bailey. See also Duncan Campbell, *Nova Scotia in its Historical, Mercantile and Industrial Relations* (Montreal, 1873), 165–71.

24. British Museum (BM), Add. Ms. 41262B, Clarkson Papers, II, fol. 8.

25. Clarkson's Mission, pp. 66–7, diary entry for 22 October 1791.

26. PRO, CO 217/63, "List of the Blacks of Birch Town"; *Diary of Simeon Perkins,* III, pp. 107, 116, 171, 285; *Diary of Simeon Perkins,* IV, pp. 213, 233, 235, 265; Bray Minutes, III, 1 November 1802, Rowland to Associates, 3 May 1802.

27. Boston King, "Memoirs of the Life of Boston King, a Black Preacher, Written by Himself, During his Residence at Kingswood-School," *Arminian Magazine* XXI (March, April, May,

June 1798): 210; PRO, CO 217/63, "List of the Blacks of Birch Town."

28. David George, "Life," p. 478; Rawlyk, "The Guysborough Negroes: A Study in Isolation," *Dalhousie Review* (Spring 1968): 26–7; SPG, Bray Associates, Canadian Papers, Elkana Morton to Associates, 20 June 1817.

29. W.O. Raymond, "The Founding of Shelburne and Early Miramichi, Marston's Diary," *Collections of the New Brunswick Historical Society*, vol. III (1907), 265.

30. *Diary of Simeon Perkins,* II, p. 238; Raymond, "Marston's Diary," p. 265; David George, "Life," pp. 479–80; PANS, Shelburne Records, General Sessions, 21 August 1784.

31. PANS, vol. 47, doc. 29, Parr to Sydney, 6 September 1784.

32. PANS, Shelburne Records, Special Sessions, 8 September 1785, General Sessions, 12 April 1786, 5 April 1791.

33. Cf. *Diary of Simeon Perkins*, II, pp. 85–7.

34. Clarkson Papers, II, fols. 15 and 19.

35. Clarkson's Mission, pp. 197–201, diary entry for 30 November 1791.

36. PANS, Shelburne Records, General Sessions, 1, 2 and 3 November 1791.

37. Clarkson Papers, II, fol. 8, "Reasons given by the free Blacks for wishing to leave Nova Scotia," and fol. 22.

38. PANS, Unpassed Bills, 1789.

39. PANS, Shelburne Records, Special Sessions, 5 August 1785, General Sessions, 12 April 1786, 5 April, 8, 11 and 19 July 1791. See also the cases of "a Negro wench Molly," 12 April 1786, and "James Singletory, his wife and child," Special Sessions, 25 August 1785.

40. Boston King, "Memoirs," pp. 209–10; SPG, Bray Associates, Canadian Papers, Blucke to Associates, 22 December 1787.

41. Clarkson's Mission, pp. 294–5, diary entry for 27 December 1791; BM, Add. Ms. 41262A

42. PANS, Shelburne Records, Special Sessions, 25 August 1785, General Sessions, 10 April 1786, 6 May 1788, 17 July 1793. See also NBM, Simonds, Hazen and White Papers, Items 238, 239 and 241, indentures of black children by the Overseers of the Poor, St John, 1787.

43. Clarkson's Mission, pp. 94–5, diary entry for 29 October 1791.

44. PANS, vol. 33, doc; 12, Sydney to Parr, 5 October 1784; PANS, Minutes of the Legislative Council, 1782–90, 9 October 1783.

45. Clarkson Papers, II, fols 15 and 21; PANS vol. 444½, Poll Tax Returns, Sydney County, 1791 and 1793; Parlimentary Papers (PP) 1796–97, vol. 102, no. 889, Wentworth to Portland, 29 October 1796.

46. Selina Thompson, "The Nova Scotians," letter number 3, *The Harbinger,* May 1812; PRO General Correspondence, America, FO 4/1, fols. 419–20, Thomas Peters to Lord Grenville, n.d. (received 26 December 1790).

47. PANB, Colonial Correspondence, New Brunswick, III, Carleton to Dundas, 13 December 1791.

48. PANS, Shelburne Records, Special Sessions, 12 and 19 May 1785, General Sessions, 3 July 1799.

49. PANS, Quarter Sessions, Guysborough County, 1785–1800, 10 October. 1787, 12 August 1789, 8 February, II and 13 August, 3 November 1791.

50. PANS, Shelburne Records, Special Sessions, 24 February, 9 June 1785, General Sessions, 3 November 1784, 14 April 1789, 12 April 1792; White Collection, VI, doc. 553, "Proceedings of the Court of Oyer and Terminer," Shelburne, 3 July 1792.

51. PANS, Halifax County Quarter Sessions, 1755–1801; MacDonald, "Memoir of Governor John Parr," p. 64.

4   From Karim M. Tiro, "Now You See It, Now You Don't: The War of 1812 in Canada and the United States in 2012," *Public Historian* 35, no. 1 (Feb. 2013): 89–97.

For public historians, the War of 1812 is a tough row to hoe. Public interest in the war is limited. The war's causes and effects are generally regarded as obscure, especially in the United States. Military heroics can always be celebrated, but both sides fumbled the fighting. The centerpiece of the Canadian War Museum's fine "Four Wars of 1812" exhibit is British general Isaac Brock's coat—a garment remarkable mostly for the clean hole made by the ball that killed Brock as he rather foolishly led his men before the enemy. The U.S. can celebrate Andrew Jackson's victory at New Orleans, but American exultation is tempered by the fact that the battle happened after the peace treaty had been signed. Even the war's name is problematic, since it fails to reflect the conflict's three-year duration. [. . .]

Although it was to be expected that commemorations would be more robust in Canada than in the United States, the extent of the differential is nevertheless surprising. In Canada, the bicentennial has been pushed so hard by the federal government as to become a minor point of controversy.[1] Meanwhile, in the United States—Baltimore excepted—you could be excused for not noticing the bicentennial at all. It is worthwhile to stop and consider the causes for this disparity, since they reflect larger issues in public history, in particular the role of government in commemoration and the tremendous importance of national grand narratives to popular historical consciousness.

The War of 1812 captures Canadians' attention more readily than it does Americans'. It always has. For one thing, the war was closer to home, at least for those in Ontario. Land battles were fought primarily on the Canadian side of the St Lawrence–Great Lakes corridor, and therefore war sites remain more proximate to Canadian population centres than American ones. Furthermore, Canadian history lacks a dramatic and unambiguous founding conflict like the American Revolution, or a destructive one on home territory. If not for the War of 1812, what would Canadian re-enactors, deprived of the rich fodder of the U.S. Civil War, do on the weekend? These are the "natural" reasons for the durability of the War of 1812 in Canadian memory.

However, the War of 1812 owes its relatively high profile to other-than-natural causes as well. From the outset, the Britons and descendants of American loyalists who comprised the provincial elite of Upper Canada seized on the American invasion of 1812 to legitimate their tight control over political, religious, and educational institutions. Revising their image from that of virtuous losers of the American Revolution to victorious defenders of homeland and Empire, these elites articulated a paternalistic and conservative cultural ideal. The political elite's power and membership did not go uncontested, so they celebrated fealty to a hierarchical social order, with the Crown at the apex, all the more fiercely. The War of 1812 occupied a prominent place in didactic literature, where the repulse of a menacing and undisciplined invasion was interpreted as an authentic, affirmative expression of loyalty to the Crown. This story line exaggerated the zeal, effectiveness, and unity of the colonists and their Indian allies, but its appeal was undeniable to elites wishing to control a potentially fractious society of anglophones, francophones, and Native peoples. When the nation was created by Confederation in 1867, the War of 1812 offered an older and more exciting origin story than one about several conferences and an act of the British Parliament.

Thus, the nationalist narrative of the War of 1812 has long been a potent force in Canadian culture. Canadian academic historians remain keenly aware of its radioactive nature, even if its half-life had passed by the 1960s. Unwilling to reify the mythic narrative, they have accordingly kept a safe distance from the bicentennial. The prevailing scholarly view is that reading the Canadian nation back into the war is anachronistic, and they point out that colonists and Indians could not really have been "fighting for Canada" when Canada did not exist yet. [. . .]

By contrast, the Canadian federal government has recognized the power of the War of 1812, harnessed it, and is trying to see how far it can go. To ensure a vigorous commem-oration, the government has spent nearly $50 million Canadian. These funds have been spent on historic sites, re-enactments, and even television advertisements and movie trailers. Recovering the older concep-tion of Canadian nationalism has great ap-peal to Conservative Party Prime Minister Stephen Harper, as it is deeply entwined with his vision of a more muscular Canada. [. . .]

For the government, the nation's more recent preoccupation with securing personal and minority rights has obscured Canada's military heritage and British identity, and the War of 1812 can help recover them. Even before the bicentennial, the government re-instituted the term "Royal" in the names of all of the nation's armed forces, and hung portraits of the Queen in all consulates and embassies. Imperial pride is an especially im-portant component of the bicentennial com-memoration because it helps counterbalance the anti-Americanism latent in the story. An-ti-Americanism is problematic for the Con-servatives, not just because the United States is by far Canada's largest trading partner, but because they admire the United States for its religiosity, its laissez-faire economic policies, and relative lack of regulation and bureaucracy.

All this has not passed without contro-versy. The bicentennial has been roundly criticized as militaristic, jingoistic, and a shameless subordination of history to politi-cal purposes. The government's emphasis on austerity in public finances has only made its generosity toward War of 1812 sites and ac-tivities stand out in greater relief. [. . .]

French Canadians in particular actively snub the commemoration. Whatever pleasure the Québécois might derive from recalling their ancestors having fought off an invasion by one group of English speakers is obviated by the deep British-imperial stamp on the memory of the war. As such, it activates la-tent resentment over centuries of British and Anglo-Canadian domination, as expressed

pithily in the motto of the province's licence plates: "Je me souviens" ("I remember"). [. . .]

Ultimately, however, in public history as in entertainment, there is no such thing as bad publicity. Prior to the bicentennial, the level of Canadian public awareness of the war had plenty of room to grow, especially among young people, according to a 2009 poll.[2] Even if the war has entered people's consciousness through the back door of satire or contro-versy, it has arrived nevertheless. If retaken today, that poll would doubtless register sig-nificantly higher levels of War of 1812 aware-ness. The government investments and the attention they have received have generated strong attendance at War of 1812 events, as well as increased visits to war sites. More-over, the public investment in the physical rehabilitation of numerous sites will secure their place as tourist attractions for several generations. Indeed, sites on both sides of the border, such as Fort Erie in Ontario and Fort Niagara in New York, are in respectable con-dition today because of Depression Era gov-ernment make-work restoration projects. In terms of developing popular historical aware-ness, investments in bricks and mortar still yield high dividends when the location is in a densely populated area or near other attrac-tions like Niagara Falls.[3]

A good place to start considering the bicentennial in the U.S. is Karl Marx's fa-mous observation that history repeats itself: the first time as tragedy, the second time as farce. But what if it was a farce the first time around? In 1812, the United States de-clared war with few resources and even less forethought. Although the war had been declared by the United States, on the Great Lakes, word reached British commanders first, enabling them to seize American goods and persons. At Detroit, Americans crossed into British territory, only to retreat and then surrender. Two hundred years later, the U.S. commemorative effort channels that day-late-and-a-dollar-short spirit. Citing a poor economy, the state of New York declined to create a commemoration-planning body until the bicentennial year had begun. In similar fashion, the National Parks Service installed a coordinator for the bicentennial only in April 2012. Needless to say, this indifference has compromised public historians' ability to take advantage of the slender window of opportunity provided by the bicentennial to raise the war's profile. Only those states, localities, and institutions connected to specific wartime events have taken care to commemorate the conflict at all. As a small state, Maryland has been able to throw itself in wholeheartedly, but New York has been slow to pay attention to a war that did not have a clear and lasting impact on its most populous areas.

[. . .]

Understandably, every state or institution has interpreted the war in terms of its involvement. This generally restricts the war's appeal to particular places, even within particular states, and does little to render the memory of a neglected war more coherent. Without an appreciation of the war's significance, state- or service-level history remains parochial. If the story in Canada is overdetermined, America's problem is the opposite: credible explanations for the war's outbreak and effects are lacking. Why is this the case?

The War of 1812's relation to America's national grand narrative is problematic. The conflict mostly involved the United States making war on border communities in Upper Canada, communities that bore no responsibility for the British violations of American sovereignty on the high seas. Many Americans looked forward to annexing whatever territory was seized. Thus, the war cannot rest comfortably within the story of a nation born of resistance to imperialism. Of course, that doesn't mean that it has not been interpreted this way. Because the war's principal foe was the familiar British Empire, Americans routinely blur it with the American Revolution. The three decades separating the two conflicts are minimized through the use of metaphors like "infant" and "adolescent" to describe the United States and underscore its innocence. The War of 1812 is often referred to as "America's Second War of Independence"—a phrase that has even apparently been trademarked by the Virginia bicentennial commission. Sequels being generally inferior to the originals, the best course of action is to ignore them. That's what usually happens.

The facts, when examined closely, are problematic. If the war's principal cause was the impressment of American sailors into the Royal Navy, as standard narratives suggest, one would expect those regions whose sons were most vulnerable to conscription to be the most supportive. However, precisely the opposite was true: It was Kentucky that led the charge, and New England opposed it bitterly. Dissenters asked why, if violations of national honor demanded a response, French depredations on American ships were not also taken up as a *casus belli*. And while the question of impressment was left unresolved by the Treaty of Ghent, that treaty did something else: It paved the way for the dispossession of Indians all along the western frontier. Although the war is commonly judged to have availed nothing, the fact remains that the U.S. added the states of Indiana, Alabama, Illinois, and Mississippi before the decade was over. Not coincidentally, if any conflict gives the War of 1812 a run for its money for the title of "a forgotten war," it is the nation's other war that caused its territory to grow dramatically: the Mexican War.

Thus, closer examination has been avoided, and the bicentennial silence is almost deafening. In 1812, no one cried more loudly for war than Henry Clay, the Speaker of the House from Kentucky. However, public tours of Clay's estate, Ashland, make no mention of his important role in getting the United States into its first official war. Some acknowledgment of his role in negotiating the Treaty of Ghent is planned for 2014. A focus on the treaty could identify it as critical moment in the development of the ethos of Manifest Destiny. Alternatively, it could simply bury Clay's stated desire to seize Canada under his later diplomatic efforts.

Because the facts of the War of 1812 resist easy assimilation into an accepted national story, they—and the war more generally—have been mostly rejected. What survive are merely random fragments—Old Ironsides, the Star-Spangled Banner—that can be made to fit and that permit the nation to take account of the conflict in a *pro forma* way. Thus, if public historians in the United States want their interpretations to gain traction with their audiences, they must engage the grand narrative, and the more explicitly the better. Public historians could begin by placing the American interpretation in dialogue with its Canadian counterpart. Both American and Canadian public historians have avoided overt chauvinism, and have consciously sought to include words expressing the motivations and sentiments of other groups. Nevertheless, they simultaneously undermine that balance by framing the conflict in David-and-Goliath terms—with opposite assessments of who was David and who was Goliath. For the Americans, it was the tale of a weak nation taking on a powerful empire; for the Canadians, it was 300 000 colonists facing invasion by a nation of seven million while their faraway British guardians were keeping the world safe from Napoleon. At Montpelier, in Virginia, the opening panel of a War of 1812 exhibit introduces the war with the subheading, "The Last Resort." At Fort George, in Ontario, the war is introduced as a war of choice, with the "United States attempting to expand its territory and strengthen its economy"; it was the work of "expansionists" who were "enflamed by *perceived* British abuses at sea" [italics mine].

This need to consider contrasting narratives applies principally to Americans. The American viewpoint is represented in the aforementioned exhibit at the Canadian War Museum and receives at least partial consideration at most other sites. The fact is that Canadians are generally aware of American views on just about everything. While the asymmetry might be attributable to the relative size of the two nations, I would argue it is, in fact, rooted in the events of 1812. Shortly after the declaration of war, citizens of Fairfield, Ohio, toasted "the Canadas." They looked forward to the people there "learn[ing] to feel the glow and animating spirit of patriotism."[4] For these Ohioans, and all Americans motivated by a sense of national mission to spread republicanism, the War of 1812 turned out to be an embarrassing failure. From that point onward, sustaining their faith in the self-evident superiority and exportability of American institutions required Americans to forget the entire episode and ignore British North America's continued existence to the greatest extent possible. (They succeeded.) In other words, from the War of 1812 to the present, Canada has not been simply overlooked; it has been repressed. Americans today have a favourable opinion of Canada, but they minimize the cultural differences between the two nations, and are always just a little surprised by its being there.[5]

Public historians in both the United States and Canada should tell a much wider range of stories than they have thus far. Without a doubt, revisiting military actions and strategies remains the first business of war commemoration. However, too much of the interpretation ends there. The recent academic literature offers some fresh avenues of interpretation. Neither the political nor military narratives capture the cross-border ties of blood and friendship that were so traumatically strained by the war, as described in Taylor's *Civil War of 1812*. Taking note of Native contributions on the battlefield is important, but so too is taking stock of what happened to Natives afterwards. As historian Francis Paul Prucha observed, "The War of 1812 was a watershed in the history of treaty making with the Indians."[6] American sites tend to ignore the connection of the war to post-war expansion. For their part, Canadians romanticize the entire relationship with Natives. The depiction of Brock and Tecumseh is at times reminiscent of a buddy film, and there is little acknowledgment of the fact that after the war Native peoples in Canada were redefined as wards and their land rights violated. Finally, in the United States, popular fixation with the national anthem is understandable. However, the real contribution of War of 1812 song, prose, caricature, and poetry was its remarkable ability to recast the nation's wartime bumbling into something that could be supported and even celebrated, a process historian Nicole Eustace has described as "a kind of emotional alchemy."[7]

The War of 1812 was ushered in by confident predictions, most notably Thomas Jefferson's proclamation that the conquest of Canada was "a mere matter of marching." Having set the bar sufficiently low, I will venture my own predictions. On the Canadian side, the novelty of the war will give way to a certain tedium, as the heroes are killed off—Brock was already dead in 1812, and

Tecumseh was killed in 1813—and the battles became simultaneously more horrific and less decisive. Nevertheless, the commemoration effort will have raised national consciousness of the war, which will be consolidated later in the decade with the World War I centennial, the Confederation sesquicentennial, and maintained over the longer term by investments in public history infrastructure.

American commemorations will spike in 2014, for the bicentennials of the attack on Baltimore, the burning of Washington, the Treaty of Ghent and, early in 2015, the Battle of New Orleans. Americans will thus bask in the warm and righteous glow of being both victim and victor, conveniently forgetting everything that came before or after. Thus contained, the war will quickly find its way back on to a high shelf. Historian G. Kurt Piehler's observation that, "Perhaps more than any other conflict in American history, the War of 1812 demonstrated the selective nature of public memory," will probably remain as true as when he wrote it in 1995.[8]

NOTES

1. I discussed early Canadian events in "Are We Having Fun Yet? Canadians Commemorate the War of 1812," *Common-Place* 12, no. 4 (July, 2012). http://www.common-place.org/vol-12/no-04/forum/tiro.shtml.

2. Randy Boswell, "Victory in War of 1812 Still Debatable," *Edmonton Journal*, Dec. 10, 2009.

3. On the long association of the War of 1812 with tourism in the Niagara Falls region, see Thomas A. Chambers, *Memories of War: Visiting Battlegrounds and Bonefields in the Early American Republic* (Ithaca, NY: Cornell University Press, 2012), ch. 5. See also Timothy S. Forest, "Epic Triumph, Epic Embarrassment, or Both? Commemorations of the War of 1812

Today in the Niagara Region," *Ontario History* 104, no. 1 (Spring 2012): 96–122.

4. *Liberty Hall* (Cincinnati, Ohio), July 11, 1812.

5. I suspect some Canadian has already noted the above but, as an American, I am unaware of it.

6. Francis Paul Prucha, *American Indian Treaties: The History of a Political Anomaly* (Berkeley, CA: University of California Press, 1994), 129.

7. Carl Benn, *The Iroquois in the War of 1812* (Toronto: University of Toronto Press, 1998), esp. 188–90; Nicole Eustace, *1812: War and the Passions of Patriotism* (Philadelphia: University of Pennsylvania Press, 2012).

8. G. Kurt Piehler, *Remembering War the American Way* (Washington, DC: Smithsonian Institution Press, 1995), 37.

Chapter 7

The Fur Trade in the Northwest

READINGS

Primary Documents

1   Fur Trade Maps, from *North of Athabasca: Slave Lake and Mackenzie River Documents of the North West Company, 1800–1821*

2   From *A Sketch of the British Fur Trade* (1815), in *The Collected Writings of Lord Selkirk 1810–1820*, vol. 2, Lord Selkirk

Historical Interpretations

3   From "'He Was Neither a Soldier nor a Slave: He Was under the Control of No Man': Kahnawake Mohawks in the Northwest Fur Trade, 1790–1850," Nicole St-Onge

4   From "Taking Indigenous Women Seriously," in *French Canadians, Furs, and Indigenous Women in the Making of the Pacific Northwest*, Jean Barman

INTRODUCTION

The fur trade has generated much historical research and commentary. The great economic historian Harold Innis viewed it as one of the activities that pushed European domination of North America northward and westward. In so doing, it created a meeting place and a site for cultural exchange between Europeans and Indigenous people. The fur trade gave birth to the Métis nation, as European men formed bonds of affection and partnership with Indigenous women, and it was a substantial contributor to the pre-Confederation Canadian economy.

It is clear that the fur trade moved the territory that would become the Dominion of Canada closer to the industrial age. The primary documents included in this chapter show how the companies involved in the fur trade conceptualized the territories on which they trapped for furs and how they sought to make their ventures predictable and steadily profitable through the efficient deployment of their capital. In other words, they sought to make what might seem like the rather disordered, outdoor pursuit of animal skins into something organized and predictable. As the selection of fur trade maps reveals, fur traders were often—initially at least—unfamiliar with the geographic environment in which they were working and were dependent upon these maps to make their way successfully in what could be a harsh environment. The excerpt from Lord Selkirk's writings provides a first-hand account of how the British viewed both the operation of the fur trade and the Indigenous men and women integral to its functioning.

As competition became most intense between the Hudson's Bay Company and its rivals, colonial endeavours (such as those at Red River) were directly affected. While maps and chronicles can tell us a great deal about the fur trade business, the historical interpretations included here illustrate how historians have fleshed out our understanding of the role that Indigenous men and women played in the fur trade and the social relationships that the trade created and sustained. In her piece, Nicole St-Onge details the experiences of Kahnawake Mohawk men who travelled far from their homes to take part in the fur trade. Meanwhile, Jean Barman challenges the male-centric fur trade narrative by showing how Indigenous women were both valued and vital participants essential to the cultivation and expansion of the western fur trade.

QUESTIONS FOR CONSIDERATION

1. What do maps tell us about the environment and about European conceptions of land in the North West?
2. What is Lord Selkirk's opinion of the way that the NWC ran their business? Did he admire them or reject their way of doing things?
3. Thinking about both the primary and secondary documents, what sort of personality type do you think might be suitable for a career in the fur trade during the late eighteenth and early nineteenth centuries?
4. Why were Kahnawake men desirable fur trade participants for French traders? What reasons did Kahnawake men have for taking part in the trade?
5. What role did Indigenous women play in fostering the fur trade? Could the fur trade have developed as it did without Indigenous female participation?

SUGGESTIONS FOR FURTHER READING

Binnema, Theodore, Gerhard J. Ens, and R.C. Macleod, eds. *From Rupert's Land to Canada: Essays in Honour of John E. Foster.* Edmonton: University of Alberta Press, 2001.

Bumsted, J.M. *Lord Selkirk: A Life.* East Lansing, MI: Michigan State University Press, 2009.

Duckworth, Harry W., ed. *Friends, Foes, and Furs: George Nelson's Lake Winnipeg Journals, 1804–1822.* Montreal and Kingston: McGill-Queen's University Press, 2019.

Francis, D., and Toby Morantz. *Furs: A History of the Fur Trade in Eastern James Bay, 1600–1870.* Montreal and Kingston: McGill-Queen's University Press, 1983.

McCormack, Patricia Alice. *Fort Chipewyan and the Shaping of Canadian History, 1788–1920s.* Vancouver: UBC Press, 2010.

Peers, Laura Lynn. *Gathering Places: Aboriginals and Fur Trade Histories*. Vancouver: UBC Press, 2010.

Podruchny, Carolyn. *Making the Voyageur World: Travelers and Traders in the North American Fur Trade*. Toronto: University of Toronto Press, 2006.

Royle, Stephen A. *Company, Crown, and Colony: The Hudson's Bay Company and Territorial Endeavour in Western Canada*. New York: Palgrave Macmillan, 2011.

Skinner, Claiborne A. *The Upper Country: French Enterprise in the Colonial Great Lakes*. Baltimore: Johns Hopkins University Press, 2008.

Van Kirk, Sylvia. *"Many Tender Ties": Women in Fur Trade Society, 1670–1870*. Toronto: University of Toronto Press, 1992.

Primary Documents

1 Fur Trade Maps, from *North of Athabasca: Slave Lake and Mackenzie River Documents of the North West Company, 1800–1821,* ed. Lloyd Keith (Montreal and Kingston: McGill-Queen's University Press, 2001), 24, 31, 64, 67, 93, and 94.

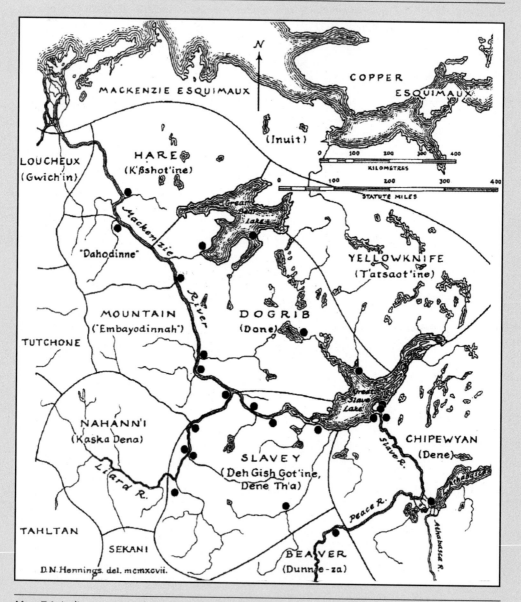

Map 7.1 Indigenous Peoples of the Mackenzie River Basin

Source: Fur Trade Maps, from *North of Athabasca: Slave Lake and Mackenzie River Documents of the North West Company, 1800–1821.* Lloyd Keith ed. (McGill-Queen's University Press, 2001): p. 24

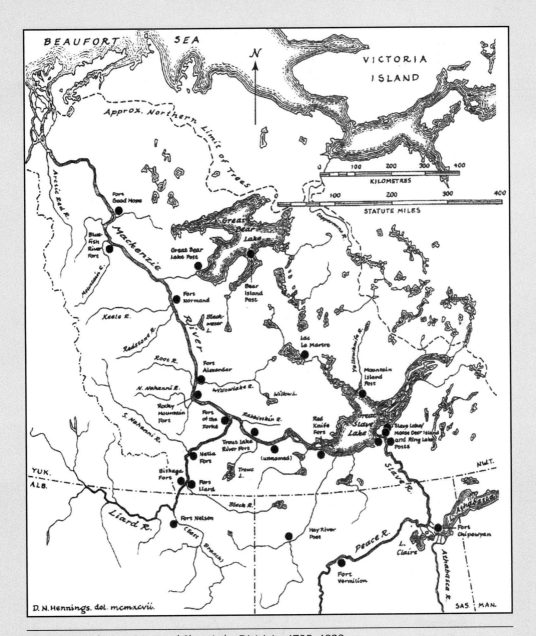

Map 7.2 Mackenzie River and Slave Lake Districts, 1795–1822

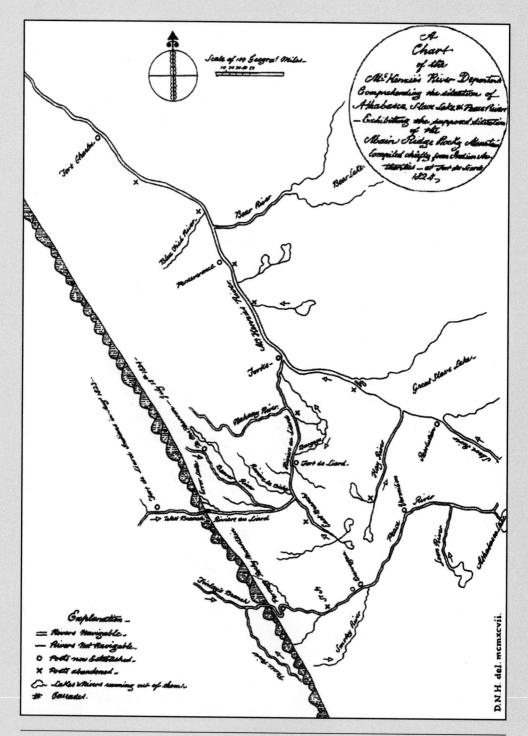

Map 7.3 Facsimile of Murdoch McPherson's map of 1824, "A Chart of the Mackenzie River Department." Redrawn to clarify details obscured in the original.

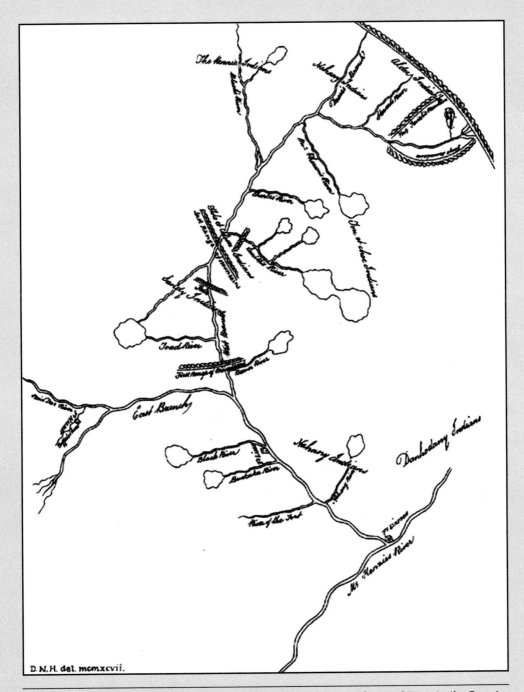

Map 7.4 Facsimile of John McLeod's map of 1831, "Expedition up the Liard River to the Francis River." Redrawn to clarify details obscured in original.

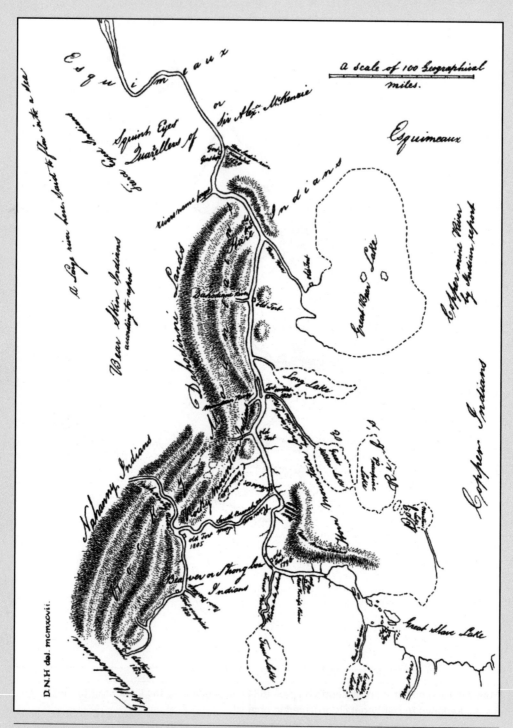

Map 7.5 Facsimile of W.F. Wentzel's map of 1821, "Chart of the countries adjacent to Mackenzies River." Redrawn to clarify details obscured in original.

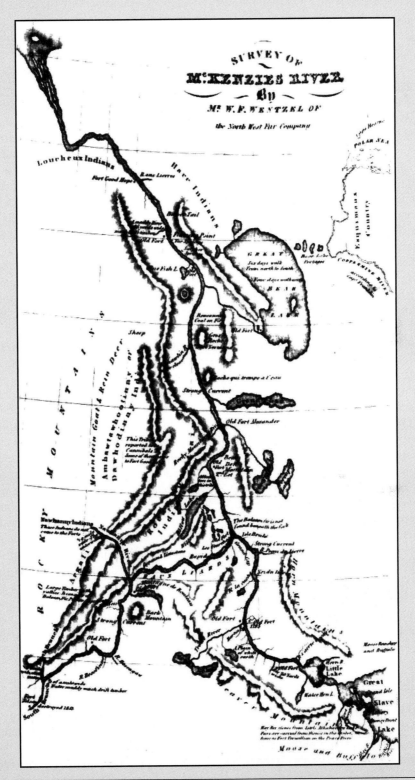

Map 7.6 Copy of W.F. Wentzel's map of 1822, "Survey of McKenzies River" (Wentzel, 1822).

2 From Lord Selkirk, *A Sketch of the British Fur Trade* (1815), in *The Collected Writings of Lord Selkirk 1810–1820*, vol. 2, *Writings and Papers of Thomas Douglas, Fifth Earl of Selkirk*, ed. J.M. Bumsted (Winnipeg: Manitoba Record Society, 1987), 48–55.

I. Remarks on the respective systems adopted in Canada prior and subsequent to the Cession of that Colony to Great Britain.— General View of the Canadian Fur Trade.—

Origin and Constitution of the North-West Company of Montreal.

The commercial benefits which were expected to accrue from the Fur Trade in Canada, formed the principal object in the original settlement of that colony.[1] For a long period that branch of trade furnished the chief employment of the colonists; but of late years the progress of population, and the increase of wealth, have given rise to other and more valuable branches of traffic.[2] The Fur Trade, however, still constitutes an important branch of Canadian commerce. An inquiry into the principles on which this trade has been conducted may be interesting, in many respects, not only to those who are connected with the colony, but to all who have turned their attention to the commercial resources, and colonial prosperity, of the British Empire: and the inquiry may be the more important, because the mode in which the Fur Trade is conducted does not appear to be generally understood, or justly appreciated, even in Canada.

While that province was in the possession of France, the Fur Trade was carried on under a system of exclusive privileges.[3] In each district of country, or nation of Indians, a licence was granted by the governor of the province, assigning to some favoured individuals the privilege of trading within the prescribed limits. The persons who obtained these privileges were generally officers of the army, or others of respectable family connection. Whatever were the motives in which this system originated, there can be no doubt that it contributed, in a very great degree, to the main object of the French government in their transactions with the Indian

nations of America: *viz.* to establish and extend their political influence.[4] Whoever possessed the exclusive trade of a district was the only person to whom the Indians could apply for such articles as an intercourse with Europeans had introduced among them; and, independent of the ordinary transactions of barter, the natives had frequently occasion to solicit favours which they could only expect from the indulgence of the privileged traders. These were generally men of liberal education, who knew how to promote the views of government; and they had the greater anxiety on this head, as it was well known that if any of them abused their privileges, or otherwise failed in promoting the general objects expected from them, their exclusive rights would be withdrawn. The conduct of the traders was at the same time closely watched by the Missionaries, whose anxious attention was directed to prevent the abuses which had been found to arise from the sale of spirituous liquors among the savages; an object in which they appear to have been in general zealously seconded by the Provincial Government.[5]

This system appears to have been wisely adapted to increase the comforts, and improve the character, of the natives; as a proof of which, we need only compare the present state of the Indians in Canada, with that in which they stood immediately after the conquest of that province by Great Britain, at which period populous villages existed in many districts, where at present we meet only two or three wandering families, and these addicted to the most brutal excesses, and a prey to want and misery.

A few years after the conquest of Canada, the former system of traffic with the Indians was laid aside, as inconsistent with the received principles of freedom of trade; and, with the exception of one district, no more exclusive privileges were granted. After the trade was thrown open to the public, the first adventurers who arrived in the Indian country made very large profits, and this circumstance soon gave rise to a keen commercial competition, the result of which, however, was very different from that which would have taken place in a civilized country, where the effect of rivalship tends only to compel the trader to supply his customers with better goods, and on more reasonable terms.[6] Among the Indians it was found that a profuse supply of spirituous liquors was a shorter and more certain mode of obtaining a preference, than any difference in the quality or price of the goods offered for sale.[7] The ungovernable propensity of the Indians to intoxication is well known, and it is easy to imagine the disorders which would arise, when this propensity was fostered by unbounded temptation. But, to comprehend the full extent of the mischief, it must be recollected, that these rival traders were scattered over a country of immense extent, and at such a distance from all civil authority, as to lead them to believe that the commission of almost any crime would pass with impunity. In such a situation every art which malice could devise was exerted without restraint, and the intercourse of the traders with each other partook more of the style of the savages by whom they were surrounded, than of the country from which they had sprung. The only difference was that their ferocity was mixed with a greater portion of cunning. Direct personal violence was perhaps seldom resorted to, because it was more easy to succeed when the object was disguised, and effected through the agency of the Indians. Those of the natives who had formed a connection with one trader might be led by him to believe the most atrocious calumnies of another, and to credit the most absurd tales of his hostile and wicked designs; and, under the influence of continued intoxication, there was no pitch of fury to which an Indian might not be roused, nor any act of ferocity which he might not be impelled to commit. Mr.

Henry, one of the first British subjects who engaged in the Canadian Fur Trade, in the very interesting account which he has published of his Travels and Adventures, observes, that on his arrival at the Grand Portage on Lake Superior, in the year 1775, "he found the traders in a state of extreme reciprocal hostility, each pursuing his own interests in such a manner as might most injure his neighbour. The consequences," he adds, "were very hurtful to the morals of the Indians." (*Page 239*).[8] The same facts are stated more at large by Sir Alexander M'Kenzie, who, in his Account of the Fur Trade, (prefixed to his Voyage through North America,) states, that "this trade was carried on in a very distant country, out of the reach of legal restraint, and where there was a free scope given to any ways or means in attaining advantage. The consequence was, not only the loss of commercial benefit to the persons engaged in it, but of the good opinion of the natives, and the respect of their men, who were inclined to follow their example; so that with drinking, carousing, and quarrelling with the Indians along their route, and among themselves, they seldom reached their winter quarters; and if they did, it was generally by dragging their property upon sledges, as the navigation was closed up by the frost. When, at length, they were arrived, the object of each was to injure his rival traders in the opinion of the natives as much as was in their power, by misrepresentation and presents, for which the agents employed were peculiarly calculated. They considered the command of their employer as binding on them, and however wrong or irregular the transaction, the responsibility rested with the principal who directed them:—this is Indian law." (*Page x.*)[9] The agents here alluded to, were the Coureurs des Bois, whom the Author had previously described, (*page ii.*) as French Canadians, who, by accompanying the natives on their hunting and trading excursions, had become so attached to the Indian mode of life, that they had lost all relish for their former habits, and native homes. Of these people the Author remarks, that they often brought home rich cargoes of furs, but that during the short time requisite to settle their accounts with the merchants, and procure fresh credit, they generally contrived to squander away all their gains. He adds, that "this indifference about amassing property, and the pleasure of living free from all restraint, soon brought on a licentiousness of manners, which could not long escape the vigilant observation of the missionaries, who had much reason to complain of their being a disgrace to the christian religion, by not only swerving from its duties themselves, but by thus bringing it into disrepute with those of the natives who had become converts to it." Sir Alexander M'Kenzie goes on to state, that from this conduct of the traders and their servants, the winter was passed among them in a continual scene of disagreement and quarrels; that the natives could entertain no respect for persons who conducted themselves with so much irregularity and deceit; that from the consequences of this licentious conduct, the traders were in continual alarm, and frequently laid under contribution by the Indians,—in short, that matters were daily becoming worse and worse, so that the merchants who furnished the traders with goods, and participated in their adventures, became disgusted with their ill success, and were with difficulty persuaded to continue their advances. The same Author specifies a few individuals, who, from greater precaution and good sense, were more successful than others, but observes, that these partial advantages "could not prevent the people of Canada from seeing the improper conduct of some of their associates, which rendered it dangerous to remain any longer among the natives. Most of them who passed the winter at the Saskatchawan, got to the Eagle Hills, where, in the spring of the year 1780, a few days previous to their intended departure, a large band of Indians, being engaged in drinking about their houses, one of the traders, to ease himself of the troublesome importunities of a native, gave him a dose of laudanum in a glass of grog, which effectually prevented him from giving further trouble to any one, by setting him asleep for ever. This accident produced a fray, in which one of the traders and several of the men were killed, while the rest had no other means to save themselves but by a precipitate flight, abandoning a considerable quantity of goods, and near half the furs which they had collected during the winter and spring. About the same time, two of the establishments on the Assiniboin River were attacked with less justice, when several white men and a greater number of Indians were killed. In short, it appeared that the natives had formed a resolution to extirpate the traders; and, without entering into any further reasonings on the subject, it appears to be incontrovertible, that the irregularity pursued in carrying on the trade has brought it into its present forlorn situation." (*Page xiii, xiv.*) "The traders," he adds, "were saved from the indignation of the natives, only by the ravages of the smallpox, which at this period spread among the Indians like a pestilence, and almost depopulated the country. By this calamity, the traders were rescued from personal danger, but the source of their profits was cut off, and very few peltries were to be obtained. Even such of the natives as escaped the contagion, were so alarmed at the surrounding destruction, that they were dispirited from hunting, except for their own subsistence." In this deplorable state of things, it is not wonderful that the traders should have been (as the Author states) very much reduced in number, and that the merchants in Canada, who supported them, having foreseen that the continuance of such proceedings would be altogether fatal to their interests, should have been inclined to form a junction for carrying on the trade in partnership. Accordingly, during the winter 1783–4, these merchants formed an Association under the name of The North-West Company, in which the leading persons were Messrs. B.

and J. Frobisher, and Mr. Simon M'Tavish, by whose influence chiefly the coalition had been brought about. The main principle of the arrangement was that the separate capitals of the several traders were to be thrown into a common stock, in consideration of which, each individual held a proportionable share of the combined adventure. In the arrangement of this co-partnership, difficulties were found, from the claims of some individuals (chiefly Messrs. Pangman and Gregory), who were not satisfied with the shares assigned to them, and who, refusing to concur in the coalition, continued to carry on a separate trade. This retarded for some time the formation of a general union, and, after that was effected, it was again dissolved by differences of a similar nature. This led, in the year 1798, to a great secession from the North-West Company, and to the formation of a New Company (known in Canada by the name of The X.Y. Company), which traded for some years in competition with the former establishment. A coalition, however, was at length effected between these rival bodies in the year 1805, at which time the North-West Company took its present shape.—The means by which this Association acquired a preponderance which has enabled the Company to secure to themselves so extensive and lucrative a trade, will be found well deserving of public attention.[10]

After the junction of the Old and New North-West Companies, the whole concern came to be divided into a hundred shares, of which a considerable proportion is held by the mercantile houses in London or Montreal, which had contributed the capital for the companies; and other shares are held by individuals who are termed *wintering partners*, and who take upon themselves the charge of managing the affairs of the Company in the interior. Of seventy-five shares assigned to the Old Company, thirty are held by one house at Montreal, the successors of those who planned the original coalition in 1783. Of twenty-five assigned to the New

Company, eighteen or nineteen are appropriated to the different houses in Montreal or London, which had contributed a capital for the undertaking. All the remaining shares are distributed among the wintering partners, some of whom possess one share, and some two. The partners hold a general meeting every summer, at the rendezvous at Fort William, at the Grand Portage on Lake Superior, where all matters are decided by a majority of votes, every share giving one vote, and the absentees voting by proxy. At this meeting, the operations to be carried on during the succeeding year are arranged, and the station to be assigned to each individual is determined; the accounts of the former year are settled; and every partner brings a statement of the transactions of the department which has been under his charge.

When a wintering partner has served for a certain number of years, he is at liberty to retire from the concern; and, without doing any further duty, to receive not only his share of the capital of the Company, but also, for seven years, to draw one-half of the profits of the share which he had held. Upon his retiring, the vacancy is filled up by the election of a new partner. The candidates for this situation must have served the Company for a certain number of years as clerks, of whom a great number are employed under the direction of the wintering partners, and are entrusted with the command and immediate management of one or more trading posts situated in the interior. The election of a new partner is decided, like the other affairs of the Company, by the majority of votes at the general annual meeting of the partners: and, as the conduct of the new partner may affect in a material degree the personal interest of every one who has a right to vote in the election, it is not likely that the choice should fall upon a person destitute of those qualifications which are considered requisite for promoting the common interest. No candidate can have much chance of success, unless he be well acquainted with the nature of the trade, the character and manners of the Indians, and the mode of acquiring influence with them. He must also be of an active disposition, and likely to pursue with perseverance and vigour any object that can tend to promote the interest of the Company. The hope of obtaining the envied station of a partner, being kept alive among all the senior clerks, excites among them an activity and zeal for the general interests of the concern, hardly inferior to that of the partners themselves. They act under the immediate inspection of those who have a direct interest in the result of their management, and are sensible that all their ability must be exerted to secure the favour of their superiors. Every wintering partner watches closely the conduct of the clerks who are under his immediate command; he is excited to this vigilance, not merely by the common interest in which he participates as a partner, but also by feelings of personal responsibility. He comes to the general meeting to give an account of the transactions of his department; and the praise or the censure of his associates is dealt out to him, in proportion to the profit or loss which has occurred in the trade under his direction, and to the success, or failure, of the plans entrusted to his management.

Nothing certainly could be devised more admirably calculated than this system, to infuse activity into every department of so extensive a concern, and to direct that activity, in the most effectual manner, and with complete unity of purpose, towards the common interest. But however much this community of interest among all the partners, and the responsibility thus imposed upon each individual, tend to keep alive an active attention to the Company's affairs, it must be admitted that they are by no means calculated to produce much respect for the rights of others:—On the contrary, the very nature of the Association, and the extensive range which their operations embrace, cannot fail to produce an *esprit de corps* not

very consistent with the feelings of propriety and justice.—This observation will be found particularly applicable to the wintering partners. In the common intercourse of civilized society the necessity of maintaining a fair character in the estimation of the public forms a continued check to that inordinate stimulus of self-interest which too often causes individuals to deviate from the principles of honour and honesty. But a wintering partner of the North-West Company is secluded from all society, except that of persons who have the same interests with himself; and if, in the pursuit of these, he should be induced to violate the rules of justice, he must feel that he is not likely to be judged with extreme rigour by the only persons for whose approbation he is solicitous. The civilized world is at so great a distance, that he cannot be very deeply affected by the chance of his conduct meeting with public reprobation; and he naturally flatters himself that his proceedings will never be investigated, or that if they should, there are so many persons to share in the responsibility, that it cannot fall very heavily on himself. In these remote situations, the restraints of law cannot operate as in the midst of a regular society.—When a plaintiff has to travel thousands of miles to find the court from which he is to seek redress, and when witnesses are to be brought from such a distance, at a vast expense, and to the total interruption of their ordinary pursuits, it must be a case of extraordinary importance, which would induce even a wealthy man to encounter the difficulty of obtaining it.[11] Every wintering partner, therefore, must naturally be aware of the extent of his power over individuals who are not rich enough to contend with the whole Association of which he is a member; and if under these circumstances, acts of injustice and oppression be committed against weaker neighbours, however greatly they are to be regretted, they cannot form a subject of much surprize.

Thus, from the very nature and organization of the Company, a conclusion may reasonably be drawn as to the line of conduct which they are most likely to pursue. That indeed may be varied in a certain degree by the personal character of the individuals at the head of the concern; but even supposing that these were men of the most honourable principles, and incapable of countenancing a systematic violation of justice, it would be with the greatest difficulty that they could restrain this tendency in others.

NOTES

1. Modern scholars might dispute Selkirk's assertion here; see, for example, Marcel Trudel, *The Beginnings of New France 1524–1663* (Toronto, 1973).

2. In general, see Fernand Ouellet, *Social and Economic History of Quebec, 1760–1850* (Toronto, 1980).

3. For a general description of the workings of the French fur trade, see Harold A. Innis, *The Fur Trade in Canada* (rev. edn, Toronto, 1956). But consult also William J. Eccles, "A Belated Review of Harold Adams Innis's *The Fur Trade in Canada*," *Canadian Historical Review* 60 (1979): 419–44.

4. Most modern scholars would agree that Selkirk here overemphasizes the extent to which the French were able to exercise their monopoly through licensing.

5. Again, Selkirk overemphasizes the success of the government in controlling matters, especially in the so-called Brandy Trade. See, for example, J.E. Lunn, "The Illegal Fur Trade out of New France, 1713–1760," *Canadian Historical Association Annual Report* (1939): 61–76.

6. For modern scholarly accounts of the changes in the fur trade after 1763, consult E.E. Rich, *The Fur Trade and the Northwest to 1857* (Toronto, 1967), 130–85; Arthur J. Ray, *Indians in the Fur Trade: Their Role as Hunters, Trappers and Middlemen in the Lands Southwest of Hudson Bay 1660–1870* (Toronto, 1974), 94 ff.

7. For recent analyses, see Ray, *Indians in the Fur Trade*, and Arthur J. Ray and Donald Freeman, *"Give Us Good Measure": An Economic Analysis of Relations between the Indians and the Hudson's Bay Company before 1763* (Toronto, 1978), 192–7.

8. Alexander Henry, *Travels and Adventures in Canada and the Indian Territories between the Years 1760 and 1776* (New York, 1809).

9. Alexander Mackenzie, *Voyages from Montreal, on the River St. Laurence, through the Continent of North America, to the Frozen and Pacific Oceans; in the Years 1789 and 1793; With a Preliminary Account of the Rise, Progress, and Present State of the Fur Trade of that Country . . .* (London, 1801).

10. For the North West Company, see Marjorie Wilkins Campbell, *The North West Company* (Vancouver, 1983); Gordon Charles Davidson, *The North West Company* (New York, 1967); W. Stewart Wallace, ed., *Documents Relating to the North West Company* (Toronto, 1934); L.R. Masson, ed., *Les bourgeois de la Compagnie du Nord-Ouest . . .* (Quebec, 1889–1890).

11. The British government attempted to deal with these questions in 1803 with the passage of the so-called Canada Jurisdictions Act, which made the courts of Upper and Lower Canada responsible for the obtaining of justice in the western territories. This legislation, of course, became one of the major bones of contention between the Hudson's Bay Company (which denied that the act applied to territory in their charter) and the North West Company backed by the Canadian government (which insisted the act did apply). In general, see A.S. Morton, "The Canada Jurisdiction Act and the North-West," *Transactions Royal Society of Canada* 3rd ser., 32 (1938): 121–38.

Historical Interpretations

3 From Nicole St-Onge, "'He Was Neither a Soldier nor a Slave: He Was under the Control of No Man': Kahnawake Mohawks in the Northwest Fur Trade, 1790–1850," *Canadian Journal of History* 51, no. 1 (Spring 2016): 1–32.

INTRODUCTION

Mohawks loom large in the *imaginaire* of French Canada. An enduring archetype of the Mohawk warrior is of a physical and savage menace to the very survival of a fledgling New France, replete with references to the Lachine and Dollard-des-Ormeaux "massacres."[1] To this day, the image of dangerous and amoral Iroquois,[2] lurking in the wood waiting to use violence to reclaim territory from those they consider invaders endures in Quebec.[3] One only has to read accounts from the French-Canadian press during the Oka crisis of the summer of 1990 to find rhetorical echoes of nineteenth-century writing concerning perceived Iroquois savagery.[4] That Mohawks were active French allies during the Seven Years' War goes unmentioned, while claims of ancient barbarous acts are repeated.[5]

The English world also promulgates the image of the fearless and clever Native warrior. Framed not quite so negatively as in the French discourse, Mohawks were repeatedly described by the British military apparatus as useful and powerful allies.[6] During the Seven Years' War and the American Revolution, the British courted Iroquois warriors as military auxiliaries.[7] During the War of 1812, with many Mohawks now living in British-held regions, some after having fled a vengeful American army during the Revolution, the colonial government capitalized on this fierce martial reputation by hiring dozens of Mohawk men to act as army auxiliaries and canoemen who took supplies into contested regions.[8]

This article argues that both these long-standing perceptions of Mohawks as men possessing superior skills as woodsmen and imbued with a fierce character informed the Montreal-area hiring practices of large fur trade concerns. An examination of hiring contracts signed by St Lawrence Mohawks indicates that they were often recruited to engage in what modern parlance terms "special ops." Large fur trade concerns specifically used Mohawks from the village of Kahnawake, relying on their warrior traditions and reputation for fierceness, to intimidate both the canoe brigades of rival companies and, farther west, potentially hostile Native peoples.[9] This article also suggests that the fur trade companies were successful in their Mohawk hiring strategies for two reasons. First, companies' desire for specialized labour led to the creation of quite generous employment clauses for engaged Mohawks and, second, companies' needs coincided with Mohawk men's wishes for exciting, potentially dangerous, and distant work that required warrior-like qualities. Mohawk men used this specialized fur trade employment to live up to their image of skilled woodsmen and strong warriors, while also meeting their families' economic needs. Even those Mohawks who eventually chose to stay in the far Northwest continued a semi-autonomous hunting-trapping warrior tradition by forming themselves into "bands of free Iroquois" who lived independently from nearby local Native peoples.[10]

[. . .]

GENERAL CONTEXT AND PULL FACTORS

Between 1714 and 1821, 35 000 men are known to have signed fur trade employment contracts in front of Montreal notaries. From the closing years of the eighteenth century to the 1821 merger of the Montreal-based North West Company (NWC) and the London-based Hudson's Bay Company (HBC), over 1300 Mohawk voyageurs who can be documented by work contracts signed up with large fur trade concerns.[11] These men originated from Sault Saint-Louis (Kahnawake) with additional small numbers from Lac des Deux Montagnes (Oka/Kanasetake) and St-Regis (Akwasasne). Added to these Mohawk voyageurs were 150 or so Algonquian or Abenake men who specialized in the Upper Saint-Maurice River Weymontachie fur trade. These numbers are conservative, as many fur trade employees prior to 1800 worked without the benefit of a written contract and not all archival notarial collections survive. Further, for this study, only contracts that were clearly identifiable as Mohawk by surname or by the labels "sauvage" or "Iroquois" affixed to their name were retained. Accordingly, contracts of residents of Kahnawake with French or English surnames and no "Iroquois/sauvage" label were not included for analysis.[12]

The present study focuses on the Kahnawake settlement that contributed by far the most eastern Native men to fur trade employment. Approximately 1100 notarized contracts from this community have survived in the notarial collections from the Montreal area held by the Archives Nationales du Quebec (ANQ). Examples of Mohawk contracts retained include those of Kahnawake's Pierre and Ignace Tegaronhonte, whose rather distinctive surnames were affixed with the label "Iroquois." Both were hired on 6 March 1798 to operate for two years as canoe middlemen and hunters west of the Red River. They were promised a total of 1000 Lower Canada (LC) *livres* each and, at least for Ignace, ownership of half his hunt's return. Each was also promised a coat, a sweater, a pair of pants, a handkerchief, two shirts, one hat, a blanket, a pair of shoes, a pair of glasses (Ignace), and a gun. Upon their return to Montreal, a second coat, pair of pants, and a hat were to be furnished. These exceedingly generous terms were not normally seen in contemporaneous French-Canadian voyageur contracts.[13] Associates of the Parker Gerrard and Ogilvy fur trade concern, a consortium that competed with the NWC for furs in the northwest region of the Great Lakes in the 1790s, hired these two men. Eventually, Parker Gerrard and Ogilvy joined the "New" North West Company (XYC) that, from 1798 to 1804, mounted a challenge to the NWC's claims of hegemony over the western fur trade.[14]

SAULT SAINT-LOUIS-KAHNAWAKE

The community of Kahnawake emerged in 1667 when ten or so Oneida settled in the general area of the Lachine Rapids, also called Sault SaintLouis, near Montreal. They were joined in 1673 by over 40 Mohawks from the village of Kaghnuwage, on the Mohawk River (present-day New York State), led by their chief, Joseph Togouiroui.[15] Sources reported two hundred warriors residing at Kahnawake by 1716. By 1736, warrior numbers were estimated to be three hundred, a figure that appears to have remained constant until at least the Seven Years' War (1756–1763).[16] Scholars contend that three factors motivated Mohawks, as well as other native populations, to move to the Montreal-area settlements. Though religious conversions attracted some, many more came due to commercial possibilities linked to a Montreal-based fur trade network, and others were lured by a desire to distance themselves from the strife and warfare that perdured in the Mohawk Valley.[17] From 1790 to the 1850s, the population of Kahnawake fell below its 1760s high mark. From twelve hundred inhabitants counted in 1763, the settlement's population fluctuated between eight hundred and one thousand well into the middle of the nineteenth century. The lowest population counts were recorded from 1800 and 1820, correlating with the marked increase in Mohawks signing up for western fur trade employment.[18]

From the 1790s onward, Kahnawake men adapted to a rapidly changing socio-economic climate that both created new possibilities and limited older economic pursuits [. . .] for men and those appropriate for women. Pursuits such as farming, which might require spending prolonged periods of time in the settlement, were deemed unsuitable for men. Tasks such as hunting, trapping, warfare, raiding, scouting, or political networking, which took men from Kahnawake for a long duration, were appropriate.[19] By the end of the eighteenth century, nearby hunting opportunities were becoming more limited, although hunting was still widely practised.[20] This growing scarcity of game might explain the interest of Mohawk men in the large Montreal-based fur trading concerns that were hiring increasing numbers on seasonal and yearly contracts. Most of the outgoing fur brigades launched from the docks at Lachine, right across the river from Kahnawake, so Mohawk men could easily seek employment for a season or longer if inclined.

[. . .]

The annual number and kinds of fur trade contracts signed in the greater Montreal region from 1790 to 1860 vary greatly.[21] The state of the international economy, fur fashions, and the level of competition between companies all played a role in determining how many men were hired each year. The contracts for the Kahnawake Mohawks, however, followed a pattern not replicated in the larger French-Canadian contract manpower pool. Although notarized contracts survive from early in the eighteenth century, formal Native contractual hires only started in the 1790s. Mohawks were hired in most years but fur trade companies sharply increased their recruitment of Kahnawake men during periods corresponding to the so-called "fur trade wars."[22] The first war, pitting the NWC and the upstart XYC, lasted from 1798 to 1804. The second, from 1815 to 1821, involved the HBC and the NWC fighting for control of the lucrative Mackenzie River basin and the western half of the Hudson's Bay watershed. Over 261 Kahnawake Mohawks signed fur trade contracts during those later years. This period of intense HBC-NWC rivalry overlapped from 1817 onward with a Montreal-area hiring push by the New York City-based American Fur Company (AFC) for its trade in the southern Great Lakes and Upper Missouri and Mississippi regions.[23] These hiring activities pressured the Montreal labour market by creating very favourable conditions for all men interested in fur trade contacts.

THE FIRST FUR TRADE WAR

From 1798 to 1804, the Montreal-based fur trade was convulsed by its first of two internecine wars coinciding with the initial documented increase in hiring of Kahnawake Mohawks. Their contracts reflected the targeted aims of the fur trade companies in hiring Mohawk men who were seen as aggressive and fast. During these six years of conflict, 317 men from Kahnawake were hired either as summer men or as multi-year winterers principally by the NWC but also by the rival XYC.[24]

An increasing number of Kahnawake men were hired in group contracts as "come-and-go" summer men to ferry supplies and furs to contested rendezvous points. On 19 September 1803, the NWC hired 20 Mohawks for a return trip to Rainy Lake, the section of their route into the Northwest that both rival companies' canoe brigades used. These men, a mixture of middlemen and those with specialized canoeing skills, could fully man at least two *canots de maîtres* (Rabaska canoes). The pay offered was enormous compared to previous years' seasonal fur trade hires.[25] A lowly middleman, usually a younger, less experienced man, received on average 300 LC livres. In the summer of 1803, middlemen were getting 450 LC livres and Mohawk steersmen and foremen negotiated salaries ranging from 600 to 750 LC livres for this trip.

Such rich sums were the equivalent of a wintering man's average wages before the onset of acute competition, and they were more generous than what French-Canadian employees received that same year from the NWC for similar work. Competition in the fur trade hiring market partly explains the generous wages. But another important factor was the danger of violent clashes with competing canoe crews who followed along the same waterways into the interior.[26] The sudden increase of Kahnawake men in the fur trade during this period points to not only an interest in the wage offered but also a willingness by Mohawks to knowingly face a higher risk of open conflict during the three-month round trip.

The second reason for hiring Mohawk men was their trapping skills, whether or not it was stipulated in their contracts. Armed with steel traps and "castoreum," they were sent by Montreal traders into areas such as the Peace River district, where competition was strong, fur-bearing animals abundant, and local Native populations had limited interest in trapping or demanded too high a price for their pelts.[27] By 1802 over 250 Indians, a majority of them Mohawk but also including some Nipissing and Algonquin, had travelled into the Northwest with NWC or XYC canoe brigades to trap in what is now northern Alberta.[28] So many Mohawk were recruited that both rival companies had to hire Iroquois interpreters to manage the men in the interior. For example, Simon Yohatorie of Kahnawake signed on with the NWC in spring 1801 for two years as a wintering interpreter at the very hefty salary of 1200 LC livres for the first year and 1400 LC livres for the second year, plus a double allotment of equipment, including a new coat, every year. More surprisingly, he had no paddling or portaging duties assigned to him in his contract.[29]

The first documented group hire of identifiable Mohawk men that can be directly linked to trapping activities in the Northwest was in November 1800 when 12 Kahnawake Mohawks signed up with the NWC. [. . .]

Kahnawake men were likely interested in this early wave of contracts for a variety of reasons. First, they were well paid to pursue favoured and respected occupations of canoeing, hunting, and trapping, thus satisfying not only economic but also cultural needs. Second, Mohawks were provided the opportunity to leave the settlement for an extended but defined period of time. The possibility of adventure, the expectation of danger, and, in the case of the multi-year contracts, the chance to explore the economic or social potential of new regions far from their home community were acceptable and desirable pathways to warrior status and male adulthood in Mohawk society. These contracts allowed them to leave as a group and function as semi-autonomous units in the interior, as they were no man's servants.

THE INTERLUDE YEARS

At the conclusion of the NWC and XYC fur trade war in November 1804, several hundred men, now deemed redundant, were let go. Some became freemen, working intermittently for the fur trade companies or going into the pemmican trade.[30] Yet even in these intervening years when the number of required employees was much reduced for the victorious NWC, Kahnawake Mohawks continued to be hired both as voyageurs and as trappers.

[. . .]

While seasonal voyageur contracts tapered off sharply for Mohawks after the end of the first fur trade war, they picked up again during the War of 1812. Interspersed within the Kahnawake fur trade hires were several canoeing seasonal contracts funded by the government. In September 1814, for example, over 70 Kahnawake men were hired for a late round-trip resupply trip to the British-held Fort Michilimackinac (present-day Mackinac Island) where the occupants had endured a long winter on short rations and a series of battles with American troops in July and August.[31] Although many French Canadians were also hired that year, few received the high salaries commanded by the Mohawks. Fewer still had Michilimackinac stipulated as their western destination. It was largely Mohawks who were attracted by the high salary offered and the very real possibility of danger.

Two earlier Mohawk group hires can be documented during the War of 1812. On 27 February 1813, 31 Kahnawake men were hired to go to Fort William (near present-day Thunder Bay, Ontario), possibly via Michilimackinac, and, if required, to proceed west of Lake Superior to Rainy Lake. [. . .] The crew included five steersmen, five foremen, and twenty-one middlemen. This was enough for a maximum of five express canoes. On this occasion, 200 French-Canadian voyageurs were also hired for the same wages and destination. For much of 1813, the British dominated the Great Lakes region, and British occupation of both Detroit and Michilimackinac likely gave voyageurs and fur traders a sense of relative security. But with the British defeat at the Battle of Lake Erie on 13 September 1813 and the American recapture of Detroit, travelling the interior waterways to Michilimackinac became a dangerous undertaking. [. . .] This peril was forcibly brought home to both the NWC and its employees when the American navy destroyed the company's depot on the north shore of the St Marys River (at Sault Ste Marie) in early July 1814, then unsuccessfully attacked Michilimackinac.

THE SECOND FUR TRADE WAR, 1815–1821

The next spike in Kahnawake Mohawk fur trade hirings coincided with the second fur trade war. Mohawk contracts crested in 1817–1818 and then ebbed as the 1821 NWC and HBC merger approached. Again, as noted for the earlier period, two types of *engagés*

were found among the Mohawks—those involved in the come-and-go summer freighting business to destinations in the Great Lakes region and the multi-year trappers and wintering men. During this second wave of hiring, many of the wintering Mohawks with contracts spanning three to six years appear to have left Kahnawake permanently. Only 18 of the 119 Mohawks that can be tracked through NWC or HBC ledger books can be traced back to the Montreal pay lists when they picked up the balance of their pay after completing their engagements in the Athabasca, English River, or Columbia regions of Western Canada. No more than a dozen Mohawks are noted in these same ledgers as dying in the west while fulfilling their contracts. Most of these men appear to have made the conscious decision of remaining in the upper country. Still, permanent relocation did not indicate a lack of concern for the kin these men had left behind in the St Lawrence Valley. Ledger books and contracts often stipulated that companies were required to give sums of money to mothers, wives, and even sisters.

The case of Kahnawake Mohawk Pierre Owayiassan exemplifies this pattern. He had been involved in both the April 1814 NWC organized trip and the following September 1814 government-sponsored trip to Michilimackinac as a middleman. On 2 December 1815, he signed a three-year wintering-and-middleman contract with the NWC for a salary of 750 LC livres, including a signing advance of 25 Spanish dollars.[32] Although the destination stated in the contract was Fort William, this was but a first stop. Owayiassan can be tracked in the NWC ledger books, working first in the English River department and afterwards in the Athabasca region, with his wages steadily increasing until by 1820 he was making 1000 LC livres per year. In the first entries covering his initial three-year contract, there are notes that the NWC gave small sums of money to his sister back east.[33]

While land pressures and depleted hunting territories were strong push factors at the onset of the second fur trade war, pull factors also existed that induced Mohawks to participate in contractual salaried employment. [. . .] Mohawk salaries and benefits remained equal or higher than those of their French-Canadian counterparts even after the waning of the second employment spike. Mohawk men commanded higher salaries due to an attractive set of skills they possessed that could be put to good use meeting the various special challenges faced in the interior by fur trade companies.

Between 1815 and 1821, at specific moments and for specific reasons, fur trade companies sought out Mohawks because of their reputation for warrior-like fierceness. [. . .] A willingness to contract out for money and adventure did not tie Mohawks to one company. Although a majority of Kahnawake contracts were with the NWC, some hired on with the HBC in those difficult pre-1821 years. One of the key problems faced by the HBC in its early efforts at recruiting in Montreal was a high rate of desertion or no-shows prior to its spring brigades departing from the docks at Lachine. During the navigation seasons of 1815, 1816, and 1817, the HBC faced unheard of desertion rates of 20–30 per cent.[34] French-Canadian men pocketed their advances of 10 to 25 Spanish dollars received at the moment of signing and then disappeared. The other new competitor hiring in Montreal, the AFC, faced this same challenge. In 1817, when the AFC hired 60 men, just 35 actually showed up on the scheduled day of departure, causing several days of delay as additional men had to be secured.[35] All companies seemed equally incapable of tracking down and prosecuting the rogues. The fur trade wars had come to the Montreal labour market. Although company men complained bitterly about Mohawk behaviour and insubordination in the Northwest, no one in Montreal complained about Mohawk desertions.

Once hired, they apparently stayed hired— at least for a price.

[. . .]

During the bitter years of the NWC and HBC fur trade war, companies persisted in hiring Mohawks as trappers and hunters. [. . .] In the spring of 1819, 19 Mohawk men departed Montreal for the Northwest to work solely as hunters for an embattled NWC that was desperate to recoup some of the tremendous losses it had incurred in the previous three years. [. . .] They all received an advance of 50 Spanish dollars (300 LC livres), but no salary was listed in keeping with the custom of earlier trapping and hunting Mohawk contracts. Once again, a detailed codicil was appended to the contract, stating that the 19 hunters—all hired for four years—would receive both a 25 per cent discount on all supplies purchased at the posts and a pre-negotiated price for their furs. [. . .]

The contract clearly named two leaders for the group: Martin Isiniaquoin (Meaquin) and Francois Xavier Teané Torens (Teanetorense). These two and several of the other men can be traced into the Columbia District and into retirement in the Willamette Valley of present-day Oregon. They seem to have remained together as a hunting band or brigade until at least 1822. Others, like Ignace Halchiaronquashe (also known as Hatchiorauquasha or John Gray), led hunting brigades in their own right. Gray eventually led a group of 12 Iroquois families to settle in Kansas City, Missouri.[36] [. . .]

AFTER THE 1821 MERGER

After the 1821 merger of the NWC and the HBC, it becomes more difficult to track voyageur contracts. With the mid-nineteenth-century increase in Montreal notaries, and the documents they produce coupled to a diminishing number of fur trade agreements, it becomes hard to locate voyageur contracts. Also, after the amalgamation, the HBC put into place cost-cutting and personnel-reduction measures. In 1821, for example, 1983 men were employed by the newly merged concern; by 1825, just 827 employees remained. This dramatic decline in personnel was engineered by a systematic closure of duplicate posts and a reorientation of most traffic to and from the interior via Hudson's Bay rather than via Montreal, as had been the case for NWC operations. This deliberate change in traffic flow meant an abrupt decline in demand for St Lawrence Valley–based voyageurs.[37]

[. . .]

Despite the merger of 1821 and the subsequent drastic reduction in personnel, HBC continued to hire Native men on multi-year contracts. In the spring of 1821, 27 Mohawks left Lachine for three-year wintering contracts with no specific locations or tasks indicated.[38] The wages remained generous—800 LC livres plus annual supplies for middlemen and 1200 LC livres for men with more specialized skills. Also, many voyageurs employed in the eastern fur trade—for example, the St Maurice River fur trade system in the 1840s and 1850s—were recruited from Kahnawake and Kanesatake.[39] In terms of the western fur trade, researcher Bruce Watson has documented the biographies of 57 Kahnawake Mohawks hired by the HBC after 1821 who pursued a life of trapping, intermixed with HBC contract work, in the Columbia and New Caledonia districts. These men eventually merged into hunting brigades with Mohawks and French Canadians already present in these regions. An initial Montreal contract can be traced for some of these Mohawks. Michel Tarantaroga, 23, and Thomas Atariatcha, 18, both of Kahnawake, signed HBC contracts in 1850 in front of Montreal notary Joseph Dubreuil to work for three years as canoemen and winterers. Both toiled in the Columbia and New Caledonia departments for years. Michel acquired a Salish wife while working for the trading concerns in the Pacific Northwest. Like many of their compatriots, both subsequently disappeared from fur trade ledgers and letters without a trace. But Alexander Ross' roster for the 1824–1825 trapping expedition into the Snake River Country illustrates the continued importance of "free" Native hunters and labourers to the smooth functioning of HBC trade in the Northwest:

> In November 1824, Alexander Ross finally inherited command of fifty-five hunters, including two Americans, seventeen Canadians, five half-bloods from east of the mountains, twelve Iroquois, two Obenaki [Abenaki], two Nipissing, one Saulteur [Ojibwa], two Cree, one Chinook, two Spokane, two Kutenai, three flatheads, two Kalispell, one Palouse, and one Snake Indian slave. Twenty-five of the trappers were married, some with sons old enough to carry a gun. In addition there were sixty-four Métis children. The brigade trailed away from Flathead post packing their outfits on horses, or dragging travois like a band of Indian.[40]

CONCLUSION

For over 60 years, the specific needs of fur trade companies for elite canoemen, occasional strong men (or at least men with such reputations), and experienced trappers coincided with the desires and expectations of Kahnawake Mohawk men. Data gleaned from Montreal fur trade contracts and archives indicate a consistent desire on the part of Kahnawake men for work that took them away from the settlement and held a degree of danger or adventure. They also preferred work that allowed them to work together amongst themselves. Mohawk men wanted to define a masculine native space for themselves within the confines of fur trade society and economy. [. . .]

NOTES

1. Desire Girouard, *Le vieux Lachine et le Massacre du 5 Août 1689* (Montreal, 1889). F.X. Garneau, *Histoire du Canada depuis sa découverte jusqu'a 1840* (Quebec, 1856), 79.

2. The Mohawks are an Iroquoian-speaking First Nation people of eastern North America. They are members of the Haudenosaunee (Iroquois) Confederacy that include the Oneida, Onondaga, Cayuga, Tuscarora, and Seneca Nations. In the eighteenth and nineteenth centuries, both English and French writers used the terms Mohawks and Iroquois interchangeably.

3. Patrice Groulx, *Pièges de la mémoire; Dollard des Ormeaux et nous* (Hull, 1998); Simon-Pierre Lacasse, 2014 (personal communication to the author).

4. J.M. Rousseau, "Les leçons de l'histoire," *Journal de Montréal*, 14 juillet 1990, édition finale. R. Pepin, "Ils doivent se civiliser!," *Journal de Montréal*, 17 juillet 1990, édition finale. The Oka crisis was a land dispute between the Mohawks and the town of Oka, Quebec. It began on 11 July 1990 and lasted until 26 September 1990. The protracted armed standoff became a symbol of native militancy and unresolved issues.

5. Recent English scholarly work does emphasize the roles of Mohawks as French allies. See for example D. Peter MacLeod, *The Canadian Iroquois and the Seven Years' War* (Toronto, 2012), ix–xvi.

6. Carl Eric Benn, *The Iroquois in the War of 1812* (Toronto, 1995).

7. Barbara Graymont, *The Iroquois in the American Revolution* (Syracuse, 1972). George S. Snyderman, *Behind the Tree of Peace: A Sociological Analysis of Iroquois Warfare* (Philadelphia, 1948).

8. Joan Holmes, *Research Concerning Kahnawake's Participation in the War of 1812* (Ottawa, n.d.).

9. Older material exists on the presence of St Lawrence Valley Mohawks in the far west. See for example Theodore Karamanski, "The Iroquois Fur Trade of the Far West," *Beaver* 62 (Spring 1982): 1–13; Trudy Nicks, "The Iroquois and the Fur Trade in Western Canada," in *Old Trails and New Directions*, eds Arthur J. Ray and Carol Judd (Toronto and Buffalo, 1980), 88–101; Jack A. Frisch, "Some Ethnological and Ethnohistoric Notes on the Iroquois in Alberta," *Man in the Northeast* 12 (Spring 1976): 51–64; John C. Ewers, "Iroquois in the Far West," *Montana, the Magazine of Western History* 13 (Spring 1963): 2–10. The historic village of Kahnawake has also known academic scrutiny though with a strong emphasis on the French period. Many of the more recent works dealing with the nineteenth century are referenced further in this article. Other works of interest are Gerald Reid, *Kahnawake: Factionalism, Traditionalism, and Nationalism in a Mohawk Community* (Lincoln, 2004) and Carl Benn, *Mohawk on the Nile: Natives among the Canadian voyageurs in Egypt, 1884–1885* (Toronto, 2009). Few studies deliberately tie the social and economic conditions experienced by Mohawks and other eastern Natives to their participation in the western fur trade. One earlier work emphasizing the outside economic forces felt by nineteenth-century Kahnawake and the participation of its men in the fur trade is Jan Grabowski and Nicole St-Onge, "Montreal Iroquois Engages in the Western Fur Trade, 1800–1821," in *From Rupert's Land to Canada*, eds Theodore Binnema, Gerhard J. Ens, and R.C. Macleod (Edmonton, 2010), 23–58. The present article builds on the earlier Grabowski and St-Onge piece.

10. Ross and editor, "Journal of Alexander Ross—Snake Country Expedition, 1824," 367.

11. Jennifer S.H. Brown, "North West Company," *Canadian Encyclopedia* (2007), thecanadianencyclopedia.ca/en/article/north-west-company/. Arthur J. Ray, "Hudson's Bay Company," *Canadian Encyclopedia* (2009), thecanadianencyclopedia.com/en/article/hudsons-bay-company/, both accessed 8 January 2016.

12. For a detailed comparison of the various clauses contained in the contracts signed by Native voyageurs as opposed to French-Canadian ones, see Grabowski and St-Onge, "Montreal Iroquois Engages in the Western Fur Trade," 27–58.

13. Nicole St-Onge and Robert Englebert, "Voyageurs Contract Database" (Winnipeg, 2011), http://shsb.mb.ca/en/Voyageurs_database, accessed 8 January 2016.

14. Marjorie Wilkins Campbell, "Ogilvy, John," *Dictionary of Canadian Biography*, http://www.biographi.ca/en/bio/ogilvy_john_5E.html; and Jennifer S.H. Brown, "XY Company," *Canadian Encyclopedia* (2006), http://thecanadianencyclopedia.com/en/article/xy-company/, both accessed 8 January 2016.

15. Commission de Toponymie du Québec, *Noms et Lieux du Québec: Dictionnaire illustré* (Sainte-Foy, 1994), 306.

16. William N. Fenton and Elisabeth Tooker, "Mohawks," in *Northeast*, ed. Bruce M. Trigger (Washington, 1978), 471.

17. Marie Lise Vien, "'Un mélange aussi redouté qu'il est a craindre': Race, genre et conflit identitaire a Kahnawake, 1810–1851" (MA diss., UQAM, 2013), 42. Audra Simpson, "To the Reserve and Back Again: Kahnawake Mohawk Narratives of Self, Home and Nation" (PhD diss., McGill University, 2003), 79.

18. Grabowski and St-Onge, "Montreal Iroquois Engages in the Western Fur Trade, 1800–1821," 27.

19. David Scott Blanchard, "Patterns of Tradition and Change: The Re-Creation of Iroquois Culture at Kahnawake" (PhD diss., University of Chicago, 1982), 210. Anthony Patrick Curtis, "Warriors of the Skyline: A Gendered Study of Mohawk Warrior Culture" (MA diss., Marshall University, 2005), 1–5.

20. Matthieu Sossoyan, "The Kahnawake Iroquois and the Lower-Canadian Rebellions, 1837–1838" (MA diss., McGill University, 1999), 20.

21. For a discussion on motives and patterns of hiring in the fur trade voyageur community, see Robert Englebert and Nicole St-Onge, "Paddling into History: French-Canadian Voyageurs and the Creation of a Fur Trade World, 1730–1804," in *De Pierre-Esprit Radisson a Louis Riel: Voyageurs et Métis/from Pierre-Esprit Radisson to Louis Riel*, eds Denis Combet, Luc Coé, and Gilles Lesage (Saint-Boniface, 2015), 71–104.

22. J.M. Bumsted, *Fur Trade Wars: The Founding of Western Canada* (Winnipeg, 1999).

23. Robert Englebert, "Diverging Identities and Converging Interests: Corporate Competition, Desertion, and Voyageur Agency, 1815–1818," *Manitoba History* 55 (June 2007): 18–23. Nicole St-Onge, "Trade, Travel and Tradition: St. Lawrence Valley Engages to the American Fur Company, 1818–1840," *Michigan Historical Review* 34, 2 (2008): 17–38.

24. St-Onge and Englebert, "Voyageur Contracts Database."

25. Grabowski and St-Onge, "Montreal Iroquois Engages in the Western Fur Trade, 1800–1821," 33.

26. Especially after 1800 and with the addition of Alexander Mackenzie to the XYC partners, the two companies engaged in ferocious competition, with forts situated side by side all along the interior waterways. This was not just a war of words, as there were also outright battles with injuries. Additionally, both companies liberally used alcohol as a means of obtaining furs from the Native populations, further adding to the general level of violence and danger found from Montreal to the Athabasca.

27. Robin F. Wells, "Castoreum and Steel Traps in Eastern North America," *American Anthropologist* 74.3 (1972): 479–84. Castoreum is a bitter, strong-smelling, creamy orange-brown substance that consists of the dried perineal glands of the beaver and their secretion. Trappers use Castoreum to attract beavers to the traps.

28. Richard Glover, *David Thompson's Narrative, 1784–1812* (Toronto, 1962), 311–12; Grabowski and St-Onge, "Montreal Iroquois Engages in the Western Fur Trade, 1800–1821," 30.

29. St-Onge and Englebert, "Voyageur Contracts Database."

30. Jacqueline C. Peterson, "Gathering at the River: The Métis Peopling of the Northern Plains," in *The Fur Trade in North Dakota*, ed. Virginia L. Heidenreich (Bismarck, 1990), 53. Pemmican is (usually) dried bison meat pounded into powder and mixed with hot fat and occasionally fruit or berries. Once prepared, the pemmican was poured into sewn skin bags. It could keep for years and became a key food staple of fur trade personnel.

31. Included in this late expedition to Michilimackinac were 17 men from the nearby settlement of Kanesatake hired as a group on 17 September 1814. St-Onge and Englebert, "Voyageur Contracts Database."

32. The Spanish dollar was widely used by many countries as international currency because of its uniformity in standard and milling

33. Entry for Pierre Ounawayashon 1816–1821, Hudson's Bay Company Archives (HBCA), F.4/32 North West Company Ledger, 1811–1821.

34. Englebert, "Diverging Identities and Converging Interests," 18–23.

35. St-Onge, "Trade, Travel and Tradition," 17–38.

36. Bruce McIntyre Watson, *Lives Lived West of the Divide: A Biographical Dictionary of Fur Traders Working West of the Rockies, 1793–1858*, 3 vols. (Kelowna, 2010), 447. The area played a major role in the westward expansion of the United States. The Santa Fe and Oregon trails ran through the area. This would have been a good place to settle for French and Iroquois former fur trade employees, as it allowed them to mix agricultural activities with more traditional pursuits of hunting, guiding, and freighting.

37. Bumsted, *Fur Trade Wars*, 232–34.

38. St-Onge and Englebert, "Voyageur Contracts Database."

39. Gyndwr Williams and Sir George Simpson, *London Correspondence Inward from Sir George Simpson, 1841–42. Edited by Glyndwr Williams. With an Introduction by John S. Galbraith* (Hudson's Bay Record Society, 1973), 43.

40. Kenneth A. Spaulding, ed., *Alexander Ross: The Fur Hunters of the Far West* (Norman, 1956), 208–9.

---

4 From Jean Barman, "Taking Indigenous Women Seriously," in *French Canadians, Furs, and Indigenous Women in the Making of the Pacific Northwest* (Vancouver: University of British Columbia Press, 2014), 107–42.

French Canadians in the Pacific Northwest fur economy took Indigenous women seriously. Men opting to stay a little longer very often—perhaps most often—did so for that reason. Origins, ambience, and reciprocity mattered, but these may have been the tipping point less often than was the intimacy that might or might not be an entryway to a sustained relationship. The presence of Indigenous women explains much of what went on in the Pacific Northwest fur economy.

[. . .]

The comfort with Indigenous peoples that accompanied French Canadians to the Pacific Northwest made them more willing than would otherwise have been the case to accommodate to Indigenous women. Once men did so, they discovered women were not alike but came from a diversity of cultures with distinctive practices and ways of living. Coastal peoples' easy access to the staples of salmon for food and cedar for most everything else resulted in more complex ways of life, based on inherited rank and behavioural protocols, than those developed by their interior counterparts, who had to spend more time making a living for themselves and their families. Among coastal groups earliest in contact with French Canadians were the Clatsops, who greeted Lewis and Clark and later the Astorians; the neighbouring Chinooks north of the Columbia River, adjacent to Fort Vancouver; and the Kalapuyans to the south in the Willamette Valley. Other posts were similarly strategically located near clusters of Indigenous peoples who would hopefully be cajoled to trap and trade. Wherever Indigenous peoples lived, they interacted not only with each other, but also with outsiders. Franz Boas and James Telt concluded on the basis of what they were told, observed, and inferred that the Okanogans, Colvilles, Spokanes, Flatheads, Pend d'Oreilles, and their neighbours had significant levels of "intercourse and intermarriage" with newcomers, "chiefly with Iroquois and French."[1] The two early ethnographers, whose occupation explains their distinguishing Iroquois from non-Indigenous Canadiens, were absolutely right in their observation.

Surviving records turn up over 400 unions occurring in the Pacific Northwest between Indigenous women and 330 of the 1240 named French Canadians. The larger number of unions than men is due to a minority engaging in sequential relationships. With such rare exceptions as Thérèse Quilquil, it is virtually impossible to track women's successive unions.

Many other unions have disappeared from view, especially if they ended before the HBC took charge in 1821 or the Catholic Church arrived in late 1838. While most records give some sense of women's origins, these might well be recorded variously over time, due to imprecision but also to families' multiple descents and to permeable boundaries between some peoples. Chinooks and Clatsops, or Chehelis, might be interspersed in respect to origin for the same woman, as were Chehelis with their Cowlitz and Nisqually neighbours, Walla Wallas and Flatheads with Cayuses, Nass with Tsimshians on the north coast, and Cowichans with Saanich on Vancouver Island (Figure 7.1).[2] Whatever the time period, records and, hence, information on relationships are sparser for some geographical areas, especially New Caledonia and north coast posts, than for others.

All the same, these accounts do give a sense of what likely occurred more generally. Most unions originated where men were stationed and were encouraged by the women's relatives seeking trade advantages. Roughly 60 per cent of the 400-plus recorded unions were with coastal women (Figure 7.2).[3] Not unexpectedly, a third of these, or 85, were with Chinooks from around Fort Vancouver and, in a few cases, Clatsops. Another 10 unions were with mainly Kalapuyan or possibly Umpqua women to the south; just over

40 with Chehelis, Clallam, Cowlitz, and Nisqually women from around the HBC post of Fort Nisqually. To the north, 50 plus unions were with women from along the Fraser River or Vancouver Island, being principally Kwantlens from the mainland or Cowichans, Kwakiutls, or Saanich from the vicinity of Fort Victoria, established in 1843, or from further north on Vancouver Island. The remaining 40 unions were with primarily Nass, Stikine, Tongas, and Tsimshian women from the north coast, where Fort Simpson operated from 1831, being joined over the next half decade by a trio of other posts.

The other 40 per cent of unions were with women from the interior—in a few cases from across the Rocky Mountains (Figure 7.3). Moving inland in today's Washington and Oregon, 70 were with Colville, Okanogan, Shuswap, Spokane, or Walla Walla women from around Spokane House, Fort Colville, Fort Okanogan, or Thompson River. Extending east into Idaho and Montana, there were 55 unions with mainly Cayuse, Flathead, Nez Perce, Pend d'Oreille, and Snake women from around one of the smaller posts or along trapping routes. Despite sparse records, 30 unions with mainly Carrier women from New Caledonia can be tracked. The remaining 20 were with women from farther away, principally Iroquois or Cree. The number of women engaged with French Canadians in the fur economy was considerable.

While it is impossible to determine women's ages when intimacy began, it is reasonable to assume puberty was the marker. The beginning of menstruation had powerful symbolic and practical significance, not only in Indigenous societies but more generally. Reflecting attitudes of the time the first Oregon law on marriage, enacted in 1843 to apply to settler society, gave that right to "all male persons of the age of sixteen years and upwards and all Females of the age of fourteen years and upwards," with those under the age of 21 needing parental consent.

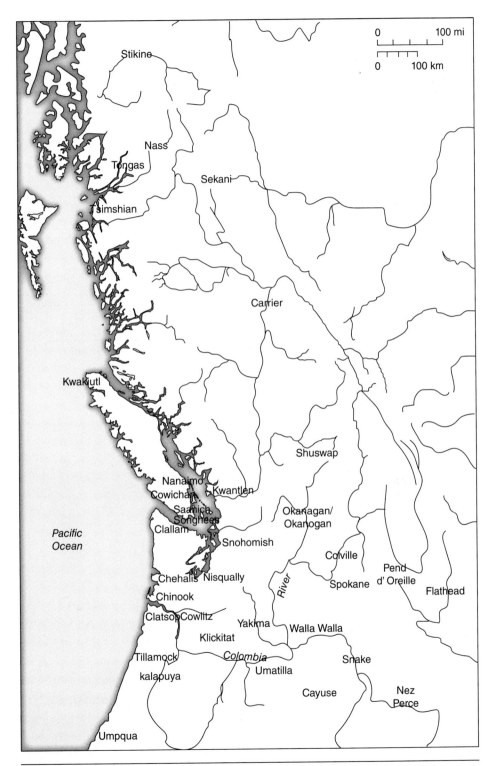

Figure 7.1 Origins of Indigenous women partnered with French Canadians in the fur economy

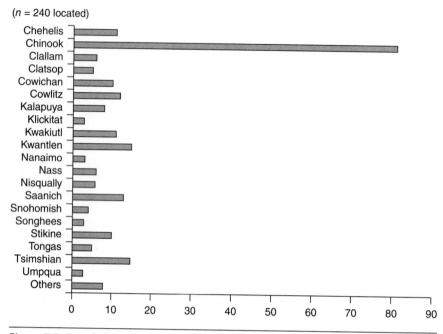

Figure 7.2 French Canadians' unions with coastal Indigenous women (*n* = 240 located)

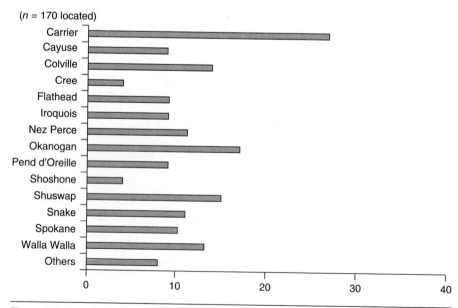

Figure 7.3 French Canadians' unions with interior Indigenous women (*n* = 170 located)

INDIGENOUS WOMEN'S PERSPECTIVES

Taking Indigenous women seriously means seeking out, so far as possible, their perspectives. Given the illiteracy of women and of almost all the French Canadians in their lives, accounts necessarily originate with outsiders. Numerous non-Indigenous, mostly male scholars have described their Indigenous counterparts as acting abominably toward evidently passive Indigenous women: "Chinook husbands, owning the bodies and wills of their women, submitted them to prostitution from which these Chinook lords took the earnings." What makes many such claims risible is their basis of authority, being in this case an early male missionary's denunciation of Chinook women as "inferior to none in profligacy, disease and extravagance," thereby justifying his intrusion into their lives, and an early newspaper's condemnation of newcomer men who dared so to consort.[4] The result is not an Indigenous perspective on women or men, but rather that of outsiders determined to control Indigenous populations in their own interest.

Some counterpoints speaking to women's agency do fortunately exist. James Strange, an early maritime trader on Vancouver Island's west coast, was simultaneously admiring of and frustrated by his encounter with local women: "The Deserved Ascendancy which the Females have over the minds and actions of their husbands, appeared accordingly in several instances to be very considerable, for my part, in my Mercantile capacity. I dreaded the sight of a Woman, for whenever any were present, they were sure to Preside over & direct all commercial transactions, and as often as that was the case, I was obliged to pay three times the Price for What in their Absence, I could have procured for One third the value."[5] Having spent much of the early 1850s among Chinooks and Clatsops, New Englander James Swan similarly took Indigenous women seriously: "Among the Clatsops and Chenooks, who live chiefly upon fish and roots, which the women are equally expert with the men in procuring, the former have a rank and influence very rarely found among the Indians. The females are permitted to speak freely before the men, to whom, indeed, they sometimes address themselves in a tone of authority."[6] Indigenous women knew their own mind.

Indigenous women engaging in intimacy with French Canadians or other newcomers did not give up one way of life for another. Not only the women themselves but also their families, as at Fort Langley, sought to use the changing circumstances in which they found themselves to their advantage as Indigenous persons. Within this exchange, women exercised considerable agency in determining what ensued over the short or longer term.

As at Fort Langley, couplings did not just happen. Not only did those in charge need to give their consent and mark the event, but each Indigenous people had its own variant of the family consent and gift giving necessary for two people to come together. An 1842 description of the Carrier of New Caledonia points to the mutual respect that underlay the ceremony: "The young man addresses himself first of all to the parents of whom he wishes to marry, and their consent decides the matter. The two families gather; the future husband gives his garments to the parents of the wife-to-be, the latter gives hers to the parents of her fiancé and both dress up in new garments brought by the parents; and that is the entire contract of marriage; that is the nuptial blessing. Sometime after, the son-in-law will make his father-in-law a present of a gun, a horse, or some other thing."[7] A daughter recalled at age 100 how her father, a son of Jean Baptiste Boucher who had arrived with Simon Fraser and never left, came to partner with a young Carrier woman remembered as Marie Tartinan, by whom he would have at least ten children. When the lost and half-starved James Boucher was rescued by Marie's family, he offered his gold watch in gratitude to her father, the chief, who reciprocated with Tartinan's hand, "much to James' surprise and delight."[8] The union was subsequently approved by the senior officer at Fort St James where James was employed as an interpreter, "for the tribe from whence they came would bring in quite a fur trade besides food supplies."[9]

[. . .]

Many of the resulting relationships reflected the impression received by the first unwed white woman to spend time in the Pacific Northwest arriving in 1837 as a missionary assistant. After conversing at length at Fort Vancouver with the families of John McLoughlin and another officer and then, not knowing French, with "six families of the laboring people . . . As well as I was able in the Chinook jargon," Margaret Bailey recorded in her diary: "It has been customary, it appears, for these servants of the Hudson's Bay Company, who are mostly Frenchmen, on settling here, to buy wives of the Indians, and for whom they pay a blanket, a musket, a horse, or more or less, accordingly as she is prized by her relatives, and with them they live in apparent tranquility without the ceremony of marriage having been performed . . . These wives and mothers appear to be attached to their husbands and children, and I have known many persons who have raised their children to maturity before an opportunity presented for them to be married. These people appear to consider the private contract they have made is equally binding as if it had been sanctified by a ceremony of law."[10] (See Figure 7.4.)

[. . .]

The spirit of reciprocity that marked the beginnings of unions was even more essential

Art Collection 2/Alamy Stock Photo

Figure 7.4 *The Trapper's Bride*, painting by Alfred Jacob Miller, 1858–59

within relationships. If they were enclosed within a male newcomer space by virtue of living with a French Canadian or other employee, women also inhabited a much larger Indigenous space. The Fort Nisqually journal recorded in the summer of 1834 the dilemma respecting Simon Plamondon, who had brought with him on being transferred there a high-ranking Cowlitz woman known as Veronique and their young family.

> Friday, July 11. All last night the Indians nigh us were singing to a medicine man who was doing his best in the killing of Plamondon's wife who has been sick for some time. I have endeavored to stop the business but believe to no purpose as she is bent on getting glowed [being made healthy] by her countryman.

The situation was so serious Plamondon was let off work, the next day "being busy at watching his wife," who was determined to have charge of her own health. As time passed, Veronique equivocated at least a bit, possibly at Plamondon's urging. "All her care is to give away property to Indian Doctors for curing her, though at times she applies to me for medicines, which are given, but the relief she gets is attributed to her Doctors." It is unclear when and how Veronique died, but the journal referred a year later to "Plomondon's deceased wife."[11]

[. . .]

At Fort Langley as elsewhere, dissatisfied women simply left, putting the male at an immediate disadvantage, for he had either to enter Indigenous space to retrieve her or to lose face. In July 1829 a woman who had been "remonstrated with" by "her husband" for talking with her mother near the gates to the post "watched her time and walked off to the [Indigenous] camp." Wanting her back, "after his work was over he followed her, & requested her return, which with the Concurrence of her relations and others around was positively refused under frivolous pretexts

that She was not Kindly treated or entirely Secured as yet with the necessary property." Reflecting assumptions of male superiority, the post's head fretted over the best course of action. If this woman was not returned, there were consequences for the other men in their relationships. It would mean "the husbands are bound down never to Correct them." The post head felt compelled to act, describing in his daily journal how he "called 5 men under arms immediately & with them proceeded to the Village when with very little gallantry in my address I ordered the lady to the Fort & acquainted the Natives that it would be best for them never to put us to Such trouble again." The woman was forcibly returned, and while there is no certainty it was the same person, a journal entry ten days later hints at what might have happened next. It noted curtly, without elaboration, how "one of our men's wives decamped this morning."[12]

French Canadians entering into intimacy with Indigenous women did not secure compliant playthings. The pride and even conceit some of the women took in their new circumstances is caught in a pithy missionary description of a trapping expedition of the late 1830s, led by Michel Laframboise from Vatennes outside of Montreal. Just before passing by the Methodist missionary settlement in the Willamette, expedition members "stopped to remove from their persons stains and traces of travel, and dress themselves carefully in their best attire," whereupon "they formed themselves in Indian file, led by Mr. La Fromboy, the chief of the party." As to what ensued: "Next [to] him rode his wife, a native woman astride—as is common with the females—upon her pony, quite picturesquely clad. She wore a man's hat, with long black feathers fastened in front, and drooping behind very gracefully. Her short dress was of rich broadcloth, leggins beautifully embroidered with gay beads, and fringed with tiny bells, whose delicate, musical tinkling could be heard at several hundred yards distance."[13]

Indigenous women were, in other words, real live human beings with all of the resulting strengths and foibles. Coastal women in particular might quarrel over their status in the social hierarchies from which they came and also in those they had entered by virtue of their partnering decisions. Thus it was on a spring day of 1814 at Fort George that Chinook chief Comcomly's daughter Ilchee, who was living with Duncan McDougall, a Pacific Fur Company officer at the very top of the hierarchy, picked a "battle" with the "woman" and children of young Iroquois steersman Ignace Salioheni. According to the officer in charge, the children were in their family's lodge "playing with some trifling things, when the former lady who is haughty and imperious, took the playthings from them and set them bawling." The affronted mother slapped Ilchee, at which "royalty was offended and a dreadful row ensued." McDougall got into the act, to the dismay of Astoria's head. "Mr. McDougall revenged the insult offered to his lady yesterday, slapping and kicking Ignace's Boy, which I conceive was very improper, for what business had she to go into Ignace's woman's tent to interfere with the children?" There is little question as to who would win out. A couple of weeks later, ostensibly because the location of their home was needed for storing goods, Salioheni's family was moved "outside of the fort . . . in the house with the Nepisangues," a group of Nipissings who had come west from the Montreal area to trap beaver and sometimes worked for the NWC as hunters.[14] For all that Ignace Salioheni was a respected steersman who had earlier guided David Thompson and was currently taking a brigade up the Columbia River, his status was no match for that of Ilchee, her husband, and also her chiefly father, who was a frequent post visitor.

Much the same story is told about Fort Langley, where Christmas was one of the few occasions in the year when women who had partnered with Indigenous Hawaiians, commonly known as Kanakas and deemed inferior in comparison to French Canadians, were permitted into the post. One year these women got into an almost immediate confrontation with "the women who were married to white men, were related to the chiefs," and on both grounds considered themselves superior. According to a son of Montrealer Ovid Allard, employed there from 1839 to 1853: "The Kanaka women were accused of passing remarks about their white sisters and then from one imaginary insult or slight the fight was on. There was no prancing or sparring. It was run and grab for the hair of the head. A regular tug-of-war ensued. Finally they were separated by their husbands and all was peace and quietness."[15] The story is also interesting for young Allard's assumption that Indigenous women took on their partners' colouring.

Indigenous women's presence was such that they would very often persuade the French Canadians in their lives, once it became possible to do so, to settle in their home territory. Half of the hundred-plus French Canadians eventually calling the Willamette Valley home would then or earlier live with Chinook, Clatsop, or Kalapuyan women. Almost all of the men settling their families around Fort Colville or Fort Nisqually did so with local women, as did their counterparts heading further afield, as to the Umpqua region of southern Oregon. In similar fashion, men north of the border put in place in 1846 almost all lived with women indigenous to the future British Columbia. Taking Indigenous women seriously was, for French Canadians, to take them seriously indeed.

[. . .]

INTIMACY'S LIMITS

Intimacy between French Canadians and Indigenous women should not, however, be idealized. Even as relationships were formed, others faltered and broke asunder. Taking French Canadians and Indigenous women seriously is to accept they each came into relationships with motives and aspirations of their own, which might or might not be fulfilled, or circumstances might intervene. Familial ties and territorial bonds mattered to indigenous women, just as chains of acquaintance did to their male counterparts.

Some individuals might feel themselves caught. At least some, if not many, men likely held to the perspective of longtime intermediary Jean Baptiste Lolo, reflecting back in 1859 to a visiting Royal Navy officer on his over a third of a century in the Pacific Northwest: "So long as she remains true to me, I will hold to her; and if she fails me—[legally] married or not—I shall discard her for another."[16] One or the other might move on, or be pushed out. Until the arrival of priests at the end of 1838, French Canadians had no legal compulsion to stick to relationships. And among at least some Pacific Northwest Indigenous peoples, according to one knowledgeable source, "divorces might be effected upon the mutual consent of the parties."[17] A paucity of information makes it difficult to know, when one or the other disappears, precisely how and why intimacy's limits were reached.

Officers in the fur economy, as modelled by Alexander Mackenzie, Simon Fraser, and others, were the most liable to move on, leaving in their wake the local women with whom they had engaged in intimacy and any offspring. Others also might have done so. Of the five Fort Langley French Canadians [. . .] who took partners almost as soon as it was permitted to do so, Pierre Therrien's relationship was cut short by his accidental death a year later, those of Étienne Pepin and Louis Ossin may have been fleeting, whereas Louis Delonie and Anawiscum McDonald wed the Indigenous women by whom they had families as soon as it became possible at the end of the 1830s.

Intimacy's limits were also reached whenever men returned home. Whereas officers could take the woman in their lives with them, as did David Thompson, it was not a possibility for French Canadians. Some, like Louis Pion, straddled both lives, even while they were in the Pacific Northwest. Employed at Astoria as a carpenter, and continuing on with the NWC as a sometime clerk in charge of Spokane House, Pion astutely balanced his allegiances. During the same time period in which he fathered William in 1816 with Mary Sukomelk, daughter of Okanogan chief Huistesmetxe, and Jean Baptiste four years later by a Spokane woman named Quichinemalese, Pion maintained ties with his hometown, as indicated by an 1820 request for the NWC to pay rent of £35.11.1 on a property there. Despite being commended as a good linguist and offered a higher annual wage, Pion went back to Quebec in 1825.[18]

Death might come without warning. As experienced by Simon Plamondon, women died in childbirth or otherwise; men in the course of their employment. The head of Fort Vancouver reported on a likely malaria outbreak there in late 1830: "Praise be to God for his great mercies only one of our men, Big Pierre [Karaganyate] died, though I am sorry to say nine of the women, two children, and several of the Indians about the place, are gone to that bourne whence no traveller returns."[19] As to what happened next, an American visitor was informed that "if a man dies, leaving a family, although the Company is not under any obligation to provide for them, they are generally taken care of."[20] [. . .]

Death made serial intimacy a matter of necessity. A Walla Walla woman named Françoise and Thomas Tewatcon, an Iroquois who had joined the NWC in 1814 and worked primarily as a trapper on Snake expeditions, had two children together by the time they wed in a Catholic ceremony in 1839. They had two more children prior to his death, whereupon, in November 1848, Françoise wed her husband's friend Paul Guilbeau, whose first Walla Walla partner Catherine, by whom he had half a dozen children, had also recently died. Now approaching 50 years of age, Guilbeau had come west in 1819 from

L'Assomption and spent a decade in New Caledonia and then time at Fort Vancouver before settling his family down in the Willamette. Within the year, Guilbeau was dead, possibly in the California goldfields, and once again Françoise rebounded. Third time around, she married the even older Laurent Sauvé, who had joined the NWC around 1817 and worked principally at Fort Vancouver as a cowherd. Sauvé, who had two daughters by a Clallam woman named Josephte who had died in 1848, himself died a decade later. As of 1880, Françoise was living with her daughter Philomene by her first marriage to Tewatcon, her Tennessee-born son-in-law, and their four children, who were farming in the Walla Walla country of eastern Oregon. Françoise's strength of character continued

on in Philomene, who by the end of the century had claimed her maternal inheritance and resettled her family on the Umatilla reservation, which had become the home of the Walla Walla people.[21]

[. . .]

Intimacy's limits were tested and sometimes reached for numerous reasons, some beyond the individuals' control, others of their making. While most are impossible to know, their range can be intuited from the examples that survive. What is clear is that Indigenous women as well as the men in their lives knew their own minds, how to get attention for their grievances, and also how to rebound in the interests of themselves and their children.

[. . .]

NOTES

1. Franz Boas and James Teit, *Coeur d'Alene, Flathead and Okanogan Indians* (Fairfield, WA: Ye Galleon Press, 1985); reprinted from Bureau of American Ethnology, *Forty-Fifth Annual Report, 1927–28* (Washington, DC: US Government Printing Office, 1930), esp. 4, 162, 179–81, 259, 286–87.

2. The origin earliest in time was in such cases preferred. The spellings of Indigenous women's origins are those most commonly used at the time as opposed to the present day.

3. The origins of a small minority of women for whom this information is unknown were assumed to be the vicinity where men were stationed at the time a woman became pregnant with their first recorded child. All totals have been rounded off to the nearest five or ten to reflect the data's imprecision.

4. Robert H. Ruby and John A. Brown, *The Chinook Indians: Traders of the Lower Columbia River* (Norman: University of Oklahoma Press, 1976), 64–65.

5. James Strange, *James Strange's Journal and Narrative* (Fairfield, WA: Ye Galleon Press, 1982), 84. For a fuller account, see Jean Barman, "Indigenous Women and Feminism on the Cusp of Contact," in *Indigenous Women*

and Feminism: Politics, Activism, Culture, eds Cheryl Suzack, Jeanne Perreault, Shari Huhndorf, and Jean Barman (Vancouver: UBC Press, 2010), 92–108.

6. James G. Swan, *The Northwest Coast; or, Three Years' Residence in Washington Territory* (New York: Harper and Brothers, 1857), 160.

7. Modeste Demers to Bishop of Quebec, December 20, 1842, in *Notices and Voyages of the Famed Quebec Mission to the Pacific Northwest* (Portland: Oregon Historical Society, 1956), 164; for a similar description, see Horace S. Lyman, "Reminiscences of Louis Labonté," *Oregon Historical* Quarterly 1, no. 2 (June 1900): 175–76.

8. Margaret Seymour as told to her granddaughter, Marguerite Hubbard, "Bearded White Men Amaze Indian Chief," "Trader's Gold Watch Won Princess Bride," and "Factor Suspects Lost Scouts Being Married," *Citizen* (Prince George, BC), June 16, 17, and 20, 1960. I am grateful to Mike Evans for bringing this source to my attention.

9. Margaret Seymour as told to her granddaughter, Marguerite Hubbard, "'Scouts Recount Story of Days with Indians," *Citizen,* June 23, 1960.

10. April 4, 1838, in Margaret Jewett Bailey, *The Grains, or Passages in the Life of Ruth Rover* (Corvallis: Oregon State University Press, 1986, original 1854), 115–16. Bailey was Margaret Jewett Smith up to the time of her marriage to medical doctor William Bailey, but for ease of identification has been named as Margaret Bailey throughout the text. The autobiographical *Grains* used the pen name "Ruth Rover" in its subtitle.

11. July 11 and 20, 1834, and November 12, 1835, in HBC, *Journal of Occurrences at Fort Nisqually, May 30, 1833–September 27, 1859*, ed. George Dickey (Tacoma, WA: Fort Nisqually Association, 1989), 1:32, 42, 2:20; also Harriet D. Munnick, "Simon Plamondon," in *The Mountain Men and the Fur Trade of the Far West*, ed. LeRoy R. Hafen (Glendale, CA: Arthur H. Clark, 1965–72), 9:321–30.

12. July 3 and 13, 1829, in HBC, *The Fort Langley Journals, 1827–30*, ed. Morag Maclachlan (Vancouver: UBC Press, 1998), 118–20.

13. A.J. Allen, comp., *Ten Years in Oregon: Travels and Adventures of Doctor E. White and Lady West of the Rocky Mountains* (Ithaca, NY: Mace, Andrus and Co., 1848), 119; also Doyce B. Nunis, Jr, "Michel Laframboise," in *The Mountain Men and the Fur Trade of the Far West*, ed. LeRoy R. Hafen (Glendale, CA: Arthur H. Clark, 1965–72), 5:145–70.

14. Alexander Henry, April 19, 20, and May 6, 1814, in Elliott Coues, ed., *New Light on the Early History of the Greater Northwest: The Manuscript Journals of Alexander Henry and of David Thompson, 1799–1814*, vol. 2 (Minneapolis: Ross and Haines, 1897), 891, 908. On Ilchee's maternal descent, see "Concumley's Followers," *Sunday Oregonian* (Portland), 17 December 1899.

15. Jason O. Allard, "Reminiscences," in Mary Cullen, *The History of Fort Langley, 1827–96* (Ottawa: Parks Canada 1979), 90.

16. R.C. Mayne, *Four Years in British Columbia and Vancouver Island* (London: John Murray, 1862), 76.

17. George Falconer Emmons, "Replies to Inquiries Respecting the Indian Tribes of Oregon and California," in Henry R Schoolcraft, *Archives of Aboriginal Knowledge*, 6 vols (Philadelphia: J.B. Lippincott, 1860), 3:212.

18. On the family see Chalk Courchane, "Jean Baptiste Peone" and "William Peone (Pion)" in "Oregon Pioneer Families," online at http://www.oregonpioneers.com.

19. John McLoughlin to Donald Manson, November 15, 1830, in John McLoughlin, *Letters of John McLoughlin Written at Fort Vancouver, 1829–1832*, ed. Burt Brown Barker (Portland: Binfords and Mort for the Oregon Historical Society, 1948), 153.

20. Charles Wilkes, *Narrative of the United States Exploring Expedition*, vol. 4 (Philadelphia: Lea and Blanchard, 1845), 392.

21. Frank Smith, family tree, online at http://www.museum.bmi.net/Picnic%20People%20M.Z/Smith,%20Frank%20A.htm.

Chapter 8

Immigration in the Early to Mid-nineteenth Century

READINGS

Primary Documents

Historical Interpretations

INTRODUCTION

One method of successful colonization is to increase the population of residents within the colonial space—but not just anyone will do. Residents who are likely to be so absorbed in their own livelihoods that they offer little opposition to the colonial administration are good candidates, as are residents likely to view the move to the colony as a step forward. In the early part of the nineteenth century, British North America had the capacity to accept such migrants, and the elites in the colonies were eager to settle newcomers on their lands. One of the ways this project moved forward was to offer subsidized ship transport and settlement assistance to willing Irish and Scottish people. Earlier in the eighteenth century, thousands from these groups had come to the territory that became the United States, so the promoters of migration to British North America were not treading entirely new ground. However, these later migrations were state-sponsored, and began to affect the demographic profiles of the receiving colonies almost immediately.

The primary documents here address all phases of the project to settle new people in the Canadas. First, an inquiry into the conditions on the ships bringing the migrants across the Atlantic conveys the sense that these passengers were considered only a notch or two above cargo. The second primary document is directed to the prospective migrants themselves, and advises them to bring certain goods along, while leaving others behind—a clear ranking of the strengths of industrial Britain and the North American frontier, as well as a commentary on the voyage.

The historical interpretations offer a view of what the experience of emigration was like for those who crossed the Atlantic seeking new lives in British North America. Elizabeth Jane Errington's reading focuses on Upper Canada, and how connected migrants were to the kin and communities they had left behind. Correspondence maintained this connection, informing potential migrants of what they might expect and helping those who had already relocated to feel like they were still part of a family, even though the possibility of daily contact had vanished. Scott See's reading on the Irish famine migration reflects on another aspect of the immigrant experience: the hostility with which many immigrants were received in British North America. Anti-Catholic prejudice was widespread among the Protestants of British North America and it was exacerbated by the large number of destitute Irish who arrived in the colonies in the mid-nineteenth century.

QUESTIONS FOR CONSIDERATION

1. What does Buchanan tell us about the experiences of these immigrants? Are officials holding to the spirit or the letter of regulations regarding passage?
2. Why might passengers be suspicious of assisted immigration schemes?
3. If you were a potential immigrant to the Canadas, how might you find Dunlop's information helpful?
4. Do you think that some of the letter writers that Errington discusses were really the best candidates for immigration after all? Why or why not?
5. How did anti-Irish nativism express itself in British North America? What factors explain the surge in nativism in the mid-nineteenth century?

SUGGESTIONS FOR FURTHER READING

Cameron, Wendy, Sheila Haines, and Mary McDougall Maude, eds. *English Emigrant Voices: Labourers' Letters from Upper Canada in the 1830s.* Montreal and Kingston: McGill-Queen's University Press, 2000.

Cameron, Wendy, and Mary McDougall Maude. *Assisting Emigration to Upper Canada: The Petworth Project, 1832–1837.* Montreal and Kingston: McGill-Queen's University Press, 2000.

Campey, Lucille H. *Atlantic Canada's Irish Immigrants: A Fish and Timber Story.* Toronto: Dundurn, 2016.

———. *Seeking a Better Future: The English Pioneers of Ontario and Quebec.* Toronto: Dundurn, 2012.

Chilton, Lisa. "Managing Migrants: Toronto, 1820–1880." *Canadian Historical Review* 92, no. 2 (June 2011): 231–62.

Elliott, Bruce S. *Irish Migrants in the Canadas: A New Approach*. Montreal and Kingston: McGill-Queen's University Press, 2004.

Errington, Elizabeth Jane. *Emigrant Worlds and Transatlantic Communities: Migration to Upper Canada in the First Half of the Nineteenth Century*. Montreal and Kingston: McGill-Queen's University Press, 2007.

Grace, Robert J. "Irish Immigration and Settlement in a Catholic City: Quebec, 1842–61." *Canadian Historical Review* 84, no. 2 (June 2003): 217–51.

Hepburn, Sharon A. Roger. *Crossing the Border: A Free Black Community in Canada*. Urbana, IL: University of Illinois Press, 2007.

Houston, Cecil, and W.J. Smyth, *Irish Emigration and Canadian Settlement: Patterns, Links, and Letters*. Toronto: University of Toronto Press, 1990.

McGowan, Mark. *Creating Canadian Historical Memory: The Case of the Famine Migration of 1847*. Ottawa: The Canadian Historical Association, 2006.

Vance, Michael E. *Imperial Immigrants: Scottish Settlers in the Upper Ottawa Valley, 1815–1840*. Toronto: Dundurn Press, 2012.

Wilson, Catharine Anne. *A New Lease on Life: Landlords, Tenants and Immigrants in Ireland and Canada*. Montreal and Kingston: McGill-Queen's University Press, 1994.

Primary Documents

1 From "Testimony of Alexander Buchanan," *Third Report of the Select Committee on Emigration from the United Kingdom* (London, 1827), 106–13.

Sabbati, 3° die Martii, 1827.
Alexander Carlisle Buchanan, Esq. called in; and Examined.

815. YOU are generally acquainted with the circumstances of the trade in the carrying of passengers between this country and the United States, as well as between this country and Canada?—From Ireland I am perfectly.

816. Have you made any comparison between the expense that will be occasioned by the restraints proposed in this Act, which has been laid before the Committee as a substitution for a former Act, and the expense occasioned by the Act of the year 1825?—I have.

817. What would be the difference of expense between the two Acts?—About 12 s. 6 d. for each passenger.

818. What do you consider would be the expense at present?—It is now perhaps 40 s. for an adult, or 3 l.

819. From what port to what port?—From Londonderry and Belfast, which are the great ports of emigration to our colonies; to the United States it is about 5 l. or 6 l.

820. What would be the expense of the poorest class of passengers from Belfast to Quebec?—About 50 s., finding their own provisions.

821. By this Act, a certain quantity of provisions is necessary?—They are; but the representations were so numerous from the poor people, that the provisions prescribed by the Act were so expensive, that the officers of His Majesty's Customs saw that it would in effect almost prohibit emigration if it were enforced, and they took upon themselves, I believe, to wave that part of the Act.

822. Do you consider that in point of fact, with respect to emigrants going from Ireland generally, the provisions of that Act have virtually been waved?—Not generally; the restriction as to numbers, and a proper supply of water, surgeon, &c. was particularly attended to by the officers of Customs, and although they waved that clause respecting a certain description of provisions, they generally made inquiry into the supply the passengers had.

823. Have you an opportunity of knowing that to be the case with respect to the south of Ireland as well as the north?—I have not.

824. Is it your impression that it has been so in the south?—I should think it has been. I dare say I have accompanied 6,000 emigrants to America myself, within the last ten years.

825. In those cases, the provisions of that Act were not enforced?—Not to any great extent; it has been the custom, for the last six or seven years, for the passengers to find their own provisions; formerly the ships found them.

826. Then in point of fact, the passengers themselves took that quantity of provisions which they thought necessary?—They did.

827. Do you imagine that the amount of provisions proposed to be required by this new Act, is greater than what is taken by the poorest of the emigrants who provide for themselves?—I do not think it is near so much.

828. The question applies to the quality as well as the quantity?—I understand it so.

829. Do the emigrants take pork or meat, for instance?—Very seldom; they take a little bacon.

830. Have the provisions which the Act prescribed with respect to tonnage, been actually observed?—They have.

831. The Custom-house officers have uniformly taken care, although they have relaxed with respect to provisions, to have the proportions of passengers to tonnage preserved?—They examine the list of passengers going out, to see that it corresponds with the licence; the licence is granted in proportion to the registered tonnage.

832. Is it the custom after the Custom-house-officer has examined the list, that passengers are taken off the coast?—I do not think it is; I have heard of trifling instances of the kind; the price paid for passage to our own colonies is so trifling, that a captain of a ship would hardly take the trouble.

833. Did you ever know it to happen in any vessel which you yourself were on board?—Never; I have repeatedly seen some relanded that have hid away on board; on the captain examining on leaving port, if he found he had any above his number, he would hove to, and put them on shore.

834. What practical inconvenience do you anticipate from allowing passengers to take with them such provisions as they may think fit, without any legislative enactment on the subject?—I think that the description of emigrants from Ireland particularly are very ignorant, and they have latterly got such an idea of the quick dispatch to America, that they would take a very short supply; they hear of packets coming over from New York to Liverpool in twenty or twenty-five days, and many of them

come into Derry, calculating upon a twenty days passage, and without a quantity of oatmeal and other necessaries in proportion, and they are obliged to provide themselves with a larger quantity before they go on board.

835. Have you ever known any inconvenience actually to arise in consequence of a deficiency of provisions?—I have not known any myself, but formerly I have understood there were very great privations suffered, and a great many lives lost, before the Passengers Act passed.

836. Is that an opinion which you have heard from so many quarters as to leave no doubt in your mind of it being the fact?—I am perfectly satisfied of it.

837. Have you not stated that these legislative regulations have, in point of fact, not been adhered to?—They have not, as regards provisions.

838. But although they were not adhered to, they were not so entirely evaded as not to leave them in considerable operation?—Decidedly not.

839. Supposing a passenger, under the expectation of a quick passage, had brought only half the food which this new Act contemplates, what would have taken place in that instance; is any inquiry made by the captain of the passenger, as to the quantity of provision he has?—Always.

840. If the quantity of provisions he had brought was manifestly under what was necessary for an average voyage, would not the captain insist on his taking more?—Decidedly, he would not receive him without.

841. With respect to the tonnage, will you state to the Committee the reason why you are of opinion that there is a necessity for requiring the height of five feet six inches between the decks, and for prohibiting all stores from being placed between the decks?—I consider it indispensable in a ship carrying at the rate of one passenger to every two tons, to reserve the entire space between decks for their accommodation, and the deck of the ship not being at least five feet and a half, it would not be proper to have it double birthed; and a ship carrying at the rate of one passenger to every two tons, will require to be double birthed, and to have six persons in each birth.

842. Are the double-decked merchant vessels usually of that height between the decks?—Generally more; there are very few that are not.

843. Then have you any reason to anticipate that ships would be built for the express purpose of carrying out emigrants, which would be of a less height between decks than the ordinary merchant vessels, or that the vessels that would be used for that purpose would probably be old merchant vessels?—Not at all; there are very few ships that trade to America that are not five feet and a half high between decks, and over.

844. Then do you conceive that there is any necessity for any regulation enforcing that which actually exists without any regulation?—The reason of that clause is, that ships carrying one to every five tons would be saved the necessity of any delay in making an application for a licence; they could take their one to five tons, and proceed on their voyage in the ordinary way; whereas if they take in a greater number than that, some restriction should be imposed.

845. Do you imagine that there will be any practical inconvenience in these regulations being enforced, either at the Custom-house at the port from which they go in England, or at the Custom-house at the port at which they land in the colony?—None whatever.

846. Do you consider that any expense would be incurred in consequence of those

regulations, which would of necessity add to the expense of the passage?—None whatever.

847. Then you are of opinion, that if those regulations were considered to be necessary, there would be no objection against them upon the ground of any real inconvenience being sustained by the trade in consequence of them?—None whatever; I am satisfied they would be approved of, both by the emigrants and the shipowners.

848. Do you entertain the opinion, that the parties going out would rather be protected by legislation to the extent proposed, than to have no legislation upon the subject?—I am perfectly satisfied they would.

849. Are the Committee to understand that they object very much to those extreme regulations, which make the expense of the passage beyond their means?—They have a great objection to being obliged to have a particular description of provisions, but that has been latterly dispensed with.

850. Then, in point of fact, has emigration from Ireland been prevented, in consequence of that part of the Act which relates to provisions?—I do not think it has.

851. As you have stated that the restrictions of this Act with respect to provisions have been virtually superseded in practice, it is presumed that emigration from Ireland cannot have been prevented by the operation of this Act?—To a very small extent; perhaps to the amount of 100 a year or 200 a year more at the outside might have gone; the difference can only be about 10 or 12 shillings in the expense. I have heard a great many statements made about the Passengers Act; as to the Act increasing the expense of passage to the United States, and amounting to a prohibition of emigration, I am satisfied that if the Act were repealed the price would not be diminished one farthing, as the American law imposes a greater limitation as to number than the British and other local regulations.

852. Supposing this Act were not to be passed, requiring the emigrant to take with him a certain specified quantity of food for 75 days, do you imagine that the emigrant could in prudence take a less quantity?—I do not think he could, for I have known instances of very fast sailing ships from Liverpool being 75, 80 or 90 days going out to New York, and frequent instances occur of ships being 60, 70 and 80 days going to Quebec.

853. You say, that you think the emigrants would not take a less quantity of provisions than that which is prescribed by the Act?—I do not think they would; they generally consult the captain; they tell the captain of the ship what quantity they have got, and if he thinks they have not got enough, they put on board more.

854. That Act provides for a certain quantity of bread, meal and flour; is that the species of provision upon which the lower Classes in Ireland live, either entirely or in a great measure?—It is generally their chief support.

855. You are not much acquainted with the south of Ireland?—Not particularly; I consider that oatmeal and potatoes form the principal food of the Irish peasantry generally; I include potatoes when in proper season, say in the spring of the year, very necessary, but in case of bad weather or other casualty, oatmeal, flour or biscuit can only be depended on.

856. You are not aware that in the south of Ireland the peasantry never taste bread from one year's end to another?—I am not aware that they never taste bread, they chiefly live on potatoes; but this Act merely says, that there shall be that quantity of that or any other wholesome food equivalent thereto; I only submit

that there should be a certain quantity of something on board, enough to keep them in life for 75 days.

857. If there were no restriction whatever by law as to the food to be taken by the passengers, do not you think that the captain of every ship carrying out passengers would for his own sake take care that no person should be taken on board who had not a proper quantity of provisions?—I think he would, or ought to do.

858. Have not you stated that that is the habit?—They generally inquire what quantity of provisions the passengers have brought; the ship is under a very heavy responsibility; I have known instances where the ship has taken on board a quantity of meal to guard against the possibility of the passengers falling short; I have done so myself, I have taken in a few tons of oatmeal, at the expense of the ship, to prevent any accident.

859. In case of a passenger falling short of provisions, would not the captain have to supply that deficiency?—Perhaps the captain might not have any to spare.

860. Does the captain generally go to sea so short of provisions?—A ship going to sea in the North American trade, if she victuals at home, may take in three or four months provisions, but what would a redundancy of a barrel of biscuit or a barrel of meal be among 300 emigrants.

861. What is the general burthen of those ships that carry 300 persons?—From 300 to 400 tons.

862. How many emigrants, according to the regulations of this Act, would be shipped on board a vessel of 350 tons?—I have put on paper a few observations with respect to the points of difference between the proposed Act and the former Act, which I will read to the Committee. In the first place, the proposed Act permits the ship to carry her full number, say one to two tons register,

children in proportion, exclusive of the crew; the former Act included the crew. Secondly, it dispenses with carrying a doctor; the former Act imposed that necessity. Thirdly, it permits the ship carrying cargo, reserving a sufficiency of space, with the whole of the between decks, for passengers, provisions, water, &c.; the former Act prohibited carrying cargo, or it was so construed by the Irish Board of Customs. Fourthly, it relieves the shipowner and captain from obnoxious and frivolous clauses and expenses that never perhaps would be resorted to, but operated in the calculation of a conscientious shipowner, not to permit his ship to embark in such trade. Fifthly, it permits the passenger or emigrant to lay in his own provisions, or to make any contract they think fit with the captain for that purpose, the captain being responsible that a sufficiency of wholesome food for 75 days of some kind is on board for each adult passenger; the former Act obliged the ship to have on board a particular description of provisions, not suited to the habits of emigrants, and of increased expense. And the proposed amended Act gives every protection to the emigrant, at the same time removing many absurd difficulties to the ship, and permits as many passengers to be put on board as could possibly be justified with any due regard to their health and lives. I shall state in my humble opinion how it operates in a pecuniary way: first, a ship 400 tons by the former Act could only carry, deducting crew, about 180 adults; now 200; difference 20, at 40 s. per head, deducting expense of water, &c. 40 l.: secondly, free from expense of doctor, at least 50 l.: thirdly, giving liberty to carry cargo, is at least worth equal to 25 l.: fourthly, I consider that dispensing with the obligation that many ships are under, to put salt provisions on board to conform to old Act, although not used equal with other matters, to 25 l.; making a total of 140 l., which on two hundred emigrants would be equal to 12 s. or 14 s. per adult; and supposing that a ship was taking in emigrants, and that plenty were offering, it would enable the ship to carry them for so much less than under the former Act, and form as much actual gain on the passage as charging so much higher, so that in fact the emigrant gets his passage for so much less, and without any loss to the ship. A ship of four hundred tons has about seventy-five feet in length of space, and twenty-six feet wide between decks; so, to have her doubled birthed, would give you about twenty-six births aside, or fifty-two in all; and allowing six persons to each birth, would accommodate three hundred and twelve persons, which a ship of four hundred tons is permitted to carry; say two hundred adults, with average proportion of children, would

at least make (if not more) the number stated, and with twenty of crew, would give on board altogether 332 persons in a space about 95 feet long, 25 to 26 feet wide, and 51–2 or 6 feet high.

863. If there were no responsibility imposed upon the captains of vessels, either with respect to provisions or with respect to tonnage, are you apprehensive that captains might be found who would be willing to incur risks from which great evils might occur to the passengers?—I am afraid many instances might occur, and unless some legislative regulation existed, I fear captains and shipbrokers would be found that would cram them into any extent, and great hardship would be likely to follow.

864. Do you know of any serious consequences that did arise previous to the passing of the Passengers Act?—I know instances where passengers were carried a thousand miles from the place they contracted for.

2 From William Dunlop, *Statistical Sketches of Upper Canada, for the Use of Emigrants: by a Backwoodsman* (London: John Murray, 1832), 14–20.

PREPARATIONS FOR EMIGRATION

When a man has determined to quit home, and settle himself in a foreign land, and he should not do so on slight grounds, much trouble and vexation may be saved by his taking a little good advice, and that we are about to give in this chapter, in so far as emigration to Canada is concerned.

It cannot be too strongly impressed upon emigrants the inexpediency of carrying to the woods of Upper Canada heavy lumbering articles of wooden furniture. All these can be procured here for far less than the cost of transport from Quebec and Montreal. The only exception to this rule is, when

a person has valuable furniture for which he cannot get any thing like a reasonable price at home; and in that case, it may be cheaper to carry it to Canada than to sacrifice it in England. [. . .] Clothes, more particularly coarse clothing, such as slops and shooting jackets, bedding, shirts, (made, for making is expensive here,) cooking utensils, a clock or time-piece, books packed in barrels, hosiery, and, above all, boots and shoes, (for what they call leather in this continent is much more closely allied to hide than leather, and one pair of English shoes will easily outlast three such as we have here,) are among the articles that will be found most useful. As a general rule also, every thing that is made of metal, (for ironmongery is very dear,) as well as gardening and the iron parts of farming tools, and a few of the most common carpenters' tools, can never come amiss; for, though a man may not be artist enough to make money as a carpenter for other people, he may save a great deal himself by having the means within his reach of driving a nail or putting in a pane of glass. A few medicines ought to be taken for the voyage, and those chiefly of the purgative kind, as ships are very frequently but indifferently furnished with a medicine chest. Among these I would recommend Anderson's, or any other of the aloetic and colocynth pills, Epsom salts, magnesia and emetics, made up in doses. If you take Seidlitz powders, or soda powders, or any of that tribe of acids and alkalies, let them be made up in phials, well stopped, not, as usual, in papers, for in that case they will get melted, or (as the learned express it) deliquate, before the passage is half over. With these phials will of course be required measures, to take out the proper proportions of each powder. Fishing and shooting tackle ought, also, to be taken; but of these I shall come to speak more at large when I treat, as I mean to do in a separate chapter, of the field-sports of Upper Canada.

In the choice of a ship, steerage passengers should look out for one high, roomy, and airy between decks; and there can be no great difficulty in finding one of that description, as a very great number of the timber ships are so constructed. A fast sailer also should be preferred; for the difference of a fortnight or three weeks in arriving at your destination may make the difference of nearly a year's subsistence to the emigrant. If he arrive in time to put in a small crop of potatoes, turnips, oats, Indian corn, and a little garden stuff, it will go a great way towards the maintenance of a family for the first year, as it will enable them to feed pigs and keep a cow, which they could not otherwise accomplish. For a similar reason, it will be to the obvious advantage of all settlers to come out in the earliest ships that sail.

To all passengers, but more especially to those of the cabin, a civil, good-tempered captain ought to be a very great inducement to sail in his ship,—as much of the comfort or discomfort of a voyage depends upon him. There are many of the regular traders between Montreal and Greenock and Liverpool who answer this description, as well as on the London and Liverpool lines to New York. And to any person who goes by the latter route, I would strongly recommend my worthy, though diminutive friend, Captain Holridge of the Silas Richards. Above all, passengers of every description should ascertain, that the captain with whom they sail is a sober man; for the most fatal accidents may occur, and have occurred, from drunkenness on the part of the officers of the ship. I prefer coming to Canada *via* Montreal, as it saves money, time, and transhipment of baggage.

It is a question often asked, how should money be taken to Canada? I reply, in any way except in goods. Not that I have not often known that mode of bringing it prove highly profitable; but it is a risk; few who come out being good judges of the price of goods at home, and none of them knowing what kind of goods will suit the Canada markets. British silver or gold make a very good investment; as the former is bought up by merchants and tradesmen, and used to purchase bills on the Treasury through the Commissariat, and the latter is remitted by the same classes to meet their engagements in England. A Sovereign generally fetches 23s. or 24s. currency, that is 5s. to the dollar;—1s. sterling passes for 1s. 2d. currency;—so that either description of bullion gives a good remittance. One great objection, however, to bringing out money, is the liability there is of losing or being robbed of it: so that, upon the whole, the better way perhaps may be, to lodge it with T. Wilson and Co. of Austin Friars, Agents for the Bank of Upper Canada, or at the Canada Company's Office in St. Helen's Place, taking an acknowledgment; and then you can draw upon the fund from Canada, receiving the premium of the day on the exchange.

People who find themselves on the outward voyage, should lay in a very considerable quantity of potatoes and oatmeal, not only because these articles are cheap, but because they have a tendency to correct the scorbutic qualities of salt meat. A few onions and leeks likewise will be found a great comfort on a long voyage, as also a good supply of vinegar and pickles.

Emigrants would find their account in bringing out small quantities of seeds, particularly those of the rarer grasses, as lucern, trefoil, &c.; for if they did not need such articles themselves, they would find plenty who would buy them at a high price. To these may be added some small parcels of potato oats, and of the large black oat of the south of Ireland for seed, as that grain, if not renewed, degenerates into something little better than chaff in the course of time.

All kinds of good stock are wanted here, and those who can afford it will always find their account in bringing such. Pigs are valuable, in many parts of this country, according to the size to which they can be fatted. Thus, supposing a hog which weighs 2 cwt. fetched twopence halfpenny per lb., one weighing 3 cwt. would fetch threepence, and so on, adding a halfpenny per lb. for each cwt. of the weight. A good bull would also be of great value; and it is my firm belief, that we have not a first-rate draught stallion in the province. I have no doubt, moreover, that a Clydesdale cart-horse, a Suffolk punch, or even a moderate-sized Flanders stallion, would be a good speculation. The best description of working cattle we have is the Lower Canadian horse, which has many of the properties and much the appearance of the Scotch galloway: he is strong, active, and indefatigable in harness, but makes a bad saddle horse, as he is often not sure-footed. A breed between this and the American horse makes a good, useful farm-horse; and it is possible that a cross between the Canadian mare and the Flanders horse would make something like the Clydesdale,—tradition asserting, that

the ancestors of the Carnwath breed sprang from a cross of some Flanders mares brought to Scotland by the Duke of Hamilton with the galloway stallions of the country.

As to dogs for household use, the English sheepdog or Scotch colley, or the lurcher, would be highly valuable, particularly if trained to bring home the cattle, which often stray in the woods and get injured by not being regularly milked. With careless settlers, indeed, one half the day is often spent in hunting up and driving home the oxen.

It has often struck me, that much time and trouble might be saved in collecting and bringing home the cattle, by taking out a few hundred weight of rock salt from Liverpool. In Cheshire they used to prepare lumps, for the purpose of putting in sheepwalks, by cutting them in the form of a ball, so that the rain ran off them without melting them. These might be put in certain places of the woods, and the cattle would not stray far from them; and they might be removed from time to time, as the pasture became scarce. Wherever there is a salt spring, or a salt "lick," as salt earth is called in this country, the deer and cattle flock to it from all quarters. A friend of mine had one on his farm, and no fence could keep off these intruders; till at last he was obliged to come to a compromise with the four-footed congress, and fairly fenced in a road to the spring, and by this species of Whig conciliation, by a sacrifice of part of his rights, saved the rest of his property.

When you arrive in the St. Lawrence, having been on shortish allowance of water, you will be for swallowing the river water by the bucket full. Now, if you have any bowels of compassion for your intestinal canal, you will abstain from so doing;—for to people not accustomed to it, the lime that forms a considerable constituent part of the water of this country, acts pretty much in the same manner as would a solution of Glauber's salts, and often generates dysentery and diarrhoea; and though I have an unbounded veneration for the principles of the Temperance societies, I would, with all deference, recommend, that the pure fluid be drank in very small quantities at first, and even these tempered with the most impalpable infusion possible of Jamaica or Cognac.

Historical Interpretations

3 From Elizabeth Jane Errington, "Transatlantic Webs of Kin and Community," in *Emigrant Worlds and Transatlantic Communities: Migration to Upper Canada in the First Half of the Nineteenth Century* (Montreal and Kingston: McGill-Queen's University Press, 2007), 136–58.

When young Harriet Pengelly finally arrived in Upper Canada, she was exhausted, bewildered, and miserable. The difficult voyage from Plymouth to New York had been followed by a slow and disagreeable journey by way of Albany and Oswego to Toronto and then west to Flamborough. "Alas! What am I come to! My heart is breaking with grief," she wrote at the end of May 1835.[1] She was almost overwhelmed by "the dirt and misery"[2] of their new lodgings; and while Robert travelled about looking for land, she was desperately lonely. "I feel very low in spirits, would I were home," she cryptically reported after a week in the colony.[3] The arrival of the first letters from home was bittersweet: "I am still very low. Wept when I read Sophy's and Uncle Irving's kind letters, such prayers for my happiness, dear friends may God bless you all."[4] To help her assuage her sense of alienation and, when Robert was away, her feeling of being "all alone in this second Siberia,"[5] Harriet reached across the Atlantic. She frequently wrote to sister Sophy and to other friends and relations in Guernsey. When not writing, she was thinking of her "absent friends";[6] and when letters arrived from home, she "felt happier than [she] had done for some time."[7]

Harriet's correspondence with home provided an emotional lifeline. It is clear from her journal that, from the beginning, she had been hesitant about emigrating to the colonies. Married in September 1834, in the space of six months she had had to adjust to life as a newlywed and to leaving her "happy home" and "dear Guernsey friends," along with all she loved "so dearly," for a foreign land.[8] Letters home were a way of maintaining contact with the familiar world of her youth. They also reaffirmed the emotional, if not physical, proximity of friends and family. On the very day the couple boarded the packet at Plymouth and also on the day they landed in New York, Harriet sent letters home.[9] Especially in the early months of her journal, Harriet's notations that she had written home often appeared in entries that recounted some disappointment, whether it was the abrupt decision of her maid Emily not to accompany the couple to America or the failure of the luggage to arrive; or, once they were in the colony, the realization that their original choice of land "was mistaken."[10]

Even after the Pengellys had bought a farm and built a home on Rice Lake and had begun to settle into the rhythms of their new lives, Harriet maintained an active correspondence across the Atlantic. She was "truly miserable" when anticipated letters from home did not arrive.[11] One "disagreeable" day in August 1835, for example, she recorded, "No letters from home, could eat no dinner— very, very unhappy."[12] Even after the couple had decided to return to Guernsey for a visit after two years and Harriet's sense of exile began to abate, letters from home remained a vital part of her daily life, something to be cherished and read "over and over."[13] As she read of the comings and goings of kith and kin in Guernsey and England, she was able to maintain a sense of belonging to a community that was far removed from her daily round of housekeeping and visiting neighbours, and at times "the awful silence of the woods of Canada."[14] [. . .]

Until her death a little more than a year after she arrived in the colony, Harriet remained emotionally rooted in a world that lay more than three thousand miles away. Although she had "the smiles and love of a very dear husband," on New Year's Day 1836 she longed for her mother's smile and "a kind mother to wish me many happy returns of the day."[15] Letters provided Harriet with the means of participating, at least vicariously, in the community of family and friends "at home" even while she was forging new friendships and becoming part of a new community at Rice Lake. For Harriet, letters were also tangible evidence that she had not been forgotten and had not lost her place in the family circle. As was the case for many around her, letters from home were a touchstone, an affirmation of who one was and, for a time at least, where one continued to belong.

Certainly, not all or even most emigrant settlers maintained such an active transatlantic correspondence. Like her husband Robert, a former British officer and a gentleman of some means, Harriet was a member of the "letter writing classes."[16] The couple could afford to travel in a cabin on a packet-ship, and Robert had the capital to buy land and hire neighbours to help build his house and clear his fields. And when they arrived in the colony with their letters of introduction to the lieutenant-governor, they became part of a society that was directly tied to London and the Colonial Office. Harriet was determined "to do without" a servant after she had sacked, for insolence, the one they had

brought from Guernsey; she hoped, she said, that work would keep her "alive in this dull disagreeable country." But the young wife obviously had considerable time on her hands.[17] She had no children to attend to and was often alone when Robert worked in the fields.

Most new arrivals had not the time, the means, or perhaps the inclination to write home so often or at such length. As George Pashley recorded in his diary, his first letters home—one to his father, a second to a friend, and the third to his "dear partner's" father—were not sent until three months after he landed in British America: "I could not get Money to Pay the Postage till then."[18] Of course, some emigrants may have chosen not to write. They wanted to sever ties with home—whether because they were fleeing from particular responsibilities (as in the case of absconding husbands) or from the court, or because they were determined to grasp the new opportunities of America and, in the process, re-invent themselves. However, it is clear that for many, re-establishing contact with home was an integral part of the process of making a new life away from home. As the new arrivals joined kin, former neighbours, and even just acquaintances who were already settled in Upper Canada and were integrated into or helped to create new families and communities and gradually become residents, the desire to maintain contact with those at home persisted. Frequently, the responsibilities attendant on kinship—coping with the needs of an elderly parent, providing aid to a young sibling or cousin, or settling disputes over parents' estates—continued to tie emigrant settlers to those they had left behind. Letters were also a means of integrating the Old World and the New, of tying the familiar domestic landscapes, people, and relationships of home into the new and increasingly familiar world of a face-to-face colonial community. On both sides of the Atlantic, receiving or sending even one brief letter reaffirmed who one was and where one fitted into the world.

The transatlantic community sustained by correspondence was for many intensely personal, and despite distance in time and space, remained surprisingly immediate. Letters became an integral part of the ongoing cycle of British emigration and were one of the central pillars of the emigrants' world. Throughout Great Britain and Ireland, they frequently became the centrepiece of discussions in family parlours, churches, and taverns about the viability of "going to America." Letters from Upper Canada that included personal accounts of the journey and life in the New World helped to make the imagined world of emigration more real and tangible; at the same time, letters that arrived in the backwoods of the colony nourished the imagination of emigrant settlers with images of familiar landscapes and faces. The arrival of family members or friends of former neighbours, sometimes years later, reinforced these rather ethereal transatlantic communities. The receipt of letters, parcels, and even newspapers—even the appearance of a complete stranger with an introduction from a former acquaintance—was enough to sustain this world, both in its tangible form and in its participants' imagination.

[. . .]

Each year, hundreds if not thousands of emigrants of all social classes and occupations wrote home to announce their arrival and to report on the state of their health and that of their companions.[19] Sometimes these first letters were sent almost as soon as the family or the individual landed at Montreal or Quebec (or, in the case of Harriet Pengelly and Anne Langton, New York). A number included a journal or an account of the voyage and a promise to write again when settled.[20] Many emigrants waited and wrote their first letters weeks or even months after they had landed, and they included some "account of Canada" or a commentary about "the state of the country" (as they had apparently promised their readers before they left home), in addition to information about their own circumstances. As William Knox's first letter home to his uncle explained, "I would have written you before this time to have acquainted you of our safe arrival in this country. But knowing that Mr George Gounlock had written to Greenhill shortly after we arrived here I told him to let you know that we were all well and I would write you as soon as we got a settlement."[21]

Not surprisingly, emigrants' first letters home varied widely in tone and content. Some had to report the death of a companion or child on the voyage or how ague, scarlet fever, cholera, or other diseases had devastated family and friends.[22] Others noted that the country was "discouraging at first" or that because of injury or ill health, they had initially had problems finding work.[23] But most letters, particularly those written after emigrants had found work or taken up land, expressed satisfaction with the country and the writer's situation; and implicitly, and often explicitly, they included assurances that they "did not repent [their] journey."[24] George Hill's mother and father must have received some comfort when their son concluded his letter, "We left you almost broken-hearted, but you may be satisfied that we have bettered our condition by coming here."[25] Perhaps most importantly, the arrival of George's letter was concrete proof that he was still alive.

For most newly arrived emigrants, the purpose of their first letter was to make contact and to renew what they obviously hoped would be an ongoing relationship with those at home. Many expected that not only would the initial recipient read their letter but that its contents and often the letter itself would be passed among "Dear Friends And Relations."[26] Mary and Arthur Stokes explicitly asked that their brothers and sisters write and they added, "Please pass this letter to others."[27] William Upton's letter to his mother asked that she give his love to all his brothers and sisters, and said, "Tell them that can write to write to me soon."[28] [. . .] Others sent salutations to specific neighbours, former employers, or members of the extended family.

[. . .]

Sending news, information, and messages to family and friends was clearly only one purpose of an emigrant's first letter home. Just as important was to urge the readers to reply as soon as possible. Almost without exception, the letters included such statements as, "I long to hear from them all"[29] or pleaded, "Please to let us hear from you as soon as convenient after receiving this; and acquaint us with all particulars, and how you all are."[30] John Luff, an apprentice and one of the Petworth emigrants, wrote to his aunt saying, "Whether we shall have the pleasure of seeing each other in this world again, lord only knows; if we should not, I wish you would join me in writing, it seems to be the only satisfaction we can truly have here."[31]

It was clearly important to those who had newly arrived in Upper Canada to know that they had not been forgotten and, indeed, that they remained part of their communities at home. For the first few weeks or months, many must have felt betwixt and between. They were no longer residents of a particular village or neighbourhood in Great Britain or Ireland; at the same time, they had few connections or commitments to new communities in America. First letters were a way of asserting their continuing relationship with communities at home; and the responses to these letters reassured them that they still had a place in the world, an identity that was firmly rooted in place and time—one which they had taken with them to America and on which they could forge new relationships. Many new arrivals therefore waited anxiously for some acknowledgement from those they had left behind.[32]

Not all (and perhaps not even most) emigrants wrote to reassure the family of their safe arrival. As many of the "information wanted" notices suggest, some men had emigrated to escape family or financial responsibilities. Even those with the best of intentions may have found that once they were in America, it

was easy to disappear, leaving wives and children at home unknowingly deserted.[33] Many more new arrivals probably did not have the ability or the means to write. Most were nonetheless determined to let those at home know that they had arrived safely and, later, to tell them how they were settling in.

Those who arrived in Upper Canada as part of a group, like John Gemmill or members of the Petworth expeditions 10 years later, or those who joined family or former neighbours already established in the colony, could always find someone to write on their behalf or, at the very least, could send greetings that would be expected to reach those at home. In the 1820s John Gemmill frequently sent messages from former shipmates and current neighbours in Lanark County, through his son Andrew, to friends and relatives in the old neighbourhood. In the summer of 1823, for example, he asked Andrew to "acquaint all Enquiring friends that Dr. Gemell John McFarline Walter Stirline James Cohune's family are all well."[34] Three years later, in a postscript to a letter, he wrote, "James Colquhoun wishes us to mention to you if you could hear anything of his brother Robert to let him know that he is well & is surprised that he has not heard from him for more than two years."[35] Andrew tracked down James Colquhoun's brother and reported back to his father. Unfortunately, the situation in Upper Canada had changed. "In your letter you desired me to let James Colquhoun know that you [had heard] from his brother," John wrote Andrew the following August, 1827. But now John had to ask Andrew to break the news to the brother that James was "no more": "He was killed in April last while at work upon his own land."[36] More often, Andrew was given a happier commission. A year after John reported James's death, he asked his son, "Give James Wrights Compliments to Mr David Strachan and Wife" and "if David Strachan be writing to his sister he may let James Wrights Relations know that he is in good health."[37]

Various members of the Petworth parties also regularly wrote home on behalf of their companions and neighbours. [. . .] James Rapson, another member of the first Petworth group, not only wrote letters on behalf of other emigrants[38] but also regularly sent his family news about his companions (some of whom were now near neighbours, and others he had heard about second or third hand), knowing that this information would be passed on.[39] For both John Gemmill and James Rapson and their friends, the world of emigration was a small world and continued to be characterized by face-to-face communication even when such conversations spanned the Atlantic. The intimacy of this world was also apparent to other Petworth emigrants who arrived in subsequent years and sought out James Rapson for advice and assistance.

In many ways, emigrant correspondence recreated and was an extension of the familiar relationships of village life. What is striking is that even with only intermittent correspondence, or with news received second or third hand and months if not years out of date, the assumption of a shared community persisted. So, too, did the apparent immediacy of the relationships. This was undoubtedly one of the factors that encouraged some family members or friends who emigrated years later to assume that a face-to-face relationship could be resumed and that they could call on those in the New World for emotional and physical support when they arrived in the colony.

Not all, of course, participated in or maintained their connections with this dynamic transatlantic community. Many new arrivals to British North America were restless and moved frequently to look for work or for better opportunities. Friends and family in Great Britain and Ireland too might move in response to local circumstances. Many on both sides of the Atlantic refused to give up hope that some lost family member or friend could be found, however. In addition to the hundreds of "information wanted" notices placed by emigrants and settlers looking for a particular individual or family, colonial newspapers sometimes printed cards of family members or friends "at home" who were hoping to get in touch with "lost" relatives abroad. In 1835, for example, English friends offered a reward to anyone who had information about Ann Hall. "A native of London," Ann had come to Canada three years earlier with a Chelsea pensioner and his wife, who had subsequently died. No one had heard from Ann since she had written in July 1832.[40] [. . .]

Often the problem for those in the British Isles was finding the beneficiary of an estate. In some instances, executors used a local agent to conduct the search. In 1829, for example, "A.B." began to look for George Long, "a Tailor by trade" who had left England 10 years earlier with his wife and four children. It was thought that he now lived "somewhere near Philadelphia" and was a farmer. His wife's family, who lived near Knightsbridge, London, were trying to contact him, for he would "hear something to his advantage."[41] In 1829 Catherine Evans of Colham, Shrewsbury, Shropshire, contacted the *Herald* office in Kingston for help finding her brother Spencer Evans, who had been discharged from the Queen's Rangers some 25 years earlier and was, she thought, now living in Upper Canada.[42] At other times, the family or its agent in Great Britain or Ireland made a direct appeal.[43] Infrequently, an anxious parent or sibling would write directly to the postmaster of the relative's last known address in America to try to track the person down.

Many emigrants and their families were determined not to lose touch. A sense of familial obligation, ongoing business affairs, or just the need to maintain the image of familiar faces and places promoted an extensive correspondence which, in a few instances, continued into the second generation. Maintaining such a correspondence had significant difficulties. Paper was often scarce, and postage, which was paid in part by the recipient, was relatively expensive and beyond the means of many.[44] Moreover mail "service" was haphazard at best. Although the larger centres in Upper Canada had postal service that linked Halifax, Quebec, and Montreal to the interior, for much of the period the most economic and quickest route for mail was through New York.[45] [. . .] Even so, to the frustration of correspondents on both sides of the Atlantic, letters were often misdirected or lost in transit.

Almost a year after arriving in Lanark, John Gemmill grew increasingly concerned that he had heard nothing from his wife Ann. He had already written twice and "had got no answer." Ironically, even this third letter, which included detailed instructions about the family's reunion, took almost nine months to reach Glasgow and arrived long after Ann had already left home.[46] The frustration with mail to Scotland persisted. In one of his first letters to son Andrew, John noted, "We are sorry to here that you have only received one letter in the course of two years. We have not been neglectfull of writting to you neither is the Country as poor but it can produce plenty of Paper but it is the post offices that must be neglectfull of not forwarding them."[47] [. . .]

In Upper Canada, some letters from home arrived at their destination only to languish because the intended recipient did not know they were there or, as often seemed to happen, because the emigrant had left the area altogether. Local newspapers regularly published lists of letters waiting to be picked up. Isaac Wilson, the pre–War of 1812 emigrant living just outside York, discovered to his dismay in 1821 that "they now have a regulation at the post office . . . to send all letters remaining unclaimed after three months down to the General Post Office at Quebec." He had not been to York for some time, and the new clerk did not know him; as a result, he explained to his brother Jonathan his letter "was sent with a raft."[48] Harriet Pengelly, on the other hand, ever anxious to receive news from home, made a point of

checking the post regularly and was always sorely disappointed when there was "none from home."[49] Mary Gapper, after deciding to marry Edward O'Brien and remain in the colony, remarked that mail sent by way of York in 1836 was delivered by "an Indian . . . who now calls regularly at very irregular times."[50]

To avoid expensive postage and problems with the mail service, letter writers on both sides of the Atlantic frequently relied on friends, acquaintances, or agents who were travelling overseas to carry their mail. It appears that a few Lanark residents returned home to visit, to fetch their family, or to go to college. Each time they left, they carried letters from John Gemmill to his son.[51] [. . .]

Personally delivered letters were a double benefit to the recipient. When the son of the Reverend William Bell from Lanark went "home" to college and delivered John Gemmill's letter, Andrew also received a first-hand account of his father and the family and could get detailed answers to the myriad questions that could not be answered by post.[52] Isaac Wilson was "pleased to inform" his brother Jonathan in the summer of 1821 "that John Barnes and his wife [had] arrived at York" and he had received Jonathan's note. "I am much obliged to you for your kindness," he wrote, "as they will afford me much information and entertainment." As Barnes had arrived with a letter from Jonathan asking Isaac to assist the bearer in any way he could, Isaac ruefully concluded that they would also afford him "some vexation, no doubt."[53] [. . .]

Entrusting acquaintances, friends, or family members with letters did not guarantee their speedy or safe arrival. Before Allanason delivered the letter, he had already spent some time travelling around America. Even so, for much of the period, "private conveyance" was less expensive and could be more reliable than the "regular" post.[54] However, sometimes the traveller or acquaintance forgot to put the letter in the post on the other side of the Atlantic or found it too much trouble to deliver it. George Pashley was disconcerted to find that his letters had not been delivered as promised. "This week I was informed that our Letters we had sent to Eng were within 2 miles of our own house because the man we expected to take them had fallen sick so they did not set off till the end of Jan."[55] Nonetheless, the imminent departure of a friend, or a visitor returning home, or the sailing of a particular ship presented an opportunity to write and make contact. [. . .]

Whether letters were mailed or sent with a traveller on the day they were written, they usually took months to reach their destinations. Correspondence between family and friends often crossed each other. News and information might be repeated in a subsequent letter when the writer realized, or feared, that the first had not arrived. This may help explain, in part at least, why some correspondents waited weeks if not months to reply to a letter; or if one arrived particularly late, saw no need to reply at all.[56] And there was, of course, the perpetual problem that writing took time and considerable thought and effort, all of which were at a premium in most new settlers' lives. What is so startling, therefore, is the sense of immediacy and often the conversational tone of many letters.

[. . .]

Of prime and increasing importance, however, was news about the health and welfare of various family members, and the primary focus of most of the transatlantic conversations revolved around family affairs. Each letter from Upper Canada began with an almost formulaic greeting. In June 1823, for example, John [Gemmill] began, "Dear son, We received your letter darted the 26TH of March on the 26 of May and the other Dated the 29 of March which Gave us Great Pleasure to hear of your Well fare and they find us all in good health at Preasant thank God for it."[57] Such almost ritualized openings were not empty rote; they were a crucial affirmation of the intimacy that existed between the writer and the recipient and a clear declaration of what was of greatest concern to both.

Each of John and Ann Gemmill's letters included references to their and their children's health; they also specifically alluded to the power of the Almighty. In November 1825, Ann and John told Andrew, "This at present leaves us in the full enjoyment of that valuable Blessing for which we have great reason to praise God."[58] The letters also always asked after family members still in Scotland, and they admonished Andrew when he did not include information concerning his sisters' welfare. "We were very much Surprised," the couple wrote in May 1823, "that you never Mention nothing about your two Sisters Margeret and Jane."[59] A month later, they asked Andrew to "be so good as to lett them know of our Welfare."[60] The Gemmills' letters presumed that the ongoing relationship between Lanark, Upper Canada, and Glasgow rested on far more than passive interaction. John expected Andrew to pass on information and to assume some responsibility for the welfare of his sisters.

At the same time, John and Ann were ensuring that Andrew remained part of the family circle in Upper Canada. Their letters reported major family events. Andrew vicariously followed his sisters as they went "out to service" and watched as the little ones, including David, who had been an infant when he left home, go to school. In 1826 Andrew heard of the marriages of sisters Ann and Mary, and in turn he related his own marriage in 1827. To John, this was an opportunity to extend the family network, and thereafter his letters included greetings to "all your [Andrew's] relations in Scotland." Two years later, while rejoicing with Andrew over the birth of his first child, John wrote, "We think that you forgot to mention her name and hope you will have a better memory when you write next."[61]

Especially in the early years, when all the children were living in the parental household, Andrew was drawn farther into life in Lanark when John's letters included notes of specific greetings from other members of the family. Sometimes, it was a brief "Jennet sends her best respects to you"[62] or, somewhat later, "Your Brothers & Sisters all join in love to you & your Family, David [the youngest son] has some recollection of you . . . but says he would know you better if you would send him the suit of cloaths."[63] Through her father's letters, Jennet, who was two years younger than Andrew, teased him about being a bachelor: "She thinks that if you do not bring a wife with you that you will remain an Old Batchelor that you would not get a Negor or Indian Squaw in the Country they will think so little of you."[64] In one of the few letters from Andrew that have survived, he replied, "Tell Janet to belief herself besides those black Ghosts of Indians."[65]

The occasion of Jennet's engagement to be married about six months later best illustrates the texture of this imagined familiar fireside. At the end of April 1824, a postscript cryptically noted, "Janet will be married before you come here so you put on spurs."[66] There may have been some hope that Andrew would arrive in time to be the best man. But John reported in November, "Since you did not come forward to be the best man, they made as merry as they could without you." And later in the same letter he passed on a message from Jennet: "As soon as you send intimation of your comming they [Jennet and her new husband] will Joyfully saddle the Tea Kettle and have everything ready to make you comfortable but they dare not put it on yet lest the bottom boil out of it before you come."[67] A year later, as John continued to hope that Andrew and his sisters would arrive, he bemoaned, "If you don't come soon, the Bottom will be out of the kettle."[68] One of Andrew's brothers, John, reintroduced the teapot to the transatlantic conversation many years later: "But my Mother says that if you don't come soon she is afraid that you have to take your tea out of the pot for the botem is out of the old tea ketel and she has got A new one and she is afraid that it will go the same way before you reach this place."[69]

The references to the familiar and domestic tea kettle—which in many Scottish homes was the symbol of welcome—helped create the illusion of a continuing and face-to-face relationship within a family divided by the Atlantic. By 1832, it must have been clear to all that Andrew and his new young family were unlikely to emigrate. Three years earlier, John had told Andrew that he "had almost despair[ed] of the realization of your wishes of our meeting again with the rest of my family around my fireside." He turned to his faith to help sustain him. The Gemmills shared an unshakable belief that "Kind Providence . . . provided all things liberally."[70] All their trials and tribulations, including family separations, were "from the Supreme Disposer of Events," John observed, and were "generally for our good."[71] Thus, he took solace that "though that [the family's reunion] may not take place upon earth, let us with the Divine assistance conduct ourselves in such a manner that we look forward to our meeting together in another and better world."[72]

In the meantime, the Gemmills created their own world—one with a tea kettle on the hob—in which, through their imagination, they shared their concerns, their triumphs, and their sorrows. And the whole family took part in the conversation that lasted for more than 10 years. After the birth of the first of Jennet's children, John told Andrew that she was "living in great hopes of her son being heir to your inheritance . . . You made this promise & she will make you keep it."[73] At the age of eight, young David was proud of the gold piece that Andrew had sent from home.[74] And when Andrew's brother, young John, wrote his first letter (and apologized for his spelling), it was sent to Andrew with the hope, wrote John, "that you are intending to pay us a visit sure that would be a hapy meting."[75] This was a world that offered all its participants emotional support—and a continuing sense of security. And for John Gemmill and his family, it provided a means of remaining part of the larger community of the extended family and friends at home in Scotland while they helped to create a new community abroad.

Frances Stewart, Mary Gapper O'Brien, and such women as Catharine Parr Traill and Susanna Moodie too maintained a regular transatlantic correspondence with family and friends in Britain. For Mary, like a young Harriet Pengelly, the arrival of letters and packages from home were a delightful treat, particularly after she had decided to marry Edward O'Brien and remain in the colony.[76] As she explained to her sister Lucy in England in 1832, "The real event of importance which glads the day is the arrival of letters."[77] [. . .] Even letters with bad news were welcomed. Mary "fretted" when letters did not arrive, and when they did they were cherished and often reread time and again.[78] In the summer of 1836, just after the birth of her third child, she wrote in her journal, "A letter from Lucy arrived a few hours after my baby & I am not very sure which was the more welcome."[79]

For women and men, both the newly arrived in the colony and those who had become well settled, letters were part of a sustained transatlantic conversation. As the Peterborough area resident Isabelle Brownlie wrote to her brother at home in a lengthy letter, "But I will tire you with my talk for I think I am talking to you but I dought I will never have the pleasure to do but if we never meet in this world I hope we will meet in the happier one."[80] Until that day, the very act of writing allowed one to enter the familiar world of family and friends. Although one might be replying to news that was months old or renewing contact after a lengthy silence, the transatlantic correspondence nearly always had a sense of immediacy. For Isabelle, as for Mary O'Brien and thousands of others, this imaginary world was as real and present as the physical world in which they now lived.

For many, the continuing connection to home was reinforced by unfinished business or family obligations. John Gemmill seems to have expected Andrew, as the eldest son, to assume some responsibilities for the two sisters who were still in Scotland.[81] John also gave Andrew authority to deal with various financial matters on his behalf. In October 1824, for example, he gave his son power of attorney to settle Ann's father's estate on the family's behalf. [. . .] Three years later, Andrew was again given authority, this time to settle a debt claimed by a former neighbour.[82] Throughout the years, John offered Andrew advice on how he might proceed, but it is clear that he had confidence in his son. Five years after the affair of the will had begun, he told Andrew, "You have at least got the better of your Uncle," and expressed his satisfaction that the estate was finally settled.[83]

Isaac Wilson, a settler in Upper Canada, too relied on his younger brother Jonathan to represent his interests at home. Isaac and Jonathan maintained a regular correspondence from the time of Isaac's arrival in the colony in 1811 until his death in 1838.[84] Like many other emigrant settlers, Isaac does not seem to have written letters per se, although Jonathan apparently did. Instead, Isaac sent home an annual or semi-annual journal that was filled with details about the landscape and local politics and described his health, his work establishing his farm, and gave news of his neighbours; and, after his sister and family arrived in 1819, their news too. In 1811 Isaac was not sure that he intended to remain in the colony. The coming of war in 1812 "confounded" his plans to travel and see something of America; it also permanently interrupted Jonathan's plan to join him in Upper Canada.[85] Isaac made a brief visit home in 1814 to settle some affairs after his father's death in 1812 and undoubtedly to see his mother. He was restless, however, and he returned to his farm outside York a year later, explaining to his brother, "I have fixed myself here for some time to come if not for life."[86] Even so, for the next 20 years, Isaac still considered himself very much part of the old household and community. He kept up to date with "the state of affairs at home"[87] from

Jonathan's letters, from newspapers Jonathan sent him, and from the first-hand reports of newly arrived emigrants or travellers who occasionally appeared with letters or packages. He also periodically offered advice to his brother about how to manage various family affairs.[88]

[. . .]

The tangible bonds of family obligations and entitlements bound many emigrants to Britain long after they had begun to settle into their new homes. Only a relative few, however, would have had an inheritance to collect or were entitled to the proceeds from an ongoing business interest. Yet sons and daughters, sisters and brothers, parents and children often continued to feel a sense of responsibility for kin—especially for their parents—on the other side of the Atlantic. Shortly after Isaac Wilson returned from his visit home, he wrote to his brother saying, "I hope my mother and you are living agreeably together in the way I left you. You must indulge her as much as you can to preserve peace among you."[89] Mother and son obviously did not live together for long. In 1824 Mrs Wilson's house was broken into. After expressing his sorrow at the damage, Isaac wrote, "It is gratifying to me to hear that things are taken care of," and he thanked his brother for his efforts.[90] Three years later, Isaac commented, "I am sorry to hear my Mother has not her health so well as usual. I think it would be better for her to try to live along with Ann or somebody than to live any longer by herself, so that she could be taken care of in case of sickness."[91] Divided by the Atlantic, there was little that Isaac could do directly for his mother, however, except provide advice and encouragement to her and his brother.

When all the children had left home, the situation could become even more complicated and worrying. For some, the problem was resolved when their parents decided to join them in America. A number of letters from Upper Canada urged parents to come, offering to send them "some assistance" for the passage.[92] Others asked friends or relations still in Britain to ensure that Mother or Father was settled and healthy. Two Petworth emigrants, for example, George and Mary Boxall, asked friends to "pray leave" their "poor mother at Henly, a sovereign" before they left.[93]

Emotional and financial support flowed both ways. John Scott's first letter to his uncle Andrew Redford was prompted by the loan of 50 pounds received from Andrew and "other kind friends."[94] Mary O'Brien periodically received monetary gifts from Aunt Sophie, for which she was always most grateful.[95] And for the first few years in the Belleville area, Fanny and William Hutton relied on funds they received from his parents to offset their growing debts. Although Fanny was a hesitant and apparently infrequent correspondent, she explained in a lengthy letter to "Dear Mrs Hutton" (as the letter began) the specific circumstances that had given rise to one particular request for assistance in this "time of trouble."[96] The details of the problems concluded with a plea for help: "The present exigency of our circumstances had prompted me to through ourselves on your kindness." If the immediate family could not lend them the "sum asked by William," she said, or "if you take a different view of our affairs from us," then she and William "would be glad" of "any suggestions which may at any time strike any of you as useful or necessary to us."[97]

Although most new arrivals could not expect financial assistance, a number did look forward to receiving parcels from family and friends at home. Isaac Wilson was "much obliged" to his brother for sending local newspapers, and he offered, "If you would like to have a newspaper from York, I could send you one."[98] Isaac also often received parcels from his brother that had been brought by recently arrived emigrants. "I believe I received everything safe," he wrote to Jonathan in 1822. "Both newspapers, one pair of good stockings, and the spectacles I find very useful."[99] Fanny Hutton, John and Anne Langton, and

Mary O'Brien were delighted when packages arrived containing cloth, books, and clothing that were often difficult to find in Upper Canada. Often as important were small tokens or presents from family and friends at home. David Gemmill's new watch, Anne Langton's pictures drawn by her brother, and other mementos became treasured possessions. They were physical representations that the recipient was not forgotten;[100] they reinforced the emotional ties to home, and they helped keep alive the images of family and friends and the landscape of their youth.

Six years after he left home, John Scott wrote to his cousin, "My heart still warms when I think on many localities in my native land I used to frequent and the friends and acquaintances I have left behind—tho' I have forgotten the names of many persons and many places, with the Poet I can still exclaim—'yet he behold her with the eyes of spirit—He sees the form which he no more shall meet—She like a passionate thought is come and gone—while at his feet the bright well bubbles on.'"[101] John Scott was certainly not the only emigrant who wrote home with vivid images in his mind. As one of his brothers wrote, "You can scarcely form any idea of a person's feeling and Emotion who has been absent from his native country so long as I have been." He explained, "Time and distance gives a sort of enchantment, a melancholy pleasure which words are quite unable to express."[102] For the two brothers, even after years away, the landscape of Scotland continued to capture their imagination and give them a connection to home. In his letters, Archibald Scott remembered walking to school with friends past local landmarks and wondered what had happened to his old schoolmaster. This was the place, he wrote, where he was born and spent his childhood: "It seems as I was then completely happy."[103]

Such racking homesickness was not shared by all in the family. John explained to his cousin in 1844 that most of his brothers

and sisters, who were all younger than he, did not "care much about seeing Scotland again." Of course, his parents could "never forget old friends, old faces and bygone times in Scotland," but after 10 years in the colony he and his siblings were "all naturalized now." John continued, "I am now become part Dutchman, part Canadian and part everything else for I live among all kinds of people and feel at home with them all."[104] A year later, he commented that he understood when many of his acquaintances who had gone home for a visit had thankfully returned "home" to Upper Canada. "They could nor remain in the Old Country" he explained, because they were "so accustomed to American habits." John felt the same and declared, "We are now, of course, all Canadians."[105]

[. . .]

Even after years away, for the Scott children and cousins living in Upper Canada, letters and newspapers from home were tangible evidence that they had not been forgotten. As William Knox wrote to his cousin in 1843, "I was beginning to think you had forgotten me altogether as it was such a very long time since I had received a Letter from Hermiston [the home farm]. I can assure you nothing for this long time gave me more pleasure than your Letter which I received last Month."[106] Letters and newspapers evoked images of home. Emigrant settlers knew that this was often an imaginary world. But they maintained the sense of a shared landscape and a shared past with those they had left behind. Although relationships were often idealized and landscapes unchanging, this increasingly imaginary world was very real in many emigrant settlers' minds. As they wrote home, they could see the faces and places of those they wrote to; they could smell the teapot brewing on the hearth and could hear the sounds of cattle or sheep, or the marketplace. This provided much of the foundation for the conversational nature of emigrant letters and the immediacy of their tone. Many, like John Scott, "fondly yet wish again to see my old Fetherlaw and my friends there."[107] In the meantime, letters would have to suffice.

[. . .]

For those who remained behind, maintaining the transatlantic community may well have been more difficult, particularly if emigrant settlers did not have the means or desire to return for a visit. But maintain it many did, and in the process they vicariously became part of the emigrants' world. For those waiting for letters from home and then responding often months and sometimes years later, the post was a vital part of their new lives. Maintaining contact over a great distance was not easy. The vagaries of the mail complicated the problems created by mobile populations and accidents, illness, or even death that abruptly ended such connections. Many emigrants, either by choice or by chance, lost touch with family at home. Many others were determined not to. Even those who did not write sent and received "reports" to and from family and friends at home. The arrival of visitors from the other side of the Atlantic certainly strengthened these long-distance relationships; for most, however, their continuing ties to home depended on the vital links of letters.

Transatlantic correspondence was an integral part of the emigrants' world. In the early years, it provided a sense of place and reassurance as they negotiated their way through a strange land. Many wrote home, either regularly or after years of silence, to renew bonds of affection. Sending and receiving letters also affirmed their identity as fathers, mothers, sisters, brothers, and cousins—in short, as part of a familial network that was rooted not in time and place but in relationships of affection and obligation. In many ways, this part of the emigrants' world rested on imagined landscapes, faces, and relationships. For the Gemmills, the Scotts, the Wilson brothers, and the thousands of others both at home and away, this transatlantic web of kin and community was central to their lives.

NOTES

1. Pengelly Family Papers, Harriet Pengelly Diary, 27 May 1835, Trent University Archives (TUA), 70–001/1/4.

2. Ibid., 26 May 1835.

3. Ibid., 29 May 1835.

4. Ibid., 5 June 1835.

5. Ibid., 8 June 1835.

6. Ibid., 10 June 1835.

7. Ibid., 14 July 1835. See also 26 August 1835, when Harriet wrote: "Received a nice long letter from Sophy . . . very, very happy."

8. Ibid., 14 March, 12 April 1835.

9. Ibid., 6 April, 8 May 1835.

10. Ibid., 26 March, 28 May 1835; also 3 March 1836, when she noted "a very disagreeable day" and that she had written three letters.

11. Harriet Pengelly Diary, 20 August 1835; also 14 August; 5, 10, 12 and 22 September, 1 October 1835.

12. Ibid., 21 August 1835. See also 27 February, 5 March 1836.

13. Ibid., 4 October 1835. See also reference to returning home, 21 July 1835.

14. Ibid., 3 January 1836. See also 16 December and 29 November 1835.

15. Ibid., 1 January 1836.

16. Charlotte Erickson, *Invisible Immigrants* (Ithaca & London: Cornell University Press, 1972) was one of the first historians to gather and analyze nineteenth-century immigrant letters. Not surprisingly, she discovered that most surviving letters were from immigrants of the literate, "middling" ranks of British society. David Fitzpatrick's ground-breaking study, *Oceans of Consolation: Personal Accounts of Irish Migration to Australia* (Ithaca & London: Cornell University Press, 1994), gathers and rests on letters from those who travelled steerage.

17. Harriet Pengelly Diary, 3 August 1835.

18. Journals of George Pashley, 2 or 3 December, Archives of Ontario (AO) MU843.

19. Jane Harrison, *Until Next Year: Letter Writing and the Mails in the Canadas, 1640–1830* (Ottawa: Canadian Postal Museum and the Canadian Museum of Civilization, 1997), 2, notes that in a somewhat earlier period, literacy, at least in Lower Canada, was relatively high. The collection of letters in Wendy Cameron, Mary McDougall Maude, and Sheila Haines, eds, *English Immigrant Voices* (Montreal and Kingston: McGill-Queen's University Press, 2000), attests to this in the Upper Canadian situation; Cameron notes that among the Petworth emigrants, about one-third were literate (ibid., xxvii–ix).

20. In addition to those in *Voices*, see letter of John Connel, 12 July 1845, National Library of Scotland (NLS), ACC7021. See also journal of George Forbes from Canada to Aberdeenshire, included in letter of 18 July 1845; Forbes's first letter was sent to "Dear Parents" on 23 May 1845 (Forbes Letters, Scottish Record Office [SRO], RH4/80).

21. William Knox to Andrew Redford, 28 October 1838, Redford Papers, SRO, GD1/815/15.

22. See, for example, the letter of Rebecca Longhurst to Mrs Weller (mother), 4 October 1832, no. 31, *Voices*, 61.

23. See letter of Simeon Titmouse to — Jackson, 11 September 1832, no. 23, *Voices*, 47.

24. William Hewitt to father and mother, William and Elizabeth Hewitt, 6 July 1836, no. 108, *Voices*, 206. See also Henry Smart to James Napper, 5 November 1832, no. 44, *Voices*, 77.

25. 5 August 1832, no. 16, *Voices*, 33.

26. This is the salutation for the letter of Richard Neal, 20 July 1832, no. 5, *Voices*, 16.

27. Letter to John Colquhoun, 10 December 1823, "Emigrant Letters," SRO, GD1/814/5. See also John Barnes to his father, 1 January 1837, no. 126, *Voices*, 246–50, which included specific directions on how and to whom it was to be distributed; also letter of Jesse Penfield to Mr and Mrs Hill, 1 January 1833, no. 50, *Voices*, 94.

28. Upton to mother, 19 September 1832, no. 27, *Voices*, 52–3.

29. William Phillips to Mrs Newall, 5 August 1832, no. 13, *Voices*, 30.

30. Simeon Titmouse to — Jackson, 11 September 1832, no. 23, *Voices*, 48.

31. John Luff to Aunt Foster, 29 July 1832, no. 11, *Voices*, 25–6.

32. References to this appear in almost all letters or journals. See, for example, letter of Richard Neal to William and Abigail Neal, 18 November 1832, no. 46, *Voices*, 79, which stated, "I have sent you a letter in July; but I have not had any answer yet: but Hope you will send me one soon." See also Edward and Hannah Bristow letter to brother, 20 July 1833, no. 82, *Voices*, 138.

33. See chapters 1 and 4 above and Elizabeth Jane Errington, *Wives and Mothers, School Mistresses and Scullery Maids* (Kingston & Montreal: McGill-Queen's University Press, 1995), chap. 3, for discussion of desertion within the colony.

34. Gemmill Family Papers, John Gemmill to Andrew Gemmill, 25 June 1823, SRO, TD293.

35. Ibid., 6 December 1826. See also a later letter, 2 May 1828, asking Andrew to find the brother of William Miller, who wanted him to write because he was "anxious."

36. John Gemmill to Andrew Gemmill, 6 August 1827.

37. Ibid., 17 September 1828.

38. See Thomas Adsett to his father, 25 June 1833, no. 71, *Voices*, 123, which ended: "Wrote by James Rapson: his wife and family are all well." Also Elizabeth Wackford to Mrs Sarah Green, 25 June 1833, no. 71, Voices, 124–5. See discussion in *Voices*, xix. The problems of literacy went both ways. For example, Charles Johnston wrote to his former employer, Thomas Tryon, Esq., announcing his arrival and asking him to pass on news to family members; he also asked Tryon to let him know how his wife's parents were, since they could not write; and he sent on a message to his brother that if he intended to emigrate, he should write and Johnston would "remain here till he comes" (Tryon of Bulwick Collection, Northamptonshire Record Office [NRO], TB869).

39. For example, his August 1836 letter concluded, "John Heather from Petworth wishes you to call at Botting's, to know how his sister is at Redhill: he is well" (James Rapson letter, 30 August 1836, no. 115, *Voices*, 214). See also Rapson letters nos. 2, 12, 38, 76, in *Voices*, and letters of his in-laws, the Tribes, Henry and Charlotte Tribe (12 February 1833, no. 54, *Voices*, 102). The annotations in the published letters of the Sussex emigrants suggest that sometimes letters were communal

undertakings, with two or three people writing individual notes to different recipients, well aware that all would read their news (*Letters from Sussex Emigrants* [Chichester, 1837], 37–41).

40. *Chronicle and Gazette*, 11 July 1835. A reward was also offered for information about James Honey, a tailor—either his current place of residence or a certificate attesting to his death (ibid., 19 August 1835).

41. *Farmer's Journal*, 13 May 1829. See also *Kingston Gazette*, 25 August 1818, looking for Alexander Langton, who had last been heard of in 1799 or 1800; *Kingston Chronicle*, 3 August 1819, looking for John Spence; *Kingston Chronicle*, 13 April 1821, looking for Donald Campbell, originally of Argyleshire, by agent in York.

42. *Kingston Chronicle*, 13 June 1829. See also *Cobourg Star*, 30 August 1843, Thomas Eyre of Cobourg and Richard Dingley, Esq., of Launceston, England, were looking for Edmund Turner Colwell, from Devon, who would learn something to his advantage.

43. See, for example, *Kingston Chronicle*, 4 July 1823, looking for William Holliday, native of Yorkshire; *Christian Guardian*, 19 April 1837, looking for "Edward, the son of Anthony and Sarah Brown" of London, who was entitled to £2000 from the estate of his maternal uncle: the solicitors were looking for him. Also *Cobourg Star*, 2 October 1844, Messrs Trehern & White, solicitors, in London were looking for John Blomfield, who had left home nine years before.

44. See discussion in *Voices*, xxxiii–xxxv.

45. See Harrison, *Until Next Year*, 125–7. David Gerber notes in *Authors of Their Lives* (New York: New York University Press, 2006) that sending letters overseas could be expensive and required planning and some knowledge of the postal system. For an intriguing discussion of "Using the Postal Service," see ibid., chap. 4.

46. John Gemmill to "Dear Wife and Family," 2 March 1822, with annotations that it was received on 23 November 1822, SRO, TD293.

47. Ibid., John to Andrew, 19 September 1823.

48. Isaac Wilson, Dear brother, 24 June 1821, Isaac Wilson Diaries.

49. Harriet Pengelly Diary, 5 September 1835, Pengelly Family Papers. In this particular sequence, Harriet became increasingly anxious, because she continued to check the mails (10 September, 12 September, 22 September, 1 October), but the long-awaited letters did not arrive until 3 October 1835. She noted similar delays and frustrations in later months.

50. Mary O'Brien Journals, 1 January 1836, AO.

51. See, for example, letters to Andrew of 1 June and 17 September 1823, SRO, TD293/1.

52. John Gemmill to Andrew, 21 June 1823.

53. Dear Brother, 24 June 1821, Isaac Wilson Diaries.

54. Wilson noted in a letter to his brother, 13 December 1834, Isaac Wilson Diaries, that he intended to send deeds home by private conveyance for exactly this reason.

55. Journals of George Pashley, February 1834, 16.

56. See Wilson letter to his brother, 26 April 1832, Isaac Wilson Diaries.

57. John Gemmill to Andrew, 21 June 1823.

58. Ibid., 21 November 1825.

59. Ibid., 21 May 1823.

60. Ibid., 21 June 1823.

61. Ibid., 8 June 1829.

62. Ibid., 17 September 1823.

63. Ibid., 6 December 1826.

64. In a remarkable passage, John passed on remarks from Jennet: "She has not got the imitation of that Black Man you sent her yet," ibid.

65. Andrew to Mother and Father, 2 October 1824, ibid.

66. Ibid., John to Andrew, 30 April 1824.

67. Ibid., 8 November 1824.

68. Ibid., 21 November 1825. This image of the kettle was also invoked by John and Caroline Dearling to Brothers and Sisters (15 July 1838, no. 134, *Voices*, 276–7).

69. Ibid., John Gemmill to Andrew Gemmill, 25 September 1832.

70. Ibid., 8 November 1824.

71. Ibid., 24 November 1829. Five years earlier, John had replied to what appears to have been a thoughtful letter from Andrew: "I take you kind advice . . . and I hope you will daily and hourly take to yourself the uncertainty of time and the precarious nature of all its enjoyments ought never to be forgot and our preparation for our eternal state ought to be our daily or hourly our constant study and employ as the basis of our Eternal felicity" (4 October 1824).

72. Ibid., 24 November 1829.

73. Ibid., 6 December 1826.

74. Ibid., 6 August 1827.

75. Ibid., 25 September 1832.

76. See Errington, *Wives and Mothers*, chap. 1, for an account of Mary making her decision.

77. Mary O'Brien Journals, AO, 13 February 1832.

78. Ibid., 15 April 1830, 14 February 1832, 13 July 1836.

79. Ibid., 25 July 1836.

80. The Miller Letters, TUA, B–70–1001, 24 March 1845.

81. See, among others, John Gemmill to Andrew, letters of 11 May and 21 June 1823, John Gemmill Family Papers, SRO.

82. Ibid., 6 August 1827.

83. Ibid., 8 June 1829.

84. Isaac Wilson Diaries. Isaac and his father had arrived in the colony in mid-1811. His father apparently returned home and John stayed. See 21 June and 19 November 1811.

85. Ibid., mentioned in letter of 24 May 1815.

86. Ibid., 30 August 1815. The letters/journal included considerable detail about the War of 1812, Wilson's sympathy with the Reformers in the 1830s, and a host of other political, social, and economic events in the colony.

87. See Isaac Wilson Diaries, 24 June 1817, 7 September 1819, and 15 November 1830.

88. See ibid., 24 June 1817 and 13 July 1822.

89. Isaac Wilson Diaries, 20 August 1815.

90. Ibid., 27 April 1824.

91. Ibid., 31 March 1827.

92. See, for example, letter of William Upton to his mother, 16 September 1832, no. 27, *Voices*, 53. See also Ann Thomas to Father, 15 October 1832, no. 37, *Voices*, 68–9; Thomas Adsett to Rev. Robert Bidsall, 21 December 1832, no. 49, *Voices*, 87–8. Charles Moore, on the other hand, in a letter to his father (c June 1833, no.

69, 110–11), told his father not to come: "It is not fit for old people."

93. George and Mary Boxall and William Tilly to family, 16 September 1832, no. 25, *Voices*, 50. See also George and Anna Hills to Father, Mother, Brother, and Sister, 8 March 1833, no. 63, *Voices*, 108–9, who "hoped" that family members would "ever be kind" to mother and father now living with them. John and Caroline Dearling to brother and sister, 15 July 1838, no. 134, ibid., 276–7.

94. Redford Papers, John Scott to Andrew Redford, 29 September 1835.

95. Mary O'Brien Journal, 20 June 1830 and 24 September 1835.

96. *Hutton of Hastings*, ed. Boyce, 2 July 1837, 57.

97. Ibid., 61.

98. Isaac Wilson Diaries, 28 October 1828. Newspapers were sent on 26 July 1830. In the early 1820s there were apparently problems having newspapers forwarded from Montreal (9 September 1820).

99. Ibid., 13 July 1822. See also 24 June 1821 and package that arrived with emigrant William Brown, 26 July 1830.

100. See, for example, Redford Papers, letter of Isabel Scott to her aunt Mrs Redford, 16 April 1840.

101. Ibid., John Scott to George Redford, 18 September 1840.

102. Ibid., undated letter, Archibald to his cousin.

103. Ibid.

104. Ibid., John Scott to cousin, October 1844.

105. Ibid., John Scott to Uncle Andrew Redford, 12 November 1845.

106. Ibid., William Knox to cousin, John Redford, 24 April 1843.

107. Ibid., John Scott to uncle Andrew Redford, 12 November 1845.

4 From Scott See, "'An Unprecedented Influx': Nativism and Irish Famine Immigration to Canada," *American Review of Canadian Studies* 30, no. 4 (2000): 429–53. © ACSUS, reprinted by permission of Taylor & Francis Ltd, www.tandfonline.com on behalf of ACSUS.

During the dreadful famine summer of 1847, as thousands of indigent Irish streamed from floating "coffin ships" to meet their fate in the cities and countryside of British North America, a growing number of people vociferously expressed fears that had been simmering for well over a decade. Disquieted members of Canada's House of Assembly, for example, unanimously agreed to address Queen Victoria with their "apprehensions" concerning the "unprecedented influx of Emigrants from Great Britain and Ireland in a state of destitution, starvation, and disease, unparalleled in the history of this province."[1] Genuine concern for the condition of the immigrants was swiftly tempered, and then virtually disappeared, as native-born and immigrant Protestants considered the possible ramifications that the accelerated introduction of large numbers of Irish Catholics would have on British North American society. Within a decade, the same Toronto newspaper that had once greeted the famine migration with humanitarian appeals for aid had hardened its opinion into a nativist resolve to bar further Irish-Catholic emigration entirely. In response to news from the United States that thousands of "unenlightened and bigoted Romanists" might slip northward across the border, the *Globe* predicted "a great calamity, dangerous to our civil and religious liberty, a calamity which every true patriot, Protestant as well as Roman Catholic, should endeavour, by all means in his power, to avert."[2]

The first clear episode of nativism—the emphatic rejection of immigrants because of their foreign identification—in pre-Confederation Canadian history was triggered by the events of the late 1840s. Strikingly, this response to the famine Irish, which was fuelled by a mixture of Protestant anxiety over the global spread of Roman Catholicism and an antipathy to Celtic peoples, has to date received little historiographical attention.[3] Yet the Canadian experience coincided with nativism in the United States, a more widely recognized phenomenon that became an integral component of nationalism and political-party formation. Canada's nativism may even have matched America's in fervour during the mid-nineteenth century, although its manifestations were certainly different.

This study seeks to identify and explain the nativist response to the famine Irish who made their way to Canada. British North American nativism was complex and varied, depending on economic, demographic, and social themes in various provinces, yet its disparate elements may be characterized by several interrelated themes. The first might be understood as a critical mass dynamic, which suggests that a dramatic number of Irish-Catholic immigrants rapidly surpassed an acceptable "threshold" when they settled among or near native-born and immigrant Protestants. The international context of anti-Catholicism, a pervasive impulse in the Western world of the nineteenth century, represents another basic principle at work. The third addresses chronology, suggesting a confluence of events as this immigrant cohort altered and was in turn shaped by British North America's political, economic, and social landscapes. Nativism was one of the tremors that rippled across North America as powerful ethno-religious plates collided in the mid-nineteenth century.

Nativism has been a recurrent social and political force in the last two centuries of American history. John Higham, who concentrated his energies on American movements, defined nativism as the "intense opposition to an internal minority on the ground of its foreign . . . connections," or a "defensive type of nationalism." Though Higham cautioned that the word "nativism," of nineteenth-century derivation, over time assumed pejorative connotations, his definition provides a durable intellectual device for analyzing a host population's reaction to immigrants.[4] [. . .]

In Canada, nativism is found in Indigenous organizations, such as the Protestant Protective Association, and imported ones, such as Ireland's ultraloyal and zealously Protestant Orange Order. Loyalty to the British Empire constituted a core element of Canadian nativism. The following argument challenges the notion that Canadian nativism was dramatically weaker than the American version in the nineteenth century.[5]

With some notable exceptions, including Native peoples, blacks, and pockets of European immigrants, the British North American colonies were relatively homogeneous well into the nineteenth century. Anglo-Saxon and Gallic influences predominated, reflecting the classic British and French "European charter groups" of colonial Canadian history. While revisionist scholars have convincingly demonstrated that a significant number of Irish Catholics were present in Canada before the years of the potato blight, most agree that the Irish famine migrants had a profound and lasting influence, especially in the principal ports of embarkation.[6] In 1847 alone, Canada absorbed approximately 100 000 arrivals, of whom roughly 90 per cent were Roman Catholics. By the time the famine abated and Irish-Catholic immigration dropped precipitously in the early 1850s, tens of thousands of newcomers had landed, ensconced themselves in urban enclaves, and moved into hinterland communities in search of farmland and work.[7]

The Maritime colonies, and New Brunswick in particular, received thousands of famine migrants. The stream of Irish peoples, which had coursed steadily during the 1840s, became floodwaters during the famine years. The 15 000 who arrived in New Brunswick during the peak year of 1847 indicated a seventeen-fold gain over 1843's figure. Immigration rates decreased dramatically after 1848, and by 1855 numbers would once again be on a par with 1843.[8] Saint John, the province's leading port, was poorly prepared to cope with the overwhelming number of immigrants. As was typical of coastal North American cities, a quarantine station in the harbour—Partridge Island—was constructed to serve as a primitive buffer between passengers with communicable diseases and local residents.[9]

Although many Irish used New Brunswick as a temporary depot on their way to the United States, approximately half of those who arrived settled in the ports or hinterland. During the late 1840s, Irish flocked to enclaves in the Saint John region; while those areas already contained some native-born and more established Irish-Protestant immigrants, contemporaries rapidly identified them as bastions of Irish Catholicism.[10] Famine immigrants also sought out towns and larger agrarian communities; many were prompted by an established provincial policy to encourage the interior settlement of badly needed farm labourers and servants who would work for "moderate wages."[11] Their migration patterns can be traced along the major river systems of the St John, the Miramichi, and later the St Croix. Large numbers of immigrants located in Fredericton, the provincial capital, where in 1851 an impressive 45 per cent of the heads of households claimed Irish birth.[12] Along the Miramichi, they settled close to established communities on the tributaries and poorer land that had been passed over by original settlers. The Irish took jobs as wage labourers in lumber mills, they set up tailor shops and clerked, and many pursued their old occupations of farming and agrarian labour.[13]

Nova Scotia's experience with famine immigrants differed in significant ways from its neighbour's. A province born of North American skirmishes in larger French and British imperial conflicts, Nova Scotia had by the nineteenth century a population that included prominent clusters of Roman Catholics. By 1827 they numbered just over 20 000 of a total population of 95 083, or 21 per cent; by the census of 1851 provincial Roman Catholics had grown to 69 634 of a total population of 257 675, or 27 per cent. While the percentage of Roman Catholics declined by the census of 1871, for the critical years around mid-century the infusion of famine Irish galvanized an anti-Catholic response in the colony.[14] This was particularly true in Halifax, Nova Scotia's major port, which had been recognized since the late eighteenth century as a city with a substantial number of Irish-Catholic residents. By 1837 fully 35 per cent of its population was Catholic; in 1851 the figure had grown to over 42 per cent. About 1200 famine immigrants arrived in 1847, a modest number by North American standards, but the increasing percentage of the city's Catholic population helped to account for growing Protestant intolerance.[15] As the provincial figures did not reflect such a dramatic immigrant surge, Halifax with its commanding Irish-Catholic population became the focal point for nativism in the colony.

Prince Edward Island's population mixture facilitated the introduction of nativist elements in the mid-nineteenth century as well. [. . .] Throughout the 1840s and 1850s, the Island experienced a population growth that surpassed any comparable period in its history. In 1841 the population stood at over 47 000; by 1861 it reached 80 857. The number of foreign-born as a percentage of the Island's total population, for example 30 per cent in 1848, was also substantial during this period. Second only to Scots immigrants, most of whom were Protestants, Irish Catholics migrated to the province around mid-century. Subsequently the Island's rate of growth began a decline that would linger into the next century.[16] Thus the nativist reaction became entrenched when immigrants, notably Irish Catholics, comprised a considerable proportion of Prince Edward Island's population.

The famine immigration's impact on Quebec rivalled or surpassed the drama found in the Maritime colonies, primarily because the St Lawrence River provided direct access to Quebec City and Montreal. Of the roughly 80 000 migrants who arrived in 1847, virtually all were channelled through the two cities.[17] While many of the immigrants pushed inland to Ontario or south to the United States, thousands located in the province. The Irish accounted for almost 44 000 of Quebec's population in 1844; by 1851–52 they had grown to 51 499.

Perhaps most importantly, they settled in great numbers in port communities where their predecessors had established a modest presence before the famine. The bulk of Irish-Catholic males gravitated to unskilled positions in the workforce; for example they comprised a key labour component in the construction of canals from the late 1820s through the 1840s.[18] Quebec City experienced an 800 per cent growth of Irish between 1821 and 1851, but probably the legacy of the famine migration was felt most acutely in Montreal. Irish Catholics represented over 20 per cent of its total population by the early 1860s and, much to the alarm of many Quebeckers, they outnumbered the Protestant Irish, Scots, and English combined.[19] The Irish eked out an existence in squalid areas that became identified with their cultural and religious traditions, such as Griffintown in the city's southwestern section along the riverbanks.[20] While Montreal housed nearly 40 per cent of Quebec's Irish by the early 1860s, substantial numbers were also drawn to smaller cities such as Sherbrooke and Trois-Rivières. Rural settlements attracted the Irish Catholics as well; individuals and families made their way along the river systems to marginal lands in the interior, including the Laurentian valley, the eastern reaches of the Ottawa River, and the Eastern Townships near the American border.[21] While some Irish Catholics undeniably became rural residents, their concentrated and explosive growth in urban locations such as Montreal contributed most to the colony's nativist reaction.

[. . .] Ontario's Irish-Catholic numbers rose dramatically in the 1830s. By 1851, Toronto's Irish Catholics comprised one-quarter of the city's population of 30 775, an increase from one-sixth in 1841; moreover they had grown at a faster rate than the other ethno-religious groups in the prior decade. The city initially absorbed over 38 000 Irish Catholics in 1847 alone, and in that year over 1000 died in the hastily erected fever sheds along the waterfront in the poorer quarters, one of which was dubbed Cabbagetown.[22] Yet one historian estimates that 35 650 abandoned the area almost immediately. The movement of peoples into the interior was kinetic and unstable; thousands of famine migrants attempted to settle on farms or find rural labour, but a significant proportion of this group returned to cities such as Toronto after they failed to procure land or employment.[23] While Irish Protestants routinely outnumbered Irish Catholics in the city that was known as the "Belfast of North America," the rapid introduction of considerable numbers of destitute Irish Catholics in the late 1840s directly contributed to a nativist response in Ontario that easily matched the fervour that other colonies witnessed.

This process essentially guaranteed that the transformation of Irish Catholics to British North America would be a doubly traumatic experience. In addition to the degradation of poverty and ever-present threat of disease, thrusting agrarian Celtic Catholics into Protestant strongholds led to massive culture shock for the immigrants and kindled a nativist reaction amongst the native-born majority. Irish-Catholic famine immigrants had dispersed throughout British North America in the late 1840s, but most had concentrated in a few urban areas close to native-born residents and more established Protestant immigrants. The combination of their decidedly "foreign" Celtic culture and Roman Catholic beliefs fuelled Canada's first significant nativist response, a phenomenon that will be brought into sharper focus by considering inter-national patterns of anti-Catholic behaviour.

Religion placed a heavy stamp on nineteenth-century peoples; it often proved a more compelling determinant of an individual's social, economic, and political status than did secular considerations. In Canada, as was the case in Europe and the United States, religious ardour cannot be understated as an important cultural and social backdrop for the Victorian age.[24] Religious beliefs often became intensified in the rigorous urban and backwoods environments of the Canadas and the Maritime colonies, where they provided a comforting refuge.[25] Religious orientation served as a keystone for both self and community identification; for the Catholic

and Protestant immigrants in North America, arguably it comprised the most conspicuous piece of "cultural baggage" that people transported to the new world.[26] The sheer intensity of religious convictions created a fertile ground for denominational conflict between Protestants and Catholics. Countless "No Popery" tracts, to cite only one example, issued forth from busy Protestant-owned presses. As the century progressed, these diatribes against the Roman Catholic Church and its adherents became intricately interwoven with racially based attacks on the Celtic Irish—the famine migration's legacy.[27]

The combination spawned one of the most powerful incentives for the nativist response in British North America, as the Irish diaspora did in Britain, the United States, and various British colonies.[28] While anti-Catholicism in Canada clearly exhibited a "derivative character," drawing sustenance from European doctrines and an international literature, it also found nourishment in local stimuli. The news of raging Papal controversies across the Atlantic, carried by the mail boats and transcribed by a robust press, touched British North America with an unmistakable poignancy. These included the "Papal Aggression" controversy, triggered by a strengthening of England's Catholic hierarchy, the authoritarian nature of the Roman Catholic church, in particular the Pope's purported authority in dictating temporal matters such as politics, pseudo-theoretical arguments about the numerous theological flaws of Catholic practices, and the perception that Catholic adherents were credulous servants who performed the bidding of priests, bishops, and ultimately the Pope.[29] Closer to home, alarmed Protestants thought of Irish Catholics as a fifth column of zealous warriors who were bent on destroying the very tenets of British North American self-identity: loyalty to the Empire and Protestantism.[30]

[. . .]

By the advent of famine migration, Canadian anti-Catholicism coursed through well-established channels. Nativism crystallized as Irish Catholics poured into the British North American colonies, giving Protestant defenders a sense of urgency that had been missing before mid-century. For example, the prolific Thomas Chandler Haliburton pointedly targeted the Irish Catholics, who were "emigrating in masses," in a classic nativist statement: Romanism "thought that if it could break down the civil power, reduce all ranks to a common level, and gradually weaken any constitutional connection between the several governments and Protestantism, it would recruit its forces from the population of its adversaries, overthrow them in succession, or perhaps overwhelm them all together."[31] Myriad editors, politicians, and Protestant votaries echoed Haliburton's points about Romanism and its purported assault on democracy.[32]

Perhaps the nativist response achieved its greatest clarity in the Maritime colonies and Ontario, where Protestant denominations enjoyed majority status. Inflated rhetoric flourished, often couched in the apocalyptic language of Papal conspiracies. One author succinctly captured the drama of the moment: "It is high time, my fellow Protestants, for us to assume in our own defence, and in behalf of our Catholic fellow subjects, a position of firm and fearless antagonism to the encroachments of the Papacy."[33] A New Brunswick newspaper noted, "perhaps a final conflict is at hand between Protestant truth and Popery leagued with Infidelity."[34] According to nativists, Catholics lied, cheated, and even murdered without remorse, secure in the knowledge that they would receive temporal forgiveness from corrupt priests. Ultimately, the conspiratorial theme became the dominant characteristic of nativist dogma in mid-nineteenth-century Canada. Fear of "the very worst kind of [Popery], *Irish* Popery," the visible spread of Catholic churches, and a general paranoia that the famine immigration signalled Catholic ascendancy, all contributed to the nativists' arsenal.[35]

Racial dogma underpinned the nativist response to the famine immigrants as well. Irish Catholics were variously characterized as the "ignorant masses" and "untameable barbarians." They comprised the quintessential "lower orders," their civility suspect because they appeared "unrestrained by any code of morals."[36] Catholics were consistently portrayed as easily duped, whereby the church hierarchy might perpetuate its "gross superstitions" or "old wives tales," and poison the minds of the "poor simple, priest-ridden" Catholic parishioners.[37] Moreover, some Protestants linked intemperance to Irish-Catholic behaviour.[38] Variations of that contention, often presented in editorials, characterized Irish Catholics as being woefully enamoured with intoxicating beverages.[39] The anti-Catholic barrage touched the minds and hearts of many individuals who naturally sought out organizations, such as the Orange Order, that would most effectively muster the Protestant vote and construct formidable defensive barriers.

Evidence abounds of the Protestants' stiffening resolve. The editorial content of Joseph Howe's *Nova Scotian* changed dramatically in the wake of the famine migration and increased confrontations between Catholics and Protestants. Whereas Howe had actively sought the readership and political support of Catholics in the years before mid-century, by the 1850s his editorials took on decidedly nativist overtones. In a characteristic attempt to draw connections between the corporate powers of the Catholic Church and Celtic proclivities, he observed: "Of the Irish Nation, or of the Irishmen in Nova Scotia, no man ever heard me breathe an ungenerous sentiment. But I am not blind to the national characteristics and foibles. I know that no people on the face of the earth have suffered more from gross misleading. Irish history teems with proofs of this assertion, and there is scarcely a City on this continent where men with some fluency, and little judgment, have not embroiled the emigrant with the resident population."[40]

[. . .]

While nativists chose from a seemingly inexhaustible supply of illustrations to rationalize their fears of Irish-Catholic encroachment, the fact that the famine immigrants settled for a time amongst the Protestant host society provided an essential rationale for Canadian nativism. A prime seed for its genesis sprouted in this atmosphere of alarm, created by the perception that destitute Irish Catholics were inundating the colonies in mid-century. The anti-Catholic reaction was most virulent in those areas that, with the possible exception of Quebec, received the greatest number of immigrants. Tensions between natives and immigrants in Quebec were tempered by the fact that virtually all of the province's French Canadians were practising Catholics. As one nineteenth-century historian observed, the "Catholic city" of Montreal was perhaps the most attractive location in Quebec for Irish Catholics to settle.[41] Quebec's case was somewhat unique, for as a general rule anti-Catholic diatribes and discord were spawned most frequently by the propinquity of Irish famine immigrants and Protestants.

Nativism was also indelibly shaped by events that coincided around mid-century. The entrenchment of anti-Catholics in the political arena, the tensions associated with struggling colonial economies, and the emergence of social institutions designed to channel and articulate Protestant goals, all provided form and substance to nativist forces. Perhaps these dynamics were most clearly signalled by the gradual removal of official anti-Catholic measures before mid-century. By 1830, in the wake of Britain's Roman Catholic emancipation measures, all of the British North American colonies had opened the franchise to adult Roman Catholic males.[42] While political tensions existed between Protestants and Catholics before the famine, they would become more widespread and varied after the 1840s.[43]

In all the colonies, the spectre of large numbers of potential Irish-Catholic voters strengthened the bonds between Protestants and political parties, especially the Conservatives, while fraternal organizations such as the Orange Order often erected the bridgework between the two. To many British North Americans, the choice between Protestant political unity and Catholic tyranny was starkly clear. Even some Liberals and Reformers shared this belief, including one politician who succinctly warned, "so long as the Protestants of this country are divided, it must be ruled by a Catholic minority."[44]

Substantial political tensions between Protestants and Catholics, for example, were clearly etched in Nova Scotia's developing political system. The tenuous coalition that had been struck between Protestant Reformers and Catholics during the 1830s all but disintegrated during the 1850s, as religious issues thoroughly infused provincial politics with an intensity that has probably not been equalled since. The Catholic political base was varied, shaped by the settlement patterns of Acadians, Irish, and Scots. Protestants, who clearly held majority status, often suppressed their denominational quarrels in order to concentrate their energies on confronting the greater Irish-Catholic peril.[45] Conservative elements, in order to undermine the alliance between Reformers and Catholics, promulgated the notion that Irish famine immigrants would have a deleterious social and economic impact on Halifax in particular and the province in general. Many asserted that Irish Catholics were incapable of behaving as loyal citizens of the British Empire.[46] The nascent Protestant Association of Nova Scotia, with ideals quite similar to those long espoused by the Orange Order, and the bitter House of Assembly Debates of 1859 epitomized the political chasm that separated Catholics, especially those of Irish ancestry, from Protestants.[47] In addition, violent episodes, the most important of which was the Gourlay Shanty riot between Scots Presbyterians and Irish Catholics in 1856, magnified political tensions.[48]

Fears of an apparent alliance between Roman Catholics and the Reform Party in

Prince Edward Island, under the rubric of tenant reform, provided a touchstone for Protestants who suspected Papal interference. For example, the *Islander*'s editor characterized his pro-Catholic counterparts of the *Vindicator* and *Examiner* as follows: "the proprietors of those papers have a common object, of far greater importance than the settlement of the land question—the attainment by the Roman Catholic Hierarchy of the supreme governing power in this island."[49] Editors encouraged Protestants to take up the "ominous war-cry," and stand "shoulder to shoulder" in a Protestant defence against supposed Roman Catholic incursions. With the party divisions increasingly being defined according to religious affiliation, and with the Catholics abandoning the Conservatives in favour of the Liberals, Protestants were drawn to the Conservatives almost by default. Dire threats of what might happen with the escalating Irish presence at the polls, evidence of the Catholics' "Godless system demanded by their Bishop," and spurious comparisons with Newfoundland's government were promulgated to convince Protestants to defend their interests in political settings.[50] A popular nativist rationale for this course of action was the 1847 election riot in Belfast, the Island's most dramatic nineteenth-century illustration of ethnic and religious confrontation.[51] In the critical year of famine immigration, it fanned the fears of Protestants who dreaded the thought of politicized Irish Catholics determining the outcome of future elections.[52]

[. . .]

New Brunswick's anti-Catholic experiences mirrored those of the other Maritime provinces. In the wake of the famine migration Orangemen and other fervent Protestants enjoyed an overwhelming political edge over the Irish Catholics, who found themselves contending with innumerable legislative and social obstacles that effectively barred them from provincial and community service.[53] The Orange Order, consisting of both native-born and Irish immigrant Protestants,

garnered support to ward off the perceived encroachments of the Irish Catholics during the 1840s.[54] Another impulse to attract Protestant voters to the Tory party yielded a remarkable marriage of interests in provincial assignments, as well as in community-level positions such as magistrates, councillors, bureaucrats, mayors, constables, sheriffs, policemen, judges, and juries.[55]

Another bedrock apprehension for anti-Catholic forces in New Brunswick, as was the case elsewhere, involved the pressing economic competition between native-born and Irish immigrants. The 1840s brought a series of depressions to New Brunswick's crucial timber industry. Irish famine immigrants, arriving during the worst years of economic distress, willingly laboured for wages far below those of the average native-born workers. Patterns of economic nativism, established before the famine, were heightened. As large numbers of Irish Catholics filtered into the colony's depressed cities and towns, unskilled native-born labourers, fearing for their jobs, greeted the penniless immigrants as anathema. The stevedores of Saint John and Portland, the day labourers in Fredericton, and the lumbermen of Carleton County and the Miramichi, all demonstrated antipathy toward the hungry Irish immigrants. This competition played an important role in the growth of nativism. Protestants called for economic segregation; merchants and employers should do business with members of their own religion, they argued. Ultimately, they hoped that ostracism would curtail Irish-Catholic immigration.[56] Thus nativists exploited a traditional fear in labour's rank and file and fashioned it into a devastating salvo in the campaign against Irish Catholics.

In Quebec, the famine immigration created similar impulses among Protestants to concentrate their modest political forces and use economic measures to ward off the perceived onslaught of Irish Catholics. The diaphanous alliance that had existed between French Canadians and Irish Catholics during the 1820s rapidly shredded during the 1830s as greater numbers of Irish caused both the French Canadians and the Protestant minority to feel socially and politically threatened. As "resentment of the Irish gradually replaced the bond of Catholicism," hostile diatribes appeared more regularly in newspapers.[57]

Tensions were perhaps most palpable in urban settings. In the ethnically concentrated environments of Montreal and Quebec City, the major point of contention between Irish Catholics and French Canadians was the establishment of separate Irish parishes. For example, by 1847 St Patrick's Church had opened its doors in Montreal, an emphatic illustration of the growing prominence of Irish Catholics. The expanding number of Irish in the workforce created another nativist fault line. As was the case in other colonies, Irish Catholics often took the most menial, lowest paying, and dangerous jobs. They toiled on canals such as the Lachine and Beauharnois, sweated as stevedores along the docks of Quebec City and Montreal, and laboured in the shipyards that dotted the St Lawrence River.[58] The infusion of large numbers of Irish Catholics exacerbated competition for employment in Quebec, but it clearly did not engender the wide-scale nativism exhibited by its western neighbour. Perhaps, as some historians have argued, the tensions between Irish Catholics and French Canadians were mitigated by the common bonds of religious identification, in spite of the rivalries noted above.[59]

Ontario's political and economic landscapes were also fundamentally transformed by the arrival of the famine Irish, and the province experienced a nativist reaction that more closely mirrored the Maritime colonies. Native responses varied according to the location of Irish-Catholic settlement and socio-political conditions; they ranged from a fear of the spread of communicable diseases to a criticism of the British government's apparently deliberate policy of depositing an unwanted human cargo in the colony.[60] Some

of the nativists' concerns were anything but fanciful. For example, the famine Irish all but destroyed the Protestant consensus in several areas, the most conspicuous location being Toronto. As more and more immigrants flooded into the province, a powerful coalition of Protestants—both native-born and immigrant—sought the political and economic means to isolate the Irish Catholics and somehow contain the spread of their religion and culture.[61] One newspaper suggested that the immigrants be transported to the interior as rapidly as possible to avoid "moral contamination" in the cities.[62]

In the hostile climate of nativism, manifested in political, economic, and social assaults, Irish Catholics struggled to survive. They were regularly vilified in the Ontario press, and through the use of tactics that were similar to those employed by their New Brunswick compatriots, Protestants assiduously worked to shut Irish Catholics out of the power structure for most of the century.[63] The Orange Order, an effective vehicle for this process, found its influence burgeoning in the decades around mid-century, its growth coinciding with the famine immigration. As one historian pointed out, despite the fact that the organization was roundly condemned by various British governors because of its vitriolic stance against Irish Catholics, it successfully forged linkages with Tory elements. As late as 1897, Irish Catholics held few municipal, police, and judicial positions in Ontario. These remained overwhelmingly the preserve of Protestants, Conservatives, and Orangemen.[64]

[. . .] Other Ontario skirmishes materialized over a host of socio-political issues. The fronts included election campaigns, the development of Sunday Schools, the use of the Bible in public education, temporal variations on the theme of "No Popery," and a rejection of famine immigrants as being unworthy and unproductive members of society.[65] Throughout all these struggles, Ontario's alarmed Protestants effectively used nativist techniques to protect themselves against the encroachment of "Irish Papists."[66]

Many Canadians believed that their future should be designed according to exacting Protestant, Tory, and British standards in the nineteenth century, and the famine Irish appeared as interlopers of the first magnitude. Political and social organizations sought to corral disparate Protestant elements in an effort to deflect the deleterious effects of Irish-Catholic immigration after the late 1840s; they formalized and legitimized nativism. The Orange Order, especially in Ontario and New Brunswick, the Protestant Alliance in Nova Scotia during the late 1850s, and the Protestant Protective Association of the 1890s, all represented societies that rose to confront the challenge of spreading Irish-Catholic interests.[67] In general, although the process was riddled with imperfections and never achieved complete success, these groups and others sought a lasting coalition between Canada's evolving Conservative parties and Protestants. Anti-Papal rhetoric, evident before the arrival of the famine immigrants, continued for the remainder of the century as "Liberal-Catholics" made modest political inroads.[68] It was periodically revitalized by events such as the Red River and North-West rebellions, the separate schools controversy, the Jesuits' Estates Act,

and episodes of collective violence, such as those generated by the fiery and charismatic apostate Charles Chiniquy, whose lectures left a trail of disturbances in the post-Confederation years.[69]

British North America experienced a nativist reaction to famine migrants in the mid-nineteenth century that rivalled the better-known American saga. Irish-Catholic males certainly had the opportunity to engage in the political process throughout most of the century, and they aggressively competed for positions in the provincial assemblies and municipalities. Still, it would be decades before they achieved a representational cohort that provided an effective counterweight to their nativist opponents. Linkages clearly took place between Conservative, Protestant, and fraternal forces to impede the perceived encroachments of Catholics in general, and the famine Irish in particular. In light of the various religious struggles in the political sphere, the intense economic competition between native-born and immigrants, the racially charged language that was bandied about in provincial assemblies, pamphlets, and newspaper editorials, the obvious attraction of nativist organizations, and the many confrontations between Protestants and Irish Catholics, Canada's history of nativism deserves closer scrutiny.

NOTES

1. *Globe* (3 July 1847).
2. *Globe* (9 February 1856).
3. Scott W. See, *Riots in New Brunswick: Orange Nativism and Social Violence in the 1840s* (Toronto: University of Toronto Press, 1993); A.J.B. Johnston, "Nativism in Nova Scotia: Anti-Irish Ideology in a Mid-Nineteenth-Century British Colony," in Thomas P. Power, ed., *The Irish in Atlantic Canada 1780–1900* (Fredericton, NB: New Ireland Press, 1991), 23–9.
4. John Higham, *Strangers in the Land: Patterns of American Nativism, 1860–1925*, rev. edn (New Brunswick, NJ: Rutgers University Press,

1988). Higham subjected his own work to a rigorous scrutiny in "Another Look at Nativism," *Catholic Historical Review* 44 (1958): 148–50; and "The Strange Career of Strangers in the Land," *American Jewish History* 76 (1986): 214–26.
5. For examples of the argument that Canada's anti-immigrant reaction was tepid by North American standards, see John White, *Sketches from America* (London: Sampson Low, Son and Marston, 1870), 355; Donald H. Akenson, *Small Differences: Irish Catholics and Irish Protestants, 1815–1922* (Montreal: McGill-Queen's

University Press, 1988), 88; and Kerby A. Miller, *Emigrants and Exiles: Ireland and the Irish Exodus to North America* (New York: Oxford University Press, 1985), 276, 323.

6. Donald H. Akenson, "The Historiography of the Irish in the United States of America," in Patrick O'Sullivan, ed., *The Irish World Wide: The Irish in the New Communities* (Leicester: Leicester University Press, 1992), 99–127; Akenson, *Small Differences*; Peter Toner, "The Irish of New Brunswick at Mid Century: The 1851 Census," in Peter Toner, ed., *New Ireland Remembered: Historical Essays on the Irish in New Brunswick* (Fredericton: New Ireland Press, 1988), 106–32.

7. Cecil J. Houston and William J. Smyth, *Irish Emigration and Canadian Settlement: Patterns, Links, and Letters* (Toronto: University of Toronto Press, 1990), 3; Donald MacKay, *Flight from Famine: The Coming of the Irish to Canada* (Toronto: McClelland and Stewart, 1990), 290–91.

8. Immigration Returns, New Brunswick Blue Books, 1840–1855, National Archives of Canada (NAC); "Report on Trade and Navigation," New Brunswick, *Journal of the House of Assembly*, 1866, Public Archives of New Brunswick (PANB).

9. Note James M. Whalen's description of the general trauma endured by immigrants in "'Allmost as Bad as Ireland': The Experience of the Irish Famine Immigrant in Canada, Saint John, 1847," in Robert O'Driscoll and Lorna Reynolds, eds, *Untold Story: The Irish in Canada*, 2 vols (Toronto: Celtic Arts of Canada, 1988), 155–6. See also W.A. Spray, "'The Difficulties Came Upon Us Like a Thunderbolt': Immigrants and Fever in New Brunswick in 1847," in Power, ed., *Irish in Atlantic Canada*, 101–26.

10. See, *Riots in New Brunswick*, 43–70; T.W. Acheson, *Saint John: The Making of a Colonial Urban Community* (Toronto: University of Toronto Press, 1985), 92–114.

11. Perley to Saunders, 22 April 1846, Correspondence, Immigration Papers, PANB.

12. William A. Spray, "Reception of the Irish in New Brunswick," in Toner, ed., *New Ireland Remembered*, 231.

13. John J. Mannion, *Irish Settlement in Eastern Canada: A Study of Cultural Transfer and Adaptation* (Toronto: University of Toronto Press, 1974), 17–27; William F. Ganong, *A Monograph of the Origins of Settlements in the Province of New Brunswick* (Ottawa: Royal Society of Canada, 1904), 73–9.

14. Census of Nova Scotia, 1851, 1861, 1871; Alexander Monro, *New Brunswick; with a Brief Outline of Nova Scotia, and Prince Edward Island* (Halifax: Richard Nugent, 1855), 319–20; Duncan Campbell, *Nova Scotia in Its Historical, Mercantile and Industrial Relations* (Montreal: John Lovell, 1873), 505; John B. Calkin, *A History and Geography of Nova Scotia* (Halifax: A. & W. Mackinlay, 1878), 88.

15. *Nova Scotian* (19 July 1852); Johnston, "Nativism in Nova Scotia," 26–27; A.J.B. Johnston, "Popery and Progress: Anti-Catholicism in Mid-Nineteenth-Century Nova Scotia," *Dalhousie Review* 64, 1 (1984): 147; Terrence M. Punch, "Irish Halifax: The Immigration Generation, 1815–1859," *Canadian Ethnic Heritage Series* 5 (1981): 6–7.

16. For dramatic evidence of Roman Catholic growth by 1861, see the detailed denominational breakdown by lots, counties, and electoral districts in the *Islander* (5 July 1861). Also note Andrew Hill Clark, *Three Centuries and the Island: A Historical Geography of Settlement and Agriculture in Prince Edward Island, Canada* (Toronto: University of Toronto Press, 1959), 83, 121. Ian Ross Robertson provided a compelling challenge to Clark's figures in "Reform, Literacy, and the Lease: The Prince Edward Island Free Education Act of 1852," *Acadiensis* 20 (1990): 55. Robertson argued that by the 1850s the Island's foreign-born population was in significant decline. Nonetheless, the compressed bulge of Irish-Catholic immigrants during the late 1840s created a population cohort that concerned Protestant elements in the following decades.

17. G.R.C. Keep, "The Irish Adjustment in Montreal," *Canadian Historical Review* 31 (1950): 39–40.

18. Ronald Rudin, *The Forgotten Quebecers: A History of English-Speaking Quebec, 1759–1980* (Quebec: Institute québécois de recherche sur la culture, 1985), 83–7; James M. O'Leary, *History of the Irish Catholics of Quebec: Saint Patrick's Church to the Death of Rev. P. McMnhon* (Quebec: Daily Telegraph, 1895), 9.

19. MacKay, *Flight from Famine,* 321.

20. Robert J. Grace, *The Irish in Quebec: An Introduction to the Historiography* (Quebec: Institute québécois de recherche sur la culture, 1993), 60–70; Herbert B. Ames, *The City Below the Hill* (1897; reprinted, Toronto: University of Toronto Press, 1972).

21. MacKay, *Flight from Famine,* 313–21; Keep, "Irish Adjustment in Montreal," 40–4.

22. Brian P. Clarke, *Piety and Nationalism: Lay Voluntary Associations and the Creation of an Irish-Catholic Community in Toronto, 1850–1895* (Montreal: McGill-Queen's University Press, 1993), 15–17; Michael Cottrell, "St. Patrick's Day Parades in Nineteenth-Century Toronto: A Study of Immigrant Adjustment and Elite Control," *Histoire sociale/Social History* 25 (1992): 61.

23. Kenneth Duncan, "Irish Famine Immigration and the Social Structure of Canada West," *Canadian Review of Sociology and Anthropology* 2 (1965): 23.

24. W.L. Morton, "Victorian Canada," in W.L. Morton, ed., *The Shield of Achilles: Aspects of Canada in the Victorian Age* (Toronto: McClelland and Stewart, 1968), 314–16; Arthur R.M. Lower, *Canadians in the Making: A Social History of Canada* (Toronto: Longmans, Green and Co., 1958), 202; William Baker, "The Irish Connection," *Acadiensis* 12 (1983): 128.

25. William H. Elgee, *The Social Teachings of the Canadian Churches* (Toronto: Ryerson Press, 1964).

26. Carl Wittke, *The Irish in America* (Baton Rouge: Louisiana State University Press, 1956), 10.

27. For useful assessments of this dynamic in Britain, see E.R. Norman, ed., *Anti-Catholicism in Victorian England* (London: George Allen and Unwin, 1968); and L.P. Curtis, *Anglo-Saxons and Celts, a Study of Anti-Irish Prejudice in Victorian England* (Bridgeport, CT: Conference on British Studies, 1968).

28. The literature on the migration of Irish in the nineteenth century is extensive. For useful collections of essays on this subject, see *The Irish World Wide* series edited by Patrick O'Sullivan, especially *The Meaning of the Famine* (London: Leicester University Press, 1997). See also Donald H. Akenson, *The Irish Diaspora: A Primer* (Streetsville, ON: P.D. Meany, 1993). The American experience is explored in Lawrence J. McCaffrey, *The Irish Catholic Diaspora in America* (Washington, DC: The Catholic University of America Press, 1997); and Arthur Gribben, ed., *The Great Famine and the Irish Diaspora in America* (Amherst: University of Massachusetts Press, 1999). For works on the Irish in the British Empire, see Patrick O'Farrell, *The Irish in Australia* (Sydney: New South Wales University Press, 1993); Donald H. Kenson, *Half the World From Home: Perspectives on the Irish in New Zealand, 1860–1950* (Wellington: Victoria University Press, 1990); and Donald H. Akenson, *Occasional Papers on the Irish in South Africa* (Gananoque, ON: Langdale Press, 1991).

29. Succinct discussions of these dynamics are found in two works by J.R. Miller: "Anti-Catholicism in Canada: From the British Conquest to the Great War," in Terrence Murphy and Gerald Stortz, eds, *Creed and Culture: The Place of English-Speaking Catholics in Canadian Society, 1750–1930* (Montreal: McGill-Queen's University Press, 1993); and "Bigotry in the North Atlantic Triangle: Irish, British and American Influences on Canadian Anti-Catholicism, 1850–1900," *Studies in Religion* 16 (1987): 289–301.

30. See, *Riots in New Brunswick,* 53–5; Johnston, "Popery and Progress," 146; Duncan, "Irish Famine Immigration," 26–7; Terrence Murphy, "The Emergence of Maritime Catholicism, 1781–1830," *Acadiensis* 13 (1984): 44.

31. *Rule and Misrule of the English in America* (London: Colburn & Co., 1851) 2: 319–21.

32. For a selection of anti-Catholic diatribes, see Rev. Robert Sedgwick, *The Papacy: The Idolatry of Rome* (Halifax: Wesleyan Conference Steam Press, 1859); Rev. Andrew King, *The Papacy: A Conspiracy against Civil and Religious Liberty* (Halifax: Wesleyan Conference Steam Press, 1859); Rev. J.L. Murdoch, *The Causes which since the Reformation Have Led to the Revival and Increase of Popery* (Halifax: Wesleyan Conference Steam Press, 1859).

33. H.M. Richey, *The Spirit of Popery, and the Duty of Protestants in Regard to Public Education* (Halifax: Wesleyan Conference Steam Press, 1859), 36.

34. *Weekly Chronicle* (18 July 1851).

35. Murdoch, *Revival and Increase of Popery,* 22 [italics in the original]; *Loyalist* (24 September 1847); *Church Witness* (6 July 1853).

36. John Earle's address, House of Assembly, 13 April 1850, in *Reporter* (10 May 1850); editorials, *Loyalist* (16 July, 17 September, 15 October 1847).

37. *Protestant and Evangelical Witness* (4 April 1863).

38. *Protestant and Evangelical Witness* (6 June 1863).

39. *Prince Edward Islander* (22 July 1864).

40. *Now Scotian* (16 June 1856).

41. John Francis Maguire, *The Irish in America* (New York: D. & J. Sadlier, 1868), 96.

42. All the other colonies had granted Roman Catholics the vote by 1810. See John Gamer, *The Franchise and Politics in British North America, 1755–1867* (Toronto: University of Toronto Press, 1969), 138–40.

43. Two notable pre-famine events that were shaped by tensions between religious and ethnic groups included the 1832 election in Montreal and a series of socio-political struggles in Bytown [Ottawa] during the 1830s. See France Galarneau, "Election partielle du quartier-ouest de Montréal en 1832: analyse politico-sociale," *Revue d'histoire de l'Amérique française* (1979): 565–84; and Michael S. Cross, "The Shiners' War: Social Violence in the Ottawa Valley in the 1830s," *Canadian Historical Review* 54 (1973): 1–26.

44. Joseph Howe, *To the People of Nova Scotia* (Halifax: n.p., 1857), 6.

45. D. Campbell and R.A. MacLean, *Beyond the Atlantic Roar: A Study of the Nova Scotia Scots* (Toronto: McClelland & Stewart, 1975), 20–3, 51–2, 55–60, 69–70, 74, 221–2.

46. Punch, "Irish Halifax," 38–9, 46.

47. For descriptions of Howe and the political struggles of the 1850s, see J. Murray Beck's various works: *Politics of Nova Scotia* (Tantallon, NS: Four East, 1985), 1: 143–6, 154; *Joseph Howe: Conservative Reformer* (Montreal: McGill-Queen's University Press, 1982), 144–5; *Joseph Howe: The Briton Becomes Canadian* (Montreal: McGill-Queen's University Press, 1983), 119–21; "The Nova Scotia 'Disputed Election' of 1859 and Its Aftermath," *Canadian Historical Review* 36 (1955): 310. The Protestant Association is addressed in *British Colonist* (18 and 25 March 1858); and Nicholas Meagher, *The Religious Warfare in Nova Scotia 1855–60* (Halifax: n.p, 1927), 191–3.

48. A description of the riots is found in *Nova Scotian* (2, 16, and 23 June 1856). The trial proceedings are included in *Nova Scotian* (22 December 1856).

49. *Prince Edward Islander* (4 March 1864).

50. *Prince Edward Islander* (17 July 1857, 12 and 19 July 1861, 6 February 1863).

51. For assessments of the clash, see *Journal of the House of Assembly of Prince Edward Island*, Appendix 1, 1847, Public Archives of Prince Edward Island (PAPEI); H.T. Holman, "The Belfast Riot," *The Island Magazine* 14 (1983): 3–7; and Ian Ross Robertson, "Highlanders, Irishmen and the Land Question in Nineteenth-Century Prince Edward Island," in L.M. Cullen and T.C. Smout, eds, *Comparative Aspects of Scottish and Irish Economic and Social History 1600–1900* (Edinburgh: John Donald, 1977), 234–5.

52. Ultimately the riot became an Island legend, as evidenced by one verse that lionized the Protestants and disparaged the Irish: "Belfast Riot," in Randall Dibblee and Dorothy Dibblee, eds, *Folksongs from Prince Edward Island* (Charlottetown: Williams and Crue, 1973), 74–8. See also *The Burning Bush and British Family Visitor* (23 June 1866).

53. House of Assembly Records, 1840–1860, PANB.

54. See, *Riots in New Brunswick*, 71–111.

55. *Carleton Sentinel* (16 and 23 July 1850, 22 July 1851, 17 July 1852, 9 July 1853); Circular from Amaranth Office, 14 January 1850, Hill to Lenentine, 31 August 1853, Resolutions from York County Lodge, 6 February 1854, Circular from James S. Beek, 17 March 1854, in Campbell Papers, PANB.

56. Saint John Common Council Report, 13 May 1840, in *Courier* (16 May 1840); Perley's Report on 1846 Emigration, in Colebrooke to Grey, 29 December 1846, Colonial Office Papers, vol. 188; *Royal Gazette* (17 March and 7 July 1847); Graeme Wynn, *Timber Colony: A Historical Geography of Early Nineteenth Century New Brunswick* (Toronto: University of Toronto Press, 1981), 155–6.

57. Mary Finnegan, "Irish-French Relations in Lower Canada," *The Canadian Catholic Historical Association, Historical Studies* (1985): 36.

58. Rudin, *Forgotten Quebecers*, 83–7, 111–13.

59. Allan Greer, *The Patriots and the People: The Rebellion of 1837 in Rural Lower Canada* (Toronto: University of Toronto Press, 1993), 158–9; Keep, "Irish Adjustment in Montreal," 45–6.

60. Pauline Ryan, "A Study of Irish Immigration to North Hastings County," *Ontario History* 83 (1991): 25.

61. One tactic employed by the Irish Catholics to cope with nativist pressure was to gather regularly in holiday celebrations. See Cottrell, "St. Patrick's Day Parades." 57–73.

62. *Packet* (24 April 1847), quoted in G.J. Parr, "The Welcome and the Wake: Attitudes in Canada West toward the Irish Famine Migration," *Ontario History* 66 (1974): 104.

63. Issues of the *Globe* throughout this period provide the mast compelling evidence in support of this point.

64. J.L.P. O'Hanly, *The Political Standing of Irish Catholics in Canada; a Critical Analysis of its Causes, with Suggestions for its Amelioration* (Ottawa: n.p., 1872), 31–3; Murray Nicholson, "The Irish Experience in Ontario: Rural or Urban?" *Urban History Review* 14 (1985): 42.

65. William Westfall, *Two Worlds: The Protestant Culture of Nineteenth-Century Ontario* (Montreal: McGill-Queen's University Press, 1989), 22, 122–3.

66. *Globe* (11 February 1856).

67. *British Colonist* (18 and 25 March 1858); James T. Watt, "Anti-Catholic Nativism in Canada: The Protestant Protective Association," *Canadian Historical Review* 48 (1967): 45–58.

68. Charles Lindsey, *Rome in Canada: The Ultramontane Struggle for Supremacy over the Civil Authority* (Toronto: Lovell Brothers, 1877), 397.

69. Pastor Chiniquy, *Fifty Years in the Church of Rome: A Record of the Life of Pastor Chiniquy* (London: The Protestant Literature Depository, 1886); Rev. Archibald Gillies, *Popery Dissected: Its Absurd, Inhuman, Unscriptural, Idolatrous and Anti-Christian Assumptions, Principles and Practices Exposed From its Own Standard Works; Being a Series of Unanswered Letters Addressed to the R.C. Bishop of Arichat, N.S.* (Pictou, NS: William Harris, 1874).

Chapter 9

Rebellions in Lower and Upper Canada

READINGS

Primary Documents

1   From "Ninety-Two Resolutions," in *Journals of the House of Assembly of Lower Canada*, 4th session of the 14th Provincial Parliament (7 January–8 March 1834)

2   From "The Seventh Report on Grievances (April 18, 1835)," in *Appendix of the Journal of the House of Assembly of Upper Canada*

Historical Interpretations

3   From "Closing the Last Chapter of the Atlantic Revolution: The 1837–38 Rebellions in Upper and Lower Canada," Michel Ducharme

4   From "From Folklore to Revolution: Charivaris and the Lower Canadian Rebellion of 1837," Allan Greer

INTRODUCTION

Like the seigneurial regime we addressed in Chapter 3, the 1837 and 1838 rebellions in Lower and Upper Canada are a touchstone in the history of the colonial period. They mark the culmination of two processes: the growth of a reform movement in Lower Canada that resented its limited influence in the colony's political life, and the growth of an alternative to unquestioned Loyalism in Upper Canada. In the case of Lower Canada, the colonial administration (especially governors Craig and Dalhousie) had made it difficult for French speakers to exercise real power in the colony, even though they formed the majority of the population. In Upper Canada, the desire among the governing group and their wealthy allies to fulfill the vision of the colony as a kind of miniature Britain led to a society that was more stratified than many citizens (reformers and radicals alike) would have preferred, and contrasted sharply with the egalitarian aura that citizens of the neighbouring United States cast about themselves.

The primary documents in this chapter illustrate the concerns reformers in both colonies had with British colonial rule during the 1830s. Although the Lower Canadian reformers conceived all their demands within the British constitutional framework, until 1828 they achieved nothing. Their failure encouraged them to adopt more radical demands (inspired by republicanism) which were embodied in the Ninety-Two Resolutions in 1834. This radicalization oriented the reformers (who were called *patriotes* in the 1830s) toward rebellion. The second primary source examined, "The Seventh Report on Grievances," shows how the Upper Canadian reformers, led by William Lyon Mackenzie, were radicals who developed a republican rhetoric in favour of reform in the 1830s. The historical interpretations considered here place the rebellions in both the international and local contexts. In his article, Michel Ducharme discusses the nature of the patriotes' and radicals' intellectual discourse and political program in the 1830s and argues that the Canadian rebellions were part of a broader movement that shook the foundation of the Atlantic world at the end of the eighteenth and beginning of the nineteenth centuries. Privileging a social approach, Allan Greer studies the politicization of the *charivaris* in Lower Canada in 1837. He shows that republican values and principles were not simply imposed on the local population by the patriote leadership, but that a popular brand of republicanism appeared in the countryside on the eve of the rebellions.

QUESTIONS FOR CONSIDERATION

1. Which of the 92 resolutions do you find most radical or confrontational?
2. How different or similar were the demands made by the patriotes and radicals in the 1830s?
3. Why did the patriotes and radicals focus on the reform of the legislative institutions in the 1830s? Why didn't they ask for the advent of a local cabinet (responsible government)?
4. How similar and dissimilar were the charivaris held in Lower Canada before and in 1837?
5. Would there have been a way to prevent the rebellions?

SUGGESTIONS FOR FURTHER READING

Buckner, Phillip A. *Transition to Responsible Government: British Policy in British North America 1815–1850*. Westport, CT: Greenwood Press, 1985.

Coates, Colin. "The Rebellions of 1837–38, and Other Bourgeois Revolutions in Quebec Historiography." *International Journal of Canadian Studies* 20 (1999): 29–34.

Creighton, Donald G. *The Empire of the St. Lawrence*. Toronto: MacMillan of Canada, 1956.

Dagenais, Maxime, and Julien Mauduit, eds. *Revolutions across Borders: Jacksonian America and the Canadian Rebellion*. Montreal and Kingston: McGill-Queen's University Press, 2019.

Ducharme, Michel. *The Idea of Liberty in Canada during the Age of Atlantic Revolutions, 1776–1838*. Montreal and Kingston: McGill-Queen's University Press, 2014.

Greenwood, F. Murray, and Barry Wright, eds. *Canadian State Trials, vol. 2: Rebellion and Invasion in the Canadas, 1837–1839*. Toronto: University of Toronto Press, 2002.

Greer, Allan. *The Patriots and the People*. Toronto: University of Toronto Press, 1993.

Jones, Benjamin. *Republicanism and Responsible Government: The Shaping of Democracy in Australia and Canada*. Montreal and Kingston: McGill-Queen's University Press, 2014.

Lacroix, Patrice. "Choosing Peace and Order: National Security and Sovereignty in a North American Borderland, 1837–42." *The International History Review* 38, no. 5 (2016): 943–60.

Ouellet, Fernand. *Economic and Social History of Quebec, 1760–1850: Structures and Conjunctures*. Toronto: MacMillan of Canada, 1980.

Read, Colin. *The Rebellion of 1837 in Upper Canada*. Ottawa: Canadian Historical Association, 1988.

Wilton, Carol. *Popular Politics and Political Culture in Upper Canada 1800–1850*. Montreal and Kingston: McGill-Queen's University Press, 2000.

Primary Documents

1 From "Ninety-Two Resolutions," in *Journals of the House of Assembly of Lower Canada*, 4th session of the 14th Provincial Parliament (7 January–18 March 1834).

1. Resolved, That His Majesty's loyal subjects, the people of this province of Lower Canada, have shown the strongest attachment to the British Empire, of which they are a portion; that they have repeatedly defended it with courage in time of war; that at the period which preceded the Independence of the late British Colonies on this continent, they resisted the appeal made to them by those colonies to join their confederation. [. . .]

9. Resolved, That the most serious defect in the Constitutional Act, its radical fault, the most active principle of evil and discontent in the province; the most powerful and most frequent cause of abuses of power; of the infraction of the laws; of the waste of the public revenue and property, accompanied by impunity to the governing party, and the oppression and consequent resentment of the governed, is that injudicious enactment, [. . .] which invests the Crown with that exorbitant power (incompatible with any government duly balanced, and founded on law and justice, and not on force and coercion) of selecting and composing without any rule or limitation, or any predetermined qualification, an entire branch of the legislature, supposed from the nature of its attributes to be independent, but inevitably the servile tool of the authority which creates, composes and decomposes it, and can on any day modify it to suit the interests or the passions of the moment. [. . .]

17. Resolved, That [. . .] the principal Agent of His Majesty's Government in this Province [. . .] has destroyed the hope which His Majesty's faithful subjects had conceived of seeing the Legislative Council reformed and ameliorated, and has confirmed them in the opinion that the only possible mode of giving to that body the weight and respectability which it ought to possess, is to introduce into it the principle of election. [. . .]

41. Resolved, [. . .] that the neighbouring States have a form of government very fit to prevent abuses of power, and very effective in repressing them; that the reverse of this order of things has always prevailed in Canada under the present form of government; that there exists in the neighbouring States a stronger and more general attachment to the national institutions than in any other country, and that there exists also in those States a guarantee for the progressive advance

of their political institutions towards perfection, in the revision of the same at short and determinate intervals, by conventions of the people, in order that they may without any shock or violence be adapted to the actual state of things. [. . .]

44. Resolved, That the unanimous consent with which all the American States have adopted and extended the elective system, shows that it is adapted to the wishes, manners and social state of the inhabitants of this continent; [. . .] and that we do not hesitate to ask from a Prince of the House of Brunswick, and a reformed Parliament, all the freedom and political powers which the Princes of the House of Stuart and their Parliaments granted to the most favoured of the plantations formed at a period when such grants must have been less favourably regarded than they would now be. [. . .]

49. Resolved, That this House and the people whom it represents do not wish or intend to convey any threat; but that, relying as they do upon the principles of law and justice, they are and ought to be politically strong enough not to be exposed to receive insult from any man whomsoever, or bound to suffer it in silence; that the style of the said extracts from the despatches of the Colonial Secretary, as communicated to this House, is insulting and inconsiderate to such a degree that no legally constituted body, although its functions were infinitely subordinate to those of legislation, could or ought to tolerate them; [. . .] [. . .]

52. Resolved, [. . .] That the majority of the inhabitants of this country are in nowise disposed to repudiate any one of the advantages they derive from their origin and from their descent from the French nation, which, with regard to the progress of which it has been the cause in civilization, in the sciences, in letters, and the arts, has never been behind the British nation, and is now the worthy rival of the latter in the advancement of the cause of liberty and of the science of Government; from which this country derives the greater portion of its civil and ecclesiastical law, and of its scholastic and charitable institutions, and of the religion, language, habits, manners and customs of the great majority of its inhabitants. [. . .]

64. Resolved, That the claims which have for many years been set up by the Executive Government to that control over and power of appropriating a great portion of the revenues levied in this province, which belong of right to this House, are contrary to the rights and to the constitution of the country; and that with regard to the said claims, this House persists in the declarations it has heretofore made. [. . .]

73. Resolved, That it was anciently the practice of the House of Commons to withhold supplies until grievances were redressed; and that in following this course in the present conjuncture, we are warranted in our proceeding, as well by the most approved precedents, as by the spirit of the constitution itself. [. . .]

75. Resolved, That the number of the inhabitants of the country being about 600,000, those of French origin are about 525,000, and those of British or other origin 75,000; and that the establishment of the civil government of Lower Canada for the year 1832, according to the yearly returns made by the Provincial Administration, for the information of the British Parliament, contained the names of 157 officers and others receiving salaries, who are apparently of British or foreign origin, and the names of 47 who are apparently natives of the country, of French origin: that this statement does not exhibit the whole disproportion which exists in the

distribution of the public money and power, the latter class being for the most part appointed to the inferior and less lucrative offices, and most frequently only obtaining even these by becoming the dependents of those who hold the higher and more lucrative offices; [. . .]
[. . .]

79. Resolved, That this House, as representing the people of this province, possesses of right, and has exercised within this province when occasion has required it, all the powers, privileges and immunities claimed and possessed by the Commons House of Parliament in the kingdom of Great Britain and Ireland.
    [. . .]

84. Resolved, That besides the grievances and abuses before mentioned, there exist in this province a great number of others (a part of which existed before the commencement of the present administration, which has maintained them, and is the author of a portion of them), with regard to which this House reserves to itself the right of complaining and demanding reparation, and the number of which is too great to allow of their being enumerated here: that this House points out, as among that number,

    lstly. The vicious composition and the irresponsibility of the Executive Council, [. . .] and the secrecy with which not only the functions, but even the names of the members of that body have been kept from the knowledge of this House, [. . .]

    2dly. The exorbitant fees illegally exacted in certain of the public offices, and in others connected with the judicial department, under regulations made by the Executive Council, by the judges, and by other functionaries usurping the powers of the legislature.
    [. . .]

4thly. The cumulation of public places and offices in the same persons, and the efforts made by a number of families connected with the administration, to perpetuate this state of things for their own advantage, [. . .]

5thly. The intermeddling of members of the Legislative Councils in the election of the representatives of the people, for the purpose of influencing and controlling them by force, and the selection frequently made of returning officers for the purpose of securing the same partial and corrupt ends; the interference of the present Governor-in-chief himself in the said elections; his approval of the intermeddling of the said legislative councillors in the said elections; [. . .]

6thly. The interference of the armed military force at such elections, through which three peaceable citizens, whose exertions were necessary to the support of their families, and who were strangers to the agitation of the election, were shot dead in the streets, [. . .]

7thly. The various faulty and partial systems which have been followed ever since the passing of the Constitutional Act, with regard to the management of the waste lands in this province, and have rendered it impossible for the great majority of the people of the country to settle on the said lands; the fraudulent and illegal manner in which, contrary to His Majesty's instructions, Governors, Legislative and Executive Councillors, Judges and subordinate officers have appropriated to themselves large tracts of the said lands; [. . .]
    [. . .]

85. Resolved, [. . .] that this House expects from the honour, patriotism and justice of the reformed Parliament of the United Kingdom, that the Commons of the said Parliament will bring impeachments, and will support such impeachments before the House of Lords against the said Matthew Lord Aylmer, for his illegal, unjust and unconstitutional administration of the government of this province; and against such of the wicked and perverse advisers who have misled him, as this House may hereafter accuse, [. . .]

86. Resolved, That this House hopes and believes, that the independent members of both Houses of the Parliament of the United Kingdom will be disposed, both from inclination and from a sense of duty, to support the accusations brought by this House, to watch over the preservation of its rights and privileges which have been so frequently and violently attacked, more especially by the present administration; and so to act, that the people of this province may not be forced by oppression to regret their dependence on the British Empire, and to seek elsewhere a remedy for their afflictions.
[. . .]

---

2 From "The Seventh Report on Grievances (April 18, 1835)," *Appendix of the Journal of the House of Assembly of Upper Canada*, 1835, vol. 1, A21-1–A21-15.

To the Honorable the Commons House of Assembly,
[. . .]

Your Committee respectfully submit the results of their enquiry, together with the evidence. If it shall appear to the House that there is just cause of complaint, and that the government has not exerted its Constitutional powers to remedy the evils from which the people desire relief, the course to be pursued is to address the Throne, stating their grievances and praying redress. If, on the other hand, the House shall be of opinion that the government is administered impartially, with sound discretion and a single eye to the general welfare; that its officers and ministers enjoy the public confidence and worthily discharge their various duties, there can be no doubt but that the Representatives of the people will mark their approbation of their conduct by cheerfully placing in their hands the small Annual Grant, which in name, more than reality, indicates a popular influence in the government.

The almost unlimited extent of the patronage of the Crown, or rather of the Colonial Minister for the time being and his advisers here, together with the abuse of that patronage, are the chief sources of Colonial discontent. Such is the patronage of the Colonial Office that the granting or withholding of supplies is of no political importance unless as an indication of the opinion of the country concerning the character of the government, which is conducted upon a system that admits its officers to take and apply the funds of the Colonists without any legislative vote whatever.
[. . .]

The patronage of the Crown, as now exercised in this Province, includes the payments of gifts, salaries, pensions, and retired allowances to the Clergy of the Methodist, Presbyterian, Protestant Episcopal & Roman Catholic orders, and to nearly the whole of the civil officers of the government, including Sheriffs, Collectors of Excise and Customs Revenue, Coroners, Justices of the Peace, Commissioners of the Court of Requests, the heads of the several departments and all in the subordinate stations under them; to Judges of the District and Surrogate Courts, Registrars of Conveyances, Wills, &c., Commissioners of Customs, Clerks of the Peace, &c. &c. These officers hold their several situations only during the pleasure of the Crown. The Royal

patronage also embraces the judicial establishment, many pensions, the nomination of the
Legislative Council, and the appointment of
its speaker and other officers,—the selection
of the officers of the House of Assembly—the
control of the Indian Department, of King's
College, and of Upper Canada College—the
appointment of the twelve District Boards of
Education, and the direction of the expenditure of public monies in aid of Emigration—
the selection of the Executive Council—the
uncontrolled management of millions of Acres
of public Lands—the appointment of 1500
commissioned Militia Officers—the sole control of the Military and Naval Forces—and
(subject to the votes of the House of Commons
in this case) the regulation of the whole Military and Naval expenditure.

The Crown also controls the expenditure
of a large annual amount of local taxation by
its power of appointing the District Magistracy during its pleasure—the justices thus
appointed select the District Treasurers and
a large number of subordinate officers, and
exercise varied and extensive civil and criminal jurisdiction. The refusal of the bench of
Magistrates of the Eastern District during the
present Session, to render to the House an account of the receipt and expenditure of the
local taxes and revenues raised from the people, and entrusted to the charge of these func-
tionaries, under the authority of several acts
of the Legislature, affords another proof that
the system under which they are appointed
requires instant revision; more especially as
the complaints of the people of that District
against magisterial peculation, as recorded
on the journals, are of long standing.

The Crown appoints the members of the
Court of King's Bench, and the Judges of that
Court regulate at their discretion the tariff
of fees to be paid therein by suitors. These
judges are dependent on the Crown for such
retiring pensions as it may see fit to award
them, if any, and enabled to look forward
with hope and expectation to the enjoyment
of other offices and situations within its gift,
by themselves and their families.

The Canada Company, the several incorporated establishments for Banking,
Canalling and other purposes, and the Harbour, Dock & Wharf Companies, in nearly
all cases, unite their patronage with that of
the local government, and steadily strive to
increase the influences of the Crown.

The Post Office Department, with about
a hundred Deputy Post Masters, is under the
solo control of the Crown—contracts are
made, and all appointments held during its
pleasure; the surplus revenue is transmitted to
England. No detailed accounts of receipts and
expenditure, have ever been laid before the
Colonial Legislature. The rates of letter postage between the different places in the Colony,
between this Colony & the others—and between Upper Canada and England, are very
extravagant. The correspondence with Europe
is chiefly carried on via: New York, which is at
once the cheapest and most expeditious route.

[. . .]

THE LEGISLATIVE COUNCIL

This body forms a part of the patronage of the
British Government; they are the nominees of
the Minister of the colonies; who can add to
their numbers at his discretion. In continually rejecting the many valuable measures
earnestly prayed for by the people, they may
be fairly presumed to act in obedience to the
power from whence their appointments were
derived. Your committee examined some of
the members of the council holding offices of
emolument under the government, and from
their answers it will readily be seen whether
they are or are not under the influence of the
Lieutenant Governors for the time being.

[. . .]

A RESPONSIBLE GOVERNMENT

The Governors of colonies, like other men,
are individually liable to all the infirmi-
ties of human nature, and in their political

capacity, when left to act without restraint, they, no doubt, sacrifice occasionally the interests and happiness of the people, to the gratification of their own passions and caprices. One great excellence of the English constitution consists in the limits it imposes on the will of a King, by requiring responsible men to give effect to it. In Upper Canada no such responsibility can exist. The Lieutenant Governor and the British Ministry hold in their hands the whole patronage of the Province; they hold the sole dominion of the country, and leave the representative branch of the Legislature powerless and dependent.

[. . .]

In Upper Canada the efforts of the Legislature have been directed towards improving the Executive Council; yet it appears on enquiry that that body affects to have done neither good nor harm—some of its individual members may, (as is asserted by Bishop Macdonell) have acquired influence near the Lieutenant Governors and misled them, but the body has few if any definite attributes, other than in the Land Granting Department, and, there, nothing but ministerial acts to perform. It is shewn in evidence by Colonel Rowan and others that the Lieutenant Governor may or may not shew the Executive Council his despatches, and may or may not ask their advice, and may or may not follow that advice after having asked it, except there be an instruction from Europe to the contrary. They are occasionally called on to report on special matters for the information of the government at home, which is often seriously and intentionally misled by them.

In the appointment to offices, and concerning the accepting or rejecting Legislative Bills, it does not appear that they have ever been consulted. Their power in the Land Granting Department has been done away in this Province by the appointment of Mr. Peter Robinson, and in Lower Canada by that of Mr. Felton, with whom the respective Governors (alone) are supposed to consult

and determine on all applications for land. The Canada Land Company monopoly too, necessarily, renders applications for grants to the government less frequent. It appears to Your Committee that the Executive Council is a nondescript with which it is folly further to contend.

There have been three classes of persons examined before Your Committee—the first, of whom Venerable Dr. Strachan is one, are of opinion that the Government is well enough as it is, and that as to responsibility it is as responsible as other Governments.

The second class desire a responsibly Ministry—some heads of departments well paid, to direct the government, to prepare bills and most of the business of the session, and to hold office or lose it according as they may happen to be in the minority or majority in the House of Assembly. This system was never attempted in any of the old colonies, but Your Committee have asked many questions with a view of ascertaining what is the public opinion concerning its practicability here; and it appears that Mr. Mackenzie, in his letters to Lord Goderich, expressed a belief that with some modifications it might be productive of a greater share of good government and public prosperity than is at present enjoyed by the people.

A third class contend for elective institutions, and affirm that while Governors come from without, and Judges are commissioned from without, favoritism towards their connexions will prevail to an extent that would destroy the influence of any set of "Ministers," constituted upon the principles desired by the second class; that the influence of Downing Street will continue to prevail as hitherto; and that the favourites of the Secretary of State will, as at present, be placed in important offices to the exclusion of better qualified men.

[. . .]

The class of persons who are in favor of elective institutions contend, that they were found to work well in the old North American colonies while in a colonial state—that the people of Upper Canada are entitled to the enjoyment of institutions equally free with those enjoyed by the old colonists during the time they were colonial, and under British protection—that few politicians are now found contending that these continental colonies, capable of containing a large population, will for a long series of years be required to submit to the inconveniences resulting from perpetual interference by the Home Government in their internal concerns—that in the House of Assembly many useful bills are proposed and carried for many successive sessions which are continually thrown out in the Legislative Council, of which the return moved for in the House of Commons by Mr. Hume and appended hereto gives particulars up to the year 1832—that it is the wisdom of the aristocracy to try to make the people fearful of themselves, by raising idle cries about loyalty, republicanism, Jacobinism, and revolution—that birth, office, or peculiar privileges ought not to give to a few superiority over the many—that the legislative council neglect and despise the wishes of the country on many important matters which a council elected by the freeholders would not—that the people, if united in claiming their privileges to constitute the second branch of the legislature, would obtain it, and that it is weakness and wavering among their representatives which alone can make them timid as to claiming the enlargement of their liberties—that the prejudices of early education, borrowed from books written by or under the authority of pensioners and salaried lawyers who have with one voice endeavoured to lull the people into the very erroneous belief that the union of church and state and the wisdom of former ages in devising great privileges for the peerage are the causes of the greatness of England, while in truth it is owing to what she has saved of popular institutions—that elective institutions are the only safeguards to prevent the Canadas from forming disadvantageous comparisons between the condition of the colonists and the adjoining

country—and that the crown of England, by its ministers, exercised no patronage in Connecticut and Rhode Island; none in the other New England States, save the appointment of a Governor; none in the proprietary governments; and that hence there is no disloyalty in freely and calmly discussing which of these modes of government that have been granted to British subjects and countries will best suit Canada.

[. . .]

The dependence of the legislative council is strikingly manifested by the facts stated in the evidence of the Honorable Colonel Clark, and the Honorable William Dickson, members of that body, before a select committee of the house of assembly during a late parliament. It appears that several legislative councillors had objected to a measure strongly urged by the executive, and its failure was inevitable. To ensure its passing, coercive means were adopted, and those members who were dependent on the government were told either to vote directly contrary to the opinions they had thus publicly expressed, or be dismissed from their offices. After this disgraceful attempt to coerce men to disingenuous and inconsistent conduct, those unacquainted with the threats which had been used were astonished at the sudden, unexpected, and unexplained change in the conduct of several members: and when this surprise was expressed to the late Honorable James Baby, (who was also an executive councillor, and the senior member) he shed tears at his humiliation, and only exclaimed "my children!" "my children!" and the late Honorable Chief Justice Powell replied to a similar enquiry of surprise, "I have received a new light within the last ten minutes."

[. . .]

We have already adverted to the circumstance of the Chief Justice being introduced into the Legislative Council, of which he is Speaker; and altho' the House of Assembly have repeatedly pointed out to His Majesty's Government, the inexpediency, in a limited community like this, of blending the judicial and political duties together, yet the same injurious system is continued. Its impropriety has been lately manifested by the result of a pecuniary negociation likely seriously to impair the independence of the judiciary and increase the distrust of the people.

[. . .]

It appears therefore that the Legislative Council, as at present constituted, has utterly failed, and never can be made to answer the ends for which it was created; and the restoration of legislative harmony and good government requires its re-construction and the elective principle.

The opinions of Mr. Fox, Mr. Stanley, Earl Grey, Lord Erskine, Mr. Ellice, Mr. Hume, Sir James Mackintosh, Mr. O'Connell, Mr. Warburton, and many other eminent British Statesmen, have been expressed in favour of elective and it appears to Your Committee that Mr. Stanley correctly describes the Legislative Council as being "at the root of all the evils complained of in both Provinces."

[. . .]

It appears to your Committee that it is more important than legislation, rendered fruitless as it is by the Legislative Council, to adopt such measures as are likely to ensure such an alteration in the system of our public affairs as seems indispensable for the peace, welfare, and good government of this important part of His Majesty's dominions. The history of all colonies shew that there has been too much inattention in the British government in the selection of Governors, it being considered a matter merely of patronage with the colonial minister, in Downing Street. Men, from the too long possession of lucrative power, whatever at first might be their relative stations soon acquire a community of interests, and thus identified in the purpose of sustaining each other in office, they have in this province made common cause against that redress of our grievances, and that conciliation of the public mind, and that economy of the public wealth, which are equally dictated by justice and wisdom.

Although the members of the Executive Council seem from their own account to render no benefit to the country, receiving however a salary from it, yet a very different duty is imposed upon them by the 31st Geo. 3rd, chap. 31, called the constitutional act, from which it appears they are appointed expressly to advice His Excellency upon the affairs of the Province. This they have never done satisfactorily. As far back as the first Session of the 10th Provincial Parliament, the House of Assembly expressed their dissatisfaction to His Excellency Sir John Colborne, in the most constitutional mode of doing so, at the opening of the Session of the Legislature; and in the following year the same sentiments were again frankly conveyed to His Excellency in the answer to His Speech from the Throne, by a solemn declaration that the Executive had long and deservedly lost the confidence of the country. In the hope of their just and constitutional wishes being attended to, the people patiently waited for relief, but the relaxation of their vigilance, which some remaining confidence in His Excellency unhappily produced, has only served to bring disappointment, and to afford a farther opportunity for the accumulation of the abuses which pervade all our institutions.

The growing condition of this part of the Empire, in population, wealth and commerce, requires there should be an entire confidence between the Executive and the Commons House of Assembly; and this confidence cannot exist while those who have long and deservedly lost the esteem of the country are continued in the public offices and councils. Under such a state of things, distrust is unavoidable, however much it is to be deplored as incompatible with the satisfactory discharge of the public business.

[. . .]

This is a state of things which, the British nation, it is presumed, cannot desire to perpetuate against us. After the right was conceded to the present United States, at the close of the Revolution, to form a constitution for themselves, the loyalists took refuge in this

Province; and, by an act passed in 31ˢᵗ year of Geo. 3. they received the charter of their liberties, conferring upon them a constitution for their peace, welfare, and good government. His Excellency, Governor Simcoe, was entrusted with the duty of putting it into operation, and in the first speech delivered by him from the throne, he made the following memorable declaration:—"I have summoned you together under the authority of an Act of the Parliament of Great Britain, passed last year, which has established the British Constitution, and all the forms which secure and maintain it, in this distant colony." And upon closing the same session he said "I particularly recommend to you to explain that this Province is singularly blest, not with a mutilated constitution; but with a constitution which has stood the test of experience, and is the very image and transcript of that of Great Britain."

It is reasonable for the people to desire to see these declarations from the throne, recorded on our Journals, faithfully observed by those in the confidence of His Majesty, and that these institutions may be made such as will secure to them their civil and religious liberties to their just extent. This country is now principally inhabited by loyalists and their descendants, and by an accession of population from the mother country, where is now enjoyed the principles of a free and responsible government; and we feel the practical enjoyment of the same system in this part of the empire to be equally our right; without which it is in vain to assume that we do or can possess in reality or in effect "the very image and transcript of the British Constitution."

The House of Assembly has, at all times, made satisfactory provision for the civil government, out of the revenues raised from the people by taxation, and while there is cherished an unimpaired an continued disposition to do so, it is a reasonable request that His Majesty's adviser in the province and those about him should possess and be entitled to the confidence of the people and their representatives, and that all their reasonable wishes respecting their domestic institutions and affairs should be attended to and complied with.

[. . .]

W. L. MACKENZIE
    CHAIRMAN.
T. D. MORRISON,
DAVID GIBSON,
CHARLES WATERS.
Committee Room, House of Assembly,
10ᵗʰ April 1835.

Historical Interpretations

3 From Michel Ducharme, "Closing the Last Chapter of the Atlantic Revolution: The 1837–38 Rebellions in Upper and Lower Canada," *Proceedings of the American Antiquarian Society* 116, no. 2 (2007): 411–28.

Half a century ago, two historians, Robert Palmer and Jacques Godechot, proposed that the late-eighteenth-century revolutions of the Atlantic World be integrated into one analytical framework. They argued that the American Revolution of 1776, the Dutch uprising of the 1780s, the unrest in the Austrian Low Countries after 1787, the French Revolution of 1789, and all of the European revolutions of the 1790s were, in fact, a single phenomenon. It was, in their view, as if one single, great revolution had shaken the Atlantic world between 1776 and 1800.[1]

Even if we can appreciate the transnational ambition of their analysis, we must recognize that this description of the so-called

"Atlantic Revolution" was really quite limited in scope, as it focused only on the United States and Europe.[2] Not a single word was said about Saint Domingue, although its unrest and revolts of the 1790s eventually led to the creation of Haiti in 1804. In fact, if we exempt the United States, it was as if the entire New World had gone missing from this Atlantic Revolution. In recent decades, historians have tried to correct this deficiency. They successfully integrated the nineteenth-century Central and South American revolutions by exploring Spanish and Portuguese colonial histories.[3] Finally, it can be said that the historical analysis of the Atlantic Revolution covers all Europe and America, between 1776 and 1840. Or can it? There is, in fact, one country's history that continues to be left out of the Atlantic framework: Canada's.

When Canadian historians have studied Canadian history at the time of the American and French revolutions, very few have tried to integrate it into an Atlantic framework. [. . .] It is true that the British North American colonies that eventually became Canada did not join the Thirteen Colonies in their revolution. It is also true that these same colonies did not take the opportunity to declare their independence during the French Revolution, or during the subsequent French Revolutionary War. This is not to say that the American and French revolutionary and republican ideals did not spread throughout the colonies during the 1780s and '90s. This is especially so in the portion of the province of Quebec that became Lower Canada in 1791. Fleury Mesplet, for instance, a French printer who had come from Philadelphia to Montreal in 1776, remained in the city after the withdrawal of American troops in May 1776.[4] Between 1785 and his death in 1794, he indirectly promoted republican ideals through his bilingual newspaper, *La Gazette de Montréal/ The Montreal Gazette*. The promotion of republican and revolutionary principles was not only the work of people within the colony.

In June 1793, Edmond-Charles Genêt, the French minister in Philadelphia, strongly urged Canadians to join the French struggle for freedom in an appeal entitled, *Les Français libres à leurs frères les Canadiens*.[5] His appeal failed to rouse his "brothers" in the colony.

So it appears that republicanism, the main ideology behind the Atlantic Revolution, did not represent a serious threat in the northern British colonies at the end of the eighteenth and beginning of the nineteenth centuries. The question arising is thus: Did republicanism or any of the key principles that inspired the Atlantic revolutionaries have any impact on Upper and Lower Canada—now Ontario and Quebec? Some distinguished scholars have argued over the years that it had a "negative" impact, Canadian history being the result of a counterrevolutionary experiment.[6] It would be interesting to discuss this question, but I will confine my paper to exploring the direct or "positive" influences of republicanism in Lower and Upper Canadian history between 1776 and 1838. I will argue that republicanism did indeed have a major "positive" impact on these colonies, although much later than in other countries around the Atlantic.

CANADA DURING THE ATLANTIC REVOLUTION (1776–1828)

In 1791, a few years after the British acknowledged American independence in the Versailles Treaty, the British government granted a new constitution to the province of Quebec. It was called the Constitutional Act in Canada, but known as the Canada Act everywhere else. One of the conscious goals of the British government in adopting the Constitutional Act was to stop the dissemination of republican principles in the province. To achieve this, the British parliament split the province into two distinct colonies: Upper Canada (now Ontario), which was mainly settled by refugees from the United

States or, as we know them, "Loyalists," and Lower Canada (now the province of Quebec), comprised of French Canadians with a vocal English-speaking minority. Thus, the Crown made sure that the Upper Canadian Loyalists could no longer complain that they were living in a French colony, while French Canadians in Lower Canada could feel less afraid of being outnumbered in their colony, could continue to live under their own civil laws, and could have free exercise of their Roman Catholic faith. This division also allowed for the granting of rudimentary parliamentary institutions to the two new colonies. The British government organized these colonial governments along the principles of "mixed" government—a system in which the king (represented by the governor or the lieutenant governor) had the executive power and in which provincial legislatures (composed of the governor, an appointed legislative council, and an elected legislative assembly) had the legislative power. The system of government conferred on Canadians in 1791 followed the usual British political system and practices, as far as colonial status would allow.

Since one of the objectives of the British government was to prevent republicanism from becoming a real threat in the province of Quebec—and thereby preventing the colony from falling into an American-style revolution—the Constitutional Act can be seen to have been a great success. It effectively prevented the spread of republican practices into the colonies. Looking at their new legislative assemblies, Canadians thought they were enjoying an excellent form of government. The fact that the assembly shared the legislative power with a British governor and an appointed legislative council did not seem to bother anyone at first.[7] On the one hand, French-speaking Lower Canadians were too busy trying to exercise their new rights in the parliamentary system to pay attention to such "details." On the other hand, Upper Canadians were too busy trying to wrestle a life out of the Ontario forests to really criticize their constitution.

If the last decades of the eighteenth century were more or less quiet in Upper and Lower Canada, things changed during the first decade of the nineteenth century. In both colonies, reform movements appeared in 1805–6, although the Lower Canadian movement was better organized, more coherent, and more efficient than its Upper Canadian counterparts. While these movements were created at the same time as the Central and South American colonies were fighting for their independence, their objectives were very different. On the whole, Canadians did not fight to obtain independence or articulate republican demands, though there were a few exceptions in Upper Canada.

Most of these reformers did not question their belonging to the British Empire or the legitimacy and form of their government. Until 1828, their demands, inspired by their reading of Locke, Blackstone, and De Lolme, aimed at gaining, for the assembly, genuine control over the executive power through a kind of ministerial responsibility, through impeachment trials, or through budgetary management, all three of which were political mechanisms that had allowed the eighteenth-century members of the British House of Commons to exercise power over the government.[8] In the end, we can say that republicanism did not have a direct or positive impact in the colonies before 1828.

REPUBLICANISM IN UPPER AND LOWER CANADA (1828–38)

Until 1828, Upper and Lower Canadian reformers, as their label implies, were not demanding revolution. But results count, and after more than 20 years of political struggles in both colonies, they had achieved nothing. By 1828, the reformers understood that they needed tougher vocabulary if they were to convince the British to reform the Canadian system. And this is how colonial reformers rediscovered the power of the republican discourse. Republican rhetoric not only gave them stronger arguments against the status quo, but it also encouraged them to question the legitimacy and the organization of the colonial political structure. After 1828, republicanism as discourse and ideology became the main source of inspiration for Lower Canadian Patriots and Upper Canadian radicals. From that moment until 1838, Canadian colonies went through a political process that corresponded to the criteria of the Atlantic Revolution. The Upper and Lower Canadian unrest of the 1830s, and its culmination in the 1837–38 rebellions in both colonies, must be considered, in my view, as the last chapter of the Atlantic Revolution, a chapter that did not end happily for Canadian republicans.

During the 1830s, all colonial republicans invoked the ideas, examples, and authority of well-known Atlantic republicans. By making these references, they were trying to gain respectability, credibility, and legitimacy. It is interesting to note that they did not often refer directly to Greek or Roman republicanism. Unlike the American patriots, the Canadian republicans did not try to connect their movement to ancient times. They were instead consciously trying to connect it to the Atlantic republican tradition that had developed during the eighteenth century. During the 1820s, their inspiration came mainly from the United Kingdom and, during the 1830s, from the United States and, to a lesser extent, from Ireland. Canadian republicans sometimes mentioned and celebrated Central and South American revolutions in their newspapers, but they were not particularly inspired by these events. Rousseauian-style rhetoric about the social contract was widely used, especially in Lower Canada, but its author was rarely mentioned or quoted extensively, nor were other French republicans. The painful memory of the Terror and the ultimate failure of the Revolution, heralded by the Restoration, led the Lower and Upper Canadian republicans to turn to Anglo-American references.

The American example was seen as useful, during the 1830s, for at least two reasons. Firstly, the American Revolution was a success and its republic an emerging power. Secondly, the Canadian republicans hoped that, by presenting their cause in a distinctly American manner, the Americans would eventually side with them, should a conflict arise between them and the British.

In 1835 Louis-Joseph Papineau, the Lower Canadian French-speaking Patriot leader, argued that if the British parliament tried to dominate Lower Canada as it had tried to dominate the Thirteen Colonies during the 1770s, many a new Jefferson or Washington would rise in Lower Canada.[9] In Upper Canada, William Lyon Mackenzie, an important radical leader, sometimes referred to Scottish heroes, such as William Wallace, Archibald Campbell (the first Marquess of Argyle), and William Russell to promote Canadian autonomy.[10] But, as in Lower Canada, it was the American Revolution and the American republic that was his real source of inspiration. In his *Sketches of Canada and the United States* (1833), Mackenzie did not hide his admiration for America's independence and institutions.

In 1836–37, the American Revolution was clearly used to encourage Canadians to fight for their rights. It had by then become "the" example to follow. In Lower Canada, the Patriots organized a boycott of British products during the summer of 1837, just as the American patriots had done during the 1770s. In October 1837, they organized a "militia" called *Les Fils de la Liberté* (the Sons of Liberty).[11] A most important public assembly was held in October 1837, a few weeks before the rebellion, which saw the adoption of many resolutions. Interestingly, the first of these was to translate the second paragraph of the American Declaration of Independence, beginning with "We hold these truths to be self-evident, that all men are created equal."[12]

At this same public assembly, a few of the Patriots urged violent actions against the state, although Papineau, their leader, was not in favour of it. He fled the colony a few weeks later, just before the rebellion. In Upper Canada, Mackenzie defended the right of Canadians to choose their form of government as a "right [that] was conceded to the present United States at the close of a successful revolution."[13] He went as far as to reprint, in the summer of 1837, in his newspaper the *Constitution,* Thomas Paine's pamphlet, *Common Sense,* first published in 1776 to promote American independence.[14] Mackenzie also wrote in his newspaper, in July 1837: "Canadians! It has been said that we are on the verge of a revolution. We are in the midst of one; a bloodless one, I hope, but a revolution to which all those which have been will be counted mere child's play."[15] By November, he published a short text entitled *INDEPENDENCE* in which he openly promoted rebellion.

The desire of Canadian republicans to connect their movement to the Atlantic Revolution, especially in its American incarnation, was clearly apparent during the 1830s.

REPUBLICANISM IN THE CANADAS: THE IDEOLOGY

Lower Canadian Patriots and Upper Canadian radicals not only appealed to the example of the republican thinkers of the Atlantic world but also adopted their ideals and principles. Therefore, they were Atlantic revolutionaries.

For Lower Canadian Patriots and the Upper Canadian radicals, as for all other republicans, freedom and equality were very closely linked. For them, individuals needed to be equal in order to be free. When republicans talked about equality, they were not talking only about equality under the law or equality of rights; they were also talking about moral equality and a certain amount of material equality. This is why both Papineau in 1823 and Mackenzie in 1833–34 were shocked

by the inequalities they saw in the United Kingdom during their visit in the metropolis.[16] Not that the Canadian republicans were social levellers; they never intended to level fortunes. But they thought that it was impossible for individuals to be free (to participate equally in political life) if there was too great a disparity between citizens, because the rich could bribe the poor and establish a form of clientelism. Amury Girod, a Swiss immigrant who came to Lower Canada in 1831, took the side of the Patriots during the 1830s, and fought as a "general" in Saint Eustache in 1837, considered that "Property is the cause of all good and all evil in society. If it is equally distributed, knowledge and power will be also . . . Liberty will sooner or later be the inevitable result."[17] Mackenzie thought much the same, and he quoted Abbé Raynald: "People of America! [. . .] Be afraid of too unequal a distribution of riches, which shows a small number of citizens in wealth, and a great number in misery—whence arises the insolence of the one and the disgrace of the other."[18]

In order to ensure the economic and social equality of citizens, these republicans envisioned a society of small landowners, all independent of one another. Mackenzie himself said: "Agriculture, the most innocent, happy and important of all human pursuits, is your chief employment—your farms are your own—you have obtained a competence, seek therewith to be content."[19] This economic independence would ensure political independence. For most Canadian republicans, life in Canada was already characterized by social equality. Their main goal was to reform political institutions to fit this social reality. In this context, colonial republicans were very suspicious of accumulation of wealth, of capitalism, of primogeniture, and of bank monopoly, which they considered detrimental to equality among citizens and might allow corruption to destroy freedom.

Canadian republicans incorporated these principles into a sophisticated set of political proposals. Considering the importance that they were giving to equality, they structured their political institutions around the idea of political equality. For them, the right of the citizens to participate in the political process was their first and most important right. The importance given to political participation implied that citizens should have the right to elect their representatives. These representatives were the only ones who could legitimately adopt laws for the well-being of all. In this context, the Patriots and the radicals concentrated their claims around the constitution of legislative power during the 1830s. Their efforts had two objectives. The first was to improve the representativeness of the Legislative Assembly in Upper Canada. In this colony, unlike Lower Canada, the radicals could not gain control of the Assembly, except between 1834 and 1836. It was clear to them that if they could not obtain a majority of the seats in the Assembly, the problem lay not in themselves but in the way that representation was framed.[20] In both colonies the efforts of colonial reformers aimed at making the legislative councils of the colonies elective, not composed of appointed members of the elite. During the 1830s, colonial republicans did not concede any legitimacy to the appointed legislative councils, the upper houses of the Upper and Lower Canadian legislatures. While a few demanded outright abolition of these bodies, most wanted to make them elective. This was the Lower Canadian Patriots' main demand. Thirty-four of the "Ninety-Two Resolutions" (the charter of Lower Canadian republicanism) adopted by their Assembly in February 1834 concerned this reform (resolutions 9–40, 51, 54).[21] Upper Canadian republicans also fought for this reform, though not with the same energy as the Lower Canadians. In its *Seventh Report on Grievances* of 1835 (the charter of Upper Canadian republicanism), a committee of the House of Assembly, chaired by Mackenzie, presented the "elective institutions [as] the only safeguards to prevent the Canadas from forming disadvantageous

comparisons between the condition of the colonists and the adjoining country."[22]

By contesting the authority of the legislative councils, the colonial republicans were contesting the existing constitutional order of the two colonies, based on the British principle of mixed government. They were demanding the reconfiguration of power relations in both Canadas according to a model of state legitimacy drawn from republican principles. They were asking the British government to acknowledge the sovereignty of the people rather than the sovereignty of parliament.

In this context, though, as in the past, Canadian republicans were loath to criticize the legitimacy of the British monarchy or the governor's presence in the colony. If they did not do so, it was because they thought that once the legislative power was made to really represent the "people," the legislature could then impose its will on the governor. The governor would then be transformed into the first of all civil servants, with no independent voice. The People would become, effectively, the Crown.

The republican discourse in both Canadas during the 1830s focused primarily on the concept of political liberty, not on those of individual rights or civil liberties. In a larger sense, Canadian republicans wanted to impose virtue. In Canada, as elsewhere in the Atlantic, virtue was one of the key words in republican rhetoric. This word had at least three meanings. First, a virtuous citizen was a citizen who was independent socially and economically: This independence was the best guarantee that he could not be corrupted and that he would be independent politically. Secondly, to be virtuous implied an ethic of simplicity and frugality. Thirdly, virtue meant the willingness of a citizen to defend the common good instead of his own personal interests; in this sense, virtue meant patriotism. Because the Canadian rebels adopted this vision of a virtuous society, they cannot be seen as classical liberals, as some have argued. They were not demanding more civil freedom, nor autonomy from the State. They aimed instead to control the state.

THE REBELLIONS AND THEIR FAILURE

The republican discourse in the Canadas during the 1830s echoed the discourses that American, Central American, Caribbean, French, and British republicans had articulated earlier in the Atlantic Revolution. The political struggles of the 1830s in the two Canadas and the rebellions of 1837–38 can be best explained by the challenge that republicanism represented for the colonial constitution. Republicans were contesting the premises upon which the authority of the colonial state rested.

In Lower Canada, for instance, by 1836–37, it had become clear to the Patriots—who controlled the Assembly—as it was also to their opponents—who controlled the Legislative Council—that their struggle could only be settled outside the framework of existing colonial institutions. The Patriots did not recognize the legitimacy of the Legislative Council, and their opponents rejected most of the reforms proposed or adopted by the Patriot Assembly. By 1837, under such conditions, neither camp could negotiate with the other. Paralysis of legislative power was the result.

Lower Canada's Patriots launched an attack on the state in November 1837. Three battles ensued. After an initial victory at Saint Denis, the British won at Saint Charles and Saint Eustache. In December 1837, Upper Canada's radicals then began their drive to overthrow the colonial government. The two rebellions were crushed, as was a second Lower Canadian uprising in November 1838 and the unrest at the Upper Canadian border with the United States. In 1837–38, superior British military might decided that the Canadas would not be republics. Just as the 1776 Declaration of Independence and the

subsequent British military defeat heralded the beginning of the Atlantic Revolution, the failure of the Canadian rebellions and the victory of British forces and Canadian volunteers, 62 years later heralded its true end.

CONCLUSION

Political life in Upper and Lower Canada became very difficult from 1828 onwards, especially in Lower Canada, where the Patriots controlled the Legislative Assembly for a decade—something the Upper Canadian radicals were never able to do. By the fall of 1837, the Patriots of Lower Canada and the radicals of Upper Canada had launched an assault on the legitimacy of the colonial state in British North America. These two groups were not simply seeking to overthrow the existing government. At a more fundamental level, they were trying to refashion the existing constitutional order of the colonies and to reconfigure power relations in both Canadas, according to a model of state legitimacy drawn from republican principles. In accordance with their republican ideals, the Patriots and the radicals fought for, among other things, the ultimate sovereignty of the people, primacy of legislative power over executive power and the economic and political independence of all citizens. In this way, the Canadian rebellions participated in the larger revolutionary movement that was fundamentally reshaping the Atlantic World at the end of the eighteenth and the beginning of the nineteenth centuries. Although Canadian uprisings occurred much later, they were not ideologically different from the upheavals that preceded them. Had they succeeded, they would have been known as the Canadian Revolution.

It is because these movements failed to overthrow the state—their leaders being better at articulating speeches and making constitutional claims than at organizing a rebellion—that the Patriots and the radicals are not often connected to the wider political and intellectual currents that were reshaping the Atlantic World at the time, even though they were clearly inspired by them and aimed to create republics in Canada. The 1837–38 rebellions may have been a failure, but they were very closely related to the complex story of the Atlantic Revolution at the end of the eighteenth and the beginning of the nineteenth centuries. They are best understood as its last chapter.

NOTES

1. Robert R. Palmer and Jacques Godechot's proposal first appeared in "Le problème de l'Atlantique du XVIIIème au XXème siècle," in *Storia Contemporanea, Relazioni del X Congresso Intenazionale di Scienze Storiche,* 6 vols (Florence: G.C. Sansoni Editore, 1955), 5: 219–39. Each wrote a history of the Atlantic Revolution: Robert R. Palmer, *The Age of the Democratic Revolution. A Political History of Europe and America, 1760–1800,* 2 vols (Princeton: Princeton University Press, 1959); Jacques Godechot, *Les Révolutions (1770–1799)* (1963; reprint, Paris: Presses Universitaires de France, 1986), 99–177.

2. Many American and European scholars have followed the path opened by Palmer and Godechot. See, among others, Bernard Bailyn, *The Ideological Origins of the American Revolution* (Cambridge: Belknap Press of the Harvard University Press, 1967); Gordon Wood, *The Creation of the American Republic, 1776–1789* (1969; reprint, Chapel Hill: University of North Carolina Press, 1998); J.G.A. Pocock, *The Machiavellian Moment* (Princeton: Princeton University Press, 1975), 333–552; J.G.A. Pocock, "The Dutch Republican Tradition," in *The Dutch Republic in the Eighteenth Century: Decline, Enlightenment and Revolution,* Margaret Jacobs and Wijnand W. Mijnhardt, eds (Ithaca: Cornell University Press, 1992), 188–93; Stephen Small, *Political Thought in Ireland, 1776–1798: Republicanism, Patriotism and Racialism* (Oxford: Oxford University Press, 2002); Annie Jourdan, *La Révolution, une exception française* (Paris: Flammarion, 2004).

3. See, among others, David Patrick Geggus, *Haitian Revolutionary Studies* (Bloomington: Indiana University Press, 2002); Jaime E. Rodríguez O., ed., *Mexico in the Age of Democratic Revolutions: 1750–1850* (Boulder: Lynne Rienner, 1994).

4. For the biography of Mesplet, see Jean-Paul de Lagrave, *Fleury Mesplet, 1734–1794: Diffuseur des Lumières au Québec* (Montreal: Patenaude, 1985); and Patricia Lockhart Fleming, "Cultural Crossroads: Print and Reading in Eighteenth- and Nineteenth-Century English-Speaking Montreal," *Proceedings of the American Antiquarian Society* 112 (2003): 23–48.

5. Genêt's text is reproduced in Michel Brunet, "La Révolution française sur les rives du St-Laurent," *Revue d'histoire de l'Amérique française* II (1957):158–62.

6. Seymour Martin Lipset, *Revolution and Counterrevolution: Change and Persistence in Social Structures* (New York: Basic Books, Inc., 1968), 31–63; and from the same author, *Continental Divide: The Values and Institutions of the United States and Canada* (New York: Routledge, 1990), 1–56, 59–60; Jerry Bannister, "Canada as Counter-Revolution: The Loyalist Order Framework in Canadian History, 1750–1840," lecture, The Liberal Order in Canadian History Conference, McGill Institute for the Study of Canada, 3 March 2006.

7. Samuel Neilson, a Whig reformer, and Fleury Mesplet, a republican, welcomed the Constitutional Act by publishing the same text promoting the new constitution in their respective newspapers: *La Gazette de Québec/ The Quebec Gazette* (23 February, 1, 8, and 15 March 1792) and *La Gazette de Montréal/The Montreal Gazette* (15 and 22 March 1792). Its author, Solon, was Jonathan Sewell, the future chief justice of Lower Canada (1808–38): John Hare, *Aux origines du parlementarisme québécois 1791–1793* (Sillery, QC: Septentrion, 1993), 46, 131.

8. In Lower Canada, Pierre Bédard was the first to ask for the introduction of a kind of ministerial responsibility in the colony in his newspaper *Le Canadien* between 1806 and 1810. In Upper Canada, this claim was first articulated by William Baldwin in 1828–29 in a petition

to the king and then in a letter to the Duke of Wellington: "Petition To the King's Most Excellent Majesty," reproduced in *Appendix to Journal of the House of Assembly of Upper Canada,* 1835, 1st session of the 12th Provincial Parliament (15 January–16 April 1835), I: 51; "William Warren Baldwin to the Duke of Wellington, January 3rd, 1829," in *Documents Relating to the Constitutional History of Canada 1819–1828,* A. Doughty and Norah Story, eds (Ottawa: J.O. Patenaude, 1935),482. Lower Canadian reformers asked for the creation of a system of impeachment trials against judges and civil servants during the 1810s. In Upper Canada, Baldwin mentioned the installation of such a system in his 1828 petition to the king. During the 1800s, in Upper Canada, and the 1820s, in Lower Canada, reformers saw the vote on supplies as their only means to influence the executive power. The confrontation between the Lower Canadian House of Assembly, on the one hand, and the governor and the upper house of the Legislature, on the other, on this issue during the 1830s paralyzed the political life in Lower Canada.

9. Papineau, "Nécessité de nommer un délégué de la Chambre d'Assemblée a Londres" (House of Assembly, 17 November 1835), in *Un demi-siècle de combats: Interventions publiques,* Yvan Lamonde and Claude Larin, eds (Montreal: Fides, 1998), 367.

10. *Constitution,* 19 October 1836.

11. See the "Adresse des Fils de la liberté de Montréal aux jeunes gens des colonies de l'Amérique du Nord," 4 October 1837, reproduced in *Assemblées publiques, révolutions et déclarations de 1837–1838,* Jean-Paul Bernard, ed. (Ville St-Laurent, QC: VLB éditeur, 1988), 216.

12. This resolution was reprinted in *La Minerve,* 30 October 1837.

13. *Constitution,* 2 August 1837.

14. *Constitution,* 19 and 26 July; 2 and 9 August 1837.

15. *Constitution,* 26 July 1837.

16. Even if Papineau was not a republican in 1823, he was shocked by what he saw in Britain. See the letters he wrote to his wife between 5 April and 22 September 1823: Louis-Joseph Papineau, *Lettres à Julie,* Georges Aubin and Renee Blanchet, eds (Sillery, QC: Septentrion, 2000), 72–91. For Mackenzie, see *Colonial Advocate,* 27 June 1833.

17. Amury Girod, *Notes diverses sur le Bas Canada* (Village Debartzch: J.P. de Boucherville, 1835), 63.

18. Mackenzie, *Sketches of Canada and the United States* (London: E. Wilson, 1833), 60.

19. *Colonial Advocate,* 9 September 1830.

20. Mackenzie began to contest the state of representation in Upper Canada in 1831. A committee of inquiry was created the same year with Mackenzie as its chair. Its report was introduced in the House on 16 March 1831. Its conclusions were predictable: "the imperfect state of the representation in the House of Assembly is and has been the cause of much evil to the Community." (*First Report on the State of the Representation of the People of Upper Canada in the Legislature of that Province* [York: Toronto Office of the Colonial Advocate, 1831, 4]). Major reforms were necessary, but this report notwithstanding, no major changes were brought to the representation in Upper Canada before the 1837 rebellion.

21. *Journals of the House of Assembly of Lower Canada,* Fourteenth Provincial Parliament, Fourth session (7 January–18 March 1834), 311–35.

22. "Seventh Report on Grievances," *Appendix to Journal of the House of Assembly of Upper Canada,* Twelfth Provincial Parliament, First Session (15 January–16 April 1835), 1: 11.

---

4   From Allan Greer, "From Folklore to Revolution: Charivaris and the Lower Canadian Rebellion of 1837," *Histoire sociale/Social History* 15, no. 1 (1990): 25–43. Reprinted by permission of Taylor & Francis Ltd. (www.tandfonline.com).

For those interested in the connections between politics and popular culture, the charivari holds a peculiar fascination. Originally an aggressive ritual directed against marital deviants, the charivari came in France to be used for overtly political purposes. "The charivari," Charles Tilly has observed, "deserves special attention because it illustrates the displacement of an established form of collective action from its home territory to new ground; during the first half of the nineteenth century French people often used the charivari and related routines to state positions on national politics."[1] But the French were not the only people who deployed the charivari form for political purposes in the first half of the nineteenth century; a broadly similar development occurred at about the same time in the former French colony of Canada. Indeed, the transition was much more abrupt in North America than in Europe. The French-Canadian charivari had long been notable for its traditionalism as to form, object, and occasion, but suddenly in 1837, when Lower Canada (now the province of Quebec) was rocked by a revolutionary upheaval, this folkloric ritual made a dramatic appearance as an important vehicle for mobilizing the population against the colonial government. Enlisted not simply to "state positions" or register "protests," the charivari form was actually used to destroy elements of the existing state structure and even to prefigure a new regime. This was displacement with a vengeance!

On the surface, there was little in the Canadian charivari custom in the years before the Rebellion of 1837 that foreshadowed its future political role. To British visitors of the early nineteenth century, it seemed a picturesque but essentially harmless practice, something that could be written up in travel books to enliven the standard account of vast forests and magnificent waterfalls. The following description was based on a charivari that occurred at Quebec City in 1817:

> Here is a curious custom, which is common through the provinces, of paying a visit to any old gentleman, who marries a young wife. The young men assemble at some friends house, and disguise themselves as satyrs, negroes, sailors, old men, Catholic priests, etc., etc. Having provided a coffin, and large paper lanthorns, in the evening they sally out. The coffin is placed on the shoulder of four of the men, and the lanthorns are lighted and placed at the top of poles; followed by a motley group, they proceed towards the dwelling of the new married couple, *performing* discordantly on drums, fifes, horns, and tin pots, amidst the shouts of the populace. When they arrive at the house of the offender against, and hardy invader of, the laws of love and nature, the coffin is placed down, and a mock service is begun to be said over the supposed body. In this stage of the affair, if Benedict invites them into his house and entertains them, he hears no more of it. If he keeps his doors shut, they return night after night, every time with a fresh ludicrous composition, as *his courtship*, or *will*, which is read over with emphasis, by one of the frolicking party, who frequently pauses, whilst they salute the ears of the persecuted mortal with their music and shouting. This course is generally repeated till they tire him out, and he commutes with them by giving, perhaps, five pounds towards the frolic, and five pounds for the poor.[2]

Though this all seemed "curious" to an Englishman, a charivari along these lines would not have looked strange to a tourist from France. The mocking, carnivalesque tone of the proceedings, the nocturnal setting, the loud and raucous noise, the masks and costumes of the participants and the elaborate, insistently public, street procession all recall French practices dating back to the Middle Ages.[3] Similarly the occasion of charivaris, following a wedding, particularly that of an ill-assorted couple, matches the customs of Canada's original mother country. There were differences, however. French customs, in this as in other matters, varied greatly from region to region. Moreover, practices seem to have evolved over the years so that, even before the emergence of the fully political charivari in the nineteenth century, charivari- type harassment, sometimes associated with other customs, was often directed against all kinds of unpopular figures such as corrupt officials, submissive husbands, or promiscuous women. The colonial ritual, by contrast, seems quite uniform and consistent, from the seventeenth century to the nineteenth and from one end of Lower Canada to the other. More faithful than their European cousins to early modern models, the French of Canada always directed charivaris at newly married couples only. This seems to be one of those areas in which a European overseas settlement functioned as a sort of "cultural museum" in which customs were distilled, purified, and preserved, even as they changed drastically or disappeared in the old country. Such resolute orthodoxy prior to the rebellion makes the politicization of the charivari in 1837 all the more surprising. What was there about this "curious custom"—annoying but hardly subversive in appearance—that lent itself to a situation of acute political strife?

Although the charivari was a custom characteristic of a pre-industrial society, it would be a mistake, in my view, to regard it as simply a throwback, an expression of a "primal ethic," hostile to market relations and punitive in its reaction to nonconformist behaviour.[4] In its Canadian guise, at least, the ritual was not part of any larger pattern of collective regulation of marriage and domestic life through public demonstrations. There was no French-Canadian equivalent of the azouade ("donkey-ride") or "skimmington," humiliating punishments inflicted in early modern France and England on submissive husbands, scolding wives, and other deviants.[5] Neither did drunks and women accused of pre-marital sex have reason to fear a charivari, as was the case in some areas of Germany and the US South. Here it was the marital match itself that was at issue, not the content of domestic life. Prior to 1837, Canadian charivaris always followed a wedding and, in every case I have examined,

the marriage was a "mismatch": either the groom was much older than the bride or vice versa, or else one of the partners had been previously married. Several accounts also mention a social mismatch accompanying the disparity in age or marital status. There was, for example, Monsieur Bellet, the target of the Quebec City charivari described above. A prominent merchant of the town, this 67-year-old widower had married his young servant girl. Just as typical was the charivari directed against a "widow lady of considerable fortune" who wed "a young gentleman of the Commissariat Department."[6]

Widowers marrying again were never the exclusive, or even the primary target of Canadian charivaris. Indeed, weddings joining widows and bachelors were far more likely to trigger a demonstration than the remarriage of men. Moreover, people of all ages and both sexes took part in the festivities, though men appropriated the starring roles. [. . .]

As far as the church was concerned, the wedding ceremony was a sacrament and therefore it could only be approached in a special spiritual state. The *Rituel* of the diocese of Quebec, a sort of priests' manual published in 1703 but still widely used more than a century later, insisted that prospective brides and grooms must "have a genuinely pure intent, looking to marriage only for the glory of God and their own sanctification, and not for the satisfaction of their cupidity, their ambition, their greed and their shameful passions." The fiancés, of course, had to take confession before the nuptials and curés were expected to impress upon them the true nature of marriage:

> Curés will inform the faithful that the purpose of this sacrament is to give to married persons the grace which they require to help and comfort one another, to live together in sanctity, and to contribute to the edification of the Church, not only by bringing forth legitimate children, but also by taking care to provide for

their spiritual regeneration and a truly Christian education. *They will above all point out to those who wish to many that persons who wed out of sensuality, seeking in marriage only sensual pleasure, or out of avarice, endeavouring only to establish a temporal fortune, commit a great sin, because they profane this sacrament,* and, in using something holy to satisfy their passions, they offend against the grace that Our Lord has attached to it.[7]

To marry for money or out of mere sexual appetite was not just morally reprehensible then, it was a serious sin for it defiled the holy sacrament of marriage.

This was all very well at the theoretical level, but how was a priest to detect such impure motives and prevent them from profaning the wedding rite? Unless candidates for matrimony made a direct confession of greed or lust, he could never be sure about their spiritual state. To refuse to marry anyone about whom he harboured suspicions would be to court disasters of all sorts (lay hostility, unsanctioned cohabitation, recourse to Protestant ministers . . .); furthermore, secular law would not allow refusal without good cause. In practice, then, the effort to ensure the purity of marriage consisted mainly of general exhortations to this effect and personal discussions, in the confessional and elsewhere, with candidates for wedlock. [. . .]

A priest had to marry an "ill-assorted" couple even if he harboured doubts about the purity of their intentions, but the crowd in the street might react differently to the outward signals of impurity, giving loud and dramatic voice to widely held suspicions.[8] The charivari might then be seen as a symbolic accusation of defiling a sacred rite. This surely is why a wink-and-nudge sexual jocularity, not to say downright obscenity, formed a central theme of most charivaris. Admittedly, sexual allusions were a feature of other carnival-type festivities but it seems to me that, beyond the general cheekiness, there was a specific and

personal charge of illicit lust implied in the charivari. It is important to emphasize, however, that it was not "immorality" as such that was being chastised. Recall that, in French Canada, charivaris were not directed against adulterers, spouse beaters, and the like. Nor, as far as I can tell, were couples of roughly the same age ever persecuted by crowds who cited other grounds for believing they were marrying out of sensuality or avarice. The immediate purpose of charivari was not to correct immorality or even to guard the sanctity of marriage against "real" impurity. It amounted, rather, to a ritualistic response to the *signs* of desecration, a public rebuke filled with accusations of lasciviousness, that aired suspicions shared by clergy and laity alike.

But more was involved than a simple clearing of the air; charivari was also, as many commentators have pointed out, a punitive procedure. Victims were punished through both humiliation and monetary exaction, two penal techniques favoured by the church and the criminal courts of the period. Public shaming was, of course, a central feature of any charivari, inseparable from the noisy charge of desecration. It recalled the *amende honorable*, a practice common under the French regime when criminals had to go through the town wearing only a shirt and stopping occasionally to beg God's forgiveness.[9] The ecclesiastical version of the *amende honorable*, much milder than that prescribed by the judiciary, involved a public confession of sin, for example by couples who had engaged in pre-marital sex.[10] Like these practices of church and state, charivari penalized people by making a public spectacle of their faults. The *amende honorable* was more than simply a penal technique, however. In the forms deployed by both priests and judges the wayward subject had to become a penitent, confessing his sin and participating in his own correction. The charivari, too, as I shall argue below, involved an important penitential element. But, before leaving the subject of the punitive aspects of charivari, let us look at the monetary penalties that, along with public shaming, were designed to make the ceremony an unpleasant experience for its victims.

Considerable emphasis was placed, by Lower Canadian crowds at least, on the payment of what amounted to a charivari fine. The sums involved were often quite substantial—50 pounds, to take one example from Montreal[11]—though the exact amount varied from case to case, depending, it seems, on the subject's ability to pay. The level of the fine was indeed the subject of elaborate and prolonged negotiation. Usually some respected local figure was employed as a mediator during the daytime intervals between the raucous visitations and he would try to establish the terms of peace and then, later, he might see that the funds were disposed of according to the agreed-upon arrangement. Meanwhile, as negotiations proceeded by day, at night the air still rang with increasingly annoying demonstrations calculated to break down the resistance and loosen the purse-strings of the unfortunate victims. The proceeds of a charivari were normally divided fifty-fifty, with half the fine going to the participants to pay for their "expenses" (i.e., celebratory drinks in the tavern) while the other half was contributed to an organized charity or distributed directly to the local poor.

[. . .]

Besides functioning as a penalty and as a means of soaking the rich, the charivari fine played a third and equally important role. It acted as a token of agreement signifying the re-establishment of peace between the targets and the perpetrators of ritual attack. In offering money, the newly married couple signified, however reluctantly, their submission to the judgment of their neighbours. Moreover, this forced gift implied a recognition—purely at the level of outward acts, of course—of the legitimacy of the charivari itself. The subjects were needled, nagged, annoyed, and threatened until they made a gesture signifying acceptance of the charivari, until they

themselves became participants in the proceedings. When victims treated the ceremony with disdain, when they refused to sue for peace or, worse still, when they called on the "forces of order" to stop the demonstration, the invariable result was that the charivari intensified. From the crowd's point of view, the offence was then compounded for, in addition to soiling the wedding rites, the subjects had also challenged its own authority to right the wrong. This is why charivaris could go on and on—sometimes for three weeks or a month—and with escalating intensity; when couples were stubborn in their refusal to pay, the custom itself became the issue and the struggle therefore raged all the more fiercely.

As soon as a fine had changed hands, however, the harassment stopped. The money served then as a token for the crowd as well as for the victim and it placed the former under an obligation to drop hostilities. [. . .] There may have been some hard feelings in the wake of a charivari, but there is no indication that, under normal circumstances, they would have been lasting. We hear, on the contrary, of a young man of Montreal who married a widow in 1833; exactly a year after his charivari he was elected for the first time as local representative to the colonial assembly.[12] Certainly there is no reason to think that Canadian charivari victims were "permanently marked" as were, according to E.P. Thompson, the targets of the less restrained sort of "rough music" dished up in the English-speaking world.[13] But then, accusation and punishment were only part of the ritual of charivari; these were but preliminaries to the treaty of peace and reconciliation, marked by the presentation of expiatory coin.

We have moved, in discussing the charivari fine, from the area of punishment to the realm of reconciliation. Except where the crowd was defeated or thwarted in its aims, the thrust of its actions seems to have been to bring about, willy-nilly, the reintegration into the community of wayward members suspected of desecration. Nowhere in the

French-Canadian record prior to 1837 does one find relentless persecution, or any apparent desire to expel or eliminate a "cancerous element" by means of charivari. [. . .]

The pre-1837 charivari was not in any clear sense oppositional. Whereas themes of social and political criticism were very much a part of charivari and carnivalesque entertainments in Renaissance Europe, in French Canada, despite the presence of anti-clerical overtones and such "ritual inversion" symbolism as cross-dressing, subversive messages were quite muted. Indeed, one might well consider the charivari a "conservative" ceremony (in so far as the vocabulary of political doctrine has any meaning in this context). Not only did it ape the procedures of priests and magistrates, it functioned as a complementary form of social control, helping to chasten deviants of a very particular sort in strictly limited circumstances. Its ultimate point of reference, moreover, was the orthodox teachings of Catholicism. Intervening when the purity of the marital sacrament was in jeopardy, the charivari crowd acted so as to restore harmony and equilibrium, in the relationship between individuals and the community as well as in that linking God and humanity.

[. . .]

Charivari presumed a sort of "people power" of the street as one of the constituents of the larger political-ecclesiastical order. It was, then, "democratic" in a literal sense. This was a combative democracy, one which had to be defended against the repressive measures of officialdom. It was nevertheless a subordinate democracy, an exercise of popular power which assumed the existence of non-popular authority in a well-regulated community. But what if the community was not well regulated and the government no longer legitimate? This was the situation during the revolutionary crisis of 1837 when the colonial regime lost the capacity to rule with the consent of the governed. At that juncture, when attempts were made to base

authority on popular sovereignty, the charivari form came to serve as a very useful vehicle for pressing the claims of the embryonic new order. This instrument of popular governance within the state (and church) became a weapon of revolt against the state.

The Lower Canadian crisis of 1837, which culminated in armed insurrection in November and December of that year, grew out of the campaign for colonial autonomy and democratic reform led by the middle-class radicals of the "Patriot party." Thanks mainly to the consistent electoral support of the bulk of the French-Canadian population, these liberal politicians managed to control the provincial legislative assembly. Opposed to the Patriots was a coalition of merchants, government officials, and settlers from the British Isles who tended to dominate all the other branches of the colonial state, including the executive, the judiciary, and the non-elective legislative chamber. Acute political conflict had brought the machinery of representative government to a grinding halt by 1836. Finally, the imperial government intervened in the following spring, hoping to end the impasse by issuing a clear refusal to Patriot demands for constitutional reform and depriving the assembly of its financial powers. The result was a storm of protest that lasted through the summer of 1837, with great public rallies, calls for a boycott of British imports and vague talk by Patriot leaders about a re-enactment of the American Revolution at some point in the future. The constant theme of radical rhetoric was that the British measures against the assembly had made colonial rule in Lower Canada illegal and illegitimate. Apart from stirring up popular indignation, however, the Patriots made no serious efforts to prepare for a war which they still believed to be many years away. Events moved toward a showdown more quickly than predicted, though, as the mobilization of the populace, particularly the inhabitants of the Montreal District, provoked repressive counter-measures which in turn led to further resistance.

As the conflict intensified in June and July, noisy demonstrations, often carried out at night by disguised bands, became common. In August newspapers began to report ritual attacks against government partisans that they did not hesitate to call "charivaris" (victims and attackers also used this term) and that did indeed seem to be closely modelled on the popular custom. This was the first appearance of political charivaris in Lower Canada and it came in two quite distinct phases. The first phase, from August to mid-October, seems to have been rather more spontaneous and popular in origin whereas, during the second phase (late October–early November 1837), the coordinating role of the Patriot bourgeois leadership became more apparent and charivaris were used for more clearly strategic purposes.

In the late summer and early fall of 1837 there were reports from several villages that a masked party gathered by night outside the home of a prominent Tory and "gave him a serenade whose chords were scarcely soothing to the ears."[14] These demonstrations resemble the politicized charivaris that became common in France under the July monarchy; indeed, they may have been inspired by European models, although I have no evidence of a direct connection. Certainly the negative serenades fit into established Canadian charivari traditions that were, of course, a French import of an earlier century; the link with native custom appears particularly in the choice of specific targets during this first phase of political charivaris. Masked revellers did not attack such obvious objects as officials or soldiers.[15] Nor did they direct their serenades against members of the English-speaking minority, even though many of the latter manifested a paranoid counter-nationalism that made them violent defenders of the British Empire. Anti-Patriot anglophones might be ostracized by their neighbours or they might find the tails and manes of their horses cut off. (This last form of harassment could certainly be placed under the broad heading of the carnivalesque, for it was a kind of symbolic castration designed to make the animal's owner a laughing stock when he rode it in public.)[16] However, attacks modelled much more closely on the charivari were reserved, in the early fall of 1837, for French-Canadian partisans of the government, and particularly for individuals who had until recently taken part in the Patriot movement but had "deserted the cause of the nation" when revolution loomed on the horizon. Members of the group—whether defined linguistically or in terms of political allegiance—who had broken ranks during an emergency when petty differences had to be forgotten, these "turncoats," were perfect targets for a treatment, the charivari, which had always served, not to attack "outsiders," but to reprove and punish the familiar deviant. Essentially expressions of hostility, these early political charivaris did not demand anything in particular of their victims, but they did probably have the effect of curbing the activities of influential French Canadians who might have been inclined to speak out in favour of the government.

Political charivaris of a special sort came to play a much more important role at a later stage of the confrontation—that is, in the two months preceding the military denouement of late November 1837. The central development of this period—one which led inexorably to the armed clash—was the breakdown of local administration in the countryside of western Lower Canada. While it awaited the arrival of additional troops from neighbouring colonies in the summer of 1837, the government had tried to stem the tide of agitation by banning "seditious assemblies," but it found that proclamations to this effect were simply ignored. Particularly in the heavily populated Montreal District, long a Patriot hotbed, giant rallies succeeded one another and often it was the justices of the peace and militia captains, upon whom the colonial authorities depended to enforce their writ, who were organizing them. The governor reacted to this flagrant defiance by dismissing "disloyal" magistrates and officers. Denouncing this move as further proof of British tyranny, Patriots who held the Queen's commission but who had been overlooked in the purge made a great show of resigning. Beginning in October, meetings were held in many parishes to set up new local administrations and, in the ensuing elections, the "martyred" officers were usually reinstated. A parallel local government, based on popular sovereignty and completely divorced from the colonial regime, was then taking shape. On 23–24 October a great public meeting held at the village of St Charles to establish a federation of six counties south of Montreal gave official Patriot approval to these uncoordinated local initiatives and urged all good citizens to imitate them.

Local government in Canada had always been rather rudimentary and subordinate to the central authorities in Quebec City. (The child of absolutism, Canada was ruled by colonial regimes—first the French, later the British—whose preoccupations were largely military and who dispensed with direct taxation and therefore with the communal institutions that could be so troublesome to western European monarchies.) By the time of the rebellion, justices of the peace and militia captains, whose responsibilities were more of a police than of a military nature, were the only important public authorities, apart from priests, in the rural parishes of Lower Canada. They were all appointed by the governor but they were definitely members of the communities they administered. Indeed, the inhabitants found various ways of "domesticating" officials who appeared in theory to be the agents of an external power. Each captain, for example, was presented with a "maypole," a tall tree trunk decorated with flags and banners and planted in the ground in front of his house, in an elaborate ceremony that implied popular ratification of the governor's choice. In the fall of 1837 many maypoles became "liberty poles" and, to mark the transformation, a sign reading

"elected by the people" was attached to a captain's mast.[17]

But what about officers and magistrates who declined to resign? There were many loyalists who tried to maintain their positions, even in areas where the population was overwhelmingly hostile to the government. From the Patriot point of view, these holdouts were the willing agents of despotism and rebels against the emergent local regimes. At a more practical level, they appeared as potentially dangerous spies and fifth-columnists at a time when war with Great Britain looked less and less remote. The issue of the Queen's commissions therefore served to personalize the struggle by identifying important enemies and bringing great constitutional conflicts down to the local level. Accordingly, loyalist officers and magistrates in massively Patriot communities came under great pressure to resign. Some suffered the fate of Captain Louis Bessette, a prosperous inhabitant whose evening meal was disturbed by the sound of axes biting into wood. Going out to investigate, he found a band of men with blackened faces in the process of chopping down his maypole. The mast crashed to the ground and a great cheer went up from the party; the house was then besieged by the noisy, stone-throwing crowd until Bessette agreed to turn over his commission.[18] The cutting down of captains' maypoles was a favourite gesture in 1837 and one rich in symbolic meaning. If the mast had originally been planted as a phallic token of respect for a patriarchal figure, Bessette's experience was, then, one of symbolic castration. At another level, however, this action should be seen as revoking the popular ratification of the captain's appointment that the maypole embodied. "You are no longer our captain," was the clear message addressed to Louis Bessette.

Whether accompanied by the severing of maypoles or not (and, of course, many of the magistrates and officers who held commissions were not militia captains), the charivari form was the preferred mechanism in the countryside south of Montreal for forcing refractory office holders to resign. National origin and previous political commitments were now (October–November) no longer a consideration. Anyone who continued to hold office was subject to attack. Dudley Flowers of St Valentin was the victim of one typical charivari, which he described two weeks later in a judicial deposition:

> I am a Lieutenant in the Militia. On the twenty seventh day of October last in the afternoon the following persons viz. C.H.O. Côté, Olivier Hébert, L.M. Decoigne, Julien Gagnon, Amable Lamoureux and Jacob Bouchard, came to my house and demanded my commission as such Lieutenant to which I made answer that I would give it up to none but the governor of the Province. Doctor Côté said that if I did not give up my commission I would be sorry for it—to which Gagnon added, "Si vous ne voulez pas vivre en haine avec nous autres rendez votre commission." Upon this they went away. About eleven o'clock in the night of the same day the same persons returned—at least I have every reason to believe that they were the same persons. . . . They began yelling in the most frightful manner. They threw stones at my house and broke the greatest part of my windows. A large stone passed very near one of my children and would have killed him if it had struck him. Julien Gagnon who had seen my barn full of oats when he came in the day time told me that I should not have to thresh them unless I gave up my commission and also said that my grain, my house and outhouses would be burnt. I saw one of the mob go with a firebrand to my barn with the intention as I verily believe of setting fire to it. But it was in a damp state from the recent rain and the fire would not take.

> On the night of the following day (28th October last) it might be about ten o'clock a masked mob, composed of about thirty or forty persons attacked my house in a similar manner . . .

> On the following day (Sunday) about seven in the evening, some sixty or seventy individuals attacked my house a third time in the same manner and with the same threats as on the former occasions but if possible with much more violence, beating kettles and pans, blowing horns, calling me a rebel, saying it would be the last time they would come as they would finish me in half an hour. They had in a short time with stones and other missiles broken in part of the roof of my house and boasted that it would soon be demolished. Fearing that such must inevitably be the case, I opened the door and told them that if four or five of their party would come in and give their names I would give them up my commission. Four or five of them did come in, disguised in the most hideous manner but refused to give their names. Finding that my life was actually in danger if I refused to comply with their requests, I handed them my commission. There were about fifteen of the last mentioned mob masked . . .

> The same persons have declared in my presence that they were determined to compel in the same manner all persons holding commissions from her Majesty to surrender them. One of these individuals told me boastingly that they had obtained no less than sixty-two commissions in one day. I firmly believe that if Doctor Côté and some of the ringleaders were taken up and punished it would have the effect of alarming the others and keeping them quiet.[19]

Many of the features of the "traditional" charivari were present in this episode: the nocturnal setting, the "hideous" disguises, the raucous serenade of blaring horns, banging pots and shouted insults. Even the lieutenant's initial encounter with the Patriot delegation recalled the negotiating process by which charivari fines were normally set: the talks were businesslike, superficially friendly but with an undertone of menace, and they were held in daylight, in an atmosphere that contrasted sharply with that of the charivari itself. Flowers resisted for some time the summons to resign but, following the example of an ordinary charivari crowd faced with a stubborn old widower, his attackers simply intensified their efforts, bringing more supporters and threatening ever more ferocious punishment on each successive evening. There were differences too, of course, notably in the stone-throwing and the overt threats of serious violence.

That the Patriots should have had recourse to the charivari custom at this juncture is not surprising. A coercive practice in which the aggressors' identities were concealed had obvious attractions at a time when arrest was still a real danger. This anonymity probably also served an equally important psychological purpose for the participants, that of overcoming inhibitions against aggressive behaviour. Indeed, the entire ritualistic package of charivari surely had this function. After all, Dudley Flowers was apparently a long-time resident of the community and he knew his attackers personally; even though he was a political enemy, the lieutenant was also a neighbour and therefore someone with whom it was important to maintain peaceful, though not necessarily cordial, relations. To turn on him with overt hostility would be to go against ingrained habits; masks and a familiar ritual may have made easier the transformation of neighbourly Jekylls into frightening Hydes.

The charivari custom offered more than simply an antidote to fears and uncertainties, however. The turning over of a sum of money was the central event of a traditional charivari and much of the pageantry was designed to extort this gift from an unwilling giver. What a perfect vehicle for forcing loyalists to resign or, more precisely, to "turn over their commissions" as the Patriot mobs usually put it. The political charivaris of this second stage of the drama of 1837 were rather blunt in declaring their intention to overcome opposition to their demands, and low-level violence, consisting mainly of stone-throwing, was common. Men like Dudley Flowers, who resisted the initial attack, were likely to have their windows broken. Captain Bessette suffered more damage than any of the other charivari victims; after chopping down his maypole, the attacking party forced its way into his house and, calling for his resignation with a deafening roar, the intruders pounded out a rhythm with sticks and clubs until his table, windows, and stovepipe had been smashed to bits. Now this toll of broken glass and damaged roofs, though severe by the standards of ordinary pre-rebellion charivaris, seems quite light considering the context of serious political crisis. Even more striking is the complete absence of personal injuries. When one places this record against the cracked heads and burned houses that resulted from, for example, the anti-Irish riots of contemporary New England and New Brunswick—not to mention the destruction wrought by crowd action in revolutionary episodes comparable to 1837—the restraining influence of the charivari form becomes all the more apparent.[20]

Of course Dudley Flowers was not impressed by the relative mildness of the treatment he received: He truly thought his life and his property were in real and immediate peril and, though he was no coward, he was frightened enough to abandon his home and flee with his family to the city shortly after the events reported in his deposition. This is because the charivari, "political" or otherwise, was designed to be frightening, particularly in the eyes of those who resisted its edicts. Before 1837, coffins and skull-and-crossbones designs hinted at deadly intentions but, during the rebellion, the threats were much more explicit. Crowds attacked stubborn magistrates and officers with talk of arson and murder. Who could be sure they were simply bluffing when, as was often the case, masked revellers were seen carrying guns as well as firebrands? Lieutenant Flowers felt he had had a lucky escape and that only the damp weather had saved his barnful of grain from the Patriot torches. He might have been less worried had he known how many other loyalists had been similarly threatened, without one single building ever being fired. The fact that he did believe himself to be in serious danger shows just how well the charivari served its theatrical purposes in the fall of 1837, when dozens of local officials capitulated to the Patriot mobs.

So far I have been discussing the way in which the charivari form was applied during the campaign of late October–early November for wholly novel political purposes. Yet, beyond the surface resemblances, there were also elements of continuity with the past in the basic functions of the ritual. For example, the extortion of royal commissions seems to have been more than simply a means of destroying the government presence in the countryside; it also had meaning in the context of the specific relationship between an individual and the community of which he was a member. In other words, this forced gift played a role analogous to that of the ordinary charivari fine in signifying the giver's submission to the authority of the collectivity. But now the community as a whole and the Patriot cause were identified. Accordingly, some charivari victims were forced to shout "*Vive la liberté!*" or to cheer for Papineau, the Patriot chief, as further proof of recognition of the incipient new regime. In accepting the victim's commission, the crowd gave its implicit assurance (sometimes it was clearly stated) that the charivari was at an end.

There was a sense, then, in which a non-resigning officer such as Dudley Flowers was treated as a sinner, a contaminating influence in a community otherwise true to new civic ideals. The charivari worked so as

to force him into the position of a penitent who had to purchase his reintegration into the fold at the price of a militia commission. Thus the admonition addressed to Lieutenant Flowers by Julien Gagnon during the preliminary visit to his home: resign your position, "if you do not wish to live in a state of hatred with us." No one expected him to become a militant Patriot overnight, but he was being offered an opportunity to make peace with his offended neighbours. It is important to emphasize that, just as conventional charivaris were aimed not against general immorality but against a specific affront to the wedding ceremony, so Flowers was targeted for a specific offence rather than some general non-conformity. Though government supporters at the time, not to mention later historians, saw the Rebellion of 1837 as stemming from a xenophobic French-Canadian hostility to English-speaking fellow-citizens, no one reproached Dudley on national or religious grounds. His "crime" was not in professing Protestantism, in speaking English, or even in believing in the Queen's majesty, but simply in retaining a commission at a time when all good citizens had a duty to resign. The atonement required of this wayward soul was just as specific and limited as the "sin" itself. He had merely to make a gesture—that of turning over his commission—that signified a renunciation of former "treason" and an acceptance of the authority of the Patriot crowd. The emphasis was on the outward act indicating a transfer of allegiance without any further surrender of personal autonomy. This was made clear to another loyalist militia officer, who proclaimed to the 50 blackened faces shouting for his resignation "that if they compelled him to give up his commissions they could not change his principles"; that is all right, came the sarcastic reply, we do not wish to alter your religion.[21]

The boast reported by Dudley Flowers of 62 political charivaris in his region alone may have been exaggerated but the basic point that, within a few weeks, dozens of resignations had been secured by this means is undeniable. By the second week of November there was, to all intents and purposes, no official government presence in most of the populous rural parishes of the District of Montreal, and an elective magistracy and militia were beginning to operate in its place. In such a situation the government naturally had recourse to its now reinforced military forces to enforce its own claim to sovereignty. The British expeditions that ventured out from Montreal were surprised at the resistance offered by the inhabitants, hastily organized through the revolutionized militia companies. The initial armed encounter at St Denis (23 November) was, in fact, a Patriot victory but, since the insurgent military effort was localized, fragmented, and defensive, the troops soon crushed their amateur opponents. What followed, in many localities, was a series of very unritualistic punitive actions; loyalists then had the satisfaction of watching flames race through the homes of neighbours who had so recently issued empty threats of arson. Turmoil continued for over a year, in Upper Canada (Ontario) as well as Lower Canada, while Patriot refugees in the northern states tried to enlist American support. But, by the end of the decade, the republican movement had been effectively destroyed.

[. . .]

For such an orthodox and mild-mannered custom, the traditional French-Canadian charivari had proved remarkably effective as a vehicle of revolt. Of course the Patriots were soundly beaten. This is hardly surprising, given the relative strength of the parties in conflict: A small colony with no external allies faced the premier imperial power on earth at a time when the latter was not distracted by serious difficulties at home or abroad. The wonder is that the inhabitants of Lower Canada were able to cripple colonial rule to the extent that they did in the fall of 1837. This is where the politicized charivari form made a crucial contribution. Serving at first, as in contemporary France, as a medium of complaint and protest, it was soon deployed as the central element in a campaign to destroy government power in the countryside and to assert a practical sort of popular sovereignty. This was a truly revolutionary role for a venerable ritual, even if the ensuing debacle did expose the military and diplomatic weaknesses of the Patriot movement.

The charivari was well suited for its insurrectional mission in a number of practical ways. The very fact, first of all, that it was a custom of collective action made it an important cultural resource when groups of people had to be assembled and organized. Since collective institutions and traditions were rather weak in French Canada, recourse to the charivari was all the more natural. Additionally, and more specifically, charivari was a more useful device under the circumstances because of the way it concealed the identity of aggressors. Above all, the traditional focus on extortion lent itself to Patriot strategies in the fall of 1837, as did the larger drama of forcing wayward individuals to make a gesture of renunciation and submission. Charivari had always been coercive, but only in a very discriminating way. Its techniques were therefore well adapted to the delicate task of exacting a particular type of obedience from certain recalcitrant individuals, all without bloodshed.

In addition to its strictly tactical role, the charivari form functioned as a framework within which the villagers of Lower Canada grappled with the moral and philosophical problems of revolt. Linked to widely held and longstanding beliefs concerning relations between the individual, the community and the cosmic order, the custom was deeply rooted in dominant political and religious ideologies. At the same time, it embodied an implicit assertion of popular rights to a share of public authority. Here was a democratic germ, and one whose claims to legitimacy were formidable. Thus, when the crisis of colonial rule came, a law-abiding peasantry that brought out its charivari masks and noise-makers in order to depose local officials could feel it was doing the right thing in the right way.

NOTES

1. Charles Tilly, *The Contentious French* (Cambridge, MA, 1986), 30.

2. John Palmer, *Journal of Travels in the United States of North America and in Lower Canada performed in the year 1817* (1818), 227–8.

3. Among the works dealing with the charivaris of early modern France, see Arnold Van Gennep, *Manuel de folklore français contemporain*, 4 vols (Paris, 1937–49), II, 614–28; Roger Vaultier, *Le folklore pendant la guerre de Cent Ans d'après les lettres de rémission du trésor des chartes* (Paris, 1965); Natalie Z. Davis, "The Reasons of Misrule" in *Society and Culture in Early Modern France* (Stanford, 1975), 97–123; Claude Gauvard and Altan Gokalp, "Les conduites de bruit et leur signification a la fin du Moyen Age: le charivari," AESC, 29e année (May–June 1974), 693–704; Jacques LeGoff and Jean-Claude Schmitt (eds), *Le Charivari* (Paris, 1981).

4. This phrase comes from Bertram Wyatt-Brown, *Southern Honor: Ethics and Behavior in the Old South* (New York, 1982), 435–6.

5. In addition to the work cited in the previous note, see E.P. Thompson, "'Rough Music': le charivari anglais," AESC 27e année (March–April 1972), 285–3; Martin Ingram, "Ridings, Rough Music and the 'Reform of Popular Culture' in early modern England," *Past and Present*, CV (Nov. 1984), 79–113; Christian Desplat, *Charivaris en Gascogne: la "morale des peuples" du XVIe au XXe siècle* (Paris, 1982).

6. Edward Allen Talbot, *Five Years' Residence in the Canadas: including a Tour through part of the United States of America, in the year 1823* (1824), 300.

7. *Rituel du diocèse de Québec, publié par l'ordre de Monseigneur l'évêque de Québec* (Paris, 1703), 347, 329 (my translation and my emphasis). Cf. Jean-Louis Flandrin, *Families in Former Times: Kinship, Household and Sexuality*, trans. Richard Southern (Cambridge, 1979), 161–4.

8. Serge Gagnon, "Amours interdites et misères conjugales dans le Québec rural de la fin du XVIIIe siècle jusque vers 1830 (l'arbitrage des prêtres)" in François Lebrun and Normand Séguin (eds), *Sociétés villageoises et rapports villes-campagnes au Québec et dans la France de l'ouest, XVIIe–XXe siècles* (Trois-Rivières, 1987), 323 (my translation). This case occurred in 1810.

9. André Lachance, *La justice criminelle du roi au Canada au XVIIIe siècle: tribunaux et officiers* (Quebec, 1978), 113–15.

10. Gagnon, op. cit., 324.

11. Talbot, op. cit., 303.

12. Robert-Lionel Séguin, *Les divertissements en Nouvelle-France* (Ottawa, 1968), 73.

13. Thompson, op. cit., 290.

14. *La Minerve* (Montreal), 10 Aug. 1837 (my translation). See also *Le Populaire* (Montreal), 27 Sept. 1837; 2, 9, and 16 Oct. 1837; *Montreal Gazette*, 30 Sept. 1837.

15. There was one exception to this pattern. A crowd that had turned out to greet the Patriot leader Louis-Joseph Papineau at St Hyacinthe, learning that the commander of British forces happened also to be staying in the town, gathered round the house where the latter was staying for a noisy vigil punctuated by catcalls and anti-government slogans.

16. Archives nationales du Québec, documents relatifs aux événements de 1837–1838 (hereafter ANQ, 1837), deposition of Robert Hall, 15 July 1837.

17. Robert Christie, *A History of the Late Province of Lower Canada, Parliamentary and Political, from the Commencement to the Close of its Existence as a Separate Province*, 6 vols (Montreal, 1866), V, 32–3.

18. ANQ, 1837, no. 257, deposition of Louis Bessette, 5 Nov. 1837.

19. ANQ, 1837, no. 146, deposition of Dudley Flowers, 3 Nov. 1837.

20. Ray Billington, *The Protestant Crusade 1800–1860: A Study of the Origins of American Nativism* (New York, 1938); Scott W. See, "The Orange Order and Social Violence in Mid-Nineteenth Century Saint John," *Acadiensis* XIII (Autumn 1983): 68–92. See also Sean Wilentz, *Chants Democratic: New York City and the Rise of the American Working Class, 1788–1850* (New York, 1984), 264–5.

21. PAC, RG4, AI, vol. 524, no. 11, deposition of Loop Odell, 17 Nov. 1837.

Chapter 10

Women in British North America

READINGS

Primary Documents

Historical Interpretations

INTRODUCTION

Converging political, economic, and social forces fundamentally reshaped British North America in the nineteenth century. From small, isolated, and weak colonies dependent on the metropolitan state, Lower and Upper Canada, New Brunswick, Nova Scotia, and eventually Prince Edward Island (to say nothing of Rupert's Land and the west coast) came to form a new entity called the Dominion of Canada. As important and noteworthy as this evolution was, it was hardly the only one. Another fundamental change was the transition from a pre-industrial to an industrial society. The advent of a new social order had huge economic and social consequences. One of these concerned the roles, rights, privileges, and expectations ascribed to men and women, both at home and in the community. It promoted the separation of the private and public spheres as the proper way to organize society. According to this discourse, women were expected to participate only in those areas of life that touched upon womanly or family welfare. But the rise of this cult of domesticity in the 1850s should not hide the fact that the place of women in the social and political life of the colonies had been more extensive in the first half of the century.

The primary documents chosen for this topic reflect the evolution of attitudes toward women in public and private life from 1808 to 1856. The first document reminds us that gender did not automatically disqualify women from voting in early-nineteenth-century British North America, even if admittedly very few women met the property qualification to be enfranchised. The property laws in Lower Canada, inherited in part from France, granted more property rights to women, and most female voters in British North America were from this colony. Though the letter to voters from Quebec County was probably intended to harm the election campaign of the candidate named, it tells us a lot about contemporary morality and expectations surrounding male–female relationships. The second primary document illustrates the emergence of the cult of domesticity in British North America. Rev. Sedgewick's lecture, a recitation of the existing boundaries between men and women and a declaration that women were to *complement* men, is notable as well because it was pitched at young men who were supposed to be forming their own systems of belief and ethics.

The historical interpretations included here reveal the lived experiences of some women from the Atlantic colonies and challenge the notion that colonial women lived a life of passive domesticity. In his article, Rusty Bitterman discusses the violence in Prince Edward Island in the context of the Escheat movement. He demonstrates that women did not shy away from violence in the 1830s as they enthusiastically participated in defending their lands from landlords' claims and joined larger community resistance. His article shows that women's lives in Prince Edward Island during the first half of the nineteenth century were different from the ideal promoted by Sedgewick. For her part, Gail C. Campbell draws on an in-depth examination of diaries to reveal how young women in New Brunswick navigated courtship. She shows how these women often had considerable freedom, which allowed them latitude to enter into relationships without parental knowledge or approval.

QUESTIONS FOR CONSIDERATION

1. What does the letter from "The Unfortunate Jeannette" suggest about attitudes toward women's participation or non-participation in political life during the early part of the nineteenth century?
2. How does Rev. Sedgewick justify not extending various rights and privileges to women, even though he seems to be in favour of all of these benefits for men?
3. Without thinking about questions of fairness or justice, were there any practical purposes for women and men maintaining these semi-exclusive existences?
4. What kinds of violent behaviours does Bitterman highlight in his article? Why were women often at the forefront of resisting rent collectors on Prince Edward Island?
5. What can diaries reveal about the lives of women in colonial societies? What are these sources' limitations?

SUGGESTIONS FOR FURTHER READING

Backhouse, Constance. *Petticoats and Prejudice: Women and Law in Nineteenth-Century Canada*. Toronto: Women's Press, for the Osgoode Society, 1991.

Bradbury, Bettina. *Wife to Widow: Lives, Laws, and Politics in Nineteenth-Century Montreal*. Vancouver: UBC Press, 2012.

Campbell, Lara, Tamara Myers, and Adele Perry, eds. *Rethinking Canada: The Promise of Women's History.* Toronto: Oxford University Press, 2016.

Chambers, Lori. *Married Women and Property Law in Victorian Ontario.* Toronto: University of Toronto Press, 1997.

Guildford, Janet, and Suzanne Morton, eds. *Separate Spheres: Women's Worlds in the 19th-Century Maritimes.* Fredericton: Acadiensis Press, 1994.

Keough, Willeen. "The Riddle of Peggy Mountain: The Regulation of Irish Women's Sexuality on the Southern Avalon, 1750–1860." *Acadiensis* 31, no. 2 (Spring 2002): 36–70.

———. *The Slender Thread: Irish Women on the Southern Avalon Peninsula of Newfoundland, 1750–1860.* New York: Columbia University Press, 2006.

McKenna, Katherine. "Women's Agency in Upper Canada: Prescott's Board of Police Record, 1834–1850." *Histoire social/Social History* 36, no. 72 (2003): 347–70.

Morgan, Cecilia. *Public Men and Virtuous Women: The Gendered Languages of Religion and Politics in Upper Canada 1791–1850.* Toronto: University of Toronto Press, 1996.

Nielson, Carmen J. *Private Women and the Public Good: Charity and State Formation in Hamilton, Ontario, 1846–93.* Vancouver: UBC Press, 2015.

Noël, Françoise. *Family Life and Sociability in Upper and Lower Canada, 1780–1870: A View from Diaries and Family Correspondence.* Montreal and Kingston: McGill-Queen's University Press, 2003.

Noel, Jan. *Along a River: The First French-Canadian Women.* Toronto: University of Toronto Press, 2013.

Poutanen, Mary Anne. *Beyond Brutal Passions: Prostitution in Early Nineteenth-Century Montreal.* Montreal and Kingston: McGill-Queen's University Press, 2015.

Primary Documents

1 "To the Electors of Quebec County," *Le Canadien*, 21 May 1808.

TO THE ELECTORS OF QUEBEC COUNTY

Gentlemen,

Although it is not customary for women to address you at election time, I hope you will forgive the liberty of an unfortunate soul who has no other resource than to appeal to your sense of justice. To whom else could I appeal? The ungrateful wretch I complain of is the Judge himself.

You know well enough, Gentlemen, the trouble I went to in working for him during the election campaign at Charlesbourg four years ago; he had suffered badly in the election in the Upper Town; and out of pity, as many of you did, I worked as hard as I could to assure his triumph. Gentlemen, you witnessed this triumph of which he boasted so much. Yet, no sooner had he won than he forgot all I had done for him, and, coward that he is, abandoned me. He had the insolence to tell me that it was I who was harming his reputation among you. Gentlemen, will you let this kind of treachery go unpunished? Will your votes in his favour reward his betrayal? Will you elect him for having broken faith with me?

The ingrate even got married, and began to frequent the Church; this was to obtain your votes. He is inconstant I assure you; I know him, he will use any means to achieve his end.

He makes promises to you, but how many promises did he make to me? He will deceive you as he deceived me. He will deceive you as he deceived the Lower Town. How many promises did he not make to the voters on the day of his triumph four years ago?

This false man has never been able to win an election except in Three Rivers. . . . What honour will you gain in electing him? The Upper Town scorned him four years ago, Deschambault had driven him out, Nicolet had driven him out. Will it be that Charlesbourg will join Three Rivers in electing him!

What will be said of Charlesbourg? What will be said of Beauport, where he is so well known? People will say that it was because he was a Judge, that it was out of fear of losing their cases in court that voters elected him. Did the Upper Town succomb to such fears? Did Deschambault and Nicolet? What now! Canadiens who never feared enemy fire in battle will become cowards for fear of losing a court case!

What an honour for Canadiens to see *their judge* running for election, to see him profane the image of the King whom he represents so unworthily? Do English judges run in elections? . . . Only Canadiens so dishonour themselves. I am a Canadienne, Gentlemen, and I would die rather than consent to such dishonour.

The Unfortunate Jeannette

---

2 From Robert Sedgewick, *The Proper Sphere and Influence of Woman in Christian Society: Being a Lecture Delivered by Rev. Robert Sedgewick before the Young Men's Christian Association, Halifax, N.S., November 1856* (Halifax: J. Barnes, 1856), 3–30.

LECTURE

The errors and blunders which are interwoven with the subject of woman's rights and woman's place in modern society are, as these points now engage public attention, to be traced either to the ignoring of the fact or the omission of the fact that in the economy of nature or rather in the design of God, *woman is the complement of man.* In defining her sphere and describing her influence, this fact is fundamental. Unless this fact be admitted as an axiom in every way self-evident, no reasoning on this subject is sound, and no conclusion legitimate, and the whole theme becomes little better than a mass of mere assumption, alike illogical in its progress and unsatisfactory in its conclusions. [. . .]

If it be thus clear that woman is the complement of man, it must follow that the sphere of the one is different from that of the other. The spheres in which they severally move are concentric indeed, and thus there must be a very great similarity between them; but there is a vast difference between diversity and opposition, and hence when it is asserted that the sphere of woman is different from that of man, it is not to be understood as if it were opposed or contrary to that of man. [. . .]

It may be worth while, therefore, to enquire what, after all, is the sphere of woman; and here it may be as well to adopt the good old way of showing what it is not, and then of showing what it is, looking at the subject negatively and then positively. [. . .]

It would never do, however, from these premises, to draw the conclusion that woman behoves and is bound to exert her powers in the same direction and for the same ends as man. This were to usurp the place of man— this were to forget her position as the complement of man, and assume a place she is incompetent to fill, or rather was not designed to fill. [. . .]

Were it not that so much is said about it in the neighboring States, it would seem utterly preposterous to assert that Parliament was the proper sphere of woman, and that she is just where she ought to be when sitting on the red benches, and is engaged as she ought to be in drawing out Bills—in explaining and defending them—in standing in the arena of angry debate, and condemning and counter-working one course of policy by justifying and furthering another, and as is thought a better. Now first of all it might be asked how are women to get there? Are they to set up as candidates for the representation and come out on the hard-shell ticket or the soft-shell ticket, on the red or the blue; and are they to appear on the hustings on the day of nomination, and, unless unanimously elected, to demand a poll? One thing is certain—he would be a sheriff indeed who succeeded in keeping the peace, on the day of election, provided the contest lay between a male and a female candidate, and much more if it lay between two female candidates. And then is it to be a mixed Assembly, are the honorable man-members and woman-members to meet together and unite their wisdom in legislating for their country, [. . .] or are the women to have a separate house and to manage the public business themselves, untrammelled by the presence, unawed by the criticism of their fellow male-members? This would be a Parliament with a vengeance. This if ever would be a speaking Assembly. And what are the powers with which such a House is to be invested? Are they to be subordinate to the other House? That would never do.

Or are they to be co-ordinate with them? That would be as unsatisfactory. Or, as probably the ladies would wish it, are they to be su-perordinate? Why, the claim would be resented as a most presumptuous invasion of the rights of men, and as utterly intolerable as fairly beyond the limits of the Constitution. [. . .]

But seriously, that the question of investing woman with similar political rights with man, and demanding of her the discharge of similar political duties, should have arisen at this time of day, after such a world-wide and a world-long experience, is indeed one of the wonders of the age.

There is a passage in one of the Lectures of Horace Mann on the powers and duties

of woman, which is every way so appropriate and withal so clear and convincing and eloquent as illustrating this point, that it deserves an acquaintanceship as extensive as possible:—[. . .]

Nothing, as it seems to be, can account for the present clamour in behalf of women voters and women office-holders but the amazingly false notions which prevail respecting the intrinsic dignity and enduring importance of education, as compared with the ephemeral tinsel of political distinctions. Respecting the clean and beautiful work of the teacher, training up characters to empyrean height and purity, as compared with the noisome and bloody work of the politician, sometimes flaying and cauterizing, and sometimes amputating and beheading, to cure or cut away from the body politic those frightful gangrenes whose very existence would have been prevented by the intelligent and faithful performance of woman's earlier and holier service. As to the idea that woman has a self evident and inalienable right to assist in the government of the race, I reply she does assist in that government now, and would to heaven she would exercise a still larger share in its administration. But this great work, like all others, is naturally divided between the sexes, the nobler government of children belonging to women, the less noble government of adults to man.

But, if the Halls of Legislature and of Congress were opened to women, they would purify them it is said. The answer to this must recognize both hypotheses respecting the sexes. First, if woman is like man, why should she not do as man has done, only aggravating and multiplying his evil works, because then the competitors would be doubled and all restraints withdrawn. But secondly, as I contend, woman is unlike man, better when she is good and worse when she is bad. Then, at least, in the present state of society, I believe that her participation in political strifes, ambitions and cupidities, would rouse to tempestuous fury all the passions that ever swept her to swiftest perdition—Men and women are yet drawn together by too many passional affinities to allow us even to hope that husbands could leave their wives, and wives their husbands, and pass for months and months, by day and by night, through all the enforced intimacies and juxtapositions of legislative life without something more than pure platonic emotions, and she who wishes her sex to encounter these perils has forgotten the wisest prayer that was ever made, "Lead us not into temptation." [. . .]

In justice, however, to the other side of this question, perhaps I ought not to omit certain collateral and incidental benefits which may be claimed to accrue should woman strip off her sex and rough it with man in the turbulence and riot of the political arena. What a beautiful school for domestic debate; prolonged not merely from morn to dewy eve, but from eve to early morn, should the father be a whig, the mother a democrat, and the daughter a third party man. On the stump, at the hustings or other bear-garden, the intimate relation of husband and wife would furnish admirable facilities for mutual impeachment and recrimination, which to bachelors and marriage haters would be intensely edifying. If husband and wife were rivals for the same office, then, no matter which party might prevail, the honour and emoluments would still come into the family, or, if both were elected to Senate or House, they might pelt each other from the opposition benches, which would be a great relief from closer quarters. [. . .] As to the parents' equal right to inculcate hostile political doctrines on the minds of their children they might make a compromise, each devoting alternate lessons on alternate days to the exposure of the other's iniquities, so that the children in the end would have a good opportunity to know the weakness of them both. [. . .]

It is now time that woman's sphere in Christian society be defined and described. [. . .] The sphere of woman is home and whatever is co-relative with home in the social economy. [. . .]

It is only at home and its co-relative situations that man finds woman to be his complement. In no other situation she can fill, in no other sphere in which she can move, will she so answer the end of her being, so far as this point goes, but at home; and this fact also, for fact it is, settles the question—what is the sphere of woman? In the camp she must either be the superior or the subordinate or the equal of man; she cannot be his complement, or, at least, she is so with multitudinous drawbacks. [. . .]

It is not the design of this lecture to treat on female education. It would seem that this point was taken for granted in the subject, and that it was admitted that, whatever the sphere, woman was qualified rightly to move in it, still the unity of the theme could not have been preserved unless some slight reference were had to this matter.

Now, there can be no doubt that the three r's, as the Irishman said, are important parts of female education, reading, writing and arithmetic. These lie at the foundation of all useful knowledge, indeed, without them the main instrumentality of acquiring knowledge is awanting, and there can be as little doubt also that the elegant accomplishments, when they can be acquired, may add very much to the usefulness of woman at home. Music and drawing, and painting and embroidery, and a smattering of French and Italian, of heavy German and clumsy Dutch, are all so many acquirements which, if once obtained, may serve to enliven a drawing room conversation and amuse and please for the nonce a drawing room party, and then they are easily retained, other things being equal, and may be exceedingly useful in various situations in life; nor can any body refuse to admit, who is willing to do woman justice, that it is quite competent and that it may be advantageous for her to dabble among the 'ologies and dive deep down into their dark regions. There is geology and ethnology and conchology and entomology, then biology and phrenology and astrology, if you will, all of them in their place somewhat instructive, all of them in their place somewhat profitable, even for a woman to know. Indeed, in certain circles of society, where these and cognate themes may happen to be the subject of conversation, a woman looks exceedingly small, if, by her silence or the irrelevancy of her remarks, she betrays her entire ignorance and the defective nature of her education; and hence the necessity and the propriety of introducing these departments of knowledge into the curriculum of our female academies and boarding-schools. But there are other 'ologies as well of which no woman, if she is to move in her sphere as she ought to, can afford to remain ignorant. There is the sublime science of washology and its sister bakeology. There is darnology and scrubology. There is mendology, and cookology in its wide comprehensiveness and its untellable utility, a science this the more profoundly it is studied it becomes the more palatable, and the more skilfully its principles are applied its professors acquire the greater popularity and are regarded with a proportionate degree of interest and complacency. Now, all this knowledge must be embraced in any system of female education that pretends to prepare woman for the duties of life.—The knowledge of housekeeping is not only not beneath her notice and regard, but is essentially necessary if she is to be at home what home expects her to be, if, in a word, she is at all to fill her place with credit to herself and comfort to those with whom she may be associated, as daughter or sister, as wife or mother, as instructress or friend, or any other relationship she may sustain to general society. And, in order that these several departments of her education may be kept in their due place and pursued according to their relative importance—that they may be purified and elevated and chastened, and thus that by their union they may subserve to the grand end of manifesting in all its varied and attractive loveliness the female character, they must be baptized, nay, permeated with the spirit and power of true religion. It has been said that man, with all his irreligion, is a religious

being. The paradox, if true at all, is eminently true of woman. There is a special unnaturalness existing and manifest between the doctrines and duties and delights of evangelical Christianity and the intellectual and spiritual process of her inner nature, and hence her aptitude for piety in its principles and practices and pleasures, hence too her attainments, and hence the vast influence which godliness exerts on herself and which it enables her to exert on others. Now, to complete her education, religion must come in—not to subsidize, but to regulate and control—not as subordinate, but as principal—not as mere *addenda* to what may be regarded as otherwise complete in itself, but as that without which nothing else is or can be complete—in short, the end of true religion, the glory of God as connected with the source of true religion; the sacrifice of Christ, must be exhibited everyday as the grand object that is to be sought by all the essential and ornamental departments of her physical and mental and moral training, according as it is written. [. . .]

Having thus ascertained the sphere of woman, and adverted to the qualifications which she behoves to possess, that she may be and do what her situation demands, the way is now prepared for the consideration of the influence she exerts in Christian society.

Now, first of all the things—the qualifications just indicated being granted—this influence is extensive, nay, universal.—Where woman is she makes herself felt, but where woman is enlightened by education, and elevated and purified by piety, she makes herself felt for good through every ramification of the body-social. Like the light and heat of the sun, which diffuse themselves everywhere, so everywhere are there indications of her presence and her spirit. From the cellar to the attic there are marks of her tidy hand and her thoughtful heart. The well ordered kitchen owns her sway. The bedroom and parlour and drawing-room confess her authority. The table, and the chimney itself, are fairly within the reach of her pervasive power and must yield to the decisions of her judgement. Children smile in her approval or grieve under her frown.—Old men regard her as a ministering spirit commissioned to cheer and comfort when every other source of enjoyment has gone. She is the light of the dwelling when the dark cloud of adversity envelopes it, and when death crosses the threshold and with ruthless hand snatches away from it the valued and the dear, it is her hand which wipes away the tear, even when her own eyes are streaming—it is her meek and quiet demeanour and calm submission which soothes and tranquillizes the bereaved mourner.

And, as has been asserted, this influence extends beyond her own proper sphere. If it be chiefly felt at home, it is nevertheless felt and acknowledged abroad. It reaches the schoolroom and college-hall. It finds its way into the workshop and the busy store. It is realized on 'Change, and even, as some of you well know, in the sweating room of the Bank. And though woman herself, as has been demonstrated, would be altogether out of her place on the red benches of the Parliament House, yet, who will deny that she makes herself felt, even in these high places of the land, and helps to modify the actings of our representatives and rulers?

And then this influence is powerful, extensive. It is mighty. It may be resisted indeed, even as the pleasant light may be excluded from some dirty room lest its filth and its disorder be made manifest. It may be resisted indeed, as the genial heat may be prevented from

radiating, and thus warming all within its scope. But, let it have fair play and full action, and just as light and heat, unchecked in their operation, reveal and revive all within their reach, so will this influence affect and subdue, and enlighten and raise, and purify and etherialize and sublimate, all and every one whose nature is capable of feeling this influence, all and every thing that, as an enchantress, she touches with her wonder working wand. [. . .]

One more general statement. This influence is refining and polishing. It rubs down the hirsute coarseness of men. It frowns vulgarity into a corner, and abashes the impudent forwardness of the pert and assuming. Where it is unknown or trodden under foot, why there is savageism untamed, there is license unbridled, there is heartless cruelty and beastly debasement; but, where it is known and felt, the savage is a savage no more, licence and libertinism tremble and flee, kindness supplants cruelty and manly dignity beastly degradation. A well educated and godly woman can make, and has made, the bully quiet and the boor mannerly, and the brawler meek and gentle as a lamb. In the presence of such a woman the lips of the profane are sealed and the tongue of the obscene is locked in his jaws. Ribaldry and scurrility are frightened into propriety, and, in spite of all that is said to the contrary, it is nevertheless true that slander herself is reft of her weapons, and, if not, yet what is as good, she is shorn of her power to use them as she chooses. [. . .]

Historical Interpretations

3 Rusty Bitterman, "Women and the Escheat Movement," in *Separate Spheres: Women's Worlds in the 19th-Century Maritimes,* eds Janet Guildford and Suzanne Morton (Fredericton: Acadiensis Press, 1994), 23–38.

In September of 1833, Constable Donald McVarish, acting on behalf of Flora Townshend, the resident owner of an estate in eastern Prince Edward Island, made his way to her property with a bundle of papers in hand. These were warrants of distress, legal documents which permitted Townshend to seize the goods of her tenants for back rents which she claimed were due. It was not to be a pleasant day for McVarish. Rents were going unpaid, as always, because tenants found it difficult to meet these costs, but growing military resistance to the entire structure of landlordism made rent resistance a political act, too. In the wake of political initiatives begun earlier in the decade, the dream of an escheat was the talk of the countryside. Members of the House of Assembly and the rural population alike were discussing the legitimacy of proprietorial claims to the colony's land and arguing that because landlords had never fulfilled the settlement obligations of the original grants of 1767, they did not in fact have valid deeds; their grants had reverted to the Crown by default. Establishment of a court of escheat, it was contended, would expose the fraudulence of landlords' claims on the Island's tenantry and permit them to gain title to the farms they had made productive. McVarish, acting for the landlords, could no longer count on deference to law officers in the rural regions in the fall of 1833. Believing that the existing land system was fundamentally flawed because the titles that supported it were invalid, rural residents balked at complying with the laws pertaining to rents.

McVarish's mission to the Naufrage region of northern Kings County took him into a region that was known for the strength of its anti-landlord sentiments—arguably, the heartland of agrarian radicalism on the Island. William Cooper, the leading advocate of the idea of an escheat, had pronounced his ideas on the flaws of proprietorial title and the rights of tenants in Kings County during the general election of 1830 and then again in a by-election in 1831. The support he received ultimately permitted him to promote these ideas from the House of Assembly. The enthusiastic response from country people in Kings County and elsewhere, expressed in public meetings, petitions, and rent resistance, marked the beginning of what came to be known as the Escheat movement. The

loaded pistol that McVarish had tucked in his pocket before leaving home probably reflected his understanding of rural sentiments in the region, as did his attempts to hide his mission from those he met and his decision to sometimes travel through fields rather than on the road. McVarish's precautions notwithstanding, he was seen and confronted by a cluster of the tenants for whom his warrants were intended. Hard words were spoken and McVarish drew his pistol. He was, nonetheless, knocked to the ground, disarmed, and conveyed to the main road. Having promised he would never return, he was released and helped on his way with a blow from a board.[1]

The person wielding the board was Isabella MacDonald, then well advanced in a pregnancy. Judging from testimony from a subsequent trial, Isabella was the most vociferous party in the altercation. McVarish claimed that the three male and two female tenants who confronted him "were all alike active and threatening," but when he pulled his pistol he aimed it at Isabella. It would seem that he perceived her as the most violent of the group. This move allowed men who were not receiving McVarish's primary attention to pull him down from behind and disarm him, in turn exposing him to Isabella's wrath. Her blow with the board was the only gratuitous violence McVarish received. Perhaps she was settling scores for his aiming his pistol at her, perhaps fulfilling the promise of violence which had prompted McVarish's move in the first place.

McVarish's discomfiture at the hands of Isabella and her companions was not an isolated incident. It cannot be explained simply as the act of a particularly forceful female tenant, a matter of personality. Again and again over the course of the Escheat movement, women assumed prominent roles in physically resisting the enforcement of landlords' claims in the countryside. This paper examines these women's behaviour and argues that the modes of resistance they employed had roots in, and were extensions of, the conditions of their daily lives. To discern this, however, it is necessary to move away from the image of rural women most commonly found in North American literature on the pre-industrial countryside. The conception of the rural woman's sphere that dominates this literature draws too heavily from middle-class experiences and sentiments and does not provide an appropriate starting place for understanding the actions of women such as Isabella MacDonald. Attentiveness to the early-nineteenth-century perceptions that gave birth to these pervasive images may, however, help us to better understand the roles rural women assumed in violent confrontations. Upper-class beliefs concerning women's sphere shaped the context in which Escheat activism unfolded. Being perceived as the weaker sex and the guardians of domesticity may have permitted women more latitude than men in their use of violence.

While it is important to recognize the significant part that women played in direct action, their participation in this form of popular politics needs to be set in the broader context of the Escheat struggle in the 1830s and early 1840s and the political changes which were occurring during this period, direct action was not Escheat's main focus. The Escheat challenge was primarily grounded in the development of a new mass politics in the formal political arena. Formal politics, unlike community-level direct action, excluded women. To examine the role of women in the Escheat movement is to be reminded that the changes associated with the rise of bourgeois democracy included the decline of an older popular politics which once afforded women a substantial place.

Direct resistance to the claims of landlords, the area of Escheat activism in which women were most prominent, occurred in two forms. There were household-level defences, such as that Isabella MacDonald engaged in, and there was larger community-organized resistance. Women were active at both levels. In the first, the members of a single household, or perhaps adjoining households,

responded defensively to the arrival of law officers. When officials attempted to serve legal papers, remove possessions, or arrest members of the household, those directly involved resisted. Women took part in such protective actions on their own and in the company of men. Catherine Renahau and her husband, John, acted together to resist the enforcement of their landlord's claims against their premises in southern Kings County in the spring of 1834. In this case, the wife and the husband were both indicted and found guilty of assaulting and wounding the constable who had arrived at their door.[2] The actions of Mrs MacLeod and her husband, Hugh, fit the same pattern. When a constable and a sheriff's bailiff came to seize their cattle in the summer of 1839, Mrs MacLeod took up a pike and Hugh an axe. Together they rebuffed the law officers. When a posse was subsequently sent to arrest the two, the entire family took a hand in attempting to prevent the high sheriff and his deputies from invading their house.[3] Charges laid against Mary and Margaret Campbell for assaulting constable William Duncan in 1834 provide some evidence that women also acted without men in farm-level defences.[4]

In addition to these sorts of spontaneous farm-level defences, tenants were involved in more broadly organized actions aimed at securing entire communities or regions from the enforcement of landlords' claims. Women figured prominently in many of these actions. Attempts to arrest the five tenants charged with repelling McVarish provoked two major community-level confrontations. In the spring of 1834, a posse was dispatched from Charlottetown to Naufrage to arrest the miscreants. They were turned back at the Naufrage bridge by a crowd, said to include "a large number of women," which had assembled in anticipation of their arrival.[5] Armed with muskets, pikes, and pitchforks, the assembly informed the deputy sheriff that they were prepared to fight and die before they would permit him to arrest the five tenants he sought. When yet another posse led by the sheriff himself attempted a similar mission the following year, women were said to make up more than one-third of the armed crowd that waited for the posse in the pre-dawn darkness and again blocked the sheriff.[6]

Women were active as well in a series of major community-level confrontations in the fall and winter of 1837–8 that, with the mass meetings being held in support of Escheat, prompted some observers to believe that the Island, like the Canadas, was on the verge of civil war. The first of these confrontations concerning land title was on Thomas Sorell's estate in northern Kings County. In September 1837, when the sheriff and his deputies attempted to enforce court orders Sorell had obtained against John Robertson, a long-time resident on the estate, they were repulsed by a crowd wielding sticks and throwing stones. As well, one ear was removed from each of the law officers' horses, which had been left at a distance from the farm.[7] Women were part of the crowd that blocked the sheriff, and they were reputed to be the primary actors in the violence.[8] Later that winter, women made up part of an armed party which assembled near Wood Islands to repel people whom they believed to be law officers initiating rent actions in that district. In a case of mistaken identity, shots were fired over the head of the rector of Charlottetown and his elite friends, who were on a baptismal mission on behalf of a spiritual lord rather than a rental mission on behalf of a secular one.[9] While the actions of the tenant group were misdirected, they nonetheless served notice that those who might attempt to enforce rent collection in the region were not welcome. On the Selkirk estate the following month, women again were active in coordinated crowd actions which blocked the enforcement of rental claims. In several locales, bailiffs attempting to seize farm goods were confronted by tenants armed with pitchforks and sticks. Men and women alike took a hand in resisting the seizure of goods and driving law officers from the communities they had attempted to enter.[10] The cumulative effect of these actions was, for a time, to bring the enforcement of rental payments to a halt across much of the Island and to force the government to consider whether it was willing to hazard deploying troops—then in short supply due to the demands made by the risings in the Canadas—in order to uphold the claims of the Island's landlords.

That rural women would be active in household defences and collective action of this sort would come as no surprise to the student of Old World popular protest. In locations on the eastern side of the Atlantic, a rich array of research has pointed to the importance of women in protest actions and has suggested ways of understanding this activity in terms of their everyday lives.[11] The evidence of female involvement in the popular resistance associated with the Escheat movement fits less easily within North American historiography and its portrayal of rural women. To be sure, the literature is broad and varied, and blanket descriptions are misleading. Nonetheless, what emerges again and again in North American descriptions of women in northern pre-industrial rural settings is the image of the farm woman as nurturing caretaker of the domestic sphere. Though her work was tiring and she was often incessantly busy, hers was an existence bounded by walls and sheltered from the coarser aspects of life. Women looked after the household and, perhaps, the adjacent garden and barns, while the men tended to rough work and public affairs.

In his late-nineteenth-century reminiscences on rural life in Ontario in the first half of the century, Canniff Haight drew the common distinctions: "The farmer was a strong, hardy man, the wife a ruddy cheerful body, careful of the comforts of her household."[12] Male muscularity was applied to the exterior world, female gentleness and diligence to the interior: "While the work was being pushed outside with vigour, it did not stand still inside. The thrifty housewife was always busy."[13] "The work" was of course male. The division is clear as well in Robert Leslie Jones's characterization of farm life on the Upper Canadian frontier. While the man of the house "split rails, built worm fences, and erected his log cabin," his wife attended to "various household industries, ranging from spinning and sometimes weaving, to the preservation of fruits by drying, and the making of butter and cheese."[14] Or, in a recent version of the theme as played out in Lower Canada: Féllicité tended to "feeding, washing, and cleaning the family, its clothes, and its house" as well as "milking the cows, making butter, and feeding the fowls." Théophile ploughed, "erected fences around the fields," and saw to "repairs to house, barn and equipment."[15] "Women's work," Christopher Clark has argued in the case of pre-industrial rural New England, "remained separate, functionally distinct from men's": "In addition to cooking, cleaning, and looking after children, women undertook the myriad tasks associated with preserving food, making and mending clothing, and keeping up their houses."[16] Or, as a classic textbook of Canadian women's history has it, farm women "scrubbed clothes on scrub boards (if they were lucky enough to have one), hauled water from the creek or the well, cooked on wood stoves, and made most of the family clothes. In addition they grew vegetables, gathered fruit, preserved and baked, and looked after their children."[17]

No doubt many "ruddy" farm women did spend their days tending to berries, butter, bread, and babies in eighteenth- and nineteenth-century North America and, no doubt, there were many households where prosperity and culture blended to create the domestic feminine sphere that is described in so much of the literature.[18] The scholarship that has given rise to this image is not incorrect. But in the absence of more nuanced studies of the experiences of women in rural settings, it has sustained misleading impressions. A

vision of country life rooted in the experiences of relatively prosperous, well-established households and heavily grounded in mid-nineteenth-century circumstances has, often enough, come to stand as a general portrait of the pre-industrial rural world. Thus, our view of the rural past tends to be too uniform and too rosy.[19] One might profitably explore the reasons for the dominance of this image and its significance to broader myths concerning rural life and North American exceptionalism. For comprehending the actions of women within the Escheat movement, the immediate problem is finding a more appropriate starting place for explaining how Mrs Macleod came to pick up a pike and Isabella MacDonald a board, and how other country women came to join in the armed groups organized to repulse law officers in Naufrage, Wood Islands, and elsewhere about Prince Edward Island in the 1830s. While some of these women no doubt tended to the domestic duties that have been assigned to the feminine sphere of rural life, there is much that these sorts of descriptions leave out, matters that go a long way toward helping us to understand how women came to participate as they did in the Escheat movement.

For most country women in Prince Edward Island in the early nineteenth century, life was much rougher and the bounds of work much broader than the prevailing images suggest. Indeed, for the rural poor, of whom there were many, the notion of a distinct feminine sphere could not have had much meaning. While there was work that was exclusively female, even in poorer households—having babies, early childcare, and so on—it is less clear that there was much work about the farm that women could avoid because it was securely outside their domain. In many rural households, particularly the poorer ones, the men were away for extensive periods earning wages in the woods, shipyards, and other sites where farm income might be supplemented.[20] Of necessity, then, women's work expanded beyond the women's sphere that is described in much of the literature. In such households, women often assumed the dominant role in maintaining the farm.[21] In farm households where life was lived on the margin, even when men were present, women often participated in heavy tasks such as clearing, planting, and harvesting. In his early-nineteenth-century observations on life in Prince Edward Island, Walter Johnstone spoke disparagingly of rural women from comfortable backgrounds who were "unable and unwilling to take the hoe, and assist their husbands in planting the seed, and raising the crop."[22] To make a go of it in the New World, immigrant women needed to apply themselves to the hard outdoor tasks of farm-making. Land-clearing work, which Johnstone described as being "the most dirty and disagreeable" and "tiresome as any I have seen in America," was shared by the entire family, women and men alike.[23] Similar observations of women's roles in the hard task of farm-making are found in the works of John MacGregor and George Patterson, who commented as well on women's part in the subsequent tasks of planting and harvesting.[24] Women, MacGregor observed, "assist in the labours of the farm during seed-time, hay-making, and harvest."[25] Getting the crops in, Johnstone noted, was the work of the entire household—"man, wife, children, and all that can handle a hoe, must work, as the season is short"—and disaster loomed for the poor if the crops were not successful.[26] It is not surprising then that Island evidence from the 1832 murder trial of Martin Doyle indicates that Martin and his wife were working side by side among the charred stumps of their field on the day that Martin was said to have shot his brother.[27] From the scattered evidence that is available concerning women's work, such was a common pattern of rural life.

The dominant image of the daily lives of rural women is inadequate not only because women's work could be much broader than it depicts, but also because the domestic sphere of work was often much narrower, too. Again and again the existing literature emphasizes the long hours that women spent, cleaning house, washing clothes, preparing meals, and spinning and weaving, No doubt long hours were spent in this work by those who possessed frame houses and ample wardrobes, ate a varied diet, kept sheep, and had spinning wheels and looms. We need to recognize, though, that many did not. In the Maritimes of the early nineteenth century, this picture of the woman's sphere pertains to the rural middle class and does not reflect the circumstances of the whole of the rural population. Indeed, for many, the physical requirements for the woman's separate sphere—multi-roomed house, kitchen and pantry, area for textile manufacture, adjoining dairy, and poultry shelters—quite simply did not exist. It did not take long to clean a one-room dwelling, assuming that this was even an objective, nor did cooking and washing absorb a day's labour when household members ate boiled potatoes and oatmeal and possessed little clothing beyond what they were wearing. We need not paint the picture this starkly, however, no matter how real it was for many, to point out that much, of the existing view of the rural women's sphere assumes material circumstances that were far more comfortable than those of much of the rural population.

As well, we must re-examine the notions of domesticity and of lives sheltered from the rough and tumble of the public world, which are commonly associated with characterizations of the pre-industrial North American farm woman, if we are to understand the behaviour of the women who were involved in direct action during the Escheat movement. In part because many Island women did engage in outdoor farm labour, they, like men, became involved in physical disputes over resources and household relations. Margaret Taylor and Jane Maclachlan fought it out with fence pickets and fists in the spring of 1830 when they differed over ownership of a piece of ground.[28] A similar physical dispute over land and fencing brought Catherine Mc-Cormack and Alexander Macdonald before a court later that year.[29] The same court session that heard the Taylor/Maclachlan case also heard the case of Elizabeth Cahill and Margaret Shea, whose personal differences had moved to the level of heaving stones.[30] As with women's work, evidence bearing on women's use of violence, or the threat of violence, in the public realm is fugitive.[31]

Certainly what emerges in the court record is but a fraction of a broader phenomenon. What percentage of the disputes where women picked up a stick or a stone or brandished their fists ultimately ended up before a judge or a justice of the peace? And what percentage of these disputes is preserved in the incomplete legal record?

In addition to engaging in direct violence, Island women were also repeatedly cited for resorting to maiming animals.[32] In this traditional form of rural retribution, livestock received the violence directed toward their owners. Vengeance was taken, or a threat communicated, by hamstringing, slashing, or otherwise mutilating the animals of an enemy.[33] There was nothing unusual in the methods used against the horses of law officers who came to Robertson's farm in the fall of 1837; they were employed against the mounts of law officers on many other occasions. Animal-maiming, by women and men, was not uncommon in intra-household disputes.

Women's participation in violent actions was not an unusual feature of the Escheat movement, nor was the targeting of law officers. Consider, for instance, the 1836 rescue of Rose Hughes from a constable's custody. Arrested near Fort Augustus in the late fall of 1836 for obtaining goods under false pretenses, she was forcibly released when the arresting constable, Angus MacPhee, was attacked by a group who had pursued him beyond the community. Though there were four men present in the rescue party, they remained in the background. The assault itself was said to be the work of nine women.[34]

We need, then, to broaden our notion of female lives and experiences if we are to make sense of women's participation in direct action during the Escheat movement. Isabella, used to hard physical labour, is unlikely to have thought it peculiar, or inappropriate, for women to use physical means to uphold their interests. When we examine the role of women in the Escheat movement, we see in part an extension of the normal patterns of work and life to meet the challenges thrown up by the land war of the 1830s. Women familiar with the rough and tumble of outdoor rural life dealt with the law officers who came to their farms as they would any other threat to their household. Accustomed to the heft of an axe and the swing of a fence picket, they applied their strengths, skills, and inclinations to the problems at hand.

Those like McVarish who were on the receiving end of these responses were caught in an unenviable dilemma. On the one hand they were, often enough, dealing with women who possessed strength, endurance, physical tenacity, and the urge to cause considerable physical harm. McVarish's choice of targets when he levelled his pistol probably showed his appreciation of women's abilities. On the other hand, he and the other law officers on the front lines of the land war were, in one fashion or another, linked to a culture which saw women differently. According to increasingly dominant middle-class and upper-class views, women were revered as submissive nurturers of the domestic sphere.[35] Historians studying women's roles in collective action in other nineteenth-century contexts have suggested that plebeian protesters may have sought to exploit such perceptions when they challenged the status quo. Women, the argument goes, enjoyed some degree of immunity in violent confrontations, or at least believed that they did, and scattered evidence does suggest they were less likely than men to suffer harm or be prosecuted for their actions. This fact may help explain their prominence in illegal protest.[36] Might this have been the case with women's participation in the direct action associated with the Escheat movement?

The evidence bearing on this question is limited, but it supports an affirmative answer. Interestingly, despite the prominent role played by women in resisting the enforcement of landlords' claims in Kings and Queens Counties in the tense fall and winter of 1837–8, none was named in the law officers' reports nor were any indicted for their actions. Only men were tried. Such preliminary screening raises questions concerning how adequately indictments and court cases document women's participation in direct action or, indeed, in other sorts of activities of this type. Were law officers uncomfortable with admitting that their lumps and bruises were the work of women or that they had been chased or intimidated by women? And, other things being equal, did law enforcement take place in a cultural context where charges against males were preferable, if an example was to be made of a few members of a larger riotous assembly? Women, it would appear, were more likely to be indicted in household-level confrontations where the numbers involved were quite small. Even when charged, however, they sometimes fared better than men. Although two women were indicted for the assault on Donald McVarish, neither served a prison term or paid a fine. The charges were dropped against Nancy MacDonald, and Isabella MacDonald, though found guilty, was pardoned by the Island's governor, Aretas Young, on account of her "being far advanced in pregnancy and having six young children."[37] All three men involved were committed to prison.

The ways in which contemporaries referred to gender when assigning meaning to incidents of Escheat-related collective action provided another window on these issues. In the wake of the resistance to the sheriff at Robertson's farm in the fall of 1836, pressure was brought on the new governor, Charles FitzRoy, to send troops into the region to sustain the civil forces in their enforcement of landlords' claims. FitzRoy sent Charlottetown's mayor, Ambrose Lane, to the region as his personal emissary to inquire into the current state of the countryside and to conspicuously make arrangements for billeting soldiers. Seeking to downplay the seriousness of the incidents that had brought Lane to the region, Robertson and his family told him that the sheriff and his assistants had never been in any real danger as "all the violence offered was by women and boys." The law officers who had beaten a hasty retreat from the mob assembled at the farm had been "unnecessarily alarmed."[38] Similarly, a dispute over the significance of the Wood Islands incident of January 1838 came, in part, to revolve around the composition of the crowd which pad assembled and fired shots over the heads of the rector's party. Those seeking to downplay the confrontation insisted that it had, in large part, been staged by women and boys. Those intent on seeing it as an indication of a broader spirit of rebellion threatening the status quo on the Island were equally insistent that the crowd had been "composed chiefly of able-bodied men."[39] What the disputants in these battles of words shared, or claimed to share, was the notion that females could not figure as real threats in violent confrontations. It is not clear whether exploitation of these perceptions of women figured into the strategic planning of household- and community-level rent resistance prior to confrontations or whether they were invoked only after the violence. Cases such as the rescue of Rose Hughes, where men were present but remained at a distance while women assaulted the constable, or the resistance at Robertson's farm, in which, according to reports, men were present but not active in the physical confrontation with law officers, suggest a conscious gendered strategy that made use of upper-class assumptions concerning women's behaviour.

[. . .] Charles Tilly has argued that [patterns of rural protest such as those on Prince

Edward Island] fit within a broader category of "reactive" collective action, locally focused efforts to protect existing rights or to uphold popular notions of justice.[40] John Bohstedt's term "common people's politics" aptly captures another facet of this type of collective action. In contexts where ordinary people were excluded from participation in formal politics, direct action provided a means for articulating plebeian sentiments; it permitted them to act as "proto-citizens."[41] As Bohstedt and others have noted, women often participated extensively in this sort of political action. "Common people's politics" tended to be an extension of plebeian life, and in locales where women "worked shoulder to shoulder with men" they also "marched shoulder to shoulder with men" in defence of their households and communities.[42] Such was the case with women's participation in the direct action associated with the Escheat movement. Local-level politics of this type was a matter for women and men alike.

This was not the case in the formal political arena. There the rules and norms that governed participation were extensions of elite and middle-class ways of life. In these circles, other notions of womanhood held sway. This would be of no small significance for the majority of women when, beginning in the late eighteenth century and extending across the nineteenth century and beyond, ordinary people about the Atlantic rim increasingly pushed themselves into, or were incorporated within, the field of formal politics. Lower-class entry into the sphere of political life was gained by compromise and by the acceptance of many of the modes of procedure that had been established by the upper classes. On the Island one thinks even of simple matters such as dress. When the Escheat leader John LeLecheur went off to Quebec to discuss the land question with Lord Durham, a fundraising campaign was necessary in order to buy him a new set of clothes. Such props were unnecessary for

engaging in political debate in Murray Harbour, but they were a part of the basic entry requirements for being taken seriously in the governor general's circles.[43] Certainly, involvement in formal politics did lead to fundamental changes in the nature of plebeian politics. As historians have noted in other contexts, one of the many prices popular forces paid for entrance into the formal political arena in the nineteenth century was the relegation of women to a sphere outside direct participation in political life. A new mass politics was emerging at the time of the Escheat movement, but as it embraced larger numbers of previously excluded lower-class elements, it also denied political expression to women.[44] On the Island, women were legally disenfranchised on the eve of Escheat's electoral victory of 1838.[45]

The involvement of women in the local politics of direct action needs to be set in this larger context. While recognizing women's participation in the "common people's politics" of the 1830s, it is important to note the transitional nature of the period and the immediate and long-term significance of the zone of political life in which women had a prominent place. Rural protest in Prince Edward Island had by the 1830s largely shifted away from direct action. A relatively broad franchise allowed many male tenants to vote; some even possessed sufficient wealth to meet the property requirements necessary for assuming a seat in the House of Assembly. The energy of the Escheat movement was directed toward exploiting the political possibilities these openings permitted. Escheat leaders sought to make agrarian voices heard in the formulation of state policy by achieving power in the legislature. This pursuit drew rural protest into an exclusively masculine sphere. The activities in which women had a substantial presence were not at the forefront of the Escheat movement, nor would they be central to the new politics that developed in the years which followed.

NOTES

1. Minutes of Naufrage Trial, Colonial Office Records [CO] 226, vol. 52, 91–4, Public Record Office, Great Britain [microfilm copies in Harriet Irving library, University of New Brunswick]. I would like to gratefully acknowledge the assistance of the Social Sciences and Humanities Research Council of Canada, whose financial support aided this research. Many thanks are due as well to Margaret McCallum for her comments on an earlier version of this paper.

2. *Royal Gazette* (Charlottetown), 24 June 1834, 3; Supreme Court Minutes, 25 June 1834; Indictments, 1834, RG 6, Public Archives of Prince Edward Island [PAPEI].

3. *Royal Gazette,* 23 July 1839, 3.

4. *Royal Gazette,* 16 Dec. 1834, 3.

5. *Royal Gazette,* 17 June 1834, 3.

6. *Royal Gazette,* 6 Jan. 1835, 3; "Council Minutes," 7 Jan. 1835, CO 226, vol. 52, 330–2.

7. Executive Council Minutes, 5 Sept. 1837, RG 5, PAPEI; *Royal Gazette,* 5 Sept. 1837, 3.

8. Hodgson to Owen, 30 Sept. 1837, MS 3744, vol. 26, PAPEI.

9. George R. Young, *A Statement of the "Escheat Question" in the Island of Prince Edward: Together with the Causes of the Late Agitation and the Remedies Proposed* (London, R. and W. Swale, 1838), 2; "One of the Party" to the editor, *Colonial Herald* (Charlottetown), 27 June 1838, 3; "O.P.Q." to the editor, *Colonial Herald,* 23 Jan. 1841, 3; "Plain Common Sense" to the editor, *Colonial Herald,* 6 Feb. 1841, 2–3; John Myrie Hall to the editor, *Colonial Herald,* 20 Feb. 1841, 2; "The Only Clergyman Resident Within the Bounds of the District" to the editor, *Colonial Herald,* 20 Mar. 1841, 3; Charles Stewart and W.P. Grossard to the editor, *Colonial Herald,* 27 Mar. 1841, 3.

10. Statement of Angus McPhee, George Farmer, and Robert Bell, 27 Feb. 1838, CO 226, vol. 55, 176–80.

11. John Bohstedt, "Gender, Household, and Community Politics, Women in English Riots, 1790–1810," *Past and Present* 120 (Aug. 1988), 88–122; Rudolf Dekker, "Women in Revolt: Collective Protest and Its Social Setting in Holland in the Seventeenth and Eighteenth Centuries," *Theory and Society* 16 (1987): 337–62; E.P. Thompson, "The Moral Economy of the English Crowd in the Eighteenth Century," *Past and Present* 50 (1971): 76–136; George Rudé, *The Crowd in the French Revolution* (Oxford: Galaxy Books, 1959); George Rudé, *The Crowd in History, A Study of Popular Disturbances in France and England, 1730–1848* (London, Serif Publishing, 1964); Olwen Hufton, "Women in Revolution," *Past and Present* 53 (1971): 90–108; John Stevenson and Roland Quinault, eds, "Food Riots. in England, 1792–1818," in *Popular Protest and Public Order: Six Studies in British History, 1790–1920* (London, St Martin's Press, 1974), 33–74; Natalie Zemon Davis, *Society and Culture in Early Modern France* (Stanford: Stanford University Press, 1975), 124–87; Kenneth J. Logue, *Popular Disturbances in Scotland, 1780–1815* (Edinburgh: Birlinn Publishers, 1979); Malcolm I. Thomas and Jennifer Grimmet, *Women in Protest 1800–1850* (London: St Martin's Press, 1982). A useful Canadian extension of this rich literature is Terence Crowley, "'Thunder Gusts': Popular Disturbances in Early French Canada," in Michael Cross and Gregory Kealey, eds, *Readings in Canadian Social History,* vol. 1, *Economy and Society during the French Regime* (Toronto: McClelland and Stewart, 1983), 122–51.

12. Canniff Haight, *Country Life in Canada Fifty Years Ago: Personal Recollections and Reminiscences of a Sexagenarian* (1885; rpt, Belleville, ON, 1971), 86.

13. Haight, *Country Life in Canada,* 46.

14. Robert Leslie Jones, *History of Agriculture in Ontario, 1613–1880* (1946; rpt, Toronto, 1977), 20–1.

15. Graeme Wynn, "On the Margins of Empire," in Craig Brown, ed., *The Illustrated History of Canada* (Toronto: Lester Publishing, 1987), 247.

16. Christopher Clark, *The Roots of Rural Capitalism, Western Massachusetts, 1780–1860* (Ithaca, NY: Cornell University Press, 1990), 274.

17. Alison Prentice et al., *Canadian Women: A History* (Toronto: Harcourt, 1988), 116. See also 76, 79, 83.

18. Hal Barron's call for the study of the extent, and timing, of the spread of the bourgeois

ideals of the cult of domesticity among "the less affluent and less 'enlightened' strata of rural society" usefully indicates a single facet of a broader challenge, that of disaggregating and more closely examining rural experiences and rural change. John Faragher's critique of stereotypes in the writing of rural women's history, and call for moving beyond these, is to the point as well. Hal Barron, "Listening to the Silent Majority: Change and Continuity in the Nineteenth-Century Rural North," in Lou Ferleger, ed., *Agriculture and National Development: Views on the Nineteenth Century* (Ames: Iowa State University Press, 1990), 16; John Mack Faragher, "History from the Inside-out: Writing the History of Women in Rural America," *American Quarterly* 33 (1981): 537–57.

19. There are, of course, exceptions to this characterization. Marjorie Griffin Cohen, for instance, notes that farm women in early-nineteenth-century Ontario frequently performed "men's work," though she tends to treat this as a temporary frontier phenomenon. *Women's Work, Markets, and Economic Development in Nineteenth-Century Ontario* (Toronto: University of Toronto Press, 1988), 69–71. As well, it is not unusual for contradictory evidence to be integrated with a more idyllic picture of the countrywoman's sphere. See, for instance, The Clio Collective, Roger Gannon and Rosalind Gill, trans., *Quebec Women: A History* (Toronto: The Women's Press, 1987), 89.

20. Rusty Bittermann, "Farm Households and Wage Labour in the Northeastern Maritimes in the Early Nineteenth Century," *Labour/Le travail* 31 (Spring 1993): 13–45.

21. When a Cape Breton farmer noted in the coal boom of 1871 that "farmers and their sons by hundreds, nay, thousands, [were] leaving their farms to the women, and seeking employment at the collieries and railways," he was describing the efflorescence of an older pattern. *Journal of Agriculture for Nova Scotia* (July 1871): 652.

22. Walter Johnstone, *A Series of Letters, Descriptive of Prince Edward Island* (1822) reprinted in *Journeys to the Island of St John*, D.C. Harvey, ed. (Toronto: Macmillan, 1955), 143.

23. Johnstone, *A Series of Letters*, 108.

24. John MacGregor, *British America* (Edinburgh: Blackwood, 1832), 329; George Patterson, *A History of the County of Pictou Nova Scotia* (1877; rpt, Belleville, ON, 1972), 223.

25. MacGregor, *British America*, 346.

26. Johnstone, *A Series of Letters*, 109.

27. *Royal Gazette*, 28 Feb. 1832, 1.

28. *Prince Edward Island Register* (Charlottetown), 15 June 1830, 3.

29. *Royal Gazette*, 13 July 1830, 3.

30. *Prince Edward Island Register*, 15 June 1830, 3.

31. See also the case of Mary Prendergast v. Ellen Prendergast, *Royal Gazette*, 3 Jan. 1837, 3; and Isabella Stewart v. Edward Wilson, *Royal Gazette*, 13 July 1830, 3.

32. *Royal Gazette*, 21 Jan. 1834, 3; 22 Sept. 1835, 3; 7 July 1840, 3.

33. For a good discussion of the tactic see John E. Archer, "'A Fiendish Outrage'?: A Study of Animal Maiming in East Anglia, 1830–70," *Agricultural History Review* 33, 2 (1985): 147–57.

34. *Royal Gazette*, 20 Dec. 1836, 3.

35. Barbara Leslie Epstein, *The Politics of Domesticity: Women, Evangelism, and Temperance in Nineteenth-Century America* (Middletown, CT: Wesleyan University Press, 1981), 67–87; Nancy F. Cott, *The Bonds of Womanhood: "Women's Sphere" in New England, 1780–1835* (New Haven, CT, Yale University Press, 1977).

36. Malcolm I. Thomas and Jennifer Grimmet, *Women in Protest 1800–1850* (London: St Martin's Press, 1982), 54; Logue, *Popular Disturbances in Scotland*, 199–203.

37. Young to Hay, 20 Mar. 1835, CO 226, vol. 52, 89.

38. Hodgson to Owen, 30 Sept. 1837, MS 3744, vol. 26, PAPEI.

39. "One of the Party" to the editor, *Colonial Herald*, 27 June 1838, 3.

40. Charles Tilly, *From Mobilization to Resolution* (Reading, MA: Rowman and Littlefield, 1978), 143–71.

41. John Bohstedt, "The Myth of the Feminine Food Riot: Women as Proto-Citizens in English Community Politics, 1790–1810," in Harriet B. Applewhite and Darline G. Levy, eds, *Women and Politics in the Age of the Democratic Revolution* (Ann Arbor, MI: University of Michigan Press, 1990), 21–60.

42. Bohstedt, "The Myth of the Feminine Food Riot," 21. See also Thomas and Grimmet, *Women in Protest*, 54–5.

43. Rusty Bittermann, "Escheat!: Rural Protest on Prince Edward Island, 1832–42" (PhD diss., University of New Brunswick, 1992), 321–8.

44. Useful views of the process are provided in Wayne Ph te Brake, Rudolf M. Dekker, and

Lotte C. van de Pol, "Women and Political Culture in the Dutch Revolutions," in Applewhite and Levy, eds, *Women and Politics in the Age of Democratic Revolution,* 109.–46; Joan B. Landes, *Women and the Public Sphere in the Age of the French Revolution* (Ithaca, NY: Cornell University Press, 1988); Allan Greer, "La république des hommes: les patriotes

de 1837 face aux femmes," *Revue d'histoire de l'Amérique française* 44, 4 (Spring 1991): 507–28; Bohstedt, "The Myth of the Feminine Food Riot."

45. They were disenfranchised by statute in 1836. John Garner, *The Franchise and Politics in British North America, 1755–1867* (Toronto: University of Toronto Press, 1969), 155.

4   From Gail G. Campbell, "From Innocent Flirtation to Formal Courtship," in *"I Wish to Keep a Record": Nineteenth-Century New Brunswick Women Diarists and Their World* (Toronto: University of Toronto Press, 2017), 95–114.

In the nineteenth century, as in our own day, adolescence signalled a new phase in young people's lives as their glances shifted more and more toward each other. Young people increasingly sought the company of their peers as they began to look to the future. What young women wrote in their diaries reflects this shift in gaze, as they reported not only their activities but sometimes their discussions with sisters and friends, their views of and interchanges with young men, their feelings as relationships evolved, and their turmoil and distress when their own feelings were not reciprocated. Their tentative posturing, innocent flirtation, and youthful crushes often emerge much more clearly in diaries than does the evolution of the more serious formal courtship that culminated in marriage.

Focusing largely on the experiences of the middle and upper classes, and the period of formal courtship that led to marriage, historians studying the history of courtship rituals in nineteenth-century British North America have portrayed young women as constrained by social mores that circumscribed their activities. In particular, the young women featured in descriptions of courtship in the early part of the century were almost always chaperoned when venturing abroad, only rarely appearing alone in public settings, and then usually in defiance of custom and without parental approval.[1]

Yet, not all historians agree with this characterization, even for the early period.[2] The diaries of young single New Brunswick women imply that they had a good deal of freedom to come and go as they wished, which allowed them to enter into relationships without their parents' prior approval, or even knowledge.

Nineteenth-century New Brunswick was a youthful society, and young women, embedded in families and neighbourhoods overflowing with young people of all ages, had rich social lives. Innocent flirtation might or might not evolve into courtship and courtship might or might not culminate in marriage. During the late 1870s and early 1880s, Lucy Morrison's sons brought home young women, their future wives among them, for croquet parties or for supper. Sometimes the couples travelled alone, sometimes in a mixed group of young people, sometimes from nearby, sometimes from a distance. Courtship occurred in casual as well as formal settings and involved only the couple or peer groups as often as it involved family or supervised church or community events. The New Brunswick experience suggests an intermediary stage for young women no less than young men: a period of innocent flirtation during which adolescents slipped into and out of more tentative informal relationships that prepared the way for, and conditioned their attitudes about, formal courtship. From innocent flirtation to formal courtship, and from courtship to marriage, New Brunswick women exhibited a significant degree of independence.[3]

[. . .]

Because young men and women were so often in one another's company, serious courtship can easily be missed in reading young women's diaries.[4] Marjory Grant's marriage to William Buchanan on 4 March 1827 comes as a surprise to the reader of her diary. And even a careful re-reading yields few enough clues about preparations for the marriage, and none at all about the nature of the courtship. On 2 February, Marjory's younger brother Absalom was sent to the store to purchase "a half dozen buttons to put on Mr Buchanan's waistcoat," suggesting that Marjory may have been making the groom a new waistcoat to wear at the ceremony. Absalom purchased porringers on the same occasion, perhaps for the new household that would soon be established. But there is no direct reference to the upcoming event in Marjory's diary. Rather, she reports travelling around the countryside with her younger sister Isabella, visiting relatives and friends. [. . .] The final two entries in her diary do indicate that some sort of celebration was in the wind. On 27 February, "Father and Mother and John's wife was down to the shore. Father got three gallons of rum and a cheese. Mother and Ann got some things over the river."[5] The following day, the family began to gather, and more supplies were purchased: "Charles came home in the evening . . . and our Jannet came in with him and brought in her baby with her—Absalom went to the shore and got one lb Tea and seven lbs sugar from Mrs Marks."[6] But it was left to Isabella, taking over her sister's diary, to announce, on 4 March, that "Marjory got married" and record the family celebration the next day: "Alexander and his wife came up,[7] eat dinner with us and James Buchanan and his wife[8] and little Mary went home and Charles went to the woods and Wm R.B. took Marjory and me to the shore and brought us

up in the evening." On 6 March, "Marjory moved out to Oak Hill."

[. . .]

If the rituals of formal courtship are often difficult to identify in women's diaries, discussion of that intermediate stage of innocent flirtation is more common. In 1873, 17-year-old Amelia Holder, enjoying what was to be her final voyage with her sea-captain father, was accompanied by her younger sister Agnes. On the homeward journey, the ship carried three passengers bound for New York: the American Consul, his wife, and their adolescent daughter, Linney. The three girls looked forward to a stopover in Barbados and the opportunities for flirtation it might afford, with Amelia noting in her diary on 28 February, "We have been talking about what we are going to do when we get to Barbadoes. We are going to try and get introduced to some nice man or a rich old one and try and marry them." Meanwhile, they practised their feminine wiles, with but limited success. Thus, one evening when the first mate, Amelia's Uncle Charles, asked the two older girls, who were heading for their favourite spot on top of the cabin, if they were "going on the house," Amelia replied, "Yes, I expect we will blow away when we get up there." And Linney teased, "You'll jump over for us won't you if we fall overboard?" When Charles replied in the negative, Linney turned to the second mate and asked, "You will won't you Mr Lowry?" Mr Lowry said yes and when Amelia took up the question and "asked who was going to jump after me . . . he said he'd jump after both of us." But Charles continued to demur, telling them that "that was the way young girls deceive young men, get them to jump over after them and then leave them to drown." [. . .]

Adolescents engaged in innocent flirtation in the hopes of attracting the attention of the object of their youthful crushes. When their tentative posturing went unnoticed or their feelings were not reciprocated, they felt the pangs of unrequited love. Emma Pitt, the only daughter in a family of seafaring men, was feeling those pangs when the *Lydia*, carrying her cousins, Amelia and Agnes Holder, arrived in Saint John on 23 April 1873. At 16, Emma had a serious crush on Fred Hatheway (referred to as "F." in her diary), a young man whose father operated the steamers that plied the St John River. In the company of her cousins, she looked around for other possible suitors, reporting a "splendid day, went over to the *Lydia* and had a stunning time. There was a whole lot of us and a Mr Saunders was there, he's very nice . . . We staid on board all night and came home in the morning . . . We went into Mr Vrooms comming home and was introduced to Mr Arnold, he's very nice too."[9] But she had not forgotten Fred, and some months later, on 12 June, she recorded that "A. and I went out walking and Fred passed us. That is the first time I have seen him for 7 months." [. . .] She continued to pine for Fred, hoping to see him when she went to meeting of a Sunday, and lamenting, "I am lonesome and I can truly say I know not why I love thee! For I don't ever see him." The following Sunday, when she saw "F. pass by walking with B.E.," she confided in anguish, "Oh! heavens I thought I should die."[10]

Back at home in Holderville that winter, Amelia Holder, too, suffered the pangs of an unrequited adolescent crush. Christmas day 1873 was a milestone for Amelia, "the first Christmas I have been home for seven years. In the evening there were a lot of young folks and we enjoyed ourselves very well. I am eighteen today. How old that seems. Pa says I am of age. I wonder where we will drift to by next Christmas. R's 26th." Things for Amelia did not "drift" in the direction she had hoped. On 19 January 1874, she confided dramatically, "My heart is broke. I shall go stick, stark, staring mad. He is going to Tyber. It was in our paper Friday. I had great hope that he was coming here . . . when the first thing strikes my eye is sailed for Tyber. I don't know exactly where that is but I think it is in the East Indies. I suppose I must give

him up now, so farewell my dreams and hopes and let us plow on in the dreary sameness of this life."

Yet perhaps we should not take such passions too seriously, for their unrequited love did not, apparently, prevent either Emma Pitt or Amelia Holder from enjoying social events.[11] [. . .]

Even in the carefully supervised setting of a Methodist ladies' academy, youthful flirtation could not be suppressed. The Mount Allison Ladies' Academy was, after all, adjacent to the Male Academy and College, and although unsupervised meetings between male and female students were strictly prohibited, such rules proved difficult to enforce. Laura Fullerton, writing in 1886, recorded several instances of infractions. On Tuesday 12 May, she noted that some of the young men from the Male Academy had been "under Min Rice's window, talking to the girls," a common enough practice, though a risky one. The following day, Laura reported that "Mr Borden had Ella & Ada Bowyer down in his office last evening, about talking from the windows and attracting attention, and this morning he had Ada Fraser and Berta Ross to his office." But the practice was too widespread to occasion very serious penalties, as implied by Mrs Archibald's injunction to all those who "had talked from window and waved to the boys . . . to come to her room immediately after closing and report themselves."[12] In an effort to monitor evolving relationships between students, the administration at Mount Allison organized mixed social events and even "Private Receptions" were regularly scheduled. In some cases, young love blossomed, and 16-year-old Laura regularly reported on budding courtships in her diary. If supervised settings could not preclude flirtation, neither could they prevent the rivalries and complications often associated with first love. Nor could the school's supervision follow students as they ranged beyond the walls of the institution. Laura Fullerton, who had not yet given her heart to any young man, became inadvertently embroiled in something of a love triangle during her Easter holiday, which she spent with relatives at Point de Bute. She had travelled by train to Aulac with a fellow student, Min Curran. There, May (with whom Min was staying) and Laura's Uncle Douglas met them. As Mr Nash, who had been courting Min at various college-sponsored social events, was also among the students spending the holidays with friends or relatives at Point de Bute, Laura was not surprised to find him among the guests when she accepted an invitation to spend the evening with May and Min. Nor was she surprised when he was kind enough to escort her home at the end of the evening. Over the course of the holidays, she spent a good deal of time with May, Min, and Mr Nash, even taking them all for a drive one afternoon when her Uncle Douglas gave her his horse and carriage. But she was discomfited when it came time to return to school and, rather than taking care of Min, "Mr N took my satchel and assisted me into the train, found a seat and sat with me coming over, took my valise from the train, seen me safe in the carriage, and then left. All results in Min being in the background and Mr N. all attentions to me. Min feels it very much, too." Laura enjoyed Mr Nash's company, and he led her to believe that Min had lost interest in him, but she was not entirely convinced, confiding to her diary that "although I had a very lovely time I was not happy. It all bothered me in a way I cannot describe. Sleep was disturbed and rest gone. One thing I am glad the holidays are over." Her worries were not without foundation, for less than two weeks later she noted in her diary that "Mr Nash and Min have made up again I think, after all he said about her too. When we got back from P. de B. he wrote her to know if she did not wish to go with him anymore, if so he wanted her to say so, and not fool him any longer. I do not know what she answered, but anyway he came over this afternoon and had Private Reception with her. So I guess they have made up again." But things did not end there.

Reflecting the unavoidable emotional undercurrents circulating among young people in even the most carefully supervised settings, the situation evolved in a fairly predictable way. After evening reception on 9 May, Laura reported that "Nash was with Min, but the girls said he would have come up to me had I bowed. However I did not and he went with Miss Curran." A few days later, the tensions bubbled to the surface. When she received a letter from Mr Nash asking for her company at the next reception, Laura, assuming that Min had broken her connection with him, agreed. However, that evening "Min came up to my room and accused me of telling Nash things about her, which thing I never did. She says she is never going with Nash again. She does not think now that I told Nash anything about her." The following afternoon, "Mr N . . . had Private Reception with Min," and the next day Laura attended a baseball match on the Academy Grounds, "mostly to see how Mr N would conduct himself. He went with Min. After a time Miss Dobson, Bell Townsend and Ada Fraser and I came home." Laura's dilemma upon discovering that Min and Mr Nash were still courting was resolved when she sought advice from Miss Black, her piano teacher. "She was so very kind and told me what to do. I was so glad I went to her. I am going to write to him, break the engagement. Miss B said she would get it over for me all right . . . I wish I had never seen him. The affair bothers me." But Laura was unsure as to what kind of letter to write, "whether to be pleasant or to be cross and let him know what I think of him. I am inclined to be pleasant, but the girls advise me not be." We do not know what kind of letter Laura sent, but the following day she reported that she "wrote to Mr N today, cancelled the engagement. I gave the letter to Miss Black." On 18 May, she received a reply from Mr N, "answered it after school and sent it by Geo. Inglis . . . I hope he will not reply."[13] Such early adolescent relationships rarely led to marriage, but the expectation of exclusivity when one was "going with" a young man set the stage for the potential shift to more formal courtship.

[. . .]

Certainly it is true that by the time most young women reached their late teens the prospect of marriage was much on their minds. Some were ambivalent, not at all anxious to give up a freedom they recognized would be constrained by marriage. Writing home in 1846, 17-year-old Mary Hill, having received news of a friend's recent marriage, commented that "it makes one feel old, to see all the playmates and companions of their childhood married. I am glad there is no news of Mary or Hannah Bixby's getting married. I should grow desperate on my return home and should wish to emigrate to a less precocious place where people do not instantly change from wild boys and girls, to sedate married persons, if they should. Is there no rumour of Achsah's getting married, so much the better.[14] I shall find some companions when I return. Hers will ever be a fresh and youthful spirit, fitted for single blessedness. The Rose will bloom on her cheek long after it has faded on those who have chosen a less carefree lot (there, is not that poetical)."[15]

Although young women themselves often grew anxious with the passing years, parents rarely encouraged early marriage.[16] Responding to her daughter's expressed concerns, Sarah Hill retorted tartly, "You must not fancy because some of your young friends are marrying at eighteen and nineteen, that you must leave school at eighteen." Telling Mary that "if your improvement should answer our expectation, and you wish it I hope your father will allow you to remain another winter at school," Sarah sought to assuage her daughter's fears, informing her that "Mary Todd who is near two years older than you, is intending to go to Jamaica Plains in the Spring to school."[17] When 18-year-old Ann Eliza Rogers made her plans to marry a man nearly 20 years her senior, we cannot know whether either her parents or her fiancé had doubts, but for whatever reason, the marriage was registered not in the spring of 1855, as Ann Eliza had planned, but in October, by which time she was well into her third trimester of pregnancy.

At 30, Sophy Bliss was old enough to know her own mind, yet her family and friends were, at best, ambivalent about her decision to wed William Carman, a 55-year-old widower. In this case, a surviving letter from Sophy's mother, Sarah, written on the day before her daughter's marriage, provides a poignant glimpse of a family struggling to come to terms with Sophy's decision. Admitting that *All I feel* would fill sheets and a task I could not get through with very well, for *you* have been my support and my comforter so long that I hardly know how to resign you and give up my right to you my good excellent daughter," she went on to assure Sophy that "you have your mother's blessing." Speaking for Sophy's sisters, among others, Sarah reassured her daughter, "You must not expect your friends to *rejoice that they have to give you up* but you will have the warmest wishes for your welfare & happiness."[18] Indeed, no diarist's record suggests that parental pressure played any role in a daughter's decision to marry.

Nonetheless, as young women came of age, they began to seek more serious relationships, shifting from flirtation to courtship. [. . .] Sadie Harper's interests [. . .] shifted from flirtation to courtship during the course of her diary. Frank Allen, the young schoolteacher whom Sadie would later marry, made his first appearance in her diary in August 1895. Soon Sadie was not only singing with him in the choir, but taking German lessons from him as well. Gradually, Mr Allen was incorporated into the Harper household's broad circle, and in early January 1896, Sadie reported, "About five o'clock Mr Allen came up then Nell, Blois, Mr Allen and myself practiced some quartettes for Lodge. He stayed to tea . . . Nell went to prayer meeting with Mama and Blois. Mr Allen and I went to Lodge where a pleasant evening was spent."[19] By March, Sadie was participating in some mild flirtation, and her diary entries suggest that Mr Allen's interest was piqued.[20] On 2 April, she reported that "Mr Allen came in on his way down from Ted's where he had been to tea, and he spent the rest of the evening here. He hadn't intended staying as he just called to leave a book for me from Ted. But he got talking and talking, and time slipped by so quickly." On 19 April, "after church Mr Allen came up again for a wonder. I don't know what struck him I'm sure. He got talking again about college life and it was after eleven when he went." Yet, while Sadie enjoyed Mr Allen's company, she gave no hint that he enjoyed any special place in her affections. When the school semester ended, Mr Allen disappeared not only from Shediac, but also from Sadie's diary. And when he reappeared, at choir practice, on 15 August, her reference to him was almost offhand: "Mr Allen is back and as bashful as ever, but it's good to have a tenor again." Even as Mr Allen embarked upon a formal courtship that becomes ever clearer to the reader of her diary, Sadie, seemingly, did not immediately recognize his intent. Thus, noting on 15 November that "Mr Allen" had asked her "to go to hear Albani with him in Moncton," she confided only, "My but I was glad as I didn't want to take my own money but rather than not hear her I would do so. It is very kind of him, I think."[21]

Because her diary for 1897 is not extant, we cannot know at what stage Sadie became as serious about the courtship as Mr Allen. But perhaps that evening was a turning point, for on 25 November, she reported, "Mr Allen and I had splendid seats . . . and oh, but I'll never forget that concert. Albani was something to dream about. She was just perfection . . . I never imagined anything like it, and tho' I couldn't understand the Italian . . . to hear her tone was enough . . . It was grand GRAND . . . That night I shall never forget, and I surely felt grateful to Mr Allen for giving me such a treat." Whatever the timing, by 1898, her heart was won and Mr Allen had become Frank. Well beyond schoolgirl crushes, at the

"pretty ancient" age of 23, Sadie, reporting private walks and private talks, reveals not only her feelings but also the tension between the desire for privacy and the desire to maintain a certain level of Victorian propriety.

Fri. Feb. 4, 1898. Nice and fine again. I sewed for most of the day. We had choir practice for a short time before tea. After tea since it had got beautiful and mild and was simply a perfect moonlight night I went and got Lena to come for a snowshoe tramp. So we had a very enjoyable one, just downtown over the drifts. After we both got home again, I practiced some solos for a while. Then Blois came in from a hockey match and brot Frank in with him. So Nell and Duff played Crokino against the Professor and me and we had a lot of fun over it. Before he left that evening we had one of our pleasant sweet little confidential talks just by ourselves. He is such a dear good fellow.

Sun. Feb. 6. Sunday was a lovely day and quite mild. Mr Matthews did not have service this morning as he did not feel well enough for two services, so thot he would take the evening one. In the afternoon we went to S.S. as usual and then had choir practice and after that Frank and I went down the track for a walk and as it was such a beautiful afternoon we enjoyed our walk so much and when we got home he came in to tea. It was his 24th birthday so he is not quite a year older than I am. Out to service in the evening and after we came home we sat and talked in the parlour for a while, while Ted and Herb and the rest of them in the house here amused themselves in the other room. Of course they teased us well for going off by ourselves but Ted's been there before often and I don't care what any of them say.

[. . .]

Sun. Feb. 13. Sunday was lovely and fine again and the walking not too bad at all. So as Mr Matthews was not having service again in the morning, Nell and I went down and heard Mr Smith preach. Frank walked up home with me afterwards and he said he was told to bring one of us back to dinner with him and as I had been up there just lately to dinner, Nell went with him this time. So we got Mr Deacon to stay with us for dinner as he had been in all morning talking to Papa. In the afternoon out to S.S. as usual and then choir practice, and afterwards Frank and I went for a lovely walk again down the track. In the evening out to church and after church as the evening was so perfect we went for a walk and when we came home we finished our talk in the parlour. As long as Mama doesn't mind, it doesn't matter a little bit to me what the other girls say.

While recognizing some intriguing, and perhaps surprising, continuities over time, the tensions both explicit and implicit in various diaries imply that shifts in attitudes and mores were subtle and required the encouragement and support of parents. But whether diarists were, like Mary Hill, reluctant to relinquish their freedom or, like Lillie Williamson, anxious to marry, young women contemplating a life of "single blessedness" had fewer career options open to them than did young men. At the same time, while the goal of courtship for both parties was marriage, the decision to wed often meant a much more significant transition for young women than for their male counterparts. For the teachers among them, it almost always meant giving up the autonomy an independent income could afford, as very few married women were employed outside the home. [. . .]

NOTES

1. See, especially, W. Peter Ward, *Courtship, Love, and Marriage in Nineteenth-Century English Canada* (Montreal: McGill-Queen's University Press, 1990), which is the standard work on Canadian courtship. Frances Hoffman and Ryan Taylor, *Much to Be Done: Private Life in Ontario from Victorian Diaries* (Toronto: Natural Heritage/Natural History, 1996), 7–40, offer a similar view.

2. See "Courtship and Engagement," chap. 1 of Françoise Noël, *Family Life and Sociability in Upper and Lower Canada, 1780–1870: A View from Diaries and Family Correspondence* (Montreal: McGill-Queen's University Press, 2003). The women cited do not appear to have been particularly troubled by either parental or societal constraints. For the United States, see Ellen K. Rothman, *Hands and Hearts: A History of Courtship in America* (New York: Basic Books, 1984), who discusses the freedom young single people had to come and go as they wished. Like Rothman, Karen Lystra, *Searching the Heart: Women, Men, and Romantic Love in Nineteenth-Century America* (New York: Oxford University Press, 1989),

also focuses on the increasing significance of romantic love in shaping the experience of courtship during the course of the nineteenth century. Noël also focuses on the role of romantic love.

3. In her study of farm women in the Nanticoke Valley in New York, Nancy Osterud also found that "couples courted within an informal, gender-mixed milieu and enjoyed relative freedom from parental supervision; they interacted in flexible and intimate, rather than stiff and stereotypical ways" (*Bonds of Community: The Lives of Farm Women in Nineteenth-Century New York* [Ithaca, NY: Cornell University Press, 1991], 11).

4. See also the discussion of the courtship of Louisa Collins in Margaret Conrad, Toni Laidlaw, and Donna Smyth, *No Place Like Home: Diaries and Letters of Nova Scotia Women 1771–1938* (Halifax: Formac, 1988), 61–80.

5. The reference here is to the shore of the St Croix River, where the village of St Stephen and the local store were located. John was Marjory's older brother; Ann was his wife.

6. Marjory Grant Diary, MC285, Provincial Archives of New Brunswick [hereafter PANB], 2, 27, and 28 February 1827. Charles was Marjory's younger brother. "Our Jannet" is a reference to her older sister, who was married to James Buchanan, a brother of the groom. Jannet, who lived at Oak Hill, in St James Parish, would stay with her parents until after the wedding; James arrived a few days later.

7. Alexander, Marjory and Isabella's eldest brother, and his wife, Mary, also lived at Oak Hill.

8. The "our Jannet" referred to in Marjory's diary.

9. Emma Alice Pitt Diary, MC827, PANB, April 1873.

10. Emma Alice Pitt Diary, MC827, PANB, 27 September; 2, 4, and 9 November 1873.

11. For a somewhat different interpretation of Amelia's unrequited love, see Ward, *Courtship, Love, and Marriage*, 159.

12. Laura Cynthia Fullerton Diary, Mount Allison University Archives [hereafter MAUA], 12–13 May 1886.

13. Laura Cynthia Fullerton Diary, MAUA, 26 April–18 May 1886.

14. Although Achsah Upton was Mary's maternal aunt, the two young women were close in age and the best of friends.

15. Mary W. Hill to Friends at Home, 10 February 1846, George Stillman Hill Manuscript Collection, MC1001, MS6/1, PANB.

16. Lee Virginia Chambers-Schiller, *Liberty, a Better Husband: Single Women in America: The Generation of 1780–1840* (New Haven, CT: Yale University Press, 1984), 17, argues that between 1800 and 1860 the view that women would be better off single than to enter into a bad marriage or compromise their integrity in exchange for a husband gained "widespread currency in newspapers, periodicals, fiction and advice books" in the United States.

17. Sarah Upton Hill to Mary W. Hill, 23 February 1846, George Stillman Hill Manuscript Collection, MC1001, PANB.

18. Sarah Bliss to Sophia Bliss, 31 May 1859, William F. Ganong Papers, 3436 5 F508, New Brunswick Museum Archives [hereafter NBMA].

19. Sadie Harper Diaries, MC286, PANB, 9 January 1896.

20. See, for example, Sadie Harper Diaries, MC286, PANB, 9 March 1896.

21. Born in Chambly, Lower Canada, Emma Albani trained in Europe, where she made her career. She returned to her native country regularly, on tours that took her across the country nine times between 1883 and 1906. Pierre Vachon, "Lajeunesse, Emma (also called Marie-Louise-Cecile-Emma)," *Dictionary of Canadian Biography*, vol. 15, 1921–1930.

Chapter 11

Indigenous Peoples in British North America

READINGS

Primary Documents

1   From "Report on the Affairs of the Indians in Canada" (1842–44), in *Appendix to the Fourth Volume of the Journals of the Legislative Assembly of the Province of Canada 1844–45*

2   "The Robinson-Superior Treaty," in *The Treaties of Canada with the Indians of Manitoba and the North-West Territories, Including the Negotiations on which They Were Based, and Other Information Relating Thereto*, Alexander Morris

Historical Interpretations

3   From "Empire, the Maritime Colonies, and the Supplanting of Mi'kma'ki/Wulstukwik, 1780–1820," John G. Reid

4   From "'An Equitable Right to Be Compensated': The Dispossession of the Aboriginal Peoples of Quebec and the Emergence of a New Legal Rationale (1760–1860)," Alain Beaulieu

INTRODUCTION

The period comprising the late eighteenth and early nineteenth centuries was one in which treaties between Indigenous peoples and colonial authorities began to institutionalize relations and to more sharply segregate the two groups. In return for certain territories, Indigenous people were to stay away from settlers who were taking up land for agricultural purposes. The nullification of Indigenous title happened along lines set out by the Colonial Office. This dictation or shaping of the terms was the prerogative of the stronger force—a pattern that continued after Confederation.

The primary and secondary sources in this chapter offer insight into the imbalanced nature of the relationship between British officials and Indigenous peoples during the colonial era, and of the ways that the British exploited this imbalance to divest Indigenous peoples of their lands and territories. The report from the early 1840s illustrates clearly that the British colonial authorities believed that they had continually treated an Indigenous population that was prone to temptation with "forbearance and kindness." The second primary document is a treaty known as the Robinson-Superior Treaty. Signed in 1850, it offered lump-sum and yearly compensation to the affected bands for the loss of their lands, and granted reserves, presumably in places that the bands wanted to continue living. John Reid's reading discusses this process (which occurred earlier in the Maritimes than in central Canada) by using the term "supplanting," which is especially appropriate because it conveys a sense that one way of life was elbowed out of the way to make room for another. His view is a bit more hopeful in that he notes that Maritime Indigenous people experienced some success in having their grievances remedied. Perhaps this was because colonization required things to happen quickly and authorities did not want to delay the process. Alain Beaulieu's account shows that the British authorities followed a different pattern in dispossessing Indigenous peoples in the St Lawrence Valley than in other parts of British North America. Following a tradition established under the French regime, the British did not conclude treaties with Indigenous people in Quebec, but instead proceeded unilaterally with the appropriation of their land.

QUESTIONS FOR CONSIDERATION

1   What goal did the British colonial administration seem to be moving toward? In other words, what changes did they hope to bring about in the relationship between Indigenous people and immigrants/settlers?

2   What did the Robinson-Superior Treaty ask of those who signed it?

3   From the perspective of Indigenous peoples in British North America, what were the possible advantages and disadvantages of being treated as individual nations?

4   What were the strategies that Maritime Indigenous people used to "negotiate" with colonial authorities?

5   How did the British dispossess Indigenous people of their land in Quebec? Why did they not conclude Indigenous treaties in the colony?

SUGGESTIONS FOR FURTHER READING

Binnema, Ted, and Susan Neylan, eds. *New Histories for Old: Changing Perspectives on Canada's Native Pasts*. Vancouver: UBC Press, 2007.

Carter, Sarah. *Aboriginal People and Colonizers of Western Canada to 1900*. Toronto: University of Toronto Press, 1999.

Dickason, Olive Patricia, with David T. McNab. *Canada's First Nations: A History of Founding Peoples from Earliest Times*. Don Mills, ON: Oxford University Press, 2009.

Fee, Margery. *Literary Land Claims: The "Indian Land Question" from Pontiac's War to Attawapiskat*. Waterloo, ON: Wilfrid Laurier University Press, 2015.

Haig-Brown, Celia, and David Nock, eds. *With Good Intentions: Euro-Canadian and Aboriginal Relations in Colonial Canada*. Vancouver: UBC Press, 2006.

Lennox, Jeffers. *Homelands and Empires: Indigenous Spaces, Imperial Fictions, and Competition for Territory in Northeastern North America, 1690–1763*. Toronto: University of Toronto Press, 2017.

Miller, J.R. *Compact, Contract, Covenant: Aboriginal Treaty-Making in Canada*. Toronto: University of Toronto Press, 2009.

———, ed. *Sweet Promises: A Reader on Indian–White Relations in Canada*. Toronto: University of Toronto Press, 1991.

Peace, Thomas, and Kathryn Labelle. *From Huronia to Wendakes: Adversity, Migration, and Resilience, 1650–1900*. Norman, OK: University of Oklahoma Press, 2016.

Upton, L.F.S. *Micmacs and Colonists: Indian–White Relations in the Maritimes, 1713–1867*. Vancouver: University of British Columbia Press, 1979.

Wicken, Bill. "26 August 1726: A Case Study in Mi'kmaq-New England Relations in the Early 18th Century." *Acadiensis* 23, no. 1 (Autumn 1993): 5–22.

Primary Documents

1 From "Report on the Affairs of the Indians in Canada" (1842–44), in *Appendix to the Fourth Volume of the Journals of the Legislative Assembly of the Province of Canada 1844–45* (Montreal: R. Campbell, 1845), Appendix EEE.

SECTION I. HISTORY OF THE RELATIONS BETWEEN THE GOVERNMENT AND THE INDIANS.

The spirit of the British Government towards the Aborigines of this Continent, was at an early date characterized by the same forbearance and kindness which still continues to be extended to them. [. . .]

Since 1763 the Government, adhering to the Royal Proclamation of that year, have not considered themselves entitled to dispossess the Indians of their lands, without entering into an agreement with them, and rendering them some compensation. For a considerable time after the conquest of Canada, the whole of the western part of the Upper Province, with the exception of a few military posts on the frontier, and a great extent of the eastern part, was in their occupation. As the settlement of the country advanced, and the land was required

for new occupants, or the predatory and revengeful habits of the Indians rendered their removal desirable, the British Government made successive agreements with them for the surrender of portions of their lands. The compensation was sometimes made in the shape of presents, consisting of clothing, ammunition, and objects adapted to gratify a savage taste; but more frequently in the shape of permanent annuities, payable to the tribe concerned, and their descendants forever, either in goods at the current price, or in money at the rate of ten dollars (£2 10s.) for each member of the tribe at the time of the arrangement. [. . .]

It has been alleged that these agreements were unjust, as dispossessing the natives of their ancient territories, and extortionate, as rendering a very inadequate compensation for the lands surrendered.

If, however, the Government had not made arrangements for the voluntary surrender of the lands, the white settlers would gradually have taken possession of them, without offering any compensation whatsoever; it would, at that time, have been as impossible to resist the natural laws of society, and to guard the Indian Territory against the encroachments of the whites, as it would have been impolitic to have attempted to check the tide of immigration. The Government, therefore, adopted the most humane and the most just course, in inducing the Indians, by offers of compensation, to remove quietly to more distant hunting grounds, or to confine themselves within more limited reserves, instead of leaving them and the white settlers exposed to the horrors of a protracted struggle for ownership. The wisdom and justice of this course is most strongly recommended by Vattel, in his *Law of Nations*, from which the following passage is an extract:—

There is another celebrated question to which the discovery of the new world has principally given rise. It is asked whether a nation may lawfully take possession of some part of a vast country in which there are none but erratic nations, whose scanty population is incapable of occupying the whole? We have already observed, in establishing the obligation to cultivate the earth, that these nations cannot exclusively appropriate to themselves more land than they have occasion for, or more than they are able to settle and cultivate. Their unsettled habitation in those immense regions, cannot be accounted a true and legal possession, and the people of Europe, too closely pent up at home, finding land, of which the Savages stood in no particular need, and of which they made no actual and constant use, were lawfully entitled to take possession of it and to settle it with Colonies. The earth, as we have already observed, belongs to mankind in general, and was designed to furnish them with subsistence. If each nation had from the beginning resolved to appropriate to itself a vast country, that the people might live only by hunting, fishing and wild fruits, our globe would not be sufficient to maintain a tenth part of its present inhabitants. We do not, therefore, deviate from the views of nature, in

confining the Indians within narrower limits. However, we cannot help praising the moderation of the English Puritans, who first settled in New England, who, notwithstanding their being furnished with a charter from their Sovereign, purchased of the Indians the lands of which they intended to take possession. This laudable example was followed by William Penn, and the Colony of Quakers that he conducted to Pennsylvania.

Nor can the friend of the Indian claim for him a monetary compensation based on the present value of the land, which has been created solely by the presence and industry of the white settlers. Its only value to the denizen of the forest, was as a hunting ground, as the source of his supply of game and furs. Of the cultivation of the soil, he then knew nothing. The progress of settlement, and the consequent destruction of the forests, with the operations of the lumberer, and fur trader, was shortly about to destroy this value; in every case the Indians had either the opportunity of retreating to more distant hunting grounds, or they were left on part of their old possessions, with a reserve supposed at the time to be adequate to all their wants, and greatly exceeding their requirements as cultivators of the soil at the present day, to which were added the ranges of their old haunts, until they became actually occupied by settlers, and in many cases, an annuity to themselves and their descendents forever, which was equivalent at least to any benefit they derived from the possession of the lands.

If subsequent events have greatly enhanced the value of their lands, it has been in consequence of the speedy and peaceable settlement of the country, by means, chiefly, of the agreements in question, and the Indians are now in possession of advantages which far exceed those of the surrounding white population, and which afford them the means, under a proper system of mental improvement, of obtaining independence, and even opulence.

These agreements have been faithfully observed by both parties. The Indians have not disputed the title of the Crown to the lands, which they have surrendered; and the annuities have always been the first charge upon the revenue derived from the sale of Crown Lands, and have been *punctually paid up to the present time.*

From the earliest period of the connexion between the Indians and the British Government it has been customary to distribute annually certain presents, consisting chiefly of clothing and ammunition. [. . .]

The practice has continued to the present time, partly owing to a renewal of the occasions which first led to it; partly to repeated, but apparently unauthorised, declarations of officers of the Government, that the system should for ever be maintained; and partly to the apprehension that its sudden discontinuance would cause inconvenience and hardships to a large portion of the race within the Province.

The British Government have always considered the Indians to be under their special charge. In the Lower Province the tribes were early converted and collected in settlements by the Jesuits, who received large grants of land from the French Crown for this service. Upon the Conquest, the Crown took possession of these estates, and thus cut off any further benefit which the Indians might have derived from them. In the Upper Province, however, Christianity and civilization had, until a recent period, made little progress among them. They were an untaught, unwary race, among a population ready and able to take every advantage of them. Their lands, their presents and annuities, the produce of the chase, their guns and clothing, whatever they possessed of value, were objects of temptation to the needy settlers and the unprincipled trader, to whom their ignorance of commerce and of the English language, and their remarkable fondness for spirits, yielded them an easy prey. Hence it became necessary for the Government to interfere. Laws were passed to prevent or limit trading with them—to hinder the sale of spirits to them—to exclude whites from their settlements—and to restrain encroachments upon their lands. Officers were appointed at the principal Indian settlements, to enforce these laws, and to communicate between the tribes and the Government; to attend to the distribution of their presents and annuities; to prevent discussion; and, generally, to maintain the authority of the Government among the tribes.

The system of dealing with them was essentially military. For a long time they were under the head of the military department, and were considered and treated as military allies or stipendiaries.

Little was done by the Government to raise their mental and moral condition. In Lower Canada the Roman Catholic Missionaries, originally appointed by the Jesuits, were maintained. In Upper Canada, until a very late period, neither Missionary nor Schoolmaster was appointed. The omission was in later years supplied by various religious Societies, whose efforts have in many instances met with signal success, and within a still more recent period the Government has directed its attention to the same object.

As the Indian Lands were held in common, and the title to them was vested in the Crown, as their Guardian, the Indians were excluded from all political rights, the tenure of which depended upon an extent of interest, not conferred upon them by the Crown.

Their inability also to complete with their white brethren debarred them, in a great measure, from the enjoyment of civil rights, while the policy of the Government led to the belief that they did not in fact possess them.*

They were thus left in a state of tutelage, which although devised for their protection

* The records of the Courts of Justice furnish undoubted evidence that the Indians are amenable to, and enjoy the protection of, both the civil and criminal laws of the Province. That they may share in, and are entitled to, all the political privileges of the whites when individually possessed of the necessary qualifications may be inferred from the fact, that John Brant, an Indian Chief of the six nations, was elected a Member of the Legislative Assembly of Upper Canada. The subsequent loss of his seat in that body, was occasioned in consequence of his not possessing sufficient Freehold property, and not on account of his origin. Mr. Justice Macaulay's, and Mr. Attorney General Ogden's opinions on this subject are given in the Appendix, No. 98.

and benefit, has in the event proved very detrimental to their interests, by encouraging them to rely wholly upon the support and advice of the Government, and to neglect the opportunities which they have possessed of raising themselves from the state of dependence to the level of the surrounding population.

It is easy, at the present day, on looking back, to trace the error of the Government, and its evil consequences; but it is only just to observe that the system was in accordance with the legislation of the times. The regenerative power of religion and education was not then as now appreciated. The effects of civilization, and the necessities arising out of it, were not foreseen. The information of the Imperial Government was very imperfect. It was not easy nor safe rashly to change a mode of treatment to which the Indians had become accustomed, and thus the system has been allowed to continue up to the present time, long after the Government has become aware of its imperfections and inconveniences.

It must also be acknowledged that the system was never fully carried out. The protection which the Government intended to throw over the Indians was not and could not be sufficiently maintained. No supervision was adequate to guard so many detached and distant bands from the evils inflicted on them by their white neighbours, aided by their own cupidity and love of spirits. Their lands were encroached upon, frequently with their own consent, bought with a bribe to the Chief. Their complaints were often adjudicated upon by parties interested in despoiling them, or prejudiced against them; and thus a system, erroneous in itself, became more hurtful from its necessarily imperfect development. Of late years, however, the government has become sensible of the necessity for introducing some change in this policy.

2 Alexander Morris, "The Robinson-Superior Treaty," in *The Treaties of Canada with the Indians of Manitoba and the North-West Territories, Including the Negotiations on which They Were Based, and Other Information Relating Thereto* (Toronto: Belfords, Clarke, 1880), 302–4.

This Agreement, made and entered into on the seventh day of September, in the year of Our Lord one thousand eight hundred and fifty, at Sault Ste. Marie, in the Province of Canada, between the Honorable William Benjamin Robinson, of the one part, on behalf of Her Majesty the Queen, and Joseph Peandechat, John Iuinway, Mishe-Muckqua, Totomencie, Chiefs, and Jacob Warpela, Ahmutchiwagabou, Michel Shelageshick, Manitoshainse, and Chiginans, principal men of the Ojibewa Indians inhabiting the Northern Shore of Lake Superior, in the said Province of Canada, from Batchewananng Bay to Pigeon River, at the western extremity of said lake, and inland throughout the extent to the height of land which separates the territory covered by the charter of the Honorable the Hudson's Bay Company from the said tract, and also the islands in the said lake within the boundaries of the British possessions therein, of the other part, witnesseth:

That for and in consideration of the sum of two thousand pounds of good and lawful money of Upper Canada, to them in hand paid, and for the further perpetual annuity of five hundred pounds, the same to be paid and delivered to the said Chiefs and their tribes at a convenient season of each summer, not later than the first day of August at the Honorable the Hudson's Bay Company's Posts of Michipicoton and Fort William, they the said Chiefs and principal men do freely, fully and voluntarily surrender, cede, grant and convey unto Her Majesty, Her heirs and successors forever, all their right, title and interest in the whole of the territory above described, save and except the reservations set forth in the schedule hereunto annexed, which reservations shall be held and occupied by the said Chiefs and their tribes in common, for the purposes of residence and cultivation,—and should the said Chiefs and their respective tribes at any time desire to dispose of any mineral or other valuable productions upon the said reservations, the same will be at their request sold by order of the Superintendent-General of the Indian Department for the time being, for their sole use and benefit, and to the best advantage.

And the said William Benjamin Robinson of the first part, on behalf of Her Majesty and the Government of this Province, hereby promises and agrees to make the payments as before mentioned; and further to allow the said Chiefs and their tribes the full and free privilege to hunt over the territory now ceded by them, and to fish in the waters thereof as they have heretofore been in the habit of doing, saving and excepting only such portions of the said territory as may from time to time be sold or leased to individuals, or companies of individuals, and occupied by them with the consent of the Provincial Government. The parties of the second part further promise and agree that they will not sell, lease, or otherwise dispose of any portion of their reservations without the consent of the Superintendent-General of Indian Affairs being first had and obtained; nor will they at any time hinder or prevent persons from exploring or searching for minerals or other valuable productions in any part of the territory hereby ceded to Her Majesty as before mentioned. The parties of the second part also agree that in case the Government of this Province should before the date of this agreement have sold, or bargained to sell, any mining locations or other property on the portions of the territory hereby reserved for their use and benefit, then and in that case such sale, or promise

of sale, shall be perfected, if the parties interested desire it, by the Government, and the amount accruing therefrom shall be paid to the tribe to whom the reservation belongs. The said William Benjamin Robinson on behalf of Her Majesty, who desires to deal liberally and justly with all her subjects, further promises and agrees that in case the territory hereby ceded by the parties of the second part shall at any future period produce an amount which will enable the Government of this Province without incurring loss to increase the annuity hereby secured to them, then, and in that case, the same shall be augmented from time to time, provided that the amount paid to each individual shall not exceed the sum of one pound provincial currency in any one year, or such further sum as Her Majesty may be graciously pleased to order; and provided further that the number of Indians entitled to the benefit of this treaty shall amount to two-thirds of their present numbers (which is twelve hundred and forty) to entitle them to claim the full benefit thereof, and should their numbers at any future period not amount to two-thirds of twelve hundred and forty, the annuity shall be diminished in proportion to their actual numbers.

———

Schedule of Reservations made by the above named and subscribing Chiefs and principal men.

First—Joseph Pean-de-chat and his tribe, the reserve to commence about two miles from Fort William (inland), on the right bank of the River Kiministiquia; thence westerly six miles, parallel to the shores of the lake; thence northerly five miles, thence easterly to the right bank of the said river, so as not to interfere with any acquired rights of the Honorable Hudson's Bay Company.

Second—Four miles square at Gros Cap, being a valley near the Honorable Hudson's Bay Company's post of Michipicoton, for Totominai and tribe.

Third—Four miles square on Gull River, near Lake Nipigon, on both sides of said river, for the Chief Mishimuckqua and tribe.

    (Signed)   W. B. Robinson.

Joseph Pean-de-chat.	His x mark.	[L.S.]
John Minway.	" x "	[L.S.]
Mishe-Muckqua.	" x "	[L.S.]
Totominai.	" x "	[L.S.]
Jacob Wapela.	" x "	[L.S.]
Ah-mutchinagalon.	" x "	[L.S.]
Michel Shelageshick.	" x "	[L.S.]
Manitou Shainse.	" x "	[L.S.]
Chiginans.	" x "	[L.S.]

Signed, sealed and delivered at Sault Ste. Marie, the day and year first above written, in presence of—

    (Signed)   George Ironside, S. I. Affairs.
                       Astley P. Cooper, Capt. Com. Rifle Brig.

H. M. Balfour, 2nd Lieut. Rifle Brig.
John Swanston, C. F. Hon. Hud. Bay Co.
George Johnston, Interpreter.
F. W. Keating.

Historical Interpretations

3 From John G. Reid, "Empire, the Maritime Colonies, and the Supplanting of Mi'kma'ki/Wulstukwik, 1780–1820," *Acadiensis* 38, no. 2 (2009): 78–97.

It has become a historical truism that the effects of the Loyalist migration to the Maritime colonies, reinforced by other substantial migrations including those of the Scots, were intensely destructive for the Native populations of the territories involved. L.F.S. Upton wrote in 1979 that "the arrival of the Loyalists completed Britain's conquest of Acadia"; the occasional "flicker of independence" notwithstanding, wholesale dispossession followed. For Upton, it quickly became clear that, "the Indians were no longer of account as allies, enemies, or people."[1] In another important and influential study, Harald E.L. Prins argued in 1996 that the Loyalist influx "overwhelmed" the Native economy, and the resulting destitution—along with the absence of support from potential diplomatic allies in France and the United States—ensured that by the 1790s, "the Mi'kmaq and other tribal nations on the Atlantic seaboard were painfully aware that the old times were over."[2] Depictions such as these are consistent with the more general historical narrative of an ongoing, far advanced dispossession of Native peoples in eastern North America as a whole. [. . .]

This article will suggest, however, that the supplanting of Mi'kma'ki and Wulstukwik by the Maritime colonies, while certainly entering a critical phase during the waning years of the "long" eighteenth century, was characterized by a complex and distinctive pattern.[3] In this substantial portion of northeastern North America there were discrete though intertwined lines of development in, on the one hand, environmental and territorial matters and, on the other hand, in those connected with military and diplomatic history. That dispossession was widespread is beyond doubt, even though a review of the evidence also suggests significant spatial variations in the scale and implications of environmental change. Yet this damaging process co-existed with the continuing Native ability to represent complaints and demands based on long-standing treaty obligations, and to extract conciliatory responses from reluctant imperial officials. Owed in part to the tensions prevailing during a period of recurrent conflicts embroiling Great Britain, France, and the United States, this persistent diplomatic capacity waned after 1815. While it lasted, it had not only carried through to a later era the practice of discussing treaty-based assertions with representatives of the Crown, but it also had continued an extended narrative of Native–imperial relations through a period that had seen a profound discontinuity in the form of greatly intensified pressure imposed by colonial settlement.

In important respects, the Mi'kmaq and Wulstukwiuk shared common or analogous histories. Interaction and intermittent military co-operation with French imperial officials characterized the late seventeenth and early eighteenth centuries for both, and reached further into the eighteenth century for Mi'kmaq who maintained a relationship with Louisbourg. The Mi'kmaw experience, and to a lesser degree that of the Wulstukwiuk, also included a relationship of general though not uninterrupted peaceful co-existence with Acadian colonists while the disruptions created by the Planter migrations of the 1760s had also proved to have limited environmental consequences.[4] When it came to the history of diplomatic relations with the British, the Mi'kmaq, along with the Wulstukwiuk and Passamaquoddy, shared a process of evolution that from 1725 onwards diverged markedly from the experience of Wabanaki neighbours. It was characterized, in particular, by the negotiation of similar and closely linked treaties in 1760–1, which marked the last major phase of treaty-making even though further negotiations and more localized treaties followed during the era of the American Revolution.[5] The Mi'kmaq and Wulstukwiuk also shared an ability to meet the pressures that arose during the 1780–1820 period by drawing on two centuries of experience not only with intercultural trade relations but also with diplomatic engagements, including citation of treaty obligations to protect essential resource harvests and the containment of agricultural settlement. The stresses imposed by colonization during this crucial transitional era were unprecedented, with the settlement of non-Native populations characterized by land hunger and a profound sense of entitlement. The results were intensely destructive, and yet there was no military defeat, no formal land surrender, and the principle of a treaty relationship that enshrined Native–imperial peace and friendship was one that—far from weakening—continued in Native political cultures to evolve and gain strength. These are the elements that demonstrate, in this geographical and cultural context as in other areas of history, that general narratives have their place but must ultimately be disciplined according to the particularities of experience.

As Upton showed many years ago, the late eighteenth century—especially the era following the closing stages of the American Revolution—saw not only profound changes in the non-Native demographics of the Maritime colonies but also an acceleration of territorial colonization and environmental change that exerted damaging and long-lasting pressures on Mi'kmaw society and economy. Subsequent studies have elaborated and re-emphasized this characteristic of the era for the Mi'kmaq, and the evidence yields little suggestion that the Wulstukwiuk experience differed significantly.[6] For all that, within a general pattern of encroachment by Loyalist refugees, Scottish rural settlers, and others there were variations. The greatest concentration of environmental pressures came with the peninsula of mainland Mi'kma'ki, where land configuration combined with encroachment and resource depletion to create by the mid-1790s a critical juncture. In early 1794, the Nova Scotia Indian Commissioner George Henry Monk wrote from Windsor to Governor John Wentworth, enclosing a petition in the name of "the Mickmack Indians." Monk had been reluctant to have the Mi'kmaw concerns addressed to Wentworth, for "their remarks and representations were such that I wished rather to discourage then [sic] to communicate them," but following a contentious meeting with Mi'kmaq from Pictou and Cape Sable and a threat that Natives would converge on Halifax to confront Wentworth directly, he finally "reduced their

Representations into the form of a Petition . . . , adhering strictly to their own Observations and remarks."[7]

Despite the possibility that Monk may have sanitized the content as well as shaping the form of the petition, its language was uncompromising even though polite. Contrasting Nova Scotia with New Brunswick, where "there are Countries back [i.e., back countries] for the Indians," the petitioners declared that "all Nova Scotia is Coast and Rivers, and that the English have taken all the Coast and Rivers, and make Roads and Settlements through the Woods every where, and leave no place for the Indians to hunt in." As a result, they continued, "a great many Mickmacks have died for want of Victuals and Cloaths."[8] As the petitioners were undoubtedly aware, there was more to the dispossession of the Mi'kmaq than simply the loss of hunting territory. Fishing was another source of repeated tension. As early as in August 1784, Charles Baker of Cumberland wrote of a conversation with the Mi'kmaw leader François Argamo, who "expressed his fears of the [Loyalist] Refugees and complained of the hardship of being drove from their hunting Grounds and fisheries."[9] Among subsequent complaints was one directed to Wentworth from the Cape Sable Mi'kmaq in 1802, that "white people set Nets intirely across the Brooks and small rivers, which intirely prevent any Fish running up the streams," while a correspondent of the Pictou *Colonial Patriot* recalled in 1828 that "we have heard . . . of a white man taking a fish from the river, and an Indian taking it from him, saying it was not his."[10] Epidemic disease was a further danger, whether smallpox and dysentery brought directly by settlers—as at Pictou in 1801—or measles, as reported at Remsheg in 1803.[11] Nevertheless, the relatively confined dimensions of the peninsula ensured that loss of territory in itself quickly became a prime threat to the Native economy and to subsistence. [. . .]

The problems in Cape Breton and on the Island of St John—later known as Prince Edward Island—were distinct although related. Settlement in Cape Breton during the Loyalist era was initially sparse, with Sydney and surrounding communities remaining small in numbers.[12] Samuel Holland's celebrated map of Cape Breton preceded the American Revolution, but in the early years of Loyalist settlement there was little territorial encroachment that would have altered his designation of the entire northern peninsula and everything directly south of it (to a point only slightly north of the Canso Strait) as "the Savage Country or Principal Hunting District."[13] Change, however, was soon precipitated through overhunting by non-Natives, although initially many of these non-Natives were not colonial residents of Cape Breton itself. While Mi'kmaw hunters responded to the earliest Loyalist settlement by selling and trading moose meat in Sydney, by March 1790 the Cape Breton Council was debating how to prevent catastrophic levels of moose kills by visiting hunters who sought hides to export to other colonies. In 1789, for instance, the council heard "near 9,000 Moose were killed in this Island . . . merely for the sake of their Skins."[14] A hastily mounted military expedition reached Cape North some weeks later and apprehended a few hunters, but by that time serious damage had been done to the stock. "The Indians . . . " reported the colony's provost-marshal, the Loyalist David Tait, in late 1792, "complain much of the whites having destroyed their Game, which is rely [sic] the case, the skin and fur trade having dwindled to very Little."[15] Less than four years later, the blame for overhunting was being put squarely on the Cape Breton settlers themselves. The colony's administrator, David Mathews, noted in the summery of 1796 that "the Native Indians were last Winter in a most deplorable situation, the Moose Deer which were their sole dependence for a Subsistence having been almost extirpated by the new Settlers."[16]

Worse was to come as Scottish settlement began. Increasing territorial encroachment eroded Native resource harvesting as well as raising related issues such as the desecration of sacred sites and the non-Native occupation of areas that even by colonial authorities had been designated formally or informally for Native use. By 1821 the Surveyor-General Thomas Crawley was taking aim specifically at Highland settlers as exemplifying "those who regardless of every principle of Justice, would deprive these inoffensive Savages of their Property."[17] In Prince Edward Island, meanwhile, the inroads made by other Scottish settlers from such tenantries as those of the former Lord Advocate for Scotland, Sir James Montgomery, led Montgomery's factor James Douglas to record in 1802 that "the Indians complain they have not a spot of ground on all these, their ancestors and their Native Coasts to make a residence upon."[18] In a previous letter, Douglas had obliquely revealed that overhunting was an issue there as elsewhere, commenting that "the White people . . . alledge in times of Scarcity which is pretty frequent with them, the Indians do not scruple to kill their Cattle slyly now and then to satisfy their hunger."[19] The heart of the matter was approached more closely in 1806, however, by the French emigré priest Jacques-Ladislas-Joseph de Calonne, who linked dispossession of the Mi'kmaq directly to the proprietary division of the Island. For "these unhappy aborigines," Calonne informed Governor Edmund Fanning, "the English government having divided up the entire Island among various proprietors, the result is that they cannot situate themselves anywhere without being quickly expelled."[20] [. . .]

In New Brunswick, which represented the imperial claim to an important portion of Mi'kma'ki as well as to Wulstukwik, patterns of dispossession were similar in many respects, though again with distinct elements stemming from both historical and geographical factors. Here, Loyalist settlement assumed prime importance, as the 15 000 or so Loyalist refugees almost instantly outnumbered the pre-existing population—Native and settler combined—by a factor of perhaps three to one.[21] Dislocation of entire Native communities resulted, among the most conspicuous being the southward migration of many Passamaquoddy following the establishment of the town of St Andrews and other encroachments.[22] By 1787, Governor Thomas Carleton felt able to offer the assurance that the Wulstukwiuk, as "a wandering tribe," had been treated with "civility and kindness" and that "the plenty of fish in summer and Moose in winter has hitherto prevented the settlement of the Whites in their neighbourhood from occasioning any inconvenience."[23] Less sanguine was the New Brunswick committee of the British-based missionary organization known as the New England Company, which in 1793 took note of a report originating in Maugerville regarding "the great decrease of their [Natives'] hunting grounds by the Settlement of the Country."[24] Some years later, Major-General Martin Hunter likewise informed London from Fredericton that, to the cost of Native inhabitants, "the wild animals of the Country are become so few as to be no longer an adequate resource." Hunter's interest, unsurprisingly, was based on military considerations, as he emphasized that the Wulstukwiuk—and, presumably, the Mi'kmaq elsewhere in New Brunswick—should be offered "some occasional relief" because their enmity would be a severe threat "in a Country where the settlements are made fronting on the Rivers, with a wilderness every where close upon the Rear."[25]

Thus, in New Brunswick and in Cape Breton, unlike in Prince Edward Island and peninsular Nova Scotia, there was a back country—even though its value for subsistence was suffering continuous erosion through resource depletion and the expansion of settlement as immigration proceeded. While in New Brunswick rivers long continued to attract settlement, thus cutting off

Native transportation routes as well as providing points of departure for the inland spread of settlement, elsewhere the building of roads represented a powerful thrust at the environmental integrity of Native economies. Among the earliest advocates of extensive road construction in Nova Scotia was Michael Francklin, an acting governor on a number of occasions during the 1760s and 1770s who had some command of the Mi'kmaw language and who served later in his career as the colony's superintendent of Indian affairs.[26] For Francklin, writing as early as 1766, roads would be the means by which "the Country will become fully explored, and the most valuable of the interior parts will be soon settled . . . ; this once accomplished . . . will render abortive every effort the Indians can make, should they hereafter be inclined to give us trouble."[27] While Francklin framed the matter in terms of projecting military force as well as economic development, a later advocate of road-building, Governor John Wentworth, was frank about its environmental consequences. "The extended roads and Settlements," Wentworth commented of the Mi'kmaq in 1793, "have been the means of destroying and driving off the wild beasts which formerly Supplied them with food and rayment." Two successive mild winters, he added, had made hunting even more difficult, "and I fear some of them perished."[28] While this represented, in one sense, an element of the particular process by which peninsular Nova Scotia increasingly became a settler space, it also represented the more general principle that road construction could lead to rapid environmental degradation with deadly consequences.

Not that these developments went unchallenged. Remonstrances directed at Officials such as George Henry Monk were frequent. One examples was a group of mainland Mi'kmaq confronting Monk; they ended a tense conversation when "they Instantly took up their Packs and went away without the usual acknowledgments," and Monk reported with some concern in 1794 that "some of the more Intelligent of them make Circuitous visits to the different Tribes, and give false reasons for such long and unusual Excursions."[29] Beyond such responses, Native strategies for offsetting the effects of settlement and environmental change included, where possible, the addition of agricultural cultivation to other sources of subsistence as well as deliberate migration. Cultivation, however, gave no protection from encroachment, as the philanthropist and would-be centralizer of Native communities Walter Bromley stated forcefully in 1822: "You will scarcely meet an Indian, but who will tell you that he has cleared and cultivated land some time or other, but that the white men have taken it from him."[30] Migration away from settlement sites and environmentally affected areas was reported by, among others, the surveyor and naturalist Titus Smith, who observed following a tour of northern Nova Scotia in 1801: "I think a considerable number of them [Mi'kmaq] have left the Province, as I have been informed at many different settlements, that there are not half so many Indians about them as there was some years ago."[31]

As a way of turning long-established and customary mobility to advantage in the context of drastically altered environmental circumstances, migration over shorter or longer distances could enable a semblance of the traditional economy to survive in places—much to the chagrin of colonial officials such as the Nova Scotia governor the Earl of Dalhousie in 1817, who deplored in the Mi'kmaq the tenacity of "their natural habits and inclination for a wandering life."[32] Even in the context of the increasing creation of reserves—systematic in Nova Scotia from 1819, more haphazard elsewhere—mobility, as Natasha Simon has pointed out, was not surrendered.[33] Yet the pressures that had characterized the preceding quarter-century had taken a heavy toll and continued to do so. Unlike previous colonizing thrusts in

Mi'kma'ki and Wulstukwik, the immigration of the late eighteenth and early nineteenth centuries was too strong and persistent to be decisively turned aside or accommodated by Native populations now drastically outnumbered. It had also been rapid. Although cultural and environmental pressures had not begun in 1782, but had a more extended past, retrospectives on the era of Loyalist and then Scottish immigration contrasted strikingly the previous availability of resources with the subsequent prevalence of poverty and ill-health.

[. . .]

Yet the rapid change in the relationship between colonization and the Native population did not necessarily extend to Native–imperial relations. Neither the Mi'kmaq nor the Wulstukwiuk experienced military defeat or made a formal surrender of territory. And both had extended experience of diplomatic relations with French and British imperial officials based on the principle of reciprocity. In these areas, there were important elements of continuity rather than discontinuity and thus a more elongated historical narrative. It is true, of course, that the overlay of colonial settlement on Mi'kma'ki and Wulstukwik during the late eighteenth and early nineteenth centuries had its own far-reaching effect on the entire process of British–Native interaction, especially in matters affecting land use and occupancy. Most noticeably at first in those areas where back countries ceased to exist, Mi'kmaw and Wulstukwiuk access to land was narrowed and Native economies hollowed out accordingly. Varying by locality, special arrangements might be made to safeguard Native use of particular areas. These included the issuing of a series of licences of occupation in Nova Scotia in late 1783 for eight tracts of land, such as the 2500 acres on the Stewiacke River that also carried for local Mi'kmaq the guarantee of "Hunting and fishing as Customary."[34] Grants of land were made to individuals such as "Benwa the Indian," who in 1810 received 140 acres on Boularderie Island in Cape Breton, while some grants to non-Natives contained survey references to lands designated—as at Pugwash—as "Indian land" or—as at Chester—as "Land Claimed by the Indians."[35] In Cape Breton, a number of land documents referred without explanation to "the Indian Line" or "the Indian Boundary," or in other cases made grants that were qualified by such statements as "if it do not interfere in the Indians Settlement."[36] More formal was the setting aside of Chapel Island for Mi'kmaw use by the Cape Breton Council in 1792 and the 10 reserves of varying size created by the Nova Scotia Council in 1820.[37] A report of the New Brunswick surveyor-general in 1803 referred to a total of some 116 000 acres "allotted to the different Indian Tribes Throughout the Province."[38] What all of these arrangements, formal or less formal, had in common was that they offered no immunity from further encroachment.

At a more general level, however, the legitimacy of the entire settlement project was frequently brought into question in Native–imperial dialogue, either explicitly or through diplomatic demands for reciprocity. The most direct statements were reported by imperial officials in Cape Breton. Lieutenant-Governor William Macarmick reported to London in 1790 that the Cape Breton Mi'kmaq were "a fierce, restless and uncontrollable Tribe continually claiming an exclusive right to the possession of the whole Island," and the Cape Breton Council supported Macarmick's assessment some weeks later in declaring that "it is well known that the native Indians have ever held up the Idea of an intrusion being made on their property by the many Settlements forming on the Island."[39] The newspaper correspondent "Philo Antiquarius" recalled that early settlers at Pictou "were constrained to submit to numerous indignities from the aborigines, who viewed their operations with no very friendly eye: these considered the settlers as usurpers of their national rights, who had encroached on their undoubted property," while the

Cumberland settler Edward Barron informed George Henry Monk with some dismay in 1784 that his Mi'kmaw informants had told him that colonization could in any event extend no further than the tidal limits of the rivers. "In that case," Barron added, "the interior of the Country can never be settled."[40] The Native demand for reciprocity, meanwhile, raised the question of legitimacy by connecting the non-Native presence with the fulfilment of promises made in return—most often, though not exclusively, in terms of the presents that underpinned diplomatic activity.[41] From the period immediately following the 1760–61 treaties, imperial officials found this connection inescapable and directly tied to the treaties. John Cunningham declared in 1767 that the purpose of his capacity as agent in Nova Scotia for distributing presents was "to supply the Tribes of Indians with Provisions and the Usual Presents in Virtue of Treaties of Peace," and a few months later the acting governor, Michael Francklin, wrote of the need to find a Roman Catholic priest to minister to Native groups "Conformable to the promises made them at their first making Peace."[42]

By the 1780s and beyond, such issues had lost none of their potency. In 1780 Lieutenant-Governor Richard Hughes of Nova Scotia noted that "the expediency of preserving the Indians in their present Sentiments of Allegiance and Tranquility (which can only be done by these Supplies) remains still in its full Force."[43] That Hughes chose to couch his observation in terms of "allegiance" during a time of warfare, and to make it explicitly contingent on the supply of presents, made his statement all the more striking. Francklin, meanwhile, who was now superintendent of Indian Affairs for Nova Scotia, confirmed that presents were essential to diplomacy. "It has ever been the Custom," Francklin reported later in 1780, "even in times of the most Profound Peace, to Assist the Indians Occasionally with Provisions from the Kings Stores, but now it is

indispensably necessary, for it is totally impossible to see, or be seen by the Indians, or can a Messenger be sent to, or from them, without an Expence of Provisions."[44] And so it continued. The later superintendent, George Henry Monk, recorded early in 1794 a conversation with the Mi'kmaw Francis Emable, who had recently found the hunt disappointing in the Canso-Antigonish region and demanded to know what measures the Nova Scotia governor proposed to take in order to ensure a living for the Native population.[45] Cape Breton Mi'kmaq, meanwhile, exerted another form of pressure. Cape Breton's acting governor, David Mathews, complained to London in 1796 that outside of the presents more readily covered by provincial funds, "they have cost me Privately double that sum; many families of them, during the last Winter, remained at my House for Weeks." A year later, Mathews again reported that Mi'kmaw visitors considered his house "a rightful home" for the leaner months of the year, or whenever they wished to visit Sydney.[46] Governor John Wentworth of Nova Scotia later reinforced the importance of reciprocity by again linking it with mutual fidelity in wartime: "The Micmacs . . . had formerly exhibited by me some assistance for their support, from His Majesty which they considered as an obligation of Loyalty. This Gratuity I discontinued toward the close of the late war and they, according to their savage customs, would not refuse presents form the French."[47]

As Wentworth implied, betrayal of reciprocity—in the view of his Mi'kmaw contacts—would jeopardize any legitimacy in the British colonial presence, which existed without a formal surrender of territory and so created a reciprocal obligation. Loss of legitimacy in turn would—for them—deserve an armed response, bringing into play the absence of any military defeat inflicted on either Mi'kmaq or Wulstukwiuk. The ability of Native forces to police the relationship affirmed in the treaties of 1760–61 had thus become evident in the era immediately following the treaties.[48] In subsequent years, and notably as Scottish and Loyalist migrations gathered force, the independent military capacity of Native groups inevitably declined. Population levels, although reliable numbers are unavailable, were clearly being affected by environmental degradation and resource depletion. Poor health and the struggle for subsistence further eroded the potential for sustaining hostilities. Governor Wentworth, in 1804, was skeptical of rumours that 2000 warriors were assembling to travel west to confront Iroquoian adversaries, "in which case they [the Mi'kmaq] must be joined by the Marisite indians of New Brunswick, and Penobscots who inhabit in the eastern districts of Massachusetts, near to Passamaquoddy. All of these cannot, I think, send more than twelve hundred Men, of which the Micmacs cannot exceed, three hundred, very inferior Warriors, badly armed in quantity and quality—almost naked—with little ammunition."[49] Whether or not Wentworth's estimation was accurate in its details—non-Native enumerations of a highly mobile population were notoriously arbitrary—the deterioration identified and its connection with colonial settlement were realities that could not be discounted. [. . .] Nevertheless, the later years of the "long" eighteenth century were characterized by extended periods of imperial warfare and almost continuous tensions between, on the one hand, Great Britain and, on the other, France and the United States. For imperial officials operating in Mi'kma'ki and Wulstukwik, who had increasing numbers of vulnerable settlements to defend as immigration accelerated, it was impossible to ignore either the localized inroads of which Native forces were capable or the potentially wider significance of such disruptions in the context of other enmities. The Cape Breton councillor and former military officer Ingram Ball, for example, worried in 1794 that in the event of war with the United States, Cape Breton might quickly find itself "in the midst

of three [fires], a French one, an American one, and an Indian one."[50]

Such considerations figured consistently in imperial approaches to Mi'kmaw and Wulstukwiuk diplomatic representations and to demands for reciprocity. Of the four colonies, Prince Edward Island was the one in which these issues surfaced the least. The Island's acting governor Phillips Callbeck reported to London during the American Revolutionary War that "the Indians avowed Dispositions to Rebellion in these parts" had meant that "I am obliged to give provisions and presents."[51] [. . .] Cape Breton, not surprisingly in view of the limited extent of initial settlement, saw much more urgently phrased assessments of the extent and the implications of shows of force by the Mi'kmaq. Macarmick, in 1790, complained of their "frequently assembling in Bodies if four or five hundred and Boasting of the Force they could procure" and remarked on "the impossibility in such case of enforcing the power of the civil authority and the Laws."[52] Some two years later, the provost-marshall David Tait declared bluntly that "the Indians talk very high" and that, in the absence of presents and the ministry of a British-supplied priest, "at present they have in their Power to destroy the whole Colony."[53] It was within this context, later in the 1790s, that the acting governor David Mathews—a Loyalist and a former mayor of the city of New York—found it necessary to submit to Mi'kmaw demands that they should stay at his house while in Sydney. [. . .]

In Nova Scotia, concerns on the part of Monk, Wentworth, and others regarding Mi'kmaw unrest arose frequently, and were consistently bracketed with a sense of urgency in offering presents. Late in 1793, for example, Wentworth directed Monk to the Windsor area, where a Mi'kmaw assembly had led to sheep seizures and, in Wentworth's view, "audacious intentions." Monk's instruction was to try to seize Mi'kmaw hostages—men, women, children—or "on the other hand and which I should prefer, if you can attach them to our cause in such a manner that the peace of our scattered inhabitants may not be disturbed by them, and also that they will join us, in case of an invasion you may promise they shall have some provisions and cloathing for their women and children." Monk, in turn, despatched an officer who downplayed the threat of "any immediate hostilities," but who also confirmed that "supplies" represented the key to resolving the situation.[54] During the ensuing winter, Monk had a series of further confrontations with Mi'kmaq who asserted, as did one group in March 1794, "that the Governor gave [sic] the Indians Blankets, Guns, Powder and everything as much as they pleased to take."[55] Although Monk was at a loss to satisfy the immediate demand, over the next two years Wentworth launched an increased distribution of supplies that he justified not only on humanitarian grounds but also on the ground that "these People would probably otherwise have been disaffected and required Coercion."[56] [. . .]

Thus, although it would be entirely wrong to portray Mi'kmaw leaders as negotiating with Nova Scotian officials from a position of strength at the turn of the eighteenth century, it remained true that they had enough remaining strengths to be able to negotiate. Recurrent periods of tension had similar results. Late in 1807 Wentworth reported that Monk had set off in an attempt to "collect and secure the obedience of these People [Mi'kmaq], and their aid in case of necessity. Otherwise, they might prove very mischievous upon the scattering unprotected settlements." Some weeks later, he commented again in the context of a possible United States invasion that "the Indians having observed there are preparations making for defence, manifested a disposition to be considered of some importance" and that immediate provision of supplies "will tend to relieve the scattering settlers from apprehensions of mischief, that might retard the Levies of Militia."[57] Even so, by April 1808, Monk

was warning that Mi'kmaq from Cape Breton and Nova Scotia were coordinating their response to the likely invasion, opting to remain neutral until they had decided who was the stronger side. Citing the threat of some to devastate Pictou, Monk cited with approval the intention of Mi'kmaq in the Cumberland area to remain neutral and perhaps even to take the British side if pressed. Since the real difficulty, in his view, lay in the undermining of the traditional economy by "the Improvements of their Conquerors," the solution lay not only in "management and relief" but ultimately in restricting the Native population to sedentary agricultural settlement. A byproduct of Monk's report, however, was to make it clear—even though Native démarches were not necessarily united or consistent, as the Cumberland example revealed—that the "Conquerors" still had some way to go before making "orderly subjects" of the Indigenous population.[58]

Governor Thomas Carleton of New Brunswick, meanwhile, was initially dismissive of both the Wulstukwiuk and the Mi'kmaq. Although 1786 saw a hostile Wulstukwiuk presence at Fredericton (during the trial of two Loyalist settlers for the murder of a Wulstukwiuk man) as well as the apprehensions of upriver settlers later that year "of being reduced to the necessity of quitting their settlement" because of Native threats, Carleton was confident of the success of forceful measures to be taken the next year "for the removal of all future apprehensions of danger, from either the insolence or any more serious unfriendliness of the Savages."[59] But the Loyalist and half-pay officer Daniel Lyman was not so sure: "On the subject of the Indians, although they are not so formidable as to threaten any ruin or imminent danger to the province, yet they are sufficiently numerous to be very troublesome, particularly if they are encouraged by our enemies. . . . I would here suggest the idea, of cultivating their friendship, by the usual mode of gaining indians."[60] Although no system of gift-giving comparable to that of Nova Scotia emerged in New Brunswick, the ensuing years saw a series of intermittent tensions that yielded equally intermittent negotiations. Carleton, finding that Wulstukwiuk interventions were capable of making communications between New Brunswick and Lower Canada "precarious and unsafe," persuaded London to authorize an additional regiment to maintain key outposts. Yet by 1794 he was warning that, in the context of tensions with the United States that might bring about an active Wabanaki alliance, "it is certainly requisite to guard against their disaffection." Carleton's chosen course was to employ a French emigré priest as a missionary, although with results that were just as unreliable as those deriving from the Protestant schools and missions maintained by the New England Company.[61] Efforts by such prominent New Brunswick figures as Robert Pagan and Ward Chipman to draw on Native expertise on the geography of the disputed border with the United States yielded respectful exchanges, notably with Passamaquoddy elders, but in 1808 Major-General Martin Hunter observed "the Indian Natives of New Brunswick," in the event of war, "would be formidable as Enemies," and that distribution of presents was needed.[62] All in all, when the War of 1812 finally began, it seemed to be a matter for profound relief to Hunter's successor as military commander in New Brunswick, Major-General George Stracey Smyth, that not only was an agreement reached "with the Indians in the neighbourhood of the County of Charlotte, for the purpose of securing their Neutrality," but also that—as Smyth had "the satisfaction to state"—similar agreements had been concluded with "the Indians of the River Saint John, Miramichi, and other parts of the Province."[63] That the negotiation of Native neutrality was cause for celebration was an eloquent comment on the persistence of an armed capacity that was residual but still significant.

When the wars ended, changes followed. As non-Native immigration continued and accelerated, the pace of dispossession quickened with it. Walter Bromley, whose primary goal was to induce "transient Indians" to "become settlers" by cultivating the land, was blunt in public statements regarding the violence with which force of numbers enabled non-Natives to take control of essential Native territories. As a part of the "gross barbarities" committed by the settlers, he reported that even a burial ground had been "lately ploughed up."[64] At the same time, the significance for imperial officials of any armed threat presented by Native warriors receded with the ending of any immediate external danger. [. . .]

From the early 1780s until 1815, a military and diplomatic continuity had been preserved that co-existed with the territorial and environmental discontinuity of that era. That Native leaders could readily capture the attention of imperial officials and make demands for reciprocity with conviction was a longstanding state of affairs that had persisted through many vicissitudes of both British and French assertions in both Mi'kma'ki and Wulstukwik. These demands had long depended on the threat, and sometimes the reality, that territory would be defended or reclaimed by force. Since the onset of Loyalist and other large-scale migrations, the threat of force had come to depend increasingly both on localized potential to disrupt settlements and on imperial apprehensions of invasion by French or US forces, following which Native intervention—local or more general—might prove crucial one way or the other. At the same time, as demands for reciprocity—or what might be seen on the non-Native side as "relief"—necessarily became more urgent and insistent, officials such as Wentworth saw no alternative but to comply even at the risk of disputes with London over budgetary excesses. As a result, the distinctive tenor of Native–imperial exchanges, far from being eroded by territorial encroachment and environmental change, was extended and entrenched. Some forms of leadership were new in style if not in substance, as in the case of the Bear River chief Andrew Meus, who spoke successfully to the Nova Scotia House of Assembly in 1821 in defence of the Mi'kmaw porpoise fishery in the Digby Gut, and subsequently journeyed to London in a less fruitful effort, according to the *Halifax Journal*, "to solicit permanent grants of land to the Indians, in order that they may become cultivators of the soil."[65] Other methods were tried and true, as when Joseph Howe complained in 1843 while he was Indian commissioner for Nova Scotia that his home was "besieged, at all hours, by Indians, who had been taught to believe that unbounded wealth was at my disposal, and that they were to be fed and clothed hereafter at the expense of the Government."[66] Rather than more general appeals to the principle of reciprocity, officials such as Howe and his successor Abraham Gesner reported more explicit references to the treaties as embodiments of the Native–imperial relationship. Gesner noted that treaty principles were "stamped upon the minds of each succeeding generation," as he had frequently been reminded by the Mi'kmaq with whom he dealt.[67]

The era from 1780 to 1820, therefore, saw the interplay of two important though distinct processes. In a territorial and environmental sense, the Mi'kmaq and Wulstukwiuk experienced rapid, unprecedented damage and constraint. Even allowing for geographical particularities, the process was abrupt and the effects long-lasting. In terms of the ability to make diplomatic use of armed capacity, however, another process drew upon a long-established pattern of Native–imperial relations in Mi'kma'ki and Wulstukwik that extended backwards in time through the treaty-making years and beyond. The two processes were not disconnected. Although colonization would ultimately erode the threat of force that underpinned Native demands for reciprocity,

the wider warfare of the era joined with the vulnerability of proliferating settlements to lend strength to these demands while the critical results of dispossession gave them added urgency. As a result, the narratives to which the two processes gave rise did not conform to any over-arching narrative of Mi'kmaw or Wulstukwiuk decline in Native–imperial affairs. Even the members of a group of Nova Scotia commissioners, which included George Henry Monk, were willing to admit in 1800 that there were moral obligations toward "the aboriginal proprietors of this country,"[68] but the claims on the Crown that were advanced from the Native side went far beyond moral obligation and with time they became more insistent and more explicitly focused on the treaties. While the realities of the nineteenth century would prove inhospitable to the realization of such claims—at least in any form that could effectively offset the depredations of land loss, economic struggle, and the social and health-related dislocations that came with them—the long version of this narrative nevertheless stretched forward into the legal evolutions of the twentieth century that would bring these issues before the Supreme Court of Canada.

That the narrative persisted was also owed in part to historical circumstances that distinguished Mi'kma'ki and Wulstukwik from other portions of North America. In particular, in contrast to most of the Aboriginal groups of eastern North America, the Mi'kmaq and the Wulstukwiuk experienced the aftermath of the American Revolution without either a forced migration or the need to deal with an entirely new imperial regime. Although the disruptions associated with colonial settlement in Mi'kma'ki and Wulstukwik were far from unusual in themselves, the long and evolutionary diplomatic response to the same Crown on the same territory was distinctive. Earlier in the eighteenth century, imperial and colonial interventions had been more complex and yet highly manageable, with both French and British regimes exerting significant but localized influences while the largely coastal and compartmentalized colonial populations of the Acadian and Planter eras had proved generally able to co-exist with Native neighbours.[69] The influx of settlers that marked the closing years of the American Revolution, an influx that only accelerated, was not manageable in the same sense. Yet the skills of those whom Wentworth referred to as "the old men," or of younger leaders such as Andrew Meus, remained relevant. Even when, after 1815, the attention of imperial officials was harder to gain and the damage wreaked by colonization was unavoidable, the demand for reciprocity was too strongly entrenched to do otherwise than persist. That it did so spoke of a narrative of Native–imperial relations that had originated long before the period from 1780 to 1820 and would extend into a future far beyond—a narrative that this limited, 40-year era confirmed rather than muted. The colonial inroads of these years had irrevocably moved the Maritime colonies away from preceding territorial and environmental characteristics and in the direction of being colonies of settlement, with all the damage to Mi'kmaq and Wulstukwiuk subsistence that these developments implied. Yet this was no simple extension of an ineluctable, continent-wide process. In this place and in an elongated span of time, there were continuities that, for whatever they might prove to be worth, accompanied the more immediate and ruinous discontinuity.

NOTES

1. L.F.S. Upton, *Micmacs and Colonists: Indian–White Relations in the Maritimes, 1713–1867* (Vancouver: University of British Columbia Press, 1979), 78, 80, 84. An earlier version of this article was presented at the Atlantic Canada Studies Conference at the University of Prince Edward Island in May 2009. The research was funded by the Social Sciences and Humanities Research Council of Canada. I thank my research assistants Emily Burton and Kelly Chaves as well as the three anonymous readers for *Acadiensis*.

2. Harald E.L. Prins, *The Mi'kmaq: Resistance, Accommodation, and Survival* (Fort Worth: Harcourt Brace, 1996), 161–3. Other authors who have put forward similar arguments include Daniel N. Paul, *We Were Not the Savages: A Mi'kmaq Perspective on the Collision Between European and Native American Civilizations*, 2nd edn (Halifax: Fernwood, 2000), and, though attributing continuous dispossession to a more extended timespan rather than identifying specific turning points, Jennifer Reid, *Myth, Symbol, and Colonial Encounter: British and Mi'kmaq in Acadia, 1700–1867* (Ottawa, ON: University of Ottawa Press, 1995).

3. In this article, I have used the terms Mi'kma'ki and Wulstukwik to refer respectively to the territories of the Mi'kmaq and Wulstukwiuk (Maliseet). Following the scheme initially set out in Emerson W. Baker and John G. Reid, *The New England Knight: Sir William Phips, 1651–1695* (Toronto: University of Toronto Press, 1998), xxii. I refer separately to the Wabanaki as a broad definition of ethnicity in the portion of the later State of Maine, extending approximately from the Saco River to the Penobscot River. Also separately identified are the Passamaquoddy who, while closely related to the Wulstukwiuk in cultural terms, occupied a territory that came to straddle the Canada–United States border, and whose population centre shifted south-westwards during the 1780s following pressure from the Loyalist migration into New Brunswick. For a thorough discussion, see William Wicken, "Passamaquoddy Identity and the Marshall Decision," in *New England and the Maritime Provinces: Connections and Comparisons*, ed. Stephen J. Hornsby and John G. Reid (Montreal and Kingston: McGill-Queen's University Press, 2005), 53–7. [. . .]

Thus, to summarize, this article will take Mi'kma'ki as extending throughout the present-day Maritime provinces (as well as to the Gaspé and Gulf islands) with the exception of the Wulstukw Valley and territories surrounding it and to the west, while Wulstukwik is defined as including the entire Wulstukw Valley—but with the proviso in both cases that the area surrounding the mouth of that river and its lower tributaries was a borderland frequented by both Mi'kmaq and Wulstukwiuk in the relevant period. The Passamaquoddy continued to occupy territory southwest of the Wulstukwiuk, but with the primary population base now on the US side of where the still-contested boundary with British North America would eventually be drawn.

4. See John G. Reid, "*Pax Britannica or Pax Indigena?* Planter, Nova Scotia (1760–1782) and Competing Strategies of Pacification," *Canadian Historical Review* 85, 4 (December 2004): 669–92 (esp. 687–8).

5. William C. Wicken, *Mi'kmaq Treaties on Trial: History, Land, and Donald Marshall Junior* (Toronto: University of Toronto Press, 2002); Rosalie M. Francis, "The Mi'kmaq Nation and the Embodiment of Political Ideologies: Ni'kmaq, Protocol and Treaty Negotiations of the Eighteenth Century" (Masters thesis, Saint Mary's University, 2003).

6. Upton, *Micmacs and Colonists*; Paul, *We Were Not the Savages*, 165–80; Prins, *The Mi'kmaq*, 153–66; Reid, *Myth, Symbol, and Colonial Encounter*, 31–45. Wulstukwik still awaits a detailed study of this era, but see Ann Gorman Condon, "1783–1800: Loyalist Arrival, Acadian Return, Imperial Reform," in *The Atlantic Region to Confederation: A History*, ed. Phillip A. Buckner and John G. Reid (Toronto and Fredericton: University of Toronto Press and Acadiensis Press, 1994), 201–4.

7. George Henry Monk to John Wentworth, 24 January 1794, CO 217/65/150, United Kingdom National Archives (UKNA); on the meeting, see Report of George Monk, 12 January 1794, Monk Papers, MG 23, Letterbook, Indian Affairs, 1783–1797, pp. 1047–51. Library and Archives Canada (LAC).

8. "Petition of the Mickmack Indians," [24 January 1794] CO 217/65/148, UKNA. See also, on Mi'kmaw exclusion from fur trapping, Julian Gwyn, "The Mi'kmaq, Poor Settlers, and the Nova Scotia Fur Trade, 1783–1853," *Journal of the Canadian Historical Association*, new ser., 14 (2003): 65–91.

9. Charles Baker to Edward Barron, 7 August 1784. Monk Papers, MG 23, Letterbook. Indian Affairs, 1783–1797, p. 1032. LAC.

10. John Wentworth to Commissioners for Relief of Indians, 28 September 1802, RG 1, vol. 430, no. 117, Nova Scotia Archives and Records Management (NSARM); Letter of "Philo Antiquarius," *Colonial Patriot* (Pictou), 11 January 1828.

11. William Nixon to Sir John Wentworth, 20 November 1801, RG 1, vol. 430, no. 88. NSARM; G. Oxley to Charles Morris and Michael Wallace, 4 February 1803, RG 1, vol. 430, no. 127, NSARM; see also Nova Scotia Council Minutes, 29 August 1801, RG 1, vol. 191, p. 80. NSARM.

12. See Robert J. Morgan, *Rise Again! The Story of Cape Breton Island*, Book One (Wreck Cove: Breton Books, 2008), 74–5; and Stephen J. Hornsby, *Nineteenth-Century Cape Breton: A Historical Geography* (Montreal and Kingston: McGill-Queen's University Press, 1992), 3–4, 25–8.

13. Samuel Holland, "A Plan of the Island of Cape Breton," [1767], Additional MSS. vol. 57,701, no. 7. British Library; see also Hornsby, *Nineteenth-Century Cape Breton*, 19–25.

14. Minutes of Cape Breton Council, 9 March 1790, CO 217/107/138–42. UKNA; also found at RG 1, vol. 319, pp. 313–5, NSARM.

15. David Tait to Evan Nepean, 4 December 1792, CO 217/109/173, UKNA.

16. David Mathews to the Earl of Portland, 7 July 1796, CO 217/112/93, UKNA.

17. Crawley to Rupert George, 5 November 1821, RG 1, vol. 430, no. 158, NSARM. For a more focused treatment of the impact of Scottish settlement, see John G. Reid, "Scots in Mi'kma'ki, 1760–1820," *The Nashwaak Review* 22/23, no. 1 (Spring/Summer 2009): 527–57.

18. James Douglas to Sir James Montgomery, 26 August 1802, Blackwood and Smith Papers, GD 293/2/20/4, National Archives of Scotland (NAS); see also J.M. Bumsted, "Sir James Montgomery and Prince Edward Island, 1767–1803," *Acadiensis* VII, 2 (Spring 1978): 76–102.

19. Douglas to Montgomery, 24 November 1800, Blackwood and Smith Papers, GD 293/2/20/2, NAS.

20. Calonne to Fanning, 16 July 1806, CO 226/21/192, UKNA (author's translation). The original French reads as follows: "ces

malheureux aborigines"; "le gouvernement anglois ayant distribué toute l'Isle entre divers proprietaires, il en resulte qu'ils ne peuvent se placer nulle part sans en etre bientot chassé." See also Claude Galarneau, "Jacques-Ladislas-Joseph de Calonne," in *Dictionary of Canadian Biography* (DCB), ed. George W. Brown et al. (15 vols to date; Toronto: University of Toronto Press, 1966–), VI: 105–7.

21. See J.M. Bumsted, *Understanding the Loyalists* (Sackville, NB: Centre for Canadian Studies, Mount Allison University, 1986), 23–35; Condon, "1783–1800: Loyalist Arrival, Acadian Return, Imperial Reform," in *The Atlantic Region to Confederation*, 184–93; and John G. Reid, *Six Crucial Decades: Times of Change in the History of the Maritimes* (Halifax: Nimbus, 1987), 61–84.

22. Wicken, "Passamaquoddy Identity and the Marshall Decision," 53; Vincent O. Erickson, "Maliseet-Passamaquoddy," in *Handbook of North American Indians*: Volume 15, Northeast, ed. Bruce G. Trigger (Washington: Smithsonian Institution, 1978): 124–5.

23. Carleton to Earl of Dorchester, 31 January 1787, RS 330, A7b, Letterbook of Thomas Carleton, vol. VII, 1786–1808, no. 2, Provincial Archives of New Brunswick (PANB).

24. Minutes of New Brunswick Commissioners, 5 March 1793, New England Company MSS, vol. 07954, Guildhall Library.

25. Martin Hunter to Viscount Castlereagh, 25 May 1808, CO 188/14/27, UKNA.

26. See L.R. Fischer, "Michael Francklin," DCB, IV: 272–6.

27. Francklin to Board of Trade, 30 September 1766, CO 217/21/357–8, UKNA.

28. Wentworth to [Henry Dundas?], 3 May 1793, CO 217/64/171–2, UKNA; see also John Parr to Viscount Sydney, 8 September 1787, CO 217/60/50–1, UKNA.

29. Report of George Monk, 12 January 1794, Monk Papers, Letterbook, Indian Affairs, 1783–1797, p. 1050, LAC.

30. Walter Bromley, *An Account of the Aborigines of Nova Scotia called the Micmac Indians* (London: Luke Hansard, 1822), 10; see also Judith Fingard, "Walter Bromley," DCB, VII, 107–10.

31. Titus Smith, "General Observations on the Northern Tour," 1801, RG 1, vol. 380, pp. 113–4, NSARM. For another example, see

Minutes of New Brunswick Commissioners, 5 March 1793, New England Company MSS, vol. 07954, Guildhall Library.

32. Draft letter of Dalhousie, 8 March 1817, Dalhousie Papers, sect. 1, pp. 26–9, NAS.

33. Natasha Simon, "Towards a Just Relationship: The Role of Treaty Negotiations in Mi'kmaq Reserve Formation in New Brunswick" (paper presented to Canadian Historical Association Annual Meeting, Saskatoon, SK, 2007), 1–2.

34. Licenses of Occupation, 17–18 December 1783, RG 1, vol. 430, no. 23½, NSARM.

35. Grant to Benwa the Indian, 22 January 1810, RG 20, ser. B, vol. 3, no. 550, NSARM; Pugwash Survey, n.d., RG 20, ser. C, vol. 86, no. 236, NSARM; "Survey of the Indians Claims at Chester by William Nelson," 25 April 1791, RG 20, ser. C, vol. 90a, no. 60, NSARM.

36. See, for example, Petition of Angus MacDonald, [1806], RG 20, ser. B, vol. 2, no. 245, NSARM; Petition of Alexander and Norman MacLeod, [1822], RG 20, ser. B, vol. 13, no. 2864, NSARM; Petition of William Mathewson, 1814, and Council endorsement, 3 October 1814, RG 20, ser. B, vol. 5, no. 1067, NSARM.

37. Minutes of Cape Breton Council, 28 November 1792, CO 217/109/20–1, UKNA; Minutes of Nova Scotia Council, 8 May 1820, RG 1, vol. 193, pp. 450–6, NSARM. On equivalent measures in New Brunswick and Prince Edward Island, see Upton, *Micmacs and Colonists*, 99–101, 114–5.

38. "State of His Majesty's Lands in the Province of New Brunswick taken from the Records in the Surveyor Generals and Auditors Office, Fredericton," 12 July 1803, CO 188/12/56, UKNA.

39. Macarmick to Lord Grenville, 30 April 1790, CO 217/107/118, UKNA; Minutes of Cape Breton Council 31 May 1790, CO 217/107/120, UKNA.

40. Letter of "Philo Antiquarius," *Colonial Patriot* (Pictou), 11 January 1828; Edward Barron to Monk, 12 August 1784, Monk Papers, Letterbook, Indian Affairs, 1783–1797, pp. 1030–1, LAC.

41. On reciprocity as a principle, see Katherine Hermes, "'Justice Will be Done Us': Algonquian Demands for Reciprocity in the Courts of the European Settlers," in *The Many Legalities of Early America*, ed. Christopher L. Tomlins

and Bruce H. Mann (Chapel Hill: University of North Carolina Press, 2001), 123–49; see also John G. Reid, "Imperial-Aboriginal Friendship in Eastern British America, 1775–1815" (paper presented to conference on "Loyalism and the Revolutionary Atlantic World," University of Maine, Orono, ME, 5 June 2009).

42. Memorial of John Cunningham, 14 December 1767, CO 217/45/3, UKNA; Francklin to Lord Hillsborough, 20 July 1768, CO 217/45/165–6, UKNA.

43. Richard Hughes to Lord George Germain, March 1780, CO 217/55/33–4, UKNA. For an example of the continuing significance of providing Crown-subsidized Roman Catholic clergy, see the comments of Governor Thomas Carleton of New Brunswick in Carleton to Dundas, 14 June 1794, CO 188/5/184, UKNA.

44. Francklin to Germain, 4 May 1780, CO 217/55/37, UKNA.

45. Report of George Henry Monk, 26 February 1794, Monk Papers, Letterbook, Indian Affairs, 1783–1797, pp. 1067–8, LAC.

46. David Mathews to the Earl of Portland, 7 July 1796, CO 217/112/93, UKNA; Mathews to Portland, 2 August 1797, CO 217/113/211, UKNA.

47. John Wentworth to Lord Hobart, 3 May 1804, CO 217/79/16, UKNA.

48. See Reid, "Pax Britannica or Pax Indigena?"; for alternative interpretations, see those cited on pages 671–2 of that article as well as the more recent John Grenier, The Far Reaches of Empire: War in Nova Scotia, 1710–1760 (Norman, OK: University of Oklahoma Press, 2008), esp. 207–15.

49. Wentworth to Hobart, 3 May 1804, CO 217/79/15, UKNA.

50. Minutes of Cape Breton Council, 30 April 1794, CO 217/110/180, UKNA. On Ball, see R.J. Morgan, "Ingram Ball," DCB, V: 53–4. I thank Jim Phillips for making the point to me regarding the increasing vulnerability of proliferating settlements.

51. Callbeck to Germain, 2 September 1777, CO 226/6/188, UKNA.

52. Macarmick to Grenville, 30 April 1790, CO 217/107/118, UKNA.

53. Tait to Evan Nepean, 4 December 1792, CO 217/109/173, UKNA.

54. Wentworth to Monk, 18 October 1793, Letterbook of Wentworth, 1792–3, RG 1, vol. 50, NSARM; George Deschamps to Monk, 4 November 1793, Monk Papers, Letterbook, Indian Affairs, 1783–1797, p. 1040, LAC.

55. Report of George Monk, 7 March 1794, Monk Papers, Letterbook, Indian Affairs, 1783–1797, p. 1072, LAC.

56. Wentworth to Portland, 8 October 1796, Letterbook of Wentworth, 1793–6, RG 1, vol. 51, NSARM.

57. Wentworth to Castlereagh, 26 October 1807, Letterbook of Wentworth, 1805–7, RG 1, vol. 54, NSARM; Wentworth to Castlereagh, 3 January 1808, CO 217/82/19–20, UKNA.

58. Report of George Monk, 23 April 1808, CO 217/82/202–5, UKNA.

59. Carleton to Dorchester, 5 December 1786, RS 330, A7b, Letterbook of Thomas Carleton, vol. VII, 1786–1808, no. 1, PANB. On the Fredericton incident, see W.S. MacNutt, New Brunswick: A History, 1784–1867 (Toronto: Macmillan, 1963), 78.

60. Memorial of Daniel Lyman, c. 1790, CO 188/4/391, UKNA; on Lyman's background, see List of MLAs, CO 188/6/141, UKNA.

61. Carleton to Dundas, 20 November 1792, RS 330 A3b, Letterbook of Thomas Carleton, vol. III, 1791–5, no. 16, PANB; Carleton to Dundas, 14 June 1794, CO 188/5/184–5, UKNA; Missionary List, 29 June 1807, CO 188/13/289, UKNA. See also Judith Fingard, "The New England Company and the New Brunswick Indians, 1786–1826: A Comment on the Colonial Perversion of British Benevolence," Acadiensis I, 2 (Spring 1972): 29–42.

62. Chipman to Carleton, 12 August 1796, CO 188/7/211–15, UKNA; Pagan to Chipman, CO 188/10/289, UKNA; Hunter to Castlereagh, 25 May 1808, CO 188/14/27–8, UKNA.

63. Smyth to Bathurst, 31 August 1812, CO 188/18/70, UKNA. On Smyth, see D.M. Young, "George Stracey Smyth," DCB, VI: 723–8; on Hunter, see D.M. Young, "Sir Martin Hunter," DCB, VII: 428–30.

64. Bromley, An Account of the Aborigines of Nova Scotia, 7–8 (and passim).

65. Halifax Journal, 27 December 1824; Petition of Andrew Meus, 16 January 1821, Journal and

Proceedings of the House of Assembly of the province of Nova Scotia, 1821, p. 36; Upton, *Micmacs and Colonists*, 88.

66.   Joseph Howe, "Report on Indian Affairs," 25 January 1843, *Journal and Proceedings of the House of Assembly of the province of Nova Scotia*, 1843, Appendix 1, p. 4.

67.   Abraham Gesner, "Report on Indian Affairs," 29 September 1847, *Journal and Proceedings of the House of Assembly of the province of Nova Scotia*, 1847, Appendix 24, p. 117.

68.   "Report of Commissioners," 15 April 1800, RG 1, vol. 430, no. 33½, NSARM.

69.   See Reid, *"Pax Britannica or Pax Indigena?"* 687.

4   From Alain Beaulieu, "'An Equitable Right to Be Compensated': The Dispossession of the Aboriginal Peoples of Quebec and the Emergence of a New Legal Rationale (1760–1860)," *Canadian Historical Review* 94, no. 1 (March 2013): 1–27. Reprinted with permission from University of Toronto Press (www.utpjournals.com).

When the British seized control of New France in 1760, they had already built a long tradition of purchasing Aboriginal land.[1] By the second half of the eighteenth century, this approach had become central to British colonial thought. Made official in the Royal Proclamation of 1763, this policy was implemented in an extensive portion of the Canadian territory. Starting in the 1780s, the British concluded land-cession treaties with the Aboriginal people living west of the Ottawa River, in what would become the colony of Upper Canada in 1791 (and then the province of Ontario in 1867). In the mid-nineteenth century, this colony's entire territory had been covered by cession treaties, some of which addressed only small portions of land while others involved immense expanses. Following Canadian Confederation, this system was extended to encompass western Canada, where Canada proceeded to carry out, over a few short decades, the largest operation of Aboriginal land purchases in its history.

The policy stipulated by the royal proclamation, however, was not applied to the Saint Lawrence Valley or to what is now the province of Quebec. Concerning these lands, the British, followed by the Canadian government, adopted a policy of unilateral appropriation, dispossessing the Aboriginal peoples without reliance on a treaty system. Long overlooked by researchers, this particularity in the British land policy has been garnering increased attention since the 1970s as a direct consequence of the growing number of land claims by Quebec First Nations. For some, the explanation lies in the French colonial past: Since the French never recognized the specific land rights of Aboriginal peoples, such rights could not have survived the French regime.[2] Others have attempted to establish that the French never denied the existence of Aboriginal land rights, but were merely deterred from formally recognizing them in treaties by situational factors.[3] The Royal Proclamation of 1763 has also been invoked both by researchers defending the thesis that the British were not required to make land-cession treaties in Quebec and by those supporting the contrary view.[4]

[. . .] The aim of this article is not to identify a standard to explain why the British did not conclude treaties—in short, to decode the past according to law—but rather to follow legal standardization in which colonial practice is inscribed through trial and error, detours, shifts in meaning, and improvisations, into a legitimizing framework. In this analysis of British legal rationales, the law is not considered in its causal dimension, as a leading factor that would explain (by creating obligations) the past or enable the identification of how things should have taken place. Instead, it is examined in its instrumental role, as a flexible tool of colonialism, which lends itself to the mutations required to justify the dispossession process.

[. . .]

The idea underlying this article is that the refusal to conclude land treaties with the Aboriginal peoples of Quebec was not the result of a pre-existing policy, but the outcome of a succession of tinkerings, in which elements of the French colonial past and British tradition were embedded. The British policy concerning Aboriginal lands in Quebec was thereby set out and implemented in a series of specific contexts, which gave rise to a new legal imaginary. The amalgamation stemmed more from fiction than from history, but it did provide the basis of a system that emerged in the 1830s, in which the creation of reserves appeared as a means of compensating Aboriginal peoples for the loss of their lands.[5]

The Royal Proclamation of 1763 holds a special place in the history of Aboriginal land dispossession in Canada. Published in the context of the Pontiac's War,[6] the proclamation established the limits of three new colonies (Quebec and the two Floridas) and also created an expansive territory, temporarily reserved "for the use of the . . . Indians." This "Indian country" included the land beyond the source of the rivers that flowed to the Atlantic Ocean and the land outside the new colonies and Rupert's Land (see Figure 1.1). The proclamation also stipulated that governors could not grant land within the boundaries of their respective colonies, which had not yet been ceded by the Aboriginal peoples. Thenceforth, the "Lands reserved to the . . . Indians" could be purchased in the name of the British Crown only "at some public Meeting or Assembly" of the Aboriginal people in question.

The proclamation resulted in the implementation of a new legal logic throughout the former territory of New France, a logic that formally recognized Native land rights. In Quebec, the document quickly acquired significant symbolic value. Aboriginal people living in the Saint Lawrence River Valley who had received copies of it regularly invoked its premise to support their land claims at the end of the eighteenth century and during

the nineteenth century.[7] Did that mean that the provisions concerning Aboriginals in the royal proclamation were applicable within the province of Quebec in 1763? The formulation of the text leaves some doubt on the subject. The passage forbidding concessions to be granted "upon any Lands whatever, which, not having been ceded to or purchased by Us as aforesaid, are reserved to the said Indians, or any of them" seems to apply only to the governors of the former colonies and not to those in the "Province of Quebec" or in the two Floridas.[8]

Some scholars interpreted this passage as revealing the inclination of the British authorities to continue the French policy of not recognizing Native rights in Quebec. However, evidence of this conclusion is very weak and in fact is practically non-existent. The historical context provides no proof to sustain the idea that Britain intended to exclude Quebec lands from the provisions of the royal proclamation. Rather, the documents elucidating the development of the British policy on this subject indicate a willingness to implement a global policy, which would apply to all North American land in its possession.[9]

If the intention of the British authorities had been to exclude Quebec from the protections afforded to Aboriginal lands, it was certainly not reflected in the instructions prepared in December 1763 for James Murray, governor of Quebec. These instructions indeed contained clear provisions on applying the royal proclamation.[10] In the colony of Quebec, the proclamation was invoked several times to refuse granting land concessions. A revealing example concerns the 1766 refusal of Governor Murray to allow merchants to settle and build in Chicoutimi, as this land was "reserved by his Maj[esty]'s Proclamation to the savages within the Province."[11] On two other occasions, the British authorities, taking support from the restrictions imposed by the royal proclamation, refused to allocate grants for lands on the northern banks of the Restigouche River.

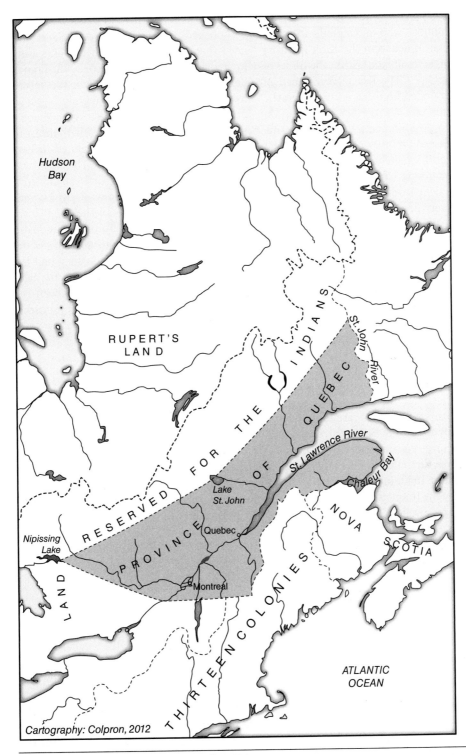

Figure 11.1 The Royal Proclamation of 1763

The first was presented in 1766 by merchant Joseph Philibot, who attempted, in vain, to execute an order from the King granting him 20 000 acres of land within the limits of the new colony.[12] The Executive Council of Quebec reminded him that according to the proclamation of 1763, the lands in question belonged to the Mi'kmaq.[13] In 1767, the same council rejected a similar request from Hugh Finlay, Scottish merchant and land owner, who was claiming lands near the mouth of the Restigouche River for the Acadians.[14]

However limited, these interventions suggest that, from the perspective of colonial authorities, the policy on the protection and purchase of Native land was applicable to 1763 Quebec. Other examples, however, indicate that the British were not inclined to extend this reasoning to all Aboriginal peoples in this colony. The groups affected by the abovementioned claim grants, namely the Innu (Montagnais) and Mi'kmaq, lived outside the centres of colonization; the British therefore had no reason to question the ancestral basis for their presence on these lands. But this was not the case for the communities living in the Saint Lawrence Valley. The Huron-Wendat had moved into the Quebec area after the Iroquois' destruction of Huronia in 1650. In the 1660s, they were followed by the Iroquois, who settled in three villages: Kahnawake, Kanesatake, and Akwesasne. The Abenakis began migrating to the Saint Lawrence Valley in the mid-1670s and settled on the southern shore of the river at the beginning of the eighteenth century, in the villages of Odanak and Wolinak. At the end of the French Regime, these villages were grouped into the Seven Nations confederacy, which also included the village of Oswegatchie (see Figure 11.2).[15]

Familiar with the history of these communities, the British knew that their presence was the result of relatively recent migration flows. This influenced their legal interpretation: If these Aboriginals were not the original occupants, they could not hope to be indemnified for any land in that location that was opened up for colonization, even if they used that land regularly. Their rights were limited to land granted to them by the French beginning in the second half of the seventeenth century. The British rapidly began to draw a distinction between Aboriginal people who, they presumed, lived on their ancestral lands, and those who had migrated to new territories relatively recently. This idea was apparently asserted for the first time in 1764 by William Johnson, who wrote to Thomas Gage that the guarantees of the 1763 Royal Proclamation regarding hunting grounds did not apply to the Iroquois and Abenakis of the Saint Lawrence Valley because they had left their traditional lands in order to settle near the French.[16] Gage, who had also been the governor of Trois-Rivières, shared Johnson's views,[17] as Guy Carleton would do a few years later in the context of a claim presented by the Iroquois of Akwesasne.[18]

In the first years after the conquest of New France, the colonial authorities had therefore outlined a territorial policy that incorporated the idea that some Aboriginal peoples in the province of Quebec had rights over their land by virtue of the royal proclamation. The French colonial past influenced this system in an incidental way, through the history of the migration of some Aboriginal people in the Saint Lawrence Valley, but not as a structuring legacy that would have determined a precise policy to follow. In this first legal framework, the concept of prior rights played a key role, as it made it possible to differentiate between two categories of rights: the rights of original land occupants, and those of the others. For a few years, this filtering mechanism led the British to consider that some Aboriginals living in the Saint Lawrence Valley did not have any specific rights over their land, aside from those that had been formally granted to them by the French.

[. . .] The first true test of British territorial policy came after the American War

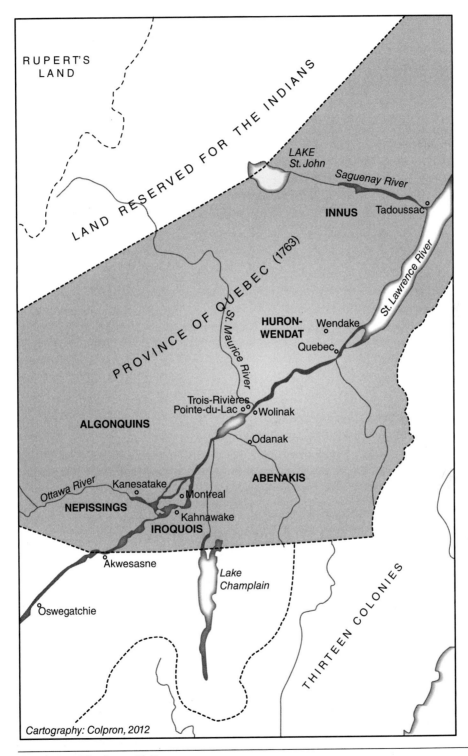

Figure 11.2 The Seven Nations

of Independence, when thousands of American Loyalists went north to seek refuge in the province of Quebec. As a result of the 1774 Quebec Act, the provincial boundaries had been extended considerably and thenceforward encompassed a large portion of the territories that had been reserved in 1763.

The Quebec Act, which abrogated the royal proclamation within the borders of the province of Quebec, contained no provisions on what procedures should be followed to purchase land from Aboriginal peoples.[19] In theory, the formal requirement to conclude treaties had disappeared. In practice however, the British authorities did not expect to change their policy on this matter. This is clearly indicated in the instructions given to Governor Guy Carleton in 1775. Article 31, which concerns portions of former Indian territory that were now within the province of Quebec, instructs the governor to ensure that the limits of any outposts in the "interior Country" be well-established and that no colonization be allowed beyond that, "seeing that such Settlements must have the consequence to disgust the Savages" and "to excite their Enmity."[20]

At any rate, the political and strategic climate did not lend itself to making significant changes on this matter. The Treaty of Paris of 1783, which put an end to the American War of Independence, had resulted in a widespread movement of discontent among the Aboriginal peoples of the interior of the continent, who could not understand how the British could have ceded their land to the Americans.[21] At one point, the British even feared that their allies would turn against them, and they launched an extensive diplomatic offensive in an attempt to decrease tensions. Caution, particularly in territorial matters, was called for to prevent the alliance from breaking up. This was particularly the case west of the Ottawa River, where a large group of Loyalists had taken refuge. To ensure that the establishment of their settlement in this sector would go smoothly, the British

rapidly concluded a few land-cession treaties, notably with the Mississauga nation.[22]

Colonial authorities apparently did not question the length of time that the Mississaugas had been in the sector; they simply assumed that they were the original inhabitants of the land and benefitted from the rights associated with ancestral occupation. But the British were not ready to follow this way of reasoning for every Aboriginal nation, as was borne out by their reaction to the protests of the Akwesasne Iroquois, who opposed the surveying of their land for the benefit of Loyalists. In support of their territorial claims, this time, the Iroquois invoked a deed given to them by the French that had been lost in a church fire.[23] While he refused to admit the legitimacy of the Iroquois claim, Governor Haldimand, "being desirous to avoid all difficulties with the Indians," chose a conciliatory course of action. In his mind, the deed being invoked by the Iroquois did not exist, but they had considered themselves "the Proprietors of that Land" for so many years that it was wiser to offer to compensate them than to insist "upon the right of the Crown."[24] The Iroquois, however, refused to give up their land in exchange for financial compensation; instead, they insisted upon preserving a specific tract of land. Haldimand would have preferred a different solution, but given the political and military tensions and the upcoming conference between Aboriginal peoples and the United States Congress, he reluctantly agreed to the Iroquois request, expressing his frustration in a letter to the British negotiator: "They must be made fully to understand and consider this as an Indulgence during the King's pleasure, no part of it ever having been granted to them."[25]

The pragmatic decision of Haldimand was a good illustration of the problem arising from the implementation of a rigid legal rationale in a context where the British still needed the military help of the Aboriginal peoples. By complying with the Iroquois request, the governor avoided creating strong dissatisfaction among useful allies. But his decision would also have an enduring (and involuntary) consequence. Paradoxically, the apparent recognition of the Iroquois' rights to the land would indeed become, in the nineteenth century, the basis for a rationale legitimizing dispossession without treaties.

This new legal logic would, however, take a few decades to fully emerge. Meanwhile, looking for a new way to justify their refusal to conclude land-cession treaties in the province of Quebec, the British would temporarily borrow certain aspects of the French legal conception. This borrowing was incited by a claim raised in the Gaspé Peninsula, as the Chaleur Bay had become an area of refuge for hundreds of Loyalists. As we have seen, in the 1760s the colonial authorities had considered this region, or at least the Restigouche River area, to be Mi'kmaq territory (or land protected by the royal proclamation) and had refused to grant some land concessions. In the 1775 instructions to Governor Carleton, London had apparently confirmed this impression by associating the Gaspé region with the "Interior Country" in which the progression of settlements should be closely monitored to avoid vexing the Aboriginal people.[26]

In the ensuing years, the colonial authorities showed some willingness to protect the rights of the Mi'kmaq in this area. For example, in 1780, Governor Haldimand wrote to Governor Nicholas Cox that the hunting privileges of the Mi'kmaq along the Restigouche River should be protected, so long as this did not interfere with commerce.[27] Two years later, Haldimand repeated that he did not want the Mi'kmaq to be treated unfairly, and he asked that steps be taken to prevent their land from being encroached upon.[28] In 1784, Nicholas Cox recommended drawing a boundary between "the hunting ground and fisheries belonging to the Savages" and the land belonging to colonists.[29] In an ordinance published the same year, he established that the colonists should pay one dollar to the Mi'kmaq to obtain the right to cut hay in the grasslands and marshes of the Restigouche River.[30] Reiterating the fact that the King wanted to protect the Indians throughout the province, Cox also confirmed that the Mi'kmaq had exclusive hunting and fishing rights along the Restigouche River.[31]

The political climate here, as in the area west of the Ottawa River, seemed to lend itself to the drawing up of a treaty with the Mi'kmaq, and in 1786, Nicholas Cox was given the responsibility, along with surveyor John Collins, of negotiating an arrangement with them. Negotiations took place over three days (29 June–1 July) in Listuguj and resulted in an agreement-in-principle. The Mi'kmaq would give up part of their land but preserve the land along the Restigouche River as well as exclusive fishing rights there. The British negotiators also promised them presents in exchange for their lands.[32] These negotiations were clearly in line with those carried out with the Mississauga[33] a few years before, and they demonstrated the will of the British authorities to continue, within the boundaries of this colony, a policy based on the recognition of the Aboriginal peoples' rights as "original occupants."

The two British negotiators showed great optimism about the agreement's chances of being confirmed by the colonial government. However, they had underestimated the importance of the economic stakes related to salmon fishing in the Restigouche River. The review of the agreement's terms in Quebec City gave rise to serious reservations, especially about the fishing rights.[34] In addition, there was pressure from an influential London merchant named John Shoolbred, who had received a concession from the King for 10 000 acres to be taken in the Chaleur Bay area.[35] After several months of dickering, the colonial authorities finally decided not to ratify the agreement negotiated in 1786.

An Executive Council committee that had been set up to look into the rights of the Mi'kmaq along the Restigouche River had concluded that it was not necessary to approve the agreement. The committee members had consulted lawyer François-Joseph Cugnet, an influential legal expert, whose opinion on the colony's early laws was in great demand at the time. Cugnet, who also occupied the positions of secretary and translator for the Executive Council,[36] convinced them that the government could allocate the land on the northern shore of the Restigouche, without concern for any potential Mi'kmaq rights, given that the French practice had consisted of allocating land "with a perfect disregard of any supposed prior title in the Indians."[37]

This was the first time that an argument based on the French judicial practice was used to reject the necessity of concluding treaties with the Aboriginal peoples in order to abolish their rights. The argument was not specific to some areas of the former French colony, but general in its formulation. If it was applicable for the Chaleur Bay area, it would also have been valid for all the territory conquered by the British in 1760. But the colonial authorities in Quebec clearly had no intention of extending this logic west of the Ottawa River, in the Upper Countries. There, the political and strategic situation prevented the implementation of a policy that, even if founded on coherent legal reasoning, would have created serious problems with the Aboriginal nations.

East of the Ottawa River, the strategic role of the Aboriginal people was less important yet not completely negligible. The bulk of the British defence was located there and, until the early decades of the nineteenth century, the Saint Lawrence Valley remained the most densely populated sector in British North America. This situation offered the colonial rulers greater latitude but did not abolish the problems stemming from reliance on French legal reasoning that denied Native land rights. This is evident in the 1787 Executive Council decision: After having refused to ratify the terms of the agreement negotiated with the Mi'kmaq the previous year, the council still decided to offer them presents in

exchange for the portion of land they seemed ready to cede in 1786.[38]

It is likely that there was some conceptual discomfort added to the specific difficulties of implementing such a legal rationale. Predicating unilateral Aboriginal dispossession on a French colonial heritage seemed particularly incongruous in the British system, which, until then, had been used to legitimize its appropriation of Native lands. Such a policy actually went against the official positions taken by the British before and after New France was conquered, positions based on the idea of negotiation and voluntary cession sealed by compensation. The Britons' self-legitimizing discourse usually played on the protective, just, and generous role of the British sovereign. This image was at the essence of the terminology regarding Aboriginal peoples in the royal proclamation, and it infused most of the official declarations concerning the protection of Aboriginal rights. Such a position was difficult to reconcile with the idea that the British need not be concerned with any rights Aboriginal peoples may have had on their land, since the French never were.

The aborted negotiations with the Mi'kmaq did not serve as a springboard for the integration of French legal logic; however, they nevertheless marked a significant step in the implementation of a Quebec-specific territorial policy. This event intensified a trend emerging in the Saint Lawrence Valley of refusing to negotiate for the purchase of Native land. Admittedly, the reasons invoked to deny the Aboriginal peoples their rights differed by area: In one case, they referred to prior migrations and in another, to the French practice of not recognizing Indian deeds. However, the result remained the same.

The non-ratification of the treaty with the Mi'kmaq emphasized the lack of a consistent territorial policy within the boundaries of the province of Quebec. The same colonial power could decide, in some circumstances, to conclude treaties with Indigenous people for the purchase of their land, and in others, to proceed unilaterally, without supporting these different approaches with a coherent legal logic. This problem was resolved in part in 1791, when the province of Quebec was separated into two colonies: Upper and Lower Canada. This division did not entirely eradicate the British policy's lack of cohesion but it did dissimulate it in part, by overlaying it with a political structure that restored a consistency of practice within each of the colonies.

Nevertheless, the fickleness of British policy remained noticeable, and the Indigenous people of Lower Canada at times highlighted it to try to soften the colonial stance. This happened, for instance, in the 1790s, during a land claim in the Upper Saint Lawrence area. While the claim was submitted on behalf of the Seven Nations of Canada, in reality, it involved only the Saint Lawrence Iroquois. At that time, as perceived by an Indian affairs agent, the Iroquois were worried by the rapid reduction of their hunting grounds, due to the arrival of the Loyalists and to the expansion of colonization in the US territory.[39]

A first request was submitted in 1794[40] and it elicited a very careful reply from the colonial government. The governor emphasized that the British policy was not to seize Native land without due consideration. He stated that if the Seven Nations were unjustly dispossessed of their land, the situation was sure to be corrected because the King "administers justice to all his children and never takes anything from them without paying the price" [translation]. Without committing formally, Dorchester nevertheless opened the door to the recognition of the Seven Nations' territorial rights. [. . .]

This response seems even more surprising when we consider that its author, Lord Dorchester, also governed the province of Quebec in 1787, when the decision to not ratify the treaty with the Mi'kmaq was made. It was also Dorchester who, in the late 1760s,

clearly rejected the idea that the Akwesasne Iroquois could have a right to the lands in the vicinity of the Saint Lawrence.[41] This radical change of perspective clearly illustrates the difficulty the British had with the instrumentalization of the French colonial past in their negotiations with the Aboriginal peoples, especially during times of crisis. Such a crisis occurred in the 1790s, when it appeared that a new conflict with the United States was on the horizon. Indeed, the Seven Nations were fully aware that this created a favourable situation for them and chose to initiate treaty negotiations with the state of New York at that time, regarding the cession of their hunting grounds south of the Canadian border.

In 1795, Dorchester had given Agent Alexander McKee the responsibility of carrying out a first inquiry into the Seven Nations' claims.[42] In July, the Kahnawake chiefs had submitted a document expounding the basis for their claims to land between the Longueuil and Kingston seigniories, "according to the partition" made by their ancestors.[43] In support of their rights, the Iroquois made reference to their immemorial occupation of the location, since "God" had "created them on these lands," and they presented their version of colonial history, in which they had welcomed the French, not vice versa. They had "never been conquered" by them, and when the "King of France" established himself on their land, he did it peacefully because the ancestors of the Iroquois shared with them the "land that the master of life" had reserved them.[44]

They were no doubt conscious of the fact that their ancestral-occupation argument had not hitherto been successful at convincing the colonial powers; therefore, the Iroquois also reminded the British that, in the past, they had purchased land from Aboriginal people who were not its original owners; these included the Mississaugas and Hurons. The Iroquois wondered why they should not benefit from the same treatment and why Governor Haldimand had not wanted to pay for their land before settling Loyalists on it. In order to put a little more pressure on the British, the Iroquois asserted that the Americans, against whom they had fought in war, were prepared to pay them for their territory on the other side of the border.[45]

The claim was submitted to John Sewell, attorney general of Lower Canada. He deemed it to be valid on certain points, but not on the extent of the land being claimed. To his knowledge, nothing would support "a pretension so unlimited." The land being claimed was within the borders of Upper Canada, but Sewell called to mind that, prior to the division of the province of Quebec, a portion of the land had been set aside for use by the Seven Nations—a reference to the 1784 negotiation between the Akwesasne Iroquois and Haldimand. John Johnson, the superintendent general of Indian affairs, knew full well the limits of that reserve, for which the Iroquois had yet to receive a formal concession. According to Sewell, a duly executed concession for this portion of land "will satisfy the seven villages, and silence their pretensions to the residue of the tract, claimed by their address and speeches."[46]

On 23 February 1797, James Green, the governor's military secretary, informed John Johnson of the opinion prepared by Sewell. He asked him to consult the attorney general on the subject and to prepare a speech in response that was to be submitted to the governor for approval.[47] The response, which was presented in June of the same year on behalf of the governor, focused on negotiations that were supposed to have taken place in 1784. In exchange for the reserve created for them, the Akwesasne Iroquois would have abandoned all their territorial claims over land in the area of the Saint Lawrence. The governor was committing to taking the necessary steps to ensure that the Akwesasne Iroquois would obtain a formal concession for that reserve, but he wanted that to put an end to all claims or representations by the Seven Nations.[48]

Despite the favourable political context, the Iroquois' argument, which clearly illustrated their capacity to force the colonial authorities to face their own contradictions, did not lead to a treaty negotiation. It did, however, trigger the first significant vacillation in the British method of analyzing Aboriginal land rights. In effect, Dorchester's response reinterpreted Haldimand's action in 1784, within the fictional framework of a negotiation, which impelled the Iroquois to renounce their rights to land in the vicinity of the Upper Saint Lawrence in exchange for the creation of a reserve. The French colonial past was not completely removed from the British discourse, which alluded to "assigned or promised" lands for the Iroquois. But this formulation remained sufficiently ambiguous to avoid aggravating the Iroquois' political sensitivity, while they continued to refer to their ancestors' sharing of the land.

The Iroquois reaction to Dorchester's response is unknown, but the lack of further claims for the land in the vicinity of the Upper Saint Lawrence intimates that the new British rationale was more acceptable, particularly because it recognized their rights, albeit only implicitly, and placed the extinguishment of those rights within a context of negotiation and renunciation. In this case, the British fiction was significantly more advantageous than the reality, since it partially reconciled both Iroquois and British conceptions, without requiring any change in practice. The idea of compensation by granting reserved land was also built on a useful illusion because, while the British affirmed that they indemnified the Iroquois for lost territories, they did so by reserving a portion of land that already belonged to them. But this fiction, which had the advantage of costing nothing, was more consistent with traditional British legal ideas, since it focused on compensation, a key concept in the ongoing process of legitimizing the dispossession of land from Quebec's Aboriginal peoples.

In the same time period, compensatory logic was apparently also applied to another area: the policy of annual gift distribution to the Aboriginal peoples. The practice, which went back to the French rule, had been taken up by the British after 1763 to ensure that they would receive the support of Aboriginal nations who had previously been allied to the French. The presents—a tangible manifestation of the alliance linking them to the British Crown—held particular symbolic meaning for the Aboriginal peoples. At the end of the eighteenth century, the colonial power was tempted to modify the primary meaning of this distribution to make it an expression of a fictional negotiation, in which the Aboriginal peoples renounced their land rights.

The argument was seemingly invoked for the first time early in the nineteenth century with the Algonquins and Nepissings, who were protesting against the arrival of lumberjacks on their hunting grounds along the Ottawa River. Philemon Wright, the merchant who had hired the lumberjacks, defended his position by repeating what he had been told in Quebec City: The Algonquins and Nepissings "have no positive rights to these lands"; by receiving "yearly gifts from the government," they had relinquished "their claims on the lands" [translation].[49] It is not known whether his interpretation corresponded to an official government position, but the idea continued to circulate and even became partly integrated by certain Aboriginal peoples in the Saint Lawrence River Valley. As evidence of this integration, in 1837, the Seven Nations of Canada described these presents in a petition as a "sacred debt" that the "Kings of France" had promised their ancestors they would respect, as "compensation for the lands" that were "given up" to them. This debt had been "confirmed by the Kings of England since the country was ceded, and paid and carried out in a timely manner since then" [translation].[50]

If the British had played a role in disseminating this interpretation, they were no longer disposed to use it in the 1830s, as a result of the high cost of the yearly gift distributions. For several years, the authorities in London had insisted on the need to radically cut these expenses. Their requests came as part of an overall review of the Indian policy, which abandoned the idea of alliances to promote the civilization of the Aboriginal peoples.[51] The decline of the Aboriginal peoples' military importance after 1815 played a role in this redefinition of the Indian policy, while the rapid progression of colonization provided a new legitimization for projects to integrate Indigenous people into the colonial world. For the British administrators, the Aboriginal people did not have much choice: if they wanted to avoid being completely marginalized, or even disappearing altogether, they had to profoundly alter their way of life and take up agriculture and sedentary life.

The position of Britain's new Indian policy helped define the outlines of a new framework to legitimize the dispossession of Aboriginal peoples in Lower Canada. The review of the Algonquin and Nepissing claim played a key role in this process. Their protests against encroachment onto their hunting grounds had begun in the 1790s and continued into the early decades of the nineteenth century, during which time they addressed a series of petitions to the colonial authorities. In particular, the Algonquins and the Nepissings were asking for the creation of a territory reserved for their use and for the payment of compensation similar to that received by the Aboriginal peoples of Upper Canada.[52]

In 1836, after several years of haggling, the colonial government finally decided to assign a Lower Canada Executive Council committee to examine the numerous requests received from the Alonquins and Nepissings. In its 1837 report,[53] the committee concluded that their claim was valid and that they were entitled to compensation. This was essentially based on the Royal Proclamation of 1763, which the Alonquins and Nepissings had cited persistently in their different petitions. In previous years, the idea that this document entitled them to compensation for their hunting grounds had received solid support from officers of the Department of Indian Affairs. However, in its use of the document for its analysis, the Executive Council committee excluded one fundamental component, namely, the obligation of using treaties to buy Native lands, and they retained only the idea of compensation through reserving land.

To support its reasoning, the committee used the precedent of the land reserved for the Akwesasne Iroquois. Whether or not they deliberately omitted the circumstances leading up to the creation of that reserve in 1784 and 1797, the committee members gave the event new meaning: that of land reserved by virtue of the royal proclamation.[54] The notion that the Saint Lawrence Iroquois were not the original occupants had totally disappeared, and so had the idea of a concession promised by the French and confirmed by the British within the framework of an indulgent policy (1784), and that of a negotiation that would have led the Iroquois to renounce their rights in exchange for their reserve (1797). All that remained was the basis on which the reserved area had been created: the royal document of 1763. The 1837 report stated that, since the Alonquins and Nepissings also cited the proclamation, it would be unjust to treat them differently: "As that Act of State has been considered sufficient to guarantee to the Iroquois of St Regis [Akwesasne] the Possession of their present Reservation, to which it is stated that they had no other Right than as Part of their ancient Hunting Grounds, the Algonquin and Nipissing tribes may have some Ground to complain if they are deprived of the Benefit of the same Protection for their Claims."[55]

The 1837 report invested the royal proclamation with new meaning, in particular, that of royal protection exercised within the context of an Aboriginal subsistence economy. At the time of the Conquest, the Crown would have indeed showed its desire "to secure to the Indians their ordinary Means of Subsistence,"[56] by placing under its control the lands that the Aboriginal peoples owned or claimed. Invested with this new meaning, the royal proclamation enabled the development of a theory of just compensation that eliminated the obligation to negotiate. For the committee, this just compensation had to be based on the adoption of measures that would maintain living conditions for Aboriginal people that were similar to those they had had before they were subjected to the impact of colonial expansion.

[. . .]

This general principle indicated a road to follow to compensate the Alonquins and Nepissings: to reserve for them "a sufficient Tract of Land . . . in the Rear of the present Range of Townships on the Ottawa River" and to promote their settlement there by offering "such Support, Encouragement, and Assistance" required to lead them "to a State of Independence of further Aid."[57]

The Executive Council committee had skillfully managed to base a unilateral policy of territorial dispossession on the Royal Proclamation of 1763. The political dimension of this document, which had been expressed in the obligation of obtaining Aboriginal consent before taking possession of their land, had vanished and been replaced by the idea of just compensation, whose measure was the creation of a reserve and the granting of government assistance to help in the transition to a sedentary and agricultural way of life. It is doubtless not a coincidence that these two elements occupied a central place in Britain's new Indian policy, which was focused on civilization.

It would seem that this reinterpretation was grounded in the fear of seeing other Aboriginal nations from Lower Canada make similar claims if the committee consented to negotiating a land-cession treaty with the Alonquins and the Nepissings. In February 1837, Duncan C. Napier, superintendent of Indian affairs, was already anticipating such demands from other Aboriginal nations if the request of the Alonquins and Nepissings received a positive response from the Executive Council committee.

[. . .]

While he did not identify the nations that might ultimately make such demands, Napier still observed that the "Hunting Grounds claimed by the Indians of Lower Canada comprise nearly the whole of the Waste Lands within the Limits of the Province."[58] The Executive Council committee was probably conscious of the broader reach that its recommendations on the Algonquin-Nepissing issue would have, and doubtless had in mind the possibility of future territorial requests coming from other nations. This would explain the effort it made to provide the basis for the principle of just compensation, which could be transposable to other claims.

The principle of just compensation set out in 1837 was approved by London two years later[59] and would become the core of the new legitimization for the territorial dispossession of Aboriginal peoples. In 1858, another commission responsible for investigating the administration of Indian Affairs fully reiterated this argument,[60] which in 1851 was indirectly expressed in a law setting aside 230 000 acres of land for the Aboriginal peoples of the former Lower Canada.[61] This law was the legal tool used to create a series of new reserves, which would, for a time, be associated to the idea of compensation for the loss of the larger hunting territories.[62]

The idea of just compensation also served as a framework for rethinking French territorial practices within a new fiction that emerged in the Bagot Commission's report. This commission of inquiry had been established in 1842 to look into the problem of the administration of Indian Affairs. [. . .] The "settlements had advanced rapidly before the conquest," wrote the commissioners, and the Aboriginal "territorial possessions . . . were therefore confined within fixed boundaries and, in several cases, were owned by virtue of letters of patent from the French Crown or from specific seigneurs" [translation]. In all of Lower Canada, according to the commission, there was only "one single place" where Aboriginal peoples "were

dispossessed without compensation of their former hunting grounds" [translation][63] and that one place was the Ottawa Valley, in the territory claimed by the Algonquins and the Nepissings.

Despite their brevity, these comments suggest that, for the members of this commission, the actions taken by the French, that is, the granting of land to the Aboriginal communities, had resulted in limiting their territorial possessions to defined spaces. These observations also indicate that, in the Bagot Commission's reinterpretation of French colonial history, the lands granted by the French Crown had had the effect of compensating Aboriginal peoples for the loss of their hunting grounds. In fact, saying that there was only one area in which the Indigenous people had been dispossessed without compensation of their former territory was equivalent to saying that the other nations had been compensated by receiving land from the French authorities.

In a way, the Bagot Commission's analysis marks the endpoint of a long process of legitimization, which used history to justify a specific way of appropriating Native land. This rereading of the French colonial past was without any real historical foundations but it provided a specific meaning for the creation of new reserves in the mid-nineteenth century. It maintained an illusion, which was all the more powerful because it could be inscribed within a historical continuity, that the reserves, whose limited boundaries express the magnitude of Aboriginal dispossession, were, in fact, compensation.

Reconstituting the convoluted path that led the British to define a specific policy regarding Native lands in the province of Quebec indicates that the French colonial past did play a role in the process. But this role had little or nothing to do with the legal interpretations put forth in the closing decades of the twentieth century that rejected the idea that there was an "Indian title" on the land in Quebec at the time of the Conquest. Although the British did flirt, in the late 1780s, with the French notion that the Aboriginal peoples' title to their lands was worthless, this temporary deviation left no significant mark on their method of legitimizing the dispossession process for Aboriginal land.

Above all, the British retained from the French a way of doing things, which consisted of appropriating Native lands without reaching treaties with them. This borrowed method established itself fairly quickly, although it is impossible to identify a specific date in the early British regime, when the decision to act in this way was formally made. This practice did not at first rest on an overall strategy. Rather, it developed from a series of specific cases where each decision reinforced the trend, creating a sort of habit, which conditioned later decisions. As they accumulated, the precedents laid out a path from

which the British surely could have deviated at any time; however, the risk of such a deviation opening the door to a series of claims created a highly effective guardrail.

[. . .]

One conclusion stands out in terms of this path: that practice determined the standard and not the reverse, at least until a new standard framework took its final shape with the theory of just compensation. Well established after 1837, this framework made it possible to reintegrate the French past into a new schema. The French colonial practice, based on the non-recognition of Aboriginal land rights, and the Royal Proclamation of 1763, the symbol par excellence of the recognition of those rights, fused into a syncretic model that coated dispossession without treaties with the varnish of compensation.

NOTES

1. For an overview of British policy related to Indigenous lands, see Stuart Banner, *How the Indians Lost Their Land: Law and Power on the Frontier* (Cambridge: Harvard University Press, 2005), 1–111.

2. This interpretation was the basis of the legal positions defended by Quebec and Canadian government prosecutors until the early 1990s. The Supreme Court of Canada rejected this interpretation in 1995. See Renée Dupuis, *Tribus, peuples et nations. Les nouveaux enjeux des revendications autochtones au Canada* (Montreal: Boréal, 1997), 59–63.

3. See, for example, W.J. Eccles, "Sovereignty Association, 1500–1783," *Canadian Historical Review* 65, 4 (1984): 475–510.

4. For an overview of different points of view on this question, see Brian Slattery, *The Land Rights of Indigenous Canadian Peoples as Affected by the Crown's Acquisition of the Territories* (PhD diss., Oxford University, 1979); Jacqueline Beaulieu, Christiane Cantin, and Maurice Ratelle, "La Proclamation royale de 1763: le droit refait l'histoire," *La revue du Barreau* 49, 3 (1989): 317–40; Paul Dionne, "Les postulats de

la Commission Dorion et le titre aborigène au Québec: vingt ans après," *La revue du Barreau* 51, 1 (1991): 128–71; Richard Boivin, "Pour en finir avec la Proclamation royale: la décision Côté," *Revue générale de droit* 25, 1 (1994): 136–42; David Schulze, "L'application de la Proclamation royale de 1763 dans les frontières originales de la province de Québec: la décision du Conseil privé dans l'affaire Allsopp," *Revue juridique Thémis* 31 (1997): 511–74; Michel Morin, *L'usurpation de la souveraineté autochtone. Les peuples de la Nouvelle-France et des colonies anglaises de l'Amérique du Nord* (Montreal: Boréal, 1997), 133–61.

5. The situation in Quebec was not uncommon in the British Empire. A similar policy of unilateral appropriation of Aboriginal lands was also in effect in the Maritime provinces, British Columbia, and Australia. These cases clearly show that the British approaches to the land rights of the Aboriginal peoples were more complex than is usually thought, the land-cessions treaties being only one method among others to legitimize dispossession. However, these cases should not be considered

in a chronological perspective with an aim to locating explanatory precedents. It is clear, for example, that for the period studied here, the case of Nova Scotia does not occur as an example that justifies the decisions made in Quebec, just as Quebec and the Maritimes are not references that legitimate or explain the decisions made in British Columbia. The same method of land dispossession can be based on different factors and legal justifications, without it being necessary to identify a precedent that serves as an explanation, except when the documentation provides support for it, which is not the case in this situation. For the Maritime provinces, see L.F.S. Upton, *Micmacs and Colonists: Indian–White Relations in the Maritimes, 1713–1867* (Vancouver: University of British Columbia Press, 1979), 37; Olive P. Dickason, "Amerindians between French and English in Nova Scotia, 1713–1763," in James R. Miller, ed., *Sweet Promises: A Reader on Indian–White Relations in Canada* (Toronto: University of Toronto Press, 1991), 48. For British Columbia, see Paul Tennant, *Aboriginal Peoples and Politics: The Indian Land Question in British Columbia, 1849–1989* (Vancouver: University of British Columbia Press, 1990). For Australia, see Stuart Banner, *Possessing the Pacific: Land, Settlers, and Indigenous People from Australia to Alaska* (Cambridge: Harvard University Press, 2007).

6. See Gregory E. Dowd, *War under Heaven: Pontiac, the Indian Nations, & the British Empire* (Baltimore: Johns Hopkins University Press, 2002).

7. For example, see Denys Delâge and Jean-Pierre Sawaya, *Les traités des Sept-Feux avec les Britanniques. Droits et pièges d'un héritage colonial au Québec* (Quebec: Septentrion, 2001).

8. Royal Proclamation, 7 Oct. 1763, in Adam Shortt and Arthur G. Doughty, eds, *Documents Relating to the Constitutional History of Canada, 1759–1791* (Ottawa: J. de L. Taché, 1918), pt I, 166–7.

9. Ibid., 27–155.

10. Ibid., see articles 60 and 62, in 199.

11. Schulze, "L'application de la Proclamation royale," 526–7.

12. King's concession to Joseph Philibot, 18 June 1766, 76977–9, vol. 157, RG1-L3L, Library and Archives Canada (LAC).

13. Slattery, *Land Rights*, 266–7.

14. Ibid., 267.

15. Jean-Pierre Sawaya, *La fédération des Sept Feux de la vallée du Saint-Laurent, XVIIe–XIXe siècle* (Sillery: Septentrion, 1998).

16. Johnson to Gage, 27 Jan. 1764, *The Papers of Sir William Johnson* (Albany: University of the State of New York, 1925), 4: 307–8.

17. Gage to Johnson, 6 Feb. 1764, ibid., 318.

18. The claim was presented in 1769. See Claus to Johnson, ibid., 7: 127.

19. The Quebec Act, s. 4, in Shortt and Doughty, *Documents*, pt I, 571–2.

20. Instructions to Governor Carleton, 3 Jan. 1775, in *Report concerning Canadian Archives for the Year 1904* (Ottawa: S.B. Dawson, 1905), 237. A "Plan for Imperial Control of Indian Affairs" was attached to the instructions to the governor. This plan, dated 10 July 1764, had been drafted by the Lords of the Board of Trade in the months following the adoption of the royal proclamation. It contained numerous provisions concerning trade with Indigenous people, and three articles (nos 41, 42, and 43) spelling out the procedures to follow when buying their lands. These articles were clearly a reworking of the provisions of the royal proclamation. The plan was also attached to instructions to Haldimand in 1778 and to those of Carleton, who had become Lord Dorchester, in 1786. See Bruce Clark, *Native Liberty, Crown Sovereignty: The Existing Aboriginal Right of Self-Government in Canada* (Montreal and Kingston: McGill-Queen's University Press, 1990), 79.

21. On the reactions of the Indians to the Treaty of 1783, see Alan Taylor, *The Divided Ground: Indians, Settlers, and the Northern Borderland of the American Revolution* (New York: Alfred A. Knopf, 2006), 111–13.

22. On the land-cessions treaties west of the Ottawa River, in what would become the colony of Upper Canada in 1791 (and then the province of Ontario in 1867), see Robert J. Surtees, "Canadian Indian Treaties," in William C. Sturtevant, ed., *Handbook of North American Indians*, vol. 4, *History of Indian–White Relations* (Washington: Smithsonian Institution, 1988), 202–7; Jim R. Miller, *Compact, Contract, Covenant: Aboriginal Treaty Making in Canada*

(Toronto: University of Toronto Press, 2009), 66–122.

23. Johnson to Haldimand, 11 Mar. 1784, 260, add. mss 21775, Haldimand Papers, British Museum. This strategy suggests that they were now familiar with the distinction, made by the British, between those who could claim the rights of "original inhabitants" and those who could not.

24. Haldimand to Campbell, 22 Mar. 1784, 1412, vol. 3, reel C-10997, RG10, LAC.

25. Haldimand to Campbell, 15 Apr. 1784, 154–5, vol. 14, reel C-1223, RG10, LAC; see also Haldimand to John Johnson, 15 Apr. 1784, 150–1, reel C-1223, RG10, LAC.

26. *Report concerning Canadian Archives for the Year 1904*, 237. At that time, the expression "Interior Country" generally designated the region situated west of the Ottawa River, but was also applied less frequently to other regions not yet opened to colonization.

27. Haldimand to Cox, 16 Aug. 1780, 70, mss 21862, Haldimand Papers.

28. Haldimand to O'Hara, 27 May 1783, 100v, mss 21862, Haldimand Papers.

29. Cox to Haldimand, 16 Aug. 1784, 133, mss 21862, Haldimand Papers.

30. Cox to Haldimand, 7 Aug. 1784, 132, mss 21862, Haldimand Papers.

31. Ibid.

32. 1785–1871, série Indiens, 1784–1900, SD8 Conseil exécutif, Provincial Archives of New Brunswick.

33. The two men invoked the treaties concluded west of the Ottawa River to convince the Mi'kmaq to cede part of their territory to the British Crown.

34. "General Observations upon the North of the Restigouche being granted to the Indians, read in Council the 2nd of March 1797," 54053–68, vol. 110, reel C-2535, series L-3-L, RG1, LAC.

35. "His Majesty Mandamus in favour of Mr John Shoolbred for lands in Chaleur Bay, June 29, 1785," 87197–202, vol. 181, RG1-L3L, LAC.

36. "Cugnet, François-Joseph," *Dictionary of Canadian Biography Online* (www.biographi.ca).

37. Minute Books on Land Matters, 13 Aug. 1787, 22, vol. A, RG1 L1, LAC.

38. Minute Books on Land Matters, 14 Aug. 1787, 8, col. A, RG1 L1, LAC.

39. "Remarques de J.B. De Lorimier sur les affaires sauvages," 22 Oct. 1793, 42–4, vol. 247, reel C-2848, RG8, LAC.

40. "Extract from minutes of an Indian Council held at Quebec 6th. February 1794," 433, pt 2, vol. 250, reel C-2849, RG8, LAC.

41. Guy Carleton was governor of the province of Quebec for a first term (between 1768 and 1778); he received the title of Lord Dorchester in 1786, at the beginning of his second term in Canada (1786–96).

42. "At a council held at Lachine with the Chiefs of the Caughnawaga's and of the Lake of the two Mountains," 26 July 1795, 222–4, vol. 248, reel C-2848, RG8, LAC.

43. "Paroles des Sauvages des Sept villages du Bas Canada . . . ," 28 July 1795, 230, vol. 248, reel C-2848, RG8, LAC.

44. Ibid., 230–1.

45. Ibid., 232.

46. Sewell to Prescott, 17 Feb. 1797, 210–12, reel H-2533, 1796–1797, Military Secretary's Entry Book, #1, vol. 17, series 1, Robert Prescott Papers, G II 17, MG23, LAC.

47. Green to Johnson, 23 Feb. 1797, 200, ibid.

48. "Lord Dorchester to the Indians, Quebec, June 5, 1797," 9238–9, vol. 10, reel C-11000, RG10, LAC.

49. "Témoignage de P. Wright," 4 Feb. 1824, in *Journal de la Chambre d'Assemblee du Bas-Canada*, 1824, Appendix R.

50. The chiefs of the Seven Nations to Governor Gosford, 3 Feb. 1837, *Copies or Extracts of Correspondence since 1st April 1835, between the Secretary of State for the Colonies and the Governors of the British North American Provinces Respecting the Indians in those Provinces*, 62, House of Commons, 1839.

51. On the new orientation of British Indian policy after the War of 1812, see John L. Tobias, "Protection, Civilization, Assimilation: An Outline History of Canada's Indian Policy," in Miller, *Sweet Promises*, 127–44.

52. See, for example, The Algonquins and Nipissings to John Johnson, 29 July 1824, 12692–3, vol. 3, reel C-11003, RG10, LAC; Speech of Algonquins and Nipissings, 31 May 1831, 32287–8, vol. 83, reel C-11030, RG10, LAC; The Algonquins and Nipissings to Mathew Lord Aylmer, July 1833, 34427–8, vol. 87, reel C-11466, RG10, LAC.

53. "Report of a Committee of the Executive Council," 13 June 1837, in *Copies or Extracts of Correspondence*, 27.

54. Ibid.

55. Ibid., 32.

56. Ibid., 27.

57. Ibid., 32.

58. Napier, "Answers to the Queries . . . ," 29 May 1837, in *Copies or Extracts of Correspondence*, 22.

59. "Copy of a Despatch from Lord Glenelg to the Earl of Durham," 22 Aug. 1839, in *Copies or Extracts of Correspondence*, 6–7.

60. Canada, *Report of the Special Commissioners Appointed . . . to Investigate Indian Affairs in Canada* (Toronto: Stewart Derbishire & George Desbarats, 1858), pt III.

61. *An Act to authorise the setting apart of lands for the use of certain Indian tribes in Lower Canada*, 14–15 Vict., 1851, ch. 106.

62. This was the perspective taken by the report of the commission in 1858 (Canada, *Report of the Special Commissioners*, pt II). See also Pennefather to Edmund Head, 4 May 1860, in "Copies or Extracts of Correspondence between the Secretary of State for the Colonies and the Governor General of Canada respecting Alterations on the Organization of the Indian Department in Canada," Ordered, by the House of Commons, to be printed, 25 Aug. 1860, *Irish University Press Series of British Parliamentary Papers, Colonies, Canada*, 23, 31; Hector L. Langevin, "On the Petition of the Algonquin Indians," Ottawa, 26 Oct. 1868, 1–3, vol. 723, reel C-13412, RG10, LAC.

63. "Rapport sur les affaires des Sauvages en Canada, 1845," s. iii, in *Journaux de l'Assemblée législative de la Province du Canada*, 1847, Appendice (T.), 3. Terres; 1. Titres aux terres.

Chapter 12

"Rushing" the Empire Westward

READINGS

Primary Documents

1   "Letter of Charles Major, 20 September 1859," in *Daily Globe*, Toronto, 2 January 1860

2   From *Journals, Detailed Reports and Observations Relative to the Exploration, by Captain Palliser*, John Palliser

Historical Interpretations

3   From "Hardy Backwoodsmen, Wholesome Women, and Steady Families: Immigration and the Construction of a White Society in Colonial British Columbia, 1849–1871," Adele Perry

4   From "'A Delicate Game': The Meaning of Law on Grouse Creek," Tina Loo

INTRODUCTION

Even before Canada East, Canada West, New Brunswick, and Nova Scotia signed on to Confederation, the other parts of North America further west, controlled as colonies or trading territories by the British or British North Americans, were attracting notice. The potential riches in British Columbia's gold fields and the expansion of the rural settlement frontier into bison range and fur trade territory captured the imaginations of British North American colonists and colonial administrators alike. Understanding what was in these territories, and understanding how these territories and their inhabitants were defined for people who would probably never visit, is central to understanding why Great Britain (and the colonies themselves) sought to expand the imperial footprint, especially when it seemed that maintaining the Empire and international alliances was becoming increasingly troublesome. (Britain had just been at war against Russia in the Black Sea region, and a rebellion was unfolding in India in 1857).

Our primary documents here represent two different kinds of reporting on the state of two separate "frontier" areas. The letter from Charles Major paints a forbidding picture of

British Columbia and is especially pessimistic about the possibility of earning a decent living in the colony. He describes a chaotic gold rush scene, one in which the authority of the Empire seems restricted to Victoria and is otherwise hardly noticeable. Though it does not deal with the rush for gold, John Palliser's commentary on the vast centre of the continent captures the same sort of expansionist spirit. He mentions deserts, but raises hopes for the regions north of the 49th parallel (the border between the United States and British/Hudson's Bay Company territory) by noting that it supported trees and grasses.

The historical interpretations urge us to think about British Columbia's colonial history, which is marked by desires to settle the land and to extract wealth from it. Adele Perry reminds us that the colonization project in British Columbia implied both the dispossession of Indigenous people and the establishment and reproduction of a settler society that was defined in racial, class, and gender terms. It is in this context that the "hardy backwoodsmen, wholesome women, and steady families" came to be seen as the ideal immigrants to Vancouver Island and British Columbia by colonial promoters. Tina Loo turns her attention to the establishment of the rule of law in the region. She reasons that even in places where it had a short history and colonial authorities desired strict enforcement, newcomers to the territory had a basic respect for the law.

QUESTIONS FOR CONSIDERATION

1. Compare Charles Major's letter to some of the correspondence that Elizabeth Jane Errington writes about in Chapter 8. Is Major trying to create the same sort of connections?
2. Judging from his report, how *scientific* do you think Palliser's expedition was?
3. How British were the inhabitants of British North America and associated territories in the late 1850s? What made them so?
4. Do you consider the informal model of miners' justice to be more suitable to areas like the BC gold fields, or were people like Governor Douglas right to push for more formal institutions?
5. How did the specific British Columbian economic and social context impact the ways in which "colonial promoters" conceptualized the kind of immigrants needed in the colony?

SUGGESTIONS FOR FURTHER READING

Barman, Jean. *French Canadians, Furs, and Indigenous Women in the Making of the Pacific Northwest.* Vancouver: UBC Press, 2015.

——. *The West beyond the West: A History of British Columbia.* Toronto: University of Toronto Press, 2007.

Fisher, Robin. *Contact and Conflict: Indian–European Relations in British Columbia, 1774–1890.* Vancouver: University of British Columbia Press, 1977.

Ishiguro, Laura. *Nothing to Write Home About: British Family Correspondence and the Settler Colonial Everyday in British Columbia.* Vancouver: UBC Press, 2019.

Loo, Tina. *Making Law, Order and Authority in British Columbia, 1821–1871.* Toronto: University of Toronto Press, 1994.

Mackie, Richard S. *Trading Beyond the Mountains: The British Fur Trade on the Pacific, 1793–1843*. Vancouver: UBC Press, 1997.

Marshall, Daniel. *Claiming the Land: British Columbia and the Making of a New El Dorado*. Vancouver: Ronsdale Press, 2018.

Owram, Doug. *Promise of Eden: The Canadian Expansionist Movement and the Idea of the West, 1856–1900*. Toronto: University of Toronto Press, 1980.

Perry, Adele. *Colonial Relations: The Douglas-Connolly Family and the Nineteenth-Century Imperial World*. Cambridge: Cambridge University Press, 2015.

———. *On the Edge of Empire: Gender, Race, and the Making of British Columbia, 1849–1871*. Toronto: University of Toronto Press, 2001.

Sandwell, Ruth, ed. *Beyond the City Limits: Rural History in British Columbia*. Vancouver: UBC Press, 1999.

Primary Documents

1 "Letter of Charles Major, 20 September 1859," in *Daily Globe*, Toronto, 2 January 1860, reprinted in Robie L. Reid, "Two Narratives of the British Gold Rush," *British Columbia Historical Quarterly* 5, 3 (July 1941): 224–7.

[From *The Daily Globe*, Toronto, Canada West, January 2, 1860.]

NEWS FROM BRITISH COLUMBIA. (From the Sarnia *Observer*.)

The following letter recently received by a person in this neighborhood, from the writer who is at present in British Columbia, was handed to us for perusal. As it contains much valuable and reliable information in reference to the country, we requested permission to publish it, which was at once granted. We therefore lay the most important portions of the letter before our readers, without further apology, satisfied that it will be read with interest by all:—

Fort Hope, Frazer River
Sept. 20th, 1859

Dear Sir:—I am afraid you will think I had forgot my promise,—but I wanted to know something about the country before writing to you. In the first place, do not think that I have taken a dislike to the country because I am not making money; the dislike is general all over the country. To give you anything like a correct idea of it would take more paper than I have small change to purchase, and more time than I could spare, and then it would only be commenced.

The country is not what it was represented to be. There is no farming land in British Columbia, as far as I can learn, except a very small portion joining Washington Territory, and on Vancouver's Island, where there is one valley of 20,000 acres; but that cannot be sold until Col. Moody's friends come out from the old country, and get what they want.

It never can be a *place*, because there is nothing to support it, except the mines, and just as soon as they are done the place goes down completely, for there is absolutely nothing to keep it up; and I tell you the truth the mines are falling off very fast. There is nothing in this country but mines—and very small pay for that; they are you may say, used up. We have been making two, three and four dollars per day, but it would not last more than two or three days; and so you would spend that before you would find more. There has been great excitement about Fort Alexander, three hundred miles above this, and also about Queen Charlotte's Island. They have both turned out another humbug like this place. A party arrived here yesterday from Alexander, and they are a pitiful looking lot. They are what the Yankees call *dead broke*. They have been six hundred miles up the river. When they got down here they had no shoes to their feet. Some had pieces of shirt and trowsers, but even these were pinned together with small sharp sticks; and some had the rim of an old hat, and some the crown. They had nothing to eat for one week, and not one cent in money. This is gold mining for you!

I expect the Frazer River fever has cooled down by this time, at least I hope so; for I do pity the poor wretches that come out here to beg. They can do that at home; as for making money, that is out of the question. Since we came here (to use the miners' term,) we have been making grub; and those who can do that, think they are doing well. If there are any making arrangements to come to this place, let them take a fool's advice *and stay at home*. I would just about as soon hear that anyone belonging to me was dead, as to hear they had started to come here. They say it wants a man with capital to make money here; but a man with money in Canada will double it quicker than he will here. And if I, or any other, was to work as hard and leave [live] as meanly, I could make more money in Canada than I can here. Since we have been on the River we have worked from half-past two and three o'clock in the morning till nine and ten o'clock at night, (you can see the sun twenty hours out of the twenty-four in the summer season.)—and lived on beans! If that is not working, I don't know what it is. Besides this you go home to your shanty at night, tired and wet, and have to cook your beans before you can eat them. And what is this all for? For *gold* of course; but when you wash up at night, you may realize 50 cents, perhaps $1.

There have been some rich spots struck on this river, but they were very scarce, and they are all worked out; and the miners are leaving the river every day, satisfied there is nothing to be made. But now that I am in the country I will remain for a year or so, and if nothing better turns up by that time, I think I will be perfectly satisfied. I have met with some that I was acquainted with, and it is amusing to see those who felt themselves a little better than their neighbors at home, come here and get out of money, and have to take the pick and shovel, perhaps to drag firewood out of the woods and sell it, or make pack-mules of themselves to get a living. I do not mean to say that it is so all over the Colony, but it is from one end of Fraser River to the other. I dare anyone to contradict what I say; and I have good reason to believe it is as bad all over the country. I saw a patch of oats here the other day. They were out in head, only four inches in height, yellow as ochre, and *not thick enough on the ground to be neighbours*. Vegetables and other things are as poor in the proportion; and as for the climate, it is just as changeable as in Canada, if not more so. I can't say much about the climate on Vancouver's Island, but I think it is rather better.

I met T.G., the carpenter, from Sarnia, who left there about a year ago. He went round the Horn, and he was ten months and fifteen days in coming here. He is cutting saw logs making a little over grub. He says he is going to write to the Sarnia *Observer*, and give this place a cutting up! There are a great many Canadians here, and they would be glad to work for their board. A man could not hire out to work a day if he was starving. I have seen some parties from California; they say times are very hard there. There are just three in our party now, H.H., J.R., and myself. There were two of the H's; one was taken sick and had to leave the river; he is in Victoria, and is quite recovered again; has been there two months, and has not got a day's work yet. I was very sick myself when I just came here, but am quite healthy now, and so fat I can hardly see to write. The rest are quite well.

The Indians are not very troublesome at the mines; they are kept down pretty well. They are very numerous here and on the Island, the lowest degraded set of creatures I ever saw.

It is estimated that the number of miners who make over wages, is one in five hundred; and the number that do well in the mines is one in a thousand. So you see it is a very small proportion. If you know anyone that wants to spend money, why, this is just the place. Anyone bringing a family here would require a small fortune to support them in this horrible place, hemmed in by mountains on all sides, and these covered with snow all the year.

I have lived in a tent since I came up the river, and I have to lie on the ground before the fire and write; it gives a very poor light, so excuse the writing. It has been raining here steady one week, and the mountains are all covered with snow; for when it rains here it is snowing upon the mountains. It is a wild looking place. You will please tell our folks you hear from me, and that we are all well. I will write to some of them in about two weeks or so. I have wrote five letters already, but I have not heard from any of them; so many letters go astray in coming here and going from this place, that perhaps they do not get them at all. Give my respects to old friends, and tell them to be contented and stay at home.

I remain, yours truly
CHARLES MAJOR.

---

2 From John Palliser, *Journals, Detailed Reports and Observations Relative to the Exploration, by Captain Palliser* (London: Eyre & Spottiswood, 1863), 7, 10–11, 16–18.

The existence of a general law regulating the distribution of the woods in this portion of the continent suggested itself to us during our first summer's explorations, and subsequent experience during the seasons of 1858–9 fully confirmed it.

The fertile savannahs and valuable woodlands of the Atlantic United States are succeeded, as has been previously alluded to, on the west by a more or less arid desert, occupying a region on both sides of the Rocky Mountains, which presents a barrier to the continuous growth of settlements between the Mississippi Valley and the States on the Pacific coast. This central desert extends, however, but a short way into the British territory, forming a triangle, having for its base the 49th parallel from longitude 100° to 114° W., with its apex reaching to the 52nd parallel of latitude.

The northern forests, which in former times descended more nearly to the frontier of this central desert, have been greatly encroached upon and, as it were, pushed backwards to the north through the effect of frequent fires.

Thus a large portion of fertile country, denuded of timber, separates the arid region from the forest lands to the north, and the habit which the Indian tribes have of burning the vegetation has, in fact, gradually improved the country for the purpose of settlement by clearing off the heavy timber, to remove which is generally the first and most arduous labour of the colonist.

The richness of the natural pasture in many places on the prairies of the second level along the North Saskatchewan and its tributary, Battle River, can hardly be exaggerated. Its value does not consist in its being rank or in great quantity, but from its fine quality, comprising nutritious species of grasses and carices, along with natural vetches in great variety, which remain throughout the winter sound, juicy, and fit for the nourishment of stock.

Almost everywhere along the course of the North Saskatchewan are to be found simply, it would be natural to infer their existence along the whole line where the Rocky Mountains run parallel and retain their altitude; but the dry areas are evidently due to other causes primarily, and they are not found above the 47th parallel in fact. It is decisive of the general question of sufficiency of rain to find the entire surface of the upper plains either well grassed or well wooded, and recent information on these points almost warrants the assertion that there are no barren tracts of consequence after we pass the Bad Lands, and the *Coteaus* of the Missouri. Many portions of these plains are known to be peculiarly rich in grasses, and probably the finest tracts lie along the eastern base of the mountains, in positions corresponding to the most desert-like of the plains at the south. The higher latitudes certainly differ widely from the plains which stretch from the Platte southward to the Llano Estacado of Texas, and none of the references made to them by residents or travellers indicate desert characteristics. Buffalo are far more abundant on the northern plains, and they remain through the winter at their extreme border, taking shelter in the belts of woodland on the upper Athabasca and Peace rivers. Grassy savannas like these necessarily imply an adequate supply of rain, and there can be no doubt that the correspondence with the European plains in like geographical position—those of eastern Germany and Russia—is quite complete in this respect. If a difference exists it is in favor of the American plains, which have a greater proportion of surface waters, both as lakes and rivers.

Historical Interpretations

3 From Adele Perry, "Hardy Backwoodsmen, Wholesome Women, and Steady Families: Immigration and the Construction of a White Society in Colonial British Columbia, 1849–1871," *Histoire sociale/Social History* 33, 66 (2000): 343–60. (Modified/shortened)

Who was in and who was out? One of the primary ways in which mid-nineteenth-century British Columbians negotiated inclusions and exclusions was through the practice and discourse of immigration. Immigration derived its social and political significance from its double ability to dispossess local peoples and establish a settler society in their stead. The settler society this process sought to build was explicitly racialized and deeply gendered. In seeking "hardy backwoodsmen," colonial promoters encouraged men committed to hard work, steadiness, and rural life; in demanding "wholesome women," they sought women who would simultaneously serve as beacons of imperial society and constrain the excesses of white men; in courting "steady families," they pursued stable units that would exemplify the virtues of the same-race, nuclear family. Together, "hardy backwoodsmen, wholesome women and steady families" were constructed as the immigrants able to transform British Columbia into the stable settler society of imperialists' dreams.

Studies of the flow of people between Europe and the Americas in the "Great Migration Era" have tended to leave a blind spot, namely their disinterest in interrogating the politicized character of nineteenth-century "new world" migration.[1] When people left Europe for the Americas or Australia, they did not simply move into large, empty spaces. Instead, they participated in a process of colonization in which Aboriginal dispossession and settler migration were irreparably linked. As Daiva Staisulis and Nira Yuval-Davis argue, migration is one of the chief ways in which settler societies constitute themselves.[2]

For individuals and families, migration was probably motivated primarily by straightforward social and economic needs, but the overarching structure of imperialism transformed these needs into imperial acts.[3] Immigration sometimes troubled and sometimes nourished the politics of empire. In either case, it cannot be separated from them.

[. . .]

Acknowledging these ties is crucial to understanding white settler colonies like British Columbia. The significance of immigration in colonial contexts derives from its central position in the very business of imperialism. Settler societies aim simultaneously to dispossess Aboriginal peoples and to replace them with relatively homogeneous settler populations, and immigration is one of the tools that has allowed them to do so. Colonies of settlement are distinguished from other kinds of colonies chiefly by their reproductive and gendered character. That colonizers *settle* implies more than residence. It denotes a reproductive regime dependent on the presence of settler women who literally reproduce the colony. Immigration must therefore provide more than non-Aboriginal bodies. Ideally, it must provide the right kind of bodies, those suited to building a white settler colony.

These connections between immigration, empire, and gender came together in mid-nineteenth-century British Columbia in an especially revealing way. Its society was the product of three sometimes conflicting imperial intentions: the fur trade, the gold rush, and the British tradition of settler colonies. North America's northern Pacific coast and the Columbia Plateau were densely populated by linguistically, culturally, and politically diverse First Nations people reliant on foraging, hunting, and fishing. The Hudson's Bay Company (HBC) began trading with local peoples in the late eighteenth century, and formal colonial authority was established in 1849 when Vancouver Island was made a British colony.

The discovery of gold on the mainland's Fraser River in 1858 precipitated the creation of a mainland colony called British Columbia. It was, according to imperial opinion, destined to be a major colony of settlement. "[N]ever did a colony in its infancy present a more satisfactory appearance," remarked one Anglican cleric. By 1866 and 1867, however, "those who once entertained most extravagant expectations began to despond."[4] Imperial downsizing followed despondency. In 1866 the two colonies were merged, retaining the name of British Columbia, and in July 1871 British Columbia joined Canada as a province, bringing the colonial period to a close.

These shifts in political form reflected widespread disappointment in British Columbia's performance as a settler colony. "The high tide of immigration expected never reached the Colony," explained Governor Frederick Seymour, "and the ebb proved much stronger than anticipated."[5] To be sure, the population expanded: There were fewer than 1000 settlers in 1855 and over 10 000 in 1871. But the settler population never rivalled the Aboriginal one, which, despite massive depopulation wrought by smallpox, likely hovered around the 45 000 mark in the early 1870s.[6]

Settler British Columbia did not grow as quickly as imperial observers hoped it would, nor did it grow in the way they had hoped. The periphery, like the metropole, defied pretences of ethnic and racial homogeneity.[7] For a supposed white settler colony, British Columbia was not very white: Chinese, African-American, Latino, and Kanaka (Hawaiian) settlers were a significant presence. Jews and continental Europeans pressed operative definitions of whiteness, and Americans unsettled the colony's claims to Britishness. In 1861 the local official for Douglas, a small gold-rush town on the mainland, enumerated 97 Chinese, 40 Americans, 20 Mexicans, 17 Europeans, and 6 "coloured" people. They dwelled amongst "About 700

Natives."[8] "It would have been difficult to find in one place a greater mixture of different nationalities," wrote German mathematician Carl Friesach after visiting Yale, another small mining town. "Americans were undoubtably [sic] in the majority—California, especially had sent a large contingent. Then followed Germans, French, and Chinese. Next came Italians, Spaniards, Poles, etc," he noted.[9]

[. . .] The diversity fostered by the gold rushes of the early colonial days diminished but never disappeared. When British Columbia entered Canadian confederation in 1871, its settler society was constituted, according to one probably conservative count, by 8576 whites, 1548 Chinese, and 462 Africans.[10]

That British Columbia's settlers were overwhelmingly male further suggested its failure to fit the norms of a white settler colony. While the female proportion ebbed and flowed over the colonial period, it never exceeded a high of 35 per cent of the white society and reached lows of 5 per cent.[11] Imperial discourse that accorded white women a special role as harbingers of empire rendered this demographic problem a political one. A popular emigration guide by "A Returned Digger," like so many others, despaired of what to do with a society so lacking in women. "The great curse of the colony," he explained, "is the absence of women. I doubt if there was one woman to a hundred men twelve months ago. I am quite sure that now, when I am writing, there must be at least two hundred men to every woman."[12] In colonial discourse, the continuing demographic dominance of First Nations people, the plurality of settler society, and its prevailing masculinity became irreparably intertwined, a three-part symbol of British Columbia's departure from dominant social norms and expectations.

Colonial promoters—a term I apply to a loose collection of journalists, politicians, officials, missionaries, and self-appointed do-gooders—looked to immigration to address the smallness, diversity, and masculinity of settler British Columbia and to render

it a prosperous and respectable settler colony. They attributed the colony's lamentable imperial performance to the sparseness of its settler society. The *British Columbian* newspaper argued that the colony's poor showing stemmed from its under-population, "because we have only a mere handful of population, a few thousand people living upon one another."[13] The colony lacked white population of nearly every description. The Victoria press noted,

> If we enter our churches, they want worshippers; our school houses want scholars; our streets and highways want pedestrians and vehicles; our merchants want trade; our traders want customers; our steamboats want passengers and freight; our workshops want workmen; our fertile valleys want farmers; our gold and silver mines want miners; in short, the two Colonies want population.[14]

While the colony had resources, wrote the *Cariboo Sentinel*, "without a population a country may remain forever a barren wilderness, dotted here and there with a few fisherman's huts and a few miners' and lumberman's cabins, and known only to the world as an inhospitable and poverty-stricken place."[15]

If colonial promoters suggested that British Columbia's ills stemmed from the sparseness of the white population, they had a related and almost boundless faith in the political potential of white bodies to make it a successful colonial enterprise. Even the most shameless boosters, however, recognized that British Columbia's distance from centres of white population meant that active state intervention was required for mass immigration to occur. If they wanted a white population, they would have to work for it, bidding it to come hither, assisting its passage, and supporting it on arrival. "To have our country filled up we must not only assist people to reach our shores, but we must show them the way to earn a living after they get here," wrote the *Colonist* in 1866.[16] The intervention of both the local and colonial state was required. "What right has the most remote of the British Colonies to expect immigration without even *asking for it*," agreed the New Westminster press, "to say nothing of *assisting* it?"[17]

Colonial promoters' demands for immigration were part and parcel of a program of asserting white supremacy in British Columbia. Himani Bannerji has recently dubbed immigration a "euphemistic expression for racist labour and citizenship policies."[18] In colonial British Columbia the process worked to exclude First Nations migrants and to minimize non-white settlers. It was difficult, although hardly impossible, to argue for the removal of First Nations with local and obvious territorial claims. Those from distant territories were easy targets for settlers committed to visions of racial segregation. The city of Victoria worked hard to control and limit the presence of the so-called Northern Tribes—people from the coastal societies of the Nisga'a, Hieltsuk, Nexalk, Kwakwaka'wakw, Tlingit, and especially the wealthy and politically powerful Haida and Tsimshian—who made annual spring visits to Victoria for trade, wage work, and festivity. In 1859 a police constable found 2235 Northern peoples, the bulk of them probably Haida and Tsimshian, living on the outskirts of Victoria.[19] As annually as they arrived, local burghers demanded their eviction. The language they used to stigmatize Northern peoples invoked the overlapping discourses of morality, criminality, and gender that have often been used to identify and marginalize immigrant groups. "Vagrancy, filth, disease, drunkenness, larceny, maiming, murder, prostitution, in a multiplied form, are the invariable results of an annual visit from the Northern Tribes," raged the *Colonist*. "We unhesitatingly declare for stopping the immigration."[20]

Those who defended the rights of Northern peoples to visit Victoria—and, by implication, their status as legitimate immigrants and thus colonial citizens—relied on another staple of immigration discourse, namely the argument that the Northern peoples' presence, however unpalatable, was sweetened by their cheap labour. When settlers demanded that Northern peoples be forcibly evicted, missionary William Duncan argued that "the driving-away policy is contrary to the interests of our Colony, which needs at least the labor of the Indians." He referred those who doubted the local need for Aboriginal labour to "the kitchens and nurseries, the fields and gardens around Victoria."[21] Governor James Douglas proposed schemes of moral and social regulation as an alternative to eviction, arguing that Northern peoples' willingness to serve as a colonial labour force made them valuable to whites. "[I]t is hardly creditable to the civilization of the nineteenth century, that so especial an element of health, as labour of the cheapest description, should be, in a manner, banished from the Colony," he explained.[22]

The sweat and toil of the Northern peoples ultimately failed to buy them a legitimate role in settler Victoria. Those who wanted racial segregation of colonial space were bolstered and legitimated by the apocalyptic smallpox epidemic of 1862, when Northern peoples were repeatedly and forcibly evicted from Victoria, a process later condoned and organized by public health legislation.[23] A brand of settler imperialism premised on the removal and containment of local peoples ultimately won out over the version that positioned them as subservient labourers for the ruling minority. [. . .]

That this process worked to include whites and exclude others is confirmed by the experience of settlers of Asian and African extraction. Douglas—himself an archetypal hybrid figure, hailing from a "creole" mother and a Scottish father and having married the half-Cree Amelia Connolly—encouraged the migration of mainly middle-class African-Americans associated with the Pioneer Society of San Francisco in 1858.

Other settlers did not share his enthusiasm. Despite the African-Americans' apparent fit with the colony's putative values of hard work, Protestantism, and respectability, their sizable presence in Victoria was regarded by many white people as a problem. Whether Victoria would replicate or challenge American-style segregation in her churches, theatres, and saloons was a significant item of debate until the black population began to disperse in the mid-1860s.[24]

It was Chinese immigration that created the most ambivalence among British Columbia's white commentators. Representations of Chinese men celebrated industriousness and sometimes located them on the colonists' side of the local imperial divide. The Grand Jury of Cayoosh (later Lillooet) told the governor in 1860 that Chinese settlers were a benefit to white traders and the government alike. The jury further requested that the state acknowledge the Chinese as settlers, asking that they "afford them every due protection to prevent their being driven away, wither by attacks from Indians or otherwise."[25]

More often Chinese men were positioned as undesirable immigrants who would imperil rather than bolster colonialism. The *Cariboo Sentinel* argued that Chinese men should not be colonists for a variety of reasons, all indicating their fundamental difference and many invoking explicitly gendered images. The Chinese, the newspaper argued, were "aliens not merely in nationality, but in habits, religion"; they never became "good citizens" or served on juries or fire companies; they never married or settled outside China and were "more apt to create immorality than otherwise"; they dealt "entirely with their own countrymen"; they hoarded their money and evaded taxes; and, lastly, they were, ironically for immigrants, "inimical to immigration."[26] No restrictions were imposed on Chinese immigration, although colonists debated ways—prominent among them being a miner's licence fee levied on Chinese men alone—designed to regulate their place within settler society.[27] Such discussions anticipated the highly organized, pervasive, and vociferous attacks on Chinese people that began later in the nineteenth century and continue to shape contemporary life and politics.[28]

The role of immigration to colonial British Columbia was thus an explicitly racial one. The "'bone, muscle, and intellect,' that is required here," explained the Victoria press plainly, "differs materially from the Indian or the African. It is Caucasian—Anglo-Saxon bone, muscle, and intellect we want."[29] Class, and the politics of respectability that so often went with it, also helped determine who would be included and who excluded. Not all white people were created equal. British Columbia's colonial promoters did not want convicts, although one, tellingly, was willing to tolerate juvenile offenders as long as they were placed on First Nations settlements.[30] When the Colonial Office inquired about the emigration of distressed Lancashire mill operatives, local officials were similarly unreceptive. Douglas replied that "this Colony offers but a poor field for destitute immigrants," warning that "instead of improving their condition, it is to be feared, that by emigrating in great numbers to this Colony, they would only be involved in a more hopeless state of distress and poverty."[31] British Columbia's officials were ultimately as fearful of organized immigration's class implications—of the shovelling out of paupers—as were others in British North America.

Immigration to this settler colony was an issue of race and class, and also very much one of gender. British Columbia's colonial failure was linked, in critics' minds, not only to the smallness and diversity of the settler society but also to the failure of increasingly hegemonic gender norms to take root there. British Columbia was home to a small, highly mobile handful of settler men living amongst a large Aboriginal society. This particular demography fostered a rough, vibrant homosocial culture created by and for young men and the widespread practice of white–Aboriginal domestic and conjugal relationships. Immigration was sought as a corrective for both. When promoters called for immigration, they called for a process that would address the society's perceived gendered deficiencies as well as its racial peculiarities.

Three gendered images dominated discussions of immigration. First, the hardy backwoodsman—a steady, hard-working man willing to meet the difficulties of colonial life and permanently settle in British Columbia—shaped discussions of men and migration. The hypothetical hardy backwoodsman was constructed in contrast to the rough gold miners who so pervaded the colony. British Columbia had two major gold rushes—the Fraser River Gold Rush of 1858 and the Cariboo Gold Rush of 1862–1863—and a host of smaller ones. Waves of young, footloose men disillusioned with the false promises of capitalist, industrial society were attracted by each strike of gold. Prevailing discourse understood these men as wandering, immoral, and anti-social. [. . .]

Miners' inadequacies as colonists became axiomatic in popular colonial discourse. [. . .] For British Columbia to fulfill its imperial potential, hardy backwoodsmen would have to replace the wandering miners. In 1859 Douglas told the Colonial Office, "The mining population are proverbially migratory and unsettled in their habits, seldom engaging in any other than their own absorbing pursuits, and therefore, it is he who tills the soil, the industrious farmer, who must clear the forest, bring the land into cultivation, and build up the permanent interests and prosperity of the Colony."[32]

The hardy backwoodsman stood in contrast not only to the wandering miner, but to another masculine drain on the colonial enterprise, the "croaker." This term, along with grumbler, was applied to men deemed unable to weather the difficulties of colonial life. Whether an erstwhile son of wealth or an urban loafer, the croaker was flummoxed by the realities of pioneering and proceeded to complain instead of work. Gilbert Malcolm Sproat, a sawmill owner, magistrate, amateur anthropologist, and promoter of immigration, described the croakers:

> [C]ertain persons came into the country who had a strong desire to make a living without taking off their coats—a desire which could not be gratified. The friends of these persons at home sent them money, which they put into silly investments. They rode to the diggings, and road [sic] back again. They hung, like mendicants, round the doors of the Government offices. They croaked in the streets, spent their time idly in barrooms, and finally disappeared.[33]

Here, the language of class is put to work in the service of gender and race: the croaker is idle and delicate, bearing the mark of both femininity and bourgeois laxity. [. . .]

Just as they repelled the weak, colonies were thought to attract the most manly of British men who stood in contrast not only to their less rugged fellows, but to the Indigenous men they alternately feminized or feared.[34] "As a rule," commented the local press, "it is the most energetic, hardy, manly, self-reliant of her sons who first people her Colonies."[35] Ideal male immigrants were hard-working, disciplined, and predisposed to rural life. The new colony, argued a supporter in 1860, "does not want the idle, the profligate, and sickly."[36] The hardy backwoodsman embraced diligent labour, especially agricultural labour, just as the gold miner rejected it. His single state meant that he was able to devote himself fully to labour, to define himself as an entirely economic being. One much-reprinted emigration guide advised, "A family is a burden till a man is established."[37] [. . .]

Yet single men, hardy or otherwise, constituted an ambivalent force for colonial promoters. Sproat thought that their tendency to wander made them a waste of public funds.[38] More fundamentally, imperial regimes were consistently troubled by the large numbers of working-class men assigned responsibility for practically enforcing them.[39] White soldiers, miners, and farmers frequently failed to meet standards of racial distance and superiority set by imperial masters. Racial concerns about young, footloose men in colonial contexts were also gendered concerns. Colonial promoters were disturbed by how regularly white men formed relationships and families with local women. Settler men who opted to remain single were also a worry. Increasingly in the mid-nineteenth century the domestic family was constructed as a necessary component of adult life. To be rendered a responsible colonial citizen who was appropriately distanced from local peoples, the hardy backwoodsman needed a wholesome woman.

The scarcity of white women in British Columbia became, along with the smallness of the settler population, axiomatic for the colony's condition. As I have argued elsewhere, white women were constructed as "fair ones of a purer caste"[40] with three related roles in the local colonial project. White women would first compel white men to reject the rough homosocial culture of the backwoods in favour of normative standards of masculinity, respectability, and permanence. "Women! women! women! are the great want," wrote aristocrat Harry Verney from London. "The normal state is man with a help meet for him, and if something is not soon done, either by the Imperial or Colonial Government, or by some philanthropists at home, I know not what will become of us. Poor man goes sadly down hill if he remains long without the supporting influence of women."[41] White women were considered to be men's collective better half, as the only force capable of ensuring their proper behaviour. Such a discourse accorded them a role, albeit a limited one, as agents in both imperialism and immigration.

White women would secondly address shortages in the local labour market and relieve overpopulation in Britain. That the supposed need for domestic servants and wives in British Columbia neatly matched fears of "surplus women" in Britain gave calls for female immigration a special efficacy. A female immigration to British Columbia, wrote one observer, "would be as great a boon to the colony as I am sure it would be to many of the underpaid, under-fed, and over-worked women who drag out a weary existence in the dismal back streets and alleys of the metropolis."[42] Immigration was thus invoked as a mechanism for simultaneously resolving the different crises of gender that troubled the metropole and the periphery.

White women's third service to the colonial project was the explicitly racial one of discouraging mixed-race sexual, domestic, and conjugal relationships. As white men's "natural" objects of desire, they would draw men away from the temptations of Aboriginal women and, in doing so, shore up the colonial project as a whole. "That many of the native women are cleanly, industrious, and faithful, we do not pretend to deny," wrote New Westminster's *Mainland Guardian*, "but, we regret to to [sic] say, they are the exceptions. With the increase of our white female population, we look for new life in our agricultural pursuits and we hope that every inducement will be offered to healthy industrious women, who are desirous of finding good husbands and comfortable homes, in this province, to come out to us."[43] This discourse was premised on the construction of white women as uplifting and on the representation of First Nations women as base and threatening that circulated throughout colonial British Columbia.

In these ways, the discourse of wholesome women emphasized the political utility of ordinary, working-class women above those who held an official role in the colonial project like missionaries' or officials' wives. Their contribution lay not in independent action, but rather in their ability to transform plebeian men. Such a discourse imbued women migrants with an agency less often acknowledged in historiography. At any rate, the sheer ideological weight of the conviction that a society lacking white women could not be a moral or even adequate one provided the motivation necessary to orchestrate immigration schemes in 1862, 1863, and 1870. Organized as joint efforts of the local elite, missionaries, and British feminists, these immigration campaigns are remembered in popular lore as the "brideships," as colony- (and, later, nation-) building enterprises. Together, the *Tynemouth*, *Robert Lowe*, and *Alpha* carried roughly a hundred women, largely teenagers from working-class and sometimes indigent backgrounds. They were putatively destined to be domestic servants, but popular discourse ensured that their real destiny lay in the marriage market. As wives of miners and farmers, colonial promoters hoped, these wholesome women would render British Columbia's fragile colonial project a stable one.[44]

The young working-class women produced by these female immigration schemes ultimately unsettled the colonial project rather than securing it. Instead of behaving as beacons of imperial rectitude, the immigrants acted like the young, working-class women that they were. Colonial promoters were deeply disappointed. By the close of the colonial period, their faith in the political usefulness of white female migration was profoundly shaken. In 1872 Sproat looked back on his experience with three separate female immigration efforts, commenting, "How to send single women to Victoria safely across the continent, and through San Francisco, is a problem which I cheerfully hand over for solution to those who are more experienced in the management of that sex than I am."[45] The fundamental problem with white female migration, he argued, was that *single* women were necessarily a moral problem. "The very delicate and difficult question of introducing single unmarried women into British Columbia might be partly solved by sending out a few, in charge of the heads of families—the women being from the same district as the

families, and thus having an addition[al] guard for their self-respect," he argued.[46]

Wholesome women, much like hardy backwoodsmen, challenged the colonial project at the same time as they bolstered it. The enthusiasm for white female migration was always tempered and eventually overwhelmed by the conviction that single women, like men, were a dangerous population that could only be properly contained by families. After the disasters of the assisted female migration efforts of 1862 and 1863, the "steady family" gained a special cachet in pro-immigration discourse that would only increase after the 20 servant-women transported on the *Alpha* in 1870 proved, like their predecessors, a disappointment to those who so sought their importation. The Female Immigration Board that oversaw this scheme recommended that the colonial government abandon the project of female immigration and shift its monies and attentions to the "assisted passages of Families, and relatives of Farmers, Mechanics, and others settled in this Colony."[47] In pledging their support for the importation of families, and not single women, members of the board endorsed the stable family as the best kind of immigration for the colony.

They were not alone in suggesting that same-race domestic families would be the best base for a settler society and thus the best immigrants. Families simultaneously constrained young women and encouraged men to be permanent and diligent settlers. The *Victoria Press* argued, "The very class which we want above all others is the married agriculturist—the man whose social circumstances will bring him to the soil, and make him a permanent as well as productive inhabitant."[48] Sproat agreed, writing that "the married farmer with modest means, and accustomed to work in the fields, is the best kind of immigrant for British Columbia."[49] The HBC supported family migration when it imported 36 married colliers to work Nanaimo's coalfields.[50] That the Colonial Office shared this familial ideal is suggested by its willingness to pay for the passage of the wives and families of the Royal Engineers, the soldier-settlers sent to enforce British claims to the mainland.[51] On rare occasions the colonial government subsidized the migration of individual families,[52] but more often used land law to buttress domestic family formation. In Vancouver Island, nuclear family formation was encouraged by laws that gave white men an additional 50 acres of free land if they were married and 10 more acres for each child under the age of 10.[53]

The overlap between immigration discourse and immigration practice was usually indirect. These demands for hardy backwoodsmen, wholesome women, and steady families were rarely parlayed into concrete action. Immigration was what colonial pundits always wanted and never got. In referring to immigrants as "mythical beings," politician John Sebastian Helmcken astutely recognized the somewhat hypnotic role immigration played in colonial discourse.[54] The mythic rather than actual character of immigration to colonial British Columbia was not for lack of heated rhetoric or wild scheming. Colonial promoters held mass meetings, struck committees, wrote passionate letters, and developed plans for using immigration to secure their imperial fortunes.[55] With the exception of the 20 servant women carried on the *Alpha* in 1870, however, the colonial government's immigration efforts were largely confined to the cheap and discursive: They subsidized mail, explored territory, printed essays, and hired lecturers to regale the masses of various urban centres. In 1861, for instance, British Columbia created an exhibit for the World's Fair designed to prove to "struggling, hard worked Englishmen how easily a livelihood may be earned here."[56]

The modesty of these efforts deeply disappointed those who considered immigration key to imperial success. They complained bitterly about the local government's apparent inability to organize immigration. In 1864 the mainland press commented that, excepting

"fifty pounds paid to a parson at Lillooet for an Essay," the colony had "not yet expended a single dollar" on immigration.[57] Five years later, the same newspaper despaired that there was not one person responsible for immigration "[a]mongst the army of officials who absorb the revenue of the Colony."[58]

If British Columbia's local government was unable, its imperial masters were unwilling. The Colonial Office argued that, given its location, British Columbia could only reasonably expect emigrants from the Australasian colonies, not from Britain, and repeatedly announced that it had no intention of ever assisting emigration to the colony.[59] When pestered to subsidize steam communication, Colonial Office staff made it clear that they lacked the requisite political will. "When this Country was supposed to be over-peopled, there was the appearance of a domestic object in schemes for using the proceeds of English taxes to encourage emigration. But that state of things has long ceased to exist," one noted.[60] Domestic issues like overpopulation fuelled the various assisted emigration schemes of the 1830s and 1840s and would again motivate major emigration schemes in the *fin de siècle*. These efforts ground to a near halt when popular economic fortunes bettered and events like New Zealand's Maori Wars and the Indian Rebellion of 1857 challenged British faith in the imperial project.

Whether in London, Victoria, or New Westminster, many doubted British Columbia's ability to attract settlers, but only a few challenged its need for a large white population. [. . .] Ultimately, British Columbia's apparent inability to attract white and especially British immigrants served not as a reason for challenging the viability of colonialism, but rather as a rationale for the colony's entry into Canadian confederation.[61] If British Columbia could not use immigration to become a stable settler colony in its own right, it would try to do so as a Canadian province. That British Columbia finally registered a white majority in the first census taken after Confederation suggests that this strategy was effective. With continuing depopulation of First Nations and the arrival of the transcontinental railroad in 1886—that tangible technology of both capital and nation and conveyor of migrants *par excellence*—British Columbia would begin to look increasingly like a textbook white settler colony, but it would continue to be haunted by a spectre of hybridity that was, in the final analysis, more nurtured by immigration than vanquished by it.

[. . .]

NOTES

1. See, for instance, Bernard Bailyn, *The Peopling of British North America: An Introduction* (New York: Knopf, 1986). For a revealing example, see the explicit definition of Ontario's Leeds and Landsdowne townships as "empty" in Donald Harman Akenson, *The Irish in Ontario: A Study in Rural History* (Montreal and Kingston: McGill-Queen's University Press, 1984), 55.

2. Daiva Staisulis and Nira Yuval-Davis, "Introduction: Beyond Dichotomies. Gender, Race, Ethnicity and Class in Settler Societies," in Staisulis and Yuval-Davis, eds, *Unsettling Settler Societies: Articulations of Gender, Race, Ethnicity and Class* (London: Sage, 1995).

3. On this point in a later period, see Stephen Constantine, "Introduction: Empire Migration and Imperial Harmony," in Constantine, ed., *Emigrants and Empire: British Settlement in the Dominions Between the Wars* (Manchester: Manchester University Press, 1990). See also Rita S. Kranidis, ed., *Imperial Objects: Essays on Victorian Women's Emigration and the Unauthorized Imperial Experience* (New York: Twayne, 1998).

4. Henry Wright, *Nineteenth Annual Report of the Missions of the Church of England in British Columbia for the Year 1877* (London: Rivingtons, 1878), 16–17.

5. British Columbia Archives (hereafter BCA), GR 1486, mflm B–1442, Great Britain, Colonial Office, British Columbia Original Correspondence (hereafter CO 60), CO 60/32, Frederick Seymour to Duke of Buckingham and Chandos, 17 March 1868.

6. All population figures from colonial British Columbia are at best guesses. These are from British Columbia, *Report of the Hon. H.L. Langevin, C.B., Minister of Public Works* (Ottawa: I.B. Taylor, 1872), 22; and Edward Mallandaine, *First Victoria Directory, Third [Fourth] Issues, and British Columbia Guide* (Victoria: Mallandaine, 1871), 94–5. Also see R. Cole Harris and John Warkentin, *Canada before Confederation: A Study in Historical Geography* (Ottawa: Carleton University Press, 1991), chap. 7.

7. Antoinette Burton, *At the Heart of Empire: Indians and the Colonial Encounter in Late-Victorian Britain* (Berkeley: University of California Press, 1998).

8. BCA, "Colonial Correspondence," GR 1372, mflm B–1330, file 620/16, John Bowles Gaggin to W.A.G. Young, 3 April 1861.

9. Carl Friesach, "Extracts from *Ein Ausflug nach Britisch-Columbien im Jahre 1858*," in E.E. Delavault and Isabel McInnes, trans., "Two Narratives of the Fraser River Gold Rush," *British Columbia Historical Quarterly* 1 (July 1941): 227.

10. British Columbia, *Report of the Hon. H. L. Langevin*, p. 22.

11. On this, see Adele Perry, *On the Edge of Empire: Gender, Race, and the Making of British Columbia, 1849–1871* (Toronto: University of Toronto Press, 2000), chap. 1.

12. A Returned Digger, *The Newly Discovered Gold Fields of British Columbia* (London: Darton and Hodge, 1862, 8th edn), 7.

13. "Our Great Want," *British Columbian*, 9 January 1869.

14. "Our Wants," *British Colonist*, 5 June 1861.

15. "Emigration," *Cariboo Sentinel*, 18 June 1868.

16. "Assisted Immigration," *British Colonist*, 11 December 1866.

17. "Population, Population," *British Columbian*, 29 May 1869.

18. Himani Bannerji, *On the Dark Side of the Nation: Essays on Multiculturalism, Nationalism and Gender* (Toronto: Canadian Scholars. Press, 2000), 4.

19. "Our Indian Population," *Weekly Victoria Gazette*, 28 April 1859.

20. "Invasion of the Northern Indians," *British Colonist*, 18 April 1861.

21. Wm. Duncan, "The Indian Question," *British Colonist*, 4 July 1861. On Aboriginal wage labour, see John Lutz, "After the Fur Trade: Aboriginal Wage Labour in Nineteenth-Century British Columbia," *Journal of the Canadian Historical Association* (1992): 69–94.

22. National Archives of Canada (hereafter NAC), Great Britain, Colonial Office Correspondence, Vancouver Island (hereafter CO 305), CO 305/10, mflm B–238, James Douglas to Sir Edward Bulwer Lytton, 25 May 1859.

23. See Perry, *On the Edge*, chap. 5.

24. For an argument for black migration to Vancouver Island, see Mary A. Shadd, *A Plea for Emigration; or, Notes of Canada West, in its Moral, Social, and Political Aspect With Suggestions Respecting Mexico, West Indies, and Vancouver's Island, for the Information of Colored Emigrants* (Detroit: George W. Pattison, 1842), pp. 43–44. On black people in Victorian society, see Irene Genevieve Marie Zaffaroni, The Great Chain of Being: Racism and Imperialism in Colonial Victoria, 1858–1871. (MA thesis, University of Victoria, 1987), chap. 4; Crawford Killian, *Go Do Some Great Thing: The Black Pioneers of British Columbia* (Vancouver: Douglas and McIntyre, 1978).

25. NAC, CO 60/8, MG 11, mflm B–83, "Address of the Grand Jury at Cayoosh to Governor Douglas," in James Douglas to Duke of Newcastle, 9 October 1860.

26. "Our Chinese Population," *Cariboo Sentinel*, 16 May 1867.

27. See, for an explanation of why they were impracticable, NAC, CO 63/3, mflm B–1489, "Speech of His Honor the Officer Administering the Government at the Opening of the Legislative Council," *British Columbia Government Gazette*.

28. On this, see Kay Anderson, *Vancouver's Chinatown: Racial Discourse in Canada, 1875–1980* (Montreal and Kingston: McGill-Queen's University Press, 1991); Patricia E. Roy, *A White Man's Province: British Columbia Politicians and Chinese and Japanese Immigrants, 1858–1914* (Vancouver: University of British Columbia Press, 1989).

29. "Indian vs. White Labor," *British Colonist*, 19 February 1861.

30. "Convict Labor," *British Columbian*, 11 January 1865; "Juvenile Offenders—Colonization," *British Columbian*, 30 May 1869.

31. NAC, CO 305/20, MG 11, mflm B–244, and CO 60/16, MG 11, mflm B–89, James Douglas to the Duke of Newcastle, 14 July 1863.

32. NAC, CO 60/4, MG 11, mflm B–80, James Douglas to Edward Bulwer Lytton, 11 July 1859.

33. Gilbert Malcolm Sproat, *British Columbia: Information for Emigrants* (London: Agent General for the Province, 1873), 4.

34. On masculinity and colonization, see Mrinalini Sinha, *Colonial Masculinity: The "Manly Englishman" and the "Effeminate Bengali" in the Late Nineteenth Century* (Manchester: Manchester University Press, 1995); Elizabeth Vibert, *Traders' Tales: Narratives of Cultural Encounters on the Plateau, 1807–1846* (Norman: University of Oklahoma Press, 1997).

35. "The Colonial Policy of Great Britain," *British Colonist*, 2 May 1863.

36. "Testimonial to D.G.F. MacDonald, Esq., C.E.," *Weekly Victoria Gazette*, 30 January 1860.

37. A Returned Digger, *The Newly Discovered Gold Fields*, p. 8.

38. BCA, Add Mss 257, file 3, Gilbert Malcolm Sproat to Lieutenant Governor, "Memo re European Immigration into B.C.," 3 November 1871.

39. See, for instance, Kenneth Ballhatchet, *Race, Sex and Class under the Raj: Imperial Attitudes and Policies and their Critics, 1783–1905* (London: Werdenfeld and Nicholson, 1980), chap. 5.

40. One of the Disappointed, untitled piece in the *British Columbian*, 7 June 1862; Adele Perry, "'Fair Ones of a Purer Caste': White Women and Colonialism in Nineteenth-Century British Columbia," *Feminist Studies* 23, 3 (Fall 1997): 501–24.

41. "Sir Harry Verney Upon British Columbia," *British Columbian*, 20 August 1862.

42. A.D.G., "British Columbia: To the Editor of the Times," *London Times*, 1 January 1862.

43. "Immigration," *Mainland Guardian*, 9 February 1871.

44. See Perry, *On the Edge*, chaps. 6–7, for an analysis of female immigration to British Columbia.

45. BCA, GR 419, box 10, file 1872/1, British Columbia, Attorney General, "Documents," G.M.S., "Memorandum on Immigration, Oct 1972," pp. 95–6.

46. BCA, GR 419, box 10, file 1872/1, "Attorney General Documents," G.M. Sproat, "Memorandum of a few Suggestions for opening the business of emigration to British Columbia, referred to as Memo C, in a letter of G.M. Sproat to the Honourable the Provincial Secretary, dated 29th August 1972," pp. 4–5.

47. BCA, GR 1372, mflm B–1314, file 955/23, "Colonial Correspondence," Wm. Pearse, John Robson, W.J. MacDonald to Colonial Secretary, 12 July 1870; E.G.A., "The Immigration Board," British Colonist, 24 June 1870.

48. "The Overland Route," Victoria Press, 16 March 1862.

49. BCA, GR 419, box 10, file 1872/1, British Columbia, "Papers Related to Immigration, 1972," G.M.S., "Memorandum on Immigration, Oct 1872."

50. BCA, Add mss E/B/M91A, Andrew Muir, "Private Diary," 9 November 1848–5 August 1850 [transcript]; Add Mss A/C/20.1/N15, James Douglas—Joseph William McKay, "Nanaimo Correspondence, August 1852–September 1853" [transcript].

51. NAC, MG 11, CO 60/9, mflm B–83, G.C. Lewis to James Douglas, 11 August 1860, draft reply, in James Douglas to the Duke of Newcastle, 12 May 1860.

52. See, for instance, James E. Hendrickson, ed., Journals of the Colonial Legislatures of the Colonies of Vancouver Island and British Columbia, 1851–1871, vol. 1: Journals of the Council, Executive Council, and Legislative Council of Vancouver Island, 1851–1866 (Victoria: Provincial Archives of British Columbia, 1980), 133–4.

53. "The New Land Proclamation for Vancouver Island," British Colonist, 8 March 1861; "Salt Spring Island," Victoria Press, 10 November 1861; Matthew Macfie, Vancouver Island and British Columbia: Their History, Resources and Prospects (London: Longman, Green, Longman, Roberts & Green, 1865), p. 205.

54. "Legislative Council," British Colonist, 4 February 1869.

55. See examples in Hendrickson, ed., Journals of the Colonial Legislatures, vol. 2: Journals of the House of Assembly, Vancouver Island, 1856–1863, vol. 3: Journals of the House of Assembly, Vancouver Island, 1863–1866, and vol. 4: Journals of the Executive Council, 1864–1871, and of the Legislative Council, 1864–1866, of British Columbia.

56. "Industrial Exhibition Circular," British Columbian, 30 May 1861.

57. "Emigration," British Columbian, 15 June 1864.

58. "What Shall We Do With Them?," British Columbian, 4 June 1869.

59. NAC, MG 11, CO 60/5, mflm B–81, T.W.C. Murdoch and Frederic Rogers to Herman Merivale, April 28, 1859; mflm 69.303, Great Britain, House of Commons, Parliamentary Papers, vol. 38 (1863), no. 430, "Emigration: Number of Emigrants who left the United Kingdom for the United States, British North America, the several colonies of Australasia, South Africa, and other Places respectively; distinguishing, as far as practicable, the Native Country of the Emigrants, 1860–1863," mflm 69-303, p. 7.

60. NAC, MG 11, CO 60/14, mflm B–87, H.M. [Herman Merivale], April 8, note en verso in T.W.C. Murdoch to Frederic Rogers, 31 March 1862.

61. BCA, GR 1486, CO 60/29, mflm B–1440, Frederick Seymour to Duke of Buckingham and Chandos, 24 September 1867.

4 From Tina Loo, "'A Delicate Game': The Meaning of Law on Grouse Creek," BC Studies 96 (Winter 1992–93): 41–65. Reprinted with permission from BC Studies.

At the end of June in 1862, 100 miners returning from the Cariboo boarded the steamer Henrietta in Douglas for the trip to New Westminster. They refused to pay for their passage, claiming that their misadventures in the upper country gold fields had left them "starving and broken," as well as broke. Despite the obvious illegality of the miners' actions, Douglas magistrate John Boles Gaggin advised the master of Henrietta to "take the men on, and on arrival at New Westminster, apply to the proper authorities for redress." Gaggin took this course of action believing, as he told the Colonial Secretary, that

> to attempt coercion with a force unable to command it would have weakened the apparent power of the Law; . . . [and] that the getting of these men out of Douglas was in every way desirable, . . . any attempt to arrest would have provoked a riot, perhaps bloodshed, and I believe I acted prudently in avoiding the least risk of this.[1]

In an effort to further justify his actions, Gaggin closed his report on a defiant note with this telling observation:

> Magistrates in these up country towns have a delicate game to play, and I believe we are all of opinion that to avoid provoking resistance to the Law is the manner in which we best serve the interests of His Excellency, the Governor. . . . [A]s it is the matter passed off without riot and without defiance of the Magistrate, though the Master of the steamer . . . was somewhat annoyed—I shall be very sorry if the cautious way I acted, with such quiet results, does not meet His Excellency's approval, but I acted for the best.[2]

The colonial government chastised the magistrate for his "want of nerve and judgment" in allowing "the occurrence of so lawless a proceeding."[3] "It appears," noted Colonial Secretary W.A.G. Young,

> that you consider yourself vested with discretionary power to temporize with your duties, and that you are unaware that, while rigidly dispensing the laws for the protection of life and property, a Magistrate may act with perfect temper and discretion.[4]

This brief episode raises questions about the social meaning of the law which I am concerned to address. Gaggin considered law to be the preservation of order—"quiet results"—and told his superiors so. From his vantage point in Victoria, Governor James Douglas saw things rather differently. The law, through its rigid application, served a more particular end by securing life and property. There was yet another perspective. Both Gaggin and Douglas considered the miners' actions "lawless," but those who boarded *Henrietta* likely did not feel the same way. Different people attached different meanings to the law, and when they used the courts to resolve their disputes these differences became apparent. As legal anthropologists argue, courts are forums in which people "bargain for reality"; not only do they dispute the "facts"—what happened—but they also dispute what constitutes legal and just action.[5]

From their arrival, British Columbia's miners possessed a reputation as a self-conscious and vocal interest group with a penchant for self-government which they learned in California's gold fields. Despite their impermanent character, California's gold mining camps developed an elaborate system of informal regulation centred on the Miners' Meetings.[6] These were elected tribunals of local miners who drafted the rules which governed behaviour in a specific locale. Their regulations covered a wide range of activities, from claim size, the technicalities of ditch widths and water rights to the use of alcohol and firearms in the camps.[7] This experience instilled the miners with a taste for local government and a certain degree of independence.[8] It was this independence that made those who streamed northward to British Columbia in 1858 to try their luck in the Fraser and Cariboo rushes so dangerous in the eyes of British colonial administrators like James Douglas and Supreme Court Judge Matthew Baillie Begbie.[9] These men considered the miners a lawless bunch and took steps to prevent local government from gaining a foothold on the banks of the Fraser River.

In September 1858, just a month after the mainland colony was formed, James Douglas issued the first Gold Fields Act.[10] It and subsequent acts created and elaborated formal government institutions and regulations specifically designed to regulate gold mining.[11] An Assistant Gold Commissioner presided over locally based Gold Commissioner's or Mining Courts. He had jurisdiction to hear all mining or mining-related disputes and to dispose of them summarily. By doing so, the Gold Commissioner's Court allowed suitors to avoid the costly delays associated with Supreme Court actions and jury trials. A locally elected Mining Board replaced the Californian Miners' Meetings, drafting bylaws which governed behaviour. Unlike the American institution they replaced, however, the decisions of the Mining Board could be overturned by the Assistant Gold Commissioner, who also possessed the power to dissolve the board at his pleasure.

Despite the early intrusion of this formal regulatory institution into the gold fields, British Columbia's miners retained a sense of themselves and their enterprise as distinct and crucial to the development of the colony. Despite their impermanent character, gold rush communities were localistic, regardless—paradoxically—of their location.[12] Miners were particularly interested in the administration of the law, watching Mining Court decisions with an eye to their own fortunes. Though the law and the courts brought British Columbia's diverse and far-flung miners together in a common process of dispute settlement, they also were the cause of much division, for they resolved differences by creating other ones. The law defined plaintiffs and defendants, assessed guilt and innocence, and ultimately, in the eyes of those involved, determined right and wrong. The potential for conflict was thus inherent in the process of dispute settlement. As will be seen, different concepts of law stood in bold relief against this structured background of formal dispute resolution.

British Columbians understood and measured their laws with a standard that was rooted in a particular geographic, social, and cultural milieu and that was not always shared by those charged with its administration. Conflicting understandings of what constituted law underlay the disputes which culminated in the Grouse Creek War (1867) and which form the focus of the following narrative.

* * *

The three cases that lay at the centre of the controversy over the colony's judicial administration were all disputes over the ownership of mining claims.[13] Each is rather unremarkable in terms of the issues of fact involved, which consisted of the recording and re-recording of claims and the placement of stakes.[14] Once the cases were appealed to the Supreme Court, however, the issues of fact in these cases became secondary to Supreme Court Judge Matthew Baillie Begbie's actions. The judge's behaviour in the three cases and public reaction to them neatly illustrate the problems associated with administering the law in British Columbia, and adumbrate the limits of formal, institutional dispute settlement.

The first of these, launched in 1865, pitted the Borealis Company against the Watson Company. After the Assistant Gold Commissioner's decision awarding a disputed claim to the Watson Company was upheld by Begbie, the Borealis Company took the case to the Court of Chancery.[15] There, sitting this time as Chancery Court judge, Begbie reversed his earlier decision, and awarded the disputed ground to the Borealis Company! By all accounts, the mining community of the Cariboo was incredulous, and the colony's three main opposition newspapers wasted no time in adding their voices to the growing cries of indignation over Begbie's ruling emanating from the gold fields. Most distressing to British Columbians was the use

Loo: A Delicate Game 385

of the Chancery Court as a court of appeal, a process that was not only expensive and protracted, but was also capricious, because decisions appeared to be unfettered by any reference to statute law. "The late decision in the Borealis & Watson case strikes me as being the most flagrant and arbitrary stretches of power that has even been committed by an individual occuping the position of Judge," wrote "Miner" to the *Cariboo Sentinel* in 1866:

. . . we have mining laws containing explicit provisions as to the manner in which claims should be taken up and held, but at the same time that any parties having money enough to stand the costs of a Chancery suit may omit to comply with these provisions and set the law at defiance; it tends to create a feeling of insecurity as the value of every title, no man is secure if he strikes a good claim, as after strictly complying with the law which he supposed to be protection and spending his last dollar in prospecting, he may find when he thinks he has reached the long hoped for goal of his ambition, that some more favoured individual had intended in taking up the same ground long previously, but had neglected . . . staking it off or recording it, a grave error certainly, but one which can be expiated by filing a bill in Equity, making a score or two of affidavits, and paying his own costs in a Chancery suit, and this is what is called "Equity."[16]

Less measured was the commentary of the Victoria-based *British Colonist*, which contended that the "endless round of litigation" in British Columbia's mining districts was "ruining claimholders, shutting up the country's wealth and causing disasters in communities hundreds of miles away from the scene of the dispute." "The risks of mining are a mere bagatelle," the newspaper concluded, "it is the risks of Begbie's Chancery Court that terrify the miner."[17]

Public indignation over Begbie's actions in the Borealis case scarcely subsided when his handling of another mining dispute again drew the attention and the wrath of British Columbians. After issuing an injunction ordering the Davis Company to cease work on disputed ground, Begbie discovered that the Supreme Court seals necessary to validate the injunction were unavailable—detained, with the rest of his luggage, on a wagon that had broken down en route to Bridge Creek. Undeterred, the judge sent a messenger to Richfield with the injunction and orders for William Cox, the Stipendiary Magistrate and Assistant Gold Commissioner there, to attach seals to the injunction in his capacity as Deputy Registrar of the Supreme Court. Cox, whose decision Begbie had overturned in issuing the injunction, declined to act as ordered, claiming that while he "entertain[ed] high respect for Mr. Begbie as Mr. Begbie and also as Supreme Court Judge," he held no commission as Deputy Registrar. Moreover, continued the magistrate,

Finding now that it is attempted to drag me into this disagreeable quarrel, and act contrary to my own conscience, I would if I actually did hold a commission as Deputy Registrar of the Supreme Court resign the post at once.[18]

Although delayed by Cox's "decisive stand," *Aurora v. Davis* came to trial before Matthew Baillie Begbie and a special jury on 18 June.[19] After deliberating until midnight, the jury awarded half of the disputed ground to each side, because "the Aurora and Davis Companies have expended both time and money on said ground in dispute."[20] According to the *Sentinel*, the jury's decision met with the general approval of the entire mining community.

There is probably no instance on record where trial by jury has been so fully appreciated. . . . We are convinced that there is not a single miner on the creek that would not gladly submit his grievances to the decision of seven disinterested fellow citizens, and thus avoid the expensive and vexatious proceedings in Chancery.[21]

Despite the satisfaction with the jury's verdict evinced by the *Sentinel*, Begbie insisted that a decision by his court "would not end the litigation, and the expense of actions in one or two other branches of this Court would be heavy on both parties." Instead of accepting the jury's verdict, the judge suggested "that the whole matter be referred to me, not in my capacity as Judge, but as an arbitrator and friend, and that whatever decision I may arrive at will be final and absolute."[22] The two sides agreed, and the following day—19 June—Begbie rendered his decision to an "anxious" courtroom. Perhaps hoping to fore-stall any criticism, the judge made it a point to downplay the irregularity of his actions and to praise the jury as an institution. "I have always had every reason to be satisfied with the findings of juries during the whole period of my own official experience in this colony," Begbie remarked; but if "a jury finds a verdict contrary to the evidence, result-ing from ignorance, fear, or any other cause it is [the judge's] privilege to set aside their verdict." Noting that "when men go to jump ground they do not see their enemies' stakes," Begbie ruled against the Davis Company and awarded all of the disputed ground to the appellant.[23]

Reaction was immediate. Five or six hun-dred miners and residents of Cariboo gath-ered in front of the Richfield Court house on a rainy Saturday night six days after Begbie's decision to discuss the administration of the colony's mining laws.[24] Amid a great many speeches lasting well into the night, the par-ticipants passed three resolutions:

RESOLVED, "That in the opinion of this meeting the administration of the Mining Laws by Mr. Justice Begbie in the Supreme Court is partial, dictatorial, and arbitrary, in setting aside the verdict of juries, and calculated to create a feeling of distrust in those who have to seek redress through a Court of Justice."

RESOLVED, "That the meeting pledges itself to support the Government in carrying out the Laws in their integrity, and beg for an impartial administration of justice. To this end we desire the establishment of a Court of Appeal, or the immediate removal of Judge Begbie, whose acts in setting aside the Law has destroyed confidence and is driving labor, capital and enterprise out of the Colony."

RESOLVED, "That a Committee of two persons be appointed to wait upon His Excellency the Administrator of the Government [Arthur Birch] with the foregoing resolutions, and earnestly impress upon him the immediate necessity of carrying out the wishes of the people."

With three cheers for "Judge" Cox, the *British Colonist*, the *Cariboo Sentinel* and the Queen (in that order), and three groans for Judge Begbie, the meeting adjourned.[25]

As a result of the mounting public pres-sure for reform, the colonial government amended the Gold Fields Act in April 1867, limiting appeals from the Mining Court to questions of law only.[26] [. . .]

The *Borealis v. Watson* and *Aurora v. Davis* cases set the stage for the final and, according to one magistrate, most "humiliating" part of this mining trilogy: the Grouse Creek War.[27] Having found Chancery and arbitration want-ing, and his government colleagues sensitive to public pressure, in 1867 Matthew Baillie Begbie found only one option remaining: to adhere to the newly amended Gold Fields Act and refuse to hear appeals from the Min-ing Courts. This course was not successful in restoring British Columbians' faith in the administration of the law. The fault was not

Begbie's, however. A less outspoken Supreme Court judge might have succeeded in blunting the sharpest barbs, but no one could have bridged the gulf between the different meanings of law created by the colony's geography.

In late April 1864, the Grouse Creek Bedrock Flume Company, a Victoria-based joint stock company, applied to Peter O'Reilly, Richfield's Assistant Gold Commissioner, for the rights to a certain portion of land on Grouse Creek. O'Reilly granted the company title for ten years provided they fulfilled the usual conditions of occupation, licensing, and recording of the claim as outlined in the Gold Fields Act. During 1864 and all of 1865 the "Flumites," as they came to be known, developed their claim, investing $20 000 to $30 000; but in late 1866 the company ran out of money, and their claim was left unoccupied from September to November. During this time—on 8 October—the Canadian Company, a locally based association of free miners, entered the Flume Company's claim, and finding it apparently abandoned, applied for rights to it. Warner Spalding, who had replaced Peter O'Reilly as interim Assistant Gold Commissioner, duly recorded the ground in the Canadian Company's name. At the beginning of the next mining season, in March, the Flumites renegotiated their lease to the Grouse Creek claim with the Crown, managing to extricate themselves from all previous conditions regulating their occupation of the ground. Inexplicably, Spalding, who had just six months earlier granted the same piece of land to the Canadian Company, presided over this renegotiation on behalf of the Crown! It was only a matter of weeks before the two companies clashed, and the dispute was taken to the district's Mining Court, again to be heard before Spalding.[28] There Spalding ruled in favour of the plaintiffs, and ordered the Canadians off the disputed ground.[29] The Canadians gave notice of appeal, but obeyed the Commissioner's order.

Though the Canadians left quietly, they were back on Grouse Creek in a month. At the end of May, Anthony Melloday and three other Canadian Company members commenced work on the Grouse Creek Flume Company's claim. This time, however, the Flumites took their complaint to the Magistrate's Court, laying criminal charges of trespass against the Canadians. The foreman, Melloday, received the heaviest sentence: one month's imprisonment The others were sentenced to 7 and 14 days.[30] [. . .]

At the beginning of July Begbie informed the two companies that he would not, in keeping with the newly amended Gold Fields Act, hear the appeal. [. . .] Undeterred, the Canadians regrouped, and now 30 or 40 strong, they again returned to Grouse Creek. Three constables and one surveyor were dispatched to eject the Canadians, but were prevented from doing so when the company's men "surrounded [them] . . . without showing any hostile disposition, or making any threats of violence, but simply claiming that as they all acted as one man, if any one was liable to arrest they all were. . . . "[31] The constables left.

Local sentiment seemed to be very much on the side of the Canadians, particularly in light of Begbie's refusal to hear their appeal—a situation that was doubly ironic, given that local sentiment, and notably the pressure of the Canadian Company's principals, John MacLaren and Cornelius Booth, had led to the 1867 amendment! Writing on behalf of the members of the Canadian Company, Booth insisted they were not "acting in opposition to the law of the land." Since they could not appeal, they were more than willing to force a new case.[32] [. . .] Booth told the same thing to a public meeting of 500 people gathered to hear "a full and truthful statement of the grievances and position of the Canadian Company." The sympathetic crowd passed a resolution recording their sympathy with the Canadians and their commitment to aid the company "by all lawful means to obtain their rights."[33]

The good will manifested toward the Canadians made itself apparent the next day, when the district's magistrate proceeded to Grouse Creek, backed this time by 25 or 30 of "the most prominent businessmen, and respectable citizens of this town" who had answered court summonses to act as special constables. Once there, the "posse comitatus" exchanged "the most friendly greetings" with the Canadians and the nearly 400 eager on-lookers who had "splashed through mud and mire, knee-deep, in haste to reach the rendezvous." All settled in for a long and what must have been anti-climactic afternoon of negotiation by letter between the two companies. In the end, with no hope of settlement, the magistrate read a writ of injunction to the Canadian Company and asked them to leave the claim. "[A] unanimous NO was returned, whereupon Mr. Ball, along with his constables, left Williams Creek, and the crowd dispersed."[34] The magistrate immediately telegraphed the governor, requesting that a detachment of marines be sent to assist him.[35] The Royal Navy refused to intervene, and Seymour, "at very considerable inconvenience to myself proceeded . . . to Cariboo."[36]

It was this stalemate that greeted the governor when he arrived in Richfield a few weeks later, on 7 August. Seymour, along with the rest of the colony, had been treated to a series of alarmist reports of "mob law" on Williams Creek from the *British Colonist* and the *British Columbian*, and no doubt expected the worst. "In our most important gold field the arm of justice hangs powerlessly by her side, while a company of men, under the most hollow and hypocritical professions of a desire to respect the law are wantonly and openly trampling it underfoot," screamed the *Columbian*:

It is simply a question of British Law vs. Lynch Law. . . . [with reference to Governor Seymour's visit] To go to the scene of strife unarmed with a force to *compel* submission will simply to be to toy with outlawry while the coveted treasure is being grabbed up.[37]

Calling for the imposition of "martial law," the *Colonist* noted that "by offering armed resistance to the mandate of a court" the Canadians were "criminals" who "went into court determined to obey the law if it was *with* them; [and] to break it if it was *against* them."[38] The *Cariboo Sentinel* took issue with its competitors' treatment of the Grouse Creek "War." "Victorians," the *Sentinel* speculated, "no doubt wrought up to the highest pitch of excitement by the graphic descriptions of the warlike attitude of the Canadians, would be surprised if they were here."

Canadians and Flumites may be seen daily in the streets of Barkerville, habited in the usual miners' garb, saluting each other without the slightest appearance of hostility.[39]

The *Sentinel's* attempts to emphasize the peacefulness of the Cariboo were not aided by the events which followed, however.

A few days after Governor Seymour's arrival, the Canadian Company strode into Richfield, not, noted one anonymous writer "in obedience to any order or summons," but at the suggestion of their leader, Cornelius Booth. Though Booth—the "Talleyrand of the band"—assured his compatriots they would not be arrested, seven of their number were. Conveyed immediately to the courthouse, the seven received three-month sentences for resisting arrest (stemming from Magistrate Ball's earlier attempt to eject the Canadians from Grouse Creek); however, with the exception of one man, all refused to go to jail. Instead, they "warned the constables not to touch any of them, and abused and black-guarded the Commissioner on the Bench!"[40] The seven told the court "that if they had treated the Commissioner to more champagne &c. they would have won their case."[41] Ball left the courtroom, and the governor requested a parley with Booth. After extracting a promise from Seymour to commute the sentences to 48 hours' imprisonment, Booth "*persuaded* his comrades to walk towards the gaol, promising them that they would not be confined three days!"[42] This concession to the form of law was continued once the redoubtable Canadians arrived at the Richfield jail. There, wrote "Crimea," "they would not allow the doors of the jail to be locked upon them and had free access to all the Court house grounds during the term of their imprisonment."[43] [. . .]

When Seymour left Richfield, he left behind conflicting impressions of what he accomplished. The Canadian Company believed they had secured a promise for a new trial, while the *Colonist* and the *Columbian* were convinced that Seymour had merely offered the services of Joseph Trutch, the Chief Commissioner of Lands and Works, as arbitrator. Added to this confusion was yet another round of vitriolic newspaper reports from Victoria, condemning the governor's actions. Claiming that Governor Seymour's negotiation legitimized the actions of the Canadian "mob," the *Colonist* predicted an end to the "security of life and property in the country."[44] The Canadians rejected arbitration, insisting that they would "accept nothing less than the law allows them": a new trial.[45] [. . .]

Seymour then appointed Joseph Needham, Vancouver Island's Supreme Court judge, as arbitrator. Needham arrived in Richfield in mid-September, prepared to try the Grouse Creek case (as well as other mining appeals) *de novo*.[46] Noting that every court had the power to suspend its rules if "any technicality arises that might tend to defeat the ends of justice," the judge began hearing evidence in the *Canadian Company v. the Grouse Creek Flume Company* on 17 September. After two weeks of testimony, Needham awarded all of the disputed ground to the Flumites. "I cannot be blind to the fact that much public excitement has existed with regard to this case," he told the court,

> but I do hope and believe that all will acquiesce in the decision of this court; I

can only say that it has been arrived at after anxious consideration, and a simple desire to administer justice according to the law. I hope, and firmly believe, that armed alone with the authority of the law, a child may execute this judgment, and that no one will here be found whose wish is not to uphold and obey the judicial tribunals of this country—tribunals which have always been regarded by Englishmen as the fountain of justice, and the bulwark of freedom.[47]

With this plea for peace, Needham ended one of the most protracted disputes in the colony's short history, and one which was noted for the bitterness engendered between island and mainland as much as for that between the rival mining factions. It also ended Begbie's stormy tenure as mining appeal court judge. After 1867 the "tyrant Judge" heard few mining cases, leaving them to his less controversial colleagues.[48]

* * *

These three cases have been discussed before by David Williams, who called them "*causes célèbres.*"[49] They were certainly that, and more, for *Aurora, Borealis,* and *Grouse Creek* illustrate the difficulty of, in Joseph Needham's words, "administering justice according to the law." The Supreme Court judge's distinction is an important one. While the Canadians and the Flumites were of one voice as to the ends of the law and the process of dispute resolution, they disagreed on how best to secure justice through the law. This was because of the variety of meanings the law in a colony as loosely organized as British Columbia. Their various definitions of the law revealed the importance of geography in determining its contours, as well as showing the limits of authority.

Despite their differences, Flumites and Canadians used the same language of laissez-faire capitalism, which linked liberty to the security of property, to frame criticisms

and to justify their actions. The New Westminster *Columbian* and the Victoria *Colonist*
contrasted "British Law" with the Canadians'
"mob rule," and predicted an end to "that
security of life and property in the country
which has ever been our proud boast."

> Capital, finding its tenure insecure, will
> fly to countries where people are made to
> respect the laws, and where possession
> of property rests upon a more stable and
> secure foundation.[50]

At the same time, the Canadian Company,
that "mob" of "footpads" and "filibusters,"
used the very same language of law and
property to predict the same ends if *its* demands were not met. "There are three things
the most despotic governments claim," Cornelius Booth told a crowd of 500 gathered
at Fulton's saloon, "namely the right to take
property, liberty and life."

> The first of these have already been
> taken from the Canadian Co., and there
> is but one step to the last. I repeat that
> these men do not wish to be looked
> upon as outlaws; they consider they have
> been unjustly shut out from having a
> hearing; and would be perfectly satisfied
> in obtaining one, even if a decision was
> given against them.[51]

The crowd agreed, as they had done in the
wake of the *Borealis v. Watson* and the *Aurora
v. Davis* cases, when they informed the colonial government that its laws and Begbie's
administration of them were driving "labor,
capital and enterprise out of the Colony."[52]
To British Columbians on both sides of the
Grouse Creek War, as well as the mining disputes that preceded it, just laws and legitimate authority were defined by their positive
effect on economic development. Begbie's
Chancery Court was viewed with contempt
not only because the laws of chancery appeared capricious, but also, and perhaps

more importantly, because of the costly delays associated with its proceedings. Jury
trials could not guarantee satisfaction either,
as *Aurora v. Davis* showed. Recourse to a jury
trial was a poor alternative to Chancery because verdicts could be set aside by an "arbitrary" judge. The "tyranny" of Begbie's court
lay in its unpredictability and inefficiency—
the two enemies of capitalist enterprise.

Just as they used the same language and
agreed on the ends that the law served, British Columbians on both sides of the Grouse
Creek war recognized the same process of
dispute resolution. The ends sought by those
who opposed the government's administration were always to be achieved with the
existing structures of formal dispute settlement. In *Borealis v. Watson*, Caribooites criticized the use of the Court of Chancery to
resolve mining appeals because its ponder-
ous proceedings were singularly unsuited
to mining activity. But what did the miners
propose as a solution? The establishment of a
Court of Appeal! Similarly, in *Aurora v. Davis*
arbitration was rejected in favour of trial
by jury. And in the Grouse Creek war, the
Canadian Company did not ask for public
sanction of extralegal action (in fact, it did
not consider that it was acting in an illegal
manner), but for "*nothing less than the law allows us*": a full hearing of its case.[53] Indeed,
as David Williams noted, both Cornelius
Booth and John MacLaren visited Begbie in
early July 1867 to ask for his intervention—
surely an indication they had not lost faith in
the legal options available.[54] Even after seven
company members were arrested in August,
the Canadians still demanded that the "tyrant Judge" or his island counterpart replace
Joseph Trutch as arbitrator.[55] Clearly, those
who took issue with British Columbia's legal
administration did not reject the structures
of dispute resolution; rather it was to the official framework of English institutions that
they looked for relief. In fact, the law might
be seen as a kind of social cement holding
colonists together.

If Caribooites agreed about the ends of the law and the institutional means of executing it, they took issue with what the law was and how to achieve justice through that law. British Columbians in other parts of the colony considered that a body of rules applied evenly and predictably ensured justice. Reflecting on the *Borealis* and *Aurora* cases, the *Colonist* pointed to Begbie's lack of legal experience as the cause of the trouble. "Unlike Judge Needham," the newspaper reported, Begbie "had no legal experience to recommend him, and it is by no means a matter of surprise that his decisions instead of partaking of that judicial clearness and point which are the universal characteristics of the decisions of English judges, should be generally rambling, disconnected and irrelevant."[56] Nevertheless, both the *Sentinel* and the Canadians dismissed the Chief Commissioner of Lands and Works, Joseph Trutch, as a suitable adjudicator for the same reasons and called for the intervention of the Supreme Court: "He [Trutch] lacks the legal acumen which is necessary to unravel those knotted points of law that are inseparably involved in the settlement of the dispute in question." [. . .][57] "Legal acumen" was not necessarily specialized knowledge, however. The valued acumen was a knowledge of community standards and local circumstance: what Caribooites wanted was law that was self-evident.

In the wake of *Aurora* and *Borealis*, Caribooites let it be known that "common sense" was the chief hallmark of just laws and just administration. The *Cariboo Sentinel* published a telling editorial emphasizing just this point by contrasting the conduct of Peter O'Reilly (the previous magistrate) with that of his predecessors and his successor, William Cox. Prior to O'Reilly's arrival, the mining court "was virtually, if not nominally, a Court of Conscience."

Then the mining laws consisted of only a few proclamations issued from time to time by the Governor, and the Commissioner supplemented these with his own judgment. Since then extensive mining laws have been passed and partially consolidated. It was not until the administration of Mr. O'Reilly that this Court, by his false pretensions to legal ability, declared itself to be a Court of Equity or Law, or both combined . . . . The policy of Mr. Cox, on the other hand, was quite different: he made no pretensions to legal ability, yet his policy was at once most agreeable to the miners; he converted this Court back once again almost wholly into a Court of Conscience, and presided in it with no little success.

Cox's success, the *Sentinel* concluded, was due to the fact he was guided by "common sense rather than a smattering of law."[58]

As the *Sentinel's* editorial revealed, common sense was an important yardstick of the law's legitimacy. Sociologists argue that common sense occupies an important place in human interaction.[59] The strength and influence of common sense lies in its "taken-for-granted" nature. Common sense is common knowledge; it is a body of truths that does not need explanation (and probably cannot be explained) for it is instantly recognized as self-evident.[60] According to sociologist Siegwart Lindenberg, common sense is a "general baseline for human interaction."[61] It is a frame of reference against which humans gauge events and understand the world as well as a "court of appeal."[62] "Common sense," argue van Holthoon and Olson, "provided the basis of appeal . . . to criticize and overthrow a more specialized and restrictive world view."[63] By appealing to a body of self-evident truths, critics attempt to show that the status quo is unnatural and illogical. But the concept could just as easily be used to buttress the existing order of things. Just as often, notes philosopher Herman Parret, "'Use your common sense,' 'Behave commonsensically'—these mean 'Be conventional,' 'Be conservative.' . . . It is used to stop argument, fantasy and originality, and it is often a *deus ex machina*, a rhetorical device to express power."[64] Given the ambiguous nature of common sense, literary critics argue that it is a powerful rhetorical device, "part of 'the formal language of ideological dispute.'"[65]

Although common sense implied a commonality of experience that cut across political, social, and economic divisions—indeed, this is part of its strength—it was rooted in a cultural and social matrix particular to a time and place. Concepts of common sense were tied to particular locales; they were, as anthropologist Clifford Geertz contended, part of "local knowledge."[66] As such, "the law . . . is not a bounded set of norms, rules, principles and values . . . but part of a distinctive manner of imagining the real."[67] Thus, when Caribooites appealed to common sense in criticizing the colonial legal administration, their meaning was clear only within their frame of reference. They wanted the law to be self-evident; however, what was common knowledge varied from place to place. Common sense dictated what was just, but because it was bounded by space and by local experience with the law, the concept had different meanings for different people. British Columbia's great distances, thin population, and poor systems of communication accentuated the localism of the colony's mining population. The mainland lacked an internal coherence that would have narrowed the variations in common sense. Its communities were uncoupled from each other, as well as the administrative centres of New Westminster and Victoria.[68] In such a geographical context a variety of concepts of law proliferated; the historian's task is to recreate that milieu so that others can appreciate it as "commonsensical."

The *Caribou Sentinel's* opposition of common sense and conscience on one hand, and law and equity on the other is important. A Court of Equity was another name for a Court of Chancery—not the miners' favourite legal institution, as Borealis showed. Initially, cases tried by equity courts had been resolved by applying the "standards of what seems naturally just or right, as contrasted with the application . . . of a rule of law, which might not provide for such circumstances or provide for what seems unreasonable."[69] By the early nineteenth century, however, the principles of equity had become a body of settled law rather than a personal and arbitrary assessment of fairness.[70] Ironically, though equitable jurisdiction evolved as a corrective to the inflexibility of the law, the Court of Chancery acquired a reputation as a morass of legal complexity and delay into which unwitting suitors could fall and never gain a settlement. When Caribooites equated Peter O'Reilly's tenure as Magistrate and Assistant Gold Commissioner with a "Court of Equity or Law," and contrasted it with Cox's "common sense," they revealed that they considered the two kinds of knowledge to be antithetical. The complexities of equity and statute law were far from self-evident truths; in fact, they were "pretensions" that caused unnecessary delays and thwarted justice. Cox's common sense cut through all this. He circumvented legal technicalities by letting "conscience" guide his decisions. In the eyes of Caribooites, Cox's "court of conscience" was the surest route to justice. Yet courts of conscience were, in legal parlance, merely another name for courts of equity or chancery![71] Why was Cox's "conscience"—his ability to apply "standards of what seems naturally just or right"—superior to Begbie's? Why, in short, was the magistrate's common sense superior to that of the Supreme Court judge?

Caribooites recognized the magistrate's decisions and actions as expressions of common sense because he was part of their community. Common sense was bounded by locale and rooted in specific constellations of social relations. Keith Wrightson shows that magistrates, constables, and jurymen were caught between "different kinds of order" in which the execution of the law had to be balanced against the more tangible pressures of familiarity in the face-to-face communities of seventeenth-century England.[72] Nineteenth-century British Columbia demonstrates the same pattern. Because the colony's magistrates were a part of the communities they administered, they quickly became enmeshed in the politics of familiarity, a situation that both aided and limited their ability to execute the law. William Cox's knowledge of miners and mining won him the admiration and support of 490 of his neighbours, who petitioned against his removal in 1866. "From the very long acquaintance we have had with Mr. Cox, and the intimate knowledge he has acquired of mining in Cariboo, we consider him much better qualified for the office than any other gentleman in this Colony"; they wrote. "Mr. Cox's conduct . . . has been such as to inspire the public with the utmost confidence in his integrity, . . . while his judicial decisions have had the effect of checking litigation."[73] These judicial decisions were often unconventional: On one occasion the magistrate settled a mining court claim by making the opposing parties race from the steps of the Richfield Court House to the disputed ground—winner take all. On another occasion Cox swore in Chinese witnesses by decapitating a chicken instead of administering the usual and less spectacular oath.[74]

Cox's "intimate knowledge" consisted of a proper understanding of community morals, and it was this empathy that underlay justice in the Cariboo. Community sentiment about what was right and wrong made it impossible to keep the Canadian Company under lock and key. Henry Maynard Ball, whose misfortune it was to preside over the Grouse Creek dispute, failed because "he had but little experience in the mining districts."[75] Familiarity also limited the ineffectiveness of enforcement. For the most part, policing was done by special constables, sworn in from the local population as the need arose. In the Grouse Creek case the special constables,

who as men of capital and business presumably stood to lose from the unrest, were of no use in ejecting their neighbours; nor could the district's jailer incarcerate the Canadians. "The public feeling was rather in favour of the Canadians," complained Frederick Seymour. "At all events no one would come forward to assist the Government in an emergency."[76]

Despite the constraints of familiarity on the execution of the law, British Columbians would have it no other way. The interventions of outsiders in their affairs were considered despotic, even when that intervention was done by a figure as magisterial as a Supreme Court judge. In this context, juries became an important bridge between law and justice. "[T]his community," reported the Richfield Grand Jury,

> owing to its isolated position, the peculiarity of its interests, and especially its national origin, has a decided preference for local trial by jury, and is extremely jealous of all verdicts by its peers. . . .[77]

The *Cariboo Sentinel* was even more direct, asserting that "a man is wrong when almost every person in the community thinks and says he is wrong."[78] When Begbie overturned the jury verdict in *Aurora v. Davis*, he not only breached what Caribooites perceived to be established practice, he also burned the only bridge between the law as a set of overarching rules and as a set of social and locally constructed norms. The judge's cavalier treatment of the jury in this and other cases led many colonists to conclude that Begbie did not consider them qualified to pass judgment on their peers. What these British Columbians objected to was not so much Begbie's failure to adhere to statute law and common law practice as the fact that he was not guided by the same self-evident truths as they were. He could not have been. The Supreme Court judge was outside their community: He resided in Victoria, visiting the colony's far-flung communities only once a year. His circuits were metaphors for his status as an outsider. Begbie's actions and decisions appeared arbitrary, particularly in a colony that lacked the social organization that would support the arbitrariness of paternal authority. Because his decisions were not necessarily commonsensical and because of the important role the law played in establishing some cohesion in the colony, Begbie's actions and decisions not only threatened the colonists' economic security but also eroded one of the few bonds tying them together.

Caribooites also considered the Grouse Creek Flume Company an outsider. Not only were the Flumites based in Victoria, headed by one of the city's largest merchants, but they also represented "big capital'" in a region where small, independent entrepreneurs were the norm.[79] The Canadians styled themselves a "company," but their Victoria opponents were the real thing. The Grouse Creek Flume Company was a joint stock venture, capitalized to the tune of $50 000. The Flumites were harbingers of a different kind of resource entrepreneur in British Columbia. By the late 1860s, most of the easily accessible surface gold in the Cariboo was gone. Continued success on the upper country creeks depended on a hydraulic process which required a substantial capital investment to construct the necessary flumes. Such an investment was beyond the means of most independent miners. Part of the support for the Canadians and the wrath directed at Begbie likely stemmed from an antipathy toward this form of large corporate enterprise that would eventually dominate resource exploitation and push out the smaller upper country operations.

Conflicting concepts of law were central to the controversies surrounding the administration of British Columbia's mining laws in the colonial period. While recent writing in Canadian legal history has cast a critical eye on the law, revealing its normative nature, few studies deal with the variety of meanings the law could take on.[80] As I have discussed, despite its detached nature, the law gained much of its meaning through the very local experiences people had with it. [. . .]

The Grouse Creek War and the events leading to it demonstrate the importance of geography in creating "local frames of awareness" that shape social meaning.[81] The law Caribooites wanted had to be self-evident; it had to be commonsensical. Because common sense was *local* knowledge, however, its meaning was spatially limited. This localism was accentuated by the colony's geography, which effectively precluded the integration of the archipelago of small settlements that was British Columbia. Geographers and sociologists have recognized that space is deeply implicated in social life.[82] Because human relations and the extension of authority are spatially as well as socially constructed, understanding what the law means involves more than contextualizing behaviour in time. Distant places like the Cariboo were uncoupled from New Westminster and Victoria, the colony's centres of authority.[83] In this spatial context, law and authority were rooted in specific and local constellations of social relations. For Caribooites, the law was more a collection of community norms than a set of hard-and-fast rules. Face-to-face relations, the politics of the personal and personality loomed large in determining authority. Being recognized as an authority conveyed more power in these localized settings than being *in* authority by virtue of some extra-community sanction.[84]

Although I have put local knowledge at the crux of understanding behaviour, local frames of reference were not the only ones that influenced the meaning of law. On Grouse Creek, common sense may have gone a long way to shape what the law meant to British Columbians, but clearly the larger framework provided by the structure, institutions, and traditions of the common law itself also played an important role.[85] Magistrate William Cox's decisions may have been commonsensical, but he and those who came before him still operated within a set of rules and procedures that at least nominally constrained action and provided a standard for measuring legality. As I discussed, British Columbians on both sides of the Grouse Creek War and the disputes that led to it never challenged the authority of the law and its institutions; instead, they took issue with their administration and looked to the existing forms of law for redress. Perhaps more important in shaping the social meaning of the law than its forms were its traditions and the expectations they created. The "rule of law" promised freedom from the dictates of arbitrary sovereigns for all, no matter their condition. The idea of the rule of law became intimately tied to the security of life and property, and became the keystone of English liberty. For British colonists, the law was an important source of unity, particularly in the years immediately following settlement. Though differences brought them before a magistrate, the British Columbians who resorted to the law were tied together in a common adversarial process that imposed a degree of structure, organization, and predictability on social relationships in a colony where such characteristics were rare commodities. More broadly, both for those directly involved in litigation and for those who perhaps afterwards discussed and criticized its administration, the law was a link to and a symbol of a common, storied, and secure past that stood in marked contrast to the new and alien environment they found themselves in. The common law conferred citizenship to colonists whose sense of place had been eroded by the experience of migration. Much of the social meaning of the law, then, was provided by the forms and traditions of the law itself—forms and traditions which had their genesis outside the locale that has been the focus of my analysis.

Although they were physically distant from the main centres of population, as well as from the rest of British North America, Caribooites were tied to another frame of reference through extensive webs of credit: the wider world of commercial capitalism. So dominant was economic activity in the collective experience of the colony that the language of laissez-faire infused British Columbians' discussions of the law and provided the standard with which they measured political authority. Begbie's actions and decisions provoked the reactions they did because they were the antithesis of what commercial capitalist enterprise demanded and defined as the criteria for legitimate action: efficiency, predictability, and standardization.

Though British Columbians on both sides of the mining disputes demanded these characteristics of the law and conceived of it as an instrument of economic development, there was room for a diversity of opinion because of the spatial context in which the law was administered. Divergent concepts of law became apparent only when the localism of the colony was penetrated by the annual circuits of British Columbia's Supreme Court. Begbie and the Supreme Court represented a different level of law and a different level of social interaction. To Caribooites, the Supreme Court judge was an outsider; his reasoning and decisions were not self-evident because he operated in a world outside the community of local interaction. To be effective, Begbie and his fellow magistrates had to balance the demands of colonial administration with local sentiment. With these conflicting demands, "administering justice according to the law" was a difficult, and sometimes impossible, task. This was Gaggin's "delicate game," and it was one that would be played over and over again amid the western mountains.

NOTES

1. Gaggin to the Colonial Secretary, Douglas, BC, 2 July 1862. British Columbia Archives and Records Services (hereafter BCARS), Colonial Correspondence, GR 1372, reel B-1330, file 621/14. For more on this episode and Gaggin, see Dorothy Blakey Smith, "'Poor Gaggin': Irish Misfit in the Colonial Service," *BC Studies* 32 (Winter 1976–7): 41–63.

2. Ibid.

3. Cited in Smith, "'Poor Gaggin,'" 45.

4. Ibid., 47.

5. For instance, see Clifford Geertz, "Local Knowledge: Fact and Law in Comparative Perspective," in his *Local Knowledge: Further Essays in Interpretive Anthropology* (New York, 1983); John L. Comaroff and Simon Roberts, *Rules and Processes: The Cultural Logic of Dispute in an African Context* (Chicago, 1981); Lawrence Rosen, *Bargaining for Reality: The Construction of Social Relations in a Muslim Community* (Chicago, 1984), and his "Islamic 'Case Law' and the Logic of Consequence," in June Starr and Jane F. Collier, eds, *History and Power in the Study of Law: New Directions in Legal Anthropology* (Ithaca, NY, 1989), 302–19. In the latter essay, Rosen notes "Law is . . . one domain in which a culture may reveal itself. But like politics, marriage, and exchange, it is an arena in which people must act, and in doing so they must draw on their assumptions, connections, and beliefs to make their acts effective and comprehensible. In the Islamic world, as in many other places, the world of formal courts offers a stage—as intense as ritual, as demonstrative as war—through which a society reveals itself to its own people as much as to the outside world" [318]. This essay shares Rosen's assumptions about the law and what it can reveal about society.

6. See Hubert Howe Bancroft, *Popular Tribunals* (San Francisco, 1887), v. 1, Chapter Ten; Charles Shinn, *Mining Camps: A Study in American Frontier Government* (New York: 1885); and on California and British Columbia, David Ricardo Williams, "The Administration of Civil and Criminal Justice in the Mining Camps and Frontier Communities of British Columbia," in Louis Knafla, ed., *Law and Justice in a New Land: Essays in Western Canadian Legal History* (Calgary, 1986).

7. Williams, 217–9.

8. See Shinn, Introduction.

9. Morley Arthur Underwood, "Governor Douglas and the Miners, 1858–1859," University of British Columbia, BA essay, 1974.

10. *The Gold Fields Act, 1859* [31 August 1859]; William J. Trimble, *The Mining Advance into the Inland Empire* (Madison, Wisconsin, 1914), 187–214, 336–7.

11. Rules and Regulations for the Working of Gold Mines under the "Gold Fields Act 1859" [7 September 1859]; Rules and Regulations for the Working of Gold Mines, issued in conformity with the "Gold Fields Act, 1859" (Bench Diggings) [6 January 1860]; Rules and Regulations under the "Gold Fields Act, 1859" (Ditches) [29 September 1862]; Further Rules and Regulations under the "Gold Fields Act, 1859" [24 February 1863]; Proclamation amending the "Gold Fields Act, 1859" [25 March 1863]; The Mining District Act, 1863 [27 May 1863]; The Mining Drains Act, 1864 [1 February 1864]; An Ordinance to extend and improve the Laws relating to Gold Mining [26 February 1864] and An Ordinance to amend and consolidate the Gold Mining Laws [28 March 1865]; An Ordinance to amend the Laws relating to Gold Mining, 2 April 1867.

12. On this theme, and more generally, the idea that mining society was not as disorganized as traditionally thought, see Thomas Stone, *Miners' Justice: Migration, Law and Order on the Alaska-Yukon Frontier, 1873–1902* (New York, 1988).

13. Williams discusses them in " . . . *The Man for a New Country": Sir Matthew Baillie Begbie* (Sidney, BC, 1977), 68–80.

14. Ibid.

15. A Court of Chancery is a court that has jurisdiction in equity; that is, it resolves disputes according to the rules and procedures of equity rather than the rules and procedures of common law. Though the principles of equity initially reflected the chancellor's own arbitrary and sometimes idiosyncratic ideas of justice (the Tudor Court of Star Chamber was the repository and dispensary of equity, for

instance), over the seventeenth, eighteenth, and early nineteenth centuries the principles of equity evolved into a more settled body of rules. Chancery never lost its negative reputation for arbitrary, protracted, and unnecessarily complex proceedings, however (see Charles Dickens' *Bleak House* [1859], for instance). Until 1870, Matthew Baillie Begbie was British Columbia's only Supreme Court judge. This meant that the division of labour in the colony's superior court was one in name only. Begbie acted as judge in assize, nisi prius, appeal, chancery, bankruptcy, probate, and admiralty cases, often in the same session.

16. Letter from "Miner," *Cariboo Sentinel*, 31 May 1866.

17. "The British Columbia Judiciary," *British Colonist*, reprinted in *Cariboo Sentinel*, 2 July 1866.

18. "Irresponsible Deputies," *Cariboo Sentinel*, 31 May 1866.

19. Ibid.

20. "Supreme Court," *Cariboo Sentinel*, 18 June 1866.

21. Ibid.

22. *Cariboo Sentinel*, 21 June 1866.

23. Ibid.

24. "Mass Meeting," *Cariboo Sentinel*, 25 June 1866.

25. Ibid. Also see "The Tyrant Judge," *British Colonist*, 28 June 1866; "Another Verdict Set Aside," and "From Cariboo," *British Columbian*, 27 June and 4 July 1866.

26. An Ordinance to amend the Laws relating to Gold Mining [2 April 1867].

27. Nind to O'Reilly, Yahwalpa, Pimpama, Brisbane, Queensland, 11 April 1868. O'Reilly Family Papers. BCARS. Add. MSS. 412, v. 1, file 6a.

28. *Canadian Company v. Grouse Creek Flume Co., Ltd.*, 27 September 1867. Archer Martin, *Reports of Mining Cases decided by the Courts of British Columbia and the Courts of Appeal therefrom to the 1st of October, 1902. . . .* (Toronto, 1903), 3–8.

29. "Magistrate's Court," *Cariboo Sentinel*, 3 June 1867. Spalding heard the case on 22 April 1867, and the order ejecting the Canadian Company was issued on 24 April.

30. Ibid.

31. "Grouse Creek Difficulty," *Cariboo Sentinel*, 15 July 1867.

32. Letter to the Editor from C. Booth, dated 13 July 1867. *Cariboo Sentinel*, 15 July 1867.

33. "Public Meeting," Cariboo Sentinel, 15 July 1989.

34. "Grouse Creek Troubles—Great Excitement," *Cariboo Sentinel*, 18 July 1867.

35. Seymour to Buckingham and Chandos, New Westminster, 16 August 1867. CO 60/28. National Archives of Canada (hereafter NAC). MG 11, reel B-97, 333.

36. Ibid.

37. "The Situation," *British Columbian*, 27 July 1867.

38. "The Grouse Greek Difficulty," *British Colonist*, 24 July 1867.

39. "The Governor and the Grouse Creek Difficulty," *Cariboo Sentinel*, 12 August 1867.

40. Anonymous letter to the Editor, dated Williams Creek, 21 August 1867, *British Colonist*, 2 September 1867.

41. Letter to the Editor from "Crimea," dated Richfield, 20 August 1867, *British Colonist*, 9 September 1867.

42. Anonymous letter to the Editor, dated Williams Creek, 21 August 1867, *British Colonist*, 2 September 1867.

43. Letter to the Editor from "Crimea," dated Richfield, 20 August 1867, *British Colonist*, 9 September 1867.

44. "The Grouse Creek War," *British Colonist*, 29 July 1867; also see "The Grouse Creek Imbroglio," 19 August 1867, and "The Patched Up Peace on Grouse Creek," 23 August 1867.

45. Resolution passed by the Canadian Company, at Booth's Saloon, Grouse Creek, 30 August 1867. Reprinted in "Grouse Creek Dispute Again," *Cariboo Sentinel*, 2 September 1867.

46. *Cariboo Sentinel*, 16 September 1867.

47. *Canadian Company v. Grouse Creek Flume Co., Ltd.*, 27 September 1867. Martin, *Reports of Mining Cases. . . .*, 8.

48. "Tyrant Judge" from "The Tyrant Judge," *British Colonist*, 28 June 1866. For Begbie and mining cases after 1867, see Williams, " . . . *The Man for a New Country,*" 80.

49. Williams, " . . . *The Man for a New Country,*" 68.

50. "The Grouse Creek 'War,'" *British Colonist*, 29 July 1867.

51. "Public Meeting," *Cariboo Sentinel*, 15 July 1867.

52. "Mass Meeting," *Cariboo Sentinel*, 25 June 1866.

53. Emphasis added. Resolution passed at a meeting of the members of the Canadian Mining Company, convened at Booth's Saloon, Grouse Greek, on the evening of the 30th August 1867. "Grouse Creek Dispute Again," *Cariboo Sentinel*, 2 September 1867.

54. Williams, ". . . *The Man for a New Country,"* 76.

55. Letter to the Editor from Cornelius Booth, dated 31 August 1867, *Cariboo Sentinel*, 2 September 1867.

56. "British Columbia's Judiciary," *British Colonist*, reprinted in the *Cariboo Sentinel*, 2 July 1866.

57. "The Grouse Creek Dispute Again," *Cariboo Sentinel*, 2 September 1867.

58. "The Administration of the Mining Laws," *Cariboo Sentinel*, 15 December 1866.

59. Frits van Holthoon and David R. Olson, eds, "Introduction," *Common Sense: The Foundations for Social Sciences* (Lanham, MD, 1987); Thomas Luckmann, "Some Thoughts on Common Sense and Science," in van Holthoon and Olson, eds, 179–98; Siegwart Lindenberg, "Common Sense and Social Structure: A Sociological View," in van Holthoon and Olson, eds, 199–216.

60. Van Holthoon and Olson, "Introduction," 3–4.

61. Lindenberg, "Common Sense and Social Structure," 202–3.

62. Ibid.; "court of appeal" from van Holthoon and Olson, "Introduction," 3.

63. Van Holthoon and Olson, "Introduction," 3.

64. Herman Parret, "Common Sense: From Certainty to Happiness," in van Holthoon and Olson, eds, 19.

65. Van Holthoon and Olson, eds, "Introduction," 8.

66. Clifford Geertz, "Local Knowledge."

67. Ibid., 173.

68. Anthony Giddens discusses the influence of space on the integration of societies. The key to integration is the extension or the "stretching" of experience over time and space (something he calls "time–space distanciation"). When people do not share common understandings of time and space the communities they live in become "uncoupled" from each other and from the central administrative state, thus posing problems for the exercise of power (i.e., the regulation of behaviour by the state). See his *A Contemporary Critique of Historical Materialism* (Oxford, 1981), 65–7.

69. David M. Walker, "Equity," *The Oxford Companion to the Law* (Oxford, 1980), 424.

70. Ibid., "Chancery," 204.

71. On courts of chancery and conscience, David Walker notes, "The Court of Chancery was sometimes referred to as a court of conscience because its jurisdiction was originally founded on relief granted by the Chancellor, as Keeper of the King's Conscience, in circumstances where equity and justice demanded it." See his *Oxford Companion to the Law*, 272.

72. Wrightson, "Two Concepts of Order: justices, constables, and jurymen in seventeenth-century England," in John Brewer and John Styles, eds, *An Ungovernable People: the English and their Law in the Seventeenth and Eighteenth Centuries* (London, 1980).

73. Petition dated Williams Creek, BC, 3 November 1866. Colonial Correspondence. BCARS. GR 1372, reel B-1355, f 1352.

74. Both examples from Margaret Ormsby, *British Columbia: A History* (Toronto, 1958), 181.

75. Seymour to Buckingham and Chandos, New Westminster, 12 May 1868. CO 60/32. NAC. MG 11, reel B-100, 368.

76. Seymour to Buckingham and Chandos, Victoria, 4 September 1867. CO 60/29. NAC. MG 11, reel B-97, 5.

77. "From Cariboo," *British Colonist*, 4 July 1866.

78. "The Administration of Justice," *Cariboo Sentinel*, 30 November 866.

79. Selim Franklin was the president of the Grouse Creek Flume Company, and J.P. Cranford was its treasurer.

80. On gender bias, see Constance Backhouse's work, including "Shifting Patterns of Nineteenth-Century Canadian Custody Law," in D.H. Flaherty, ed., *Essays in the History of Canadian Law* (Toronto, 1981), v. 1, 212–48; and "Nineteenth-Century Canadian Rape Law, 1800–1892," in Flaherty, ed., *Essays in the History of Canadian Law* (Toronto, 1984), v. 2, 200–47; on class bias in enforcement, see Michael Katz et. al., *The Social Organization of Early Industrial Capitalism* (Cambridge, MA, 1982), Chapter Six; and Nancy Kay Parker, "The Capillary Level of Power: Methods and Hypotheses for the Study of Law and Society in Late-Nineteenth-Century Victoria, British Columbia," University of Victoria MA thesis (history), 1987.

81. Geertz, *Local Knowledge*, 61; cited in Aletta Biersack, "Local Knowledge, Local History: Geertz and Beyond," in Lynn Hunt, ed., *The New Cultural History* (Berkeley, 1988), 82.

82. According to geographers Jennifer Wolch and Michael Dear, space impinges on social practices in three generalized ways: First, social relations are *constituted* through space; they are *constrained* by space; and they are *mediated* by space. For instance, to understand law and authority we must look at how geography influences the construction of legal institutions (the constitutive role of space); how distance hinders or facilitates the imposition and articulation of law and legal institutions (the constraining role of space); and finally how space facilitates the construction of the social meanings of the law (the mediating role of space). See Michael Dear and Jennifer Wolch, "How Territory Shapes Social Life," in Wolch and Dear, eds, *The Power of Geography: How Territory Shapes Social Life* (Boston, 1989), 9.

83. Giddens, *A Contemporary Critique of Historical Materialism*, 65–6.

84. Stephen Lukes, "Power and Authority," in Tom Bottomore and Robert Nisbet, eds, *A History of Sociological Thought* (New York, 1978).

85. On this theme see Greg Marquis, "Doing Justice to 'British Justice': Law, Ideology and Canadian Historiography," in W. Wesley Pue and Barry Wright, eds, *Canadian Perspectives on Law and Society: Issues in Legal History* (Ottawa, 1988), 43–69.

Chapter 13

The Emergence of Métis Identity

READINGS

Primary Documents

1 From "J. Halkett to Earl Bathurst, 3 June 1818," in *Correspondence in the Years 1817, 1818, and 1819, between Earl Bathurst and J. Halkett, Esq. on the Subject of Lord Selkirk's Settlement at the Red River, in North America*

2 From "Declaration of the People of Rupert's Land and the North West," Fort Garry, December 8, 1869, in *The Collected Writings of Louis Riel*, vol. 1, Raymond Huel, ed.

Historical Interpretations

3 From "Within the Grasp of Company Law: Land, Legitimacy, and the Racialization of the Métis, 1815–1821," Michael Hughes

4 From "Prologue to the Red River Resistance: Pre-liminal Politics and the Triumph of Riel," Gerhard Ens

INTRODUCTION

The Métis in western Canada were, initially at least, the offspring of relationships between fur trade workers and Indigenous women. The dominant characteristic of the earliest of these relationships was that the men tended to be French-speaking, thanks to employment practices in the trade. Over time, however, this early pattern became less dominant—English-speaking men also fathered children, Métis entered into relationships with Indigenous, European, or other Métis people—to the point that there are several possible paths to being Métis today. Ancestry may have assisted in the creation of this distinctive group, but it is not the only element constitutive of this new ethnic identity. After all, many people in the St Lawrence Valley who had Indigenous ancestors never considered themselves or were considered Métis. Kinship networks, economic activities, and cultural factors also played a role in the advent of what came to be known as the "New Nation" in the 1860s.

At various times in Canadian history, especially on the prairies, "mixed-blood" people and their interests have driven events. The primary documents and historical interpretations in this chapter illustrate how the Métis found themselves between First Nations and European-origin societies, connected to each but not belonging wholly to either. To the extent that their presence served the dominant order, they were tolerated, but they tended to be most comfortable in communities of their own, pursuing jobs that could take advantage of their "between-ness." The fur trade had been their genesis, and until the middle of the nineteenth century, it had much to do with the trajectory of Métis life. Halkett's strong denunciation of the Métis as the hired thugs of the North West Company and opponents of Lord Selkirk's colonization scheme at Red River during the later 1810s shows how easily racial animosity and commercial competition could bleed together. The "Declaration of the People of Rupert's Land and the North West" shows how Métis reacted to the Hudson's Bay Company's surrender of Rupert's Land to the Dominion of Canada in 1869. They strongly contested the transfer of what they considered their land and asked to be treated as a "sovereign" people. In his article, Michael Hughes shows how the efforts of the Hudson's Bay Company and the North West Company led to the construction of the Métis as a racialized community as early as the 1820s. Finally, Gerhard Ens provides background to the 1869–70 Resistance, showing how divisions and doubts existed within the Métis community—divisions that were directly related to questions of identity.

QUESTIONS FOR CONSIDERATION

1. What is Halkett's attitude toward the Métis in the Red River region? Why does he hold this attitude?
2. Why did the Métis resent the ways in which their territory was transferred from the Hudson's Bay Company to the Dominion of Canada?
3. Why do you think people were and are so fascinated by racial or ethnic origins?
4. How did the Hudson's Bay Company's and the North West Company's competing versions of events at the Seven Oaks battle contribute to the development of Métis identity?
5. Ens presents us with a picture of Red River society on the eve of the resistance there. Compare and contrast the competing ideals of community that Ens describes.

SUGGESTIONS FOR FURTHER READING

Adams, Christopher, Gregg Dahl, and Ian Peach, eds. *Métis in Canada: History, Identity, Law and Politics*. Edmonton: University of Alberta Press, 2013.

Andersen, Chris. *"Métis": Race, Recognition, and the Struggle for Indigenous Peoplehood*. Vancouver: UBC Press, 2015.

Devine, Heather. *The People Who Own Themselves: Aboriginal Ethnogenesis in a Canadian Family 1660–1900*. Calgary: University of Calgary Press, 2004.

Ens, Gerhard J. *Homeland to Hinterland: The Changing Worlds of the Red River Métis in the Nineteenth Century*. Toronto: University of Toronto Press, 1996.

———and Joe Sawchuk, eds. *From New Peoples to New Nations: Aspects of Métis History and*

Identity from the Eighteenth to the Twenty-First Centuries. Toronto: University of Toronto Press, 2015.

Foran, Timothy P. *Defining Métis: Catholic Missionaries and the Idea of Civilization in Northwestern Saskatchewan, 1845–1898.* Winnipeg: University of Manitoba Press, 2017.

Hogue, Michel. *Métis and the Medicine Line: Creating a Border and Dividing a People.* Regina: University of Regina Press, 2015.

Macdougall, Brenda. *One of the Family: Métis Culture in Nineteenth-Century Northwestern Saskatchewan.* Vancouver: UBC Press, 2010.

Reid, Jennifer. *Louis Riel and the Creation of Modern Canada: Mythic Discourse and the Postcolonial State.* Winnipeg: University of Manitoba Press, 2012.

St-Onge, Nicole. "Uncertain Margins: Métis and Saulteaux Identities in St-Paul des Saulteaux, Red River 1821–1870." *Manitoba History* 53 (October 2006): 2–10.

———, Carolyn Podruchny, and Brenda Macdougall. *Contours of a People: Métis Family, Mobility, and History.* Norman, OK: University of Oklahoma Press, 2014.

Stewart, W. Brian. *The Ermatingers: A 19th Century Ojibwa-Canadian Family.* Vancouver: UBC Press, 2008.

Primary Documents

1 From "J. Halkett to Earl Bathurst, 3 June 1818," in *Correspondence in the Years 1817, 1818, and 1819, between Earl Bathurst and J. Halkett, Esq. on the Subject of Lord Selkirk's Settlement at the Red River, in North America* (London: J. Brettell, 1819), 34–45.

Seymour Place, January 3, 1818.

MY LORD,

I take the liberty of again addressing your Lordship on the subject of the British Colonists at the Red River, in consequence of intelligence recently received from that quarter. The last accounts from the interior of North America communicate the satisfactory information that Lord Selkirk has succeeded in re-establishing the settlers upon the lands from which they had been twice driven by the North-West Company of Montreal.

Having left Fort William as early in the last summer as the state of the river navigation would admit, Lord Selkirk proceeded into the interior, and arrived at the Red River in the month of June. In the preceding winter he had taken measures to enable a small party of the settlers, who had been driven away in

the summer before, to return in safety to the Settlement; and, upon his arrival there, he found that they had again begun to re-establish themselves, and to cultivate the lands which had been assigned to them. Under the circumstances in which they were placed, their agricultural operations were, of course, much circumscribed; and the horses of the Settlement having been carried away, or destroyed, by their opponents, they were prevented from putting so much land into tillage as they otherwise would have done. They had sowed, however, above sixty acres of grain. The crops of the former year had been destroyed by the persons employed by the North-West Company, who, after Mr. Semple and twenty of his people were killed,—the surviving settlers driven away,—and their habitations reduced to ashes—turned their horses loose into the fields of wheat, and other grain, for the purpose of laying them waste. The malicious satisfaction which the Company's adherents felt in thus destroying the promising crops of the Settlement, was, however, somewhat damped by the circumstance of nearly fifty of their horses having died in consequence of the surfeit. The European cattle and sheep, which had been sent to the Settlement, as a breed, were also destroyed by the persons employed by the North-West Company, whose brutality, throughout the whole of these transactions, was such as scarcely to be credited.

A few days after the 19th of June, the day when Mr. Semple and his followers were put to death without quarter by their opponents, Mr. Archibald Norman McLeod the magistrate, one of the Company's principal agents, together with several of his partners, accompanied by a considerable number of the half-breeds who had been engaged in the slaughter of the 19th, rode to the spot, and, having assured these half-breeds that they had done well, the party, with loud shouts and laughter, began to exult over, and even to kick the dead bodies which had remained upon the ground. On the side of the North-West Company, only one person, a half-breed, had fallen. His body was buried, and a paling placed round his grave; but the bodies of the settlers, (with the exception of a few who had been brought away and interred by some native Indians), were all left unburied on the spot, and were afterwards devoured by dogs. In the following spring their bones were collected, and interred by Captain D'Orsonnens, who, at Lord Selkirk's request, had proceeded to the Red River with a party of the new colonists in the preceding winter.

Shortly after Lord Selkirk had arrived at the Settlement, he was joined by a large portion of the remaining settlers who had been driven away in the summer before. Contrary to the expectations of the North-West Company (who had exulted in the idea that these colonists must have been all compelled to go back to Hudson's Bay for the purpose of returning to Europe), they had passed the autumn and winter towards the north end of Lake Winnipic, and at the Saskatchawan. Having heard that Lord Selkirk had arrived in North America, and was proceeding into the interior, they trusted that now they would not be entirely forsaken, and that means would be found to enable them to return with safety to the Red River.

By the latest accounts from that place it appears, that these settlers, together with the new ones who had recently arrived from Canada, (including the discharged men of the De Meuron and Watteville regiments), were establishing themselves, with every reasonable prospect of success. During their route, they had invariably experienced the friendly offices of the Indian population; and the native tribes in the immediate neighbourhood of the Red River, have formally and solemnly declared their intention to support them. With respect to the miserable race termed Metifs, Half-breeds, or Bois-brulés, a band neither in the slightest degree formidable from their numbers, nor their courage, even a large portion of these have now declared that they mean to support the Red River Colony. It cannot, indeed, be expected that such banditti are to be trusted, while within the sphere of the influence and bribes of those who originally hired them to commit acts of aggression against the colony, and afterwards remunerated them for their hostility. But if the North-West Company, by whom they were so employed, can be restrained, by the interference of Government, from again instigating these ignorant and deluded people to renew the outrages against their fellow-subjects, there can be no doubt of the Settlement remaining henceforward secure and undisturbed. Without some adequate interference, however, it can scarcely be expected that the Company's partners in the interior, will be induced to relinquish their endeavours to cause it final destruction. Their rancour towards the colony has, in all probability, increased in proportion to their disappointment, in being twice baffled in their hopes to effect a permanent dispersion of the colonists.

A sufficiency of documents, I should suppose, has been submitted to your Lordship in the course of the last two or three years, fully to satisfy His Majesty's Government, that, from the commencement of the Red River Colony, there existed, on the part of the North-West Company, a determined resolution to destroy it. If that fact be admitted,—and I do not hesitate in asserting, that it is impossible for any person who will investigate the matter with attention, to entertain the slightest doubt on the subject,—every thing which ensued must appear a natural consequence of such determination. If the Company, in following up their resolution, happened not to succeed in their attempts to destroy the Settlement in one way, they were ready to try it in another. They began by endeavouring to instigate the native Indians against the colonists; but in this they completely failed. Their next proceeding—in addition to bribing and seducing a considerable portion of the settlers to desert from the colony, and break their contracts—was to hire, arm, and array their half-breed dependents, and make them, under the personal direction of partners and clerks of the Company, attack the colonists, burn their houses, and drive them by force from the Settlement. And, at the very time they were planning and executing these measures, their agents and principal partners were addressing memorials to Government, in which they boasted of their humanity and kindness towards these people, whom they were thus shamefully oppressing.

I have the honour to be,
My Lord,
Your Lordship's obedient
And humble Servant,
J. HALKETT.

Earl Bathurst,
&c. &c. &c.

2 From "Declaration of the People of Rupert's Land and the North West," Fort Garry, 8 December 1869, in *The Collected Writings of Louis Riel, vol. 1: 1861–1875,* ed. Raymond Huel (Edmonton: The University of Alberta Press, 1985), 42–4.

DECLARATION

Of the People of Rupert's Land and the North West

WHEREAS, it is admitted by all men, as a fundamental principle that the public authority commands the obedience and respect of its subjects. It is also admitted that a people when it has no Government is free to adopt one form of Government in preference to another to give or to refuse aliegance [sic] to that which is proposed. In accordance with the first principle the people of this Country had obeyed and respected that authority to which the circumstances surrounding its infancy compelled it to be subject.

A company of adventurers known as the "Hudson's Bay Company" and invested with certain powers granted by His Majesty (Charles II.) established itself in Rupert's Land, AND IN THE NORTH-WEST TERRITORY for trading purposes only. This Company, consisting of many persons, required a certain constitution. But as there was a question of commerce only, their constitution was framed in reference thereto. Yet, since there was at that time no government to see to the interests of a people already existing in the country, it became necessary for judicial affairs to have recourse to the officers of the Hudson's Bay Company. Thus inaugurated that species of government, which, slightly modified by subsequent circumstances, ruled this country up to a recent date.

WHEREAS, this government thus accepted was far from answering the wants of the people, and became more and more so as the population increased in numbers, and as the country was developed, and commerce extended, until the present day, when it commands a place amongst the Colonies; and this people ever actuated by the above mentioned principles, had generously supported the aforesaid government, and gave to it a faithful allegiance; when, contrary to the law of nations, in March, 1869, that said Government surrendered and transferred to Canada all the rights which it had or pretended to have in this territory, by transactions with which the people were considered unworthy to be made acquainted.

AND WHEREAS, it is also generally admitted that a people is at liberty to establish any form of government it may consider suitable to its wants, as soon as the power to which it was subject abandons it, or attemps [sic], to subjugate it without its consent, to a foreign power; and maintain that no right can be transferred to such foreign power. Now, therefore,

1st. We, the Representatives of the people in Council assembled at Upper Fort Garry, on the 24th day of November, 1869, after having invoked the God of nations, relying on these fundamental moral principles solemnly declare in the name of our constituents and in our own names, before God and man, that from the day on which the Government we had always respected, abandoned us by transferring to a strange power the sacred authority confided to it, the people of Rupert's Land and the North-West became free and exempt from all allegiance to the said Government.

2d. That we refuse to recognise the authority of Canada, which pretends to have a right to coerce us and impose upon us a despotic form of government still more contrary to our rights and interests as British subjects than was that Government to which we had subjected ourselves through necessity up to a recent date.

3rd. That by sending an expedition on the 1st of November charged to drive back Mr William McDougall and his companions coming in the name of Canada to rule us with the rod of despotism without a previous notification to that effect, we have but acted conformably to that sacred right which commands every Citizen to offer energetic opposition to prevent his country being enslaved.

4th. That we continue and shall continue to oppose with all our strength the establishing of the Canadian authority in our country under the announced form. And in case of persistence on the part of the Canadian Government to enforce its obnoxious policy upon us, by force of arms, we protest before hand against such an unjust and unlawful course, and we declare the said Canadian Government responsible before God and men for the innumerable evils which may be caused by so unwarrantable a course.

Be it known, therefore, to the world in general and to the Canadian Government in particular, that as we have always heretofore successfully defended our country in frequent wars with the neighbouring tribes of Indians, who are now on friendly relations with us, we are firmly resolved in future not less than in the past, to repel all invasions from whatsoever quarter they may come.

And furthermore, we do declare and proclaim in the name of the people of Rupert's Land and the North-West that we have on the same 24th day of November, 1869, above mentioned, established a Provisional Government, and hold it to be the only and lawful authority now in existence in Rupert's Land and the North-West, which claim the obedience and respect of the people.

That meanwhile we hold ourselves in readiness to enter into such negotiations with the Canadian Government, which may be favorable for the good government and prosperity of this people.

In support of this declaration, relying on the protection of Divine Providence, we mutually pledge ourselves on oath, our lives, our fortunes, and our sacred honor to each other.

Issued at Fort Garry this 8th day of December in the year of our Lord one thousand eight hundred and sixty-nine.

(Signed,) JOHN BRUCE, President.

LOUIS RIEL, Secretary.

Historical Interpretations

3   From Michael Hughes, "Within the Grasp of Company Law: Land, Legitimacy, and the Racialization of the Métis, 1815–1821," *Ethnohistory* 63, no. 3 (July 2016): 519–40. Permission conveyed through Rightslink.

On 19 June 1816 a coalition of Métis and North West Company (NWC) forces attacked a party of Scottish settlers and Hudson's Bay Company (HBC) personnel at the Red River colony near present-day Winnipeg, Manitoba. The conflict, later known as the Battle of Seven Oaks, resulted in the deaths of 21 people, including the colony's governor, George Semple. The roots of the conflict can be traced back to 1811 when the company granted Lord Selkirk the Colony of Assiniboia.[1] Selkirk asserted HBC sovereignty over the area by establishing an agricultural colony at Red River and settling it with over one hundred displaced Highland Scots travelling in family units.[2] The colony suffered from lack of preparation, harsh weather, and starvation in its early years. To secure provisions, the colony's previous governor, Miles MacDonell, issued the Pemmican Proclamation in 1814, ordering a halt to the export of pemmican from the District of Assiniboia, the grant of land in which the colony was situated, to procure enough provisions for the struggling colony.[3] The NWC sought to limit HBC activities on lands west of the colony because the Métis used them to hunt buffalo, process their meat, and trade the pemmican to the NWC, which used these provisions to feed its agents trading in the lucrative Athabasca country. MacDonell inflamed relations further with the NWC and Métis when he forcibly seized pemmican from Métis hunters who were resisting his commands.[4] Believing that the HBC intended to disrupt their trade, the NWC temporarily dispersed the colony once prior to the Seven Oaks battle. The NWC's resolve to reclaim control of the territory strengthened after the HBC re-established the colony

with new settlers.[5] In 1815 the HBC retaliated by burning Fort Gibraltar, the NWC's post on Red River, and in 1816 the NWC and Métis regrouped with the intent of driving off the colonists, leading to Seven Oaks.[6] Considering imperial strategy and Métis livelihood, the actions of the companies and the Métis illustrated the multiple claims to land at Red River.[7]

In the five years following Seven Oaks, the NWC and HBC engaged in a paper war to impress on British and Canadian publics their version of events.[8] Gerhard Ens has recently argued that each company developed competing discourses to blame its rival for the attack.[9] Each claimed legitimacy while accusing its opponent of advocating crime and disorder. However, there was a deeper agenda. Herein I argue that the two companies' campaigns reveal two visions of imperial rule rooted in competing views of land, race, and family. Company discourses are crucial to understanding the competing legal orders in the northwest. The discourses of both companies justified their actions and condemned their competition in ways that reflected each company's institutional structure. In so doing, both companies sought to define which company would control British jurisdiction and who would be categorized as subjects.

Both companies' rhetoric changed throughout the 1810s in response to major events, such as Seven Oaks, court proceedings in Canada, and parliamentary debate in London.[10] During these years company partisans published more than 30 pamphlets and books in the Canadas, Great Britain, and the United States.[11] [. . .] Following the Battle at Seven Oaks, the attacks became more incendiary as both companies articulated their versions of the events to discredit the claims of their competitors. [. . .]

The central issue for each party was controlling lands around Red River. Basing its claims on its vast experience trading in "Indian country," the NWC argued that it was the sole legitimate authority in the region. The NWC rested its legal assertions on the provisions included in the Canada Jurisdiction Act (CJA), passed by Parliament in 1803, which extended the jurisdiction of Upper and Lower Canada over British territories outside the colony's borders.[12] Based on the Royal Proclamation of 1763, the CJA established a new legal and geographic entity, "Indian territories," which resembled the Indian country designated in 1763.[13] [. . .] Asserting that the areas around Red River qualified as "Indian territories," the NWC believed their alliance with the Métis strengthened their claims against the HBC. The NWC argued that their agents had formed stable relationships with Indigenous peoples and that these alliances constituted a form of legitimacy based on prior usage. The HBC, on the other hand, began to racialize all peoples of mixed background as "half-breeds" in their intention to disqualify the Métis from claiming either land or an Indigenous identity.

[. . .]

Hierarchy defined the organizational structure of the HBC. It sought to expand colonial rule through the implementation of a racialized division of labour and an expansion of a legal system that the company administered within the boundaries of "Rupert's Land." It claimed ownership over Rupert's Land by right of discovery, enshrined in their 1670 charter that granted the company monopoly access to a territory encompassing all the lands that drained into Hudson's Bay.[14] While the NWC believed the HBC's century-old charter was invalid because it had never been implemented, Selkirk disagreed.[15] In the HBC's view, the NWC was a band of criminal trespassers who had invaded the HBC's realm and fomented murderous violence. The HBC contended that its charter allowed the company to exercise jurisdiction over NWC, so long as its rule was "not contrary or repugnant" to the laws of Great Britain.[16] [. . .]

In a dialogic process with the NWC, the HBC began to categorize all peoples of mixed descent, including the Red River Métis, as "half-breeds." [. . .] By analyzing company usage of the category "half-breed" in the context of the rivalry, I contend that the HBC pamphleteers represented an early attempt to imbue the category "half-breed" with political meaning. Rather than representing Métis as an independent Indigenous nation with claims to the soil, the HBC argued that the "half-breeds" were British subjects who both enjoyed the protection and faced the penalties of British law. HBC officers also referred to the Métis as the "Bois Brulés" and "Metiss," but their racialized understanding of the "half-breed" as an apolitical group informed their usage of the other categories.[17]

HBC writers argued that the patrilineal descent of the Métis trumped any connection that they may have maintained with their Indigenous mothers and families. The legitimacy of these "country marriages," or marriages à la façon du paye, was the source of legal ambiguity and doubt.[18] HBC officers, including Governor George Simpson, who took control of the company following its merge with the NWC, refused to recognize his own country marriages as legitimate.[19] HBC partisans maintained that only legally recognized marriages were legitimate. Despite the prevalence of country marriages, the HBC dismissed and even stigmatized any role Indigenous women played in Métis families. The HBC view of "half-breed" family structure was so deviant in its gendered composition that it characterized the Métis as an entirely male group, the "bastard sons of Indian concubines."[20] The HBC therefore made a direct link between family structure, legitimacy, and title to land. By racializing the Métis as "half-breeds," they manufactured the idea that the Métis were totally severed from their kinship connections with their Indigenous relations.

The NWC sought to become the dominant and perhaps sole company trading in the "Indian territories." Its agents countered the HBC insistence that their 1670 charter granted them exclusive rights to land and territories that encompassed a landmass running from Quebec to the Rocky Mountains. Company representatives saw the HBC as criminal aggressors who violently and illegally sought to destroy NWC trade. The categories "half-breed" and "Indian" assumed vastly different meanings in NWC publications. Whereas the HBC sought to prove to readers that the "native Indians" approved of its settlement project, the NWC argued that they opposed Selkirk's plan. The NWC contended that the "Indians" and "half-breeds" represented independent political and military forces with whom only its agents could negotiate, because HBC agents were ignorant in Native diplomacy. The NWC disavowed any responsibility for Seven Oaks, which was rather the product of the actions of an "independent" Indian nation.

The conflict reveals a major legal transformation in the British fur trade. French and later British traders had long relied on alliances with autonomous Indigenous communities. Indigenous peoples could exercise enough power within these diplomatic relationships to force the colonizers onto a "middle ground" on which all parties were required to recognize one another and to negotiate and adapt to each other.[21] European powers would negotiate with their Indigenous allies to wage war or make peace; likewise, Indigenous peoples would participate or withdraw as they saw fit. The 1810s signalled the legal decline of that older system. NWC rhetoric defended this older model of the fur trade by arguing that it had conducted the trade and formed alliances with Natives decades before the HBC asserted its territorial claims. However [. . .] it was becoming

clear that the imperial government would no longer accept this model of the fur trade. [. . .] The system that had relied on alliances with Indigenous peoples and their autonomy within the trade gave way to one bounded by civil regulations. [. . .]

The Battle of Seven Oaks represented a moment of coalescence around a shared, distinct Métis ethnic and perhaps national identity. The Selkirk colony posed new threats to Métis social and economic life due to its central location along the fork of the Assiniboine and Red Rivers. The Métis had a stake in the fur trade conflict. They were defending their access to resources along the river, including hunting grounds and fisheries. For the Métis, the battle represented a "collective defensive reaction to the activities of the competing fur trade companies that coveted trade routes and favored wintering sites" at the fork.[22] While any claims to land and national identity are complicated by the utterly self-serving rhetoric of the NWC, it appears that the Métis were acutely aware that the HBC incursion threatened their livelihood. Métis and NWC arguments that the HBC had dispossessed the Métis of land around Red River concerned the HBC enough to racialize the Métis to legitimize company rule. While the NWC may have played a key role in the first articulation of a Métis "nation," Métis resistance to HBC settlement meant that the HBC would need to fashion legal arguments that removed any doubt that any legitimate opponents existed. Therefore Indigenous agency—embodied by Métis actions, articulated in NWC propaganda, and imagined by the HBC as a threat—shaped the rhetorical strategies of the HBC in their attempts to claim the northwest.

Company officials articulated these strategies in 1817 when the Colonial Office investigated the explosion of violence. John Sherbrooke, governor-in-chief of British North America, dispatched William Coltman to serve as JP in "Indian territories" and equipped him with the power to recommend charges against subjects who had committed crimes. During his investigations Coltman was in constant communication with the companies and Métis participants and took depositions from these parties. Consisting of 314 folio pages, the report was read by administrators from both companies, legal officials in Canada, and eventually the political elite in London and was put to seemingly contradictory uses. The NWC attorney Samuel Sherwood used the report's finding of a private war in his defense of NWC actions in the courts of Lower Canada in 1818.[23] In 1819 the Coltman report was appended to the "Blue Book," Papers Relating to the Red River Settlement, presented to Parliament. [. . .] By 1821 evidence in the Blue Book convinced Parliament to grant the HBC legal rights to Rupert's Land and the western Indian territories, support the combination of the two companies, and clarify Canadian jurisdiction over western lands.[24]

Within the report, NWC testimony contended that the "half-breeds" constituted an Indian tribe "entitled to property in the Soil, to a flag of their own, and to protection from the British Government."[25] Coltman equivocated with the NWC on this point.[26] He wrote: "They evidently acted in the first instance under a mistaken sense of right, and an impression that the Settlers were invaders of the natural rights of themselves and of the North West Company."[27] He continued that "their claims to the soil jointly with the Indians (in favor of which the evidence before me shows that plausible grounds might be assigned) as evidently strongly impressed on them" by the NWC partners.[28] Coltman found that the "half-breeds" had long lived along Red River with their Indian relations and were "established as chief" by the time the first traders arrived from Montreal after the Seven Years' War.[29] From this position of local authority, they "levied heavy contributions on those who came into the country to trade" and opposed HBC encroachments on their lands and its legal regime.

The Métis asserted that the HBC had encroached on their Native rights to lands around Red River. After the Pemmican Proclamation and subsequent 1815 dispersal of the Scottish colony, Coltman reported that Cuthbert Grant, the Métis leader, had temporarily struck a deal with the HBC to allow HBC trader John McLeod to visit the colony once a year equipped with three canoes to trade. Coltman wrote that "this was the first year the Half Breeds began to talk of a recompence for their lands."[30] In 1816, after HBC officer Colin Robertson established the colony a second time, Alexander Fraser was "ready to come down and chastize the colonists."[31] In his description of Seven Oaks, Coltman added that Cuthbert Grant openly admitted that his people sought to destroy the Scottish colony because "their pretensions were inconsistent with the rights of natural justice, both in respect of themselves, and of the north west company, and had been the cause of continued disputes from nearly the first establishment of the Colony."[32] [. . .] HBC officers would later expend considerable energy attacking the connection between the Métis and the NWC to convince the imperial government and British public that its view of legal jurisdiction was correct.

Proclaiming the charter's supremacy, HBC administrators rejected the argument that the "half-breeds" constituted an independent Indian nation, and they protested Coltman's report.[33] They argued that the "half-breeds" were invented by NWC management to wreak havoc on the colony. HBC writers pinpointed the year 1812 as the "signal for a train of nefarious proceedings, ending in the first distraction of the colony."[34] At this point, the "half-breeds" were in the company's employ as military auxiliaries and labourers. One HBC agent contended: "The Half-breeds, who before the summer had always been classed along the Canadian Engages of the NWC & had never been heard of as a separate body of men, were now brought forward and started to call themselves a nation of Indians." HBC proponents argued that, by the time of Seven Oaks, Métis forces became "organized in a systematic Manner, & with the distinct avowal of the illegal purpose of driving the Settlers from their lands." [. . .] The HBC rejected the idea that the two companies had entered into a kind of warfare rather than being the victims of crimes committed by the NWC and their "half-breed" workers.

Coltman agreed with the HBC that the "half-breeds" had colluded with the NWC to eject the HBC and the Red River colony from the interior. He viewed the HBC as the initial instigators, but he also faulted the NWC for furnishing the "half-breeds" with the weapons required to mount an attack and for using the idea of Indian warfare to wash their hands of the violence.[35] It was particularly reprehensible that the NWC encouraged "the nearly savage force consisting of the mixed population or half breed Indians of the Country" to kill British subjects.[36] Yet Coltman decided not to bring any of the participants, from the NWC, HBC, or the "half-breeds," to Montreal to stand trial for the violence at Seven Oaks. He found that the affair was the product of the "disturbed state of the country" born of the rivalry that resembled "private hostility or war."[37] Coltman's attempts to find a compromise between the two companies ran counter to Selkirk's project of bringing the NWC and its allies to justice. [. . .]

THE NWC CAMPAIGN

NWC publications criticized the HBC for assuming that the 1670 charter was still valid and that it had granted them the right to establish a private legal system at Red River. Ridiculing the HBC pretense that King Charles II could grant "a domain exceeding in extent the kingdom of England," they stated that the HBC "had equal power to assign him a similar kingdom on the moon" a century and a half earlier.[38] [. . .] NWC supporter Adam McAdam [. . .] asserted that the charter was legally similar to other charters from the seventeenth century, such as the Massachusetts Bay Charter, that were no longer recognized as binding.[39]

The NWC viewed actions taken under the charter, such as the Pemmican Proclamation, as illegal. [. . .] Alexander MacDonell asserted that Miles MacDonell intended the Pemmican Proclamation to prevent HBC rivals from moving across the Red River area. He stated that "free Canadian hunters and Half-breeds" were labouring "in their usual and peaceable occupations" when they were "taken prisoners by men with fixed bayonets, for no other cause than being suspected by Miles of being favourably inclined towards the North-West Company."[40] Ellice labelled Selkirk a "fell tyrant, presuming upon impunity" whose actions were not "mere venal trespasses" but "real acts of pillage and robbery, in justification of which, he has not one inch of legal ground to stand upon."[41]

NWC spokesmen argued that relations between the two companies were peaceful prior to the colonization of Red River. The new Red River colony represented nothing less than an abuse of legal privileges, and the disruption understandably fomented retribution from neighbouring Indians and "half-breeds." Alexander MacDonell wrote: "The Agents of the North-West Company have never attempted to conceal, that the aggressions of Lord Selkirk, produced acts of reciprocal violence and retaliation, which it was neither sought nor attempted abstractly to justify."[42] HBC militarization at Red River ignited local "Indians and Half-Breeds" to seek vengeance and protect their property. Alexander MacDonell asserted that Miles MacDonell endeavoured "to persevere in his attempts to maintain it by force, and the resistance occasioned by his interference with the rights and properties of the Half-Breeds and Natives."[43]

NWC partisans argued that the HBC fabricated the friendly relations that the company had formed with Natives other than the Métis at Red River. McAdam wrote that "the Indians; none of these will ever acknowledge the authority of Lord paramount Selkirk."[44] He ridiculed HBC claims that the company had protected the interests of the Indians. The HBC could not "be otherwise than in a state of hostility with the Indians" due to Selkirk's agents, "who came to seize these lands from their ancient proprietors" and to confiscate the food and resources gathered there.[45] Alexander MacDonell reported that "the common high road was also obstructed, and the free Canadian hunters and Half-breeds in their usual and peaceable occupations were chased, and taken prisoners by men with fixed bayonets, for no other cause than being suspected by Miles of being favourably inclined towards the North-West Company."[46] He asserted that Seven Oaks illustrated growing Native disapproval of the colony. However, Indigenous resentment was not instantaneous but cultivated by HBC misdeeds. The HBC encouraged violence by intimidating the NWC's Indigenous allies, by attacking the NWC Fort Gibraltar on the Red River, and by seizing Métis pemmican.[47]

NWC agents argued that they alone possessed the knowledge and experience to negotiate with the "savage" nations of the interior, including the "half-breeds." They viewed Indigenous communities as potentially violent but also as "free and independent people" who held title over their lands.[48] NWC publications contended that "Indians" made the colony unsafe due to their natural propensity to steal and pillage the white settlers. One publication included a letter from the NWC to Henry Goulburn, undersecretary to the Earl of Bathurst, in which the company used the spectre of Indian war to suggest that conditions in the interior declined to the point that Parliament should intervene. "The Indian hatchet once raised, will not discriminate between Settler and Trader," wrote NWC proprietors. "We only trust they may be enabled by their united endeavours to conciliate the Natives, and to ward off the danger with which his Lordship's indiscretion has threatened them."[49] Adam McAdam asked a rhetorical question in the Montreal Herald illuminating the pitfalls of HBC absolutist pretensions. "How can rival traders," he wrote, "with a few servants, whose whole profits, and very personal security depend on the good will of the natives, exercise a despotism over a hundred times their number of roving Indians, whom they only see occasionally?"[50] Legal authority should emanate from Parliament, not the HBC, who allowed its colony to be attacked by a group they considered an independent Indian nation. NWC discourse promoted a model of jurisdiction that resembled the conditions established by the Proclamation of 1763. The NWC represented the HBC as overreaching and inexperienced, while NWC agents were skilled diplomats who were needed to negotiate with autonomous Métis and Indigenous communities.

The NWC positioned themselves as defenders of the Indians and Métis and opponents of an HBC colonization scheme that would illegally dispossess Indian and "half-breed" peoples. Alexander MacDonell, an NWC agent who organized much of the resistance against the HBC, wrote that the NWC "had always considered the natives as the lawful owners of the soil; that we were determined never to admit the claims of the Hudson's Bay Company."[51] [. . .]

The author of another pamphlet argued that the CJA was derived from the Royal Proclamation of 1763, which prohibited British subjects from purchasing land "within Indian territory." The pamphlet concluded that the Royal Proclamation of 1763, much like the CJA, supported the interests of fur traders over settlers. Ellice penned a mock speech by an Indian warning his community that the HBC planned to displace the Natives in a manner similar to the US government. He declared: "Look at what has happened amongst other nations of Indians, by a similar proceeding of the Americans. They drive the nations from place to place after signing their lands in succession." Ellice conveyed to his audience that the British government and by extension the NWC intended to protect Indigenous lands against the HBC's intrusion.[52]

NWC representatives asserted that the "half-breeds" were Indigenous peoples with a long history of participation in the fur trade. A footnote in one publication stated that

> an impression is attempted to be made, that these latter people are a race only known since the establishment of the North-West Company; but the fact is, that when the Traders first penetrated into that country, after the conquest of Canada, they found it overrun by persons of this description, some of whom were the chief Leaders of the different Tribes of Indians in the Plains, and inherited the names of their Fathers, who had been the principal French Commandants, and Traders of the District.[53]

The publication argued that the "half-breeds" had established themselves at Red River in the eighteenth century and had claimed the provision trade for themselves. McAdam stated: "The bastards, the savage half breed, are frequently spoken of.—That is to say, in polite English, some of the white men from Canada and Hudson's Bay, have sometimes left a child behind them in those countries; they are very few in proportion to the other natives, and are much beloved by them."[54] NWC partisans argued that Métis constituted a coherent Indigenous community with claims to land that trumped the HBC arguments. The NWC did not see the Métis residing on "Indian territories" as separate from their Indigenous families, and thus they could legitimately claim land in a space not legally designated for white settlement. It should be noted that the NWC arguments were undoubtedly self-serving: Métis sovereignty would mean that the NWC would have an ally around Red River and could continue to dominate the region. Their model of authority, however, differed greatly from the absolutist claims made by the HBC in that they recognized the Métis as constituting an Indigenous people.

THE HBC PROJECT

HBC arguments about colonization were linked to Selkirk's larger project of establishing a vast agricultural hinterland and a comprehensive system of laws and government, all administered by the company. The HBC argued that the NWC, lacking any desire to colonize the area, had created an area in which "oppression, violence, and fraud, had been continually exercised, in the intercourse between the natives and the traders." The establishment of an HBC colony, on the other hand, would facilitate in the "detection and punishment of frauds or crimes . . . by substituting habits of sobriety and regular industry in the stead of the savage and licentious manners which had before prevailed."[55] Furthermore, Selkirk viewed the fur trade as a hindrance to the true development of "Indian territories" as an agrarian hinterland that would benefit the empire far more than a string of fur trade posts commanded by Canadians with questionable respect for British laws. To counter arguments that the HBC would illegally appropriate Indigenous lands, Selkirk reprised his role as a humanitarian and cited "native Indian" depravity to suggest that his intervention would improve the lives of Indigenous peoples by breaking their oppressive bonds with the Canadian traders.[56]

After Seven Oaks, the HBC attacked NWC legitimacy by arguing that the NWC represented nothing more than a criminal organization that encouraged its employees to trespass on HBC lands, murder its employees, and steal its property. In his published narrative John Pritchard asserted that he had observed NWC servants abuse Indigenous peoples with lethal force for "very slight offences," such as avoiding debt or hunting for competing companies.[57] Other materials incriminated the NWC by narrating the events in the 1810s that led both to the multiple expulsions of the settlers and to Seven Oaks. Lord Selkirk believed that the first Montreal traders were so enticed by enormous profits that they engaged in commerce that "was very different from that which would have taken in a civilized country."[58] [. . .] John Halkett stated plainly that the NWC goal "was to hire, arm, and array their half-breed dependents, and make them, under the personal direction of partners and clerks of the Company, attack the colonists, burn their houses, and drive them by force from the Settlement."[59] He also narrated the after events at Seven Oaks in graphic detail. After the NWC partners and Archibald McLeod arrived at the scenes they congratulated the "half-breeds" for their conduct. They then "began to exult over, and even to kick the dead which had remained."[60] Taken together, these publications contended that the NWC's lack of respect for British civil society had resulted in a number of atrocities horrifying to the British public.

[. . .] HBC writers identified specific leaders who led the unprovoked assault against British subjects. John Halkett wrote that NWC agent Cuthbert Grant gathered "half-breed" accomplices from all branches of the trade to commit violence and that Simon McGillivray led a party of "half-breeds in their expedition against the Red River" prior to Seven Oaks.[61] Several accounts related that the NWC issued Duncan Cameron a military uniform and appointed him "sub-deputy sheriff" with the privilege to issue warrants.[62] John Pritchard stated that the NWC mobilized the "Half-Breeds" even prior to Seven Oaks in 1816, as evidenced by Peter Pangman's attacks against the settlers in 1815.[63] In 1816 Cameron and Alexander MacDonell marched around in military uniform "at the head of a tumultuous rabble of half-breed servants, and others, to the great terror of the peaceable settlers."[64] The legal privileges provided to the NWC under the CJA had done nothing more than mobilize the "half-breed" "rabble" to commit violence against the HBC.

To undermine the contention that the "half-breeds" constituted an independent nation, the HBC exploited British concepts of legitimacy to assert that "half-breeds" possessed no valid territorial claim within Rupert's Land. HBC publications regarded the "miserable race termed Metiss, Half-breeds, or Bois Brules" as "neither in the slightest degree formidable from their numbers, nor their courage."[65] Pritchard argued that Peter Pangman, identified as a "half-breed," had been "a leading man in these outrages, and was one of the pretended chiefs of the half-breeds or *new nation*."[66] One publication made the connection between legitimacy, land, and nationhood clear: "These are the illegitimate progeny of the partners, agents, traders, clerks, voyageurs, and servants, of the North West Company, by Indian Women. They have always been much under the control of that company."[67] Peter Pambrun believed the "half-breeds" had no connection to place or community. In a deposition following Seven Oaks he remarked that "a great number of the men, commonly called Brules, Metiss, or half-breeds, viz. [were] the bastard sons of Indian concubines, kept by the partners or servants of the North-West Company."[68] By attacking the legitimacy of their parentage, the HBC also attacked Métis claims to legitimacy as a distinct people and to land. By privileging the "half-breed's" relation to their fathers, company representatives erased the connections that bound the Métis to their Native kin. HBC propaganda therefore advanced a distorted view of Indigenous kinship that eliminated any argument that the company had acted unlawfully when it colonized Red River.

HBC spokesmen went further to discount Métis claims by characterizing the "half-breeds" as a lawless menace that combined the worst qualities of "civilization" and "savagery." Referred to here as the "bois brules," one pamphlet stated that

the appellations which are given to the spurious offspring of the partners, clerks, and servants of the company . . . are designation[s] calculated for disguise, by which persons unacquainted with the demi-christian origin of the "bois brules," might be induce[d] to suppose that they were some powerful Indian nation. The fact is, however, that many of these have received from the lamentable care of their parents the rudiments of education.[69]

HBC proponents writing as Archibald MacDonald stated that the colony was attacked by the "half-breed Indians (Spurious descendants of the Canadian servants of the North-West Company, by Indian women), together with those of the settlers who had previously joined them."[70] The publications also criticized the use of Native symbols throughout the conflict. Pritchard noted that, following the Pemmican Proclamation, the "half-breeds on horseback, with their faces painted in a most hideous manner, and in the dresses of Indian warriors, came forward and surrounded using the form of a half-moon."[71] As the NWC introduced this particular idea to the Métis, the HBC would take it as evidence that the Métis lack the power to define themselves. The HBC argued consistently—during the conflict and well after—that the emergence of a separate Métis identity resulted totally from external stimuli and influence and that their claims against the company were nothing more than performance.

The idea that the "half-breeds" constituted a "spurious" people allowed HBC authorities to invalidate any claims the Métis had as either "civilized" or, more critically, Indigenous peoples. The HBC maintained that Selkirk had received the blessing of local "Natives" to establish the colony. One publication claimed that the "native Indians" were always friendly toward the colonists, and if not, the change in relations was undoubtedly owing to NWC interference.[72] Prior to Seven Oaks, Lord Selkirk articulated this view that most Native families traded with the HBC before the NWC interfered and that the NWC viewed alliances

with their rivals as "crime" deserving the "severest vengeance."[73] HBC publications argued that at Seven Oaks only three "Indians" participated, firing no shots, and that their primary role was as "spectators."[74] These statements legitimized the HBC colonization scheme, undermined the NWC position that the Red River colony of Scottish settlers disrupted relations, and separated "native Indians" as distinct from the "half-breeds."

CONCLUSION

In 1821 the HBC view of territorial sovereignty would triumph when the company merged with the NWC, thus concluding the battle over what shape legal ordering would assume in the northwest. The NWC strategy of basing its territorial claims on its alliance with the Indigenous communities, including the Métis, ended when the company was absorbed by the HBC. After 1821 the HBC ruled by a hierarchy of dependence, an inchoate legal infrastructure and civil society based at Red River, and more emphasis on international borders. The shape of that colonial order emerged during the company rivalry. Arguing in dialogue with the Métis and their NWC allies, the HBC invented the category of "half-breed" to undermine Métis claims to cultural and political distinctiveness, as well as to deny their kinship with their immediate Indigenous relations. In their view, "half-breeds" were a depoliticized and homogeneous group of marginalized dependents subject to colonial rule; they were, by definition, ineligible for nationhood or the status of an independent people. Once their NWC allies amalgamated with the HBC, the only advocates for Indigenous sovereignty in Rupert's Land would be the Métis themselves. Their resistance to absorption into the empire as British subjects and their claims to land in the HBC holding would persist throughout the company era.

NOTES

1. For an analysis of how representations of Seven Oaks circulated in Canadian historiography to naturalize Anglophone settler society, see Lyle Dick, "The Seven Oaks Incident and the Construction of a Historical Tradition," *Journal of the Canadian Historical Association* 2, no. 1 (1991): 93–119; Gerhard Ens, "The Battle of Seven Oaks and the Articulation of a Metis National Tradition, 1811–1849," in *Contours of a People: Metis Family, Mobility, and History,* eds Nicole St-Onge, Carolyn Podruchny, and Brenda Macdougall (Norman: University of Oklahoma Press, 2012), pp. 92–112; and J.M. Bumsted, *Lord Selkirk: A Life* (East Lansing: Michigan State University Press, 2009), 201.

2. Ens, "Battle of Seven Oaks," 95.

3. Semple preceded MacDonell in 1815. Dale Gibson, "Company Justice: Origins of Legal Institutions in Pre-Confederation Manitoba," *Manitoba Law Journal* 23 (1995): 259.

4. Ens, "Battle of Seven Oaks," 94.

5. Ibid., 98.

6. Gibson, "Company Justice," 260.

7. Ens, "Battle of Seven Oaks," 93–102.

8. J.M. Bumsted, *Fur Trade Wars: The Forming of Western Canada* (Winnipeg: Great Plains Publications, 1999), 245. He refers to these competing discourses as a "war of words."

9. Ens, "Battle of Seven Oaks," 102–4.

10. E.E. Rich, *The Fur Trade and the Northwest to 1857* (Toronto: McClelland and Stewart, 1967), 238–41.

11. For an outline of this publication history, see Bumsted, *Fur Trade Wars,* 245–57.

12. For information about the Canada Jurisdiction Act and its shortcomings, see Hamar Foster, "Long-Distance Justice: The Criminal Jurisdiction of Canadian Courts West of the Canadas," *American Journal of Legal History* 34, no. 1 (1990): 14–37; Gibson, "Company Justice," 257–64; Russell Smandych and Karina Sacca, "The Development of Criminal Law Courts in Pre-1870 Manitoba," *Manitoba Law Journal* 24, no. 2 (1996): 209; Desmond Brown, "Unpredictable and Uncertain: Criminal Law in the Canadian North West before 1886," *Alberta Law Review* 17, no. 3 (1979): 501–4; Kathryn Bindon, "Hudson's Bay Company Law: Adam Thom and the Institution of Order in Rupert's Land, 1839–54," in *Essays in the History of Canadian Law,* vol. 1, ed. David Flaherty (Toronto: University of Toronto Press, 1981), pp. 44–45.

13. Foster, "Long-Distance Justice," 9.

14. Gibson, "Company Justice," 257; Frank Tough, "Aboriginal Rights versus the Deed of Surrender: The Legal Rights of Native Peoples and Canada's Acquisition of the Hudson's Bay Company Territory," *Prairie Forum* 17, no. 2 (1992): 229–30.

15. Gibson, "Company Justice," 257.

16. Ibid., 253.

17. Recent scholarship has criticized historiography for confusing the Red River Métis with other racially mixed fur trade communities throughout the Great Lakes. See Chris Andersen, "*Moya 'Tipimsook* ('The People Who Aren't Their Own Bosses'): Racialization and the Misrecognition of 'Métis' in Upper Great Lakes Ethnohistory," *Ethnohistory* 58, no. 1 (2011): 37–63.

18. Jennifer Brown, *Strangers in Blood: Fur Trade Company Families in Indian Country* (Vancouver: University of British Columbia Press, 1980), 90–92.

19. Ibid., 125–26. Brown notes that attitudes changed when the introduction of the clergy and Christian marriage signalled attempts at social ordering and a move toward racial hierarchy while offering institutional recognition of these marriages.

20. John Halkett, *Statement Respecting the Earl of Selkirk's Settlement at Kildonan, upon the Red River, in North America; Its Destruction in the Years 1815 and 1816; and the Massacre of Governor Semple and His Party* (London: Brettell, 1817), app., xlvii.

21. Richard White, *The Middle Ground: Indians, Empires, and Republics in the Great Lakes Region, 1650–1815* (New York: Cambridge University Press, 1991).

22. Carolyn Podruchny and Nicole St-Onge, "Scuttling along a Spider's Web," in *Contours of a People: Metis Family, Mobility, and History,* eds Nicole St-Onge, Carolyn Podruchny, and Brenda Macdougall (Norman: University of Oklahoma Press, 2012), p. 61.

23. Bumsted, *Lord Selkirk,* 394.

24. Gerald Friesen, *The Canadian Prairies: A History* (Lincoln: University of Nebraska Press, 1984), 83; Rich, *Fur Trade*, 238.

25. CO (Colonial Office, National Archives) 42/181, "Mr. Coltman's Mission to the Indian Territory," fol. 37.

26. CO 42/181, fols. 37–38.

27. CO 42/181, fol. 15.

28. Ibid.

29. CO 42/181, fol. 100.

30. CO 42/181, fols. 107–8.

31. CO 42/181, fol. 119.

32. CO 42/181, fol. 140.

33. CO 42/181, fol. 244.

34. CO 42/181, fol. 58.

35. CO 42/181, fol. 244.

36. CO 42/181, fol. 246.

37. CO 42/181, fol. 310.

38. Samuel Wilcocke, *A Narrative of Occurrences in the Indian Countries of North America, since the Connexion of the Right Hon. The Earl of Selkirk with the Hudson's Bay Company, and His Attempt to Establish a Colony on the Red River; with a Detailed Account of His Lordship's Military Expedition to, and Subsequent Proceedings at Fort William, in Upper Canada* (London: McMillan, 1817), 5.

39. Adam McAdam, *Communications from Adam McAdam: Originally Published in the "Montreal Herald," in Reply to Letters Inserted Therein under the Signature of Archibald MacDonell, Respecting Lord Selkirk's Red River Colony* (Montreal: Gray, 1816), 19.

40. Alexander Greenfield MacDonell, *A Narrative of Transactions in the Red River Country, from the Commencement of the Operations of the Earl of Selkirk till the Summer of the Year 1816* (London: McMillan, 1819), 21.

41. Ellice, *The Communications of Mercator upon the Contest between the Earl of Selkirk, and the Hudson's Bay Company, on One Side, and the North West Company on the Other, Republished from the Montreal Herald* (Montreal: Gray, 1817), 47–48.

42. MacDonell, *Narrative of Transactions*, vii.

43. Ibid., 38–39.

44. McAdam, *Communications*, 11.

45. Ibid., 43.

46. MacDonell, *Narrative of Transactions*, 26.

47. Ibid., 77.

48. Ellice, *Communications of Mercator*, 56.

49. Wilcocke, *Narrative*, app., 60.

50. McAdam, *Communications*, 34.

51. MacDonell, *Narrative of Transactions*, 67.

52. Ellice, *Communications of Mercator*, 30, 53.

53. Wilcocke, *Narrative*, 148–50.

54. McAdam, *Communications*, 41.

55. Samuel Gale, *Notices of the Claims of the Hudson's Bay Company and the Conduct of Its Adversaries* (Montreal: Gray, 1817), 66.

56. Thomas Douglas, Earl of Selkirk, *A Sketch of the British Fur Trade in North America, with Observations Relative to the North-West Company of Montreal* (London: Ridgeway, 1816), 16, 118.

57. John Pritchard, Pierre Chrysologue Pambrun, and Frederick Damien Heurter, *Narratives of John Pritchard, Pierre Chrysologue Pambrun, and Frederick Damien Heurter, Respecting the Aggressions of the North-West Company, against the Earl of Selkirk's Settlement upon Red River* (London: Murray, 1819), 3.

58. Selkirk, *Sketch*, 4.

59. Thomas Douglas, Earl of Selkirk, *A Letter to the Earl of Liverpool from the Earl of Selkirk, Accompanied by a Correspondence with the Colonial Department (in the Years 1817, 1818, 1819), on the Subject of the Red River Settlement in North America* (London: Printed by J. Brettell, 1819), 83.

60. Ibid., 80, 81.

61. Selkirk, *Letter*, 65.

62. Ibid., 98.

63. Pritchard, Pambrun, and Heurter, *Narratives*, 54.

64. Ibid., 14.

65. Selkirk, *Letter*, 81.

66. Pritchard, Pambrun, and Heurter, *Narratives*, 18.

67. Halkett, *Statement*, 19–20.

68. Ibid., app., xlvii.

69. Gale, *Notices*, 45–46.

70. Archibald MacDonald, *Narrative Respecting the Destruction of the Earl of Selkirk's Settlement upon Red River, in . . . 1815* (London: Brettell, 1816), 10.

71. Pritchard, Pambrun, and Heurter, *Narratives*, 27.

72. Gale, *Notices*, 70–71.

73. Selkirk, *Sketch*, 43.

74. Halkett, *Statement*, 118.

4 From Gerhard Ens, "Prologue to the Red River Resistance: Pre-liminal Politics and the Triumph of Riel," *Journal of the Canadian Historical Association* 5, no. 1 (1994): 111–23. Permission conveyed through the Copyright Clearance Center.

The Red River Resistance of 1869–70 is usually thought to have begun in October of 1869 with the stopping of the Canadian survey, the formation of the Métis "National Committee" led by Louis Riel, and the blockade of the road to Pembina. As well, most historians credit Riel with taking the initiative in formulating a Métis response to the Canadian plan to acquire Rupert's Land. What these accounts miss is the vibrant debate and conflict within the Métis community about what their response to Confederation should be. The first coherent plan of assuring Métis rights was formulated in July 1869 and was opposed by Riel. It was not until Riel had defeated this first plan and its leaders that he assumed leadership of the movement against annexation.

It is this early "pre-liminal"[1] phase of the Red River Resistance—July through October 1869—that this paper proposes to examine in some detail. During this period, two Métis groups, one led by William Dease and the other by Louis Riel, were locked in a power struggle. It was a struggle on a symbolic level in which the two sides offered different paradigms of Métis "communitas"[2] as the basis on which to present their case to the Canadian government. The struggle occurred at the grassroots level involving such tactics as negotiation and coalition formation. It was not until Riel had defeated William Dease for the leadership of the Resistance and consolidated his basis of support among the French Métis that he felt strong enough to initiate the breach of October 1869. The analysis offered here concentrates on the activities of individuals vying for power within very limited political settings, and is interested in how those who achieved power carried out the consciously held goals of the group.

It is my contention that the initial Métis conflict between Dease and Riel not only set the tone for the larger Resistance to come but determined, to a large extent, the problems Riel and his faction would have in building a consensus in the Colony. To this end, the paper will explain the nature of this power struggle, the opposing paradigms of Métis communitas, the tactics Riel used to defeat his rivals, and the implications that this power struggle had for Métis unity in the Colony after October 1869.

The few historians who have examined this early period of the Red River Resistance in any detail have tended to denigrate the Métis that opposed Riel. W.L. Morton, in his extended introduction to Alexander Begg's journal, tried to show that the true nature of the Resistance was revealed in the conflict between the Métis "half-articulated demand for corporate rights . . . and the intention of the Canadian authorities to grant individual rights in due course."[3] In his view, it was the "new nation" of the Métis which was "the central and dynamic protagonist of the Red River Resistance."[4] To make this argument Morton downplayed the role the Catholic clergy had in championing Riel's leadership,[5] and implied that those Métis opposed to Riel were dupes of the Canadians in Red River.[6] To have accorded the Métis opponents of Riel some volition and legitimacy would have undercut his argument that Riel was the undisputed leader of the French Métis in Red River.

Philippe Mailhot's account of the same period provides a much more accurate account of the role the Catholic clergy, especially that of Father Ritchot. Based on a detailed reconstruction of Ritchot's journal, Mailhot details the active part he played in directing Riel's Resistance.[7] Mailhot's account, however, closely follows Ritchot's partisan perspective. While Mailhot does not completely endorse Ritchot's argument that Dease's actions were directed by John Christian Schultz,[8] he does note that Dease's proposals mirrored those of the Canadian Party,[9] and that Dease and his party were not up to the task of directing the Resistance to annexation.[10] What both Morton and Mailhot overlook are the antecedents to the Dease proposals, and the active role the Catholic clergy had in discrediting the Dease party.

The first major Métis response to the news of the impending transfer of Rupert's Land to Canada came during the summer of 1869. In response to the vitriolic demonstrations of the Canadians in the Colony,[11] and in order to protect their land rights, a number of Métis called a large public meeting. This group included some of the traditional Métis leadership in the Colony such as William Dease, Pascal Breland, and William Hallet. Dease was the son of John W. Dease and Jenny Beignoit, and had been born in 1827 at Calling Lake. He settled at Red River and married Marguerite Genthon. The couple and their large family lived and farmed in both St Vital and St Norbert. By 1869 Dease was a prominent French-Métis trader and farmer, and member of the Council of Assiniboia. An indication of Dease's close connection to the various Native communities around Red River was his fluency in French, English, Ojibwa, and Sioux.[12] Pascal Breland, a son-in-law of Cuthbert Grant, was a hunt and trading chief of numerous hivernant villages, the patriarch of St François Xavier, and was also a member of the Council of Assiniboia in 1869. William Hallet was the most prominent English-Métis chief of the annual buffalo hunt with close family ties to numerous French-Métis families.[13]

These men placed an advertisement in the *Nor'Wester* inviting all Métis to meet at the Court House on 29 July 1869 to discuss what the Métis response should be to the proposed transfer of Rupert's Land to Canada.[14] At this meeting, William Dease quickly took the initiative and advanced what might be termed an "Aboriginal Rights" paradigm for Métis rights.[15] Dease called on the Métis to defend their rights to land in the Settlement, and disputed the validity of the Earl of Selkirk's purchase of the same from the Indians. The Métis, he said, should demand the £300 000 that Canada was about to pay to the Hudson's Bay Company. To this end the Métis should form a new government in the Colony to displace the HBC, and make their case to the Canadian government. While the first proposal elicited considerable support, the call to form a new government did not and the meeting broke up with no clear plan of action decided.

Historians have generally regarded this first initiative as a failure and attributed its lack of success to the notion that Dease and Hallet were dupes of John Christian Schultz and that their program too closely resembled that of the Canadians in the Settlement— perceptions which apparently put the Métis on guard and restrained them from supporting Dease and his proposals.[16] However, this view is based on an entirely uncritical acceptance of the comments of Fathers Dugast and Ritchot,[17] both of whom were themselves not only steadfast partisans in the conflict but had also been the first to draw attention to the similarity between Dease's proposal and the Canadians' plans in order to undermine the former. The meeting of July 29, consequently, was not a failure, but merely the opening round of a debate that would continue until early October.

Looking at the history of the Red River Settlement in a little longer perspective, it is also clear that the Dease proposal, far from being inspired by Schultz's Canadian faction in Red River, was an Aboriginal rights position designed by the traditional leadership of the Métis. Indeed, the Métis position as presented by Dease had been worked out nearly a decade earlier, in 1860, when it seemed likely that Red River would become a Crown Colony, a possibility which raised questions about Indian title, Hudson's Bay Company jurisdiction, and individual land rights in Red River.[18]

Debate over who had title began in 1860 when Peguis, the Saulteaux Chief, challenged the HBC claim to land in the Red River Settlement with the simple argument that the Indians had never sold it to Lord Selkirk and the Hudson's Bay Company.[19] That prompted the Métis, under the chairmanship of Pascal Breland, to hold a large meeting at the Royal Hotel near Fort Garry to discuss their position. The most eminent Métis traders and hunters—William Dease, Urbain Delorme, Pierre Falcon, William Hallet, George Flett, and William McGillis—all spoke, and all agreed that, the treaty being one of friendship, not sale, the HBC had not received title to the Red River Settlement by treaty with Peguis in 1817. Indeed, it was their view that the Métis had a legitimate claim to the land and, moreover, that their claim should have priority; they were descendants of the Cree, the first residents of the area, while the Saulteaux had arrived in the Red River region only shortly before 1817. Accordingly, the meeting concluded with an agreement by all present that since no proper arrangements had been made with the Native tribes of the region and since the Métis were now on the land and the immediate representatives of the first tribes in the region, the Métis should use every legitimate means to advance their claim for consideration in any arrangement which the Imperial Government might see fit to make. The meeting then adjourned until May, when the various Indian chiefs and wintering Métis would be in the Colony.[20]

This second gathering confirmed the conclusions of the first, and a statement was taken from André Trottier, one of three witnesses to the 1817 Selkirk Treaty, who swore that the Chiefs had not sold the land but only rented it to Selkirk for 20 years.[21] The controversy died down when it became clear that Crown Colony status was not forthcoming, but it subsequently flared up again in 1861 when the HBC decided to exact payment for all lands occupied in the Colony at the rate of 7s 6d per acre. If this payment was not received, the HBC warned, these lands would be sold to the first purchaser, in which case all improvements would be lost to the present occupiers. While the threat was soon withdrawn, it provoked an indignant reaction in several parishes where the Métis reaffirmed that no monies would be paid, that the HBC had no right to the land (never having purchased it in the first place), and that it was the Métis themselves who had a very palpable right to it, being the "descendants of the original lords of the soil."[22] While arguably minor incidents, these indignation meetings illustrate that the traditional Métis leadership had worked out a theory of Aboriginal rights as early as 1861 and were already using it to defend their land claims in Red River. It was a position that owed nothing to the Canadians in Red River, and it was this theory that Dease reiterated in July 1869.

Given Riel's opposition to Dease and his party, it is important to delineate Riel's paradigm of Métis communitas and the sources for it. That Riel should have assumed leadership of the Métis in 1869 is somewhat surprising. His father, who had been a leader of the free-trade movement in 1849, was fondly remembered in Red River, but Louis Riel Jr had no natural constituency among the Métis. He had left the Settlement at the age of 13 in 1858 to attend school in Montreal and had only returned to the Colony in the summer of 1868. He did not farm; he did not participate in the buffalo hunt; he did not trade; and, on his return to Red River, he refused his friend Louis Schmidt's suggestion to begin freighting to St Paul. Indeed, from his return to Red River until he assumed leadership of the Resistance, it is not clear that Riel did very much of anything. The one report of his activities, albeit from an unsympathetic observer, George R. Winship, gives the impression that he was just an ordinary town loafer who lived entirely off his mother. Winship, who had arrived in Red River about the same time as Riel, also noted that Riel was never known to earn anything himself by manual labour, preferring to hang around saloons a good deal "waiting for something to turn up for him to do suitable to his tastes."[23] Those historians who even bother to question why Riel rose to the leadership of the Métis usually point to his education as putting him naturally in the forefront. While this reasoning is plausible, it would not have carried much weight with the Métis buffalo hunters, merchant traders, or Métis councillors of Assiniboia.[24]

In fact, Riel's true constituency in 1869 was the Catholic Church, and it was through the Church that most of his influence would come. The most recent study of the Catholic Church's role in the Resistance leaves off deciding whether Riel or Catholic priests directed the Resistance, but clearly proves that Father Dugast (the main teacher at the St Boniface College) and Father Ritchot (the parish priest of St Norbert) were close partners with Riel in deciding Métis strategy in 1869–70.[25] With Archbishop Taché out of the Settlement, Dugast and Ritchot took the lead in guiding their Métis flock. Both men were secular priests who had been born in Quebec and shared a French-Canadian nationalism that saw the French Métis sharing a common history, language, and culture with the *Canadiens*. Ritchot in particular felt very threatened by the recent arrivals from Canada and feared for the religious rights of the Métis.[26] Furthermore, both men condemned the traditional buffalo-hunting economy of the Métis, hoping to win them over to a settled agricultural way of life.[27] It is therefore not surprising that the two men distrusted the traditional Métis leadership and their Aboriginal-rights justification for Resistance in 1869. For his part, Ritchot personally disliked William Dease (though Dease was a Catholic) and regarded him as a man "sans princippe et aussi hignorant qu'orgueilleux."[28] Father Dugast, meanwhile, criticized Dease's Aboriginal-rights justification of Resistance in a report to Taché, calling Dease a fool and adding that if the

details of the assembly of July 29 were heard in Canada, the Métis would all be taken for a band of lunatics.[29]

For Dugast and Ritchot, then, Riel most closely represented their ideal for the Métis of Red River. Attending the College of Montreal, he had been educated by the Sulpician fathers (who trained their students "as a Catholic and French-Canadian elite, proud of their difference from the English majority of North America"[30]) and so was steeped in the twin tenets of patriotism and religion. As Riel wrote in 1874, "The French-Canadian Métis of the North (West) are a branch of the French-Canadian tree. They want to grow like that tree, with that tree; they never want to be separated from it, they want to suffer and rejoice with it."[31] Accordingly, it is easy to understand why Ritchot viewed Riel as a "jeune homme du pays (et de talent)."[32]

With this paradigm of Métis communitas in mind, the events during and after the assembly of July 29 become more explicable. Following Dease's speech, John Bruce, who would later become the first president of Riel's "National Committee," took the floor and castigated Dease for advocating revolt. As a magistrate and member of the Council of Assiniboia, Dease should be the first to defend the government of the country, Bruce contended, and all such intrigues should be opposed. Apparently Bruce's arguments found their mark and the assembly broke up without endorsing Dease's plan of action. Father Dugast's lengthy report of this meeting makes it clear that Bruce had been carefully coached in his address.[33] Most of the evidence suggests that Ritchot, Dugast, and possibly Riel, had done the coaching and, indeed, Ritchot later admitted that he had advised his parishioners to be on their guard, and that he considered the object of the meeting to be of a dangerous character.[34] As well, both Ritchot and Dugast went out of their way to paint the Dease initiative as being inspired by John Christian Schultz.

Further meetings followed in August as the Métis continued to debate the position they should take to protect their rights considering the proposed transfer to Canada.[35] The Dease initiative, however, had collapsed by early October and with it the Aboriginal-rights paradigm of Métis communitas. Writing later, Ritchot attributed the collapse of this early movement to a failure of leadership (the leaders being bought off by Canadian transportation contracts), to the Protestant clergy's interceding with the English Métis to accept the transfer, and to the greed of some French-Métis merchants who saw Confederation as an economic opportunity.[36] While there was some truth to Ritchot's assessment, more important was the determined opposition of Riel, Ritchot, and Dugast, and their elaboration of another paradigm of Métis communitas that carried more emotional weight with the French Métis.

By the end of August, the French Métis had increasingly come to see Confederation as the annexation of Red River by Protestant Orange Ontario and, consequently, as a threat to their religious rights.[37] News that William McDougall would be the new governor of the territory only raised the fears of the French-Catholic clergy and the many French Métis who viewed him as one with the other Canadians in the Colony (John Schultz, Charles Mair, John Snow, and J.S. Dennis), all of whom were widely distrusted.[38] Moreover, by this time there were also rumours circulating that McDougall was a "priest murderer."[39]

Dugast, writing to Taché, recounted a conversation between the Métis and John Snow that clearly showed the mindset of the time. Snow, who had been sent from Canada to build a road from Fort Garry to Lake of the Woods, tried to calm the fears of the Métis of Pointe-de-Chêne, but they would have none of it. They replied that he was friendly now that he was weak, but that they knew how the English had treated the Catholics of Upper Canada. "You are orangemen and you are all alike."[40]

How these sentiments and rumours were spread remains unclear, but these sentiments were undoubtedly shared by the Catholic clergy who, by October 1869, increasingly justified resistance to Canada in terms of protecting French and Catholic rights in Red River and who closely supported Riel, clearly the ascendent Métis leader. Thirty-five years later Dugast was to write:

> In reality he [Ritchot] was the soul of the movement. It was he who launched it and without him the movement would not have taken place. . . .
>
> It was M. Ritchot and I who not only guided but who drove on that opposition to the Canadian government—this is the real truth. I did not say it in my book because all truth is not suitable for publication. I say it to you. The ignorant métis would never have thought of vindicating their constitutional rights if M. Ritchot and I had not made them aware of them. Without M. Ritchot and me the movement remains inexplicable.[41]

With Dease's initiative in disarray, and with the active support and encouragement of Ritchot and Dugast, Riel moved to take the lead. Along with Baptiste Tourond and a few other Métis, he stopped the Canadian survey on 11 October as it approached the river lots of the Parish of St Vital, an action which, given the increasing fears and paranoia of the French Métis, won him considerable support. Then, when news arrived of the imminent arrival of McDougall in Pembina, Riel and his faction—which by this time included many of the younger and more militant boatmen of the Colony—took steps that would breach the established order, and initiate a period of crisis in the Red River Settlement. On October 20, Riel and his men met in the home of John Bruce where they organized a "National Committee" and made plans to stop McDougall from entering the Settlement. All was planned with the approval and knowledge of Ritchot.[42] The next day "la barrière" was erected across the Pembina trail at St Norbert, and all incoming and outgoing traffic was stopped and searched.

This act overturned the status quo, directly challenged the Council of Assiniboia's legitimacy, and threw the Colony into an uproar. Already humiliated by the combined efforts of Riel, Ritchot, and Dugast, and aware that most Métis still did not agree with the precipitous and resolute action Riel and his men had taken, William Dease now took an uncompromising stand against Riel, arguing that McDougall should be permitted to enter the territory and hear the Métis complaints. Sensing that support for Riel's course of action was slipping, Ritchot called for an assembly of Métis to meet in St Norbert on October 24 to resolve the divisions among the people. At this meeting, Dease and his supporters threatened to dismantle the barricade across the Pembina trail and only the intercession of Ritchot quieted the following uproar. Ritchot calmed the assembly by asking if they did not agree that Canada had treated the Colony with a lack of respect, and if it was not proper that some resistance be made. Even Dease's men could not disagree with this, and Ritchot eventually persuaded the majority of the Métis at the assembly to agree to back the path taken by Riel. Most of the rest agreed to stay neutral.[43] Dease, however, was not satisfied and continued his opposition.

The following day Riel was summoned before the Council of Assiniboia and asked to abandon his plans to prevent McDougall from entering the Colony. When Riel refused, the Council approached Dease and asked if he could raise enough French Métis to overturn the decision taken on October 24 and force Riel's men to disperse.[44] Dease moved quickly to raise a group of men to attend another meeting at St Norbert on October 27, at which both sides repeated their arguments for or against Riel's strategy. While Ritchot later claimed that he had not taken a leading role, another account, almost surely based

on intelligence supplied by Dease, noted that Ritchot had declared "in favour of the stand taken, and called upon the insurgents to maintain their ground."[45] Still another of Dease's party testified that Ritchot had "raved and tore his gown addressing the assemblage in the most frantic and excited manner."[46] The appeals of Ritchot and Riel together convinced even 20 of Dease's 80 supporters that Riel was right, Ritchot observing later (with an almost palpable disdain) that Dease had been supported by only George Racette, six Indians, and a handful of others.[47] Defeated, Dease and his supporters left the ground to Riel.

Riel had won. While Dease would continue to oppose Riel throughout the winter and spring of 1869–70, and other prominent French Métis would slide back and forth between neutrality and opposition, Riel never again lost the support of most of the French Métis. The Council of Assiniboia met for the last time on October 30, agreeing there was nothing more they could do.

Usually treated as a minor and almost inconsequential interlude, the Dease/Riel conflict played a major role in defining the nature of the Métis Resistance in 1869–70. On a symbolic level, it was a battle over whether the Resistance would be grounded broadly on a concept of Métis Aboriginal rights and led by the traditional Métis leadership, or whether the Resistance would be more narrowly a defence of French and Catholic rights in the settlement and led by the young Riel. To be sure, the Resistance had many other facets not touched upon here, and there were other reasons (class, economic, familial, and generational) why many French Métis opposed Riel;[48] however, unless one understands the symbolic nature of the Dease/Riel conflict, one cannot understand how key participants understood the events in which they were involved. Those Métis leaders who had been upstaged by Riel, and sometimes badly mistreated,[49] were never able to accept his leadership.

Later in the Resistance, Riel tried to bridge the chasm that had developed between his followers and those of Dease, who continued to enjoy a good deal of support among the Métis in both Red River and in St Joseph[50] and whose help Riel needed if he hoped to build a consensus around his leadership. Writing to Dease in St Joseph, where he had sought refuge from Riel's men after they had surrounded his house, Riel pleaded with his opponent to join forces:

We have been in hostility till now, but I am certain it was not our intent to have bloodshed, among friends and relatives, or to strike terror or mourning in the lives of the Métis along the R.R. . . .

Mr. Dease when have I ever done you any harm. If just recently our soldiers surrounded your home, it was with the intention of bringing you here to accept our word of honour and assuring us that you would do all in your power to restore peace & public safety. . . . I beg you this favour, let us re-unite and join hands. . . . Mr. Dease, I beg of you, why are you so opposed to us, after we have already discussed and aired these problems. My personal ambition is a thing not in my heart, and if I am capable of doing something it will be for the good of all. I do not ask for a reward, but only for that support and sustenance before all Métis.[51]

Dease, however, remained unmoved.

Riel also tried to broaden the scope of the Resistance after October 1869 to win over the support of the English Métis, but it never lost the French and Catholic tinge it had acquired in the period from July through September. This made it extremely difficult for Riel to build any settlement-wide consensus. After Riel and his men seized Upper Fort Garry in November of 1869, they raised a flag adorned with the fleur-de-lis and the Irish Shamrock. This ceremony was carried out by a Catholic priest who was attended by 60 of the scholars of the Roman Catholic seminary in St Boniface.[52] This symbolism was not lost on the English Métis. By allying himself so clearly with the Catholic clergy to defeat the Dease faction, Riel would never be acceptable as a leader to anything more than a small minority of English-Protestant Métis.

The Riel/Dease conflict also has some implications for the question of whether the Métis of 1869 were concerned with their Aboriginal rights. Thomas Flanagan, in a useful study of the political thought of Louis Riel, has argued that the question of Aboriginal rights played no role in the public debates of the 1869–70 Resistance. Riel's strategy in 1869, he argued, was to present the Métis as civilized men with rights equal to those of any British subject.[53]

Riel wanted the Colony to enter Confederation as a Province with institutions modelled on those of Quebec: local control of land and natural resources, responsible government, a bilingual Governor, bilingualism in the legislature and courts, and a tax-supported system of Protestant and Catholic schools.[54]

This is an accurate assessment of Riel's paradigm of Métis communitas in 1869. It does not, however, accurately describe competing paradigms that were part of the public debates on resistance before October 1869.

This paper has argued that the idea of Métis Resistance in 1869 did not spring from the brow of Riel alone and that, as early as July 1869, other Métis leaders such as William Dease had proposed another paradigm of resistance that was based on a theory of Aboriginal rights. This Aboriginal-rights paradigm, however, was opposed by Riel and his clerical advisors, Fathers Ritchot and Dugast, in their struggle to gain the leadership of the Métis Resistance. Their strategy consisted of stressing a defence of French and Catholic rights threatened by the Canadians in the Colony. With the triumph of Riel and defeat of Dease in the Assembly of October 27, the Aboriginal-rights paradigm disappeared from public view in Red River. It is interesting to note, however, that once Riel was in control of the Resistance in Red River, Father Ritchot utilized an Aboriginal-rights argument to rationalize the Métis Children's land grant (section 31 of the Manitoba Act) in his negotiations with the Canadian Government in Ottawa in 1870.[55]

NOTES

The author would like to acknowledge and thank John Foster, Tom Flanagan, Gerald Friesen, Paul Chartrand, and Allen Ronaghan, who read an earlier draft of this paper and made a number of useful comments and suggestions.

1. This term is borrowed from the anthropologist Victor Turner who pioneered a processual approach to studying political conflict as social drama. From his study of symbol and ritual, Turner outlined a three- or four-stage process by which social dramas unfold. In this process, the first phase of a social drama was a period of "separation" or "breach" that Turner refers to as a pre-liminal phase. This phase is comprised of symbolic behaviour signifying the detachment of the individual (or group) from either an earlier fixed point in the social structure or from an established set of cultural conditions. This is a period when the norms that govern social relations between persons or groups within the same social system (village, chiefdom, university department) break down. Such a breach is signalled by an overt or deliberate non-fulfillment of some crucial norm governing the intercourse of the parties. See Victor Turner, *Dramas, Fields, and Metaphors: Symbolic Action in Human Society* (Ithaca, 1974), 13–42.

2. This is a term that Turner uses to describe the bond uniting a people over and above any formal social bond.

3. W.L. Morton, Introduction to *Alexander Begg's Red River Journal and other papers relative to the Red River Resistance of 1869–70* (Toronto, 1956), 3. Morton's introduction runs from page 1 to 148. The section dealing with the events from June through October 1869 are found on pages 31 to 55.

4. Ibid., 3.

5. Ibid., 50–1. Morton argues that some of clergy approved of Riel's aims, but only followed the Métis and did not instigate or lead the Resistance. It is interesting to note that while Morton included one of Father Dugast's letters of 1869 (29 August 1869) in his collection of documents, he left out the more interesting ones (those of 14, 24, and 31 August 1869) which deeply implicated Dugast and Ritchot in the actual planning of Riel's campaign for the leadership of the Métis.

6. Ibid., 33.

7. See Philippe R. Mailhot, "Ritchot's Resistance: Abbé Noël Joseph Ritchot and the Creation and Transformation of Manitoba" (PhD diss., University of Manitoba, 1986), 14–62.

8. Schultz had arrived in the Red River Settlement in 1861, and was the acknowledged leader of the Canadian faction openly advocating annexation to Canada.

9. Philippe R. Mailhot, "Ritchot's Resistance," 21–2, 48.

10. Ibid., 29–30, 47.

11. Among other activities that were alarming the Métis, the Canadians were staking out land, they freely denounced the Americans, Fenians, and Métis in the Colony, they ran up the Canadian flag as if a symbol of conquest, and the Métis were openly and contemptuously spoken of as cowards. Hudson's Bay Company Archives (HBCA), A12/45, William McTavish to W.G. Smith, 24 July 1869, fo. 269–70. HBCA, RG 1, Series 4/8, William McTavish to Joseph Howe, 14 May 1870, 2.

12. State Historical Society of North Dakota, A26, Albert E. Dease Papers.

13. Two of William Hallet's sisters married French Métis and converted to Catholicism.

14. *Nor'Wester*, 24 July 1869. It was later reported that Pascal Breland had not given permission to use his name on the invitation.

15. While no minutes exist for this meeting it can be reconstructed using the various

accounts that do exist. See Archives de l'archevêché, Saint-Boniface (AASB), Dugast to Taché, 29 juillet 1869, T6695–6698; HBCA, A12/45, William McTavish to W.G. Smith, 10 August 1869, fos. 282–3; and Provincial Archives of Manitoba (PAM), MG3 B14, M151, Ritchot's Narrative of the Resistance, volume 1.

16. George F.G. Stanley, *Louis Riel* (Toronto, 1963), 56–7. W.L. Morton, "Introduction," to *Alexander Begg's Red River Journal*, 32–4.

17. AASB, Dugast to Taché, 29 juillet 1869, T6695–6698; PAM, MG3 B14, M151, Ritchot's Narrative of the Resistance, volume 1.

18. See "Red River a Crown Colony," *Nor'Wester*, 28 February 1860.

19. This debate can be followed in the pages of the *Nor'Wester*. See "Native Title to Indian Lands," 14 February 1860; "Peguis Refuted," 28 February 1860; "The Land Question," 14 March 1860; "The Political Condition of the Country," 28 April 1860; "Peguis Vindicated," 28 April 1860; "The Peguis Land Controversy," 14 May 1860; "The Land Question," 14 June 1860; "The Halfbreed Meeting," 28 June 1860; "Paketay-Hoond on the Land Question," 28 June 1860; "The Land Controversy," 28 June 1860; "The Last Half-Breed Meeting," 28 September 1860.

20. "The Land Question," *Nor'Wester*, 14 March 1860.

21. "The Land Question," *Nor'Wester*, 14 June 1860.

22. "Indignation Meetings," *Nor'Wester*, 15 June 1861.

23. PAM, MG 3 B15, George B. Winship Account of 1869–70 (typescript).

24. See, for example, Philippe Mailhot, "Ritchot's Resistance," 30.

25. Ibid., 31.

26. A.G. Morice, *History of the Catholic Church in Western Canada*, Vol II (Toronto, 1910), 10.

27. Philippe R. Mailhot, "Ritchot's Resistance," 9–10.

28. PAM, Ritchot's Narrative of the Resistance, volume 1, 16.

29. ASSB, Dugast to Taché, 29 juillet 1869, T6695.

30. Thomas Flanagan, *Louis "David" Riel: Prophet of the New World* (Toronto, 1979), 7.

31. Louis Riel writing to the President of the Saint Jean-Baptiste Society of Montreal, 24 June 1874. Quoted in Thomas Flanagan, "The Political Thought of Louis Riel," in A.S. Lussier (ed.) *Riel and the Métis: Riel Mini-Conference Papers* (Winnipeg, 1979), 140.

32. PAM, Ritchot's Narrative of the Resistance, volume 1.

33. AASB, Dugast to Taché, 29 juillet 1869, T6697.

34. Canada. Parliament, House of Commons, *Sessional Papers*, 1874, No. VII, "Report of the Select Committee on the Causes of the Difficulties in the North West Territories in 1869–70," Appendix No. 6, Testimony of Noël Joseph Ritchot, 20 April 1874.

35. AASB, Dugast to Taché, 31 aout 1869, T6778–6780.

36. PAM, Ritchot's Narrative, volume 1.

37. HBCA, A12/45, W. McTavish to W.G. Smith, 2 November 1869, fo. 313–14.

38. This sentiment is clearly visible in the letters written by Father Dugast to Taché in the AASB. See his letters of 14 Aout 1869, T6734–37; 24 Aout 1869, T6764–67; and 31 Aout 1869, T6778–80.

39. HBCA, RG 1, Series 4/8, W. McTavish to Joseph Howe, 14 May 1870, 13. The basis of this rumour had to do with McDougall's role in the Manitoulin Island Incident of 1862–3 in Canada. For an explanation of this incident and its bearing on McDougall's reputation among the Métis, see Neil Edgar Allen Ronaghan, "The Archibald Administration in Manitoba, 1870–1872" (PhD diss., University of Manitoba, 1987), 61–85.

40. AASB, Dugast to Taché, 31 Aout 1869, T6781.

41. Archives du Collège Sainte-Marie, Fonds-Immaculée-Conception, Dugast to Fr. Joseph Grenier, 15 April 1905. Quoted in W.L. Morton (ed.) *Alexander Begg's Red River Journal*, 51n. Morton quotes this letter only to dismiss it as inaccurate citing as reasons that it was written 35 years after the fact, that Dugast possessed a flair for inaccuracy, and that Dugast was a vain and garrulous man. A close reading of Dugast's correspondence written in 1869, along with Ritchot's Narrative, suggests exactly the opposite.

42. See Ritchot's Narrative, vol. 1. These events and Ritchot's influence on them is described in some detail in Philippe Mailhot, "Ritchot's Resistance," 31–9.

43. PAM, Ritchot's Narrative, vol. 1, 22–5.

44. PAM, Minutes of the Council of Assiniboia, 25 October 1869.

45. Canada. Parliament, House of Commons, *Sessional Papers* 1870, No. 12, "Correspondence and Papers Connected with Recent Occurrences in the North West Territories." Letter of J.S. Dennis to William McDougall, 27 October 1869. That Ritchot took an active role at this meeting is also backed up by Ritchot's subsequent actions during the Resistance. In December of 1869, after Riel and his men had seized Fort Garry, they began to run low on supplies and approached the Hudson's Bay Company for an advance. William McTavish, the presiding HBC officer, refused the request and told the Métis to leave the fort. This caused a dilemma for the Métis Council and Riel. Their choices at this point were to either abandon the Resistance or forcibly seize HBC property. In the meeting held to decide their course of action, Ritchot took a prominent role advising the Métis to continue their course. Their case was already before the Canadian government, he argued, and soon the present ministry would fall and the demands of the Métis would be secured. With this encouragement the Métis decided not to disperse and the HBC stores and safe were broken into. See HBCA, A12/45, William McTavish to W.G. Smith, 11 December 1869, fos. 328–9.

46. Canada. Parliament, House of Commons, *Sessional Papers* 1870, No. 12, "Correspondence and Papers Connected with Recent Occurrences in the North West Territories."

47. PAM, Ritchot's Narrative, vol. 1.

48. See Chapter 5 of Gerhard J. Ens, "Kinship, Ethnicity, Class and the Red River Métis" (PhD diss., University of Alberta, 1989).

49. Many of the Métis who opposed Riel were later imprisoned by Riel including William Dease, Baptiste Charette, William Gaddy, William Hallet, and Gabriel Lafournaise. Hallet was kept in chains in an unheated room through the worst of the winter.

50. St Joseph was a Métis community just across the US border near the present-day town of Walhalla, North Dakota.

51. Louis Riel to William Dease, 15 February 1870. Reprinted in G.F.G. Stanley (general editor) *The Collected Writings of Louis Riel/Les Écrits Complets de Louis Riel, Vol. 1* (Edmonton, 1985), 52.

52. HBCA, A12/45, William McTavish to W.G. Smith, 11 December 1869, fo. 328–9.

53. Thomas Flanagan, "The Political Thought of Louis Riel," 150–2. See also his "Political Theory of the Red River Resistance: The Declaration of December 8, 1869," *Canadian Journal of Political Science* XI, 1 (March 1978): 153–64; and "The Case Against Métis Aboriginal Rights," *Canadian Public Policy* IX, 3 (September 1983): 316–7.

54. Ibid., 139.

55. For Ritchot's use of this argument see his Ottawa journal published in W.L. Morton (ed.) *Manitoba: The Birth of a Province* (Winnipeg, 1965), 140–2.

Chapter 14

Confederation and Anti-Confederation

READINGS

Primary Documents

1   From *Parliamentary Debates on the Subject of the Confederation of the British North American Provinces*, George Brown

2   From *Parliamentary Debates on the Subject of the Confederation of the British North American Provinces*, A.A. Dorion

Historical Interpretations

3   From "Tax Revolt in Nova Scotia in the 1860s: Fairness and Region," in *Tax, Order, and Good Government: A New Political History of Canada, 1867–1917*, Elsbeth Heaman

4   From "Confederation as a Hemispheric Anomaly: Why Canada Chose a Unique Model of Sovereignty in the 1860s," Andrew Smith

INTRODUCTION

Confederation is the worst-kept secret in Canadian history. We have referred to it in earlier topic introductions, and students frequently foreshadow it in essays focusing on the 1840s or even earlier. We know the outcome, and want to dissect the past so that we can better explain how predictable (or perhaps shocking) the result was. We do this regardless of how important the constitutional changes brought about in 1867 actually were for people living in the newly confederated colonies. For some, like those who got access to a railway as part of the package, Confederation was life-changing. It affected their livelihoods, their prospects, and their sense of being linked to the rest of the world. For others, such as those who remained relatively isolated from the reconfigured state's gifts or demands, life went on much as it had before.

The debate surrounding Confederation was passionate and continued well beyond the 1860s. As the primary documents make clear, Confederation's proponents believed that the scheme could solve many of British North America's persistent problems and pave the way for future expansion. George Brown, perhaps Canada West's keenest expansionist, argued that Confederation would bring justice to the inhabitants of the future province of Ontario, who suffered, he believed, under a grievous "French domination" in the Province of Canada, and that it would allow for the annexation of the northwest. Others were more wary. Many of Confederation's opponents indeed regarded the scheme as undemocratic or unwieldly. A.A. Dorion, in particular, mentions several reasons why the arrangements for Confederation seemed to be rather too hastily made.

The historical interpretations included in this chapter complicate the story of the merger by placing Confederation in the local and international contexts. Elsbeth Heaman challenges the notion that an inherent conservativism led the Atlantic colonies to be cool to the union proposal by examining the impact of Confederation's proposed fiscal arrangements on New Brunswick, Nova Scotia, Prince Edward Island, and Newfoundland. She reveals that the complicated system of taxes, subsidies, and consolidation of tax power in the federal realm that was part of the merger was sufficient to entice only two of the four colonies to join Confederation in 1867. Andrew Smith provides a broad view of the Confederation process, adopting a hemispheric approach for his analysis of the push for Confederation. Smith recognizes the strong desire of British North Americans to remain part of the British Empire, and he shows how political developments of the 1860s in the United States and Latin America shaped the form that Confederation—and the ongoing British connection—would take.

QUESTIONS FOR CONSIDERATION

1. Was Brown right to argue that the Confederation scheme would bring justice to both English- and French-speaking Canada and that it had been endorsed by the electorate?
2. Dorion's speech introduces us to some of the potential problems associated with the creation of a new nation from the provinces of British North America. What were some of these?
3. What are the advantages and disadvantages of being linked politically (e.g., as part of a federation like Canada) with distant places that might not share the value systems that predominate in your community?
4. What were the financial concerns that the Atlantic colonies had with Confederation? Why did Nova Scotia and New Brunswick elect to join the union? Was it the correct decision?
5. How did political events in the western hemisphere impact Canada's path to Confederation? Did Brazil or the United States have a greater impact on the eventual form of the union?

SUGGESTIONS FOR FURTHER READING

Buckner, Philip. "Beware the Canadian Wolf: The Maritimes and Confederation." *Acadiensis* 46, no. 2 (2017): 177–95.

———. "The Maritimes and Confederation: A Reassessment." *Canadian Historical Review* 71, no. 1 (1990): 1–30.

Laforest, Guy, Eugénie Brouillet, Alain-G. Gagnon, and Yves Tanguay, eds. *The Constitutions that Shaped Us: A Historical Anthology of Pre-1867 Canadian Constitutions.* Montreal and

Kingston: McGill-Queen's University Press, 2015.

Martin, Ged. *Britain and the Origins of Canadian Confederation, 1837–67.* Vancouver: UBC Press, 1995.

———, ed. *The Causes of Canadian Confederation.* Fredericton: Acadiensis Press, 1990.

Miller, Bradley. "Confederation in Court: The BNA Act as Legal History." *Canadian Historical Review* 98, no. 4 (2017): 708–26.

Moore, Christopher. *Three Weeks in Quebec City: The Meeting that Made Canada.* Toronto: Allen Lane, 2015.

Morton, W.L. *The Critical Years: The Union of British North America 1857–1873.* Toronto: McClelland and Stewart, 1964.

O'Flaherty, Patrick. *Lost Country: The Rise and Fall of Newfoundland, 1843–1933.* St John's: Long Beach Press, 2005.

Romney, Paul. *Getting It Wrong: How Canadians Forgot Their Past and Imperilled Confederation.* Toronto: University of Toronto Press, 1999.

Silver, I.A. *The French-Canadian Idea of Confederation, 1864–1900.* Toronto: University of Toronto Press, 1997.

Smith, Andrew. *British Businessmen and Canadian Confederation: Constitution-Making in an Era of Anglo-Globalization.* Montreal and Kingston: McGill-Queen's University Press, 2008.

Waite, Peter B. *The Life and Times of Confederation, 1864–1867: Politics, Newspapers, and the Union of British North America.* Toronto: Robin Brass Studio, 2001.

Primary Documents

1 From George Brown, in *Parliamentary Debates on the Subject of the Confederation of the British North American Provinces* (Quebec: Hunter, Rose and Co., 1865), 84–6.

LEGISLATIVE ASSEMBLY

Wednesday, February 8, 1865

The Order of the Day for resuming the debate on the Resolution for a Union of the British North American Colonies, having been read,—

Hon. GEORGE BROWN rose and said: Mr. SPEAKER, it is with no ordinary gratification I rise to address the House on this occasion. I cannot help feeling that the struggle of half a life-time for constitutional reform—the agitations in the country, and the fierce contests in this chamber—the strife and the discord and the abuse of many years,—are all compensated by the great scheme of reform which is now in your hands. (Cheers.) The Attorney General for Upper Canada, as well as the Attorney General for Lower Canada, in addressing the House last night, were anxious to have it understood that this scheme for uniting British America under one government, is something different from "representation by population,"—is something different from "joint authority,"—but is in fact the very scheme of the Government of which they were members in 1858. Now, sir, it is all very well that my honorable friends should receive credit for the large share they have contributed towards maturing the measure before the House; but I could not help reflecting while they spoke, that if this was their very scheme in 1858, they succeeded wonderfully in bottling it up from all the world except themselves—(hear, hear)—and I could not help regretting that we had to wait till 1864 until this mysterious plant of 1858 was forced to fruition. (Hear, hear, and laughter.) For myself, sir, I care not who gets the credit of this scheme,—I believe it contains the best features of all the suggestions that have been made in the last ten years for the settlement of our troubles; and the whole feeling in my mind now is one of joy and thankfulness that there were found men of position and influence in Canada who, at a moment of serious crisis, had nerve and patriotism enough to cast aside political partisanship, to banish personal considerations, and unite for the accomplishment of a measure so fraught with advantage to their common country. (Cheers.) It was a bold step in the then existing state of public feeling for many members of the House to vote for the Constitutional Committee moved for by the last session—it was a very bold step for many of the members of that committee to speak and vote candidly upon it—it was a still bolder thing for many to place their names to the report that emanated from that committee,—but it was an infinitely bolder step for the gentlemen who now occupy these treasury benches, to brave the misconceptions and suspicions that would certainly attach to the act, and enter the same Government. And it is not to be denied that such a Coalition demanded no ordinary justification. But who does not feel that every one of us has to-day ample justification and reward for all we did in the document now under discussion? (Cheers.) But seven short months have passed away since the Coalition Government was formed, yet already are we submitting a scheme well-weighed and matured, for the erection of a future empire,—a scheme which has been received at home and abroad with almost universal approval.

Hon. Mr. HOLTON—(Ironically) hear! hear!!

Hon. Mr. BROWN—My hon. friend dissents from that, but is it possible truthfully to deny it? Has it not been approved and endorsed by the governments of five separate colonies?—Has it not received the all but unanimous approval of the press of Canada?—Has it not been heartily and unequivocally endorsed by the electors of Canada? (Cries of hear, hear, and no, no.) My honorable friend opposite cries "no, no," but I say "yes, yes." Since the Coalition was formed, and its policy of Federal union announced, there have been no fewer than twenty-five parliamentary elections—fourteen for members of the Upper House, and eleven for members of the Lower House. At the fourteen Upper House contests, but three candidates dared to show themselves before the people in opposition to the Government scheme; and of these, two were rejected, and one—only one—succeeded in finding a seat. (Hear, hear.) At the eleven contests for the Lower House, but one candidate on either side of politics ventured to oppose the scheme, and I hope that even he will yet cast his vote in favor of Confederation. (Hear, hear.) Of these twenty-five electoral contests, fourteen Upper House elections embraced no fewer than forty counties. (Hear, hear.) Of the 130 constituencies, therefore, into which Canada is divided for representation in this chamber, not fewer than fifty have been called on since our scheme was announced to pronounce at the polls their verdict upon it, and at the whole of them but four candidates on both sides of politics ventured to give it opposition. (Cheers.) Was I not right then in asserting that the electors of Canada had, in the most marked manner, pronounced in favor of the scheme? (Hear, hear.) And will honorable gentlemen deny that the people and press of Great Britain have received it with acclamations of approval?—that the Government of England have cordially endorsed and accepted it?—aye, that even the press and the public men of the United States have spoken of it with a degree of respect they never before accorded to any colonial movement? Sir, I venture to assert that no scheme of equal magnitude, ever placed before the world, was received with higher eulogiums, with more universal approbation, than the measure for the acceptance of the Canadian Parliament. And no higher eulogy could, I think, be pronounced than that I heard a few weeks ago from the lips of one of the foremost of British statesmen, that the system of government we proposed seemed to him a happy compound of the best features of the British and American Constitutions. And well, Mr. SPEAKER, might our present attitude in Canada arrest the earnest attention of other countries. Here is a people composed of two distinct races, speaking different languages, with religious and social and municipal and education institutions totally different; with sectional hostilities of such a character as to render government for many years well-nigh impossible; with a Constitution so unjust in the view of one section as to justify any resort to enforce a remedy. And yet, sir, here we sit, patiently and temperately discussing how these great evils and hostilities may justly and amicably be swept away forever. (Hear, hear.) We are endeavoring to adjust harmoniously greater difficulties than have plunged other counties into all the horrors of civil war. We are striving to do peacefully and satisfactorily what Holland and Belgium, after years of strife, were unable to accomplish. We are seeking by calm discussion to settle questions that Austria and Hungary, that Denmark and Germany, that Russia and Poland, could only crush by the iron heel of armed force. We are seeking to do without foreign intervention that which deluged in blood the sunny plains of Italy. We are striving to settle forever issues hardly less momentous than those that have rent the neighboring public and are now exposing it to all the horrors of civil war. (Hear, hear.)

Have we not then, Mr. SPEAKER, great cause of thankfulness that we have found a better way for the solution of our troubles than that which has entailed on other countries such deplorable results? And should not every one of us endeavor to rise to the magnitude of the occasion, and earnestly seek to deal with this question to the end in the same candid and conciliatory spirit in which, so far, it has been discussed? (Loud cries of hear, hear.) The scene presented by this chamber at this moment, I venture to affirm, has few parallels in history. One hundred years have passed away since these provinces became by conquest part of the British Empire. I speak in no boastful spirit—I desire not for a moment to excite a painful thought—what was then the fortune of war of the brave French nation, might have been ours on that well-fought field. I recall those olden times merely to mark the fact that here sit to-day the descendants of the victors and the vanquished in the fight of 1759, with all the differences of language, religion, civil law, and social habit, nearly as distinctly marked as they were a century ago. (Hear, hear.) Here we sit to-day seeking amicably to find a remedy for constitutional evils and injustice complained of—by the vanquished? No, sir—but complained of by the conquerors! (Cheers by the French Canadians.) Here sit the representatives of the British population claiming justice—only justice; and here sit the representatives of the French population, discussing in the French tongue whether we shall have it. One hundred years have passed away since the conquest of Quebec, but here sit the children of the victor and the vanquished, all avowing hearty attachment to the British Crown—all earnestly deliberating how we shall best extend the blessings of British institutions—how a great people may be established on this continent in close and hearty connection with Great Britain. (Cheers.) Where, sir, in the page of history, shall we find a parallel to this? Will it not stand in an imperishable monument to the generosity of British rule? And it is not in Canada alone that this scene is being witnessed. Four other colonies are at this moment occupied as we are—declaring their hearty love for the parent State, and deliberating with us how they may best discharge the great duty entrusted to their hands, and give their aid in developing the teeming resources of these vast possessions. And well, Mr. SPEAKER, may the work we have unitedly proposed rouse the ambition and energy of every true man in the continent of America, and mark that island (Newfoundland) commanding the mouth of the noble river that almost cuts our continent in twain. Well, sir, that island is equal in extent to the kingdom of Portugal. Cross the straits to the main land, and you touch the hospitable shores of Nova Scotia, a country as large as the kingdom of Greece. Then mark the sister province of New Brunswick—equal in extent to Denmark and Switzerland combined. Pass up the river St. Lawrence to Lower Canada—a country as large as France. Pass on to Upper Canada,—twenty thousand square miles larger than Great Britain and Ireland put together. Cross over the continent to the shores of the Pacific, and you are in British Columbia, the land of golden promise,—equal in extent to the Austrian Empire. I speak not now of the vast Indian Territories that lie between—greater in extent than the whole soil of Russia—and that will ere long, I trust, be opened up to civilization under the auspices of the British American Confederation. (Cheers.) Well, sir, the bold scheme in your hands is nothing less than to gather all these countries into one—to organize them all under one government, with the protection of the British flag, and in heartiest sympathy and affection with our fellow subjects in the land that gave us birth. (Cheers.) Our scheme is to establish a government that will seek to turn the tide of European emigration into this northern half of the American continent—that will strive to develop its great natural resources—and

that will endeavor to maintain liberty, and justice, and christianity throughout the land.

Mr. T.C. WALLBRIDGE—When?

Hon. Mr. CARTIER—Very soon!

Hon. Mr. BROWN—The hon. member for North Hastings asks when all this can be done? Sir, the whole great ends of this Confederation may not be realized in the lifetime of many who now hear me. We imagine not that such a structure can be built in a month or in a year. What we propose now is but to lay the foundations of the structure—to set in motion the governmental machinery that will one day, we trust, extend from the Atlantic to the Pacific. And we take especial credit to ourselves that the systems we have devised, while admirably adapted to our present situation, is capable of gradual and efficient expansion in future years to meet all the great purposes contemplated by our scheme. But if the honorable gentleman will only recall to mind that when the United States needed from the Mother Country, and for many years afterwards their population was not nearly equal to ours at this moment; that their internal improvements did not then approach to what we have already attained; and that their trade and commerce was not then a third of what ours has already reached; I think he will see that the fulfillment of our hopes may not be so very remote as at first sight might be imagined—(hear, hear.) And he will be strengthened in that conviction if he remembers that what we propose to do is to be done with the cordial sympathy and assistance of that great Power of which it is our happiness to form a part. (Hear, hear.) Such, Mr. SPEAKER, are the objects of attainment to which the British American Conference pledged itself in October. And said I not rightly that such a scheme is well fitted to fire the ambition and rouse the energies of every member of this House? Does it not lift us above the petty politics of the past, and present to us high purposes and great interests that may well call forth all enterprise to be found among us? (Cheers.)

2 From A.A. Dorion, in *Parliamentary Debates on the Subject of the Confederation of the British North American Provinces* (Quebec: Hunter, Rose and Co., 1865), 245–69, 690–5.

HON. MR. DORION—But, sir, I may be asked, granting all this, granting that the scheme brought down is not the scheme promised to us, what difference our bringing in the provinces at once can make? This I will endeavor to explain. When they went into the Conference, honorable gentlemen opposite submitted to have the votes taken by provinces. Well, they have now brought us in, as was natural under the circumstances, the most conservative measure ever laid before a Parliament. The members of the Upper House are no longer to be elected, but nominated, and nominated by whom? By a Tory or Conservative Government for Canada, by a Conservative Government in Nova Scotia, by a Conservative Government in Prince Edward Island, by a Conservative Government in Newfoundland, the only Liberal Government concerned in the nomination being that which is controlled by the Liberal party in New Brunswick, whose fate depends on the result of the elections that are now going on in that province. Such a scheme would never have been adopted if submitted to the liberal people of Upper Canada. When the Government went into that Conference they were bound by the majority, especially since they voted by provinces, and the 1,400,000 of Upper Canada with the 1,100,000 of Lower Canada—together 2,500,000 people—were over-ridden by 900,000 people of the Maritime Provinces. Were we not expressly told that it was the Lower Provinces who would not hear of our having an elective Legislative Council? If, instead of going into Conference with the people of the Lower Provinces, our Government had done what they pledged themselves to do, that is, to prepare a Constitution themselves, they would never have dared to bring in such a proposition as this which is now imposed upon us by the Lower Colonies—to have a Legislative Council, with a fixed number of members, nominated by four Tory governments. Why, taking the average time each councillor will be in the Council to be fifteen to twenty years, it will take a century before its complexion can be changed. For all time to come, so far as this generation and the next are concerned, you will find the Legislative Council controlled by the influence of the present Government.

HON. MR. DORION—The honorable member for Lambton says that makes no difference. It makes just the difference that we are to be bound by the scheme or by a Constitution enabling the Council to stop all measures of reform, such as would be desired by the Liberal party; if the honorable member for Lambton thinks that makes no difference, I beg to differ from him, and I believe the Liberal party generally will. The Government say they had to introduce certain provisions, not to please themselves, but to please the provinces below, and they have pledged themselves to those provinces that this House will carry out the scheme without amendment. Does not the honorable member see the difference now? If the two Canadas were alone interested, the majority would have its own way—would look into the Constitution closely—would scan its every doubtful provision, and such a proposal as this about the Legislative Council would have no chance of being carried, for it is not very long since the House, by an overwhelming majority, voted for the substitution of an elected for a nominated Upper Chamber. In fact, the nominated Chamber had fallen so low in public estimation—I do not say it was from the fault of the men who were there, but the fact is, nevertheless, as I state it—that it commanded no influence. There was even a difficulty in getting a quorum of it together. So a change became absolutely necessary, and up to the present moment the new system has worked well; the elected members are equal in every respect to the nominated ones, and it is just when we see an interest beginning to be felt in the proceedings of the Upper House that its Constitution is to be changed, to return back again to the one so recently condemned. Back again, did I say? No, sir, a Constitution is to be substituted, much worse than the old one, and such as is nowhere else to be found. Why, even the British house of Lords, conservative as it is, is altogether beyond the influence of the popular sentiment of the country. Their number may be increased on the recommendation of the responsible advisers of the Crown, if required to secure united action or to prevent a conflict between the two Houses. From the position its members occupy, it is a sort of compromise between the popular element and the influence or control of the Crown. But the new House for the Confederation is to be a perfectly independent body—these gentlemen are to be named for life—and there is to be no power to increase their number. How long will the system work without producing a collision between the two branches of the Legislature? Suppose the Lower House turns out to be chiefly Liberal, how long will it submit to the Upper House, named by Conservative administrations which have taken advantage of their temporary numerical strength to bring about such a change as is now proposed? [. . .] I venture to prophesy, sir, that before a very short time has elapsed a dead-lock may arise, and such an excitement be created as has never yet been seen in this country. (Hear, hear.) Now, if this Constitution had been framed by the members of our Government, we could change some of its provisions. [. . .] But no, the Constitution is in the nature of a compact, a treaty, and cannot be changed. (Hear.)

I now come to another point. It is said that this Confederation is necessary for the purpose of providing a better mode of defence for this country. There may be people who think that by adding two and two together you make five. I am not of that opinion. I cannot see how by adding the 700,000 or 800,000 people, the inhabitants of the Lower Provinces, to the 2,500,000 inhabitants of Canada, you can multiply them so as to make a much larger force to defend the country than you have at present. Of course the connection with the British Empire is the link of communication by which the whole force of the Empire can be brought together for defence. (Hear, hear.) But the position of this country under the proposed scheme is very evident. You add to the frontier four or five hundred more miles than you now have, and an extent of country immeasurably greater in proportion than the additional population you have gained; and if there is an advantage at all for the defence of the country, it will be on the part of the Lower Provinces and not for us. And as we find that we are about to enter into a very large expenditure for this purpose of defence—this having been formally announced in a speech delivered by the President of the Council at Toronto—and as Canada is to contribute to that expenditure to the extent of ten-twelfths of the whole, the other provinces paying only two-twelfths, it follows that Canada will pay ten-twelfths also of the cost of defence, which, to defend the largely extended country we will have to defend, will be much larger than if we remained alone.

[. . .]

This I contend, then, that if the military and naval defences of all the provinces are to be provided for by the General Government, and if you have to increase the militia for this purpose, the Lower Provinces will pay only their proportion of two-twelfths, and Canada, while obtaining no greater defensive force than at present, will have to pay five times as much as we are now paying. (Hear, hear.) Why, sir, take the line dividing New Brunswick from Maine and you find it separates on the one side 250,000, thinly scattered over a vast territory, from 750,000 on the other, compact and powerful. These 250,000 Canada will have to defend, and it will have to pledge its resources for the purpose of providing means of defence along that extended line. (Hear, hear.) And, if rumor be true, the Intercolonial Railway, this so-called great defensive work, is not to pass along Major ROBINSON'S line. The statement has been made—I have seen it in newspapers usually well informed—that a new route has been found that will satisfy everybody or nobody at all; and while I am on this point I must say that it is most singular that we are called upon to vote these resolutions, and to pledge ourselves to pay ten-twelfths of the cost of that railway, without knowing whether there will be ten miles or one hundred miles of it in Lower Canada, or whether it will cost $10,000,000 or $20,000,000.

HON. MR. DORION—In 1862, when the question of the construction of this road was before the country, what was the cry raised by honorable gentlemen opposite? Why, that the MACDONALD-SICOTTE Government had pledged itself to build a railway at whatever cost it might come to; and those who were loudest in these denunciations, were the very gentlemen who have now undertaken to build the road without knowing or even enquiring what the cost of it will be. (Hear, hear.) This, if I remember right, was the purport of a speech made by the Hon. Attorney General West at Otterville. (Hear, hear.) I was satisfied, sir, at that time, to press my objections to the scheme and retire from the Government; but my colleagues were denounced without stint for having undertaken to build the railway and pay seven-twelfths of its cost, and now the House is asked by the very men who denounced them to pay ten-twelfths of it, without even knowing whether the work is practicable or not. (Hear, hear.) [. . .] It is folly to suppose that this Intercolonial Railway will in the least degree be conducive to the defence of the country. We have expended a large sum of money—and none voted it more cordially and heartily than myself—for the purpose of opening a military highway from Gaspé to Rimouski; and that road, in case of hostilities with our neighbors, would be found of far greater service for the

transport of troops, cannon and all kinds of munitions of war, than any railway following the same or a more southern route possibly can be. That road cannot be effectually destroyed; but a railway lying in some places not more than fifteen or twenty miles from the frontier, will be of no use whatever, because of the readiness with which it may be attacked and seized. An enemy could destroy miles of it before it would be possible to resist him, and in time of difficulty it would be a mere trap for the troops passing along it, unless we had almost an army to keep it open. [. . .] Sir, I say it here candidly and honestly, that we are bound to do everything we can to protect the country—(hear, hear,)—but we are not bound to ruin ourselves in anticipation of a supposed invasion which we could not repel, even with the assistance of England. [. . .] The best thing that Canada can do is to keep quiet, and to give no cause for war. (Hear, hear.) Let the public opinion of this country compel the press to cease the attacks it is every day making upon the Government and people of the United States; and then if war does come between England and the States—even if from no fault of ours—we will cast our lot with England and help her to fight the battle; but in the meantime it is no use whatever to raise or keep up anything like a standing army.

[. . .]

Now, sir, when I look into the provisions of this scheme, I find another most objectionable one. It is that which gives the General Government control over all the acts of the local legislatures. What difficulties may not arise under this system? Now, knowing that the General Government will be party in its character, may it not for party purposes reject laws passed by the local legislatures and demanded by a majority of the people of that locality. This power conferred upon the General Government has been compared to the veto power that exists in England in respect to our legislation; but we know that the statesmen of England are not actuated by the local feelings and prejudices, and do not partake of the local jealousies, that prevail in the colonies. The local governments have therefore confidence in them, and respect for their decisions; and generally, when a law adopted by a colonial legislature is sent to them, if it does not clash with the policy of the Empire at large, it is not disallowed, and more especially of late has it been the policy of the Imperial Government to do whatever the colonies desire in this respect, when their wishes are constitutionally expressed. The axiom on which they seem to act is that the less they hear of the colonies the better. (Hear, hear.) But how different will be the result in this case, when the General Government exercises the veto power over the acts of local legislatures. Do you not see that it is quite possible for a majority in a local government to be opposed to the General Government; and in such a case the minority would call upon the General Government to disallow the laws enacted by the majority? The men who shall compose the General Government will be dependent for their support upon their political friends in the local legislatures, and it may so happen that, in order to secure this support, or in order to serve their own purposes or that of their supporters, they will veto laws which the majority of a local legislature find necessary and good. (Hear, hear.) We know how high party feeling runs sometimes upon local matters even of trivial importance, and we may find parties so hotly opposed to each other in the local legislatures, that the whole power of the minority may be brought to bear upon their friends who have a majority in the General Legislature, for the purpose of preventing the passage of some law objectionable to them but desired by the majority of their own section. What will be the result of such a state of things but bitterness of feeling, strong political acrimony and dangerous agitation? (Hear, hear.) [. . .] But, sir, respecting the defences of the country, I should have said at an earlier stage of my remarks that this scheme proposes a union not only with Nova Scotia,

New Brunswick, Prince Edward Island, and Newfoundland, but also with British Columbia and Vancouver's Island. Although I have not been able to get the information from the Government—for they do not seem to be very ready to give information—yet I understand that there are despatches to hand, stating that resolutions have been adopted in the Legislature of British Columbia asking for admission into the Confederation at once. I must confess, Mr. SPEAKER, that it looks like a burlesque to speak as a means of defence of a scheme of Confederation to unite the whole country extending from Newfoundland to Vancouver's Island, thousands of miles intervening without any communication, except through the United States or around Cape Horn. (Oh!) [. . .]

So far as Lower Canada is concerned, I need hardly stop to point out the objections to the scheme. It is evident, from what has transpired, that it is intended eventually to form a legislative union of all the provinces. The local governments, in addition to the General Government, will be found so burdensome, that a majority of the people will appeal to the Imperial Government for the formation of a legislative union. (Hear, hear.) I may well ask if there is any member from Lower Canada, of French extraction, who is ready to vote for a legislative union. What do I find in connection with the agitation of this scheme? The honorable member for Sherbrooke stated at the dinner to the delegates given at Toronto, after endorsing everything that had been said by the Honorable President of the Council:—

We may hope that, at no far distant day, we may become willing to enter into a Legislative Union instead of a federal union, as now proposed. We would have all have desired a legislative union, and to see the power concentrated in the Central Government as it exists in England, spreading the aegis of its protection over all the institutions of the land, but we found it was impossible to do that at first. We found that there were difficulties in the way which could not be overcome.

Honorable members from Lower Canada are made aware that the delegates all desired a legislative union, but it could not be accomplished at once. This Confederation is the first necessary step towards it. The British Government is ready to grant a Federal union at once, and when that is accomplished the French element will be completely overwhelmed by the majority of British representatives. What then would prevent the Federal Government from passing a set of resolutions in a similar way to those we are called upon to pass, without submitting them to the people, calling upon the Imperial Government to set aside the Federal form of government and give a legislative union instead of it? (Hear, hear.) Perhaps the people of Upper Canada think a legislative union a most desirable thing. I can tell those gentlemen that the people of Lower Canada are attached to their institutions in a manner that defies any attempt to change them in that way. They will not change their religious institutions, their laws and their language, for any consideration whatever. A million of inhabitants may seem a small affair to the mind of a philosopher who sits down to write out a constitution. He may think it would be better that there should be but one religion, one language and one system of laws, and he goes to work to frame institutions that will bring all to that desirable state; but I can tell honorable gentlemen that the history of every country goes to show that not even by the power of the sword can such changes be accomplished. I am astonished to see the honorable member for Montreal West helping a scheme designed to end in a legislative union, the object of which can only be to assimilate the whole people to the dominant population. In that honorable gentleman's own country the system has produced nothing but a dissatisfied and rebellious people. Is it desirable that in

this country then we should pass a measure calculated to give dissatisfaction to a million of people? You may ascertain what the cost of keeping down a million of dissatisfied people is by the scenes that have been and are now transpiring on the other side of the line, where a fifth of the people of the United States has risen and has caused more misery and misfortune to be heaped upon that country than could have been wrought in centuries of peaceful compromising legislation. Sir, if a legislative union of the British American Provinces is attempted, there will be such an agitation in this portion of the province as was never witnessed before—you will see the whole people of Lower Canada clinging together to resist by all legal and constitutional means, such an attempt at wresting from them those institutions that they now enjoy. They would go as a body to the Legislature, voting as one man, and caring for nothing else but for the protection of their beloved institutions and law, and making government all but impossible. The ninety Irish members in the British House of Commons, composed as it is of nearly seven hundred members, by voting together have caused their influence to be felt, as in the grants to the Maynooth College and some other questions. It would be the same way with the people of Lower Canada, and a more deplorable state of things would be the inevitable result. The majority would be forced by the minority to do things they would not, under the circumstances, think of doing. This is a state so undesirable that, although I am strongly opposed to the proposed Federal union, I am still more strongly opposed to a legislative union. Those who desire a legislative union may see from this what discordant elements they would have to deal with in undertaking the task, and what misery they would bring upon the country by such a step. (Hear, hear.) I know there is an apprehension among the British population in Lower Canada that, with even the small power that the Local Government will possess, their rights will not be respected.

How, then, can it be expected that the French population can anticipate any more favorable result from the General Government, when it is to possess such enormous powers over the destinies of their section of the country? Experience shows that majorities are always aggressive, and it cannot well be otherwise in this instance. It therefore need not be wondered at that the people of Lower Canada, of British origin, are ready to make use of every means to prevent their being placed at the mercy of a preponderating population of a different origin. I agree with them in thinking that they ought to take nothing on trust in this matter of entering upon a new state of political existence, and neither ought we of French origin to do so, in relation to the General Government, however happy our relations to each other may be at present.

[. . .]

I contend that the local constitutions are as much an essential part of the whole as the general Constitution, and that they both should have been laid at the same time before the House. (Hear, hear.) We ought, besides, to have a clear statement of what are the liabilities specially assigned to Upper and Lower Canada. (Hear, hear.) It is well that Upper Canada should know if she has to pay the indebtedness of Port Hope, Cobourg, Brockville, Niagara, and other municipalities which have borrowed from the municipal loan fund, and what these liabilities are; and it is important for Lower Canada to be told what are the amounts they will be required to tax themselves for. We ought, besides, to obtain some kind of information upon the subject of the Intercolonial Railway, what is the proposed cost, and what route is to be followed; and before these facts are before the House, we ought not to take it upon ourselves to legislate on the subject. Still further, the people of the country do not understand the scheme. (Hear, hear.) Many members of this House, before hearing the explanations which have been offered, were, and others are still, in doubt as to the bearing of many of

these resolutions. [. . .] I owe an apology to the House for having offered such lengthened remarks on this question, and I have to thank honorable members for having so kindly listened to them. (Cries of "go on".) I will simply content myself with saying that for these reasons which I have so imperfectly exposed, I strongly fear it would be a dark day for Canada when she adopted such a scheme as this. (Cheers.) It would be one marked in the history of this country as having had a most depressing and crushing influence on the energies of the people in both Upper and Lower Canada—(hear, hear)—for I consider it one of the worst schemes that could be brought under the consideration of the House; and if it should be adopted without the sanction of the people, the country would never cease to regret it. (Hear, hear.) What is the necessity for all this haste? The longer this Constitution is expected to last, the greater the necessity for the fullest consideration and deliberation. [. . .] There are three modes of obtaining the views of the people upon the question now under discussion. The most direct one would be, after debating it in this House, to submit it to the people for their verdict, yea or nay. The second is to dissolve the House and appeal to the people. The third is to discuss and pass the resolutions or address to a second reading, and afterwards leave it open to the public to judge of its merits, by meeting and discussing it, and sending in petitions and instructing their representatives how to vote upon it when they came to Parliament at the next session. Any one of these methods would elicit the views of the people. But to say that the opinions of the people have been ascertained on the question, I say it is no such thing. (Hear, hear.) We have heard one side of the question discussed, but we have heard none of the views on the other side; and yet the feeling, as exhibited in some parts of the country, has been unmistakeably in favor of an appeal to the people. Some fifteen counties in Lower Canada have held meetings and declared for an appeal before the scheme is allowed to pass; and when honorable gentlemen on the other side have held second meetings, they have been condemned more conclusively than at first. (Hear, Hear.) [. . .]

There is no hurry in regard to the scheme. We are now legislating for the future as well as for the present, and feeling that we ought to make a Constitution as perfect as possible, and as far as possible in harmony with the views of the people, I maintain that we ought not to pass this measure now, but leave it to another year, in order to ascertain in the meantime what the views and sentiments of the people actually are. (The honorable gentleman was loudly cheered on resuming his seat.)

Historical Interpretations

3 From Elsbeth Heaman, "Tax Revolt in Nova Scotia in the 1860s: Fairness and Region," in *Tax, Order, and Good Government: A New Political History of Canada, 1867–1917* (Montreal and Kingston: McGill-Queen's University Press, 2017), 56–87.

In 1864, politicians from the United Province of Canada turned to the other British North American provinces for help in breaking their political deadlock. A growing plurality of Upper Canadians believed themselves under-represented and overtaxed, and they demanded constitutional reform that would either increase their representation or decrease the fiscal transfers. A plurality of Lower Canadians rejected all proposals for reform. Together, the two pluralities appealed to Atlantic Canada to join the union and break the deadlock. Because the political deadlock was a product of unequal fiscal relations, those had to be addressed as well. How would the Atlantic provinces figure in the kind of fiscal transfers that had provoked the political stalemate? The answer was clear. All four Atlantic provinces were consuming provinces; all four could be expected to pay more than their share of customs. Because the Atlantic provinces inhabited a "reluctant land," more marginal than that of the central Canadian agricultural heartland, they imported much of their basic food-stuffs and manufactures.[1] Their debt loads were also below that of Canada. By uniting with them, Canada could increase its revenues and its credit. Local economies might be struggling in some places, but union, its advocates argued, would lead to regional prosperity. Opponents of Confederation had a variety of arguments, but taxes were one of their strongest lines of attack. In a relentless barrage of speeches and newspaper articles, leading anti-Confederation voices argued that, regardless of other benefits, the BNA Act would appropriate much more than a few farthings and would draw them toward the centre of power. [. . .]

There was a very obvious, common-sense problem with the fiscal project as it was formulated and sold to the people. On the one hand, the Canadian tariff would extract surplus revenue from the people; on the other hand, the method of returning that revenue—subsidies to the provincial governments—fell far short of what was fair or necessary. Both observations were unambiguously true, and Nova Scotia was particularly hard hit by the formula worked out in Quebec. The Unionist finance minister, James MacDonald, insisted that provincial responsibilities would be much reduced and revenues more than adequate. Historians disagree. Historian Phillip Buckner makes the point pithily: The fiscal deadlock at Quebec was only broken when "Tupper came up with a formula that deliberately underestimated the needs of the Nova

Scotia government in order to arrive at a figure—an annual grant of eighty cents per capita—acceptable to the Canadians. This decision ensured that the Maritime provincial governments would be left with wholly inadequate resources."[2] Writing during the 1920s, at a time of serious regional economic downturn, J.A. Maxwell confirmed the "Anti" argument that Nova Scotia lost 90 per cent of its revenue in Confederation but only about 55 per cent of its spending responsibilities.[3]

If the flow of money from Ottawa to Halifax was clearly spelled out and clearly restrictive, the flow of money from Halifax to Ottawa—the tariff—was murkier. Rates were never perfectly comparable, but Nova Scotia and Prince Edward Island had a general tariff of 10 per cent and New Brunswick 15 per cent, while the Province of Canada was at 20 per cent, lowered to 15 per cent in 1866 in preparation for union.[4] Debates about how the Canadian tariff would affect the Atlantic region were speculative and empirical, grounded in ongoing debates about how existing tariffs worked. Antis saw much evidence for quasi-imperial and predatory taxation, and they launched a tax revolt against it. Much more than just a prelude to "better terms," the agitation against Confederation was also a critique of fiscal imperialism. Whereas the Unionist camp filled their newspapers with glittering predictions of state-driven wealth, the Antis filled theirs with grim warnings of state-driven poverty. In the process, they dissected the meaning and consequences of regionalized poverty. These were self-conscious political agents enjoying extraordinary liberties, and in asking whether they could continue to enjoy them, the anti-Unionists developed a clear-sighted analysis of how power operated in an increasingly imperial world.

The Quebec scheme, critics argued, would extract "tribute" from the peripheries and pull power and wealth to the political centre. That's what empires did, and that's what Canada was designed to become.

Confederation supporter Thomas D'Arcy McGee had once, as an Irish radical, espoused the "commonplace" view that "monopoly capitalism was the driving force behind the empire." In the 1860s, many expatriate Irish papers still took that view, but McGee had changed his tune and now championed both the British and Canadian unions.[5] When McGee insisted that this would be a partnership of equals, like the Mohawk Confederacy, the anti-Unionist Halifax *Morning Chronicle* responded that the Mohawk Confederacy beautifully served "Indian tribes occupying contiguous hunting grounds" but would confer no such benefits on the Atlantic tribes should they choose to join. A Mi'kmaq chief would wisely respond with summary violence "if three of his young men had gone off to Canada and spent a month dancing and feasting and swallowing firewater, and had then come back with a proposition to put out the council fires, dishonor the tribe, and pay tribute forever to the Cocknawagas."[6] Maritimers saw freedom being sacrificed to imperial exigencies. [. . .]

For there to be a tax grab there had to be something to tax and a state apparatus that lent itself to the grabbing thereof. All four Atlantic provinces were consuming provinces, but there were other considerations that made each of them more or less taxable. Neither Newfoundland nor Prince Edward Island had the kind of wealthy landowning classes that provided Burke's ballast. The small populations were mostly poor fishing and farming folk without much investment in the land. Newfoundland had a large Catholic minority that looked more like those shivering peasants in the Saguenay than the Protestant yeomen that the *Globe* continually exalted. In Prince Edward Island's case, the land was largely owned by absentee landlords. Politics there revolved around projects of escheat, aimed at seizing the land from the landowners, that metropolitan authorities were continually repressing and suppressing. Thus, appropriately for a colony with few landowners, the local franchise required not property but three days of statute labour on the roads.[7] So, while both Newfoundland and PEI were heartily invited to join the projected union, neither could provide a solution to George Brown's problem.

What of New Brunswick and Nova Scotia? Did they most resemble Upper or Lower Canada? The evidence was mixed but tended toward an Upper Canada resemblance. Both boasted wealthy, conservative, landed classes, a loyalist heritage, and a moderate path to responsible government, and both could be expected to oppose such Americanisms as a universal male franchise. Actually, Nova Scotia had recently abolished its property franchise for an assessment franchise and then abolished that franchise in favour of something approximating manhood suffrage, but no one seemed to like it. The Reform/Liberal government led by the champion of responsible government, Joseph Howe, had introduced legislation to restore property qualifications that would disenfranchise one voter in four, but then had to call an election before it took effect. The electorate that Howe was in the process of disenfranchising ousted him, but the new Conservative premier, Charles Tupper, sustained the restricted franchise. Nova Scotia was ostentatiously opting for property over people. Arguments for manhood suffrage were more marginal in the more conservative political culture of New Brunswick, where the premier, Leonard Tilley, was a moderate liberal with a reputation for fiscal soundness.[8] Tupper and Tilley formed enduring alliances with John A. Macdonald. They were politically like-minded: pragmatic, liberal-conservative politicians who based their platforms on economic development.

Reform liberals were less cohesive. They had fewer material interests in common and more occasion to quarrel. Take George Brown and Joseph Howe: Both advocated responsible government in the 1840s and small-state, liberal governments largely in the hands of the middling people in the 1860s. Brown had

good reason to look hopefully to Nova Scotia for supporters. But the reasons why Brown should look to Nova Scotia to fix Canadian politics were reasons why Howe should reject the invitation. There was the fatal flaw: Confederation served Brown by precipitating his province out of the union's straitjacket, but if Brown were in Nova Scotia, wouldn't he see Confederation as precipitating his colony *into* a straitjacket? That was how Howe understood things. Confederation was designed to check Macdonald's fiscal cronyism, but a cynic might find little evidence of a successful check. Why would any self-respecting liberal sign up? Howe voiced objections that Brown, were he in Howe's shoes, would probably have voiced. Delegates to the Charlottetown and Quebec conferences knew that Upper Canadians did not actually want to raise heavy taxes from the Atlantic provinces and that Brown hoped Maritimers would help him lower Canadian tariffs. He said so in the debates and in the Globe: "In the Confederation . . . the free traders of the West in conjunction with those of the Maritime Provinces will surely be able to secure a tariff as low as that of Nova Scotia."[9] But to believe that taxes would indeed go down required faith that the Antis lacked.

Arguments against Confederation as a tax grab were voiced early and often. Tilley had boasted during the constitutional debates that New Brunswick had a surplus that year of half a million dollars. Such boasts played very well in selling New Brunswick to Canada but less well in selling Canada to New Brunswick. When Tilley introduced the deal at a public meeting in Saint John in mid-November, his fiscal explanations fell flat.[10] Tilley described the basic terms, 80 cents a head and an additional top-up of $63 000 resulting in local revenue of $354 000, as more than enough to cover local purposes. He argued that industrialization in New Brunswick would reduce imports and taxes on imports, but the subsidies would not decline because they were fixed by law. There was much to criticize in this. The attack was led by the Saint John *Freeman*, an Irish-Catholic newspaper published by Timothy Anglin. His biographer remarks: "In very long, amazingly detailed, and cogent articles, Anglin poured scorn on the arguments and figures of Tilley."[11] He demonstrated that Confederation would raise an extra quarter of a million dollars annually from New Brunswick, and half a million from Nova Scotia. But even that would not meet Canada's fiscal needs. Any idiot could see that the Intercolonial to the east, the western extension of canals and railways, and the projected new military spending must all drive expenses far beyond existing levels. Canada would need millions more per year and would look to the Atlantic region for much of it. [. . .]

Nova Scotia Unionists gamely defended tax hikes. At the first public meeting for the returned delegates in early December 1864, Liberal (soon to be Liberal-Conservative) Jonathan McCully predicted glorious prosperity and was followed by Liberal (soon to be Liberal-Conservative) Adams Archibald who pooh-poohed predictions of higher taxes, but still admitted that if Nova Scotia was to be part of the Intercolonial Railway, "Your tariff must be raised." Tupper, up next, argued that Confederation would benefit Nova Scotia rather than cost it revenue, but he also argued for more railways and higher taxes.[12] The Nova Scotia Antis zeroed in on these claims and levelled damaging criticisms.[13] A turning point came on 30 December at a meeting organized by Andrew Uniacke, a Halifax merchant, for the "Let Alones" to have their say. The running themes of the five-hour meeting were fiscal transfers and economic decline. Joseph Howe attended the meeting but did not speak. Less than two weeks later, the first of Howe's "Botheration Letters" appeared in the Halifax *Morning Chronicle*. The paper was edited by Jonathan McCully, who was anti-Tupper but pro-Confederation; he was dismissed and William Annand made the paper a standard-bearer against Confederation. Howe

had welcomed the idea of Confederation in 1864, but he rejected the terms hammered out in Quebec as a political and fiscal assault on Nova Scotia. He couched his response in terms of the classic rights of the British subject, which was to say the British taxpayer. To exercise those rights, Nova Scotians needed control over their taxes, but the scheme provided no such agency either locally (because the provincial legislature would be too weak) or federally (for lack of numbers). [. . .]

In his first Botheration Letter, describing Nova Scotia's representation in Ottawa, Howe saw his hard work in getting responsible government being undone. The province's delegates to Ottawa would be too few and too politically divided to influence policy. Tupper and McCully, erstwhile rivals, had united around Confederation to be "friends from the teeth outwards" but once in Ottawa, "our members will be no longer unanimous, but split into two factions each following the fortunes of its leader, and each trying to bargain with the minister for the patronage and control of Nova Scotia." Thus divided, they would be easily controlled by a "little knot of politicians 800 miles away."[14] The second letter contrasted a divided Nova Scotia with a united French Canada: "Ever since the Union of the two Provinces, the French Canadians, by sticking together, have controlled the Legislation and Government of Canada. They will do the same thing in a larger Union, and, as the English will split and divide, as they always do, the French members will, in nine cases out of ten, be masters of the situation." Local governments would be too weak to object: "The Provincial Parliaments will have scarcely more dignity than the City Council, and of this we are quite sure, that neither Mr Archibald, Mr McCully nor Dr Tupper would take a seat in ours, were it offered free of costs and charges."[15]

Given those imbalances of power, the argument continued in the third letter, Canada would steamroller its tariff over Nova Scotia interests. Canada was to Nova Scotia as Britain was to Canada: an industrial powerhouse that would devastate the infant industries of the undeveloped partner. Whereas Nova Scotia got its revenue by taxing rum, Canada made its own rum and taxed manufactures. No reversal was likely because "a powerful party exists in Canada who advocate protection to Colonial manufactures." The Canadian tariff, applied to Nova Scotia, would wipe out existing revenues and injure Nova Scotia's trade with other British and colonial partners. It would devastate Nova Scotia's "noble fleet of ships and annually extending foreign trade."[16] [. . .]

What cared the metropolis for colonial poverty? What claims had poor regions upon the metropolis? Howe identified poverty as a regionalized product of empire. This is not to suggest that he took the pauper's point of view or that he saw a heinous plot against Nova Scotia. But historical precedent established an economic and political pattern of self-reinforcing inequality. This was a confrontation between political economy as theory and as practical experience. It grew from the same soil as British historical economics, inaugurated around the same time in a series of articles analyzing land tenure and impoverishment in Ireland comparative to England and continental Europe that T.E. Cliffe Leslie, a professor at Queen's College in Belfast, built up into an argument for inductive economics as against deductive, liberal political economy.[17] No such rigorous intellectual orientation characterized the anti-Confederation analysis of empire and poverty, but there was, nonetheless, an insistence that the two were not accidentally but systemically conjoined. This was very much a mid-Victorian debate about poverty, but it was a remarkably frank and sympathetic rendering of poverty's outlook.

[. . .]

Maritimers, like Canadians, posited a mutually reinforcing politics of identity and interest. The Unionists insisted that Maritimers would be crucial power-brokers in a divided Canada. Tilley made the claim in November 1864: "It is asked—Will you not impose heavier taxes? No. Heavier taxes would not be imposed. It seems taken for granted that the Canadian tariffs must be adopted. He repudiated the idea. For a number of years the Government of Canada had been sustained by very small majorities; and will it be said that forty-seven members, the representatives from the Lower Provinces, would not have some voice in the question of Tariff."[18] Archibald made the same claim two years later: Local taxes would go into a common Canadian purse that Nova Scotia would have a right to share in, and "we shall be in a position to assert that right." Canadians were divided by "differences permanent in their nature, and such as to create the elements of opposing parties." Sharing qualities of each, Nova Scotia could vote according to self-interest.

[. . .]

The Antis saw fantasy at work. Anglin ridiculed Tilley's claims that not just the Maritimes but even Prince Edward Island could alone "turn the balance." The claim was that Maritimers could ally with Upper Canada to keep Lower Canada in "perpetual subjection," or with Lower Canada to "keep Upper Canada in check." But the underlying theory was incoherent, argued Anglin. The federal Parliament was supposed to be organized around economic interests rather than identities. If that turned out to be true, if French Canadians, relieved "of anxiety about religion, language and laws, send representatives to the General Parliament to look after only their commercial and political interests, the state of affairs in which four or fifteen could turn the scale would be at an end, and we would find the representatives from the Montreal district at least uniting with the Upper Canadians in forcing on us those schemes for the development of the West for which we indeed would have to pay more than a share, but from which Montreal would derive great benefit, while we gained absolutely none."

On the other hand, if French Canadians felt as endangered as ever and the conflicts that had so long raged and injured Canada persisted, "should we not hesitate to involve ourselves in those quarrels and plunge into the vortex in which Canadian politics are now engulfed?"[19] Maritimers would do better to avoid the Canadian morass and build the Intercolonial themselves.

New Brunswickers were convinced, and in 1865, they voted Tilley out of office. Anglin's attacks won him a place in the new anti-Unionist government of A.J. Smith.[20] Confederation seemed to be dead in the water. In Nova Scotia, Tupper responded with a resolution in favour of Maritime union, but the debate that followed focused entirely on the pros and cons of the Quebec scheme. In defence of Confederation, Tupper also styled himself as an outraged taxpayer who combatted direct imperial taxation.[21] But where Unionists made fuzzy predictions of wealth and unity, the Antis responded with long, detailed fiscal analyses. Annand argued that Canada "knows that we have a surplus revenue, that we are a largely consuming people, and would be a valuable acquisition to the central treasury." Galt had said that, as well as that a Canadian tariff would increase taxation on the lower provinces from $2.5 million to $3 million. The difference would be paid by Nova Scotia because New Brunswick already paid high taxes and Prince Edward Island was too small to make much difference. Annand quoted the *Globe's* remark that "There can be no doubt that (under Confederation) the Lower Provinces would be heavy tax-payers." Taxes would rise 50 per cent and revenues shrink by $178 000 from a pre-Confederation budget of half a million dollars. Would the cuts be to roads, bridges, or schools? Archibald McLelan followed Annand with an even longer analysis of debt allowances, revenues, and subsidies. Currently, Nova Scotia had "the largest sum of any of the Colonies for local purposes, per head $1.96, but under the Quebec arrangement will have

the least—$1.12¼." Nova Scotia would pay double per capita what Canadians paid in customs. Confederation would "surrender to Canada the power to tax us to any extent that their extravagance may render necessary." He predicted a $782 560 transfer to Ottawa from the outset.[22]

Nova Scotians did not come cold to these debates. They had their own debates about their own taxes and tariffs. Like Cartier in Quebec, Tupper was imposing compulsory and highly unpopular centralized school taxes. He shrugged off that unpopularity. Governments must force modernity on recalcitrant populations, and it was enough, he argued, to have the "intelligent sentiment of the country" on side in regard to education, the franchise, and Confederation.[23] But, objected the opposition, Tupper's school taxes benefitted the rich disproportionately. They were too onerous and "did not provide sufficiently for the poorer sections" of the province. Tupper defended the higher tax and admitted the burden on the poor, but, he explained, it was "almost impossible . . . to frame any law that did not more or less benefit the rich and populous sections." When the opposition urged indirect rather than direct taxes to pay for schools, the attorney general responded that "the indirect tax was the dearest that a man ever paid" and that grumbling only persisted because people were "continually being stirred up" by the opposition.[24] The Confederationists wanted to keep lucrative and demoralizing taxes out of the hands of locals by removing them to Ottawa, even as they admitted that wealthy, populous central regions must disproportionately benefit from centralization of taxation and spending.

What of Nova Scotia's experience with its own tariff? Did it protect or injure the poor? Grain for bread must be imported and was more cheaply imported from the United States than from Canada, even after the Americans ended reciprocity. Should the colony unilaterally remit the duty on American flour, enabling the poor to buy cheap bread, or should it keep up a retaliatory duty and buy Canadian flour? Where Tupper and Archibald defended a duty, Liberals replied that the price of flour was "enormous," devastatingly so in the poor western counties. Archibald McLelan argued that "it was very hard that the poor people should have been obliged to pay a tax of $28 000 during six months on flour at a time when it was up to the exorbitant price of $8 or $9 a barrel," and William Blackwood that "it was the duty of the Legislature to impose as few burthens as possible upon the masses." Bread was only the beginning. Nova Scotians must also buy expensive Canadian manufactures.[25]

[. . .]

Joseph Howe saw identical causes operating to impoverish the workingman and the region. Canadian financial distress constituted the "secret history of Confederation," and the revenues of Nova Scotia would go to Canada's creditors. Distress in Nova Scotia would grow while the means to relieve it would shrink: "You are generously permitted to maintain 'the poor,' and to provide for your 'hospitals, prisons and lunatic asylums.' We have it on divine authority that the poor 'will be always with us,' and come what may we must provide for them. What I fear is that, under confederation, the number will be largely increased, and that when the country is taxed and drained of its circulation, the rich will be poorer and the industrious classes severely straitened." Worse, poverty would provoke violence: "If you take away from us £100,000 a year you will find it tell on our finances, cripple the discounts of the banks, check commercial enterprise, limiting the comforts of poor, diminishing the wealth of the rich. I am not sure that we will be content to bear it until we are reduced to milk and potatoes; before that comes we will take up our rifles, but I do say that what has happened to Ireland—the drawing of the life blood out of her is just what is likely to happen to us."[26] This was not traditional British rule but something very different, Howe

argued in a letter. The imperial metropolis, though it had controlled some casual revenues, rarely interfered with inferior patronage and "could levy no new taxes." The new "Downing Street at Ottawa will appoint our Governors, Councillors, and Judges—will have unlimited powers of external and internal taxation—At the start, will control and dispense a surplus revenue, drawn from Nova Scotia alone, of £234,000 or nearly twenty times the highest amount that the Colonial Secretary ever dispensed. And besides Downing Street never took a pound out of the country. If sometimes lavishly expended, the Casual revenue was all spent in the Country which raised it, but the Finance Minister of Canada may, annually, draw out of Nova Scotia an enormous sum and spend it where he likes. That our nineteen members will afford us any protection it is in vain to hope."[27] By undemocratizing Nova Scotia, Howe was returning to older mechanisms of political responsiveness that he saw Canadians actively dismantling. Ottawa would be more unaccountable and unresponsive to Nova Scotia electors than anything previously seen there.

Neither Canadian nor British politicians could remain entirely deaf to the grievances. It was becoming clear that Prince Edward Island and Newfoundland would not accept any version of the deal on offer, but that Nova Scotia and New Brunswick might. New Brunswick's opposition was eroded partly by British diplomatic pressure, partly by disappointing talks around trade and railway construction with the United States, and partly by a new Fenian threat that brought down Timothy Anglin. The Fenians, or Irish Republican Brotherhood, were founded in Dublin in 1858 and aimed to lead Ireland out of British union. When the movement was violently repressed in Britain in 1865, Fenian veterans of the American Civil War threatened to strike back in British North America, prompting panicked reinforcement of borders there. In New Brunswick, the Fenian panic triggered an outpouring of hostility toward

Irish Catholics and their sympathizers, above all Anglin. The *New Brunswick Reporter* asked "whether Mr Anglin is to rule this Province, or this Province to rule Mr Anglin; whether loyalty or Fenianism is the chief power in the land?" The vitriol won them a by-election and Anglin's resignation.[28] Unionists realized that the loyalty cry could swing a general election and forced one in April 1866, shortly after a Fenian raid materialized against Campobello. Leonard Tilley won 33 of 41 seats. The openly Anti forces won only three seats, all of them representing large Acadian populations. Confederation was then approved in the New Brunswick legislature by a vote of 38 to 1. Nativism overwhelmed the argument from regressive taxation, and not for the last time.

New Brunswick and Nova Scotia were now both in Unionist hands. William Miller, an anti-Unionist representing Richmond, suggested that better terms might effect a compromise. In London that December, delegates from New Brunswick, Nova Scotia, and Canada met to adjust the terms. There were ten changes on subjects ranging from the pardoning power to control of fisheries. Slightly better fiscal terms were now offered to New Brunswick and Nova Scotia: Their revenue of 80 cents per head would not be capped at the 1861 census but allowed to rise until the population reached 400 000. As well, there would be an increased subsidy of $80 000 to Upper Canada, $70 000 to Lower Canada, $60 000 to Nova Scotia, and $50 000 to New Brunswick.[29] In the ensuing debate in Nova Scotia, where the Antis had flagged Upper Canadian gloating over the first fiscal deal, the Unionists could now flag Upper Canadian dismay at the second. For Adams Archibald, the better terms proved that Nova Scotia controlled the balance of power. He quoted George Brown on the new arrangements that gave Upper Canada 60 cents per capita, Lower Canada 74 cents, Nova Scotia 88 cents, and New Brunswick $1.10: "Nothing could be more scandalously unjust to Upper Canada than this." Nothing

except, perhaps, the new distribution of seats in the upper house, about which Brown declared: "The thing is utterly unfair." So many outraged expostulations proved that Maritimers, too, could form a political combination. Other pro-Confederationists pointed to Cape Breton, where grumbling over its annexation had died away as locals demanded and obtained fair treatment: "If Cape Breton gets justice it is because we are bound to have it—because there is not a government in this country that would dare to ignore the claims of that island for a single year."[30] Unpersuaded, Annand insisted that revenue would drop from $800 000 in 1866 to $585 000 in 1868. Even people unfamiliar with constitutional treatises "well understand transactions in money in which their pecuniary interests are involved." McLelan concurred: Confederation was a tax grab. "In Lower Canada there were over a million of people paying comparatively nothing to the revenue. The great difficulty of Canadian finances arose from the fact that while these people contributed little or nothing, they claimed an equal share of the revenue." Nova Scotia would make up the difference, as shown by a comparison of current taxes on tea, sugar, molasses and flour, "the necessaries of life to the poor man."[31]

The unspoken Unionist rejoinder was that those taxes would find their way back to Nova Scotia, if not as subsidies, then as patronage spending. Macdonald's hand was all over the BNA Act. Because local governments were intended to check federal spending by championing local ratepayer interests, Macdonald had every interest in ensuring that they were as underfunded as possible. A fiscally beleaguered province could only carry opposition to Ottawa so far. There can be little doubt that the combination of a rich federal government and a poor provincial one was intended to make federal rather than provincial patronage carry more weight. Macdonald would be highly motivated to buy off Nova Scotia handsomely, as he had always bought off Quebec handsomely—that was the crux of the Unionist argument about the balance of power. But the Nova Scotia Antis saw weakness rather than strength in those covert dealings, and they also predicted that Maritimers could not long sustain the unity that had secured French Canada its concessions. Both views had truth to them. Macdonald stocked his government with important Maritime power-brokers and put them in control of the tariff. Early industrialization in Canada was consciously steered toward the industrialization of the Maritime provinces. But as Canada expanded westward in the twentieth century, as Anglin had foreseen, Maritime economic and political influence dwindled.

Confederation passed, despite popular hostility in Nova Scotia, because established authority backed it. The Antis could only ask for consideration, and they did not receive it. Joseph Howe was disgusted by the official indifference that greeted the Anti agitation and petitions in Britain and no less disgusted by the indifference in the new Dominion when, on the eve of the new Parliament's inauguration, he travelled to Ontario and gave speeches that the press ignored. But once Confederation was in force, elections gave the Nova Scotia Antis an overwhelming majority in the local legislature and an overwhelming preponderance among Maritime members of the federal Parliament. Tupper was the lone Confederationist returned to Ottawa, and Macdonald had to name such defeated Unionist candidates as McCully and Archibald to the Senate.

In Nova Scotia, Premier Annand's government rallied resistance and pursued repeal of the union. As ever, this was a battle fought on many fronts: public meetings, newspapers, legislative resolutions, and delegations. Agitators invoked the spectre of tax resistance that threatened to explode into "violence and bloodshed."[32] Much of the fire emitted from Martin Wilkins, the attorney general, who won his seat in Pictou on a strong Anti platform and, early in 1868, produced a manifesto against the forced scheme. Confederation was

tyranny because it wrested taxes from Nova Scotia without its consent, and taxes, for Wilkins, were the measure of free political agency. "Before the British America Act was imposed upon us Nova Scotia was as free as the air. How could the people of this country be taxed? There was no power to tax them except this House, their own servants, whom they commissioned to tax them. Is that the state of things now? Have we any power over the taxation of this country? Does not the Act in question confer upon Canada the fullest power of taxing all the property of Nova Scotia at their arbitrary will?" Britain had no power to tax Nova Scotia and, therefore, no power to impose the BNA Act.

[. . .]

Wilkins's remarks coincided with the release of the first Dominion tariff, which raised taxes on many Nova Scotia staples. Del Muise remarks that it "came like the fulfilment of some biblical prophecy."[33] There was also an unprecedented new stamp tax that even Tupper and D'Arcy McGee opposed as a tax on knowledge. But Macdonald insisted that although people wanted their papers free, government must "resist popular feeling."[34] Repeal meetings soon began to spread across Nova Scotia and then New Brunswick. One rural meeting that drew 250 people to the courthouse in Barrington, Shelburne County, Nova Scotia, unanimously resolved that luxuries were undertaxed, necessities overtaxed, and such a policy "must prove disastrous to the poor and middling classes."[35] While the Antis felt vindicated, the Unionists were deeply embarrassed by the new taxes and flooded Macdonald's inbox with protestations. These letters and Macdonald's responses to them merit scrutiny because they show the covert networks of influence and suasion at work. Grievances voiced by enemies must be categorically rejected, but those voiced by friends must be addressed if not redressed. Macdonald's reply to those informed and detailed letters conveys exactly how he reckoned with the problem—both real and potential —of poverty in the Maritime region. It will come as no surprise to the reader that he dismissed it outright as a matter for federal politics. But he was forced to compromise to carry the province. [. . .]

NOTES

1. Cole Harris, *The Reluctant Land: Society, Space, and Environment in Canada before Confederation* (Vancouver: UBC Press, 2008).

2. Phillip A. Buckner, "The 1860s: An End and a Beginning," in Phillip A. Buckner and John G. Reid, eds, *The Atlantic Region in Confederation: A History* (Toronto: University of Toronto Press, 1994), 376.

3. J.A. Maxwell, *A Financial History of Nova Scotia, 1848–1899* (PhD dissertation, Harvard University, 1926), 84–5.

4. J. Harvey Perry, *Taxes, Tariffs and Subsidies: A History of Canadian Fiscal Development,* 2 vols (Toronto: University of Toronto Press, 1955), vol. 1, 26.

5. David A. Wilson, *Thomas D'Arcy McGee: Passion, Reason, and Politics 1825–1857* (Montreal & Kingston: McGill-Queen's University Press, 2006), vol. 1, 259–60; e.g., Toronto *Irish Canadian*, 10 August 1864.

6. Halifax *Morning Chronicle*, 25 January 1865.

7. Sean Cadigan, *Newfoundland and Labrador: A History* (Toronto: University of Toronto Press, 2009); Rusty Bitterman, *Rural Protest on Prince Edward Island: From British Colonization to the Escheat Movement* (Toronto: University of Toronto Press, 2006); Ian Ross Robertson, *The Tenant League of Prince Edward Island, 1864–1867: Leasehold Tenure in the New World* (Toronto: University of Toronto Press, 1996); Colin Grittner, "Working at the Crossroads: Statute Labour, Manliness, and the Electoral Franchise on Victorian Prince Edward Island," *Journal of the Canadian Historical Association* 23, 1 (2012): 101–30.

8. Grittner, "Privilege at the Polls." Information in the DCB, 22 vols (Toronto: University of Toronto Press, 1959–), available online: www.biographi.ca/en/index.php (accessed on 12 November 2016).

9. Toronto *Globe*, 8 October 1866, quoted in R.T. Naylor, *The History of Canadian Business, 1867–1914* (Montreal & Kingston: McGill-Queen's University Press, 2006; reprint), vol. 1, 31;

Christopher Moore, *Three Weeks in Quebec City: The Meeting that Made Canada* (Toronto: Allen Lane, 2015), 221.

10. P.B. Waite, *The Life and Times of Confederation 1864–1867: Politics, Newspapers and the Union of British North America* (Toronto: University of Toronto Press, 1962), 236.

11. William M. Baker, *Timothy Warren Anglin 1822–96: Irish Catholic Canadian* (Toronto: University of Toronto Press, 1977), 68.

12. Nova Scotia, *Debates and Proceedings of the House of Assembly* (Halifax: Joseph C. Crosskill, 1867), 85, 96–7.

13. Delphin Andrew Muise, "Elections and Constituencies: Federal Politics in Nova Scotia, 1867–1878" (PhD dissertation, University of Western Ontario, 1971), 39; Kenneth G. Pryke, *Nova Scotia and Confederation* (Toronto: University of Toronto Press, 1979).

14. Halifax *Morning Chronicle*, 11 and 14 January 1865.

15. Halifax *Morning Sun*, 13 January 1865.

16. Halifax *Morning Sun*, 13 January 1865.

17. T.E. Cliffe Leslie, *Land Systems and Industrial Economy of Ireland, England, and Continental Countries* (London: Longman's, 1870), beginning with "The State of Ireland," published in *Macmillan's Magazine*, February 1867; G.M. Koot, "T.E. Cliffe Leslie, Irish Social Reform, and the Origins of the English School of Historical Economics," *History of Political Economy* 7, 3 (Fall 1975): 312–36.

18. Saint John *Morning Freeman*, 19 November 1864.

19. Saint John *Morning Freeman*, 28 January 1865.

20. William M. Baker, "Squelching the Disloyal, Fenian-Sympathizing Brood: T.W. Anglin and Confederation in New Brunswick, 1865–6," *Canadian Historical Review* 55, 2 (June 1974): 142.

21. Nova Scotia, *Debates and Proceedings*, 10 April 1865, 208–14.

22. Ibid., 11 April 1865, 235 and 17 April 1865, 256.

23. Nova Scotia, *Debates and Proceedings*, 9 March 1866, 63 and 18 March 1867, 15; this is also J.A. Maxwell's assessment of Tupper, *Financial History of Nova Scotia*, 38. On Cartier, see Brian J. Young, *George-Etienne Cartier, Montreal Bourgeois* (Montreal & Kingston: McGill-Queen's University Press, 1981), 90–1.

24. Nova Scotia, *Debates and Proceedings*, 1865, 183–4, 194, 206–8.

25. Nova Scotia, *Debates and Proceedings*, 1867, 70–2.

26. Halifax *Morning Chronicle*, 29 May 1867; Speech at Dartmouth, 22 May 1867, Joseph Andrew Chisholm, ed., *The Speeches and Public Letters of Joseph Howe* (Halifax: Chronicle, 1909), vol. 2, 514.

27. Howe to Marquis of Normandy, 22 November 1866, in Burpee, "Joseph Howe and the Anti-Confederation League," *Transactions of the Royal Society of Canada* 3, 10 (1917), 440–1. Burpee calls the argument an obvious fallacy.

28. William M. Baker, *Timothy Warren Anglin 1822–96: Irish Catholic Canadian* (Toronto: University of Toronto Press, 1977).

29. In J.H. Gray, *Confederation, or, The Political and Parliamentary History of Canada* (Toronto: Copp, Clark, 1872), vol. 1, 385–7.

30. Nova Scotia, *Debates and Proceedings*, 19 March 1867, 36 and 51.

31. Ibid., 12 April 1867, 126.

32. Halifax *Morning Chronicle*, 31 August 1868.

33. Muise, "Elections and Constituencies," 110.

34. *House of Commons Debates*, 20 December 1867, 337.

35. Halifax *Morning Chronicle*, 21 January 1868.

4 From Andrew Smith, "Confederation as a Hemispheric Anomaly: Why Canada Chose a Unique Model of Sovereignty in the 1860s," in *Remaking North American Sovereignty: State Transformation in the 1860s,* eds Jewel Spengler and Frank Towers (New York City: Fordham, 2020).

In the early 1770s, virtually all of the western hemisphere was subject to or claimed by a European sovereign.[1] The Atlantic revolutions that began in the Thirteen Colonies in the 1770s swept away this system of sovereignty.[2] By the 1860s, the British North American colonies were a hemispheric anomaly in the sense that they were the only large regions of the American mainland that were still part of a European colonial empire. In other words, the model of sovereignty in place in present-day Canada was distinctive among the large countries of the hemisphere. As has been demonstrated elsewhere, the federation of the British North American colonies between 1867 and 1873 was intended to preserve this rather unusual status.[3]

[. . .]

The hemispheric approach adopted here has several key elements. First, it is comparative and seeks to understand the experience of present-day Canada in light of parallel developments in other western hemisphere countries. Second, it is interested in the connections between Canada and these countries. [. . .] There were substantial trade ties between present-day Canada and Latin America and even an attempt, in 1866, to negotiate a free-trade agreement linking British North America and the other monarchical territories of the western hemisphere.[4] Moreover, as is shown below, Canadians in the 1860s were aware of political developments in Latin America and referenced them in the Canadian constitutional debates of that decade. Because many Canadians in the 1860s adopted a hemispheric approach, it behooves the historians who study them to follow suit. Third, the hemispheric approach developed here involves highlighting race and class. Recent comparative research on the century after the Atlantic Revolutions suggests that the politics of nation building in many western hemisphere countries was connected to the question of how far to apply the "contagious" ideas of liberty and equality, which had originally been used by white colonial elites opposed to the policies of European monarchies, to other ethnic and socio-economic groups.[5] In the United States, Brazil, Cuba, Mexico, Argentina, and other New World countries in the nineteenth century, a central issue was whether poor whites and the descendants of Africans and Amerindians were to be considered full citizens, or indeed citizens at all.[6] This dynamic was the common denominator linking the politics of nation building in these countries. [. . .]

SOVEREIGNTY

[. . .] The Canadian Constitution of 1867, which was an act of the British parliament, produced a state that was quasi-sovereign in that it possessed a degree of internal sovereignty while not yet enjoying juridical personhood in the eyes of the international community.[7] In 1865, a Canadian politician accurately described the powers of the British parliament over the colonies, remarking that is has "sovereign and uncontrollable authority in making, confining, enlarging, restraining, repealing, revising and expounding of laws."[8] [. . .] Most Canadian legislators agreed that the state of affairs whereby ultimate sovereignty (that is, the right to alter the constitution) lay (somewhere) in London should continue. When a politician declared during the debates on Confederation that "our first act should have been to recognize the sovereignty of Her Majesty" he was cheered by his fellow legislators.[9] When discussing the division of powers between the future federal and provincial governments, the prevailing view was that most sovereign powers should be exercised by the national government: The U.S. system of states' rights and state sovereignty should be avoided at all costs.[10] [. . .]

SOVEREIGNTY AND CANADIAN CONSTITUTIONAL POLITICS IN THE 1860s

Had British North Americans expressed a clear preference for independence in the 1860s, the British parliament almost certainly would have granted this request, thereby terminating its sovereignty over northern North America. In 1837–38, British troops had brutally crushed a republican rebellion in Lower Canada just as they had earlier tried to crush the American Revolution and would subsequently crush anti-British risings in India and elsewhere. Then, in the 1840s, the British gave internal home rule ("Responsible Government") to their colonies of white settlement in North America and Australasia.[11] By the 1860s, Britain had abandoned any notion of holding on to her remaining North American colonies by force. Indeed, a sizeable proportion of the British political class now thought that continued British sovereignty over the country's North American colonies was a net burden for the British taxpayer.[12] [. . .]

As has been shown in other publications, the federation of the British North America colonies in the 1860s was intended as a means of keeping the colonies British.[13] That the intention of the creators of the 1867 Constitution was to strengthen rather than to diminish the colonies' ties to Britain is suggested by the arrangement of the Quebec Resolutions of 1864, which were a draft outline of the constitution of 1867. The very first of these resolutions declared the delegates' belief that the "present and future prosperity of British North America will be promoted by a Federal Union under the Crown of Great Britain." The third resolution stated that "in framing a Constitution" the delegates' decision-making had been shaped by their wish to perpetuate the connection with the mother country and to replicate her political institutions "so far as our circumstances will permit."[14] [. . .]

Observers in the United States agreed that the federal constitution drafted at the 1864 Quebec City conference was a measure that would help to keep Canada in the Empire.[15] The *New-York Tribune* condemned the delegates in Quebec City for their "submissiveness" to England, noting that they had been "very anxious to affirm their loyalty to the British Crown."[16] Some in the United States saw the proposed federation of the North American colonies as a threat to America's republican institutions. For instance, the *New York Herald* denounced England for planning to foist a Brazilian-style hereditary viceroy on the poor people of British North America.[17] The *New York Times* also recognized that the promoters of Confederation wished to draw closer to Britain, although it sneered that "the 'monarchical principles' on which it is ostensibly said that the new Federation is to be based" did not extend so far as to induce Canadians to pay for a large standing army in peacetime.[18] The *Advertiser*, a newspaper in the border town of Calais, Maine, regarded the plan to federate British North America as unimportant because it would involve no change to the colonial status of the provinces. It remarked that the colonists "do not propose to separate themselves from Great Britain. If they did the movement would be one of great significance. And so long as they remain as Provinces it is of not the slightest political consequence whether they unite or remain separate."[19]

MONARCHISM AND CANADIAN POLITICAL CULTURE IN A HEMISPHERIC PERSPECTIVE

Most contemporaries recognized that the aim of Confederation was to keep the colonies within the British Empire. Canadians' evident loyalty to the Crown was driven, in part, by a belief in the benefits of monarchical political institutions over their republican alternatives. This belief that blended constitutions that included monarchical institutions were generally superior was seen in the ideas of Thomas D'Arcy McGee. In the 1840s, he had participated in an armed uprising that sought to create a sovereign Irish republic.[20] He became a fervent advocate of the British connection after arriving in Montreal. In the 1860s, McGee waxed poetic on the great blessings British sovereignty had brought to Canada. Given that the

republican experiment that had begun in 1776 was being severely tested at this time, McGee's argument resonated with many of Queen Victoria's subjects in northern North America.[21] In 1863, he proposed a permanent viceroy for Canada on the Brazilian model, suggesting that one of Queen Victoria's younger sons should become Canada's king.[22] McGee's decision to use Brazil as a constitutional model shows that at least some Canadians in the 1860s were thinking in hemispheric terms. In speeches in the Canadian parliament, McGee denounced the republican institutions of the United States and proclaimed his preference for the ancient establishment of monarchy. In 1858, he declared that "my native disposition is reverence towards things old and veneration for the landmarks of the past." He explained away his flirtation with republicanism as due to the excesses of British rule in Ireland. He also declared that he was "as loyal to the institutions under which I live in Canada as any Tory of the old or the new school."[23]

McGee believed that without the stabilizing forces of monarchy and active government, New World societies would inevitably degenerate into anarchy as individuals in the western hemisphere lacked the customary and legal restraints common in the more hierarchical societies of Europe. In his 1865 book on federal government, he observed that the people of Canada, "like all other American communities (when compared with European countries) have necessarily very decided democratic tendencies within them." By democracy, McGee meant an unruly mob. It was, he said, the task of the present generation of British North Americans to see that "authority is exalted" and that the best way of doing so was to strengthen the power of the central executive in any future British North American federation. "Executive impotency" should be avoided. Although McGee conceded that the U.S. Constitution of 1789 was "a vast advance on the previous Articles of Confederation" it nevertheless provided for too weak a government due to the compromises nationalist statesman such as Alexander Hamilton had been forced to make with "state jealousy" and the "wild theories of the demagogues of the day," by which he meant Thomas Jefferson. Again adopting a hemispheric frame of reference, McGee regarded the Empire of Brazil as perhaps the best-governed nation in the hemisphere, attributing that country's relative peace and stability to its monarchical institutions.[24] The fact the Brazil's prosperity was based on slavery went unmentioned by both McGee and by the British North American politicians who visited that country in early 1866 on a trade mission.[25] Like many British North Americans, they were largely indifferent to the question of the rights of black people and the struggles then underway throughout the hemispheric about the rights of people of African descent.

EVIDENCE FOR POPULAR SUPPORT FOR REMAINING WITHIN THE BRITISH EMPIRE

Elite opinion in British North America in the 1860s was generally hostile to the idea of a complete break with Britain. It is hard to assess with a high degree of certainty the extent to which this attitude was shared by non-elite Canadians (for example farmers, lumberjacks, petty traders, and members of the emerging urban working class), as methodical public opinion polling did not reach Canada until the 1930s. However, as far as we can tell, most ordinary colonists shared the elite's belief that remaining in the British Empire was normative. On the eve of the 1864 constitutional convention in Quebec City, reporter Charles MacKay assessed colonial attitudes to the British connection for the readers of the *Times of London*. He said that of the three basic options open to the colonists (for example, joining the United States, becoming an independent republic, or remaining within the Empire), the vast majority of Canadians favoured the latter. MacKay based this statement on conversations he had had all over the Province of Canada. In the course of a 1200-mile journey through the

colony, he had "interchanged ideas" on this issue with men at all levels of society, from stagecoach drivers and farmers to merchants and "members of the legislature of every political party." MacKay said that the desire to remain British subjects was shared by French Canadians, descendants of the old United Empire Loyalists, and more recent immigrants from the British Isles, the three main groups in the Canadian electorate. MacKay summed up the situation: "Canadian loyalty is not a thing of light account."[26] [. . .]

Identification with Britain was, of course, stronger in some localities than in others. Richard Cartwright, a politician first elected to the Canadian parliament in 1863, discussed this issue in his memoirs. He recalled that attitudes toward the United States had been much more positive in western Upper Canada than in the old United Empire Loyalist settlements along the St Lawrence River. In his parliamentary constituency, Lennox and Addington, many voters were the grandsons of the pro-British refugees who left the Thirteen Colonies during the American Revolution. In such communities, there was a strong sense of loyalty to Britain. Cartwright's own grandfather was one of these refugees. In regions of Canada that were settled in the nineteenth century, the political culture was quite different: Cartwright recollected that when a business trip took him to the area west of Toronto in 1856, he had been surprised and even "disgusted" by the widespread "sentiment in favour of union with the United States."[27] Many farmers and others in that region thought that joining the United States would bring prosperity.

OPPOSITION TO THE PREVAILING DESIRE TO REMAIN WITHIN THE BRITISH EMPIRE

While it appears that a majority of British North Americans wished to remain part of the British Empire, there was nevertheless substantial dissent from this view. Some wished to become part of the United States, the Great Republic. Others wished to form an independent Canadian republic, an option that would have brought Canada into line with the many small independent republics that had emerged out of Spain's empire in the western hemisphere. Advocates of the latter option had few allies outside of Canada. However, those Canadians who favoured so-called "continental union" had allies in Washington, at least for a brief period in the 1860s.

[. . .]

In the aftermath of the election of Abraham Lincoln, a Republican, in November 1860, many southern states left the union and recalled their congressional representatives. This change in the sectional balance in the Senate allowed for the issue of the acquisition of Canada to be re-opened. In January 1861, as state after state in the lower south announced its secession, the *New York Herald* proposed that the northern states let the south depart in peace and instead concentrate on annexing British North America as compensation. The editor of the *Herald*, who had once lived in the North American colonies, reasoned that a union between the free-soil states and the slavery-free British provinces would be a more natural one than the former union between North and the slave-holding South.[28]

Some senior Republicans supported this idea. Lincoln's Secretary of State, William Henry Seward, proposed the annexation of Canada in a confidential memorandum for the president in early April 1861, shortly before the first shots of the Civil War were fired at Fort Sumter.[29] Seward, who was from New York State, had first advocated the peaceful acquisition of Canada in an 1857.[30] In 1857, he had condemned the Southerners' opposition to annexing Canada, declaring that it would have been better had the United States expanded northward into British America rather than southward into Mexico. Speaking of his recent tour of Canada and Labrador, he said that he had found the "inhabitants

vigorous, hardy, energetic, perfected by the Protestant religion and British constitutional liberty." [. . .]

The start of the Civil War in 1861 put the issue of northward expansion on hold. Few Canadians wished to join a country that was racked by civil war. After the surrender of the Confederacy in April 1865, Canadian interest in annexation quickly revived, due in part to Washington's announcement of its intention to abrogate the 1854 Reciprocity Treaty, which had given colonial natural products duty-free entry into the Republic. In the summer and autumn of 1865, there was a lively debate in Canada on the advisability of joining the United States. The *Montreal Trade Review* observed that a rapid change in Canadian thinking about Annexation had taken place since the capture of the Confederate capital of Richmond in March: "what was three months ago regarded as rank disloyalty is now the most frequent topic of discussion and advocacy."[31] In 1865, the *Globe* attacked two other newspapers in Upper Canada, the *Galt Reporter* and the *St. Catharines Post*, for supporting Annexation on the grounds it would improve local economic conditions. In an editorial written in response to a piece in the *Galt Reporter*, the *Globe* stated that it was a fallacy to suppose that Confederation, Annexation, or any other constitutional change would restore prosperity. The *Globe* said that the previous autumn's poor harvest would have been bad under any political system. It compared the Galt newspaper to a "quack" doctor selling a cure-all pill.[32]

[. . .]

The discussion of "continental union" was encouraged by John F. Potter, the United States consul-general in Montreal. In 1866, the Massachusetts Congressman Nathaniel P. Banks introduced a bill to provide for the admission of the eastern British North American colonies as states, each with two senators. According to this bill, Rupert's Land was to be given the status of a territory similar to Dakota.[33] Congressman Banks does not appear to have regarded the incorporation of a predominantly French-speaking territory (Lower Canada) into the United States as problematic, an attitude that can be related to his earlier experiences as military governor of Louisiana, a state in which linguistic politics had become connected with the racial politics of Reconstruction during the 1864 state constitutional convention.[34]

[. . .]

A few businessmen in Canada, most notably Orrin S. Wood, the chief executive of the dominant telegraph firm, endorsed the continental union concept. He was fired by the firm's board of directors for publicly advocating Canada's peaceful incorporation into the United States.[35] Many of the Canadians who opposed Canada's continued membership in the British Empire were trade unionists or self-described socialists who opposed the power of the bourgeoisie. In 1864, the labour activist T. Phillips Thompson proposed that the British North American colonies unite under a republican constitution. Thompson did not want the British North American colonies to become part of the United States, and instead envisioned a separate sovereign nation freed of the entanglements of the British Empire. Thompson took issue with Thomas D'Arcy McGee's view that Canada could become sovereign while still remaining part of the British Empire and subject to the jurisdiction of the imperial parliament. [. . .]

Thompson appears to have thought that his vision of a just and egalitarian society required the attainment of full sovereignty by the people of British North America and republican political institutions. The chief problem with monarchy, he felt, was that it was linked to aristocracy and inequality more generally. Thompson regarded the various recent proposals for the creation of a Canadian order of nobility as highly undesirable, observing that "already we have too much of the aristocratic feeling" and Canada's elites looked down on "the farmer and the mechanic." In his view, it should be

"our aim to repress rather than encourage this feeling, which the establishment of an aristocracy would assuredly tend to strengthen and develop."[36] As did his opponent McGee, Thompson adopted a hemispheric frame of reference, doing so when he noted that in addition to being the only monarchy in South America, Brazil was the sole nation on that continent that still permitted slavery.[37] Thompson stressed that he favoured a union of the British North American colonies but insisted that it have a republican form of government, not a hereditary head of state.

[. . .]

WHY DID MOST CANADIANS SUPPORT REMAINING IN THE BRITISH EMPIRE RATHER THAN THE ALTERNATIVES?

British North Americans who advocated joining the United States or republican nationhood were a small minority. We therefore need to explain why so many British North Americans in the 1860s supported remaining in the British Empire when other constitutional options were open to them. First, their status as British subjects offered them a degree of military protection against the Army of the United States and the Fenians, an Irish-American paramilitary organization that attacked the Canadian border in the 1860s.[38] This status also offered British colonial subjects considerable consular protection when they travelled abroad, as the recent Don Pacifico affair has vividly illustrated.[39] Second, the American Civil War had discredited the U.S. experiment with democracy and republicanism in the eyes of many Canadians. The U.S. concept of state sovereignty was widely regarded in Canada as the cause of the Civil War, which is one of the reasons the Canadian constitution of 1867 provided for a very strong central government and weak sub-national governments.[40] Third, Canadians were aware of the chaos in other republican countries in the western hemisphere. Only the Empire of Brazil stood out as a beacon of stability in a sea of republicanism, as McGee argued. One can well understand why McGee's interpretation of events elsewhere in the hemisphere would have reinforced his monarchism. In 1864, as British North America's political leaders were about to frame their plan for a federation within the British Empire, the War of the Triple Alliance was breaking out in Latin America. This conflict pitted Paraguay, a former Spanish colony, against two other former Spanish colonies, Argentina and Uruguay, along with Brazil. When the war concluded in 1870, perhaps 400 000 were dead.[41] This conflict was reported in Canadian newspapers and likely would have reinforced the idea that the republics of Latin America were a hotbed of instability and violence. Canadians already had a negative view of republican institutions thanks to the recent civil war in the United States.[42] Those Canadians who adopted a hemispheric frame of reference had additional data points to support their existing political views, monarchical or republican.

In accounting for the widespread nature of the preference in favour of remaining in the Empire, we also have to integrate race and ethnicity into our analysis. As was mentioned previously, there were some in the United States, particularly the Radical Republicans, who would have welcomed the British North American provinces into the United States. However, there were many who were opposed to this option. In some cases, this opposition was rooted in an ethnic-nationalist definition of who could be a U.S. citizen. [. . .] The ethnic nationalist definition of U.S. citizenship, of course, excluded black and Chinese individuals, but it also excluded, albeit less virulently, non-Protestants and those who were not of Anglo-Saxon or closely related stock.[43] British North Americans who were not of Anglo-Celtic ancestry were able to observe this pattern, which helps to explain why so many of them wished to remain under British sovereignty.

British North America in the 1860s had a large population of non-Protestant, non–Anglo-Celtic people, namely the French Canadians. Although many regions of British North America were overwhelmingly white, Protestant, and Anglo-Celtic, some in the United States perceived Canada as a motley crew of non–Anglo-Saxon, biologically inferior people. This was certainly the view that *Frank Leslie's Illustrated Newspaper* in New York took in an editorial on whether the incorporation of Canada into the United States was desirable. This editorial said that it was opposed to any further "territorial aggrandizement" by the United States save for the annexation of the slave colony of Cuba. Canada, the editor reasoned, had too many non–Anglo-Saxon people living in it to be worthy of "admission into the Union." This editorial, which strangely did not specify what was to happen to the existing population of Cuba, claimed that so much "incongruous rubbish" had already entered the United States as to make the annexation of "squalid hyperboreans" undesirable. [. . .]

The evident reluctance of some Anglo-Saxon Protestants in the United States to take over a territory associated with Roman Catholicism and the French language is part of a broader pattern. U.S. historians often associate the ideology of Anglo-Saxon supremacy with Manifest Destiny and the desire to engross as much territory as possible. The reality was more complicated: As Eric T. Love demonstrated in *Race over Empire*, a sense of superiority over non-white and non–Anglo-Saxon people prompted many in the United States to recoil from proposals to annex particular territories. Indeed, this sentiment contributed to the decision of Congress to block the territorial expansion plans of the Grant administration. The politics of race influenced U.S. hemispheric diplomacy in the Reconstruction Era, when U.S. legislators considered proposals to annex Alaska, the Virgin Islands, and part of the island of Santo Domingo.

With the exception of the purchase of Alaska in 1867 and the acquisition of the unpopulated Midway Islands, most of these proposed expansions of U.S. territory failed, in part because of congressional opposition to including additional non-white majority territories in the United States. The predominant view in the North was that the country already had enough problems connected to the semi-tropical and racially mixed states of the former Confederacy.[44] [. . .]

An ethnic-nationalist definition of U.S. citizenship was liable to antagonize potential supporters of continental union in Canada. Indeed, we know that the anti-Catholic, anti-Irish chauvinism rampant in the United States in the 1850s converted the aforementioned Thomas D'Arcy McGee from a republican into an ardently loyal subject of Queen Victoria.[45] Speaking during a somewhat earlier wave of anti-Catholic sentiment in the United States, a French-speaking Roman Catholic legislator famously declared that "le dernier coup de canon tiré pour le maintien de la puissance anglaise en Amérique le sera par un bras canadien" (the last cannon shot in defence of British power in the America would be fired by a French-Canadian hand).[46] Advocates of a British identity for Canada were promoting an inclusive, civic-nationalist definition of Britishness that attracted many whites who were not of British ancestry.

In 1861, John A. Macdonald declared that he considered "every man who says that he is in favour" of the British connection as belonging "to my party, whatever his antecedents may have been."[47] [. . .]

CONCLUSION AND DIRECTIONS FOR FUTURE RESEARCH

The course of Canadian political history in the 1860s resulted in a constitutional settlement whereby British North America remained under British sovereignty. The other options that were open to British North Americans in the 1860s, becoming an independent republic or joining the United States, remained roads not taken. As the older historiography on Canada in the 1860s has shown, a host of factors helped to produce this outcome. [. . .] However, it is important to recognize that contemporary ideas about racial and ethnic hierarchies did shape the drawing of the political map of northern North America in the 1860s in a fashion that has not been acknowledged by previous scholars. By bringing race back into the story of Canadian Confederation in the 1860s, we can develop a better understanding how the Canadian federation was created and the subsequent evolution of the Canadian nation-state. [. . .]

NOTES

1. Lauren Benton, *A Search for Sovereignty: Law and Geography in European Empires, 1400–1900* (Cambridge: Cambridge University Press, 2010); Jack P. Greene, "Negotiated Authorities: The Problem of Governance in the Extended Polities of the Early Modern Atlantic World," in *Negotiated Authorities: Essays in Colonial Political and Constitutional History* (Charlottesville: University of Virginia Press 1994), 1–24. I would like to thank Jay Sexton and Marise Bachand for commenting on earlier drafts of this paper.

2. John Lynch, ed. *Latin American Revolutions, 1808–1826: Old and New World Origins* (Norman: University of Oklahoma Press, 1994).

3. Andrew Smith, "The Reaction of the City of London to the Quebec Resolutions, 1864–1866," *Journal of the Canadian Historical Association/Revue de la Société historique du Canada* 17, no. 1 (2006): 1–24.

4. Andrew Smith and Kirsten Greer, "Monarchism, an Emerging Canadian Identity, and the 1866 British North American Trade Mission to the West Indies and Brazil," *Journal of*

Imperial and Commonwealth History 44, no. 2 (2016): 214–40.

5. Lester D. Langley, *The Americas in the Age of Revolution, 1750–1850* (New Haven: Yale University Press, 1996), 58, 176, 232.

6. A.W. Marx, *Making Race and Nation: A Comparison of South Africa, the United States, and Brazil* (Cambridge: Cambridge University Press, 1998); Mara Loveman, *National Colors: Racial Classification and the State in Latin America* (Oxford: Oxford University Press, 2014); Edward Telles and René Flores, "Not Just Color: Whiteness, Nation, and Status in Latin America," *Hispanic American Historical Review* 93, no. 3 (2013): 411–49.

7. Philip Noel-Baker, *The Present Juridical Status of the British Dominions in International Law* (London: Longmans, Green, 1929).

8. *Parliamentary Debates on the Subject of the Confederation of the British North American Provinces, 3rd Session, 8th Provincial Parliament of Canada* (Quebec: Hunter, Rose & Co., parliamentary printers, 1865), 220.

9. Ibid., 33.

10. Ibid., 433, 440.

11. Phillip Buckner, *The Transition to Responsible Government: British Policy in British North America, 1815–1850* (Westport: Greenwood Press, 1985); Peter Cochrane, *Colonial Ambition: Foundations of Australia's Democracy* (Victoria, Au.: Melbourne University Press, 2006).

12. Bernard Semmel, *The Liberal Ideal and the Demons of Empire: Theories of Imperialism from Adam Smith to Lenin* (Baltimore: Johns Hopkins University Press, 1993), 17–38.

13. See Smith, "Reaction of the City of London."

14. "Quebec Resolutions," in *Confederation: Being a Series of Hitherto Unpublished Documents Bearing on the British North America Act*, ed. Sir Joseph Pope (Toronto: Carswell, 1895), 38–52.

15. Andrew Smith, *British Businessmen and Canadian Confederation: Constitution-Making in an Era of Anglo-Globalization* (Montreal: McGill-Queen's University Press, 2008), 91–108.

16. "The Canadian Federation," *New-York Tribune*, October 20, 1864, 4.

17. In its reply to the *New York Herald*, the *Toronto Globe* stated that people in British North America would decide for themselves whether the federation's chief magistrate would be named "Governor," "Viceroy," "President,"

or "King." "English Designs on America," *Toronto Globe*, September 15, 1864, 2.

18. "The Canadian Confederation: Imperial Designs," *New York Times*, October 23, 1864, 4.

19. Quoted in "Confederation: What Our Neighbours Think," *Saint John Weekly Telegraph*, December 7, 1864, 3.

20. David Wilson, *Thomas D'Arcy McGee: Passion, Reason, and Politics, 1825–1857* (Montreal and Kingston: McGill-Queen's University Press, 2008), 259, 328, 4.

21. Thomas D'Arcy McGee, *The Crown and the Confederation: Three Letters to the Hon. John Alexander McDonald, Attorney General for Upper Canada* (Montreal: J. Lovell, 1864).

22. McGee, "A Plea for British American Nationality," *British American Magazine* 1 (August 1863), 337–45, 342. For the possibility that Canada might acquire a permanent hereditary viceroy chosen from among Victoria's sons, see "The Vice-Royalty," *Saint John Morning News*, October 21, 1864, 2.

23. Thomas L. Connolly, *Funeral Oration on the Late Hon. Thos. D'Arcy McGee: Delivered in the Metropolitan Church of St. Mary's, Halifax, Nova Scotia on Friday 24th April, A D. 1868* (Halifax, N.S.: Compton, 1868), 12.

24. Thomas Darcy McGee, *Notes on Federal Governments, Past and Present* (Montreal: Dawson, 1865), 51, 52, 44, 34.

25. Andrew Smith and Kirsten Greeg, "Monarchism, an Emerging Canadian Identity, and the 1866 British North American Trade Mission to the West Indies and Brazil," *Journal of Imperial and Commonwealth History* 44, no. 2 (2016): 214–40.

26. "Canada and the Canadians," [London] *Times*, October 22, 1864, 9.

27. Richard Cartwright, *Reminiscences* (Toronto: W. Briggs, 1912), 20.

28. L.B. Shippee, *Canadian-American Relations, 1849–1874* (New Haven: Yale University Press, 1939), 183.

29. Robin W. Winks, *Canada and the United States: The Civil War Years* (Baltimore: Johns Hopkins University Press, 1960), 4–5, 33–34; Glyndon G. Van Deusen, *William Henry Seward* (New York: Oxford University Press, 1967), 535–37.

30. Shippee, *Canadian-American Relations*, 184.

31. "The Effect on Canada," *Montreal Trade Review*, April 2, 1865, 141.

32. "Gloomy Minds," *Toronto Globe*, May 17, 1865, 2. See D.F. Warner, *The Idea of Continental Union: Agitation for the Annexation of Canada to the United States, 1849–1893* (Lexington: University of Kentucky Press, 1960), 43.

33. Fred Harvey Harrington, *Fighting Politician: Major General N.P. Banks* (Westport, Conn.: Greenwood Press, 1970), 179.

34. Shirley Brice Heath, "Language and Politics in the United States," *Georgetown University Round Table on Languages and Linguistics* 28 (1977): 267–96.

35. Wood returned to the United States after his dismissal. See O.S. Wood to President and Directors, July 15, 1865, in Montreal Telegraph Company papers in Canadian National Railways Company Fonds, R231–386-4-E, sub-sub-series in Library and Archives Canada.

36. T. Phillips Thompson, *The Future Government of Canada: Being Arguments in Favour of a British American Independent Republic* (St Catherine's: Herald Press, 1864), 13.

37. Ibid., 9.

38. Hereward Senior, *The Last Invasion of Canada: The Fenian Raids, 1866–1870* (Toronto: Dundurn, 1991); Phillip Buckner, "British North America and a Continent in Dissolution: The American Civil War in the Making of Canadian Confederation," *The Journal of the Civil War Era* 7, no. 4 (2017): 512–40.

39. Abigail Green, "The British Empire and the Jews: An Imperialism of Human Rights?" *Past & Present* 199, no. 1 (2008): 175–205.

40. Garth Stevenson, *Ex Uno Plures: Federal-Provincial Relations in Canada, 1867–1896* (Montreal and Kingston: McGill-Queen's Press, 1993).

41. Harris Gaylord Warren, *Paraguay and the Triple Alliance: The Postwar Decade, 1869–1878* (Austin: University of Texas Press, 2014), 31–32.

42. S.F. Wise, "The Annexation Movement and Its Effect on Canadian Opinion, 1837–67," in S.F. Wise and Robert Craig Brown, *Canada Views the United States: Nineteenth-Century Political Attitudes* (Seattle: University of Washington Press, 1967).

43. Eric Foner, "Who Is an American? The Imagined Community in American History," *Centennial Review* (1997): 425–38.

44. Eric Tyrone Lowery Love, *Race over Empire: Racism and U.S. Imperialism, 1865–1900* (Chapel Hill: University of North Carolina Press, 2004).

45. Wilson, *Thomas D'Arcy McGee*, 321–28.

46. Étienne-Paschal Taché speech on the Militia Bill, April 24, 1846, quoted in Jacques Monet, *The Last Cannon Shot: A Study of French-Canadian Nationalism 1837–1850* (Toronto: University of Toronto Press, 1969). Translation by author.

47. Macdonald, "Remarks on the Composition and Policy of the Brown-Dorion Government," in *Address of the Hon. John A. Macdonald to the Elders of the City of Kingston* (Kingston, Canada: West 1861), 95.